FRAMINGHAM STATE COLLEGE

3 3014 00137 5684

D1507593

BOOKS BY ANTHONY HOLDEN

Laurence Olivier
Of Presidents, Prime Ministers and Princes
Prince Charles

LAURENCE OLIVIER

LAURENCE OLIVIER

Anthony Holden

ATHENEUM · NEW YORK · 1988

Framingham State College
Framingham, Massachusetts

First published in Great Britain by George Weidenfeld &
Nicolson Limited

Copyright © 1988 by Anthony Holden Limited

All rights reserved. No part of this book may be
reproduced or transmitted in any form or by any means,
electronic or mechanical, including photocopying,
recording or by any information storage
and retrieval system, without permission in
writing from the Publisher.

Atheneum
Macmillan Publishing Company
866 Third Avenue, New York, N.Y. 10022

Library of Congress Cataloging-in-Publication Data
Holden, Anthony,————
    Laurence Olivier/Anthony Holden.—1st American ed.
    p. cm.
    Bibliography: p.
    Includes index.
    ISBN 0-689-11536-9
    1. Olivier, Laurence, 1907–   . 2. Actors—Great Britain-
    -Biography. I. Title.
    PN2598.O55H6 1988
    792′.028′0924—dc19
    [B]   88-14672
                                                      CIP

Macmillan books are available at special discounts for
bulk purchases for sales promotions, premiums, fund-
raising, or educational use. For details, contact:

Special Sales Director
Macmillan Publishing Company
866 Third Avenue
New York, N.Y. 10022

First American Edition

10 9 8 7 6 5 4 3 2 1

Printed in the United States of America

PN
2598
O55
H6
1988

For

JOHN DAVID MORLEY

in memory of Cuchulain

Contents

Illustrations		xi
Foreword		xv
Prologue		1

PART ONE: "Some Are Born Great"

1	1907–24	9
2	1924–8	27
3	1928–31	47
4	1931–5	66
5	1935	84

PART TWO: "Some Achieve Greatness"

6	1936	101
7	1937	113
8	1937–9	129
9	1939–41	150
10	1941–4	169
11	1944–5	184
12	1945–7	201
13	1947–8	224
14	1948–52	246

15 1952–5   271
16 1955   287
17 1955–6   301
18 1956–8   314

PART THREE: "Some Have Greatness Thrust Upon Them"

19 1958–62   333
20 1962–3   349
21 1963–4   363
22 1964–7   384
23 1967–73   403
24 1973–83   426
25 1983–7   446

Chronology   454
Notes   470
Bibliography   482
Index   492

Illustrations

Between pages 42 and 43

Childhood: Olivier aged eight (*BBC Hulton Picture Library*)

First theatrical steps: aged twelve, as a matador (*National Film Archive*), and aged fourteen, as Katharina in *The Taming of the Shrew* (*BBC Hulton Picture Library*)

The beetle-browed young actor, aged twenty, as Uncle Vanya and Tony Lumpkin for Birmingham Rep, 1927 (*both photographs from Weidenfeld Archives*)

Matinee idol: as Beau Geste, 1929 (*BBC Hulton Picture Library*), and in his first film, *The Temporary Widow*, 1929 (*Weidenfeld Archives*)

Marriage at twenty-three to Jill Esmond, 1930 (*BBC Hulton Picture Library*)

1930–31: Success with Noël Coward in *Private Lives* (*Tom Graves*) leads to Hollywood where Jill is a bigger star (*National Film Archive*)

First Shakespeare: Romeo (*photograph by Cecil Beaton courtesy of Sotheby's London*) and Mercutio (*Weidenfeld Archives*), 1935, leads to Hamlet at the Old Vic (*Victoria and Albert Museum*) and a film of *As You Like It* with Elisabeth Bergner, 1936 (*National Film Archive*)

Enter Vivien Leigh, with Olivier in *Fire over England*, 1936 (*National Film Archive*), and *Hamlet* at Elsinore (*Mander and Mitchenson*)

More success at the Old Vic: as Toby Belch, 1937, and Coriolanus, 1938 (*both photographs by Angus McBean, Harvard Theatre Collection*)

Hollywood stardom: in *Wuthering Heights* with Merle Oberon, 1939, and *Rebecca* with Joan Fontaine, 1940 (*both photographs: National Film Archive*)

1940–41: with Vivien in a screen success, *Lady Hamilton* (*National Film*

Archive) and a stage disaster, *Romeo and Juliet (The New York Public Library*)

Between pages 138 and 139

The newlywed Oliviers in a 1941 studio publicity photo (*Kobal Collection*)

After a year in the RNVR (*Fox Photos*), Sub Lt Olivier RN directs and stars in *Henry V*, 1943 (*Tom Graves*)

1944–5: A triumphant return to the Old Vic as Richard III, Sergius, Hotspur and Justice Shallow (*all photographs © John Vickers*)

'Oedipuff': as Oedipus and Mr Puff (*both photographs © John Vickers*)

Receiving his knighthood (*Keystone Press*)

The blond director and star of *Hamlet* knocks out a stunt man (*National Film Archive*), contemplates a camera angle (*Tom Graves*) and is knighted at thirty-nine, while squire of Notley Abbey (*photograph by Cecil Beaton courtesy of Sotheby's London*)

Olivier and Vivien leave for an eventful tour of Australia, 1949 (*© John Vickers*)

In *The School for Scandal* and *The Skin of our Teeth* (*both photographs © John Vickers*)

Seeing Vivien off on her disastrous trip to Ceylon (*National Film Archive*)

Vivien plays Cleopatra to Olivier's Antony (*Rex Features*) and Caesar (*Angus McBean, Harvard Theatre Collection*)

A dashing flop as Macheath in *The Beggar's Opera*, 1952 (*National Film Archive*), but a triumph as director and star of *Richard III*, 1954 (*Tom Graves*)

Between pages 234 and 235

Forcing the smiles with Vivien, both onstage in *The Sleeping Prince*, 1953 (*Tom Graves*), and offstage (*Tom Blau, Camera Press*)

The great 1955 Stratford season: as Malvolio (*Angus McBean, Harvard Theatre Collection*), Macbeth (*Weidenfeld Archives*) and Titus Andronicus (*Angus McBean, Harvard Theatre Collection*)

Fun and games for charity: with Vivien and Danny Kaye in *A Night of a Hundred Stars* (*Popperfoto*) and dressing up in drag (*© Terry O'Neill*)

Directing and co-starring with Marilyn Monroe in *The Prince and the Showgirl*, 1956: onscreen (*Tom Graves*) and off (*Popperfoto*)

1957: *Vita nuova* onstage as Archie Rice in *The Entertainer* (*British Lion/National Film Archive*) and off with Joan Plowright (*Weidenfeld Archives*)

1961: With his new wife, Joan Plowright, on Broadway (*Weidenfeld Archives*)

In *Becket*, at first in the title role with Anthony Quinn, then as the King with Arthur Kennedy as Becket (*both photographs © Friedman-Abeles*)

Two new theatres to run: Chichester, 1962 (*Pierre V-Manery*) and the National Theatre of Great Britain (*BBC Hulton Picture Library*)

1963–4: Three early roles at the National Theatre: Astrov in *Uncle Vanya* (© *John Vickers*), Othello and Solness in *The Master Builder* (*both photographs from Weidenfeld Archives*)

Between pages 330 and 331

1967–71: At the National Theatre as Edgar in *The Dance of Death* (*Rex Features*), Shylock, 1970 (*Kobal Collection*), and James Tyrone in *Long Day's Journey into Night* (*Zoë Dominic*)

Three worlds, three roles: in *Sleuth* (*National Film Archive*), as Big Daddy in *Cat on a Hot Tin Roof* (*Kobal Collection*) and in the House of Lords as the theatre's first peer (*Zoë Dominic*)

At seventy, putting a brave face on debilitating illness (*Nobby Clark, Camera Press*)

Taking the children to school in Brighton (*Rex Features*)

1966–81: A gallery of screen cameos as The Mahdi in *Khartoum*, the Russian prime minister in *Nicholas and Alexandra*, Sir John French in *Oh! What a Lovely War*, Mr Creakle in *David Copperfield*, the Duke of Wellington in *Lady Caroline Lamb*, Dr Christian Szell in *Marathon Man*, Julius in *A Little Romance* (*Keystone Press*), General Douglas MacArthur in *Inchon* (*Weidenfeld Archives*) and Zeus in *Clash of the Titans* (*Camera Press*) (*uncredited photographs: National Film Archive*)

Theatrical history is made as Sir Ralph Richardson, Sir Laurence Olivier and Sir John Gielgud play their only scene together in the film of *Wagner* 1981 (*London Trust Prods Ltd*)

Lord and Lady Olivier attend Richardson's memorial service, 1983 (*Tom Graves*)

1981–2: Three last great television roles as Lord Marchmain in *Brideshead Revisited* (*Granada Television*), Clifford Mortimer in *A Voyage round my Father* (*Thames Television*) and King Lear (*Zoë Dominic*)

1987: Lord Olivier celebrates his eightieth birthday with his wife and children (*Alistair Morrison, Camera Press*)

At eighty, Olivier can still pull off his lifelong disappearing trick, complete with Cheshire Cat smile (*Alistair Morrison, Camera Press*)

Foreword

Around the time of his seventieth birthday, in a letter to a perfect stranger, Laurence Olivier brooded over the prospect of writing a reluctant account of his life – less, it seems, for any self-gratification than to forestall the attempts of others to write it for him.

Olivier did not want his story told, by himself or anyone else. His letter began by confessing to a profound dislike of himself, a self-hatred so powerful as to make him reluctant to contemplate the effort of memory involved in any account of his life or career. To dredge into his own past would be too painful; to help anyone else do so, if only in private conversation, would be even worse. There was too much, it seemed, of which to be ashamed.

He would prefer his past to remain off limits, quarantined behind a fragile *cordon sanitaire*. But the future looked no better. After a wearisome sequence of professional disappointments, and a debilitating series of major illnesses, Olivier could no more bear to look forward than to look back. His working life was already confined to the depressing artificiality of film and television studios, rather than the inspiriting exertions of live theatre. Now he began to wonder if even camera work was beyond him.

Would he ever act again? Olivier was in remarkably confessional mood, doubly so when writing to someone he had then never met.[1] The surprised stranger in receipt of this remarkable document, in the summer of 1977, was myself – the immediate cause of these candid confessions being merely the happy chance that I was born on Olivier's fortieth birthday, in the hot midsummer of 1947, while the recently knighted actor was filming his historic *Hamlet*. So although it is now some years since Olivier bashfully removed his date of birth from *Who's Who*, I for one have always known what's what.

His seventieth birthday, my thirtieth, happened to fall while I was writing the Atticus column of the London *Sunday Times*. I wrote to Olivier pointing out this charming coincidence and boldly suggesting that he enter into the spirit of it by granting me an exclusive birthday interview. At the time I was writing a biography of the Prince of Wales, to which Olivier had made a helpful contribution. Who knows: perhaps, as an ardent admirer, I might "do" him next?

Well, he did not particularly want to be "done", thanks very much. He could not have said so more charmingly, but left little or no room for further attempts at persuasion. In the fullness of time Olivier did, indeed, write his own account of his life and work, so personal a book that he threw out the ghost-writer assigned to help him (Mark Amory), so confessional that it caused his friends to cringe with embarrassment. Was this the real Larry? It was not the Larry they knew. Or was it? When was he role-playing and when was he not? Said his son Tarquin, privately, to friends: "It says absolutely nothing and gives everything away."

The book, of course, did well, so well that Olivier the actor, director, impresario and peer, ever anxious to be considered versatile, thought it time to become a best-selling author too. Another volume, *Olivier on Acting*, appeared two years later – less mawkish than the first, thanks to the work of another amanuensis (Gawn Grainger), less "actor-y" backstage preciousness, more red meat, more specifics. The greatest player of our time was doing what he had vowed he never would: passing on the tricks of his trade. But between them the two books still did not add up to a comprehensive, let alone objective, account of one of the most extraordinary lives, in any profession, of this century. That was my case to our mutual publisher and friend, Lord Weidenfeld, who persuaded Olivier that I had a point. And so this book came, over several years, to be written – though I met its subject only at the beginning of my work, strictly socially, at the Garrick Club.

So I should emphasize right away that this is neither an official nor an authorized biography, still less an account which Olivier has in any way sanctioned or approved. Nor would I wish it to be. When writing histories of the living, I have learnt the hard way, too close a personal relationship with one's subject can be a dangerous privilege. Lord Olivier has known of my work and given sundry friends, colleagues and acquaintances his permission to talk to me – perhaps the most valuable assistance any living and obsessively private subject of a biography can give its author.

The fact that so many of his professional colleagues felt in need of Olivier's permission to talk to me says a good deal about his standing. As is the case with royalty – which, in theatrical terms, I suppose he is – friends and acquaintances value their place in the charmed circle too highly to risk banishment. So the list which follows is a selective way of expressing my thanks to some of the many people who have responded generously to my requests for assistance. Of the 200 and more people approached – a frightening number of whom, alas, have died since I began my work – the following are those to whom I have most reason to be grateful for their time, conversation or correspondence, and in many cases hospitality: Joss Ackland, Mark Amory, Harry Andrews, Eileen Atkins, Sir Richard Attenborough, Maxine Audley, Lauren Bacall, John Badham, Felix Barker, Dr Kathleen Barker, Jill Bennett, Elisabeth Bergner, Colin Blakely, Michael Blakemore, Claire Bloom, Robert Bolt, John Boulting, Melvyn Bragg, Kenneth Branagh, Stuart Burge, Desmond Cecil, Richmond Crinkley, Michael Croft, Hume Cronyn, Constance Cummings, Ian Dalrymple, Keir Dullea, Anne Edwards, Laurence Evans, Leslie Evershed-Martin, Douglas Fairbanks Jr, Richard Fleischer, Gwen Ffrangcon-Davies, Brian Forbes, Greer Garson, Sir John Gielgud, Gawn Grainger, Graham Greene, Kenneth Griffith, Julian Hale, Sir Peter Hall, Rex Harrison, Nigel Hawthorne, Charlton Heston, Sir Harold Hobson, Ian Holm, Anthony Hopkins, Jeremy Irons, Jeremy Isaacs, Russell Jackson, Derek Jacobi, Georgina Jumel, Danny Kaye, Arthur Kennedy, J. W. Lambert, Ian McKellen, Lord and Lady Miles, Sarah Miles, Jonathan Miller, Sir John Mills, Terence Morgan, John David Morley, Sheridan Morley, John Mortimer, Zero Mostel, Michael Mullin, David Niven, Peter O'Toole, Richard Pasco, Daniel Petrie, Denis Quilley, Diana Rigg, Tony Rocca, Nicola Russell, Sebastian Shaw, David Susskind, Jessica Tandy, Dorothy Tutin, Kathleen Tynan, Hugo Vickers, Alexander Walker, Irving Wardle, Arnold Wesker, Lord Wilson of Rievaulx, Bridget Winter, Peter Wood.

Direct and indirect quotations from those interviewed and willing to be named are identified in the source notes on pages 470–81. I much regret that some of those approached, including Garry O'Connor and John Cottrell, two theatrical biographers preparing their own future works on Olivier, felt unable to meet for an exchange of views. O'Connor, indeed, has expressed the daunting opinion that "There exists no outstanding and complete biography of Olivier for the simple reason that the total of the man, his life and his work, is still too great to be embraced by any one individual."[2] Any *soi-disant* biographer of Olivier will, however, always be grateful to the pioneering work of Felix Barker (1953) and the subsequent studies by John Cottrell (1975), Thomas Kiernan (1981) and Melvyn Bragg (1984), as well as the two *festschrifts* edited by Logan Gourlay (1973) and Garry O'Connor (1987), and the pictorial surveys of Olivier's career compiled by Margaret Morley (1978), Robert L. Daniels (1980) and Robert Tanitch (1985). There are also several volumes on Vivien Leigh, notably those by Alan Dent (1968), Anne Edwards (1977) and Alexander Walker (1987), as well as a forthcoming one by Hugo Vickers. My specific debts to these and other books consulted, all of which are listed in the extensive bibliography on pages 482–91, are made clear in either the text or the source notes. I hope I may be forgiven any inadvertent omissions.

I must also thank, for their patient and invaluable help, the staff of the Academy of Motion Picture Arts and Sciences in Los Angeles; the libraries of the BBC in London, both television and radio; the British Film Institute; the British Museum; Colindale Newspaper Library; the Shakespeare Research Centre, Stratford-upon-Avon; the Society for Theatre Research, London; the Museum of London; the National Film Archive; Granada Television; Thames Television; the press office of the National Theatre of Great Britain; and International Creative Management Ltd.

In 1984–5 Deborah Holmes spent a year working as my research assistant, between London and both coasts of the United States; her help in conducting numerous interviews and amassing a wealth of documentary source material proved invaluable. I am also grateful to the theatrical omniscience of Martin Tickner, who combed the text for factual errors, to Laurence Evans for double-checking the chronology, and to the Society for Theatre Research for assistance with the bibliography.

Some material from a draft of the book was adapted into a series of three articles in the London *Observer* to mark Olivier's eightieth birthday in May 1987. I am grateful to the editor, Donald Trelford, and deputy editor, Anthony Howard, for their helpful suggestions at the time.

For their friendship, encouragement and patient professional advice, especially when my work took longer than envisaged, I am grateful to John Curtis, Juliet Gardiner, Hilary Rubinstein and George Weidenfeld in London; and Alfred Knopf Jr, Tom Stewart and Georges Borchard in New York. The meticulous editing of Linda Osband (UK) and Elmer Luke (US) improved the manuscript beyond recognition.

Finally, my sons Sam, Joe and Ben will be very pleased to know that it is at last finished. In the closing stages their feelings about the seemingly interminable nature of my work were not unlike those of Peter Ustinov's three-year-old daughter Andrea, born while he was working with Olivier on a somewhat protracted film. Asked what her father did for a living, she replied simply: *"Spartacus."*[3]

CHISWICK, LONDON, 1987

"All I ask, as an audience, is to believe what I see and hear. An actor, above all, must be the great understander, either by intuition, observation or both, and that puts him on the level with a doctor, a priest or a philosopher ....

"There are many dimensions in the art of acting, but *none* of them are good and interesting unless they are invested with the appearance or complete illusion of truth. The difference between truth and the illusion of truth is what you are about to learn. You will not finish learning it until you are dead."

Laurence Olivier, to Old Vic School students, in 1947

LAURENCE OLIVIER

Prologue

Is anybody there? It is a question often asked about all actors, their supreme representative this century being Laurence Olivier. There are those who think not, who argue that within the countless different Oliviers they have known and worked with, praised and criticized, worshipped and reviled, there lies an empty shell, even a hollow man, a vacuum waiting to be filled by circumstance.

There are many more who say: Yes, of course *somebody* is there, but who? No one, least of all the man himself, can tell. "I'm not sure what I'm like," he has said, "and I'm not sure I want to know."[1] Behind that bland, unremarkable exterior – now old and sadly frail, once a furious force of nature – there apparently co-exist too many different Oliviers for the real one to be found.

His long lifetime of astonishing achievement is based entirely on a supreme skill at turning into other people, a bewildering variety of them, while wilfully refusing ever to be himself. Offstage as on, Olivier's life has been one long disappearing trick. The only clue he leaves behind is the smug, Cheshire Cat smile of an inner self which has yet again evaded capture.

One result is a curious personal anonymity. Though one of the most looked-at faces of this century, Olivier has been able throughout his life to walk down a street, travel on public transport, even stroll around his own London club, quite unrecognized. The ghost-writer of his memoirs got off to a bad start by failing to recognize his celebrated employer at their first meeting: "The man who came through the right door at the correct time was too short for Henry v, too urbane for Archie Rice, too ordinary for Richard iii."[2] By then, of course, Anonymous had become an offstage role as honed and polished as any other. But Olivier has always been neither

1

tall nor short, neither fat nor thin, neither handsome nor ugly – which is why he can, with such relish, assume any shape or appearance he pleases.

Here is a man who has climbed all the worldly pinnacles his profession has to offer, then invented a few more to challenge his old age, entirely by donning disguises. A man who could move thousands, even millions to tears with a look, a sound, a syllable, who could raise them out of their own worldly gloom with a gesture or a grin, a swash or a buckle. A man capable of great intuitive understanding of the human soul and of communicating that understanding to vast, unseen audiences, yet seemingly unable to rationalize it, to apply it to his own or others' real lives.

No one has ever truly known him, least of all himself. Friends and fellow professionals talk variously of a lovable, hateable, intimate, distant, charming, ruthless, masculine, feminine, young, old chameleon – a different person each time they meet him. Even his three wives describe a man permanently on a stage, whether in a public place or the privacy of his own home. Asked how she can tell when her husband is acting and when he is not, Joan Plowright, the last Lady Olivier, replies: "Larry? Oh, he's acting all the time."[3]

The man himself offers more sinister, even less illuminating evidence: "I am far from sure when I am acting and when I am not. Or, more frankly, when I am lying and when I am not. For what is good acting but convincing lying?" It is a great deal more, as he well knows. The art of acting is also more than – another of his infuriating, self-deprecating definitions – "the childhood game of pretends". Olivier of all people knows that a truly great actor is more than just a great pretender. Such jokes are merely self-obscuring screens behind which to duck and weave. Describing the new Shakespeare Theatre at Stratford, Ontario, to Olivier, Christopher Plummer told him that it was "impossible to lie" when acting on its arena stage. "My God," said Olivier, "what are we going to do?"[4]

In 1965, though nearly sixty, Olivier was giving one of his most ambitious Shakespearean performances: Othello, at the National Theatre of which he was founder-director. One evening his performance transcended even its normal heights, so much so that his fellow actors, as the audience still cheered, formed a backstage arcade to applaud him all the way to his dressing-room.

The Moor swept past in grim silence, slamming the door behind him. Anxious lest they might somehow have offended the great man, the company delegated Iago – in the shape of Frank Finlay – to make sure he was all right. Through the keyhole Finlay called: "What's the matter, Larry? It was great!" Back came the momentous reply: "I know it was great, dammit, but I don't know how I did it. So how can I be sure of doing it again?"[5]

By his own confession, Olivier has never been an intellectual actor. His own phrase for what he does is "working from the outside in". When preparing a role, he has always tried to hit on some external starting-point – be it a false nose, a wry smile, a specific person or just a pair of old boots – as a prop on which to build the rest of his performance, which then follows instinctively. His performing creed has always been: "The best way of preparing yourself for something is to do it."[6]

Olivier's love of elaborate make-up and other, more radical facial alterations has always amounted to another series of masks behind which to hide. He admitted as much to Michael Caine, when they began the filming of *Sleuth* together. "I'm not like you," Olivier told his awestruck co-star. "You can act as yourself; I can never act as myself. I have to have a pillow up my jumper, a false nose, or a moustache or wig. I can't do it; I cannot come on looking like me and be someone else like you can."[7]

Many years earlier, Olivier said much the same thing to Spencer Tracy, one of the few great contemporaries with whom he never worked: "I admire so much about you, Spence, but nothing more than the fact that you can do it *barefaced*."

"I can't act", replied Tracy, "with stuff all over me."

"But don't you feel as if they're looking at *you*?" Olivier persisted. "Don't you feel naked?"

"Only", replied Tracy, "when I have a lousy line."[8]

In a long lifetime of false noses, Olivier has always been least credible while wearing his own. When disguised merely as himself, as for instance in his memoirs, there was an inconsistency, a mawkishness, a confusion of half-truth, waning memory and wishful thinking which amounted, amid moments of painful candour, to a cry for help. His friend Peter Ustinov, while reading Olivier's own account of himself, kept wishing he would "put on a false nose and be himself again".[9]

If he had known who he was, he might have done. But Olivier has always seemed most himself when transformed into someone else. In his long career as an actor he assumed no fewer than 194 different stage, screen or television identities. Offstage, there seem to have been even more.

Before taking the American writer Terry Southern to meet Olivier, Kenneth Tynan explained: "Now, what you've got to realize about Olivier is that he's like a blank page and he'll be whatever you want him to be. He'll wait for you to give him a cue, and then he'll try to be that sort of person."[10]

All his life he has needed this escape from himself, this assumption of alien features and gestures, to come fully to life. At Ralph Richardson's memorial service in 1983 the nondescript, bowed and shrunken figure who had to be helped to his seat in hushed reverence, in the midst of yet another debilitating illness, turned into a neo-Henry v – voice booming, catch in the throat perfectly timed – when required to read the lesson.

During one rehearsal for Olivier's Othello, a drunk and disruptive West Indian stagehand had to be forcibly ejected from the Old Vic auditorium; angry scenes followed outside the theatre before anyone realized that this suddenly satisfied grin, in fact, belonged to "Sir", alias "the boss": "Just practising, don'tcha know." While being shown around the new Chichester Festival Theatre, a group of tourists grew annoyed with one of their

3

number, who complained long and loud that it was all a conspicuous waste of public money; when they suggested that he take up his complaint with Olivier, then the theatre's artistic director, the great man himself cast off his disguise with all the satisfaction of a Sherlock Holmes or a Houdini.

"Olivier", said Gielgud, "is a great impersonator. I am always myself." A master of disguise, an impersonator – a player, all too literally, more than an actor? Says Sir Peter Hall, Olivier's successor as director of the National Theatre: "Acting is not imitation but revelation of the inner self. This is not what Larry does or sets out to do. He is a performer."[11] Olivier himself has said:

> The more intelligent of my young colleagues, in ceaseless talks pathetically seeking some rationalization of our lives, agree that their choice of *métier* was to satisfy an urgent need to "express themselves".... I have to confess, rather shamefacedly, that I have never been conscious of any need other than to show off.

Olivier's lifelong need to be loved shows as much in these mock-denials of his own hard-wrought gifts as in, for instance, his legendary kindness to young actors awed by his presence. Up to a point: fierce professional jealousy would soon surface whenever anyone else threatened to make a success of a role he considered annexed, private property, let alone to steal a stage, a film, even a public meeting from him.

He has never been a man to cross. When Derek Jacobi, one of his discoveries, revived Olivier's celebrated double-bill of Oedipus and Mr Puff, he received a telegram from the great man saying simply, "You cheeky bugger."[12] It was a more genuine greeting, perhaps, than the letter received by Ian Holm, when playing Richard III at Stratford-upon-Avon, after reviews had mentioned his name in the same breath as his mentor's. "I shan't of course be coming, dear boy," was the gist of it. "But I see they say you do this when I did that, and I see they say you don't do that where I did this." The effect was to put Holm right off his performance for days.[13]

For some fifteen years the name of Olivier was sufficiently celebrated to be marketed by Benson & Hedges Ltd as an elegant cigarette, one of the first with a filter-tip. On the forlorn day in 1973 when the brand was finally withdrawn, he overheard an excited group of young spear-carriers at the National saying, "Look, there goes Nicol Williamson."

"So he does," mused Olivier. "I wonder if he'll be a cigarette one day?"

If proud to be immortalized as a cigarette, Olivier had other, bolder aspirations. "In his complex way," says the playwright John Osborne, "he is a self-conscious man, very aware of his role in the history of the twentieth century and his place in the English hierarchy. Up to a point, I think, his attitude is that he is making history, particularly English history." Olivier once said that his goal was "to fascinate the public in the same way that they might follow a boxer or a cricket player". This is partly due, as Osborne points out, to Olivier's "very secure poetic sense of history.... When he went in to bat he felt he was batting for England."[14]

But Olivier also wanted to be a popular hero, admired as much for colourful behaviour off the field of play as for bravado on it. Like any supreme sportsman, he craved appreciation of his masterful technique as much as the apparent effortlessness concealing it: "My life's ambition has been to lead the public towards an appreciation of acting, so that they will come not merely to see the play, but to see acting for acting's sake." Above all he hoped to be recognized for representing his country in some glorious way, by giving flesh to the thwarted dreams of the common man.

So it is significant that Olivier's one failing as an actor has been an inability to play ordinary people, men with no visible distinguishing marks, with no glittering worldly successes to offset their common human failings. A condition of his constant flight from himself has been the chance to become a mighty figure, albeit a flawed one, by night. If by day he impressed as, for instance, a committee chairman, while he was running the National Theatre, it was because he was turning in an impeccable impersonation of a thousand committee chairmen. If people who met him in middle age thought he looked like a retired bank manager, the effect was calculated. Once the ringing name of Laurence Olivier was attached, the transformation of that bank manager's bland features into those of a third-rate music-hall comedian or a drunken old actor, a Moorish general or a Venetian Jew, seemed all the more remarkable.

The very name was enough to ensure that he would be, at the least, different. What's in a name? The combination of Laurence with a "u" and O-liv-i-er, both meticulously à la française, had an innate ring of its own sufficient to give him the early confidence he needed. In later life Olivier himself proved as much with his wild impersonations of Laurence *Oliver*, an outrageous vulgarian midway between Bottom and Archie Rice, who had haunted his early years in the shape of many a programme misprint. "It was hilarious," said Sir Ralph Richardson. "Had Larry been born Laurence Oliver, he would never have grown up to be the actor he was. An actor, perhaps, but hardly one with his dash and sweep. 'Oliver' sort of stumbles off the tongue, whereas 'Olivier' flows and soars. The name is very much a reflection, even a function, of the man. Thank God his forebears maintained the name Olivier when they came to England, rather than changing it to Oliver."[15]

Once spelt right, celebrated and adorned with titles, the name simply became another handy disguise behind which to hide. If life on the run was the answer, the perpetual search for escape routes would take him in as many directions as possible. Versatility not just as a performer, but as a professional, has always been Olivier's greatest aspiration and his proudest boast. After 121 stage roles, fifty-seven films and fifteen television portrayals, he turned eighty as a hologram, sharing West End billing with a succession of pop stars in the space-age musical *Time*. It is typical of Olivier to be the first actor in the history of his craft to ensure that he can appear on the stage posthumously.

Offstage, meanwhile, he has been director of thirty-eight stage productions, six television plays and six films, the first director to film Shakespeare successfully. He has been actor-manager, impresario, entrepreneur, patron of rising talent. He has been wartime rallying-point for the nation, its unofficial ambassador overseas. He has been founder-director of Britain's National Theatre, realizing a dream as old as Shakespeare. He has been the youngest actor ever to be knighted, the first to be elevated to the peerage, the first to join the Order of Merit.

He has defied death not merely in courting wilful professional dangers, but in defeating a series of major illnesses which would have seen off lesser men. He has been a failure as one husband and a success as another, a failure as one father and a success as the next. In life as in art, Olivier was always sure to learn from his mistakes and overshadow them with a swift return to success. As famous a lover offscreen as on, it was only after several attempts that he finally conquered the role of paterfamilias. To work with, he could be "both a god and a monster", says Sir Peter Hall. "I suspect that God is rather like Olivier."[16]

Onstage, as J. B. Priestley put it, "No English actor, living or dead, can begin to compete with him. A Garrick, a Kean, a Henry Irving, merely enjoyed a small local reputation when compared with his. His career has been fantastic, as if a young actor had been visited by a wild dream."[17]

Offstage, meanwhile, the Olivier story is that of a born actor who has spent his long life auditioning to be himself, the one role he could never quite pin down.

PART ONE

"Some Are Born Great"

"Although his traffic in entertainment can lead one to forget it, the great actor is one of nature's miracles. He brings aspects of music, poetry, literature and sculpture within the capacity of a human being and transmits them to the crowd...."

Laurence Kitchin, *Mid-Century Drama*

"I believe I was born to be an actor."

Laurence Olivier, *Sunday Times*, 3 November 1963

CHAPTER 1

1907–24

On 20 July 1971, while Baron Olivier of Brighton was making his maiden speech in the House of Lords, he heard on his left the unmistakable sound of "an ancient, tremulous, aristocratic whinny: 'An aaaahc-tah?' "

It was only twelve years before Olivier was born that Henry Irving became the first actor-knight in the history of their profession of "rogues and vagabonds". Even Irving's honour had itself had to wait twelve years while Queen Victoria's Prime Minister worried whether to raise the theatre to such a level of respectability might not be "too audacious", and Irving himself worried lest it might "impair" his relations with other actors.[1]

Within a century of Gladstone's doubts Olivier had raised his profession's social status beyond the House of Lords to the Order of Merit, the traditional preserve of those likely to be remembered by posterity. When asked what OM stood for, he would simply say, "Old Man". Thespian respectability had, meanwhile, proved catching – so much so that in the 1950s a hapless traffic cop found himself up against a lofty performance from the theatre's most notoriously reckless driver: "I, my dear man, am Sir Ralph Richardson. Beside me sits Sir Cedric Hardwicke. And behind me Sir Laurence Olivier." In one of their favourite anecdotes, both Olivier and Richardson relished the change of accent for the immortal reply: "I don't care if you've got the whole of King Arthur's ruddy round table in there. You're getting a ticket!"

For years, according to Peter Ustinov, Olivier had been telling people that his one remaining ambition was to be the theatre's first peer.[2] Yet when Prime Minister Harold Wilson first offered him ermine in 1968, he turned it down. A knighthood, by now a commonplace theatrical distinction, he considered gallant and glamorous, a peerage merely "stuck-up". It took two years of Wilsonian intrigue to persuade Olivier to accept this "least selfish" of honours[3] – on the grounds that it would enable him to speak up on behalf of his professional constituency, rather than merely to add more self-gratifying ribbons to his chest.

Yet Olivier has never spoken in the House of Lords since his maiden speech – a performance so characteristically florid that the notices were mixed. He may well have regarded the show as closed by the first-night critics. But this fundamental ambivalence, this wilful contrariness – about both himself and his roles in offstage life – runs deep in his nature, almost as deep as his fiercely proud Englishness. The mock-modesty involved in fighting shy, like Irving, of being raised above his fellow professionals is typical of Olivier's quintessentially Anglo-Saxon ways. When he played Henry v at the Old Vic in 1937, Charles Laughton came backstage to say: "Do you know, Larry, why you're so good in this part? Because you *are* England!" The story remains to this day one of the proudest boasts of this Anglo-Catholic minister's son, for all his suave French name and his pride in his dashing Huguenot ancestry.

There are still a few Oliviers to be found today in the Pyrénées-Atlantiques region of Gascony, but none at all in the mountain village of Nay, just south of Pau, where a Huguenot branch of the family made its home until the beginning of the sixteenth century. All his life Laurence Olivier's father clung to a romantic vision of his French forbears amid the huddled masses fleeing across the Channel after the revocation of the Edict of Nantes. But the Rev. Gerard Olivier fathered a son celebrated enough for these matters to be investigated; and the evidence indicates that they escaped first to Holland, whence the Rev. Jourdain Olivier came to England in 1688 as chaplain to King William of Orange.

Most Gascons today have a few *oliviers* in their gardens; the name simply means "olive tree", though it was originally coined to describe one who plants, tends, picks or sells olives. With Jourdain, however, there began generations of Olivier family service to the church rarely interrupted before the beginning of this century and Laurence's defection to the stage. He was the first Olivier, according to his cousin William, the family historian, to enter the theatrical profession in 400 years of traceable Olivier history.[4]

But the links between the church and the stage have always been strong. Distinguished theatrical names from Vanbrugh to Thorndike also came from clerical stock. Laurence Olivier's father, Gerard, was the youngest of the ten children of the Rev. Henry Arnold Olivier, rector of Poulshot in Wiltshire. The Oliviers were immensely proud of their long-standing service to the church, tracing it from Jourdain, William of Orange's chaplain, to his son Jerome, minister of the French Chapel at the Savoy in 1721. There was a break of only one generation – Jerome's son Daniel became a prominent diamond merchant in the City of London – before the next Daniel Olivier became rector of Clifton, Bedfordshire. He married a clergyman's daughter and bred another, but his second son turned out to be a military man; a footnote in British history remembers the High Sheriff of Wiltshire, Colonel Henry Stephen Olivier, for raising a troop of mounted volunteers known as "Olivier's Horse", to help put down the Rick Riots and agrarian revolts in southern England which preceded the Great Reform Bill of 1832. The Colonel bred three clergyman sons, the eldest of whom was Laurence's grandfather.

The Rev. Henry's children made an interesting assortment, a tribute to the enlightened liberal upbringing he seems to have given them. Laurence's Uncle Henry was an army colonel, his Uncle Herbert a portrait painter of modest renown. But the most eminent was his Uncle Sydney, one of the founders of the Fabian Society, friend of George Bernard Shaw and the Webbs, who went on to become Governor of Jamaica, Secretary for India in Ramsay MacDonald's Government and the first Labour peer. In his own maiden speech in the House of Lords some fifty years later, the second Baron Olivier referred to his uncle as "incomparably more deserving, virtuous, illustrious, and in service to his country richer than I can ever hope to be".[5]

Even Gerard Kerr Olivier, who was eventually to become the latest Olivier to devote his life to the church, started in a somewhat more Bohemian vein. While a Winchester schoolboy of sixteen, summering with his parents in Italy, he was told by his Italian singing coach, a celebrated tenor named Lamberti, that his voice was good enough to train for the opera. When he came home with this exciting news, his mother coldly handed him one lira, with the rider that it was all the money he would ever get if he entered that "monstrous" profession.

To the apparent relief of his parents, Gerard instead went up to Merton College, Oxford, to prepare for holy orders. But again the Bohemian streak seems to have prevailed. By his second year he had joined the university dramatic society, run up embarrassing debts and decided to abandon the church. On the surface a cold and remote parent, Gerard never confided in his son why he was eventually sent down. There was a family legend that it had something to do with his being caught driving a coach-and-four with some abandon down Oxford High Street. But Laurence always remained sceptical about this theory, and later reached the private conclusion that Gerard was withdrawn because his own father was no longer prepared, once he had turned his back on the church, to pay off his debts.

Gerard was sent instead to Durham University, where he won an undistinguished degree (a Fourth in Classics) and began a handy career as a cricketer, which was to lead to a brief spell playing at county level for Hampshire. Still sceptical about his faith, he turned to the usual resort of those with middling degrees, county cricket caps and no great motivation to do anything else: schoolmastering. It was during his four years as an assistant master at Boxgrove School, a preparatory school in Guildford, Surrey, that he met and fell in love with the headmaster's sister-in-law, Agnes Crookenden, a pretty and vivacious brown-eyed girl who in 1900 became his wife. Agnes Crookenden's sister, the headmaster's wife, believed that there was more to the marriage than met the eye: "Gerard's interest in my sister was mixed half of masculine attraction and half of concern for his career. Gerard had settled down to being an educator and had great ambitions for himself. He was a slight but commanding chap, not terribly outgoing in private but very authoritative in a classroom of young boys." Gerard's interest in Agnes was certainly sincere, but her sister was sure that it did not fail to occur to him, when choosing his wife, that a girl from a family of educators could be a great asset:

> Originally, I think, he hoped to succeed my husband at Boxgrove. But when that failed to come to pass, because of Gerard's young age and certain youthful indiscretions he had not yet lived down, he rather abruptly decided to establish his own school. He and Agnes were married. Then, with some financial help from the family, the two of them leased a small building in Dorking and opened a school of their own. Of Gerard's really, since it was his way of fulfilling his ambition to become a headmaster as soon as he could.[6]

One of the reasons Agnes accepted Gerard's proposal, and was prepared to endure a four-year engagement while they saved enough money to open their own school, was that she had vowed never to marry a clergyman. She was to enjoy three years of marriage, and the birth of her first two children, before discovering that she had done so by mistake. The Oliviers embarked on their married life at Tower House, Dorking, which they bought with their meagre savings and filled with just enough pupils to cover household expenses. Their eldest child, Sybille, was born there, as was their elder son, Gerard Dacres (always called Richard or "Dickie"), before 1903 saw Gerard Olivier suddenly heed the call he had spent his youth and early manhood shunning. To Agnes's dismay Tower House was sold and, after a brief spell as an assistant at the nearby Church of St John the Evangelist, Holmwood, her husband took up a humble curateship at St Martin's, the parish church of Dorking.

The servants were dismissed and much of the furniture sold, as the Oliviers moved into the more modest surroundings of 26 Wathen Road, just off the busy Dorking High Street. Next door lived the local chimney sweep. The semi-detached, three-bedroom Victorian house still stands today, with no blue plaque to indicate that this century's most distinguished actor was born there in the summer of 1907.

It was the year Rasputin began to gain influence at the court of Czar Nicholas II, while Lenin left Russia to found his newspaper, *The Proletarian*. In Paris Picasso painted *Les Demoiselles d'Avignon* and the Cubists held their first exhibition. It was the year Grieg died and Mahler wrote his eighth symphony. The year 1907 was a year of only modest interest to historians, in Britain as around the world. Rudyard Kipling won the Nobel Prize for Literature, while on 21 February, in York, Mrs Constance Auden gave birth to a son called Wystan. On 18 December, Mrs Emma Harris was also to give birth to a son, Christopher, who on becoming a playwright would adopt his mother's maiden name of Fry.

And on 22 May, at 26 Wathen Road, thirty-six-year-old Mrs Agnes Olivier presented the local curate with his second son. The child was named Laurence after his earliest traceable ancestor, Laurent, and given his father's middle name of Kerr. Father Gerard, intensely proud of the family's Huguenot ancestry, insisted that all Olivier names be spelt *à la française* (though in time Laurence was to be saddled with the family nickname of "Kim").

In his memoirs, the new arrival describes the circumstances of his birth with such vividness that he might have been taking notes. His father, it seems, was cooking sausages at the time – which happened to be 5 a.m. – when the family physician, Dr Rawlings, walked in with the unwashed, new-born infant. The Rev. Gerard Olivier held his new son "with a sense of slight disgust". It is the beginning of an unequivocally harsh portrait of his father, a man to whom "saving was a craving", who even made his sons share his bathwater, in stark contrast to the loving care Olivier lavishes on "my heaven, my hope, my entire world, my own worshipped Mummy", who was to die when he was only twelve. According to his sister, Agnes on her death-bed made her reverend husband promise to be "as kind as he could" to Laurence, her "baby", who "became aware of some signs of this effort as time crawled by".

"Everything about me irritated him," writes Olivier of his father, for whose understanding he would eventually have cause to be considerably grateful. But the first few years of his life were unsettled and nomadic. Olivier would never remember the house in which he was born; he was barely two when the family was already on the move, first to a somewhat smarter Dorking residence called East Dene, with a vista of open countryside. Only a year later, however, its comforts were exchanged for the slums of London's Notting Hill, where Gerard's missionary zeal had led him to accept a less comfortable appointment as a curate attached to St James's Church, working out of a tin-roofed mission hut. It was becoming a habit with the Rev. Olivier to put his own professional inclinations before the private wishes and comforts of his wife and family. Olivier's brother, Dickie, said in later years:

> My father was a man who was never satisfied with the status quo. As he gained confidence in his powers as a clerical orator, he envisaged greater and greater evangelical challenges for himself. He was not interested in aspiring to a high office within the church. Rather, he was obsessed with delivering the church's message to those most likely to be indifferent to it. Which is why, much to the consternation of my mother, he leapt at the chance to transfer to Notting Hill.[7]

Laurence was just three, and might have looked forward to a more comfortable middle-class upbringing, had his father not severed his ties with Dorking. The Oliviers had become accepted and popular in this epitome of English bourgeois towns, where "the Rev." had made his mark at the local cricket club.[8] The records show that he topped the batting averages in 1902, scoring a century against local rivals Reigate, and a doughty forty against a visiting MCC side, helping his team to hold them to an honourable draw. Agnes Olivier had put down solid enough roots, including a popular role in the local community, to have overcome her initial objections to her husband's new calling. The older children were content at the local school, to which Laurence would have followed them, at least at first. But it was not to be.

Nor was his father's life in Notting Hill, ironically enough, to be as professionally happy as it had been in Dorking. With the characteristic zeal of the convert, Gerard practised an enthusiastically "high" version of the Anglican ritual, burning a good deal of incense and preaching vivid, histrionic sermons. He also preferred to be addressed as "Father" and toured his parish in the cassock and black hat of a Catholic priest. All this did not go down too well with the parish fathers of Notting Hill, who had no reason to prize him for his cricketing talents. Gerard's vicar took a particularly dim view of his unorthodoxy and finally gave the recalcitrant curate an opportunity – which he defiantly shunned – to resign. The Olivier family had spent only one year in their new home, 86 Elgin Crescent, from whose bedroom windows Laurence could just see the bright lights of the White City exhibition, before Gerard arrived home one evening to report that he had been sacked.

It was not this bleak news, but a needle pricking her finger, which prompted Agnes Olivier to swear in front of young Laurence. The moment is remembered in the family archives for moving the three-year-old boy to complete his first sentence: "Why did you say damn for, Mummy?" There followed an itinerant summer, as the turbulent priest trailed his family behind him from one holiday position to another in assorted British seaside towns. It was Christmas before he found another living which suited him – back in London, to the children's dismay, this time in Pimlico, as first assistant priest at the Church of St Saviour's. For the next six years, the family home was to be 22 Lupus Street, SW1.

Laurence was just five. For the next few years, he tells us, his mother constantly had to spank him for lying, an "inveterate and seemingly irresistible sin", which he now thinks of as "some initial practice in what was to become my trade". The bug, clearly, had already bitten him. For it was here in Lupus Street that he first dragged a huge wooden chest up the many stairs to his top-floor bedroom and ranged it across the window, whose curtains he drew around it to create a makeshift stage. At first he played at clergyman, solemnly mimicking his father's Sunday rituals in front of a toy altar, drawing his eiderdown about him as vestments; on the bedroom door appeared a grandiose notice proclaiming "St Laurence's Shrine". Soon, however, he was giving the family full-scale performances of moments from plays he had seen at his brother's choir school; Dickie would join him in scenes from *Box and Cox* and in the Hubert and Arthur scene from Shakespeare's *King John*. For footlights he would use candles set in cigarette tins, lovingly made for him by his father, who – to everyone's surprise – seemed thoroughly to approve of the entire proceedings.

Gerard Olivier could see that his son's sense of theatre derived from his own ecclesiastical style. In time, his father hoped, Laurence might follow him into the church. Olivier later recalled:

> My father was an effective preacher, and as a boy, sitting watching him and others in the pulpit, I was fascinated by the way a sermon was delivered. Those preachers knew when to drop the voice, when to bellow about the perils of hellfire, when to slip in a gag, when suddenly to wax sentimental, when to turn solemn, when to pronounce the blessing. The quick changes in mood and manner absorbed me, and I have never forgotten them.[9]

By the age of seven, according to a childhood memoir written by his sister Sybille, Laurence was precocious enough to render long scenes from Shakespeare, with or without his brother's assistance, with or without an audience. If the family heard the shrill piping sounds from the top floor, they knew their youngest member was rehearsing for his next production.

Olivier grew desperate for his father's approval. Said his sister:

> He tended always to be quiet and withdrawn when Father was in the house, and then burst out into his other much more ebullient self when he was gone, by way of compensation. Of course, Mother and Father themselves

15

were a right opposite pair, and this may have had something to do with Larry's being first one way, then the other. Despite his attachment to Mother, he was in awe of Father. He wanted so for Father to like him. So he would often act like Father, whether intentionally or unconsciously – I suppose in the hope that he would gain Father's approval, or at least soften his disapproval.[10]

But Olivier's mother was determined not to have another clergyman in the family. "In order to deflect him, Mother encouraged Larry to turn his mock-sermonizing into recitations of monologues from well-known plays," said Sybille.[11] Olivier himself says he "played shamelessly" to his mother.

> She would mouth the words with me, and whenever I stumbled she would urge me on, applauding deliriously when I got it right and suffocating me with hugs at the end. Soon she started to invite other people in to watch me perform – neighbourhood ladies, relatives and the like. And it was always the same at the end – much applause, most of it polite, I'm sure, and a great deal of hugging and "Isn't-he-darling" sort of praise. I suppose you could say that I decided at a very early age that acting was for me.[12]

It was 1914 and, as the world went to war, it was time for Laurence to go to his first proper school. The year before, he had spent a few disastrous weeks as a boarder at a small prep school in Blackheath, where he wept so copiously that his soft-hearted mother had brought him back home. Next he had attended another prep school nearer his home, in Cliveden Place, near Sloane Square, called Mr Gladstone's School. "I believe my mother must have picked this place because it was only a penny bus fare from Pimlico, where we lived," he recalled, "and I think she must have had a horrid shock when she got the first term's bill, because I was whipped out of the place pretty smartly and sent somewhere else."

It was during his short career at Mr Gladstone's that the young Olivier enjoyed a seminal, almost mystical, experience he was to recall sixty-five years later in a *festschrift* marking the twenty-fifth anniversary of the English Stage Company at the Royal Court Theatre, Sloane Square, where he himself was to enjoy one of his finest hours in 1957 as Archie Rice in John Osborne's *The Entertainer*:

> I was coming out of Sloane Square tube station one day and I glanced up a passage beside it that I had never taken much notice of before. To my astonishment I saw, gathered around what I later knew to be a stage door, a group of men and women with paint on their faces. But what truly amazed me was the extraordinary clothes they were wearing. I stared and stared at them, dumb-founded. I simply could not believe my eyes, that people could get themselves up in such a fashion. I rushed into school and told a couple of boys, "There are some of the weirdest people you ever saw in your life up

that passage." They laughed uproariously at me. "Why, you stupid fool, that's a theatre," one said. "They must have been just actors – they wear those sort of things – just out for a breath of fresh air. It's hellish hot in those places, I believe."[13]

From Mr Gladstone's School, Laurence went on to a local day school in Graham Terrace, the Francis Holland Church of England School for Girls, which had one junior day class for boys. It was to be the next in a trail of prep schools attended by the boy, largely because his mother had set her heart on sending him to the choir school of All Saints in Margaret Street, near Oxford Circus, where his brother Dickie was already a pupil. But Laurence kept failing the voice exams. Each new prep school would be regarded as a strictly temporary measure until he finally won his place at All Saints, to which end Agnes herself continued coaching her son at the piano. In the meantime, he devised various ingenious methods of playing truant from Francis Holland, including imaginary "lunches" with a Miss Finlayson on nearby Ecclestone Bridge. When the headmistress, Miss Sheppard, finally asked his mother why it was necessary for young Laurence to slip off so often to see this mysterious figure, Agnes again felt obliged to administer the slipper.

At the age of nine, Olivier finally won the place his mother so coveted for him among the fourteen-strong choir of All Saints. For Agnes Olivier, said her older son Richard, it was a double-edged moment. Boarding-school was to prove the making of young Laurence, but only by liberating him from his mother's apron-strings. "For the first time he showed a need to break the bonds, if only tentatively, of Mother's attachment to him. To say that he was ready to emerge full speed ahead from the emotional cocoon she had wrapped him in would be to overstate it, of course. But he did begin to show signs – not of resentment, but of a young bird ready to test its wings." Already, when Dickie came home for the school holidays, his younger brother would "beat me about the ears with incessant questioning about what it was like. Mother would gaze upon us sadly, almost as if she knew she was losing her precious Larry. But she had too much sense to make a fuss about it. She was still number one in his eyes. But he had rather quickly come to realize that there was another world, a vastly more varied world beyond the one he knew, which was centred on Mother."[14]

The young Olivier who arrived at All Saints was a moody, rather solitary figure, who took little trouble to make friends. He quickly became unpopular and was cruelly mocked for his ineptitude on the sports field. Said Laurence Naismith, an All Saints contemporary who also went on to become an actor:

17

It was strange, because Larry was naturally athletic, had good co-ordination, that sort of thing. But when it came to games, he was as awkward as a cow trying to balance on a wire. I suppose this was because he had never been allowed to play sports before. By the time he started playing at All Saints, the other boys were way ahead of him in basic physical skills and they thoroughly rejected him, laughed him off the fields or only picked him to play if they were desperate for one last body to make up a side. Naturally he did not take to this treatment very well. In reaction he became quite a nasty young man, which only made him further disliked.[15]

Young Laurence became determined to find another school activity in which to make his mark.

A very high Anglican church, All Saints encouraged flamboyancy among its clergy; Olivier remembers the sermons as "very dramatic, very effective ... a bit theatrical". Irving had recently given the theatrical profession such a "canopy of respectfulness" that staff and pupils alike were very proud of the school's close links to the stage. Sunday services had all the ritual of a theatrical performance and all the props: "six blazoned candlesticks, a crucifix, the Host with a lamp in front of it". Laurence began as a "boat boy", carrying an incense-filled boat down the aisle in procession; one of the few unrealized ambitions of his life was to become the thurifer, at the head of this procession, "the man who swung the incense and made extraordinary juggling cavortions – depending on the height of the theatricality and his nature, he could make the censer do really wonderful things if he chose". When Olivier revisited All Saints at the age of seventy-five, for a television retrospective, the camera caught him weeping; and one of his few failings as an actor has been a lifelong inability to fake tears.

Once at All Saints, said Dickie, Laurence

certainly missed Mother at the beginning, and there were moments when he wished he could flee the school. But in all he adjusted well, probably more easily because I was there, a familiar face. It was as though he instinctively recognized that the time had come to stop being the protected little brat and make something of himself in the world of his peers. I dare say the adjustment was much more painful and difficult for Mother. She was left alone at home with Father, while the school kept Larry much too busy to dwell overlong on thoughts of home.[16]

The regime at All Saints was rigorous: long choir practices took up as much time as normal school lessons, meaning that all the children had to be boarders and the holidays were shorter than those of most other schools. To compensate, various "treats" were arranged during term-time, among them an annual Christmas visit to the Theatre Royal, Drury Lane, set up by the Duke of Newcastle, a churchwarden of All Saints and patron of the school. The Duke would take a block of seats in the dress circle so that the boys' parents and friends could join them at a pantomime.

And so it was by courtesy of this munificent aristocrat, at Christmas 1916, that nine-year-old Laurence Olivier made his first visit to the theatre. Dressed in Eton jacket with white tie and waistcoat, he and his schoolmates saw two popular comedians of the day, Stanley Lupino and Will Evans, in *Babes in the Wood*. Lupino, to the boys' delight, even made impromptu cracks about the choir boys up in the gallery. After the performance, the Duke took them all backstage to meet the cast, and the young Olivier had his first sniff of a theatrical dressing-room.

Among the five assistant priests on the staff of All Saints was a talented amateur actor called Father Geoffrey Heald, who, with the support of the vicar, H.F.B. Mackay, ensured that the school's strong theatrical tradition was maintained. Early in Laurence's days there, Heald cast him as a policeman in what was only a light-hearted burlesque, but he noted with approval that the boy, who had made himself a papier mâché helmet for the occasion, nevertheless took the whole business very seriously. The following year, mounting a Christmas term production of *Julius Caesar*, Heald at first gave Olivier the part of First Citizen.[17] But he so shone in rehearsals that, although he was the smallest boy in the cast, Heald soon promoted him to Brutus. The original Brutus, an older boy named Ralph Forbes who went on to become something of a film star, was switched to Cassius; he and Laurence would together have to murder Olivier Senior, brother Dickie, who was cast as Caesar.

Heald, according to Sybil Thorndike, was a bold and innovative director, using the aisles as well as the full width of the stage, sowing in young Laurence an urge to look beyond convention and tradition. In later years Heald was to say that he had never come across a child who so quickly and naturally mastered the arts of diction and deportment; Olivier, in turn, was to remember Heald as "extremely lively, highly artistic". The ten-year-old boy clearly gave a remarkably mature performance. Among the first-night audience, equally remarkably for a schoolboy production, was the great actress Ellen Terry, then seventy, accompanied by Lady (Herbert Beerbohm) Tree and the young Sybil Thorndike, already a family friend of the Oliviers through her own clergyman father.

Ellen Terry apparently enjoyed herself so much that she asked to come again on the second night, after which she was introduced to the cast onstage. Young Laurence – who had earlier confessed, amid giggles, that he had never heard of the great lady – was given the privilege of escorting her down from the stage. He remembers her saying to him: "Oh, don't you love it? Don't you just *love* the words?" That night Ellen Terry wrote

in her diary: "The small boy who played Brutus is already a great actor."
Sybil Thorndike recalled: "He had been on the stage for only five minutes
when we turned to each other and said, 'But this is an actor – absolutely
an actor. Born to it.'"

The extraordinary legend of Olivier's star-studded stage debut does not
stop there. Bishop Temple, then Rector of St James's, Piccadilly, later to
follow his father as Archbishop of Canterbury, declared himself to have
been so moved that he wept. When the production was revived some nine
months later, it was graced by the presence of another of the theatrical
grandees of the day, Sir Johnston Forbes-Robertson. Legend has it that
Forbes-Robertson took Laurence's father aside and told him: "My dear
man, your son *is* Brutus." Olivier, pointing out that Sir Johnston would
anyway have been "courtesy itself" on seeing his father's dog-collar,
modestly says he has never believed this story. But in a letter to Heald,
Forbes-Robertson did observe that "Brutus delivered his oration to the
citizens with a pathetic air of fatalism which was poignantly suggestive –
remarkable in one so young."

Recalling that "quite a fuss" was made at All Saints over his performance
as Brutus, Olivier later denied that it was "some sort of epiphany, wherein
I discovered my true calling as an actor". He had worked hard at it, he
said,

> because I wanted so badly to be good and not seem an amateur. . . . I felt I
> was in a constant no-holds-barred competition with the other boys, and
> since I was such a bloody dud at sports and other things, I felt that if I
> mucked up there I would for ever be a total outcast. So, yes, I did set out
> to distinguish myself, or at least save myself from embarrassment. And I
> suspect that I used a lot of tricks I had learned about realism from the play-
> acting I had done with my mother and sister at home.

But he had been brought up to believe that acting was not a calling to
which a boy of his circumstances should aspire.

> Which is not to say that the experience wasn't an epiphany of another
> sort. . . . It gave me a much more secure perception of myself than I had ever
> had before in a personal sense. Call it ego, self-esteem, self-confidence –
> whatever you wish. Having been made to feel rather worthless for so many
> years, it was a tremendous shot in the arm.[18]

The following Christmas saw Larry – as people were already beginning
to call him – as Maria in scenes from *Twelfth Night*, which again drew
praise, though he himself remembered it sixty-five years later as "extremely
forced". His family, meanwhile, was on the move again, this time to
Letchworth in Hertfordshire, where his father had taken up a more
comfortable living at the Church of St Michael's and All Saints, which

came complete with a handsome Queen Anne house. Any pleasure the children may have taken in a more comfortable home, despite the chore of having to make new friends yet again, was abruptly shattered in March 1920, when Agnes Olivier died, quite suddenly and unexpectedly, of a brain tumour. She was only forty-eight.

Laurence had last seen her two weeks before, lying in bed, paralysed down one side. He had not been told of the seriousness of her condition and recalls no suggestion that he might never see his mother again; so he just kissed her as he would at the end of any normal weekend and returned to All Saints. "I often think, and say, that perhaps I've never got over it," he told Kenneth Tynan in a BBC television interview nearly half a century later:

> Anyway, my father had to take over, not knowing me very well. I think to him I was rather an unnecessary child. He could look at my sister eating a lot of porridge, and my brother eating a lot of porridge, with comparative equanimity, but when I was eating a lot of porridge it annoyed him intensely. My sister says I simply got on his nerves, poor man. I don't blame him at all because I was probably very fat and absolutely brainless. However, when my mother died he had to take care of me: my brother was at school, and my sister was, I think, already half way out into the world.[19]

Their mother's death cast a long and heavy shadow over the young lives of her three children, especially Laurence, who had been her "baby", who had depended on her and who was still wary of his more distant, dour and somewhat eccentric father.

Agnes Olivier, a handsome woman with a touch of the gipsy about her looks, was remembered by those who knew her as a smiling and generous friend, whose laughter filled the Olivier home with a charm its pater-familias sometimes lacked. Gerard moved to a smaller home very quickly, complaining again of money problems, though the children noticed that he could now afford a cook and that a little alcoholic refreshment made its first appearance around the house. But the new home lacked the grace and *joie de vivre* they missed in their mother. In her last illness, as throughout her life, Agnes had displayed patience, courage and humour. These last two, if not always the first, were qualities she had already bequeathed to her youngest child – as well as a dash of those gipsy looks.

Many years later, Olivier told Kenneth Tynan of the "utter desolation" he had felt after his mother's death: "He had entertained thoughts of going down to Chelsea Bridge, jumping off and drowning himself in the Thames. He said that ever since then, whenever he crossed Chelsea Bridge, or passed by it, he always thought of his mother and his suicidal feelings." But the sudden loss of his mother's affection, and his father's failure to replace it,

21

would combine to forge the deep ambivalence in Olivier's character which would prove his making as an actor. After long discussion with Olivier, Tynan came to the conclusion that

> had it not been for his father's neglect, he would never have discovered the drive in himself to succeed in the theatre as he did. It was not just external drive he was talking about – an "I'll-show-him" motivation. What he really meant was that in acting he discovered a way in which he could delve into and express emotions that he never dared to, never knew how to do, in real life.[20]

Because of the death of his mother, said Tynan, Olivier all his life nursed "a pipeline to a childhood pain we can only guess at".[21] Tynan's own guess, as Olivier's colleague, friend and most eloquent interpreter, was characteristically perceptive:

> From everything I've learned of Larry, from himself and others, he is the product of a fortuitous, almost ideal melding of two distinct, powerful genetic inheritances. The one is what I would call his exterior gifts: his voice, his physical aspect, his athleticism, his daring, his self-absorption and his single-minded devotion to his work, all of which make for that compelling presence he has as an actor. These he clearly gets from his father. Yet had he possessed these alone, he would merely have been a competent actor. What served to ignite and transform all those traits into something unique were his interior gifts, which are what I believe he got from his mother. By these I mean his perception, his instinctive intelligence, his intuition for the absolutely right gesture and movement, his ability to plumb character, his powers of observation and mimicry, his clearly feminine sensitivity and emotional expanse. Evidently Larry's mother was a woman in whom all these traits powerfully reposed. I say "reposed" because, as a woman raised in Victorian times and married to a man of Larry's father's rather tyrannical temperament, she never had a chance to really exercise her gifts. In the end, the only way she expressed them was by passing them on to her son.[22]

It may also be due to his mother's posthumous influence that Olivier has always displayed a decidedly feminine streak, both in his character and in his acting. "I may be rather feminine, but I'm not effeminate," he once said – with rare self-perception – to the critic Michael Billington, who was "very struck by his slightly raffish coyness". The sheer sexuality of Olivier's stage presence was to become one of the hallmarks of his career; but throughout his life, offstage as on, that sexuality has been capable of a marked ambiguity. Olivier's legendary charm derives from carefully cultivated, very feminine techniques of persuasion and allure; offstage, he is capable of all the male equivalents of eyelash-fluttering winsomeness. Onstage, as Billington put it in an excellent essay on this theme, "he can be masculine or feminine but never neuter".[23] He was to bring female guile, vulnerability and mischievousness to all the most masculine of Shakespeare's epic heroes; his eyes, always his most powerful physical asset, were to bring similar ambiguity to several rugged rogues of the giant screen. Both as a man and as an actor, Olivier's sensibility has always been fed by the pipeline of pain he maintained to his childhood, for ever rooted in this appalling moment. In his own view, both romantic and self-dramatizing, Olivier has never really recovered from the shock of losing his mother when he needed her most.

The Olivier who now returned to All Saints was a more solitary figure than ever. Laurence Naismith remembered that

> Larry was capable of alternating bouts of almost hysterical good cheer and despondence, mixed further with frequent expressions of rude behaviour. He went through a period when he was an inveterate show-off. At times he was an immature clod who conducted himself in the most boorish way. At other times he would disport himself in an elegant manner that was well beyond his years. He kept us all off balance in our attitude towards him. As I remember it, he had no close friends throughout his stay. No one could trust him to be constant. He would be your great pal one day, and then turn around and rather compulsively try to humiliate you the next.

After the young Olivier's success in *Julius Caesar*, said Naismith, "one got the feeling that Larry was on stage all the time, that his whole life in school was devoted to testing out roles. It was impossible to tell the real Larry Olivier from some character he was temporarily playing."[24] Richard Olivier also sensed the actor in the making:

> You must remember that in many ways my brother was a highly emotional boy by nature, which he got from our mother, and that his emotions were constantly stifled at home by Father. Once in school and away from Father, he was better able to let his emotions run free. The fact that he went overboard at times was simply akin to a wild animal being suddenly let out of a cage.... Larry *was* incorrigible for a while, but soon he got control of himself and learned to, as it were, "edit" his behaviour.[25]

At All Saints the following year Laurence put in, according to contemporary accounts, his most precocious stage performance yet – as Katharina in *The Taming of the Shrew*, to Geoffrey Heald himself as Petruchio. Ellen Terry was again among the theatrical notables in the audience; this time she noted that she had "never seen Kate played better by a woman, except Ada Rehan". It is the only one of those schoolboy performances of which we ourselves can still get a taste today, from the remarkable photograph which survives of a determined, haughty Katharina, whose dark, smouldering, thirteen-year-old eyes are already issuing a formidable challenge to the camera.

The young actor Denys Blakelock, later to become one of Olivier's closest friends, also found himself in the All Saints audience that night. Larry, he wrote, "was not good-looking as a boy; he had a rather dark, glowering look, which was admirably suited to the Shrew. As to his acting ... I can only say that the impression he made on that very professional audience was something quite exceptional."[26] Sybil Thorndike's verdict was:

> I saw Larry in all those productions at All Saints and was impressed most of all by his wonderful Katharina. His Shrew was really wonderful, the best Katharina I ever saw.... You know, some people are born with technical ability. And Larry was. He didn't have to work hard enough at technical things because he knew it all from the start. Johnny Gielgud had to work much harder. He wasn't technically equipped as Larry was. Larry was from a little boy.

The following year, after Laurence had moved on to his public school, St Edward's, Oxford, this production was selected to take part in a schools' festival on the sacred stage of the Shakespeare Memorial Theatre, Stratford-upon-Avon. Gerard had chosen St Edward's because of its connections with the church and the preponderance of old boys who went into the ministry. But Laurence's steps were already headed in a different direction fast assuming inevitability.

It was at the end of his second term, just before his fifteenth birthday, that he played Katharina in Stratford during the annual week of celebrations for Shakespeare's birthday. He led the procession to the parish church for the traditional birthday service and that afternoon met the American actor James Hackett, who called a halt to his *Othello* rehearsal to allow the schoolboys their own rehearsal time onstage. Heald observed the excited reverence with which young Olivier took his first steps on a famous professional stage; but he was also pleased to note that when the big moment came, the excitement calmed into a professional self-discipline, which Heald attributed to the experience of church service and ritual instilled by All Saints. Similarly, young men who have sung all the great hymns and masses have a head start in matters of diction and enunciation, so that the young actors had no difficulty coping with the acoustics of that mighty auditorium. (This was the Shakespeare Theatre which famously burnt down the following year, 1923, so that in later years Olivier was unique among his profession in having trod its hallowed boards.)

There were no names in the programme, but the press cuttings next morning were unanimous. *The Times* critic expressed "wonder at lines so well and clearly spoken", adding that one boy's performance as Katharina had "a fire of its own.... You felt that if an apple were thrown to this Katharina she would instinctively try to catch it in her lap, and if apples give her pleasure we hope with all gratitude that someone will make the experiment." The *Daily Telegraph*, meanwhile, got quite carried away. "The boy who took the part of Kate made a fine, bold, black-eyed hussy badly in need of taming. I cannot remember seeing any actress in the part who looked it better." The critic in question, W. A. Darlington, later recalled in his memoirs that he had gone to the theatre that afternoon only "on impulse, because I was feeling bored and livery".[27]

Olivier returned to St Edward's with reluctance. He was not at all happy there. It was not just because he had really wanted to go to Rugby – or, like his brother, to Radley. His was not the kind of temperament which easily wins the pack popularity required to be content at these merciless English institutions, where an individualist tends to be marked out as a pariah. So he knew better than to boast about spending the school holidays mincing about onstage dressed as a girl, however celebrated the theatre. Even those heady press cuttings had to stay firmly in his pocket, whence he would take them out to savour in the rare corners of solitude afforded by public school life.

Inevitably for an All Saints boy Olivier had been recruited for the school choir as soon as he arrived and, before long, he was designated soloist. This was not the best way of becoming a popular figure, as he desperately wanted: "I confess that the wish for this treacherous glory – popularity – had and has been obsessive all my life." Instead, he tells us, he was soon known as "that sidey little shit Olivier", and was a popular target for the attentions of both adolescent homosexuals and sadistic prefects. Even his attempts to live up to his father's cricketing prowess went sadly wrong when L. K. Olivier, last in for his house with eight runs needed to win, was out for three – clean bowled by a contemporary named Douglas Bader, later to pass into legend as the legless air ace of the Second World War.

In the last of his three years at St Edward's, Olivier was horrified to find himself cast as Puck in the Christmas production of *A Midsummer Night's Dream*. "*Puck*, to that audience?" But it was here, at the age of sixteen, that he discovered something within himself, "a small, sharp poniard of steel", to prove useful throughout his career as it prompted a still, small internal voice: "So that's *it*, is it? *This* dismally wretched part, this *utterly hopeless, so-called* opportunity. Okay. *Right*. In that case – I don't know yet how, but I'll knock their bloody eyes out with it *somehow*." Unabashedly he danced up and down the aisles, back and forth through the audience, making surprise entrances, his face lit by two torch-lamps strapped to a harness around his chest. It proved another early triumph; the review in the school magazine thought Puck "far the most notable" member of the cast; a little too robust, perhaps, but "he seemed to have more 'go' in him than the others". From that week on Olivier suddenly found himself what he had always wanted to be: popular. Two more lessons were thus learnt – one about the nature of "stardom", and the other that "Shakespeare could look after himself and look after, too, the actor who trusts him."

A few days later it was the end of term and another trauma was in prospect: his elder brother Dickie was departing for four years in India as a rubber planter. The younger Olivier was distraught; first no mother, now no brother. That unhappy day in January 1924, after seeing Dickie off at Fenchurch Street, Laurence spent in miserable silence. In the bath that evening, second into the water now instead of third, he asked his father how soon he might be allowed to follow Dickie out East. Previous thoughts about his future, when he could steer Gerard away from the church, had centred around the Merchant Navy and forestry. Now rubber planting was the height of his ambitions; all he wanted to do was join Dickie, whom he considered the mainstay of his life, as soon as possible.

"Don't be such a fool," was the Rev. Gerard Olivier's quite unexpected reply. "You're not going to India, you're going on the stage."

CHAPTER 2

1924–8

The acting profession, only recently learning to live with its new-found respectability, boasted just two training colleges in the 1920s, both in London. The Royal Academy of Dramatic Art in Gower Street had been founded by Sir Herbert Beerbohm Tree in 1904, followed two years later by the Central School of Speech Training and Dramatic Art, tucked away in one of the corridors which snake around the labyrinthine interior of the Royal Albert Hall. The Central School's founder, principal and presiding genius was Miss Elsie Fogerty, "Fogie" to generations of students and friends, a small but determined Irishwoman of such formidable character that George Bernard Shaw once said of her: "She will get her way; there's nobody that can stand up to her."[1] Fogie, according to one of her many successful ex-pupils, "looked like a dignified cross between Queen Victoria and Mr Punch".

Elsie Fogerty (1866–1945) had herself been an actress who trained in London and Paris and made her first professional appearance in 1879, at the age of thirteen. But her particular interest in the problems of diction, and the correct enunciation of the language she loved, led her to abandon a career on the stage for one helping others to master its basic skills. She adapted and produced a number of Greek plays and wrote several manuals of speechcraft, including the influential *The Speaking of English Verse*. As principal of the Central School for forty-one years, from its formation to her death, she undoubtedly played a major part in establishing the reputation of the contemporary English stage, envied the world over for its clarity of diction and the music of its verse-speaking – a tradition which has begun to wane only with this latest generation of players. If some of her ideas on stagecraft were a little dated, her insistence on correct diction was much more important in shaping many a famous theatrical future.

Never seen without a fur hat and stole, Fogie became the focus of great respect and affection from her profession. She ran the Central School as a non-profitmaking business, scratching a modest living by giving private lessons to aspiring young actors, though too soft-hearted to charge the less well-off. Among those "patients" of Elsie Fogerty who protested that he never received a bill for her services was the young John Gielgud.

Always very secretive about her age, Fogie once told her students that as a girl she had been patted on the head by Garibaldi, which sent them all rushing to their history books to see when he had visited England. Shortly after her death in 1945, in her eightieth year, Olivier himself wrote:

> All her working life she preserved exactly the same appearance, that of a forceful, handsome, though smallish woman of about forty. Her past and present seemed always to be one with her. Only after the flat in Queensberry Place had been bombed did it appear that all was not well: quite suddenly she seemed to be withering like a barked tree that has lost contact with its roots. This change was remarked upon by many of her old friends, and that all of a sudden she should look more or less what must have been her age surprised us strangely.[2]

In June 1924, shortly after his seventeenth birthday, Olivier took a day's leave from St Edward's to attend auditions at the Central School. His father had genuinely astonished him by advocating a career in the theatre. That night in January, alone in the house together after Dickie's departure for India, the two had enjoyed a long and candid conversation – the first such, perhaps, in Olivier's young life, certainly the first since his mother's death. He realized that his father was not altogether the remote, cold fish he had always thought him, heedless of his youngest child's feelings and aspirations. The Rev. Gerard had, in fact, been thinking over his talented son's future very carefully. But paternal support for a career on the stage came at a price; Olivier's father now set him a formidable target. Merely securing a place at the Central School would not be good enough; he must win both a scholarship to cover his tuition fee *and* a £50-a-year bursary. A churchman's meagre stipend would not be enough to set him up in London. If unsuccessful, he would have to abandon all further hopes of becoming an actor.

Olivier still vividly recalls that June day over sixty years ago. Filled with horror at the prospect of performing alone on the vast Albert Hall stage in front of a packed house of thousands, he was relieved to be guided to a small and dingy back room. There an audience of one sat alone – a tiny, round lady in her late fifties, scarcely visible behind a battered old table

in a pool of inadequate light. As his audition piece Olivier had prepared
Jaques's celebrated soliloquy from *As You Like It*, "All the world's a
stage...", which he proceeded to deliver as forcefully as his young talent
knew how. Anxious to show that he had no inhibitions about physical
expression, he had practised a dramatic gesture to suit each line; as it
progressed, moreover, his rendering grew ever louder and more agitated.

At the end Miss Fogerty called Olivier down and told him without
further ado that the scholarship was his. Well, thank you, but what about
the bursary? Elsie Fogerty said she might be prepared to discuss that in a
moment. First, she had to point out that his delivery had been, how could
she put it, over-gesticulative. Young Olivier attached, perhaps, too much
importance to the need for physical action. For instance, "When you say
'sudden and quick in quarrel', it is not necessary to make fencing passes."
She let her hand fall languidly from her shoulder to her lap: "Sans *everything*.
Yes?"

During his recitation Olivier had noticed Elsie Fogerty shading her eyes,
above and beneath, the better to assess his looks. Now she gave him a piece
of advice which for years was to affect his preparation for every role he
undertook. Placing the tip of her little finger on his forehead, against the
base of his unusually low hairline, she traced a vertical line down to the
bridge of his nose, pausing in the deep hollow of his browline. "You have
weakness", she said, "... *here*." Behind his slightly shy eyes, beneath the
beetle brows of which he was already gloomily aware, the young would-
be actor immediately felt the force of that remark. It was to haunt his first
few years on the stage and to prove the beginning of a lifetime of false
noses.

Fogie's new recruit gulped and again raised the matter of the bursary,
explaining that for his father it was, together with the scholarship, a *sine
qua non* of his attendance at the Central School. His sister Sybille had
already been a pupil there – an undistinguished one, but apparently a
favourite of Fogie's – which Olivier subsequently believed to have helped
his case at this tense moment.

"Do you mean", asked Elsie Fogerty, "that without our bursary you
cannot become an actor?" He nodded. After "a suitable show of hesitation", she granted Olivier this Holy Grail, and he was able to go home
and inform his father that both conditions had been duly met. The fact
that Father Olivier expressed merely satisfaction, more than any visible
enthusiasm or joy, his son generously attributes to "the confidence of his
predictions". The rather more brutal truth is that he won the bursary
because Elsie Fogerty was anxious to enrol more male students, of whom
at this time there were only six among seventy girls at the Central School.

That summer, after leaving St Edward's, Olivier found himself an attic bedsitter in Castellain Road, Paddington, and embarked on a life so Spartan that he remained, to his professional dismay, miserably thin. "My arms hung down like wires from my shoulders."[3] Had he chosen to live at home and commute the thirty-five miles from Letchworth to the Central School, he would not have found himself so stretched for cash that he had to swallow his pride and ask his father to swell the bursary with an allowance of £1 a month, thus giving him the meagre sum of some twenty-five shillings a week for bed, board and travelling expenses.

But it was not just the commuting which made Olivier reluctant to go home. He was shaken by his father's sudden and unexpected decision to remarry. Quite apart from his idolatry of his dead mother, Olivier's strong Anglo-Catholic beliefs – carefully instilled by his father – were enough to make him resent the emergence of a stepmother.

Gerard, who had himself for years preached the virtues of celibacy, once again found himself unpopular with his parishioners. He had met his new wife, Isobel, in the romantic surroundings of a cruise to Jamaica, as fellow members of a Mission of Help; at the same time he had just accepted a new position as rector of St Paul's, Brighton. But the burghers of Brighton, once they heard the news, withdrew the offer, which led to a lurid press debate of some embarrassment to the Olivier family, soon reeling under such tabloid headlines as "CUPID V. CONGREGATIONS" and "SHOULD VICARS WED?" Gerard, as always, firmly stood his ground, thus losing a highly attractive living. It was to be two difficult and penurious years before he found another, as rector of Addington, near Winslow, Buckinghamshire, which was to prove his last.

Olivier remembers his young self at the Central School as a lazy student, "particularly idiotic in my inattention to most of the lectures.... I just wanted to get on with the *acting* – natural enough, but how senseless; these studies would not come my way again, except as spare-time pleasures." But Fogie's famous slogan – "Breath, note, tone, word" – was already edging more power into his thin tenor voice. Then skills such as fencing and deportment joined diction on the school curriculum, and his evenings were spent in front of the mirror at his lodgings practising make-up and disguise with sufficient imaginative powers to bewilder his fellow lodgers. On the few occasions he could afford to go to the theatre, he would seek out his favourite actress and pin-up, Gladys Cooper, or the actor of the moment, Gerald du Maurier – the only lustrous stars in an otherwise barren theatrical firmament.

The West End of the mid-1920s was a dispiriting desert of timid man-agements, profiteering middle-men and tired old ham performances at the end of the *bravura* tradition. The acting highlights of the 1924 season were John Barrymore's Hamlet, du Maurier and Cooper in Frederick Lonsdale's

The Last of Mrs Cheyney and the emergence of Sybil Thorndike and Edith Evans as actresses of the front rank. Noël Coward, who had dashed off *Hay Fever* in an inspired three-day burst, posed as the angry young man of his day with *The Vortex*, while a sometime Irish navvy called Sean O'Casey premiered his new play *Juno and the Paycock*. Chekhov's overdue recognition arrived with productions of *The Cherry Orchard* and *The Seagull*. But theatre-goers' tastes were symbolized more by the cult popularity of the song "I want to be happy" from *No, No, Nanette*, which began its record-breaking run of 665 performances at the Palace Theatre in March 1925. For an aspiring actor, Olivier has recalled, "there honestly wasn't anyone to admire; except one had to admire du Maurier as a technician".[4] Close study of du Maurier's celebrated "naturalness", however, was to prove somewhat counter-productive: "Actually Gerald du Maurier, brilliant actor that he was, had the most disastrous influence on my generation because we really thought, looking at him, that it was easy; and for the first ten years of our lives in the theatre nobody could hear a word we said."

In 1924 one of Olivier's Central School teachers, Henry Oscar, declared that he had "no inner fire". Nevertheless it was Oscar who gave Olivier his first London part, the tiny one of The Suliot Officer in his own production of Alice Law's *Byron* at the Century that November, and two Shakespearean walk-ons (with twenty-two lines between them), Master Snare and Thomas of Clarence in *Henry IV, Part II*, three months later. But the young Olivier's "unfortunate" face – a mass of hair from widow's peak via beetle brows to his first, emergent moustache – combined with his lack of physical grace or self-discipline to produce "an invisible wall of discomfort", as Oscar put it, around his every performance. Even Elsie Fogerty herself, in a rare moment of pessimism, is said to have declared that he would be "better off on a farm". He was rather young for his age, more than a trifle cocky in class, and the best that could be said of him was that he displayed, if nothing else, "flair".

That was certainly what Athene Seyler thought when she came to the school to judge its annual Gold Medal, to be awarded on the strength of a production of *The Merchant of Venice* in which Olivier played Shylock to Peggy Ashcroft's Portia. Miss Seyler – to co-star with him ten years later in the film *Moscow Nights*, and thirty years later in Peter Brook's *The Beggar's Opera* – adjudged that Olivier gave "no great character performance", but displayed intelligence behind the words, a concentration of purpose and "a quality of latent power" she found difficult to define. Above all, she noted, this young Shylock "did not hand you his whole performance on a plate; he left it to you to discover *him*".[5] She awarded the Gold Medal jointly to Olivier and Ashcroft, though a disappointed Olivier admits that "nothing of metal ever emerged". He has since said, with the confident modesty of the established celebrity, that the medal was "wafted my way by Elsie, who may well have felt a need to justify the old scholarship/bursary embarrassment".

Some years later, when Olivier's career was still in its early, matinee idol stages, Elsie Fogerty bracketed him with Peggy Ashcroft, of all the students who passed through her hands, as standing out in "possessing the peculiar combination of intelligence and feeling which gives assured success". But she continued, with characteristic shrewdness: "Like all actors whose whole personality seems to pass into the character he is playing, there are times when he does not prepare himself sufficiently for the climax of the play."[6]

Elsie Fogerty remained devoted to Olivier all her life, sending him a sprig of white heather and two four-leaf clovers when he joined the navy in 1941, and in the year of her death, 1945, urging all she met to see his film of *Henry V*. As the actress Isabel Jeans reports:

> For weeks after she saw the film her first – and final – words every time one met her would be "Have you seen Henry Five?" Even my husband and I – although, in fact, we had taken her to see it – were invariably asked this challenging question. The deep impression it made on her had completely obliterated the circumstances in which she had seen it.[7]

Fogie, who in fact rather disapproved of films, would say: "Larry is the only producer who has created a real film in England."

In his vacations from "The Hall", as the Central School was known to its students, Olivier supplemented his slender income by finding work at St Christopher's School theatre near his former home in Letchworth Garden City. Though he looks back on the work as "semi-amateur", it was professional enough to look good on his embryonic *curriculum vitae* and to earn him £4 a week, at first as second assistant stage manager and general understudy in a play for children, *Through the Crack*, by Algernon Blackwood and Violet Pearn. None of the cast ever defaulted, so Olivier never left the wings. When he secured a seat for his father's former cook, Amy Porter, he told her: "You won't actually see me 'up there', but when you hear the bell during the interval in the tea-room, you will know *my* finger will be on it."

He had found the job through Edith Craig, Ellen Terry's daughter, who was producing the season. Not only had the play already been cast by the time he contacted her, but the programmes had even been printed. He solved the little matter of his name's omission by getting some labels printed declaring that the Assistant Stage Manager was one Laurence Olivier, and gluing them all in himself one by one.

His willingness to work at so menial a level was rewarded the following

Easter, when St Christopher's audiences were privileged to witness the professional stage debut of Laurence Olivier, cast as Lennox in a not undistinguished production of *Macbeth* by Norman V. Norman, a formidable actor-manager "trying out" a last come-back in the safety of the Home Counties before essaying the West End. Lady Macbeth was played by Norman's wife, Beatrice Wilson, whose performance in the part Olivier still rates almost as highly as that of his second wife, Vivien Leigh (opposite his own Macbeth at Stratford thirty years later). There is, alas, no trace of any printed comment on the Olivier debut; but it is interesting to note that another emerging actor only three years older, John Gielgud, was at the time already enjoying excellent notices as Romeo at Barry Jackson's Birmingham Rep.

On graduating from the Central School, Olivier had no idea what kind of actor he wanted to be. All he did know was that experience was essential. So he began the footsore and soul-destroying round still familiar to young unknowns: trudging from agent's office to agent's office in the Leicester Square–Charing Cross Road–Shaftesbury Avenue triangle and buying advertisements in the trade press. "Laurence Olivier at liberty" read the discreet announcement in each week's issue of *The Stage* (still with us today), *The Era* (not) and Thursday's *Daily Telegraph* – still regarded as the paper with a special relationship to the theatrical profession, even though it no longer carries the weekly theatre page where Olivier paid three shillings a line to announce his availability. In rare moments of respectable employment the Olivier "card", as such notices were known, would boast "*The Farmer's Wife* No. 1 Tour – Next Week, Plymouth" or even (1926) "Birmingham Rep. Next Week, *Uncle Vanya* (name part)". It was worth every penny of his three shillings a line – even if the result was that he was often able to afford only half a sandwich for supper at the coffee-stall beside Warwick Avenue tube station, near his digs.

One day in 1925 the investment paid off with an invitation to read a part for Julian Frank, known as a "lucky" manager (which, mumbles Olivier, "usually meant that *he* was lucky, not you"). The role, exotically named Armand St Cyr, was in a sketch called *The Unfailing Instinct*, written by Frank himself as a curtain-raiser for his then star turn, Ruby Miller; her current hit, *The Ghost Train* by Arnold Ridley (many years later, as an actor, to become a national favourite in *Dad's Army*), was thought to be slightly too short to give provincial audiences the value-for-money they expected. Olivier got the part – that of a star-struck interviewer written in to feed the great lady some good lines. It was in this unlikely role, at the Hippodrome, Brighton, in the autumn of 1925, that Laurence Olivier made what he himself (still contemptuous of Letchworth as "semi-amateur") regards as his "unquestionably" professional debut.

Whereby hangs a tale he is extremely fond of telling. Most actors have their debut anecdotes, and Olivier's is a classic of the genre. Not to put too fine a point on it, he did the only thing any new actor must avoid, in the great dictum of Noël Coward, to achieve some vestige of plausibility: he tripped over the scenery.

It would, of course, have to be a charity gala night, with a star-studded Sunday evening audience, and such great contemporary names on the bill as Harry Lauder, George Robey and Alice Delysia – not to mention Ruby Miller, the only "legit" in the show, whom all the comics and unicyclists were thus watching with reverence from the wings. As he arrived at the stage door, Olivier was warned by the door-keeper that this was an "old-type" set, with a door-frame which was the same width top, sides and bottom. In Dressing-Room No. 12, a kindly old actor made the same point, as did the call-boy who escorted Mr "Oliver" to the wings. There the stage manager pointed out how easy it was to trip over these door-frames if you were not careful. He was waved away impatiently: "This", thought Olivier, "was getting tedious." On his cue he crashed straight through the door-frame, tripped headlong over the offending threshold, and found himself prostrate amid the footlights and the most thunderous laugh of his career. "In the many years between then and now I have delightedly played in numerous comedies.... I have flattered myself that I could generally fetch the size of laugh that I thought I, or the comic situation, merited, but ... never, never in my life have I heard a sound so explosively loud as the joyous clamour made by that audience." There were dark looks from Miss Miller, who silenced the unwelcome laughter with all the skill of an orchestral conductor. And when, his few lines over, the chump named in the programme as "Lawrence Oliver" successfully negotiated the exit, there was a smattering of ironic applause. Next day the local paper wryly commented: "Mr Oliver makes a good deal out of a rather small part."

There followed an all-too-brief tour, in which he combined a walk-on part as a policeman with another stint as assistant stage manager, and then another spell among that perennial majority of the acting profession, the unemployed. But it was only a few weeks later, in early October, that a portentous handwritten notice was sent out from Castellain Road, at his landlord's suggestion, to all potential agents and interviewers: "Mr Laurence Olivier begs to thank you for your extreme kindness in the matter of his employment, but is anxious that you should not trouble yourself more than is necessary and therefore wishes to advise you that he has been engaged by the Lena Ashwell Players."

Lena Ashwell, an actress of some renown by now in her mid-fifties, had turned to actress-management in a spirit of somewhat doomed philanthropy. Taking Shakespeare to the masses was her creed, the only trouble being that the masses did not much seem to want him. Undeterred, the Lena Ashwell Players trod a regular weekly path from Fulham and Battersea Town Halls on Mondays and Tuesdays to Shoreditch and Camberwell on Fridays and Saturdays. Members of the company had to pay their own fares to all these venues – quite a consideration for one living in Maida Vale on some £2 10s a week. Sometimes they would venture as far into the London suburbs as Deptford Baths, where Olivier himself first christened this motley crew of played-out veterans and young hopefuls "the Lavatory Players" – a reference to the impromptu changing-rooms provided, the stage being a precarious patchwork quilt of boards laid over the public swimming-pool. Maybe this was why Olivier was never able to take his role as a Lena Ashwell Player as seriously as his colleagues, a professional failing which was to lead all too soon to his downfall.

School matinees were another hardy perennial of the Ashwell itinerary, and it was at one such, at a girls' school in Englefield Green, Surrey, that Olivier went too far. Flavius, after all, does not have too much to do in *Julius Caesar*, and his first thought was to pull down the makeshift curtain which served as a backcloth, guaranteeing the audience an exciting glimpse of pink flesh as the disrobed female members of the cast scuttled for cover. This feat he never, alas, achieved. But he was already developing a reputation as the company giggler, when the girls of Englefield Green were privy to the second early hiccup in his career. As Philip Leaver, the hapless actor playing Marullus, mounted a beer crate on the emphatic line, "Knew you not Pompey?", he was so emphatic that the long pants beneath his toga fell down around his ankles and then wrapped themselves around the beer crate, completely immobilizing him. Far from going discreetly to his aid Olivier, helpless with laughter, backed off into the wings, leaving the crowd of Roman citizens to disperse uncertainly until the curtains came to the rescue of a tongue-tied and red-faced Marullus. It so happened that Lena Ashwell herself, who usually preferred to play the aloof, elusive manager, was out front that afternoon. Next morning she called Olivier to her office and fired him.

So he was forced to do what his young pride had resolved at all costs to avoid: ask the help of his father's friends, among whom was numbered Canon Thorndike, whose daughter Sybil was making herself quite a name. Her St Joan had been one of the hits of the 1924 season. Now, in partnership with Bronson Albery, she had set up in management with her husband Lewis Casson, the only director for whom she would work. Back on the poverty line, Olivier sought an audience with Casson and bluntly asked him for work, any work. "All right," said his father's friend, who had heard from the vicar of All Saints that he had seen Olivier in the street looking pitifully thin. "Spear-, halberd- and standard-bearer, all the understudies you can undertake without looking ridiculous, and second assistant stage manager in *Henry VIII* at the Empire in Leicester Square, at a salary of £3 a week."

Olivier pleaded for £4, in vain. He needed a new suit – actors of his degree, in those days, had to provide their own clothes for modern-dress roles – but could save nothing from £3 a week in London digs. Miserable, he was reminded of his father's advice about London: "You can either walk everywhere and save bus fares, or bus everywhere and save shoe-leather. You'll have to try it and see which is cheapest." But at the end of his second week at the Empire, Olivier's pay packet mysteriously contained £4 rather than the previous week's £3. He never discovered any reason for this unexpected rise other than the legendary kindness of the Cassons.

Olivier felt he had at last found a niche with a reputable and worthwhile company; but he took considerable pride in his prompt corner work and wondered at times whether he did not really prefer stage management to acting. Although it is on record that, on at least one occasion, he inevitably rang down the curtain at the wrong moment, Olivier's proud boast throughout his career has been that he has never come across a better stage manager than he himself once was. He even made himself somewhat unpopular among the company by superciliously "shush"ing offstage actors who chatted in the wings. So it was not a good move, when he took to the stage as a crowd control officer at Anne Boleyn's wedding, to play the part with such gusto as to knock one of the leading players off his feet. The young upstart was plainly told to curb his over-enthusiasm.

The following March, none the less, the name of Laurence Olivier (spelt right at last) appeared in the Empire programmes as Second Serving Man in *Henry VIII*. When a few matinees of Shelley's verse drama *The Cenci* were added to the company's repertoire, he was given the small part of an elderly servant to Orsino (played by Arthur Wontner), in which he made enough of a mark for Sybil Thorndike to mention it frequently in later years. It was not Olivier, however, but an even younger actor who caught the attention of the critics in this production: Jack Hawkins. Others in the company included Olivier's first employer, Norman V. Norman (as Henry VIII), and the first woman with whom he was to decide that he was in "love" – a purely innocent puppy love of course, blithely oblivious to the fact that the lady in question was quite recently and happily married. Playing Anne Boleyn in *Henry VIII* was Angela Baddeley, at twenty-one the elder of two "ravishing" theatrical sisters who were to break many a heart, among them that of Olivier's fellow spear-carrier Carol Reed, later the celebrated film director, whose natural father Sir Herbert Beerbohm Tree was among the notables who came to see the show. As Queen

Katharine, Sybil Thorndike recalled, her train was carried by two future knights: "They were both wonderful boys ... and they were both in love with the same girl, Angela Baddeley. They used to quarrel like mad, and I would say 'You shut up, you two, and attend to what you're doing.'"

In the London of the Roaring 20s, of course, it was the fashion to fall in love with love, and the romantic young Laurence Olivier was very much in spirit with the times. Those who knew him in these early, devil-may-care days recall a sequence of hopeless passions, all of them wide-eyed and from-a-distance, all of them unrequited, all of them a part of growing rather late into maturity. Not until her eightieth year did Dame Peggy Ashcroft reveal how narrowly she missed the chance of becoming the first Mrs Olivier. "Many years later Larry told me that when we went to tea with a member of the repertory company in his digs in Birmingham, and our host had retired to the lavatory, the sudden pulling of the chain had prevented him from proposing." The opportunity, added Dame Peggy wistfully, "never recurred"; but she chose not to disclose whether she would have accepted the young Olivier.[8] In his next job he was to fall in love again, with another newly and happily married actress called Muriel Hewitt, whose husband Olivier at first found, perhaps not surprisingly in the circumstances, rather irksome.

But with Ralph Richardson, in time, he was to forge the great friendship of both their long lives. They were brought together by a remarkable man named Barry Jackson, a wealthy, stage-struck idealist who had given up a career in architecture to devote himself to the theatre. At a time when the West End was devoting itself to more and more frivolous pursuits, Jackson was running a highly enterprising repertory company from a purpose-built new theatre in Birmingham.

The son of the founder of the Maypole Dairies chain, Jackson had been christened Barry after Barry Sullivan, his father's favourite actor, and was brought up to love the theatre. With the money he inherited when only twenty-seven, he founded the Birmingham Repertory Company in 1919. It was Jackson's eclectic determination which quickly won his company its reputation for daring repertoire and for giving their first chance to almost every young actor or actress of the period who subsequently went on to prominence.

It was Sybil Thorndike, almost a surrogate mother since the death of his own, who steered Olivier towards Jackson's Birmingham. He emerged from his first professional stage work, according to Denys Blakelock,

> throbbing with a desire to make something of himself in the West End. Perhaps he was a wee bit overbearing, perhaps he believed out of some youthful conceit and impatience that he had learned all he needed to learn and was ready to explode full-blown on to the theatrical scene. I know he

suffered a rude surprise. He was all over the place auditioning for roles, but he was turned down time and again.

It was, at this stage, Olivier's looks which let him down. He had grown enormously in self-confidence, and was already working hard to build up his body and add *gravitas* to his voice; but he was still thoroughly dishevelled-looking, even wild in appearance, with absolutely no sense for clothes. "It was a time when the modern plays being done in the West End were all frothy comedies and fey farces, and the only actors producers were looking for were the slicked-hair, dashing, glib types," said Blakelock. "Finally he went back to Sybil Thorndike in despair and said: 'What can I do?' Sybil put him straight. She said: 'Forget the West End for a while. Have you heard of Birmingham?' "[9]

In 1924, five years after Jackson had founded the Birmingham company, the city proved so ungrateful – by turning up in scant numbers to an adventurous production of an obscure play, George Kaiser's *Gas* – that he promptly moved its centre of operations to the Kingsway Theatre, London. Loud public protest coaxed him into reopening his Birmingham theatre the following year, but the link with the Kingsway remained. And it was on the Kingsway stage, early in 1926, that a penniless and painfully thin Olivier auditioned for nothing less than the title role in another adventurous Jackson production, *The Marvellous History of Saint Bernard*, by a then fashionable French dramatist, Henri Ghéon. He did not, of course, get it. Even the offer of first understudy to the actor who did, Robert Harris, was withdrawn in favour of Denys Blakelock. Olivier himself had done enough to catch the eye of Jackson's casting director, Walter Peacock, who was later to become his agent, but finished up only with the tiny part of A Minstrel.

It was, however, work; and it was an entrée to a world of professional discipline, friendship and wide-ranging experience, which was to prove the launching-pad for his career. The Birmingham company was then the pre-eminent group with which any aspirant actor could hope to serve his apprenticeship. Lilian Baylis had yet to be persuaded to stage Shakespeare at the Old Vic; and the fledgling Stratford company, formed in 1919 under the directorship of William Bridges-Adams, was still stuck in the late nineteenth-century habit of "singing" Shakespeare in almost operatic style. Jackson's mercurial set-up, moreover, kept three touring companies permanently on the road and transferred its Birmingham successes to any one of three London theatres – the Royal Court, the Kingsway and the Regent – which gave a young actor a metropolitan showcase for his talents.

Birmingham's main rival in Olivier's day was the Liverpool Repertory Company, then going through an innovative period. But Jackson's Birmingham was as pre-eminent in the 1920s as the Royal Shakespeare Company in the 1960s – blazing a trail in 1925 with the first modern-dress Shakespeare anywhere, known to theatrical history as "the plus-fours *Hamlet*", which revolutionized Shakespeare production in this country. Even so, it was to be another ten years before Olivier himself challenged Gielgud's "singsong" Shakespeare in the famous 1935 *Romeo and Juliet*, and it was not until 1938 that Tyrone Guthrie staged Alec Guinness's modern-dress *Hamlet* at the Old Vic.

Olivier has always looked back on his apprenticeship at Birmingham as the *sine qua non* of his subsequent achievement. The decline of the repertory system in Britain, he still believes, has deprived younger actors of the chance to enjoy a broad enough grounding to their careers. Denys Blakelock, one of Olivier's young contemporaries at Birmingham, recalled that it was

> much more than just a performing organization. Being there was like going every day to the most advanced school of theatre in the world. One was thoroughly immersed in the theatre and learned more in a week about acting styles and dramatic history than one would in years of plodding around the West End. The company was loaded with competition, and it created an atmosphere in which everyone tried to outdo everyone else, not just in performing ability but in theatrical knowledge and sophistication as well. Larry took to this competition like a fish to water. Some people were eventually defeated by it, but it excited him enormously and drove him on with ever more intensity to stand out.[10]

The Birmingham programme managed to get two "i"s in its new recruit's name, but also treated him to two "l"s. Not that The Minstrel was a big enough part to win Laurence "Ollivier" any critical attention. The production of *Saint Bernard* was warmly enough received when it opened on 27 April 1926, but was rudely interrupted by the General Strike, which closed down all but essential services for twelve days in May. Olivier (who is today fed up with people telling him he was on the wrong side) promptly donned plus-fours and signed on as a gateman on the London underground, for which he was paid £5 a week – only £1 10s less than he was earning at the Kingsway. *Saint Bernard* was to return for only a few more performances; a bitter curtain speech from Jackson after the last performance rebuked his handful of paying customers for being so few in number.

Jackson's Birmingham company subsidized loss-leaders like these with a remarkably heavy touring programme, often with several different casts performing the same play simultaneously around the country. Their big current hit was Eden Phillpotts's *The Farmer's Wife*, which had a dashing juvenile lead on which young Olivier had his eye. First, however, he was dispatched to Clacton-on-Sea to replace a minor player in a Welsh comedy, D. T. Davies's *The Barber and the Cow*, whose merits may be judged by the exchange which ended the second act:

> "The cow has fallen into a coma."
> "That wasn't a coma. It was a full stop."

Leading the company was Cedric Hardwicke, the biggest name on Jackson's books at the time, who remembered the young Olivier as "very noisy; he had no trace of subtlety; he shouted every part".[11] Among the supporting cast were Richardson and his wife. Three future knights of the theatre in one provincial touring company: Clacton did not know its luck. Nor did Olivier, who thought Richardson pompous and aloof, while Richardson for his part considered the young Olivier (with some justification) rather gauche – "a cocky young pup full of fire and energy". Olivier was, moreover, openly flirting with his wife.

Richardson, nevertheless, offered him a lift to their next port of call, Bridlington, mainly to show off his gleaming new Austin 7. Olivier and Muriel, known to her husband and close friends as "Kit", squeezed into the front passenger seat alongside him, and were chatting and laughing so happily that they scarcely noticed Richardson's concern when the water temperature needle reached boiling. Cursing his passengers' lack of concern, Richardson leapt out and almost scalded himself as he investigated the state of the radiator. Steam was belching out by the time he found an oblivious Olivier at his side, asking him for a word in private.

"What the devil is it, Laurence?"

"I wanted to ask, Ralph, if it was all right with you if I called Muriel 'Kit'."[12]

It was perhaps just as well that *The Barber and the Cow* was a doomed enterprise, and this awkward trio soon involuntarily disbanded. Olivier was transferred to another Birmingham company touring even further afield. At least he now had the part he was after in *The Farmer's Wife*, the lovesick young farmer Richard Croaker (whom Richardson himself had played some eighteen months before). For six months he toured the length and breadth of Britain, a gruelling stint which was to prove invaluable in two ways. He read Stanislavsky for the first time; as *My Life in Art* was passed around the company, Olivier found it "a source of great enlightenment". And he managed to pick up some decent notices in the local papers along his tortuous route; Wimbledon thought him "capital", Clifton "excellent", Southend "clever" and Edinburgh "artistic". By the end of the tour Olivier had made enough of an impression to be engaged as a juvenile lead by the repertory company proper.

He was to make his mark as Tony Lumpkin in *She Stoops To Conquer*, the title role in *Uncle Vanya*, Jack Barthwick in John Galsworthy's *The Silver Box* and Parolles in a modern-dress *All's Well That Ends Well*. But he might have deprived himself of the chance, had not Jackson's producer that season, W. G. Fay, shown greater sympathy with the high spirits of youth than Lena Ashwell. Still only nineteen, Olivier had not yet shed his naïve eagerness to make his fellow actors laugh on stage, or "corpse". One day, he would have this heretical habit well and truly drummed out of him by Noël Coward. Not yet, however, and it was in a mood which he now cringes to recall that Olivier decided to play a trick on one of the company's most valued stalwarts, Melville Cooper, who was playing the central part of The Burglar in one of Eden Phillpotts's less inspiring curtain-raisers, *Something To Talk About*.

Surprised by this intruder at a country house party, Olivier's decidedly minor character, a monocled aristocrat, is asked, "Who are you?", and should have replied: "We are Conservatives." On the show's last night he decided to "improve" his line to "We are Freemasons, Frothblowers and Gugnuncs" (current jargon which, he assures us, seemed wildly funny at the time).[13] A few of the audience laughed; Melville Cooper managed to contain himself to a smile; the one person who thought the whole thing screamingly funny, and was not slow to show it onstage, was Olivier himself. Summoned before Fay the next day, he was given a lecture he never forgot, both about the irresponsibility of such behaviour towards his fellow professionals and the slur cast on Jackson's reputation. "Sir Barry", Fay told him in no uncertain terms, "did not open a music-hall." The culprit, suitably chastened, considered himself lucky not to have been fired again.

Doubly so, when a few months later he was winning praise from George Bernard Shaw himself as a Parolles described by the critic J. C. Trewin as "an amiable, too smart young man, a *sommelier*'s scourge".[14] In John Drinkwater's *Bird in Hand* he was chastised by the *Birmingham Post* for one "out of character" moment – "his sentimental kissing the door of his sweetheart's room" – but more favourable reviews were beginning to accumulate. It was a tiny part in a bold new play by Elmer Rice, *The Adding Machine*, which finally brought him to London.

With his usual persistence Jackson chose *The Adding Machine*, his most outlandish production of the year, to open his 1928 Royal Court season. Anxious to make his mark, but with no "talkies" as yet to help him, Olivier cast around for a way to polish up his New York (East Side) accent. After seeing Denys Blakelock one night in *The Silver Cord* at the St Martin's, Olivier went backstage and begged to be introduced to the star of the production, the distinguished American actress Clare Eames. She proved remarkably generous with her time, taking Olivier through his part over and over again. His boldness paid off when, despite murmured dissent from the curmudgeonly W. G. Fay, Olivier was adjudged to have "by far and away the best Americanese". This early display of a lifelong pursuit of perfection also enabled him, for the first time, to catch the eye of a major critic, St John Ervine of the *Observer*: "Mr Laurence Olivier as the young man who accompanies Judy O'Grady into the graveyard gave a very good performance indeed – the best, I think, in the play. He had little to do, but he *acted*." Fay promptly punctured his pride by telling him to take no notice of "that Ervine ... he knows noth'n'". Audiences seemed somewhat baffled by Rice's space-age satire, but crusty old Arnold Bennett offered mild approval in his *Evening Standard* column: "I feared the worst, but it turned out quite well." Clare Eames was even more impressed; she told Denys Blakelock: "Larry looks down at me with the eyes of a conqueror."[15]

Olivier, believed Clare Eames, was "just beginning to be conscious of the dynamic power that was in him". With his success in *The Adding Machine*, it began to go to his head. He became unpopular with Jackson's leading directors, especially Fay and Ayliff, for constantly questioning their ideas and with his fellow actors for offering to improve on their performances. One of Birmingham's leading ladies of the time, Eileen Beldon, later testified that

> Larry Olivier made himself generally obnoxious. Frankly, I couldn't stand him. More than once I pleaded with Jackson to get rid of him. He was slovenly and hi-falutin. Of course, I realize now that he was just a young boy trying to prove himself, and that much of his behaviour came from the fact that he was so scared and felt so far out of his element. At least, that's what Larry told me recently. I have no reason to doubt it.[16]

For a while Olivier's brashness paid off, as he managed to emerge unscathed, even praised, from some indifferent Birmingham productions. Few were enamoured of Jackson's next venture, a modern-dress *Macbeth*, in which Olivier alternated between a double-breasted City suit and silk dressing-gown as Malcolm. The Scottish play spawned its usual trail of disasters: on the eve of the opening night, the dress circle of the theatre caught fire, and during one of the first week's performances the scenery collapsed. But it was the production itself, by Henry Ayliff, that was the biggest disaster. Jackson, who had admitted to doubts that *Macbeth*, rooted as it is in a primitive, barbarous Scotland, could work in a contemporary setting, gracefully told the first-night audience: "Experiments do have their failures."

For the title role, which he had had difficulty casting, Jackson had finally made the eccentric choice of Eric Maturin, a light, drawing-room-comedy actor who had never even so much as seen *Macbeth* in the theatre.

Childhood: Olivier aged eight

(LEFT) First theatrical steps: aged twelve, as a matador, and (ABOVE) aged fourteen, as Katharina in *The Taming of the Shrew*. (BELOW LEFT) The beetle-browed young actor, aged twenty, transformed (CENTRE) into Uncle Vanya and Tony Lumpkin for Birmingham Rep, 1927

Matinee idol: (ABOVE) as Beau Geste, 1929, and (ABOVE RIGHT) in his first film, *The Temporary Widow*, with Lilian Harvey, 1929. (BELOW) Marriage at twenty-three to Jill Esmond, 1930

1930–31: Success with Noël Coward in *Private Lives* (ABOVE) with Adrianne Allen and Gertrude Lawrence leads to Hollywood (BELOW), where Jill is a bigger star than Olivier

First Shakespeare: Romeo (ABOVE LEFT) and Mercutio (ABOVE RIGHT) opposite Gielgud 1935, leads to Hamlet at the Old Vic (BELOW LEFT) and a film of *As You Like It* with Elisabeth Bergner, 1936

(ABOVE) Enter Vivien Leigh, with Olivier in *Fire over England*, 1936, and *Hamlet* at Elsinore, 1937. (BELOW) More success at the Old Vic: as Toby Belch, 1937, and Coriolanus, 1938

Hollywood stardom: in *Wuthering Heights* with Merle Oberon, 1939 (ABOVE), and *Rebecca* with Joan Fontaine, 1940

1940–41: With Vivien in a screen success, *Lady Hamilton*, and a stage disaster, *Romeo and Juliet*

The doomed nature of the enterprise also seemed to take the heart out of the other central performances, so that Olivier was lucky enough to be one of only a handful in the cast to earn critical warmth as a reasonably convincing Shakespearean. One eyewitness who could still recall Olivier's Malcolm nearly sixty years later was the actress Jessica Tandy: "It was the first time I became aware of him, and quite a while before I got to know him. The production was pretty dire, but whenever he came on as Malcolm the whole stage came to light. I have never forgotten it."[17]

The good luck which any young career so desperately needs at this stage had come his way. Olivier's success as Malcolm prompted Jackson and Ayliff to cast him as Martullus in a revival of Shaw's *Back to Methuselah*, which Jackson had bravely premiered in 1923, despite its huge length and distinctly uncommercial atmosphere. ("Mr Jackson," Shaw had asked him, "are your wife and children provided for?") Olivier was dismayed to see the name of Ralph Richardson also in the cast list; ever since Clacton they had still regarded each other with intense suspicion. At the first few rehearsals there was a stony silence between them, which Olivier found too uncomfortable to bear. As the group broke for lunch one day, he proposed to a surprised Richardson that they go and have a drink. At a pub next door to Sloane Square tube station the jokes began to flow and past misunderstandings were quickly forgotten, as the seeds were sown for the most momentous theatrical partnership of the century. All her long life Gwen Ffrangcon-Davies would remember the "March of the Children" sequence, in which she was "lifted out of an egg by Laurence Olivier and Ralph Richardson, both playing young boys".[18]

According to the critic Harold Hobson, Olivier went "unnoticed".[19] But Jackson and Ayliff were sufficiently impressed to offer him his first leading role in London, the title part in Tennyson's *Harold*, a month before his twenty-first birthday. John Gielgud, who had already played the Royal Court as Rosencrantz or Guildenstern – he cannot remember which – in the "plus-fours *Hamlet*", recalls being disappointed; he had hoped to be offered Harold himself.[20] Richardson, too, found himself for the first time playing a supporting role to Olivier. It was another daring choice of play: a nineteenth-century verse drama noted for its untheatricality, distinguished only by the cutting edge of its rhetoric, never before performed on the "legitimate" stage. Tennyson himself had admitted to complete ignorance of "the mechanical details necessary for the modern stage", and Henry Irving had adjudged the piece "quite impossible" to produce effectively. For the first time since Tennyson wrote his epic in 1876, audiences – torn, according to a contemporary account, between respect and mockery[21] – could hear:

... the ring
Of harness and the deathful arrow sing,
And Saxon battleaxe clang on Norman helm.
Here rose the dragon-banner of our realm:
Here fought, here fell, our Norman slander'd King.

Olivier – who today is still fond of crying "Oh Tostig, Tostig, what art thou doing here?" – learnt his 3,000 lines in a week. He was still too young to carry off so huge a role with the authority it needed, but he could already, as Trewin put it, "spark off Saxon fire". In that Sunday's *Observer* his first public champion, St John Ervine, established Olivier's base-camp on the theatrical map:

> Mr Laurence Olivier, the Harold, varies in his performance, but he is excellent on the whole and has the makings of a very considerable actor in him. His faults are those of inexperience rather than of ineffectiveness. The good performance he gave in *Macbeth*, added to the good performance he gives in *Harold*, makes me believe that when romantic and poetic drama return to their proper place in the theatre, Mr Olivier will be ready to occupy the position of a distinguished romantic actor.

Esmond Knight, who was to become a close colleague, testifies that "the reason he got such good notices during that season at the Court was that he had the temerity and the sauce to do amazingly inventive things".[22]

Olivier's last role with the Birmingham Rep at the Royal Court, which he regarded as a "trick ... to test how conceited I might have become with all the recent promises of glory", was the "miserably" small one in another Ayliff modern-dress Shakespeare – this time *The Taming of the Shrew*, a play much better suited than *Macbeth* to an updating (which this time had already been tried and tested in New York). Rather in the manner of the contemporary Royal Shakespeare Company, the comedy was turned into a romp, complete with a rebellious Ford car onstage ("Come on, in God's name," roared Petruchio) and press photographers, even a movie camera, at the wedding scene. The principal parts were carried off with great panache by Scott Sunderland and Eileen Beldon, but it was Ralph Richardson who stole the show as Tranio, a cheeky Cockney chauffeur in morning-coat and silk hat.

Olivier's role was merely that of The Lord in the Christopher Sly prologue. But he had "seen the trick a mile off and took it like a lamb".[23] Richardson had reason to doubt this whenever the production called for him to turn Olivier's way. This was one of those authentic play-within-a-play *Shrews*, which left the onstage audience in view throughout the show – ineffably boring for the actors, who passed the time by pretending to sleep or making funny faces whenever those in mid-speech, notably Richardson, caught their eye. What would those people in the box, especially Olivier, be up to next? In the account of Richardson's biographer, Garry O'Connor,

> they changed make-up, fidgeted, whispered behind their hands, pulled faces, waved – but nothing they could do put Richardson off his stroke. One night, however, they sat absolutely still – elbows resting on the front of the box – just watching him and doing nothing. This began to tease Richardson, make him nervous.... Concentration wavered.... Finally he could take no more and corpsed in full view of everybody.

The other advantage to Olivier of being onstage throughout the evening was the chance to show off his handsome profile, now embellished by a new Ronald Colman moustache. The relatively ugly duckling who had joined the Birmingham company two years before was now, as he approached his twenty-first birthday, described by his co-star Gwen Ffrangcon-Davies as "this ravishing creature". It was, as Denys Blakelock put it, an amazing metamorphosis. Pre-Birmingham, the "usually rather pale" Olivier had had

> a mass of thick, black hair which grew rather low on his forehead, ending in a sort of widow's peak. This hair was then apparently quite unmanageable. He couldn't get it to part, he couldn't get it to behave at all. He was rather sensitive about it and hated people remarking on it. His eyebrows, too, were very thick and black, and grew in profusion right across his rather broad nose; and his teeth, especially the two mid-front, were set particularly wide apart.[24]

Now, however,

> he had somehow got his hair to part at last; he had had the gaps between his teeth filled in, his eyebrows trimmed and straightened, and he was beautifully and rather gaily dressed. He had stopped short at his nose, though he has since made up for this by remodelling it with nose-clay into one shape after another in almost every part he has played in the last twenty-five years.

As only the closest friends can, Blakelock adds a coda which could be taken harshly, but should rather be read as an affectionate, even envious, tribute to a young man determined to make his mark: "All this is an example of that application and detailed attention to the job, without which no artist can hope to attain to any position of enduring importance, much less make for himself a name that will last beyond his lifetime."

It was also an early sign of Olivier's unquenchable ambition. As he looked around for a part which would prove his next stepping-stone to stardom, Olivier had another, equally urgent, priority: marriage, preferably to someone who could lend more lustre to his promising-looking career. He was soon to find both. And in both roles he was to be grievously miscast.

CHAPTER 3

1928–31

"Genteel poverty", Olivier once said, "is probably the most fertile ground for ambition that there can be. 'Because', you seem to say, 'I want to get out, I'm going to get out. When I get out of this I will show them, I will show them, I will show them.'" It was in June 1928, a month after his twenty-first birthday, that he got his chance to show them, by beginning the long, hard climb out of his background, away from his family, further and further from his roots.

Olivier found himself doing another odd job for Sir Barry Jackson at London's Royalty Theatre: taking over the lead role in one of Birmingham Rep's long-running West End successes, John Drinkwater's *Bird in Hand*. The juvenile roles he already knew well. Now he was playing the lead part he had had his eye on: Gerald Arnwood, the squire's son who proposes to the innkeeper's daughter. It was to prove highly appropriate, for the innkeeper's daughter, originally Peggy Ashcroft, had also been recast. Joan Greenleaf was now played by a pretty, dark-haired girl of twenty named Jill Esmond, the daughter of famous theatrical parents. Within three weeks of meeting her, Olivier had proposed offstage as well as on.

Though six months younger than Olivier, Jill was more theatrically experienced. A graduate of the Royal Academy of Dramatic Art (RADA), she had already been on the stage for six years. Her father, who had died when she was fourteen, was H. V. Esmond, a celebrated actor-manager and playwright of the era; her mother was Eva Moore, an actress-producer equally celebrated in her own right. Olivier, in uxorious mood anyway, was by no means averse to the prospect of marriage into so theatrical a family; in his own words, he decided that "with those antecedents, though not *dazzlingly* attractive, she would most certainly do excellent well for a wife". It may have been, as he concedes, "incredible presumption", but "I wasn't going to wait for anyone better to come along."

The object of his affections was more mature and more cautious. This romantic young man's headlong pursuit seemed to her to stem more from some deep-seated longing for marriage than from any great feelings towards her personally. Jill's reply to his first, impetuous proposal was to suggest a six-month "get to know each other" engagement; in fact it was to take her a good two years to accept him. For those first six months, however, while the run of *Bird in Hand* continued, life was rosy for both of them. Her mother invited Olivier to give up the squalor of his London digs for a room in their riverside home at Hurley, in Berkshire, so he was seeing Jill at home all day as well as acting passionate love scenes with her every evening. But strictly onstage: in his early twenties Olivier still clung to the religious convictions instilled in him by his father. He himself chose to reveal to the world that, for all the many infatuations of his youth, he was a virgin when he married.

Professionally, meanwhile, with the longed-for promotion from juvenile lead to matinee idol still on the drawing-board, he was in need of more luck. And this time it was to come in unusual guise. Olivier's early life provides ample proof of the truism that careers of this scale, in their fledgling stages, need to be as blessed in their bad luck as in their good.

There was a backstage buzz of excitement at the Royalty one night as word got around that the audience included Basil Dean, perhaps the most prominent producer of the day, certainly the most controversial, and thus the man on whose coat-tails every young actor hoped to make his name. Dean had run the Liverpool Repertory Company until 1913 – an inspiration to Barry Jackson in founding Birmingham six years later – and had gone on to run the Theatre Royal, Drury Lane, and then the St Martin's. He had scored notable successes with *Hassan*, complete with its memorable Delius score, and *The Constant Nymph*, which he co-dramatized himself. Dean was a Cecil B. de Mille of the theatre, whose penchant for the big effect – through the latest stage gadgetry, elaborate sets and dazzling lighting – sharply divided both critics and audiences. The text usually took second place to the grand gestures in a Dean production, but his showmanship was enough to guarantee good box office.

It was known that Dean was planning an extravaganza of epic proportions even by his standards, a swashbuckling production of P. C. Wren's *Beau Geste*, and that he was on the lookout for a dashing young actor to play the title role. For Olivier and his rivals, all of whom desperately preened their Colman moustaches, it was one of those legendary theatrical chances-of-a-lifetime. Olivier knew his name was one of literally hundreds on Dean's talent-spotting list, but he had also heard (wrongly, as it transpired) that his beetle brows had already ruled him out. That night he went onstage determined to give a performance Dean could not ignore; then he sat back and waited, none too optimistically, for a summons from the great man.

Months went by before he was finally called for an audition, which he attended with newly plucked brows and a score of other hopefuls. Dean was not going to be rushed into a decision. Olivier felt he stood a good chance; but even by December, when he was delighted to be invited to read *Geste* at a run-through, there was no official word that the part might be his. In the meantime, a month before, he had been offered an apparently much less attractive role, which very nearly altered the entire course of his career.

The Incorporated Stage Society had been founded in 1899 by a group of philanthropic theatre-lovers (including, by coincidence, his Uncle Sydney, the first Lord Olivier) to try out new plays which stood little chance of being seen in the commercial theatre. They were to have West End casts and to be mounted in West End theatres, which meant only one or two performances on Sunday nights, as most participants were working elsewhere the rest of the week. It was under the auspices of this respected but distinctly uncommercial organization that James Whale, a little-known actor/director who had admired Olivier in *Bird in Hand*, came backstage to tell him he was about to direct a new war play by an author named R. C. Sherriff. On offer was the part of Captain Henry Stanhope in a play called *Journey's End*.

The fee for the entire enterprise, three weeks' rehearsal for just two performances, would be a mere £5. The play, by a thirty-two-year-old Surrey insurance clerk of whom nobody had heard, was a gloomy account of life in the trenches of the First World War – scarcely in the gay mood of the times. It had an all-male cast, no romance, not even a particularly heroic theme, and came just ten years after a war everyone was still trying to forget. No one expected the Stage Society's production to attract much attention, let alone to earn a West End production. Already it had been turned down by every major London management, and the part of Stanhope rejected by half-a-dozen leading actors. Yet Olivier accepted. Why? Partly because he had always regretted, in a romantic sort of way, that he had been too young to fight in France. But more importantly because Basil Dean had seen him only as a moon-faced lover; now he could see him playing a soldier, a leader of men. This could be his path to Beau Geste.

It was a risk. But risk-taking was in Olivier's nature, as Ralph Richardson testified at the time:

Laurence was driving my car; we were going down to Brighton, just the two of us, and were on the Croydon by-pass; after the aerodrome there was a steep hill with a wicked crossroad at the bottom. Now, of course, there are plenty of traffic lights; then, there were none. Laurence approached this crossroad at about 50 mph, which was almost as much as the car would do, and he went bang over it. I was absolutely horrified and could not speak for a time. When I could, I said, "Laurence, never, never, as long as I live, will I forgive you for that." Laurence was cheerful: "It is a well-known thing, Ralphie," he said, "that when you get to a point of danger, you get over it as quickly as you can."

The subsequent progress of *Journey's End* towards the unlikely status of minor twentieth-century masterpiece occupies one of the more touching corners of recent theatrical history. A huge critical and popular success in its first week, it was within months being performed all over the world, in twenty-seven different languages, and was swiftly *en route* to Hollywood via Broadway. Many an actor was to make his name in it and to earn a swift passage to stage or screen stardom, while Sherriff – whose seventh effort this was for his Kingston Rowing Club friends to perform on their amateur theatrical nights, and even *they* had turned it down – soon found himself transformed from a £6-a-week insurance clerk to Hollywood's highest-paid screenwriter.

When subsequently invited to fly west to write a screenplay for Remarque's *All Quiet on the Western Front*, Sherriff declined on the grounds that he had already spent enough time in the US for the Broadway run of *Journey's End* and must now get home to his mother. He went on to write numerous renowned screenplays, including *The Invisible Man*, *The Four Feathers*, *Goodbye Mr Chips*, *Mrs Miniver*, *Odd Man Out* and *The Dam Busters*. At the time, however, though aware that Whale had deliberately chosen an unknown for the lead so as not to intimidate the rest of the cast, Sherriff had never before met a professional actor.

At the first run-through, in a shabby upstairs room over a Charing Cross Road shoe shop one cold November morning, he thought them "an ordinary looking lot of men: what you might see any evening waiting on Waterloo Station for a train home". Olivier was

> sitting over the small bleak fire, trying to warm himself. There wasn't any central heating and the room was very cold. He looked slighter and paler than he had appeared onstage: not at all like the tough, drink-sodden company commander that I had visualized. He looked bored and restless. I got a feeling that he wished he hadn't come.[1]

In the event Sherriff was to consider Olivier's performance "magnificent"; he "couldn't imagine a production of the play without him".

Such luminaries as Shaw had read *Journey's End* with a yawn. But Olivier had had the sixth sense to see that the part of the war-weary company commander, who resorts to the bottle in an attempt to disguise his growing cowardice, could give him the opportunity to show off the broader powers he believed himself to possess.

The response to the play's first performance, at the Apollo Theatre on the evening of Sunday, 9 December 1928, gave scant indication of the phenomenal success ahead. Among the notables in the audience was Barry Jackson, who admired Olivier's performance, adorned by the uniform, Sam Browne belt, revolver and holster Sherriff himself had worn in the trenches. The play, the first to suggest that not everyone in stage khaki need be a hero, was a moving monument to the dead of Flanders. But Jackson and all the other impresarios present still believed it to stand no chance in the commercial theatre. When the critics came to the second and final performance the next afternoon, however, their response surprised everyone.

Personal praise for Olivier was soon drowned in a tide of acclaim for Sherriff's play, which broached the post-war disillusion expressed in poetry by Robert Graves, Siegfried Sassoon and Edmund Blunden. The legendary Hannen Swaffer of the *Daily Express* eulogized *Journey's End* as "this greatest of all war plays". And the most influential critic of the day, James Agate of the *Sunday Times*, called it "a work of extraordinary quality and interest which brings one into touch with the greatest experience known to living man". Agate threw the weight of his weekly radio broadcast behind the play's "extraordinary significance and merit" and against the London managements who were refusing to stage it. It was months before one lone impresario, Maurice Browne, agreed to a run at the Savoy, which was to last 600 performances. Stanhope was played not by Olivier, but by Colin Clive, who also went on to beat him to the part in the screen version.

For while the London managements were dithering over *Journey's End*, Olivier's tactics had at last succeeded in persuading Basil Dean that he had found his Beau Geste. Dean had been so impressed by *Journey's End* that he had thought of producing it himself, but shared every other management's reservation not only that there were no women in the play, but also that there was nothing to attract women to go to see it. There may have been young or youngish men who would go – but how many, as the critic W. A. Darlington put it, would "choose it as an entertainment to which to take their womenfolk"? Dean, who later described the decision as "the most dismal mistake of my career",[2] opted instead for his soldier-play of a very different kind, in which an unrequited Great Lover sets off to join the French Foreign Legion – a tale with all the romantic-heroical glamour Sherriff had deliberately eschewed.

51

Framingham State College
Framingham, Massachusetts

The battle for the part of Beau Geste had, in the end, come down to two contenders: Olivier and a fellow actor in *Journey's End*, Maurice Evans. Evans played Raleigh, the subaltern who is shot in the back and dies in Stanhope's arms. The two friends, who shared a dressing-room that momentous evening, both gave this climactic scene all they could, for they knew very well what was at stake: Basil Dean was out front again.

Dean came backstage immediately after the performance and asked Evans – in a gesture Olivier described as "the most vulgarly unkind thing I had as yet witnessed" – to leave the room. Evans bowed out gracefully, leaving Dean to offer Olivier the part of Beau Geste there and then. "It was generally felt", wrote Darlington, "that he had earned his promotion and was now a made man. I do not remember one person suggesting that this lucky young man, faced by two alternatives each attractive in its way, had not picked the right one."[3] Dean himself planned *Beau Geste* as "a mighty Wurlitzer of a production". It was to have a cast of 120 including Marie Lohr and Madeleine Carroll, and his most ambitious special effects yet, including a full-scale battle scene complete with a real Maxim gun, climaxing with Olivier's funeral on a Viking pyre genuinely set on fire. How could it go wrong?

All too easily. However successful the novel, it was absurd to ask a London audience to keep straight faces as all these ex-public schoolboys donned cartoon uniforms and slapped each other on the back with cries of "Stick to it, old boy". And how could anyone believe that the elegant hero would really swap his dinner-jacket and the civilized comforts of his ancestral manse at Brandon Abbas for the squalor of the barrack-room at Sidi-bel-Abbès?

The production, which opened at His Majesty's in the Haymarket just a week after *Journey's End*, was dismissed as "badly planned", "chaotically staged", "absurdly overlong". Said *The Times*: "Mr Laurence Olivier deserves prizes in the fifth form ... though he did his best to make life tolerable, this life was altogether too long and too slow and too shamelessly false to the sense and humour of the most romantic existence." Dean recalled the first-night reception as "rapturous", but the painful truth is that a relief fireman, alarmed by the all-too-realistic flames from Olivier's funeral pyre, rang down the emergency curtain too soon. By the time he had got it up again, half the audience had left, and it was nearly midnight before the rest stumbled numbly out into the street. Dean, who described Olivier at this time as "a darkly resolute young man, with a well-placed speaking voice and a reserved manner", compared this "bravura" performance favourably with that of Ronald Colman, who had played Geste in the (silent) movie the year before. Even he, however, said later that "Larry had given little sign of the latent powers that were to carry him to pre-eminence."[4] But the cruellest cut, from Olivier's point of view, was the judgement of the revered Agate, who had so admired his Stanhope and who now thought he had rightly made Geste an ass – "but not a commanding ass". The acting laurels were again awarded instead to eighteen-year-old Jack Hawkins as his brother John, "an actor with a future".

During rehearsals, his name in lights and his salary £30 a week, Olivier had bought himself the successful actor's ritual camel-hair coat and taken a room in a large house in Pembridge Villas, North Kensington, in anticipation of a long run. But as *Journey's End* packed them in at the Savoy, *Beau Geste* closed in under a month, losing its backers the then huge sum of £24,000. Olivier was distraught. He had turned down a subtle, demanding part in a successful drama for a shallow, bravura flop. Over lunch with the American critic Sewell Stokes, he picked at his food sullenly: "Just my luck, I suppose, to miss the chance of a lifetime. Colin Clive's got rave notices. I'm sure he deserves them. Best choice for the part, I expect. But how I wish I had the part!"[5]

Years later Sherriff read a theatrical anthology in which Olivier named Stanhope as the favourite part he had ever played. The playwright, nevertheless, thought Clive "more rugged and restrained" in the role, while the actor-critic Robert Speaight considered that "no one else could have played the part as well as Clive; even Olivier had not played it as well".[6] But Speaight also observed that Colin Clive was "an actor of one part only". And as Clive progressed towards Hollywood, Olivier soon had cause to understand what is meant by good bad luck. As the son of an army colonel, educated at Sandhurst, Clive might have been born for the part of Stanhope; but in Hollywood, where in the 1920s he commanded average earnings of $100,000 a year, he could never shake the typecasting. A withdrawn, shy man who could not handle stardom – and who, like the character who had made him famous, sought solace in drink – he was dead after just six years there, at the age of thirty-seven.

Olivier, meanwhile, at least had the consolation of the leading role in Dean's next extravaganza, *The Circle of Chalk*. Now he was a Chinese prince called Po who falls in love with a damsel in distress, a tea-house girl sold into slavery, played by the great silent movie star Anna May Wong. Olivier gave free rein to his fascination with make-up, disappearing behind enormously high cheek-bones, cunningly slanted eyes and a brow so deep it seemed never to end. All too predictably, the show was another disaster. As soon as the great Anna May opened her mouth, her squeaky American voice shattered any attempt at illusion; Olivier himself, recovering from laryngitis, sang his song in an inadvertent falsetto; the scenery turntable jammed; and when two coolies slipped on the lacquered stage, another leading actor was propelled headfirst across the footlights into the arms of the orchestra. Again, Dean looked back on the production as fondly as he could: "Olivier, in a gorgeous primrose silk robe as the prince, spoke, sang and made love delightfully, although at this period of his career over-inclined to reticence. I hoped the part would be some compensation for his great disappointment in choosing Beau Geste instead of Captain Stanhope." And *The Times* was not too unkind: "There are discreet and dexterous sketches by Mr Laurence Olivier."

But it was to prove the second of seven successive flops in which Olivier was involved while he watched Clive and the *Journey's End* companies ruefully:

> [It was] brilliantly successful wherever it played, in New York, Chicago and in as many tours as Maurice Browne chose to send it on; the Blue Company, the Red, the Green, the Pink, the Purple – until he ran out of colours. That was the kind of dazzling whirligig a theatre success could sometimes achieve in the 1930s until about Munich time. That was what I had renounced.

As he struggled from flop to flop, however, he gained "not only experience but a happy collection of critical remarks and first-night approbation which constantly remarked, to my delight, upon my versatility". Hence again his good fortune even in bad. *The Circle of Chalk*, which like *Beau Geste* closed within a month, was followed by two more short-lived London dramas, *Paris Bound* (at the Lyric with Herbert Marshall and Edna Best) and *The Stranger Within* (at the Garrick with Olga Lindo and Roland Culver). Even in a play admired by the critics, and even in a performance which culled warm notices, Olivier could not find himself a box-office success. It did him no harm at all, however, that his name had appeared in large letters outside five different London theatres in as many months, and was becoming familiar to audiences and managements alike.

The result was both a steady income, at last, and his first invitation to Broadway, where English actors were scoring a string of notable successes in the seventy-four theatres then open in New York. Olivier was offered the satisfying part of Hugh Bromilow in Frank Vosper's thriller *Murder on the Second Floor*, already a proven success in London. Vosper himself was playing Bromilow in London and suggested Olivier "represent" him across the Atlantic at the Eltinge Theater. It was not only the bright lights of Broadway which beckoned an excited Olivier; somewhere among them, still enjoying the continuing success of *Bird in Hand*, was his intended, Jill Esmond.

Their months of separation had been part of the "trial period" imposed by Jill. Now, when he surprised her backstage on the evening of his arrival, it was soon clear to them both that they had waited long enough. In the heady atmosphere of Broadway stardom, with Olivier on a ten-week guarantee of $500 a week, they lived the high life and agreed to marry as soon as they were both back in England.

Ten weeks later, it was Olivier who found himself sailing home first, fresh from yet another failure. There appeared to be a jinx on his professional, if not his private, life. Despite its success in London, *Murder on the Second Floor* bombed on Broadway, closing after five weeks and attracting none of the Hollywood talent scouts who might have offered him the chance to stay across the Atlantic. Insult was added to injury when he tested for the part of Stanhope in the film version of *Journey's End*, only to be told that it too had gone to Colin Clive, now inseparably associated with the part in the public mind.

So Equity rules dictated that he must return home, barred from accepting another Broadway role within six months, at the end of his ten-week guarantee – the second five of which he spent putting a brave face on his role as unemployed adjunct to a more successful and more famous fiancée. Jack Hawkins, also in New York at the time, recalled that although he was evidently

> going through a bad patch, [Olivier] always remained in good spirits, and as ever he was a splendid companion.... He consoled himself with the company of an extraordinary dog that he bought from a man in the street. The animal reminded me of two extremely dirty brown face flannels knotted together, but Larry assured me it was a very rare Portuguese wolf-hound. Sadly, it had to go because it developed an addiction to bathtub gin and was constantly fainting.[7]

He had left London in July, expecting an open-ended American life in love with Jill. Now it was barely September and he was back, while she remained in New York committed indefinitely to *Bird in Hand*. There followed a sustained period of unemployment; for several months he was, in the time-honoured theatrical euphemism, "resting". For a few weeks he rented Ralph Richardson's London flat while he too enjoyed success on Broadway. Then to conserve funds, Olivier paid his first sustained visit in years to his father and was delighted to forge a strong and affectionate bond with his stepmother, Isobel Buchanan Olivier, whom he called (after her initials) "Ibo". She was to give Gerard ten more happy years before his death in 1939, although Olivier later chose to reveal that her waning interest in sex after the age of fifty had apparently soured his father's later life. Isobel herself survived her husband by another two decades; in the illnesses of her later years she was frequently visited by her fond stepson, who tried in vain to persuade the doctors to accede to her whispered requests that she be "let go".

December 1929 saw the end of Olivier's involuntary "rest", with a promising-looking return to the West End in the strong part of Jerry Warrender, the shell-shocked pilot in Frank Harvey's play *The Last Enemy*, which he himself described as "uncomfortably poised between Heaven and Hampstead". Among his co-stars were Frank Lawton and Athene Seyler, who had so admired his Shylock at the Central School. In the words of the critic William Macqueen-Pope, Olivier played "a wild, impetuous young man who came back from the dead. His entrance, straight through a seemingly solid door, was a big thrill and was backed by a fine performance."[8] *The Times* almost agreed: "Mr Lawton and Mr Olivier, so long as the guardian angels do not trouble them, are admirable...." But the most significant notice came from Ivor Brown in the *Observer*:

> As the airman Mr Laurence Olivier gives a rendering of the first lustre, as vivid in its nervous brutality as in its later gentleness.... This actor, who be it remembered after some fine work with Sir Barry Jackson's team was first in the part of Stanhope in *Journey's End*, has during the past year given a series of consistently brilliant performances in consistently ill-fated plays. May this one break the unlucky series. At any rate, his time will come.

The Last Enemy – too depressing, alas, for Christmas theatre audiences – joined Olivier's lengthening roll-call of failures after just ten weeks, which was a long run by his current standards. He was already committed to one week at the Arts Theatre in John van Druten's *After All*, with Elissa Landi and Cathleen Nesbitt, which saw *The Times* still championing him: "The delicate contrasts which the dexterous sketches of character afford are continually delightful. Of these contrasts the utmost is made by Mr Olivier...." But he was then to undergo eight months without another stage part – the longest period of inactivity in his entire career. He did manage to chalk up his first two film roles, but only under the auspices of the British Quota Act, which decreed that a proportion of British-made films be shown amid the flood-tide of imports from Hollywood. As a result, the British products were lacklustre and soon forgotten.

Olivier's first film part, for which he earned £58, took him to Berlin – his first flight, which took eight hours from Croydon – to play the juvenile lead in an Anglo–German production called *The Temporary Widow*. Retitled *Murder for Sale* in the US, it was a vehicle for the dancer Lilian Harvey, who was big box office in Germany. Olivier's few weeks away gave him his first taste of opera; he tucked in thirteen (including *Carmen* twice) in as many evenings, before enjoying a brief lakeside holiday with a group including Felix Aylmer. Back in England he played an anonymous Man in another quota production – four days' work for £60 – called *Too Many Crooks*, with Dorothy Boyd, Bromley Davenport, Mina Burnett and Arthur

Stratton. The experience and the movie were so powerful that Ellen Pollock, making her screen debut, does not even remember Olivier being in it.

The fees from both movies were set aside against his and Jill's wedding day. Just a month before, on 18 June, a note in Olivier's diary recalls another momentous appointment in that summer of 1930, which was at last to alter his fortunes dramatically: "10 a.m.: Noël Coward."

Already, at thirty, the toast of London – with *Hay Fever*, *The Vortex* and *Bitter Sweet* to his credit – Coward was sitting up in bed in his Chelsea home in Japanese silk pyjamas, still eating his breakfast, when Olivier arrived. Immediately calling him "Larry", Coward told him with quiet confidence that he was about to produce his greatest success yet, a new four-handed comedy called *Private Lives*, and that he, Larry, could make his name with the part of Victor Prynne. Chucking "Noëlie"s around the room with excited abandon, Olivier thanked him kindly and took away the script. A few days later he was back, telling Noëlie that he would rather play the leading role, Elyot Chase.

Coward laughed himself stupid. He had, of course, written the two main parts, the divorced couple Elyot and Amanda, for himself and Gertrude Lawrence. Written in four days, while he was recovering from 'flu in Shanghai, *Private Lives* was an unashamed vehicle for the heady box-office talents of Noël and Gertie. Victor (Amanda's second husband) and Sybil (Elyot's new wife) were there merely as foils to these two sparkling characters; in Coward's own words, they were "extra puppets ... little better than ninepins, slightly wooden and only there at all in order to be repeatedly knocked down and stood up again".[9] Crestfallen, proud young Olivier was all set to turn him down. But Coward, who had admired him in *Paris Bound* the previous year, needed him. Though Victor was a bore and a prig, the poor soul playing him had to be handsome enough for Amanda to have married him in the first place. Coward also knew that only exciting actors could play bores effectively. With a shrewd mixture of calculation and candour, he told Olivier that he could ill-afford to turn down so glitzy a shop-window as a huge London success at this difficult period in his career. Besides, he was getting married soon, wasn't he? He would need the money. In short: "Don't be such a bloody fool, dear boy. I'll get you fifty quid a week for playing Victor. Rehearsals start in a fortnight."

They were already under way on 25 July, when Olivier and Jill Esmond were married at All Saints, Marylebone: the ceremony was conducted by the vicar, Rev. Mackay, still there from the groom's choir schooldays. It was, as Olivier had hoped, one of the high society occasions of the year – but more because of the bride than the groom. Not only was Jill an ever-rising star in the theatrical firmament, but she had returned from Broadway to go straight into another London hit, taking over from Kay Hammond in the long-running *Nine Till Six*. She had ensured her wedding maximum publicity, moreover, by vouchsafing her own, very bold for their day, views on the subject of matrimony to the *Daily Herald*. Under the heading "WHAT I THINK OF MARRIAGE", Jill set forth arguments which may be commonplace today, but were then advanced enough to have given even her husband-to-be a moment's pause:

> Victorian girls must have looked forward to marriage as a partial escape from a domestic cage. Today marriage is in some ways more like an entrance into a cage.... Many of our elders are fond of talking about the "rights" and "duties" of husbands and wives, as though marriage were a business contract with obligations set forth in black and white. If ever the man I married behaved decently towards me, or I towards him, only because it was laid down in an unwritten marriage contract, I should feel it was high time we parted.
>
> Not that I expect married life to be one long romantic dream. It is impossible that the first careless rapture should last for ever, and luckily too, for nobody could endure such a mental condition for long. Sooner or later, but inevitably, one settles down on an even keel. There is a mutual readjustment. And if one could look forward to that readjustment and see it clearly and dispassionately under conditions of the present day, then the first problem of modern marriage is as good as solved.[10]

The piece had attracted a great deal of attention and caused Olivier a hard time among his friends. In a follow-up interview on the eve of their wedding, Jill was asked whether she still stood by her view that "I should certainly have secrets and friends unknown to a husband of mine, and I should sometimes have a holiday from him as well as work"? Certainly, she replied, adding that she saw no reason why a wife should not support her husband. "She might, for instance, be a better wage-earner, while he might want to take up some sort of work not likely to bring in any money for some time." At the time she was the bigger earner, but she had a very realistic view of her future husband's potential; as she told another newspaper thirty years later: "When we were courting I was, I suppose, the bigger name. But I was always, *always* conscious that his potential was enormous. I always knew he was the much more important person...."[11]

Olivier himself, scarcely a progressive thinker in such matters at any time in his life, was quietly alarmed by all this, though naturally entering into the spirit of things by thinking it "utterly splendid". Jill Esmond's strength and separateness of character did not bode well for marriage to a confused young man with only two things on his mind: sex and success. It was her name, not his, in the headline of *The Times*' report of their wedding next day. But the vicar's son who had shared his father's bathwater, and who had only recently graduated from down-at-heel bedsitterland, was happily aware that he had come a long way in a short time that summer Saturday, as flashbulbs recorded his capture of a beautiful and famous bride amid a galaxy of show-business guests: Jack Hawkins, the Ralph Richardsons, Nora Swinburne, Frank Lawton, Richard Goolden, Alison Leggatt, Margaret Webster.[12] Among the wedding presents was a Persian necklace of black pearls and brilliants from Princess Marie-Louise, stagestruck grand-daughter of Queen Victoria.

[Lady Fripp, a friend of Jill's mother, lent the newlyweds her house at Lulworth Cove for their honeymoon. But Her Ladyship also lent the couple her two unmarried daughters as "hostesses", which added an extra edge of tension to an already strained atmosphere. Again we have Olivier's own description of the physical events of the wedding night, which were scarcely earth-shaking. After some inconclusive fumbling, groom turned away from bride with what he himself calls the "dazzlingly selfish" thought that his wife did not "suit" him. He then lay awake realizing, on Night One, that it had all been a "crass mistake".

A less impetuous man might have read the omens some months before and called the whole thing off. Only weeks before their wedding, according to Olivier, Jill had told him that she was in love "elsewhere" and "could not and did not try to deceive herself into believing that she was in the slightest degree in love with me". Nor did he know that he was not the only suitor to have met Jill off her ship in Liverpool on her return from New York; according to another actor who had shared the voyage with her, Jill had been waving simultaneously to Olivier and another potential groom waiting on the dock above him, and asking her companion's advice as to which she should marry. But Olivier persuaded himself that he would soon put things to rights, "by proving such divine perfection as a husband that any such petty difficulties could be outfaced".

But all too soon he grew resentful of her mother's possessiveness. It had led to a family row before the wedding, when his father had refused to marry the couple, as Jill's mother wished, at the Chapel Royal, Savoy, for the reason that "it is known that divorced people are able to be married there". Gerard had thus been barred from conducting his son's wedding service at all, attending only as a guest, and a guest who got a frosty reception from his son's new mother-in-law. When the couple arrived home from their honeymoon, therefore, to find Jill's mother on the doorstep, having just been "in to furnish a little", the marriage was already on course for the rocks. "Did I really think that a possessively adoring mother would allow the darling of her life to enter a new home that boasted no stick of furniture except a double bed? Yes . . . I really did think that."

Olivier's rush into marriage, he reflects, had been "nothing more commendable than a convenient passport for a rush into bed" – a rush that proved utterly ineffectual, doubly so in view of his discovery that "the idea of bearing children did not find any welcome in my bride's eyes". When a son, Tarquin, was born six years later, he was not to be blessed with the happiest of childhoods. The main effects of marriage on Olivier were his discovery of contraception and his abandonment, for ever, of his religion.

Olivier's father had bequeathed him more than just a stylish surname. An upbringing steeped in the rituals of religion – from Gerard's high church, histrionic pulpit to the incense-laden rites of his son's church choir school – had bred both Olivier's sense of theatre and his zealous fervour about everything he has ever undertaken. It also, however, endowed him with a deeply felt but only half-understood belief in external forces, in a judgemental divinity, which came to amount to little more than nervous, self-doubting superstition. Once he abandoned the Christian God, his father's God, Olivier developed a crippling propensity for guilt. For the rest of his life he would be prone to bouts of deep and frightening self-disgust, most acute during periods of surprised happiness. Ever since this turning-point of his youth, Olivier's insatiable craving for worldly success has always been shadowed by a fear of its consequences for his immortal soul.

The prospect of commercial success at last in *Private Lives* should have been able to take his mind off the misery of the mutual mistake he and Jill had made. But Olivier was none too happy about that, either. It was not just that he took an immediate dislike to his co-ninepin, Adrianne Allen. As the pre-West End run made it clear that the foursome had a hit on their hands, Olivier was miserable – despite the more than welcome money – to find himself in yet another frivolous part. He was playing, what's more, a loser – a dull, priggish, deserted husband. Not the kind of image he was after at all. Where were all the romantic leads, the grand-scale heroic roles he knew would suit his good looks and mercurial stage presence? His career, as well as his young marriage, seemed to be stuck firmly in the doldrums.

With the engaging candour of youth, he bared his heart in a flirtatious interview with an attractive female reporter when the tour reached Manchester. He told the bemused girl, to whom this young man seemed to have the world at his feet:

Only fools are happy.... I suppose it is because they don't really know what they want in life, and so very little pleasure that comes along they regard as a paradise of happiness. I somehow can't get that way. I always examine things so very closely that immediate pleasures are dwarfed by my insistence on ultimate benefits. I want events to go my way and don't want to be driven by events....

Then, with more than a hint of self-love, he laid into Victor Prynne and others:

> I have with very few exceptions always had parts that I have not liked. They have not always been difficult parts, but I have not been too fond of the characters I have had to portray.... I hate the part I am playing now, for instance. I don't mean that I hate playing the part of Prynne, but I think it is a most hateful character. Audiences, you know, find it very difficult to dissociate the actor from the part he is playing, but I do hope Manchester is different. I dearly wish they wouldn't think I am actually what I appear on stage.[13]

"S.P.", the initials-only author of the article, kept expressing astonishment at such self-searching, adding confidence that "the time is not far distant" when Olivier would "become a really brilliant luminary in the theatrical firmament". But to add to the misery of the poor, unappreciated young actor moping in the Midland Hotel, she even managed to spell his name *Lawrence*. (As in turn, even more gallingly, did Noël Coward in the account of the tour in his first volume of memoirs, *Present Indicative*, published seven years later.)

Oblivious at the time of his friend's private agonies, Coward revelled in the *Private Lives* tour as "swathed in luxury.... The touring days of the past belonged to another world. Assurance of success seemed to be emblazoned on the play from the first; we had few qualms, played to capacity business and enjoyed ourselves thoroughly. We felt, I think rightly, that there was a shine on us."[14] It was first-class trains and hotels all the way. Adrianne Allen recalled being "slightly shocked" as the foursome's first meal together, on the train to Edinburgh, ended with a rather drunk Olivier throwing bits of bread at Coward and then "anything stickier he could lay his hands on, until the two of them turned the fight into a Mack Sennett custard-pie comedy".

In London *Private Lives* opened the new Phoenix Theatre to the effusive rapture of a black-tie society audience who were utterly in thrall to its sophisticated marital banter. With seat prices at a stunning £2 4s 6d, it was the London opening of the year and won the sniffy reviews to which Coward had become accustomed while breaking box-office records. Mrs Patrick Campbell enthused backstage about Noël's "little hummings at the piano"; T. E. Lawrence wrote to Coward of his "superb prose"; and even the curmudgeonly Arnold Bennett dubbed him "the Congreve of our day".

But the two lesser characters, as they had feared, got rather short shrift. "Mr Laurence Olivier and Miss Adrianne Allen handsomely pretend to absence of brains and breeding" was all Agate could bring himself to say.

Even Coward felt somewhat mortified:

> Adrianne played Sybil with a subtle tiresomeness and a perfect sense of
> character, more character actually than the part really had.... Larry
> managed, with determination and much personal charm, to invest the
> wooden Victor with enough reality to make him plausible. I frequently felt
> conscience-stricken over them both, playing so gallantly on such palpably
> second strings.[15]

When John Mills visited him backstage on the first night, after what he
remembers as "one of the few evenings in the theatre which have stood out
vividly in my memory", Coward asked his view of Olivier's performance.
"Well," said Mills, "I couldn't believe that anyone as good-looking as that
could be such a rivetingly good actor." Said Coward, as Mills remembers
it: "I'll tell you something: with my unmatched, priceless perception and
without the aid of a crystal ball, in my much-sought-after opinion that
young man, unless something goes radically wrong, will before long be
acknowledged as our greatest actor."[16]

There was little evidence for this in Olivier's daytime work during the
London run of *Private Lives*, playing Straker, the male lead but yet another
cold fish, in the low-budget British film *Potiphar's Wife* (US title: *Her Strange
Desire*). Adapted by Edgar Middleton from his stage comedy, but now
billed a "sex drama" by the moguls of British International Pictures, it
recounts the saga of an aristocratic wife (Nora Swinburne) who is bored
with her husband and takes up instead with her chauffeur (Olivier); when
he grows indifferent to her, she brings charges of assault. Though Olivier
won moderate praise, the film was condemned for its immorality and "bad
taste" – less of a guarantee of box-office success in the 1930s than it is
today. At the time Olivier was "very, very thin and a bit gauche",
remembers his co-star, Nora Swinburne.[17] "Very jolly and nice, but he
had no magic in those days." Added her husband, Esmond Knight: "He
was like a roaring sort of peasant boy."[18]

Coward had already established his oh-so-chic "golden rule" never to
play in any role for more than six months, divided between London and
New York. So after only twelve weeks at the Phoenix, to a chorus of
complaint from disappointed Londoners, he took himself, Gertie and Larry
off to wow Broadway. Audiences who believed that *Private Lives* could not
survive without "Noël-and-Gertie" were proved very wrong and have
been ever since. Coward's biographer, Sheridan Morley, while hailing
Coward and Lawrence as "perhaps the definitive light-comedy partnership
of the century, and never better expressed than in this one play", argues
that *Private Lives* "represents Coward's greatest claim to theatrical immortality". Royalties from the play to the Coward estate prove to this day

that scarcely a week goes by without someone deciding to produce the play somewhere in the world; perhaps the most celebrated revival of recent years, apart from that in Hampstead which launched Coward's own renaissance in his homeland in 1963, was that mounted on Broadway twenty years later as a vehicle for the much-married-and-divorced partnership of Richard Burton and Elizabeth Taylor.

For Olivier, still obsessed by the irony of a commercial success at last in so demeaning a role, the New York transfer was to prove a crucial turning-point. For one thing, Adrianne Allen had become pregnant (the resulting baby being the actor Daniel Massey, who was to play his godfather Noël Coward in the 1968 movie about Gertrude Lawrence, *Star!*). Adrianne was to be replaced across the Atlantic by his wife Jill. Secondly, in so surefire a commercial hit, the chances were that Hollywood talent scouts would be all over him. And so it was to prove – a confusingly upbeat end to a year he would always regard as one of his most miserable.

As Olivier sailed off to New York with the glitzy Noël Coward roadshow, he barely registered the fact that his friend Ralph Richardson had joined the Old Vic company to complement the ever more assured John Gielgud in some major Shakespearean partnerships. Gielgud, who had made his Old Vic debut at the age of seventeen, was still its "child prodigy" eight years later, having in this last season alone played Romeo, Antonio, Richard II, Oberon, Orlando, Macbeth, Hamlet, Hotspur, Prospero and Mark Antony (twice), as well as several other non-Shakespearean roles. But classical acting was as yet a consummation Olivier did not consider especially, let alone devoutly, to be wished. He was more intent on making his name as a matinee idol, of the swashbuckling Fairbanks persuasion, as a swift passport to Hollywood.

The other major bonus of this first association with Coward was that "The Master" (as his friends reverently referred to him) had fast surpassed even Elsie Fogerty and Barry Jackson on the roll-call of Olivier's theatrical mentors. Not merely theatrical, for he had set Olivier off on a lifetime's reading, prescribing *Wuthering Heights*, *Of Human Bondage* and *The Old Wives' Tale* by Arnold Bennett as "three of the best" to shape his tastes. During the run of *Private Lives* Coward proved himself, meanwhile,

> a great mind-opener and very inspiring to work for ... he was probably the first man who took hold of me and made me think ... he taxed me with his sharpness and shrewdness and brilliance, and he used to point out when I was talking nonsense, which nobody had ever done before. He gave me a sense of balance, of right and wrong.[19]

Coward did one other thing for Olivier, which he regards as "priceless": he taught him not to giggle on stage. "By trying to make me laugh outrageously, he taught me how not to give in to it. My great triumph came in New York when one night I managed to break Noël up on the stage without giggling myself."

It was a long and somewhat tedious process for Coward to rid Olivier of the schoolboy habit which still clung to him.

> Larry was a terrible giggler onstage and I had to stop him. It's one thing to have an actor's joke, but it's not very fair on the audience. If I did anything in the part that was at all funny, Larry would be in fits of laughter instead of being cross, so I said "From now on I'm going to try and make you laugh, and every time you do so, I'll kill you." He got so angry with himself for falling for it, and I ruined several of his performances, but it was worth it.[20]

Coward's technique was to invent a dog called Roger, invisible but always onstage when he and Olivier were playing a scene together. Roger belonged to Elyot, but was immensely attracted to Victor, especially his private parts, both before and behind, to which he apparently did "unmentionable things" in full view of the audience. "Down, Roger!" Coward would cry, or "Not in front of the vicar!", until merely a shocked "*Roger!*" would be enough. At length Olivier could take it without a hint of a smile, so much so that he began to get his own back. "A friend of mine has a house on the edge of Cap Ferrat" went one of Victor's lines in the play. "On the *edge*?" ad-libbed Coward. "Yes, on the *very* edge," replied Olivier, straight-faced, which got such a good laugh that Coward wrote it into the script.

Olivier's final test came in a joint Noël–Gertie assault one evening in New York, during the breakfast scene towards the end of the play. As Coward describes it:

> When Amanda spluttered over the coffee, Victor had to slap her hard on the back. One day she choked and turned round to him and said, "You great clob!" "Clob?" I said, and she replied, "Yes, clob." To which I added, "The man with the clob foot!" And, of course, Larry had to restrain himself from giggling. I had finally cured him.[21]

Private Lives opened in New York in January 1931, at the Times Square Theater, and proved as successful as it had in London. Jill, in Coward's view, succeeded Adrianne Allen "excellently", while the New York critics "resented the thinness of the play less than the London critics, and enjoyed the lightness of it more.... We strained every nerve to justify the almost overwhelming praise that was most generously lavished upon us." Though Walter Winchell thought it "something to go silly over", the reality seems to have been slightly different; there was praise for the performances but cool reviews for the play itself, best summarized in the view of the man from *Variety*: "Mr Coward and Miss Lawrence are a couple of cooing meanies.... Coward seems kinda grouchy over their scrapping ... he goes to the piano and starts to sing." Olivier, wrote John Mason Brown, "did nicely enough in a supplementary part Mr Coward had forgotten to write".[22] And Brooks Atkinson wrote: "He and Jill Esmond served the humiliating function of being straightman and straightwoman for the comic extravagance of Noël Coward and Gertrude Lawrence.... It was not a glamorous engagement for Olivier, but it was an experience."[23] For Olivier, moreover, it was an experience which had paid off. Thanks to the showcase of *Private Lives*, the East Coast talent scouts were encouraging him to peel off and head west.

"Hahlleewood," sneered Noël Coward as Olivier took his leave. "You've got no artistic integrity, that's your trouble; this is how you cheapen yourself." But Hollywood was the "Ultima Thule" of Olivier's dreams – so much so that when Jill developed acute appendicitis in New York and was rushed to hospital, he did not trouble to stay at her bedside. Racing ahead on the pretext of fixing a home and a car, he found a pretty three-bedroomed house on the top of Look-Out Mountain, with a view across Tinseltown to the Pacific, and settled down to what were to prove two utterly wasted years.

CHAPTER 4

1931–5

I t was the Oliviers' good fortune – or so they thought – to have been in a Broadway hit at just the moment Hollywood talent scouts were combing the New York stage, ever more desperately, for actors who could speak at all plausibly in front of a camera. The end of the silent movie era had taken many a great name with it; like Anna May Wong, Olivier's co-star in *The Circle of Chalk*, numerous stars of the silver screen had only to open their mouths to find their career in ruins. The moment had not yet arrived when a Lana Turner could be "discovered" sipping soda at the fountain of a downtown drugstore. The stage was the talent scouts' only hunting-ground; good looks and an acceptable speaking voice were quite as important as mere acting skills.

And an English accent was regarded as a positive asset, so much so that a British colony began to sprout in Hollywood, with the English stage suffering not so much a brain drain as a gold rush. Charles Laughton, Claude Rains, Leslie Howard, Ray Milland and Cary Grant were among scores of British actors who headed west in the 1930s, some of them never to return. In the immortal words of another, Sir Cedric Hardwicke: "God felt sorry for actors, so he gave them a place in the sun and a swimming-pool; all they had to sacrifice was their talent."[1]

Suddenly, to the bemusement of the West Coast, there were cricket clubs and polo teams, afternoon tea parties and a general sense of superiority over the natives – as the writer Sheridan Morley dubbed it, a "Hollywood Raj". Perhaps the shrewdest Briton to pass through Hollywood in the 1930s was one who did not stay, J. B. Priestley, who noted after a brief visit:

66

Its trade, which is in dreams at so many dollars per thousand feet, is managed by businessmen pretending to be artists, and by artists pretending to be businessmen. In this queer atmosphere, nobody stays as he was; the artist begins to lose his art and the businessman becomes temperamental and overbalanced.[2]

Several major studios tested Olivier and Jill while they were in *Private Lives*, with a particularly close interest shown by MGM, who had bought the film rights to the play. (In the end, the leading roles went to Robert Montgomery and Norma Shearer; even Noël Coward and Gertrude Lawrence were not considered big enough box-office names.) It was still Jill Esmond who was the hotter property, as witnessed by a cable from a young talent scout named David O. Selznick to his boss at Paramount, B. P. Schulberg:

> PLEASE WIRE INSTRUCTIONS CONCERNING LAURENCE OLIVIER AND JILL ESMOND. OPINION HERE DIVIDED, WITH MAJORITY BELIEVING ESMOND MORE DESIRABLE FOR STOCK THAN OLIVIER. HOWEVER, FELIX YOUNG AND MYSELF ARE THE ONLY TWO THAT HAVE SEEN OLIVIER APART FROM TEST AND WE BOTH CONSIDER HIM EXCELLENT POSSIBILITY. MY OWN FEELING IS THAT, IN SPITE OF THEIR UNQUESTIONED MERIT, THEIR SALARY IS WAY OUT OF LINE FOR BEGINNERS, ESPECIALLY AS WE HAVE NO PARTS IN SIGHT FOR EITHER. WOULD RECOMMEND HAVING NEW YORK TRY TO USE THEM....[3]

But Paramount made no offer. In the hope of swift advancement, both Olivier and Jill eventually signed with RKO Radio, a new studio anxious to promote its own fresh talent. Both were on $700-a-week contracts for three pictures in two years. "We thought we were the luckiest people in the world," he recalled, "and I suppose we were."[4] But the studio records show that while Jill was regarded as a fine prospect for leading female roles, her husband presented more of a problem. In the words of one RKO executive: "He has no chance – he tries to look like Ronnie Colman, but his face is too strong and his looks are too rugged rather than weak and suave. When it comes to rugged actors, we don't need Englishmen. We've got plenty of Americans around to handle those parts."

Once signed and on the payroll, nevertheless, a "property" was duly promoted. A still extant clip from 1931 shows RKO allowing an obsequious young Olivier to promote the fledgling British industry in "talking pictures" (still only six years old): "May a comparatively young English actor offer his very humble congratulations to those who have initiated this enterprise. Hollywood has set a high standard of production, but I know perfectly well that the British brain and the British capital embodied in these and the other British studios will make the British picture Hollywood's most successful rival." Thereafter, however, RKO required Olivier to become thoroughly transatlantic, and he was soon to be found looking uncomfortably macho in sundry baseball poses for the fan magazines. If he were to be RKO's answer to Ronald Colman, he would be packaged with a difference: this suave, moustachioed Englishman was recast as an all-American boy at heart. So the studio was none too pleased when Olivier rather contradicted the party line by joining the new Hollywood cricket club, founded by the only former England cricket captain to have turned movie actor, C. Aubrey Smith.

Here Olivier was to renew old friendships and forge new ones. Among his circle were James Whale and Colin Clive, whose success with *Journey's End* had transformed their lives. Whale had been working for Howard Hughes and was now about to direct a celluloid version of Mary Shelley's horror classic *Frankenstein* (in which he was launching another new English actor, William Pratt, who had been persuaded to change his name to Boris Karloff). Clive, his life gradually disintegrating, was still soldiering on in sundry stiff-upper-lip officer roles. Olivier even found friends dating back to his schooldays at All Saints: Ralph Forbes, Cassius to his Brutus in that *Julius Caesar* so admired by Ellen Terry, had made his name in the movie version of *Beau Geste* and was fortunate enough to be married (though not for much longer) to Ruth Chatterton, voted "the finest actress on the screen" by readers of *Movie Fan*. There was the English character actor Anthony Bushell, another founder-member of the cricket club; and there was the Canadian Raymond Massey, fresh from a Broadway triumph as Hamlet, now making his screen debut as Sherlock Holmes. But Olivier's closest new friend was an American, Douglas Fairbanks Jr, whose marriage to Joan Crawford was at the time on its last legs. From mawkishly vodka-ridden evenings at Hollywood's Russian Club, bemoaning the fact that their wives did not understand them (when not plotting a Soviet counter-revolution), these two prototype "hellraisers" began an intimacy which was to last all their lives.[5]

It was not long before an excited Olivier learnt that his co-stars in his first American film would be the great Erich Von Stroheim and the sultry Lily Damita, breaker of many a noble heart, though her own was to be severely battered by six stormy years of marriage to Errol Flynn. Add Adolphe Menjou, and he had won fourth billing to a formidable trio, under the directorship of Victor Schertzinger. The material, alas, was less formidable. Originally entitled *The Sphinx Has Spoken*, from the extravagant romance of that name by Maurice de Kobra, the movie which finally emerged as *Friends and Lovers* did little to help any of their careers. Olivier's first Hollywood picture, in his own words, "died the death of a dog". It lost RKO $260,000. And *Picturegoer* added insult to Olivier's private injury by reporting that his performance as Nichols was "precious".

He later made this first experience of working with a great Hollywood star sound like a rather poignant black comedy.

> Von Stroheim was preoccupied with a bit of business throughout the rehearsals. To appear ultra-sinister, he was to wear a black patch over one eye and a monocle over the other. But which ornament for which eye? He kept reversing black patch and monocle for Schertzinger's approval. He was a worker, but off the set he seemed to be distracted, worried, lost.

Years later when Olivier saw Von Stroheim in *Sunset Boulevard*, it struck him as an uncanny echo of the German's real life, even in 1931, "the fallen giant of the silent era, dazed by his fall".[6]

The next offer seemed more promising: male lead to the *femme fatale* of the day, Pola Negri, in a real-life Ruritanian drama about Queen Draga, wife of King Alexander of Serbia. The script called for Negri's execution by firing squad, and for Olivier to be thrown out of a window, to whose sill he clung until his fingers were crushed by rifle-butts – thus precipitating a fine instance of Hollywood's beloved death-from-a-great-height, not to mention the end of the Serbian monarchy. There were Fairbanks-like prospects here, it seemed, until Olivier was struck down by jaundice and had to withdraw.

The jaundice was immediately followed, appropriately enough, by a film called *The Yellow Passport*, adapted from the old English melodrama *The Yellow Ticket*. Lionel Barrymore took over the part played onstage by his brother John seventeen years before, the secret police "heavy" in a torrid Czarist melodrama which cast Olivier (on loan from RKO Radio to Fox) as an idealistic English journalist entangled with Elissa Landi. He himself looks back on it as "really quite all right", while the *New York Times* of the day granted that he portrayed Julian Rolphe "quite persuasively". Again, however, *Picturegoer* complained that "if it were not for the acting of Elissa Landi and Lionel Barrymore, this picture would be of little entertainment value".

So 1931 had seen him off to an uninspiring start in pictures, and both the Oliviers began to feel a dispiriting sense of wasted time. There were months of languid inactivity, much of it spent on the party circuit, between films. Most of the community were quite content with so undemanding a way of life, but Olivier and Jill were young and impatient, full of energy and ambition. The opportunities they were passing up back home began to trouble them. "The studios didn't seem to understand when we complained," said Jill. "We were receiving our weekly cheques. What had we to grumble about? That was their attitude." Olivier was also haunted by something David O. Selznick had once said: "If you are primarily concerned with something that is usually called personal artistic integrity, you don't belong in the business of making commercial pictures. You should get yourself a paintbrush or a typewriter."

The next year, 1932, was to prove even worse: for Olivier played only one part, and that was another disappointment. It looked at first like a "truly promising picture": *Westward Passage*, adapted by its director Robert Milton from a novel by Margaret Ayer Barnes, which saw him entangled in an on-off lovematch with Ann Harding. Miss Harding, he wrote home to his family, was "angelic", the complete antithesis of the usual Hollywood star, suggesting that his part be written up, that camera angles, lighting and close-ups favour him as much as herself; but to little avail. *Picturegoer* (in the shape of Lionel Collier) went for him again: Olivier "fails to make an attractive character out of Nick Allen.... The role should have been an expression of young love's dream as imagined by an impetuous and volatile lover. Instead Olivier tends to make him a 'bounder'." But the performance wrung his first "excellent" out of the *New York Times* and *The Cinema* went so far as "effervescent". Olivier, who had felt the part presented "splendid opportunities", found himself feeling "the stir of optimism". But it was not to last: "Conditions were against any seed becoming fertile."

As soon as his main work on *Westward Passage* was complete, Olivier flew down to Mexico to join his two boozing pals, Douglas Fairbanks and Robert Montgomery, on a fishing holiday – only to find himself arrested at Ensenada airport by two Mexican policemen incapable of enough English to explain why. Once he had been led off to the local jail, where his passport was confiscated, officials managed to communicate that a 1,000-peso fine would see him on his way. With nothing like that amount on him, Olivier was clapped behind bars. He was angrily demanding the means to cable the British consul in Mexico City when who should appear, grinning smugly, but Fairbanks and Montgomery, who had bribed the police to take part in an elaborate practical joke. They duly congratulated their friend upon his acting skills. But when Olivier learnt that the arresting officials could speak perfectly good English, he was horrified. Only he knew that his papers were *not*, in fact, in order; he had left in too much of a hurry even to organize a Mexican visa.[7]

Hollywood may have partied its way through the Depression, but for the studios times were growing very lean. It was a common occurrence for the proverbial men in black from the "front office" to arrive on a film set after just a few scenes had been shot, and for thumbs to be drawn across throats as yet another picture fell victim to the collapse of yet another bank. RKO Radio, going through its own economic crisis, desperately brought in that same cable-happy, philosophizing talent scout David O. Selznick, now all of thirty years old, as vice-president in charge of productions. The first thing he did was to set up a "Story Cabinet", with sub-committees in charge of finding scripts which would appeal to women, to young people, to the elderly, to sports fans, to theatre-goers. Then he cut all salaries in half.

Olivier found this "a pointedly dismal sign of the times" and determined to head for home, where he had the offer of what seemed a decent film part opposite Gloria Swanson. *Friends and Lovers* and *Westward Passage* had between them lost RKO over $500,000, so the studio was not going to go out of its way to persuade him to stay. The contemporary verdict of one of its headhunters was crushing:

> The reason that Olivier never became the great movie star many people thought that he should have been ... was because he has no screen personality. He transforms himself magnificently onstage, but on screen all that comes through is his basic personality, which he himself has called "hollow". That hollowness may be just right for a stage actor, who uses his roles to fill himself in; but it is his hollowness that the camera captures.

The fact that Selznick shared this view – that Olivier had huge potential as a stage actor but just did not light up the screen – made it all the easier for the young, frustrated actor to grow homesick.

Such sentiments were not, however, so easy for his wife, who had tentatively been promised a path to real Hollywood stardom as Sydney Fairfield in Clemence Dane's *A Bill of Divorcement*, originally produced for the stage with huge success by Basil Dean. The catch, of course, was that she would have to renew her contract with Selznick at his new bargain-basement rates, in her case $750 a week. Olivier was in the throes of trying to talk her out of it, with little success, when one day he was summoned to Selznick's office for reasons he cannot now remember. The appointment anyway proved more important for what happened before Selznick arrived.

Rather than leave Olivier kicking his heels outside, Selznick's secretary told him to go on in and make himself at home in the vice-president's empty office. Few young hopefuls offered such an opportunity would restrain themselves from snooping around the great man's desk – and there, tucked in the blotter, Olivier saw a document of great significance to Jill's true prospects at RKO. It was the draft of a contract for a young unknown called Katharine Hepburn, whom Selznick proposed to sign for $1,500 a week, rising to $2,500 over three years. Olivier had already, also by mistake, seen Hepburn's screen test. Clearly she was to be RKO's answer to MGM's Garbo. And with *A Bill of Divorcement* the only major script currently scheduled at the studio, there seemed little doubt as to who would finally be playing Sydney.

Jill still took some persuading. Hungry for success, she simply did not want to believe what Olivier was telling her; and besides, Hepburn had yet to sign that contract. Though they were ill-matched and agreed that their careers must come before their marriage, these relative newlyweds had, nevertheless, come to display considerable professional affection towards each other. Jill finally decided to swallow her pride and return to England with her husband. Both were proved right later that year, when *A Bill of Divorcement*, also starring John Barrymore, did indeed prove the vehicle that launched the formidable screen career of Katharine Hepburn.

Olivier returned to England in the highest spirits, only to face yet another disappointment. At Ealing Studios, whose management was desperate for the financial injection, Gloria Swanson was herself producing *Perfect Understanding*, yet another marital melodrama, as the supposed vehicle for her translation from Movie Queen of the 1920s to ditto of the 1930s. Under the direction of Cyril Gardner, Olivier played Nicholas Randall, Swanson's husband, whose belief that marriage can be independent and free of jealousy the film set out to disprove by somewhat predictable means. "Tedious" was the verdict of the *New York Times*, though it again singled Olivier out for praise as giving "a sterling performance in a none-too-fortunate role". But the film was a total flop, even worse than the Hollywood mediocrities from which he had fled. It was, he told a journalist some years later, quite simply "the worst film ever made".

Another, yet greater body-blow followed almost immediately when he and Jill teamed up again with Gertrude Lawrence for a quickie movie called *No Funny Business* – a United Artists regurgitation of *Private Lives*, all broken marriages and Riviera moonscapes, disguised only thinly enough to avoid accusations of plagiarism. If Olivier had not yet squared up to the subtle demands of the silver screen, the great Gertie Lawrence made no concessions at all. The result, yet again, was a disaster – its supreme accolade to this day being that this is one of the few Olivier films to merit no mention in his autobiography. *Monthly Film Bulletin* allowed that he looked "somewhat unhappy as the conventional juvenile lead of the period", while conceding that the film had "a certain fascination as a period piece". But the *New York Times* did not mince words:

> *No Funny Business* deserves some sort of booby prize for its success in reaching such a devastating level of mediocrity. One of the less distinguished products of the recently rejuvenated British film studios. The pace is laboriously slow, the camera static, the recording bad and the direction gifted with a supreme talent for telegraphing its intentions several scenes ahead. It is all excessively silly and makes almost no sense or any point.

Olivier found himself utterly disillusioned with the world of films and determined to have nothing more to do with it. He would return to the stage as soon as a half-decent opportunity presented itself. His sometime mentor Basil Dean – still, it seems, a shade guilty about the *Beau Geste* episode – was an expert witness to this low-point in Olivier's early career. *Perfect Understanding*, he recalled, had "the young Olivier making an early film appearance in a leading part, but showing little sign as yet of those gifts of emotional power and bravura comedy that were later to carry him to the very top of English acting".[8]

Neither as an actor nor as a self-manager had Olivier yet hit his stride. As a performer he was still limited, though showing signs of the versatility which would later be his hallmark; as master of his own fate, relying on a sixth sense which was to prove as crucial to his career as his other innate talents, he was making all the wrong decisions. Opportunism and a youthful lust for fame and fortune had been obliterating any more modest wish to learn his trade slowly and carefully, and to carve a gradual, phased ascent to the top. He had not even established base camp. The decision to return to the stage, in something less than a star part, was the best he had yet made. And the opportunity that came along to give him the chance was more than half-decent.

In April 1933 he was offered a middling part in Keith Winter's *Rats of Norway*, one of those very British plays dealing with the curious moral world of an English private school, in this case a preparatory school near Newcastle. It was not a leading role, but it afforded Olivier the chance to work with his friend Raymond Massey and his childhood idol Gladys Cooper – who had, to his delight, personally sought him for the part. Olivier made a quietly powerful impact as Steven Beringer, an idealistic young schoolmaster corrupted by his elders, so much so that the veteran *Sunday Times* critic Harold Hobson later included it in a list of just seven occasions in his theatre-going life when he had felt himself to be in the presence of greatness. "The feeling", he wrote, "was *coup de foudre*, a thunderclap."[9]

Hobson, a man of unpredictable enthusiasms habitually couched in the most purple tones, waxed lyrical:

Olivier's moment came when, as a young schoolmaster, he stood looking out through a great window on to a cheerless lawn, and murmured to himself, in memory of a vanished world in which kindness and that charity which is love still existed, and even perhaps Parthenophil was not lost, these simple and heartbreaking words:

Four ducks on a pond,
A grass bank beyond,

73

A blue sky of spring,
White clouds on the wing:
What a little thing,
To remember for years –
To remember with tears!

I saw Olivier twice in *Rats of Norway*. ... What remained with me when the play was over was less the tragedy of defeat than the sheer, sad beauty of the regret in Olivier's voice that the fine, untroubled peace of morning should descend to the ruin and destruction of night.

Hobson went round to tell Gladys Cooper how moved he had been. "She looked", he tells us, perhaps not to our surprise, "amazed."[10]

Olivier felt elated to be back in the theatre – "like a man brought round from some kind of asphyxiation, I was an actor again". He was not alone at the time in believing that stage acting and film acting were two very different crafts. But he was wrong. "We know now that this is not by any means a true assessment," he later wrote. "The truth is infinitely subtler. They call for the same ingredients in different proportions." It was to be years yet before he would become capable of regarding screen acting with anything but the most dismissive scorn. He was not to make another American film until *Wuthering Heights* in 1939; but first came one near and very tantalizing miss.

Hollywood was already on his trail again. The first offer was easy enough to turn down: a one-year contract with MGM, offering forty weeks' work for $40,000. Details as to casting, directors and co-stars – no doubt gruesome – were unstipulated. Two days after receiving his refusal, the same studio was back; this time the cable from his Hollywood agent carried an impossibly tempting message:

HAVE ONE PICTURE PROPOSITION LEADING MAN OPPOSITE GARBO GREAT PART
STARTING IN TWO WEEKS ANSWER IMMEDIATELY.

On offer was the leading role opposite Greta Garbo, then at the very peak of her incomparable screen career, in her forthcoming epic *Queen Christina*. On the basis of Olivier's showing in *Westward Passage*, Garbo herself had asked for him as her screen lover. Granted this useful intelligence he was careful to haggle at some length before signing a $1,500-a-week contract and travelling west again, amid publicity on a scale he had not known before. Reporters mobbed him on his departure from Waterloo, as if Garbo's choice of an English leading man were some kind of national honour. "This", declared the London *Evening Standard*, "is the big part that Larry Olivier has deserved for so long."

Little did the *Standard* know that Olivier himself was still in the dark about the exact nature of the part; it was not from MGM, his employers, but from a London film writer that he discovered he was to play a Spanish envoy to the seventeenth-century Swedish court, with whom the Queen would fall in love and share a romantic incognito journey disguised as a man. Even more ominously, cables from the director, Rouben Mamoulian, indicated that the contract safely in his pocket might guarantee nothing but money. All would depend on "whether or not, once in costume and make-up and in the actual studio, he could hold his ground in experience and authority opposite Garbo".

Olivier was both surprised and horrified to find that the first scene scheduled for production was the most torrid love duet in the entire film, requiring him to establish an immediate and powerful screen rapport with an actress whom he had yet to meet. When introduced on the set next morning, he found Garbo disturbingly cold and charmless; smoking languidly, she failed to remove her dark glasses and made no attempt at polite conversation. All too soon they were swept into the first take, when Olivier as Don Antonio was to meet Garbo in her boudoir and "discover the warm, tender woman beneath the boyish masquerade".[11] The director explained, as Olivier recalled it, that "I was to come forward, grasp Garbo's slender body tenderly, look into her eyes and, in the gesture, awaken passion within her, that passion for which she is later to give up the Swedish throne." He gave it everything he could, "but at the touch of my hand Garbo became frigid. I could feel the sudden tautness of her, her eyes as stony and expressionless as if she were marble."

Quite what went wrong remains, as is so often the case with Garbo, shrouded in mystery, although it seems that the Siren sensed the truth: Olivier was afraid of her. The movie-going world now knows that she finally settled for her customary co-star, John Gilbert, in place of Olivier – an act the Hollywood history books describe as "unusually generous", given that Gilbert's own career had foundered since his falsetto voice and Utah accent made him yet another silent screen star destroyed by the talkies. The fan magazines, moreover, had humiliatingly chronicled his long, vain string of attempts to make Garbo his wife. Olivier himself has ingenuously said: "I just didn't measure up.... She had an enormous image to the public. And me, I was just grovelling like a puppet ... not the way to play her great lover.... I simply wasn't up to her – a horrible experience."[12] The evidence of the director, Mamoulian, would seem to confirm this: "Although he had qualities that suited the part, he didn't have enough maturity, skill and acting weight to match Garbo's. In short, he was too young and inexperienced."[13]

The most candid (and highly engaging) explanation we have is again Olivier's own. He realized in the first two weeks, "with ever-increasing apprehension", that he was not making the best of himself. "Something was stopping me. I was too nervous and scared of my leading lady. I knew I was lightweight for her and nowhere near her stature, and began to feel more and more certain that I was for the chop." So he made up his mind to find some way of reaching friendlier terms. Before work started one morning he came across Garbo sitting on an old chest.

> I went boldly up to her and said the three or four sentences that I had made up and practised: but no utterance came from her. I began to flounder and grab at anything that came into my head: some sayings of Will Rogers, of Noël [Coward] – anybody – anything at all, until I came to a wretched end and stopped, pale and panting. After a breathless pause, she slid herself off the chest sideways saying, "Oh vell, live'sh a pain, anyway."

He knew then that "the end was not far off". That evening Garbo disappeared from the set early, and Olivier was asked if he would mind saying his off-screen lines to the continuity girl instead. "I'd *rather*," he replied, relieved at his own candour – not unlike that, it would seem, of the condemned man. Next morning the producer, Walter Wanger, gave him the bad news for which he had prepared himself. "We are crazy about you here at MGM, and we want to put you under contract. But it's just that in this particular part ..." The official line put out by the studio was that Garbo had found him "not tall enough".

Despite the phenomenal success of *Queen Christina*, now a cult movie even by Garbo standards, and despite the considerable public humiliation when his firing hit the newspapers, hindsight suggests that Olivier was again fortunate in his ill-fortune. Had he shared Garbo's triumph, there would have followed the inevitable long-term contract with MGM and major screen stardom, and he might never have returned to the stage. Though irked by the mention of only one Olivier, Jill, in the 1934 edition of the British film annual *Stars of the Screen*, he himself professes to have been relieved at the way things worked out with Garbo: "The part, even in John Gilbert's hands, was a hopelessly unsuccessful one."

Whether or not this is special pleading, history records that, to Wanger's evident relief, Olivier was only too happy to collect the money and run. Years later, Olivier learnt through the director George Cukor that Garbo regretted the whole episode and admitted that he had been treated rather badly. It is certainly documented that in the late 1940s she wanted him for a film she proposed to make – but never did – on the life of Georges Sand.[14]

After the *Queen Christina* fiasco, Olivier unhesitatingly turned down a chance to star as a silver screen Romeo to Norma Shearer's Juliet – declaring that Shakespeare would "never work on film" – and headed instead to Hawaii for a vacation with Jill at the Royal Hawaiian Hotel, Honolulu. A broken toe while surf-riding was the major incident here until a cable arrived inquiring "WOULD YOU BE INTERESTED IN METRO CONTRACT FIFTEEN HUNDRED FORTY WEEKS IN ONE YEAR GUARANTEE?" It was without difficulty that Olivier told the delivery boy, "No Reply." He was certainly relieved not to have to return to England immediately and face those reporters again at Waterloo, for he and Jill were now New York-bound to work for one of the most controversial directors of the day, Jed Harris,[15] in an equally controversial new play.

Mordaunt Shairp's *The Green Bay Tree* was one of the first stage works to deal forthrightly with the subject of homosexuality, delicate box-office material in the mid-1930s. It was a characteristically bold move on the part of Harris to couple it with a production of *The Lake*, a more sentimental British success by Dorothy Massingham and Murray Macdonald. Harris had flown to Hollywood to suggest to Katharine Hepburn, already a major star, that she should show her respect for her craft by returning to the Broadway stage in both. In *The Lake* she would have the lead; in *The Green Bay Tree*, as the only woman in the cast, she would be fourth or fifth in the rankings – a fine indication to her public that Hollywood stardom had not gone to her head. It was an ingenious argument, but Miss Hepburn was in no mood to be persuaded.

"I know what you're thinking," said Harris. "This sonofabitch is trying to promote me. He's got a play with nobody in it, and he'd like to shore it up. So he's trying to con me into it with all these crazy arguments.... Am I right?" Miss Hepburn replied: "You're a mind-reader."[16]

She finished up doing only *The Lake*, a disaster famous above all for Dorothy Parker's remark – made in the interval, not, as legend has it, in a review – that "Miss Hepburn runs the full gamut of her emotions from A to B." And Jill Esmond had a degree of revenge for *A Bill of Divorcement* when she won Hepburn's role in *The Green Bay Tree*, which turned out to be a huge success for all concerned. Olivier was particularly arresting in the play's central scene, which called for him to be "beaten into slavish submission by his benefactor's abnormal attraction for him".

He earned his finest notices yet, with Brooks Atkinson raving in the *New York Times*: "Olivier's Julian is an extraordinary study in the decomposition of a character. His ability to carry a character through from casual beginnings to a defeated conclusion, catching all the shades of meaning as he goes, is acting of the highest quality." Said another reliable critic, Stark Young: "It is a long time since so subtle, fluent and right a performance has been seen in this town."[17] But again Olivier was not happy. He did not like himself in the part, largely because he felt uncomfortable playing a homosexual. Above all, he hated the overbearing Jed Harris, who had provided him with "the most miserable month of rehearsals in my life". When Hepburn herself went backstage to congratulate him – humiliated in Harris's other production in the same week that she won her first Oscar for *Morning Glory* – Olivier told her: "I hate Jed so, I have to get rid of all my drive to kill him."

Harris's methods, it has to be said, did seem to get results, but he was universally disliked in the theatrical profession as a notorious bully to all his casts, no matter how distinguished. For *The Green Bay Tree*, he set out to get two macho, virile young men to play the two leading homosexuals; the ploy succeeded brilliantly, but at great cost to all egos concerned, as Olivier's co-star, James Dale, agreed: Jed Harris "thought himself wonderful, and we all cordially disliked him, all and sundry. And he depressed Olivier beyond words. But then Jed Harris would have depressed anybody . . . we had four weeks of this man, rehearsing every day, and it was one of the most unhappy experiences for both of us."[18]

Indeed it was Harris's universal unpopularity that was eventually to earn him two niches in stage history more memorable than any of his own numerous hit shows. Harris was said by Walt Disney to have inspired the cartoon character of the Big Bad Wolf; and when Olivier, ten years later, was planning his memorable Richard III at the Old Vic and casting about for the most hateful person he could call to mind, he decided to model his demonic king on what he could bear to remember of Jed Harris.

The bad taste Harris left in his mouth, and his young unease at finding himself in the part of a limp-wristed, submissive homosexual – however praised and commercially successful the production – had Olivier longing for release from what looked like being a long-running hit. The opportunity came after twenty weeks, in March 1934, when Noël Coward invited him home to take the lead in a play he would direct himself.

S. N. (Sam) Behrman's *Biography* also marked the end of Coward's long association with C. B. Cochran and his first venture into production with his business partner Jack Wilson. An American comedy of manners which had already proved itself a hit on Broadway, it provided Olivier with the role of a publisher's editor who goads an autobiography out of a celebrated society painter played by Ina Claire, the sometime Mrs John Gilbert, who had created the part in New York. Olivier, who had seen and admired his co-star in the American production, knew that Coward had personal doubts about the play and had decided against acting in it himself. So he was doubly alarmed to see how frenetically fast a production his director demanded. The piece was too cool for such a pace, thought its leading man, and he was to be proved right when – against all the odds – it bombed, closing after barely a month and proving the only real flop in Ina Claire's lustrous career. As Richard Kurt, wrote Ivor Brown in the

Observer, Olivier worked "as well as any man could to hold our interest in this boor; he feels his way into the very heart of roughness, and it is not his fault if, at the close, we are tired of the fellow and his raucous, self-righteous ranting at the world".

After yet another flop, Olivier at least had the consolation of the high life back in his new home, the studio house in Cheyne Walk, Chelsea, which had been the last home of the painter James Whistler. To ease the monotony of their marriage he and Jill lavished their Hollywood earnings on sumptuous furnishings chosen for them by the society designer of the day, Arthur de Lissa; they laid out the most elegant of London gardens, scattered tapestries and bronzes around, and even gave pride of place to a ring-tailed lemur, which sat caged in the minstrels' gallery overlooking the river. Here they hosted many a stylish party, prompting Noël Coward to remark that "the trouble with Larry is that he has such illusions of grandeur". For an actor who had yet to score his first real success in a leading rôle, the part he wrote for himself in life did, indeed, rely much more on his highly polished personal charm than on his track record, which was showing no immediate signs of improvement.

Next came the first of two last-minute stand-in roles, when an unhappy Ralph Richardson pulled out of rehearsals for *Queen of Scots* (written by Gordon Daviot, alias the novelist Josephine Tey, for Gwen Ffrangcon-Davies), complaining that he was miscast as the swashbuckling, amorous Bothwell. Richardson was really, it seems, rather shy of the love scenes with Miss Ffrangcon-Davies. Only a week before the opening Olivier leapt at the chance, and to considerable effect. He may have been, in one immortal judgement, "more Hollywood than Holyrood". But Agate praised his Bothwell as "an excellently conceived and executed portrait ... except that I think he is a little too light, especially in the voice, which has the tennis club, will-you-serve-first-partner-or-shall-I? ring about it". Miss Ffrangcon-Davies remembered:

> He played it brilliantly and he looked absolutely divine. He was almost too handsome, really, for Bothwell. All the ladies who have ever played with Larry fell under his spell. He was marvellous to work with – and when it came to the clinches, you didn't have to worry. That was the good part.

The production was further memorable to Olivier for the number of long-standing friendships it initiated: with Gwen Ffrangcon-Davies herself; with Mercia Swinburne, George Relph's wife; with the director Margaret Webster; with the designers, Elizabeth Montgomery, Percy and Sophie Harris, the three talented girls known collectively as Motley; with two newcomers, James Mason and George Devine, both in peripheral roles; and especially with two other young actors, Glen Byam Shaw and

79

Campbell Gullan, with whom he formed a three-member club called, after his character, The Bothwellians. The club rules, as he describes them, were undemanding:

> There must have been four scenes in the last act; after the first, Gully [Campbell Gullan] would be finished, and his office was to get the [whisky] bottle, the soda and the glasses ready on the tray. Glen would be off the stage five minutes after scene two; he would pour out the drinks. They would sit talking and staring at them for the four minutes or so that it took me to be through with the third scene.... The pleasure of fulfilment owes much, if not all, to the durance of the waiting upon it. I am sure that the wait before I burst in upon them was to those friends a dedicated vigil.

Above all, however, *Queen of Scots* introduced Olivier to a professional partnership which was to alter his career dramatically – and not before time – the following year. The play was directed by the "young meteor" of the Old Vic, John Gielgud, who had played opposite Gwen Ffrangcon-Davies in Daviot's previous historical epic, *Richard of Bordeaux*. Although Gielgud, then thirty to Olivier's twenty-seven, describes the production as "only a moderate success",[19] he had made due note of Olivier's young, brash talent and was to seek it out again with vastly more substantial consequences. As Olivier had inherited the part from Richardson, who had, in fact, suggested him to Gielgud as his replacement, this modest production in its way brought together for the first time the remarkable triumvirate of actors who between them were to have such an immense impact on their craft over the coming half-century – and whose private friendships, with their loyalties and their rivalries, their jealousies and their generosities, their ups and their downs, were to be equally illustrative of the art of great acting.

But the Gielgud–Olivier partnership was not to catch fire quite yet. The younger and vastly less distinguished actor first had another breach to leap into, even less exalted than a part in which Ralph Richardson had felt ill-at-ease. Noël Coward wanted him to play the young lead in *Theatre Royal*, a comedy by Edna Ferber and George S. Kauffman about a celebrated but absurdly self-important family of American actors; it was, in fact, a thinly veiled satire on the First Family of the American theatre, the Barrymores. (In the United States the play had been named *The Royal Family*, a title deemed too *risqué* for production on an English stage still saddled with the supervision of the Lord Chamberlain.) Especially galling for Olivier was the fact that Coward wanted him only for the three-week, pre-West End provincial tour, as a £100-a-week favour to his old friend and mentor. When the play came into town his character, Tony Cavendish, would be taken over by the actor who had created him in New York, Brian Aherne, at present detained in Hollywood.

Olivier, of course, had other ideas. His part was an outrageous take-off of John Barrymore, and thus a rare opportunity to combine his talent for mimicry with some bravura physical acting – and stage gymnastics – of the most extravagant kind. He set out to play the part with such gusto and daring that Aherne would never have the nerve to take it over.

Olivier succeeded triumphantly, indulging himself in the Fairbanks-style high jinks he had coveted for so long, climaxing in a memorable eight-foot leap over a balcony which unnerved audiences, not to mention the rest of the cast, night after night. He had already endeared himself to its most distinguished member, Dame Marie Tempest, during a violent fencing scene, when his sword slipped his grasp, flew across the stage and struck the formidable eighty year old upon her ample bosom. Relishing the spirit of his performance, Dame Marie became Olivier's staunchest supporter, treating Aherne with her haughtiest indifference when he arrived to claim his role. Poor Aherne, when he saw Olivier's performance, became even more ill-at-ease: "I was deeply impressed and terrified to watch him jump from the upper landing over the banisters and down on to the stairs below. Could I possibly do it? I thought not."[20]

Several sleepless nights later, with Marie Tempest refusing to re-rehearse, Aherne's problem was unexpectedly resolved when Katharine Cornell telephoned from New York with the attractive proposition that he return to play Mercutio to her Juliet, in a cast that also included Basil Rathbone (as Romeo), Edith Evans, Orson Welles and the young Tyrone Power. "Noël released me and I left at once, thankful that I wouldn't have to attempt that jump." This, at least, was the account given by Aherne in his memoirs, but one of Coward's biographers suggests that the director had been up to some skulduggery of which Aherne never knew. Once Coward realized how sensational Olivier's performance was, he is said to have made a transatlantic call to Guthrie McLintic, Cornell's husband, who was to direct her as Juliet, suggesting that Aherne would be perfect for Mercutio. The only loose end to Coward's plot was that Olivier was looking forward to what looked like an even better part in the new Keith Winter play, *Ringmaster*. On learning this Coward took Olivier for a walk, during which there ensued a conversation, as Olivier recalls it, along these lines:

COWARD: "Suppose Brian were to break his leg?"
OLIVIER: "He won't break his leg."
COWARD: "But supposing he did, then you'd have to play, wouldn't you?"
OLIVIER: "What about *Ringmaster*?"
COWARD: "Fuck *Ringmaster* and leave it to me."[21]

Olivier's arrival in London in *Theatre Royal*, in what was hailed as his outstanding performance to date, signalled the biggest impact he had yet made on the West End. He earned rave reviews and standing ovations for the sheer athleticism of his performance, and he thoroughly enjoyed himself, playing the role with what the theatre historian Audrey Williamson remembered as "harebrained charm".[22] He had been playing Cavendish at the Lyric for almost two months when, perhaps inevitably, he misjudged the leap one night and broke his ankle.

So Olivier began 1935 on crutches. But as luck – again – would have it, his part in *Ringmaster* was still available and required him to spend the evening in a wheelchair, as the landlord of a Torbay guest-house who terrorizes his lodgers. He made good use of his involuntary infirmity, acting out painful movements with a realism which made audiences wince, and ending the performance in an agonized writhing which brought them to their feet. Despite an impressive cast, including his wife Jill, Dame May Whitty, Colin Keith-Johnston, Nigel Patrick and Cathleen Nesbitt, under the direction of Raymond Massey, the final curtain came down after only a week. Audiences had proved enthusiastic, but the critics had appreciated the performers more than the play. Ivor Brown, however, was growing impatient with Olivier's delivery: "I wished he would not clip his speech and throw away the last words of a sentence; it was a continual strain to hear him." On the terminal Saturday night, after six curtain-calls, Olivier found himself for the first time required as leading actor to make a curtain speech: "We as characters have unfortunately died tonight," he said, to cries of "Don't take it off!" "But we hope that, brief though our appearances have been, we will live in your memories."

Closure after eight performances was the shortest run Olivier had yet suffered in London. It was doubly embarrassing because he was fast becoming a minor celebrity, invited to lunch with Sir James Barrie, to drinks with Sir Gerald du Maurier, and even, as best-known old boy, to judge the passing-out exams at the Central School. But his next venture, which also marked his debut as an actor-manager, was not to fare much better than his last. For *Golden Arrow*, a modish play featuring the then rare distinction of an unmarried couple living together, Olivier teamed up with the manager who had stuck his neck out over *Journey's End*, Maurice Browne. Browne soon became unhappy with his partner's wish to direct as well as perform, and began to fear that Victor Cunard's play was too slow-paced and frothy to stand much chance. Olivier disagreed violently, took over sole management of the enterprise, had the proud words "Laurence Olivier presents" printed on a playbill for the very first time and was soon proved emphatically wrong.

The play was really very threadbare, but Olivier was too caught up in his first taste of directing to notice. With the enthusiastic approval of his cast, which included Helen Hayes and Cecil Parker, he was attempting to pioneer a new method of direction, based on his own frustration with directors who spent the first few days worrying over the tiniest inflections and practising all sorts of experimental moves. It gave the actor no time, he argued, to grow into his part. So after a read-through on the first day, he began by blocking certain moves for each act, right or wrong, and sticking to them at least for now; he then took his cast straight through an entire act per day and the whole play on the fifth. Only then, when the actors had come to grips with their characters, did he begin to modify his original thoughts. This was for many years to remain, as a director, the basis of his approach.

Despite (or perhaps because of) its director's other bold experiments, such as a party scene in which everyone talked at once as a gesture to "naturalism", *Golden Arrow* lasted just two weeks and proved notable mainly for the first of the many "discoveries" Olivier was to make as director or actor-manager. In the role of an American girl he cast Enid Garson, a twenty-year-old redhead from County Down with a BA degree from London University, but little acting experience; in later years, when she changed her first name to Greer and went on to an Oscar-winning Hollywood career, co-starring with Olivier in *Pride and Prejudice*, she was to vindicate his curtain speech declaring her to possess "undeniable and obvious potentialities". Though showing early signs of his now familiar archness, the speech was hailed by Agate in the *Sunday Times* as the only worthwhile thing Olivier had said onstage all evening.

"I wish there were something more positively interesting to record about that first Olivier production," said Denys Blakelock, who had had a minor role in it. "But the play, though witty and entertaining, was very lightweight and did not give him much chance to stretch his imaginative powers."[23] It had been a lean five years since *Private Lives*, during which Olivier's marriage had proved as uninspired as almost every stage and screen project he had tackled. "It's no good," he told Emlyn Williams over a midnight coffee at Lyons Corner House in the Strand. "I'll never make it. I'm washed up."[24]

But around the next corner lay the chance to play the classical roles which were to point him towards greatness. Denys Blakelock, who knew him so well at the time, sensed the significance of the moment. Despite his erratic career, twenty-seven-year-old Olivier was then "at his most smart and sophisticated – quite a different personality from what we know today". He had travelled far already since 1928 and "the days when Clare Eames had said 'Larry looks down at me with the eyes of a conqueror.' The conqueror had arrived. The building of his empire was about to begin."

CHAPTER 5

1935

"**T**oo kind, dear boy, too kind" was all Sir John Gielgud would say, a smile playing around his lips, to the suggestion that but for him Laurence Olivier might never have become a classical actor. "That's really for you to say, not me."[1]

The record shows that Olivier had displayed little interest in Shakespeare before 1935, when Gielgud suggested alternating the roles of Romeo and Mercutio with him, to Peggy Ashcroft's Juliet. He had not even been Gielgud's first choice. Yet this would prove to be his first step towards stealing Gielgud's crown.

In November 1934, while Olivier was leaping nightly over the banisters of the Lyric Theatre, an even more startling theatrical phenomenon had been taking place outside the New Theatre in St Martin's Lane. For the first time in living memory, people were queueing in the West End to see Shakespeare. In his second attempt, at the age of thirty, John Gielgud had lovingly crafted a Hamlet so compelling, so poetic, so in command of its audience's emotions that *le tout Londres* found itself in his thrall. The critics had been lukewarm – "Everest half-scaled" was Agate's verdict – but for once theatre-goers chose to ignore them. Bronson Albery, Gielgud's partner in the venture, had planned a run of six weeks which extended eventually to six months and a total of 155 performances, second only in the entire history of *Hamlet* performances to Henry Irving's 200 some sixty years before. Those critics conscientious enough to return after the first night soon began to realize the significance of the production, Gielgud's own. J. C. Trewin, for one, hailed it as "the key Shakespearean revival of its period".

Although the text makes it clear that Hamlet's age is around thirty, it is a twentieth-century phenomenon for audiences to prefer their Hamlets to be in the bloom of youth. Traditionally, until the 1920s, an actor was expected to have built a reputation before he squared up to the role: Forbes-Robertson played the part for the first time at the age of forty-four, Irving at thirty-seven, Barrymore at forty, and few others had tackled it before thirty-five. So Gielgud's previous Hamlet, at the age of twenty-six, had been a trail-blazer in itself; when it transferred from the Old Vic to the Queen's in 1929, even though for only a short run, it was itself making theatrical history. And Agate was impressed: "I have no hesitation in saying that it is the high watermark of English Shakespearean acting in our time."

At the time, Olivier was floundering in his post-*Beau Geste* run of seven consecutive flops. By Gielgud's second Hamlet, he had appeared only in modern-dress roles, apart from Bothwell, throughout his erratic first decade in the commercial theatre. It can be argued that Olivier was moving with the spirit of the times; accentuated by the talkies' hunger for contemporary themes, the demand of the late 1920s and early 1930s was for "naturalness" and novelty, experiment and innovation. But if it required an actor of unusual nerve and dedication to earn his living in doublet and hose, while displaying a fine indifference to the twin totems of Hollywood and megabucks, the supreme example of that actor was to be found in John Gielgud. He was scarcely revolutionary in his techniques, apart from his desire to surround himself with the best available actors, rather than follow the great actor-managers in employing mere competents who would ensure their own pre-eminence. But in both his Hamlets, Gielgud strove to perfect the traditional approach – reflective, poetic, almost musical – at the expense of any major reappraisal of the work. So when he invited his brash young contemporary to join him in more West End Shakespeare, he little knew that he was signalling a clash of cultures which was to resound through the British theatre for the rest of the century.

Neither the play nor his co-star had been Gielgud's first choice. Already he had reduced Terence Rattigan to tears by abandoning plans to produce his version of *A Tale of Two Cities* (after a plea from the veteran actor Martin Harvey, who had made the part of Sidney Carton his own in *The Only Way*). When the suggestion of *Romeo and Juliet* came up, Gielgud had conceived the production around himself and Robert Donat, the new toast of the English cinema after his success as Richard Hannay in Alfred Hitchcock's *The Thirty-Nine Steps*. But Donat, another dedicated actor determined not to abandon the stage for cinema work alone, had long been planning his own production. Olivier's willingness the previous year to take over from Richardson at such short notice, and with such effect, in Gielgud's production of *Queen of Scots* now paid off – despite the fact that he had shown little interest in, or aptitude for, the classical theatre. As Gielgud and Albery cast around for a swift replacement for Donat, they knew just where to turn. At first, to Gielgud's consternation, Olivier hinted that he too was planning his own production, with his wife Jill as Juliet. But he was "generously", as the ever gracious Gielgud put it, prepared to abandon his own plans for the chance to play with his great contemporary.

So Gielgud, by both his art and his persistence, had single-handedly created the favourable climate in which Olivier could now seize upon his first chance of a major classic role on the London stage. Fortune was again smiling on Olivier: for him, the timing of Gielgud's offer could not have been more perfect. Despite himself, he had just clocked up yet another indifferent film, *Conquest of the Air*; for all his reservations about screen acting, Olivier had not been able to resist the financial security of an Alexander Korda contract when offered it the previous April. The Hungarian-born Korda's London Film Productions was riding high on the success of Charles Laughton in *The Private Life of Henry VIII*, and a mini-Hollywood was burgeoning at his fast-expanding studios on the edge of London, at Denham in Buckinghamshire, where many actors now bought large, suitably vulgar homes. Olivier joined Laughton, Richardson, Massey, Leslie Banks, Merle Oberon and Maurice Chevalier among Korda's leading stars. It was with this first rush of money to the head that Olivier had financed his abortive *Golden Arrow*.

Two months later he was earning what he had already lost in another Russian spy drama, *Moscow Nights* (retitled *I Stand Condemned* in the United States), which was an unashamed remake of the successful French version, *Nuits Muscovites*. Despite the presence of Athene Seyler, Penelope Dudley Ward and the grand old man of French cinema, Harry Baur – not to mention the screen debut, as Soldier in Hospital Bed, of one Anthony Quayle – it fell very flat; the innovative camera techniques, flagrantly copied from the French version, lost their panache in Anthony Asquith's translation. As Olivier put it, "Even the title sounded better in French." In the role of Captain Ignatioff, yet another dashing, moustachioed rescuer of a damsel in distress, Olivier caught the attention of the *Observer* critic: "Such pleasure as I got ... was largely due to Mr Olivier's recurrent appearances on the screen." But the consensus was best expressed by the novelist Graham Greene, then film critic of the *Spectator:*

Completely bogus. ... This absurd romantic spy-drama of wartime Russia opens with Volga boatmen and carries on with every worn-out property of a Hollywood Russia, even to the gipsy orchestras. The direction is puerile, no one can drop a glass or a tray without Mr Asquith cutting to a shell-burst. But he has been well-served by his players, by M. Harry Baur [...] and Mr Laurence Olivier as an embittered young front-line officer who loves a young society nurse engaged to the profiteer.[2]

So it was another timely rescue for this comfortably-off but more-miss-than-hit performer when Gielgud and Albery made him the up-market offer he could not refuse. Gielgud was excitedly basing his production on a highly successful *Romeo* he had directed for the Oxford University Dramatic Society three years before, at the invitation of its then president, George Devine, later to be the founding father of the English Stage Company at the Royal Court. It had used methods Gielgud had absorbed at the Old Vic from Harcourt Williams, himself a disciple of Harley Granville-Barker: "a purge on Bardic rhetoric, continuity of action and the principle of designed production".[3] As designers, then and now, Gielgud used the Motleys, the talented three-women team Olivier had first met during *Queen of Scots* and was often to employ himself in later years. Gielgud asked them to reproduce the triple-arched scheme they had designed for Oxford, which placed the balcony with due prominence in the centre and gave Gielgud as director "the advantage of simplicity and speed".[4]

Only three weeks were available for rehearsals, as Gielgud was simultaneously (and most unhappily) filming *The Secret Agent* for Hitchcock by day. Had there been longer, it is entirely possible that this historic production might never have reached the stage, for it was clear from the first that the two actors were totally at odds in their approach to the part of Romeo. Gielgud's reputation had been built on the lyrical, reflective, euphonious school of Shakespearean acting; Olivier was trying to make his as a feet-on-the-ground naturalist, all flashing eyes and fire-and-brimstone. Where Gielgud rolled the lines around his tongue and let Romeo's poetry resound mellifluously to the rafters, Olivier spoke verse as he had always been taught and has always believed to be correct – "to speak it as if that is the way you speak naturally". He saw Romeo, moreover, not as the traditional moon-faced idealist, but as a tousle-haired sixteen year old, at once impetuous and hesitant, in the desperate grip of a love all too recognizably adolescent. Gielgud had never intended the alternating of roles to be competitive, but that was what it inevitably became: the kind of theatrical sport popular a century before, when two rival young actors of different styles sought to outdo each other and seize the initiative in a contest that would continue indefinitely elsewhere, on separate stages.

The English stage bore a great tradition of the exchange of roles, but more often of Othello and Iago than Romeo and Mercutio; Mercutio, after all, dies half-way through the play. Whatever the parts, it invariably becomes a bit of a prizefight. It was almost a century since Macready and Phelps exchanged Iago and Othello, without damaging either of their reputations; forty years later Irving and Edwin Booth met on the same heavyweight bill, which resulted in damage from which Booth's career never recovered. A celebrated example of more recent years was the swapping of Othello and Iago by Richard Burton and John Neville at the Old Vic in 1956. Burton was praised much more for his Iago than his Othello, which – like Olivier's Romeo – was criticized for making the verse sound like prose. While Burton went on to a celebrated career as an actor who preferred lucrative movie roles, expensive wives and celebrity *per se* to the distinguished stage reputation he could have had, Neville proved as outstanding a theatre administrator as an actor, notably at the Nottingham Playhouse and subsequently at Stratford, Ontario. Olivier, when he came to cast his Othello at the National Theatre in 1964, was careful to choose as Iago a young company member, Frank Finlay, who would be in no danger of stealing the show from him.

Back in 1935, in caustic mood, Agate summarized the entire project as rather like a game of golf: "The two actors put themselves in the position of two golfers engaging not in a match by holes, but in a medal round, the par of the course being the ideal performance of the character."[5] The problem was that "the par of Mercutio is pretty well known", whereas "the par of Romeo is something upon which the best analysers of golf-courses have never agreed".

By inviting Olivier to open as Romeo, Gielgud adopted a high-risk strategy which appeared to vindicate his own approach to romantic acting: his Mercutio took the first round on points when the production opened at the New on 17 October. Olivier came on looking every inch an Italian Renaissance prince straight out of the Uffizi Gallery, his gestures restless with the impetuosity of hot-headed youth. Descriptions of that moment dwell on the vivid impression he gave of confused, impulsive, romantic adolescence, with much romantic subtlety of detail. Jessica Tandy recalls how Olivier "worked for ages to bend his fingers back so that in the balcony scene the visual line from fingertips to neck would be pure. Already he understood style in a way few actors do." Other moments which lingered in the memory, according to Audrey Williamson, included "his tender fingering of Juliet's balcony, as if the stone were a sentient part of her ...", "pale, haunted at the cry 'I am fortune's fool ...'", "his blanched prevision of doom over Tybalt's body ... authentically clairvoyant on:

> My mind misgives
> Some consequence, yet hanging in the stars
> Shall bitterly begin his fearful date
> With this night's revels."

But this Romeo, if he had "the warm sun of Italy in his face and veins", alas displayed in his voice "some of the hard edge of the North". The richness of the Olivier voice was already discernible, waiting to be mined, but buried beneath clipped speech and too rudimentary a feeling for words. Olivier's Romeo was roundly condemned for its mangling of the beauties of Shakespeare's verse; verdicts ranged from "His blank verse is the blankest I have ever heard", to "Mr Olivier plays Romeo as if he were riding a motor-bike."

He was absolutely crushed. "When the sledge-hammer of opprobrium struck its blow from every critic to a man, I was so shocked that it was all I could do to get myself on to the stage for the second performance." After taking a long walk with Glen Byam Shaw, who was playing Benvolio, Olivier went straight to Bronson Albery's office and offered to give up the part immediately. Albery would not hear of it; and as the run continued, as Olivier had hoped, "bit by bit and one by one eminent writers began to take some trouble to come to my defence".

Agate was at his most contradictory. In a piece which ended by declaring Olivier's Romeo "the most moving I have ever seen", he complained bitterly about his "modernity and clipped speech". The performance, he declared,

> suffered enormously from the fact that the spoken part of the poetry eluded him. In his delivery he brought off a twofold inexpertness which approached virtuosity – that of gabbling all the words in a line and uttering each line as a staccato whole cut off from its fellows. In his early scenes this Romeo appeared to have no apprehension of, let alone joy in, the words he was speaking....

Olivier's respect for the text seemed virtually non-existent:

> Throughout one wanted over and over again to stop the performance and tell the actor that he couldn't, just couldn't, rush this or that passage ... what is the use of Shakespeare's writing such an image as "The white wonder of dear Juliet's hand" if Romeo is not himself blasted with the beauty of it?

But to Trewin, Olivier's Romeo so caressed certain phrases ("Look, love, what envious streaks Do lace the severing clouds in yonder east") as to be matched by "no other player in remembrance". He had "won half his battle as soon as Romeo, olive-skinned, impetuous, adolescent, entered straight from Renaissance Italy, a world of hot sun, sharp swords and brief lives". For Darlington, "Olivier's young lover was so impassioned that he upset the balance of the balcony scene. One felt sure that this Romeo would never have consented to stay down in the garden speaking blank verse; he would have swarmed up a pillar and taken Juliet in his arms, and where would your Willie Shakespeare have been then...?"

An awed Richardson told Gielgud: "He stands against the balcony with such an extraordinary pose that this animal magnetism and vitality and passion come right over." To most, that "animal magnetism" was enough to staunch any doubts about Olivier's diction. Here was a Romeo who was wildly enough in love to be ready for death – a quality Gielgud was to find hard to reproduce. The director Tyrone Guthrie, renowned for his shrewd eye, wrote to Olivier (who had yet to meet him):

> This is Fan Mail! Have been deeply thrilled and moved by R & J, and especially with your Romeo. I believe the critics are right who fault you for not getting full value out of the verse. I didn't feel this at the theatre, but thinking it over as I go to bed now I believe it's true. But it doesn't matter. Your performance had such terrific vitality – speed and intelligence and *muscularity* – a lyric quality pictorially, if not musically. It has been a very exciting evening.

Guthrie's letter was to lead in time to an historic partnership. But Olivier treasured even more a letter from an anonymous admirer, whom he never met:

> When the interval came I was almost in tears and could not control my voice to answer anything more than a monosyllable when my companion spoke to me. I do not think I ever wish to see this play again lest my memory of Olivier be dimmed. Here was the true youth untouched by love, with all the shy hesitancies of inexperience when he first set eyes on Juliet at the feast. He flowered into such beauty of feeling and movement that my heart ached for him, knowing what was to follow.[6]

As Gielgud prepared for the change-over, which required considerable re-rehearsal, he was growing more miserable by the day on the set of *The Secret Agent*. Hitchcock had persuaded him to accept the role of Somerset Maugham's reluctant spy on the grounds that the character was a modern-day Hamlet, a man hesitating over a number of very difficult decisions. But Gielgud had not enjoyed the filming at all, partly because he detested his director's penchant for practical jokes, more because he found the chronic waste of time on a film set enervating. "Alfred Hitchcock", he said at the time, "has often made me feel like a jelly and I have been nearly sick with nervousness." Later he recalled: "I had to get up very early in the morning and was always fidgeting to get away by five or six for the evening performance, so I grew to dislike working for the cinema.... I did not have much confidence in my talent as a film actor, and I thought when I saw the film that it was rather poor...."[7]

At the end of November, when he was scheduled to take over as Romeo, Gielgud was at a particularly tiresome stage of filming: lying under piles of train-wreck rubble for four days of complex reshooting and sitting for hours in front of a blank screen while Lake Como was back-projected behind him. Olivier, meanwhile, was mugging up on Mercutio by seeking the advice of his friend Richardson, who was playing the role on tour in the United States. Richardson wrote to Olivier from Boston:

I can't tell you how to play Mercutio; you should be much better than me ... but as you ask me I will tell you my experience of it. Be careful not to hurry the "Mab" speech, as I did at first from over-anxiety to be bright. It is a speech that depends on detail, and if all the points are made will seem enormously brilliant, but if slightly rushed is just dull. The second scene plays itself. I play it with a sort of lazy humour and come on yawning and blowing pip-squeaks after the party – but don't forget the sudden delicacy of "If love be blind, love cannot hit the mark". The next scene you should do extremely well – here I am as rapid as can be – the real "Mercutio" tremendously smart and as full of full-up light and life as I can make him. You should try to produce a different key every time you come on – and wear your clothes in a different way. I have a tremendous circular scarlet cloak of fine red flannelette; this I can do a great many things with....

The letter ended with advice Olivier was still able to quote by heart many years later:

I hope you are not bored with all this, my dear boy – but one thing more – the greatest difficulty is to keep sober enough in the one hour twenty-five minutes wait you have before the end to take your curtain-call without falling into an orchestra pit. This takes years of skill and cannot be over-estimated, as much of the effect of the poetic "Mab" speech may be lost by such an incident....[8]

When the dread role-swap came, as Gielgud remembered it, "the only trouble came in our scenes together, when we kept on trying to speak on each other's cues".[9] But the consensus was that Olivier was altogether better suited to Mercutio. One especially successful moment came when he taunted Juliet's nurse, played by Edith Evans; on the line "A sail, a sail ...", he mortified her by lifting the hem of her skirt with the point of his sword. In contrast to Gielgud's lyrical rendering of the Queen Mab speech, Olivier was "a Mercutio all dash and swagger, a Mercutio well pleased with himself, a Mercutio who had perhaps walked too much in the heat of the sun and was a little mad".

The contrast between their styles now became so conspicuous that Agate accused them both of "a clash of magnanimities that is almost embarrassing", with Gielgud "going to the length of not letting us see what he thinks of Mr Olivier's diction in the Queen Mab speech, and Mr Olivier tempering Mercutio's death agony to permit us a glimpse of

Romeo's contrition". And Olivier's Mercutio? "There is plenty of honest rock about it, though he turns on the poetry in the way that athletic young fellows turn on their morning bath...."

There was no doubt, however, that Olivier's Romeo had been much more in love with Juliet than Gielgud's, who seemed to be rather more in love with himself. Wrote Agate:

> Mr Olivier's Romeo showed himself very much in love but rather butchered the poetry, whereas Mr Gielgud carves the verse so exquisitely that you would say the shop he kept was a *bonne-boucherie*. Yet is this Romeo ever really in love with anyone but himself? ... I have a feeling that this Romeo never warms up to Juliet until she is cold.

As Juliet, Peggy Ashcroft, caught in the middle of the growing controversy, had rather liked Olivier's less musical approach to the verse and his "more realistic" approach to the love scenes.[10] But she found that Gielgud seemed to carry the audience along with him more whole-heartedly. As Herbert Farjeon put it, "Mr Olivier was about twenty times as much in love with Juliet as Mr Gielgud is, but Mr Gielgud speaks most of the poetry far better than Mr Olivier." It fell to Agate, in his influential radio programme, to issue a suitably magisterial verdict: "If Romeo were just a lovesick gumph, occasionally falling into a deeper trance in which he speaks unaccountable poetry, then Olivier is your Romeo. But if it is a question of playing Shakespeare's analytical and critical lover, then Gielgud's the man."

An unhappy Gielgud was cheered by a letter from his mentor Harley Granville-Barker, declaring the production "the best bit of Shakespeare I've seen in years".[11] But the great man was careful not to be caught comparing the two players. Other critics rather ducked the issue too, by declaring that Edith Evans anyway stole the show as the Nurse – in Darlington's description, "as earthy as a potato, as slow as a cart-horse and as cunning as a badger". Gwen Ffrangcon-Davies recalls how unhappy both men were in tights, Olivier because his legs were so thin and Gielgud "because he is knock-kneed". Nobody was totally happy, but the production packed them in at the New until the end of March, closing after 186 performances, the longest run of the play on record since it was first performed in 1597.

What of the evidence of the two protagonists themselves? In his own memoirs, written only twelve years later, Gielgud chooses not to dwell on the first night, with Olivier as Romeo, saying merely that it "opened with great success". When the time comes for him to take over, however, he recalls:

Larry had the advantage over me in his vitality, looks, humour and directness. In addition, he was a fine fencer, and his breath-taking fight with
Tybalt was a superb prelude to his death scene as Mercutio. As Romeo, his
love scenes were intensely real and tender, and his tragic grief profoundly
touching. I had an advantage over him in my familiarity with the verse,
and in the fact that the production was of my own devising, so that all the
scenes were arranged just as I had imagined I could play them best.... I
enjoyed the lightness and gaiety of [Mercutio].... But I was again disappointed with my performance as Romeo and resolved after this to be done
with it for ever.[12]

Twenty years later, in an American television interview, Gielgud offered
a more generous, self-effacing judgement:

I was very busy enunciating all the poetry very beautifully, but I was very
cold aesthetically compared with him. And I was struck then, as we all have
been since, by his extraordinary power and originality, and the way he
dashes with a part, and really wrings its neck without self-consciousness or
worrying whether he's attractive or good or bad, or what. He's a great
performer without caring, you feel, what is said. He doesn't act with the sort
of caution and fear that some of the rest of us have.[13]

With the benefit of hindsight, Olivier candidly confessed that it had
seemed to him Gielgud was going through a phase of over-adjusting to
what was expected of him, too conscious of his beautiful voice and his
lyrical gift, at the expense of reality:

It made me rebellious. It made me think that Shakespeare was now being
handled in a certain way, and because of the extremely strong influence that
a man of John's power and gifts would have on a company, all the company
would be going that way. So when I entered this company I rather cut
across it, thinking in my innocence that they'd say "Ah, this is the real one,
because the other's not quite right."

But of course it never works like that. I think John rather leant towards
my kind of naturalism, but it didn't alter his own convictions. All it did was
that I saw him going a little further into the expected field of florid elocutory
renditions. By that time he had almost settled for singing it, which I didn't
like. As soon as I see someone acting in Shakespeare and singing with a
tremolo in his voice, I just want to go out, because he's not trying to persuade
me that anything real is going on at all. He's just saying "Listen to my
beautiful voice" and "Do listen to this glorious cadence I'm about to give
you now."[14]

It was the beginning of a lifelong rivalry, often a somewhat terse and
jealous one. As recently as 1986 Olivier said, quite wrongly, of Gielgud:
"He harks back every now and again to how terrible I was as Romeo, but
that was over forty-five years ago now. Surely you don't have to harbour

unpleasant thoughts about people for forty-five years?"[15] They never again acted together onstage. Gielgud was to direct Olivier as Malvolio at Stratford twenty years later – again a not altogether happy experience – and they would in their veteran years become a much-sought-after cameo duo (or, with Richardson, trio) in assorted, often not very distinguished, big budget movies. Much has been written of the respective merits of their acting styles, with Olivier broadly winning the palm for excitement and "animal magnetism", Gielgud for intellect and lyricism. But one of the most succinct comparisons came from Olivier himself in a television interview with Kenneth Tynan in 1967:

> I've never thought of myself as quite the same actor as he is.... I've always thought that we were the reverses of the same coin, perhaps. I've seen, as if you had a coin, the top half John, all spiritual, all spirituality, all beauty, all abstract things; and myself as all earth, blood, humanity; if you like, the baser part of humanity without that beauty. I've never been interested in that side, though naturally I've had to develop something of it in order to be an actor at all. But I've always felt that John missed the lower half and that made me go for the other....[16]

Then, turning specifically to the 1935 *Romeo*:

> I suppose I must have sensed a sort of possible rivalry between us that might last all our lives. I don't know. But whatever it was, when I was playing Romeo I was carrying a torch, I was trying to sell realism in Shakespeare. I believed in it with my whole soul and I believed that Johnny was not doing that enough. I thought that he was paying attention – to the exclusion of the earth – to all that music, all that lyricism, and I was for the other side of the coin. I dived for that.

Tynan himself had already made his own eloquent attempt at the comparison, contrasting them in terms of Burke's *Enquiry into the Nature of Ideas upon the Sublime and the Beautiful*, equating Gielgud with the Beautiful and Olivier with the Sublime. "One thinks of Olivier", he wrote, "in terms of other species, of panthers and lions; one thinks of Gielgud in terms of other arts, of ballet and portrait painting."[17] The contrast between them was reminiscent of that drawn by Dr Johnson between Milton's ability to carve a colossus out of granite and his inability to carve heads on cherry-stones. "For the larger, shattering effects of passion, we look to Olivier; for the smaller, more exquisite effects of temper, to Gielgud."

Twenty years later, when Michael Redgrave was leading the next generation of Shakespearean actors, Tynan was to compare the three in an even more telling metaphor:

There is, you see, a gulf fixed between good and great performances; but a bridge spans it, over which you may stroll if your visa is in order. Mr Redgrave, ignoring this, always chooses the hard way. He dives into the torrent and tries to swim across, usually sinking within sight of the shore. Olivier pole-vaults over in a single animal leap; Gielgud, seizing a parasol, crosses by tight-rope.

What should not be forgotten, amid all this competitiveness, is Olivier's admission that but for Gielgud and this production he might never have become a classical actor at all. Tempted at the time by management as well as acting, he had it in mind to devote himself to modern plays by writers like J. B. Priestley. Certainly the effect of the *Romeo* experience on Olivier was that he felt he had earned his spurs in the classical theatre and could now go on to higher and yet bolder things without endangering whatever West End career the future might hold. The following season at the Old Vic, at Guthrie's invitation, he was to prove his point, tackling four major Shakespearean roles and establishing himself as a classical actor of the first rank.

The final irony of this historic production, which altered the performance and production styles of Shakespeare throughout the English-speaking world, is that both men considered themselves failures in the part of Romeo. But his now won Olivier a major Shakespeare enterprise of a very different breed, hailed by one of the popular papers as "the most coveted prize in screen acting in the country today" and by Ralph Richardson as "the artistic satisfaction of £600 a week": the part of Orlando, opposite the celebrated German actress Elisabeth Bergner, in her husband Paul Czinner's film of *As You Like It*. Bergner had been so impressed by Olivier's Romeo that she told Czinner: "That is the man I want as my partner."[18]

Olivier still had fundamental doubts about the filming of Shakespeare, reinforced by conversations with Gielgud, who had turned down several Hollywood offers to film his *Hamlet*. But the money was much too tempting – thirteen weeks of filming, at a then vast salary – and, as he said at the time, the opportunity to work in any medium with Bergner, a most accomplished and then major star, was more than welcome. He said in a studio interview:

I have always wanted to play Shakespeare decently, not with genius – God forbid – just decently and intelligently. I had hoped to do it with Romeo – no, good heavens, not a screen Romeo, but in the theatre. Perhaps I did. I don't know. Anyhow I don't believe I can have been nearly as rotten, or half as good, as the critics made out. In the meantime I hope I can do something with Orlando, something reasonably intelligent. No one can play with Bergner without learning something from her.

That was to be his first disappointment. Bergner did not take to him: "He was *not* charming or friendly to work with. He could be inspirational, but he treated us both – me and my husband – as foreigners." Only the presence on set of the eminent Leon Quartermaine, she believed, kept Olivier from "grandstanding". So Olivier barely met Bergner, who took to sleeping late and arriving on the set in mid-afternoon, by which time Olivier was anxious to get away and rest before an evening onstage as Mercutio. It was very much in character that he trained with professional wrestlers to make Orlando's wrestling bout as realistic as possible, but all the realism he could muster was not enough to disguise how ill-suited this particular play was to the screen. Olivier soon found that film could not convincingly convey his mistaking Rosalind for a boy, and tried to make up for it by adding an edge of madness to Orlando's high spirits. He was also disturbed by the inevitable demand that scenes be filmed out of any coherent order. It was not until he actually saw the picture that he would realize the full extent of Bergner's Teutonic accent on Shakespeare's English, so agonizing that one smart critic felt moved to note that "even Olivier's insufficient command of verse seemed satisfactory in comparison".[19]

Czinner had tried to assuage Olivier's initial doubts by assuring him that the text would not be abused. No less a figure than J. M. Barrie had been called in to adapt it; Barrie would hang around the set in solitary state, puffing his pipe smoke into many a shot. But Czinner was inevitably proved wrong. As with all these early experiments in filming Shakespeare, the director felt a need to suit an action to every word, to introduce constant movement where the text stood contentedly still – to fail, in short, to let the words work their magic. As Graham Greene put it in his *Spectator* review:

> Dr Czinner ... seems to have concluded that all the cinema can offer is more space: more elaborate palace sets and a real wood with room for real animals. How the ubiquitous livestock (sheep and cows and hens and rabbits) weary us before the end, and how disastrously the genuine English woodland is spoilt by too much fancy, for when did English trees, in what is apparently late autumn, bear clusters of white flowers?[20]

Greene also found another good reason to object to the filming of Shakespeare:

> Horns and cuckolds have been heavily censored, the streak of poison which runs through the comedy has been squeezed carefully out between hygienic fingertips, and what is left, apart from Arden and absurd delightful artificial love, is Shakespeare at his falsest, Adam and church bells and good men's feasts and sermons in stone, all the dull didactic unconvincing images. That,

I think, is the chief objection to Shakespeare on the screen: the British Board of Film Censors will see to it that only the school versions of his plays are produced....

As an Orlando "sullen, brooding, a little oafish", Greene found Olivier's performance "even more satisfying" than Bergner's. The *Daily Telegraph*'s Campbell Dixon was one of the first critics to wax lyrical: "I have said before that Laurence Olivier seems to me to be one of the most brilliant actors in the world.... His triumph as Orlando is all the more striking for its contrast to his glamorous Romeo and his fiery Mercutio." If Olivier was proving nothing else, he was displaying early signs of the versatility which he would make the hallmark of his career.

When the film was (rather optimistically) reissued in 1949, the promotion capitalized on Olivier's recent knighthood – the first and one of the very few times he has been unable or unwilling to prevent himself appearing on a poster as *Sir* Laurence Olivier. The respective fortunes of his and Bergner's careers, moreover, were reflected by the hoisting of his name alone above the title. For all its weaknesses, *As You Like It* now has a reputation as something of a cult movie among celluloid Shakespeare buffs – "treasured", according to the American critic Robert L. Daniels, "as a modest and airy delight".[21] Neither the film, however, nor Miss Bergner, rate a mention in Olivier's autobiography.

So it was back in a hurry to the theatre and to a meeting which was to prove all too momentous. Olivier and Richardson, both now high earners, were anxious to try a management partnership, to which end Richardson had commissioned J. B. Priestley to write them a play. The result was the curiously titled *Bees on the Boat-Deck*, a satire on contemporary England rather in the manner of *Heartbreak House*, with which Priestley was so pleased that he too came in on the financing of the production. With a cast of only ten and a single set, the production costs amounted to £2,000, split equally between the three of them. Olivier again ensured that his part called for the maximum of athletic prowess, including a daring slide down a rope to the eponymous boat-deck, during which he more than once burnt his fingers. Ivor Brown enjoyed himself hugely – "I have not seen Laurence Olivier better than in the raillery and comic invention of the Second Officer" – but Agate hated every minute of it: "Mr Olivier is even less happy, for his second officer is no second officer at all, but a young gentleman from behind the counter of a bank." The public did not warm to it, either, perhaps because Priestley's rather heavy-handed contemporary satire soured the otherwise enjoyably light-hearted froth of the comedy. It lasted only four weeks at the Lyric, to Olivier's surprised dismay. His new career as an impresario had as yet proved rather dismal. After seeing both *Golden Arrow* and *Bees on the Boat-Deck*, Harold Hobson summed up: "The bankrupt firm had become a doomed ship, and Olivier and Richardson went down with her."

During one matinee of *Bees*, when Richardson had become so depressed that he was scarcely even trying any more, he was perplexed to hear Olivier whispering urgently to him: "Come on, Ralphie, stop groaning." Richardson sensed that there was somebody out front whom Olivier wanted to impress. He thought at first that it must be Ivor Novello, who was conspicuous in one of the stage boxes. But when they reached the interval, and Olivier said with a huge grin "Can we stop now?", Richardson realized that it was not so much Novello as his companion who was exercising his friend's considerable emotional energies. She was a young actress, new to the West End, whose name was Vivian Holman. She was shortly to change it to Vivien Leigh.

Just as his professional life had again hit the doldrums, Olivier's private life was taking a guilty but exhilarating new turn. As for Mrs Holman, she knew exactly what she wanted and had set out single-mindedly to get it. It was already nearly two years since, as a strikingly pretty twenty-one year old, married with a one-year-old daughter, she had attended a performance of *Theatre Royal* with a girlfriend. Vivian had watched the wild, histrionic antics of young Laurence Olivier as the madcap Tony Cavendish with ever widening blue-green eyes. She turned to her friend and said: "That is the man I'm going to marry."

"Don't be ridiculous," came the reply. "You're both married already."

"That doesn't matter. I'm still going to marry him one day."[22]

PART TWO

"Some Achieve Greatness"

"Anyone who has been an actor any length of time does not
know whether he has any true emotions or not."

Sir Cedric Hardwicke

CHAPTER 6

1936

For a descendant of Huguenots with a French-sounding name, Laurence Olivier has always been extraordinarily British. The more he has grown towards the status of national institution, the more fiercely patriotic have become his instincts, his pronouncements and, indeed, his way of life, pottering around his country garden at weekends, memorizing the Latin names of all his flowers.

Even at the end of 1935, when success of a kind was at last beckoning him, Olivier would regretfully count the cost in terms of the more orthodox pursuits of English youth which he had sacrificed to his theatrical aspirations. A sizable slice of Olivier desperately wished he had been educated at Eton and Oxbridge, changed the guard outside Buckingham Palace, walked to work in the City in pinstripes and a bowler hat. They were cosily familiar roles which spoke to him of history and continuity, of elegance and refinement, of a quintessentially British pursuit of languid excellence.

If all that had now passed him by, he decided, it was not too late to live such a life by proxy. A son could live it for him. Though his marriage had never really recovered from its awkward beginnings and had long since idled along in a state of inoffensive mutual boredom, he had persuaded Jill that a child might give them the incentive to breathe some life into it. Now approaching thirty, she in turn allowed her natural maternal instincts to overcome her rather more mature human doubts.

It seems hard on the child in question, Tarquin Olivier, today a discreetly successful businessman in his early fifties, living in contented obscurity, to say that the decision was a disastrous one. But Olivier made it for all the same, wrong reasons he had made his decision to marry. He had met and fallen in love with Vivien Leigh before Tarquin was even conceived; and he was to leave Jill Esmond for her just ten months after the child was born. Only in the last twenty years has Olivier managed to establish any kind of rapport with his son, and that an intermittent and uneasy one.[1]

But it was in confident mood, intent on bequeathing posterity a creature in his own image, that Olivier dined with Jill at the Grill Room of the Savoy Hotel, London, in the late summer of 1935. Across the room sat Mrs Vivian Holman, being entertained to dinner by John Buckmaster, Gladys Cooper's son, one of many doomed gentleman moths then attracted to this particular flame. Mrs Holman's presence was no coincidence. Having read in a fan magazine that Olivier frequently dined at the Savoy Grill, she had specifically asked poor Buckmaster to squire her there. This was not her first attempt to meet Olivier in this enterprising way, but that night she looked like succeeding. Seeing the Oliviers, and eager to impress, Buckmaster proudly pointed them out – "Good friends of mine, don't you know?" – then wryly observed: "Doesn't Larry look an odd little thing without his moustache?"[2]

To her escort's dismay, Vivian became remarkably exercised in the defence of a man she had never met. "He doesn't look funny at all," said the lady indignantly; she then proceeded to spend the rest of the evening in rather absent mood, desperately hoping the moustacheless star would come over to say hello on his way out.

Olivier, on a wave from his friend, naturally did so. He did not let on that he had already seen "the possessor of this wondrous, unimagined beauty" on the London stage. When formally introduced to her, he noticed that she took his hand very firmly and held his eyes with a very determined gaze. By the time they were all outside together, waiting for taxis, he had courteously invited Mrs Holman to a party he was throwing that weekend at his new country house at Burchett's Green, near Maidenhead. "Just", as he himself put it, "like any first act of the period, isn't it?"

Vivian Hartley had married Leigh Holman in 1932. She was a drama student in her first term at RADA, he a successful young barrister; they had met the previous Christmas in Torquay, at the South Devon hunt ball. Within months she was pregnant and thus compelled to give up her RADA career. But for now she was content: Leigh kept her in considerable style in a Queen Anne house in Stanhope Street, Mayfair, once the home of Lynn Fontanne; he gave her plenty of money to spend on clothes and shared her delight in their little daughter Suzanne, born one month prematurely on 12 October 1933.

Vivian's nature, however, was outgoing, restless and ever in search of fresh experience, new pleasures to explore. Any man would have had trouble keeping up with her, especially one working so hard simply to keep her. She may have vowed already that she would never have another baby – it was "too messy" a business. But those who knew her well thought it only a matter of time before she would have another husband.

Vivian Mary Hartley was born in Darjeeling, India, on 5 November 1913. Her parents were not surprised to be told by the doctor that theirs was a particularly beautiful baby; her mother had turned to face Mount Kanchenjunga just before the birth, having been advised by the Indian ayah that this would guarantee her child's "perfection of face".[3]

Gertrude and Ernest Hartley had been married for two years. She was a devout Irish Catholic, he a well-to-do exchange broker, based in Calcutta, and an amateur actor of reputedly outstanding talents; Vivian's first recorded appearance alongside him in amateur theatricals was at the age of three, singing "Little Bo Peep". Ernest's business did so well that he was able to retire young, and felt he now deserved to enjoy himself. Vivian was sent to a convent school in Roehampton, where she played Mustardseed in *A Midsummer Night's Dream*, Miranda in *The Tempest* and made an early determination to become an actress, then spent her teens with her parents on a prolonged Grand Tour of Europe. She was educated at a series of schools in Switzerland, Paris and Bavaria, emerging from her Swiss finishing school an elegant, cultured and stunningly beautiful eighteen year old, still as stage-struck as she was determined to squeeze out of life everything that it might have to offer her.

Leigh Holman was an adoring husband, but he offered Vivian little of the challenge she relished. As she began her first few tentative steps into the theatrical profession, there were three young matinee idols who commanded the hearts of British womanhood (who lived in blissful ignorance of the sexual preferences of two of them): Noël Coward, Ivor Novello and the young Laurence Olivier. Like many another of her age, the *ingénue* Miss Hartley fell in love with Olivier across the footlights of *Biography*, *Queen of Scots* and finally *Theatre Royal*; unlike most, she then set out to win him. When she had been to see Olivier in *Theatre Royal*, the sum total of Vivian's acting experience was one line – "If you are not made headmistress, I shan't come back next term" – spoken in a fetching gymslip in a Gaumont-British film starring Cicely Courtneidge as the headmistress in question. Though she had delivered her ringing words with the broadest range of emotions she could muster, it was to be some time before Vivian Holman's talents were noticed.

Her husband certainly did not take her early career as seriously as she did. He was both hurt and astonished when she abandoned him in Copenhagen just as they were about to embark on a "second honeymoon" –

an elaborately planned yachting holiday in the Baltic – on the off chance of a walk-on part as a giggling schoolgirl in that same first film, ironically entitled *Things Are Looking Up*. By the time he returned, having completed the trip alone, she had not yet managed to get on the set and had spent the time staying with her friend Clare Sheridan in Sussex.

It was, of course, Leigh Holman's incredulity that she could leave him on holiday for what he called "a lark" – the half-chance of hanging around as an extra, for a paltry guinea a day – which had largely made her do it. Shortly after his return, however, she did manage to talk her way into the front row of the walk-on parts, and even earned herself that one line, thus hoisting her pay to thirty shillings. No more work resulted, however, and Vivian might have languished indefinitely in the doldrums had not an enterprising young agent named John Gliddon had a bright idea. It was time, he told an actress friend, Beryl Samson, that England had its own "star discovery" system, modelled on Hollywood's, where pretty girls who could speak at all presentably might be catapulted to stardom, making a lot of money for themselves and everybody around them in the process. Did she know anyone suitable?

So Beryl Samson introduced Gliddon to Vivian Holman, who bought a new summer frock and wide-brimmed hat for the occasion. With her kittenish good looks, those blue-green eyes and her cultured vowel sounds, she bowled Gliddon over. All that was needed, he said, was a new name. Vivian Holman would not do; nor would Vivian Hartley. How about April Morn? Even Vivian was appalled by that. On the bus ride home with Beryl, she decided to solve the problem with what also looked like a good domestic move: she would make use of her husband's first name and call herself Vivian Leigh.

Gliddon then launched her on the time-honoured round of lunch, tea and dinner at the Ivy, the Ritz and the Savoy, interspersed with the smart parties and star-studded functions at which so photogenic a protégé was bound eventually to catch somebody's eye – especially given the high demand for quota movies, known in the trade as "quota quickies". Before long, sure enough, came the inevitable phone call from Alexander Korda, whose Denham studios were busy making stars out of mildly talented but strikingly beautiful women such as Wendy Barrie, Diana Napier and Merle Oberon (later to become Korda's wife). Gliddon escorted Vivian to the interview, which she felt sure would set her dainty foot firmly on the first rung of the ladder to fame. But Korda was none too impressed. She was exquisite, yes, he told Gliddon afterwards, she was charming, but she was not *unique*. Barrie was "pure", Oberon "exotic", Napier "a beetch". He could not discern in Miss Leigh any single quality that would give him a unique epithet of that order, and unique epithets were Korda's stock-in-trade.

Vivian was devastated, but Gliddon quickly managed to get her a part – the role of leading lady, no less – in a British and Dominions quickie called *The Village Squire*. It was a week's work at eight guineas a day – and was quickly followed by another, as a secretary, in an equally forgettable Elstree product called *Gentleman's Agreement*. Both films drew dire reviews, making the exposure, which Gliddon naturally considered useful in itself, somewhat double-edged. It drew painful attention to a question which was to haunt Vivien Leigh's entire career, even after she had won an Oscar in her first Hollywood movie. Sure, the camera adored her, but could she act?

David Horne, her leading man in both movies, evidently thought so, for he invited her to play his young, flirtatious wife in his next venture, a Florentine romance called *The Green Sash*. The stage, thought Gliddon, would be an even sterner test of Vivian's still very limited talents. It is doubtful if he would have gone along with the idea had the play not been opening at an obscure theatre called simply the Q, buried away at Kew, in the outer reaches of South London. Vivian emoted away to her own satisfaction and earned a first notice in *The Times* (whose anonymous critic was then Charles Morgan) which could have been a lot worse: "The dramatists have given so vague a sketch of Giusta that Miss Vivian Leigh has little opportunity for portraiture, but her acting has a precision and lightness which should serve her well when her material is of more substance."

However modest these beginnings, Vivian was thrilled to be able to think of herself as a professional actress with screen and stage performances to her credit. Leigh Holman was not. The run of *The Green Sash* was only two weeks, but he resented the way her new life disrupted their domestic routine. His wife was still asleep when he left for work in the mornings, having rarely come home much before dawn, and had left for the theatre by the time he got back. He could not see why she should want to chase such flimsy work, with such meagre rewards. He did not want to go to all those parties – and she did not seem to want to do much else. "I feel tied," she told her friend Patsy Quinn, meaning she felt tied down. The pursuit of Olivier began.

As soon as she had met Olivier, and convinced herself that they were in mad and mutual love, Vivian's once strong feelings for her husband diluted to rather bored affection. Another part in another humdrum Ealing movie, an Associated Talking Pictures vehicle for Gracie Fields called *Look Up and Laugh*, only made domestic matters worse. The picture was directed by Basil Dean of *Beau Geste* fame, as much a martinet on the film set as in the theatre. He was so brusque with Vivian – complaining, to her mortification, that her neck was too long – that warm-hearted Gracie

Fields felt obliged to comfort her. "Don't worry, love," she said, "you've *got* something." Neither the director, nor the lighting cameraman, nor the film critics appeared to agree. Vivian had yet to rate a mention in a film review and yet to win a regular studio contract. One early fan was Ealing's casting director, Aubrey Blackburn, who tried to get Vivian officially on the books, but Dean vetoed any such idea.

Again Leigh Holman hoped that would be that. *Look Up and Laugh* had taken his wife away from him for another four weeks. But the very day after shooting ended, she was off again with Gliddon to meet another impresario, this time the former actor and critic Sydney Carroll, who was about to stage an adaptation by Ashley Dukes of a German comedy called *The Mask of Virtue*. It was to be directed by Maxwell Wray, a close colleague of Korda's, who had turned for help to Aubrey Blackburn. The central role, a strong and difficult one, was that of Henriette Duquesnoy, a prostitute masquerading as an innocent young virgin. He had approached Peggy Ashcroft, Anna Neagle, Diana Churchill and Jane Baxter, but all were unavailable. When he told the Ealing casting director that the girl had to be "spectacularly beautiful", Blackburn had immediately suggested Vivian Leigh. Ten other girls were sitting with her outside Carroll's Charing Cross Road office that afternoon while Gliddon went in to plead her case. Yes, she had only one professional appearance on stage to her name, he said, and yes, it was in an obscure play in an obscure theatre. But if "spectacular beauty" is what you're looking for....

Wray left the office for a moment and took a nonchalant walk down the hall. When he came back, he told Gliddon and Carroll: "If Vivian Leigh is the girl dressed in black sitting at the far end of the table in the outer room, then as far as I'm concerned, the part is cast." All that remained was for Sydney Carroll to make one tiny but significant suggestion: would she mind changing the spelling of her first name from Vivian to Vivien? It seemed so much more feminine. Of course not; she quite agreed. And so Vivian Hartley Holman finally became Vivien Leigh.

Carroll and Wray knew they were taking a big risk, but had no time to look further. Could the girl act? Rehearsals did not bring much reassurance. "I didn't know a thing," she told an interviewer twenty-five years later. "Every day they nearly fired me because I was so awful."[4] At the Ivy restaurant one day she overheard another member of the cast saying, "She's so terrible – she'll have to go." But Wray proved a diligent and creative director. He watched her closely to divine what he considered her better points – a certain grace when she moved, an extraordinary beauty in repose – and tried to build her performance around them. By the time of the opening night, 15 May 1935, he felt confident enough to invite Korda to join him in the stalls.

Vivien Leigh's performance that night enraptured everyone. Contemporary accounts suggest that she radiated across the footlights a feminine version of that same "animal magnetism" discerned by Ralph Richardson in Olivier's Romeo. As her biographer Anne Edwards reconstructed it:

> No matter what else was happening on stage it was difficult to tear one's eyes away from her. She was lighted and costumed so that with the magnificence of her classic long neck and her ivory skin and perfect face, she looked in repose like a Florentine painting. There was a lilting beauty to her voice even if it lacked range and she had a curious vulnerability that brought instant sympathy to her role.

Her range was still clearly very limited, her inflection unpredictable and her voice immature, but the consensus, in the elegant words of one critic, was that "her grace was like a magic cloak, and her whole performance so took the senses and lit up the stage as to make criticism unchivalrous".

Such thoughts did not, of course, deter Agate. "Miss Leigh", he wrote that Sunday, "has incisiveness, *retenue* and obvious intelligence. She gives to this part all that it asks except in the matter of speech. If this young lady wants to become an actress, as distinct from a film star, she should at once seek means to improve her overtone, displeasing to the fastidious ear." Vivien took such seasoned advice in deadly earnest and went at once to a voice coach, later (thanks to Olivier) to Elsie Fogerty.

When Olivier himself had seen *The Mask of Virtue*, he decided that it was not "chiefly on account of her promise as an actress" that Vivien attracted attention in the role:

> Apart from her looks, which were magical, she possessed beautiful poise; her neck looked almost too fragile to support her head and bore with it a sense of surprise, and something of the pride of the master juggler who can make a brilliant manœuvre appear almost accidental.... She also had something else: an attraction of the most perturbing nature I have ever encountered. It may have been the strangely touching spark of dignity in her that enslaved the ardent legion of her admirers.

"Even a Hungarian can make a mistake," Alexander Korda told Gliddon on the first night, after he had visited Vivien in her dressing-room and conceded that she *did*, after all, have that uniqueness he was looking for. Next morning's newspapers heralded a new star – literally, for once, of the "overnight" variety – and by the following week Vivien had a five-year, £50,000 Korda film contract. Readers were told she was still only nineteen years old, though in truth she was all of twenty-one.

Vivien revelled in her new-found fame, which only made her husband more uncomfortable. Every day brought lunch at the Ritz or the Savoy, a photo session or an interview. And every night saw her dragging Leigh to some party, from which, as often as not, she would let him go home without her. One day that autumn, naturally enough, she went to see Laurence Olivier's Romeo, the most blatantly sexual acting she had ever seen. Their brief meeting at the Savoy and her own newfound celebrity now gave her the confidence to go backstage to congratulate him; he responded graciously that he had admired her in *The Mask of Virtue*. Did she have any plans? Well, she had just had a big disappointment: Korda had abandoned his film of *Cyrano de Bergerac*, in which she was to have played Roxanne to Charles Laughton's Cyrano. But she had just been offered the part of Jenny Mere in Clemence Dane's dramatization of a Max Beerbohm story, *The Happy Hypocrite*, opposite Ivor Novello. Olivier murmured his approval, which was enough to decide her to accept the part. He was astonished by her beauty; but managed, given his huge ego and his actor's skill, to hide the fact. As she kissed him farewell – "on the shoulder", as he remembers it – he did, however, suggest that they meet for lunch.

It took place at the Ivy, but was not quite the kind of lunch Vivien had envisaged. Still the respectable married man, Olivier had brought Gielgud along, which led them down Memory Lane to the day Vivien had auditioned for the part of the Queen in his Oxford production of *Richard II*, while an oblivious Olivier waited in his dressing-room for that evening's performance. But he managed to tell enough self-deprecating anecdotes, with enough wit and style, to wriggle her more firmly than ever on to his hook. He seemed obsessed, to her dismay, with the classical theatre, surprising her by his insistence that she audition for Gielgud. Tackling the great classical roles had not occurred to Vivien before this lunch. Now, of course, it became a major, and seemingly obvious, goal.

First, however, fate in the shape of Alexander Korda was to bring them together in the kind of intense professional relationship which would seal the events to come. It would take more than three months, starting that August, to film *Fire over England*, an extravagant love story set in the time of Elizabeth I (Flora Robson) and the Spanish Armada. Since the huge international success of *The Private Life of Henry VIII* three years before, Korda had been anxious to mount another costume drama. This one, adapted from an A. E. W. Mason novel, had the advantage of an unashamedly patriotic theme, in time of war, at a moment when similar stormclouds were gathering over Europe. For the first but not the last time, this Hungarian-born Anglophile was consciously doing his bit for the morale of the British people.

Olivier and Vivien played the two central young lovers: Michael Ingolby, a young naval officer who has escaped from Spanish clutches after seeing his father burnt at the stake, and Cynthia, one of the Queen's ladies-in-waiting. Before shooting began, they had still never met alone. When first they bumped into each other at Denham, in the corridor outside the studio canteen, Vivien demurely said how thrilled she was to be working with him. "We'll probably end up fighting," laughed Olivier, who was less enthusiastic about the whole project. "People always get sick of each other when they're making a film."

They were to disprove that rule with a vengeance. Even when Jill bore Olivier a son shortly after filming began, it became obvious to all around them, as work progressed, that Olivier and Vivien were twin souls being drawn into an uncontrollable mutual passion. Olivier had never before been physically unfaithful to Jill – if for no other reason than his single-minded pursuit of success – but now he more than made up for lost time.

Their love scenes in the film still bear eloquent witness to what was going on offscreen. They were spending more and more time apart from the rest of the cast, disappearing alone together at meal breaks (usually, at Denham, a communal business), rest periods and, increasingly, after work for the day had finished. In Vivien Leigh's own words:

> It was during the making of *Fire over England* that Larry and I . . . fell in love. Alex Korda was like a father to us – we went to him with every little problem we had. We usually left convinced that he had solved it – or that we'd got our way, even when we hadn't. Well, one day we went to him and said, "Alex, we must tell you our great secret – we're in love and we're going to be married." He smiled and said: "Don't be silly – everybody knows that. I've known that for weeks and weeks."[5]

"This thing", in Olivier's own words, "was as fatefully irresistible for us as for any couple from Siegmund and Sieglinde to Windsor and Simpson. It sometimes felt almost like an illness, but the remedy was unthinkable; only an early Christian martyr could have faced it." As he began to feel pity for Jill, then pain, then guilt, "Virtue seemed to work upside-down: love was like an angel, guilt was a dark fiend. At its every surge *Macbeth* would haunt me: 'Then comes my fit again.'"   .

It was for his love of his craft as much as his co-star that Olivier, as always, insisted on doing all his own stunts in the film – including an especially dangerous one during a sea battle which, according to Flora Robson, "sent up the producer's blood pressure".[6] A galleon had been built in a field at Denham, where the night-time battle scene was filmed – naturally – at night. Olivier was required to leap from one galleon to another, throw a lighted firebrand along the petrol-soaked deck, then dive overboard into a hidden safety net as the deck burst into violent flames. After one of several takes the hosing system failed to put out the fire; the water instead rolled along the deck with burning petrol floating on its surface, causing him to slip and fall heavily overboard in his haste to escape the advancing flames. Erich Pommer, the director, thinking Olivier had broken his neck, tried to insist that he use a stand-in. But Flora Robson, who had watched "appalled" as the flames had chased him overboard "with a crunch", told Pommer: "He would feel a fraud to be praised for a scene he had not done himself." "All film acting", replied the director flatly, "is a fraud." But he was persuaded to let Olivier persist.

Though now a major West End star, Olivier had yet to register a major impact in any of his films. He was far from being the biggest name on Korda's books; Charles Laughton, recently Captain Bligh and Rembrandt, and Robert Donat, about to make *Knight without Armour* opposite Marlene Dietrich, were far better known and indeed far better paid. Donat was already suffering severely from the chronic asthma which was to end his life so prematurely. Had Donat not insisted on continuing to work regardless – with the help of cocaine tablets – Korda intended to make Olivier Dietrich's co-star, as soon as he had finished *Fire over England*.

As for Vivien, few people knew that she had even been in a film. Korda, however, decided it was time to promote more names from his stable, and these two young lovers would be the beneficiaries. Besides Flora Robson, the film had a strong cast including Raymond Massey as King Philip of Spain, Leslie Banks as the Earl of Leicester, Robert Newton as a Spanish grandee, and Olivier's despairing old Central School tutor, Henry Oscar, as the Spanish ambassador. Also on hand as a bearded spy in what he later thought "a film of some distinction" was the young James Mason. He was killed off in the first reel of the film, to enable Olivier's character to take over his false beard and dangerous mission; as Mason recalled, "Mine, as can be seen, was a vitally important role, but after one day's and one night's shooting it was all over."[7]

The film was well directed by William K. Howard from a strong script by Clemence Dane and Sergei Nolbandov. So Korda threw the full weight of his publicity department behind it, turning *Fire over England* into the grand scale of commercial success that he knew heavy promotion could bring a strong product. Only at the lavish Hollywood launch, at Grauman's Chinese Theater in Los Angeles, did amused American critics point out that this "quintessentially English" costume drama was "presented" by a Hungarian, produced by a German and directed by an American, with a Chinese cameraman, a Russian art director, a Russian co-writer and a French costume designer.

It was Flora Robson's film, but Olivier and Vivien drew enthusiastic praise. "One of the most notable pictures of the year," declared *Picturegoer*'s Lionel Collier – convinced at last – "a really finely produced and directed historical romance which is a real credit to British studios ... the lovers are extremely sympathetically portrayed by Vivien Leigh and Laurence Olivier." Even Graham Greene in his *Spectator* column, despite being scathing about Flora Robson and sceptical that Elizabeth Tudor "would have allowed quite so much kissing and cuddling in her presence", declared *Fire over England* "the best production to come from Denham yet".[8] The acting was "far better than we are accustomed to in English films.... Laurence Olivier can do the hysterical type of young romantic hero with ease." Somehow Greene managed to avoid mentioning Miss Leigh.

It was early in the filming of *Fire over England*, when he and Jill were spending a desultory weekend with their new baby at her mother's country home, that Olivier found among the other house guests the rising young director Tyrone ("Tony") Guthrie. Guthrie, who had run the Old Vic during the famous Laughton season of 1933–4, had been invited to take charge again that autumn. Although the Old Vic had forsworn anything which might remotely resemble a star system, Guthrie was shrewd enough to know that a dashing young leading man would do no harm at the box office. He had seen Olivier's Romeo and been impressed enough to write to him that self-styled "fan letter", despite the discordant chorus of critics. Now, he suggested, it was time for Olivier to tackle Hamlet – an eye-catching Hamlet, what's more: an uncut text. Why should Shakespeare be cut to two and a half hours, as opposed to four and a quarter, as if time spent in a theatre seat were costed like time spent in a taxi? It was an insult as much to the audience as to the author, argued Guthrie. It was the ideal opening for Olivier, the launch-pad for a really distinguished career.

Olivier hesitated. The time had come, it seemed, to make a final choice between matinee idolatry, film stardom and the more *serioso* but less lucrative attractions of classical distinction. At twenty-nine, he was still unsure which he really wanted. But he was also, he admitted to Guthrie, a little frightened. He still smarted from the Romeo reviews and looked back on that performance as a disaster. What if he passed up more lustrous, mass audience opportunities, only to fail again? It was a very tempting offer, but he would like time to think.

Guthrie returned to London confident that he had the makings of an outstanding season. Olivier, meanwhile, asked around for advice. A crucial figure in the process was Harcourt Williams, who had run the Old Vic for many years and whose counsel to accept carried much weight. Jill was too preoccupied with their baby to take much interest. The one person left to consult was Ralph Richardson, who, with his delightful lack of self-interest, would give the verdict that mattered most. A transatlantic call brought the characteristic response: "Full-length *Hamlet*? I think it's a very good idea, dear boy."

And so the beginnings of Olivier's unparalleled theatrical eminence began against a background, in his own words, of "two years of furtive life, lying life. Sneaky. At first I felt a really worm-like adulterer, slipping in between another man's sheets, the studio or theatre dressing-room game blessed by generations of randy actors, but unprotected from sudden intrusion." Fifty years later, in 1986, a visitor to his home found Olivier in his eightieth year watching an old Vivien Leigh movie and confessing with tears in his eyes: "This, this was love. This was the real thing."[9] Yet even after all these years — whether with the benefit or the curse of hindsight — this hugely acclaimed artist, showered with every honour his craft has to offer, still needed to feel his way to the loftiest and most contrived of self-justifications:

> Artists are supposed to suffer, it is part of their gift. The office of drama is to exercise, possibly to exhaust, human emotions. The purpose of comedy is to tickle those emotions into an expression of light relief; of tragedy, to wound them and bring the relief of tears. Disgust and terror are the other points of the compass.

Over the next two years Olivier was to bring all these grand apophthegms to proof — both on and off the stage.

CHAPTER 7

1937

T
hroughout the twentieth century the Old Vic has always held a
special place in the hearts of London theatre-goers. This unlikely,
often unkempt, out-of-the-way old playhouse, stranded on the
wrong side of the Thames in a less than salubrious area, has hosted
many of the great performances of our time in its stately auditorium. For
the last seventy years, moreover, the name of the Old Vic has been all but
synonymous with that of William Shakespeare. Twenty-five years after
Laurence Olivier first set foot in the place in 1937, the Old Vic's umbilical
association with Shakespeare would make it the natural first home for
Britain's fledgling National Theatre, under his directorship, while grander
premises were under interminable construction on the South Bank.

It was not always thus. When it first opened in 1818, the Royal Coburg
Theatre was expressly forbidden to stage the works of Shakespeare, its first
attempt to do so resulting in prosecution.[1] For the first sixty years of
its life the Old Vic was a melodrama theatre, the haunt of prostitutes,
pickpockets, gin-soaks – the roughest clientele in town. But all that changed
in 1880, when the theatre's lease was acquired by Miss Emma Cons, a
God-fearing social worker dedicated to the cause of Temperance. Her one-
woman crusade against the evils of drink swiftly transformed this foul-
smelling fleapit into the Royal Victoria Coffee House and Music-Hall
Foundation, where respectable Victorians could thrill to concerts, extracts
from opera, Sunday afternoon religious addresses, "penny lectures" by
distinguished speakers – and, just occasionally, a vaudeville act, but only
of the most wholesome variety. In 1912 Miss Cons handed the management over to her assistant, her sister's daughter Lilian Baylis, who was to

113

become one of the legendary figures of twentieth-century British theatre.

By the time of Olivier's arrival in her orbit in 1937, Lilian Baylis had already founded the Old Vic Shakespeare Company (in 1914) and the Sadler's Wells Theatre (in 1931) as a home for opera and ballet. Always shrewd in her choice of collaborators, it was Baylis's advancement of Ninette de Valois which led to the foundation of the hitherto unimaginable English Ballet Company. Already her tireless, religiously motivated work to bring culture to the masses had been recognized with the award of the Companionship of Honour and an honorary degree from Oxford University.

Thrift was her watchword: ever haggling, borrowing, bargaining, she wanted nothing for herself, only for her theatre, for the maintenance of its artistic standards and its reputation as "The People's Theatre". "Oh God," she would pray, "send me a good actor, and cheap!"[2] – to answer "a crying need of working men and women who want to see beyond the four walls of their offices, workshops and homes into a world of awe and wonder". Gradually, however, and inevitably, as she watched every performance from her own stageside box, where she carried on with her paperwork on a hidden kitchen table, Baylis watched the intellectual bourgeoisie take over from The People as the Old Vic's natural clientele.

It was not unusual for that clientele to catch the smell of kippers or sausages wafting across the stalls as Baylis cooked her afternoon tea on a gas-ring in the prompt corner. The critic Ivor Brown described this natural eccentric as "an odd little Empressario, with her fire of faith, her queer face, her spluttering speeches, and her vanities of cap and gown". She would pray for divine guidance daily, taking all her many backstage problems straight to God and insisting on moral rectitude from all her employees, actors or not. "Are you pure, dear boy?" she is said to have asked one young spear-carrier. "I'm not narrow-minded or anything, but I won't have anything going on in the wings." She would speak with equal directness to the mighty. "Hurry home now, dear," she said to Queen Mary after a matinee, "you've got to get the King his tea."

Baylis was sixty-two, grey-haired, bespectacled and rather stout when Olivier first met her, with a squint in one eye and a slight speech impediment caused by paralysis in one side of her mouth. Known equally for her wrath and her generosity, she was to lavish more of the latter on Olivier, though she snapped at his helpful suggestion that a theatre bar might swell funds: "My dear boy, don't you realize that if it hadn't been for drunken men beating their wives, we wouldn't have this place."[3] At the end of their first meeting, to an actor she was paying £20 a week, and who had recently been commanding £500–£600 a week in films, she said: "Of course you really oughtn't to come here at all when you can get so much money elsewhere, but still that's your business." From that moment, Olivier told his first biographer, Felix Barker, he adored her.

To her new young protégé, Lilian Baylis became the mother-figure he unconsciously sought in most older women, to replace the mother he had missed so sorely since the age of twelve. He was often to reminisce fondly of the times Lilian Baylis tucked him up backstage beneath an eiderdown before the rigours of his uncut, four-and-a-quarter-hour *Hamlet*. When he returned to the Old Vic in the early 1960s, as founder-director of the National Theatre, Olivier converted her former office into his own dressing-room and renamed it the Baylis Room,[4] which it remains to this day. In the corner stands her old desk, which, sentimentally, he had retrieved from storage and returned to its proper place in her memory.

While Olivier was finishing the filming of *Fire over England*, Guthrie began the 1936–7 Old Vic season with *Love's Labour's Lost*, *The Country Wife* and *The Witch of Edmonton*. The season's other stars were both women: Edith Evans and the American actress Ruth Gordon; the rest of the company included such young novices as Alec Guinness, Alec Clunes, Isobel Scaife, Evan John, Michael Redgrave and his wife Rachel Kempson. As Christmas approached, their immersion in the great domestic drama of the Royal House of Denmark was set against a real-life one across the River Thames in the House of Windsor, where King Edward VIII was agonizing between his throne and the woman he loved.

Guthrie, already known as a highly cerebral director, had spent much of the year deep in the study of the works of Sigmund Freud. Himself the son of a dead father who remained something of an enigma to him, Guthrie was particularly fascinated by one paper by Freud's biographer, Dr Ernest Jones; it discussed two plays, Shakespeare's *Hamlet* and Sophocles's *Oedipus*, both of which deal with royal successions, the "sins of the father" syndrome and a son's sexual feelings towards his mother. Striking many a chime in Guthrie's own inner turmoil, Jones argued that Hamlet hesitates to kill Claudius at prayer because he is subconsciously "in love" with his mother and thus, perhaps, even jealous of the new king's sexual relations with her; his motives might, therefore, be rather less pure than the text suggests and less banal than the "need for more proof" traditionally argued by literary critics. "The whole picture", wrote Jones, "is not, as Goethe depicted it, one of a gentle soul crushed beneath a colossal task, but one of a strong man tortured by some mysterious inhibition."[5]

Lilian Baylis, no prude for all her devoutness, was all in favour of the Freudian approach. When innocent young actresses could not summon up the sexuality required for *Measure for Measure*, she had been known to say: "Now, dears, all we can do is go on our knees and pray for lust."[6] Lust, she knew, was good box office; and so, it seemed, would be this new approach to Hamlet. It would require mature acting from a twenty-nine year old to convince his audience that he loved his mother only just this side of incest; but British motherhood would surely flock to see it.

Guthrie patiently endured a long correspondence with a pained Michael Redgrave, who was complaining (in a "cocksure" way he himself later found "outrageous") that Olivier had got all the best parts. Guthrie had offered him Horatio; he replied that he would rather play Laertes, who "should be a young soldier, very forceful and physically bigger than Hamlet, bursting with health and proper pride". Guthrie replied: "Laertes by all means if you prefer, though I'd call Horatio the better part." The rest of the cast included Robert Newton as Horatio, Dorothy Dix (succeeded, because of illness, by Esme Church) as Gertrude, Francis L. Sullivan as Claudius, George Howe as Polonius, Cherry Cottrell as Ophelia, Marius Goring doubling the Player King and Fortinbras, and Alec Guinness as Osric.

Before rehearsals began, Guthrie and Olivier paid a call on Dr Jones in Harley Street to discuss how his theories could be put into practice. Olivier, who had also been studying John Dover Wilson's *What Happens in Hamlet*, recalled how Jones offered "an impressive array of symptoms: spectacular mood-swings, cruel treatment of his love and, above all, a hopeless inability to pursue the course required of him". The Oedipus complex could there-fore, Olivier concluded, "claim responsibility for a formidable share of all that is wrong with him. There is great pathos in his determined efforts to bring himself to the required boiling-point, and in the excuses he finds to shed this responsibility." In rehearsals Olivier further argued that Hamlet, apart from his "involuntary pusillanimity", had a weakness for dramatics.

This would be reasonable if the dramatics spurred him to action, but unfortunately they help to delay it. It is as if his shows of temperament not only exhaust him but give him relief from his absorption in his purpose – like an actor who, having spent his all in rehearsal, feels it almost redundant to go through with the performance.

Guthrie has left us a vivid description of Olivier at this time, on the threshold of fame:

Offstage he was not notably handsome or striking, but with make-up he could achieve a flashing Italianate, rather saturnine, but fascinating appear-ance. The voice already had a marvellous ringing baritone brilliance at the top; he spoke with a beautiful and aristocratic accent, with keen intelligence and a strong sense of rhythm. He moved with catlike agility. He had, if anything, too strong an instinct for the sort of theatrical effect which is striking and memorable. From the first moment of the first rehearsal it was evident that here was no ordinary actor, not everyone's cup of tea – no very strong personality can be that; not necessarily well-cast for Hamlet, but inevitably destined for the very top of the tree.[8]

The first night, on 5 January 1937, was an unusually tense one for Olivier. Apart from the fact that the cast had never achieved a complete run-through of the play – not even at the dress rehearsal, which was all-night chaos because of the complexities of Guthrie's lighting scheme – Olivier was up against several sources of antagonism. There was the traditional Old Vic audience – smelling, to him, of "boiled eggs and dead cats" – who regarded him as a matinee idol *arriviste*, denying their regular favourites their due advancement; there were the Gielgud devotees, all ears rather than eyes; and there were those who would simply like to see a rather flash young actor humbled by the Bard. On he streaked, in Robert Speaight's description, "meteoric, on a stage where Gielgud's *legato* still lingered", but Olivier "conquered the Gielgud loyalists with his portrait of a man whose weakness was to do too much rather than too little, and with too many minds to make up rather than one which he could not make up at all".[9]

Guthrie, pacing around anxiously at the back of the dress circle, sensed an antagonism in the audience right from the start. Fearing for both his production and its leading man, he looked on in an agony of apprehension as the action approached Hamlet's arrival on the battlements to watch for his father's ghost. Olivier, it seemed, also felt the audience's antipathy, for he proceeded to play the scene in a way he never had in rehearsals: staying downstage, soft-voiced, almost feline, he drew the audience towards him, straining for his every intonation, and for the rest of the evening had them in his thrall. Guthrie knew at once that here were the makings of true, instinctive theatrical greatness.

Olivier's Hamlet bore both the strengths and the weaknesses of his Romeo. Visually, he was stunning: he shaved the hair from the side of his head, plucked his eyebrows, painted the skin beneath his eyelashes white to catch the light and drew a faint line beneath his eyes, from the tear ducts down over his cheek-bones. (When the photographer Angus McBean remarked on these elaborate preparations, Olivier told him: "Oh yes, tired boy stuff, don't you dare remove it with your bloody retouching, old boy.") But the verse speaking was still rough-edged, with a tendency to rush the big speeches and reach for puzzling emphases. The passions again ruled the intellect; here was no scholar Hamlet, more the frustrated man of action with a flashing temper. But it had a Renaissance drive and flexibility of mood which contrasted sharply with some other recent, over-sentimentalized and bowdlerized performances. At least one observer noted how "it fitted certain of those aspects of Elizabethan 'melancholy' first brilliantly analysed in the character of Hamlet by [A.C.] Bradley".[10]

As so often with his most memorable performances, one line lingered above all others in the minds of those present as catching the mood of the actor's achievement. In this *Hamlet*, it was Olivier's cry of "I do not know why yet I live to say this thing's to do", the outcry of one in an intolerable dilemma, his hand itching for his sword. Guthrie's good sense – and his good luck – was to go for the Freud–Jones interpretation with an actor who would anyway have presented a strong Hamlet, thrashing around in frustration at such unwonted, inexplicable inaction, rather than the traditional weak, hesitant young scholar. The portrayal of weakness and indecision has never, then or since, been Olivier's forte.

As Peter Ustinov later put it (of Olivier's film of *Hamlet*, prefixed as "the story of a man who could not make up his mind"): "Of all actors, he is the most difficult to imagine as one who has not made up his mind."[11] To a pedantic Michael Redgrave, it was quite simply wrong: "On the contrary he *did* make up his mind, as thoroughly as anyone in his unique cir- cumstances could." Even for Harcourt Williams, the Old Vic guru to whom Olivier had turned for advice, this was a problem: "Olivier's per- formance was provocative.... I found him intensely interesting, a shade too acrobatic, and belonging to that class of Hamlet that makes it not so easy to accept 'How all occasions do inform against me'. It takes a Forbes- Robertson or a Gielgud to explain that side of Hamlet's character."[12]

Olivier made much of the scene regarded by Ernest Jones as so central, lifting his sword above Claudius's head "with all the demoniac intention of assassination; then his sword-arm dropped as if dragged down by some unseen leaden force, and throughout the whole of the rest of the speech – with its merest shell of excuse for his own inaction – he paced the stage with a restless and uncomprehending exasperation". In the closet scene, moreover, he smothered his mother in an utterly lascivious kiss, which she wiped away with horror. Even the innocent question to Ophelia, "Where's your father?", was loaded with a significance conveying his obsession with the relationships of children and parents.

It was all wasted on the audience, of course. Olivier felt it worked, for it gave his performance a consistency, but few among either theatre-goers or critics divined the Freudian overlay. Even Dr Jones, alas, was not satisfied. In a rather sniffy letter to Guthrie, he wrote:

> I was present at the first three acts last evening, having unfortunately to leave after that time.... One very serious fault was the old custom of playing Polonius as a clown, though I have never before seen the terrible gaffe of having Laertes and Ophelia giggling at each other....
>
> Now for the Prince of Denmark. You will not, of course, expect me, who have known Hamlet himself, to be content with any human substitute. Mr

Olivier played well and understandingly the scenes with the Queen. But temperamentally he is not cast for Hamlet. He is personally what we call "manic" and so finds it hard to play a melancholic part....

Then I hastily concur on the severe strictures which have been passed on his gabbling the words, to the ruin of the beautiful and sonorous poetry and philosophy they are meant to convey.... Hamlet is thinking aloud, not chatting to bystanders....

ps: You will not of course convey my opinion to Mr Olivier while he is still playing the part.[13]

Agate, in cantankerous mood again, came up with one of his most celebrated apophthegms: "Mr Olivier's Hamlet is the best performance of Hotspur this generation has seen." He conceded that Olivier had "a well-turned head, a pleasing, youthful face, a magnificent voice of bow-string tautness and vibrancy marred by a few commonplace intonations ... good carriage, a spring, pantherine gait and the requisite inches". But he also noted "a modern, jaunty off-handedness which is presumably a legacy from parts of the Beau Geste order". Olivier's Hamlet, in short, "excelled any Hamlet of recent years" in its "pulsating vitality and excitement". But "Mr Olivier does not speak poetry badly. He does not speak it at all."

After Claudius has stormed out of the play scene, Olivier's "Why, let the stricken deer go weep" was accompanied by a tremendous leap from the throne to the mimic stage below, and thence down to the footlights in high hysteria. To Agate, this was "a matter for the most compelling admiration". But at the beginning of the play his was "the honest, frank perplexity of a modern young man at Oxford or Cambridge, whose annoyance that his mother should have remarried with indecent haste is not going to prevent him from helping himself that afternoon to a hundred of the best off the sister University's bowling".

For Alan Dent of the *News Chronicle*, later to become Olivier's textual collaborator on his Shakespeare films, this was "an admirable prose Hamlet – swift, sardonic, passionate.... He is handsome in presence, and in his general bearing so bloody, bold and resolute that it is inconceivable that he could allow any philosophic qualm or query to stand between him and immediate regicide." He dealt with the philosophy "as he does with the poetry of the part. He construes and intelligently shows all the meaning of the great soliloquies, but seldom begins to reveal any feel for their poetical or even their metrical quality."

Fifty years on, these notices sound almost like praise. Critics were so hellbent on the lyrical tradition of Shakespeare that Olivier's determined "naturalism" was simply ahead of its time. To many, as with his Romeo, the sheer physical excitement of Olivier's acting outweighed any deficiency in his verse speaking. But at least two of his fellow actors, who both went

119

on to become similarly distinguished knights of the theatre, were unable to grasp or accept the Shakespeare revolution he was pioneering.

The truth, said Michael Redgrave (Laertes),

> was that I thought he was a bad Hamlet – too assertive and too resolute. He lacked the self-doubting subtleties the part demands. Every actor, even one as gifted and versatile as Olivier, is limited in his range of parts by his own temperament and character. The very boldness of Larry's personality, his natural drive and his pragmatism make him unsuitable to play an introspective, wavering character like Hamlet.[14]

When Redgrave himself finally came to play Hamlet (in 1949, at the age of forty-one), he "so strongly rejected the 'pathological' interpretation of Hamlet, as in some way the victim of an Oedipus complex, that I used every possible occasion to stress his love for his father".

Alec Guinness, who understudied Olivier as well as playing Osric, was "outraged at the gymnastic leaps and falls required by his example. I never liked the performance or Guthrie's production, but it was huge box office...."[15] Looking back at it with "wiser hindsight", however, Guinness realized "it was necessary for Olivier to do what he did – and it laid the foundations for his becoming a truly great actor". Characteristically, Olivier fought the duel with Redgrave's Laertes so intensely as to be a real threat to life and limb. Stuart Burge, the Player Queen, thirty years later to direct the film version of Olivier's *Othello*, recalls how one night Olivier's aggression sent Redgrave's sword flying out into the darkness:

> It flew straight into Lilian Baylis's stage box, nearly killing one of the governors. Everybody was trying to contain their laughter, but the problem was that the fight could not continue without the sword. I crawled offstage and hid behind the box, hoping for it to be handed to me, but the governor was too stunned to retrieve it. After what seemed like an eternity, I heard Miss Baylis say, "Oh give them back the sword, so they can finish and we can all go home."[16]

If the young Olivier brought anything to Hamlet, and indeed to Shakespeare performance, it was virility. He had set out to make the Prince of Denmark a figure full of Elizabethan zest for life, a dashing, acrobatic young man who glorified in his prowess as a swordsman – in what Ivor Brown summarized in the *Observer* as his "muscularity". This Hamlet, wrote Brown, in the notice which Olivier found most satisfying, was

> a master of riposte with tongue as with sword. His prose banter is admirably taken, springing quick from a quick mind. There is more of thistle and sword-grass than of sensitive plant in his composition. This means, of course, that the kind of pathos so richly established by Mr Gielgud is not there. That is inevitable: no one Hamlet can be all Hamlets, and Mr Olivier

succeeds in the prose of Hamlet of which Mr Gielgud (playing a cut version) was somewhat shy. Of course there are glimpses, and acute ones, of the tender spirit; there are soliloquies in verse which are spoken with fine cadences, but the dominating impression is of "the flash and outbreak of a fiery mind" and of a steely body too. The weakness here is that you begin to suspect that such a Hamlet would have put through his murderous work without so much self-security and hesitation.

It was in the stage-door pub, late in the *Hamlet* rehearsals, that Olivier himself suggested to Guthrie what he would like to do next: Sir Toby Belch in *Twelfth Night* – a total contrast, by way of a chance to show off both his versatility and his mastery of the art of disguise. Together they began to piece together the rest of the cast, using the best of the *Hamlet* company. Alec Guinness would make a splendidly gauche Sir Andrew Aguecheek; Marius Goring could contrast his stolid Fortinbras with a spritely Feste. Already wracked by marital guilt, Olivier suggested his wife Jill for Viola. But the part went to Jessica Tandy, with Jill playing Olivia. Orsino would be played by Leo Genn.

The Old Vic neither planned nor rehearsed very far ahead in those days, and the run-up to *Twelfth Night* was a rushed and chaotic affair. The production was not much helped by Guthrie's bright idea of doubling Viola with Sebastian, which led to some complex scenes for Jessica Tandy, with a mute actor miming Sebastian on the occasion she had to meet him. Into his elaborate costuming Olivier built a pouch, ostensibly filled with sack, in fact containing a script from which he could remind himself of his next lines as he stood in the wings waiting to enter.

His make-up was the first of the many elaborate, at times outrageous, disguises of which he was to prove so fond. A veritable pile of false noses surmounted the real thing; false bags were glued under his eyes; pads of sponge were concealed in his mouth to puff up the cheeks. Add a long, straggling moustache, and it became a family joke between him and his sister Sybille that he had modelled Sir Toby on their Uncle Herbert, the portrait painter. Olivier entered into the role with almost too much gusto; Guthrie became concerned about "some rather grotesque overplaying". Jessica Tandy laughingly remembers how "very naughty" he was during his duel with her as Sebastian: "He would keep prodding me in the chest. He loved that."[17] Alec Guinness found himself caught in a highly competitive stage partnership, with more and more business being added each night in the constant battle for more laughs.

Guthrie summed it up tersely as "a baddish, immature production of mine, with Olivier outrageously amusing as Sir Toby and a very young Alec Guinness outrageous and more amusing as Sir Andrew". To Trewin, Olivier's Belch was "like a veteran Skye-terrier, ears pricked for mischief", while Guinness's Aguecheek was "a walking wraith".[18] This Belch, according to Farjeon, "thinks life consists of falling down. ... There is no core to this Sir Toby, nor is he master of the revels, just a sodden butt and a bit of a puppet."[19] Audrey Williamson described Olivier's Belch as "riotously convivial ... with a disarming lovableness ... a Falstaff in embryo". It was the nearest he would ever get to playing Shakespeare's gargantuan Sir John, a role he would always regard as belonging personally, *in perpetuo*, to Ralph Richardson.

With *Hamlet* and *Twelfth Night* doing good box office, Lilian Baylis was delighted with Guthrie's management of her theatre and urged him in the spring of 1937 to consider a special production of some sort to mark the Coronation of the new King, George VI, that May. Whenever the subject of a National Theatre came up, after all, she would always say "We *are* the National Theatre." The obvious offering would seem to be *Henry V*, a flag-waving burst of patriotism finely tuned to the occasion. The only problem was that both Guthrie and Olivier considered themselves pacifists.

Olivier, particularly, loathed the character of the King, with his exultation in warfare and his "scoutmaster" humour. In rehearsal he and Guthrie toyed with the notion of a debunking production, holding the play's blatant jingoism up to ridicule. But that would scarcely have been appropriate to the times, with a new and popular King succeeding his brother after the only abdication in British history; even a hint of irony would have ill-become the Old Vic's reputation as a surrogate National Theatre at a moment when the monarchy needed all the support it could get. Olivier had no choice but to make what he could of a character he despised.

So it is not surprising that he opened in the role rather half-heartedly, fighting shy of Henry's great St Crispin's Day clarion-cry, despite a supporting cast of 100 and a sea of Motley's finest flags and banners around him. He was a cool and calculating Henry, witty and sensitive in the bilingual love scene with Katharine, but unconvincing as a gung-ho man of war. As the run progressed, however, the performance developed enormously. Gradually Olivier found the majesty of the poetry casting its own spell. "The words", he said, "worked their own medicine." Again it had been Richardson to the rescue, with the seasoned advice that however much Henry might be a "cold bath" king, Shakespeare had given him the voice and eloquence of a poet, and this was how he should be played. "You say he is a scoutmaster. Yes, if you want, but he is the exaltation of scoutmasters. Shakespeare does this to everybody. Without Shakespeare, Macbeth would be a rather common murderer, instead of which he's a great poet."

Once he had shed his initial cynicism, Olivier's "Lion King" was soon enthralling audiences so much that Baylis and Guthrie doubled the run from four to eight weeks, and box-office records began to go. Guthrie was impressed by the change in Olivier and came to regard this as one of his best productions. As Katharine, Jessica Tandy

> hardly ever missed going to the wings to watch Larry's soliloquy before the battle, "Upon the King ...!" How marvellously and powerfully he played it! Hardly speaking above a whisper, but with what ease and depth! The audience held their breath. Fortunately we have his performance preserved in his own production of the film – but I shall never forget the live performance.[20]

It was the first time Olivier impressed the distinguished Shakespeare scholar Laurence Kitchin, who had heard him complaining contemptuously about student make-up at the Central School, "a matinee idol martinet" whose Hamlet he deliberately avoided. But his Henry v came as a shock:

> There sat the King as the prelates got down to expounding his claim to the throne of France, and there was I, ready to watch a matinee idol's growing pains. Having seen [Godfrey] Tearle and Richardson, I expected to learn nothing new about the part. Sooner or later the legalistic drone would end and Henry would ask, in the stately manner of Tearle, or as near as a classical novice could get to it: "May I with right and conscience make this claim?" It would, of course, be essential that the claim was just. Any doubt, and Henry would call off the war at once: if the play was not staunchly and reputably patriotic, it was nothing. And then I noticed that the King was getting restive. Olivier was showing the same cross impatience with the prelates as he had shown to the students about their make-up four years ago. Generations of persecuted schoolboys were being vindicated by a Henry who had no more time for that dreary speech than they. That was the revolution, consolidated when Olivier spoke the enquiry very clear and fast on a rising, hectoring inflection. It was plain that he was going to war anyway. Right and conscience were being given the value they had in 1937 when speeches relative to the international situation were made.[21]

One memorable night Charles Laughton came backstage to tell Olivier how moved he had been. "Do you know why you're so good in this part?" asked Laughton, swelling to his grandest Churchillian proportions. "Because you are England!"

The Danish Government seemed to agree. At the end of this first triumphant Shakespeare season, it invited Olivier to lead the Old Vic company to Denmark as the first English actor to perform Hamlet before the Danish royal family at Elsinore itself, on the very ramparts of Kronborg Castle. It was to prove the beginning of a tradition maintained by John

Gielgud (1939), Michael Redgrave (1950) and Richard Burton (1954).
The trip would be memorable in a number of ways, but Olivier was careful
to ensure as much in advance by persuading Guthrie to take on a new
Ophelia, to replace Cherry Cottrell, in the comely shape of that rising star
Miss Vivien Leigh.

Vivien had been to see his Old Vic Hamlet no fewer than fourteen times,
at a period when her own career, after that first heady success in *The Mask
of Virtue*, seemed to have become becalmed. She had clocked up two more
films and two stage comedies, but without the spectacular success she had
come to crave, perhaps even to expect. *Dark Journey* was an overly complex
spy movie with Conrad Veidt, directed by Victor Saville at Denham,
whose plot even she found hard to follow; while in *Storm in a Teacup*,
adapted for the screen from James Bridie's play, she showed such early
promise as a light comedienne, opposite Rex Harrison, that there was brief
talk of the two forming a celluloid partnership. The most memorable thing
about the first night of *Because We Must*, a poor vehicle for her return to
the West End stage, was that she happened to give all her fellow members
of the cast copies of a new American novel she had just read, *Gone with the
Wind*, with whose heroine she felt a strong and urgent sympathy. When
the play closed within a month, all that was on offer was a tiny part in a
humdrum farce called *Bats in the Belfry*; it returned her to the orchestrator
of her first triumph, Sydney Carroll, and to its venue, the Ambassadors,
but in a role so modest – all she had to do was drop a tray – that she had
become badly depressed.

Vivien was prepared to accept such humble, almost demeaning, work
because she knew she needed more experience. Even Olivier himself,
though he did not tell her until years later, still had doubts about her
talents as an actress. He had fallen in love with some sort of elusive, lyrical
theatrical beauty across the footlights of *The Mask of Virtue*, but seeing her
in these mediocre modern comedies began to fill him with doubts. The
main quality to draw on, he decided, was her sheer determination, her will
to succeed. The time they spent together was devoted to voice coaching,
movement and an array of director-to-actress advice, as much as to the
illicit making of love.

Elsinore – in Guthrie's words, "no picnic"[22] – turned into an episode
worthy of the Keystone Cops. The performances, arranged by the Danish
Tourist Board to inaugurate a new annual festival, were scheduled to take
place in the courtyard and on the battlements of the castle, which domi-
nates the sound dividing Denmark from Sweden. The Tourist Board, not
being the most experienced of theatrical managers, had not quite grasped
the significance of the messages from London about the set, lighting and
backstage arrangements. When the cast arrived in Denmark a week before

the opening night, the locals had laid on 100 blond-haired cadets to make up Fortinbras's army. But a new set had been built which bore no relation to their production, and the Danish powers-that-were had not anticipated that their visitors would need time and space to rehearse.

As the castle was open to visitors all day, and the authorities unwilling to close it, the only option was to rehearse at night. It was May, and the daytimes were sunny and pleasant: Olivier, Vivien and their colleagues slept, played tennis and boated on the sound. By night, unfailingly, it poured with rain, which made something of a mockery of the Danish insistence that a huge posse of axe-wielding, steel-helmeted firemen be present at all rehearsals in case of mishaps during the nightly midnight-to-six shift. As the actors got progressively more cold and miserable, finding the open air a startlingly enervating place to work, and as the rain grew ever stronger, Lilian Baylis was having the time of her life: after being unwell for some time she was now loving being Abroad, staying in a hotel, exploring the strange new foreign food and looking after her "little ones". As was only to be expected, she also shared the rigours of their after-dark sessions, dispensing sandwiches and lemonade – and, on one memorable evening, a keg of rum – from the comparative shelter of a battlement window.

On the night of the opening, with the royal party approaching by special train from Copenhagen, the heavens opened wider than ever. At 7.30, with the performance due to begin at eight, the rain was coming down, as Guthrie put it, "in bellropes". He held an urgent council of war with Baylis and Olivier, and it was unanimously agreed that an open-air performance had become impossible. The only thing for it, royalty or no royalty, was to play in the ballroom of their modest hotel, the Marienlyst – in whose garden the original Hamlet supposedly lies buried.

There was, of course, no stage in the hotel ballroom and no time now to build one. As Olivier conducted a rush re-rehearsal, using the centre of the room as the focal point of the action, it looked to Guthrie rather like a circus. For the first time he realized the potential of a phrase which had yet to be coined – theatre-in-the-round. Nightmarish though this emergency was, it sowed in Guthrie's mind the startling notion of dispensing with the proscenium arch. As Olivier and his fellow actors discovered new exits and entrances, Guthrie enlisted the drama critics of the *Daily Telegraph*, *Dagbladet* and *Paris-Soir* to help him rearrange 900 seats around the sides of the ballroom. Miss Baylis meanwhile kept the royal family, the diplomatic corps and sundry other VIPs at bay in the hotel lobby.

The performance was not their best, but the audience proved very sympathetic. After a couple of hours, half-way through a very long and tiring play, the strains of constant improvisation began to tell on the cast; and the final scene, as Guthrie remembered it, was "a shambles, but not quite in the way the author intended". Those journalists present came away with more positive memories. "The remarkable thing", wrote George W. Bishop, the *Telegraph* critic who had helped with the furniture, "is that it came off. It was as if a travelling band of players – as had visited Kronborg nearly 400 years before – had improvised a performance in an inn yard or local hall."[23] For Ivor Brown it was

> as good a performance of *Hamlet* as I have ever seen. The words, the story, the driving emotional pressure of the play were clear and compelling. Indeed the very smallness of the stage and the nearness of the audience round about – during the duelling one feared for the nobility and gentry in the front row – seemed to intensify the excitement which *Hamlet* never fails to produce.[24]

If only by accident, studio theatre also appears to have been born that night, even though Guthrie thought his cast could have done with more exits and entrances than the hotel manager would allow them to use. (When, next morning, the director inquired what was behind one particular door, of which the manager had been especially protective, it turned out to be a pair of nesting blue-tits and their young.) Quixotic though the entire episode was, it was to prove the inspiration for such later Guthrie landmarks as the conversion of the Edinburgh Assembly Hall into the spectacular theatre-in-the-round still in use at the annual Festival today, and his establishment in North America of the Stratford Theatre, Ontario, and the Guthrie Theatre in Minneapolis.

It was in Elsinore that Olivier celebrated his thirtieth birthday and came to grips with the biggest crisis yet in his young life. For a year now he and Vivien had been leading the "furtive, lying" life of illicit lovers, though increasingly unable to disguise their feelings from those around them. This time his wife had accompanied him, and in Denmark he had found himself making love to Vivien "almost within Jill's vision". There were limits to furtiveness; there were also limits to the amount of guilt they were prepared to inflict on themselves, or pain on their partners. It was doubly cruel, for both marriages were fond and affectionate, with a degree of mutual respect. But they finally resolved that the time had come, on their return, to tell their respective spouses of their love. They did so one synchronized evening that June.

Neither Jill nor Leigh was particularly surprised. Both had seen it coming for the better part of a year. It seemed best to all concerned that the break be immediate; both Olivier and Vivien moved out virtually overnight, leaving their children behind them. Suzanne Holman was to say in later years that she felt she had scarcely known her mother; her father, who remained an important constant in Vivien's life, took on for his daughter the status of a martyred hero.[25] It was to be many years before Tarquin Olivier established any kind of relationship with his father, who remained – when his work permitted him the time and emotional energy – deeply riddled with guilt. Neither of the deserted partners ever remarried, and both stalwartly refused all temptations to make public their true feelings about the way in which they had been pretty ruthlessly used as stepping-stones to stardom.

For the shell-shocked lovers, there was little time for remorse. The first task facing them was to complete a film they had begun before travelling to Denmark. Their three pre-Elsinore weeks back with London Films at Denham, on the set of *Twenty-One Days*, had given Olivier the chance to coach Vivien in the role of Ophelia, a task he set about with particular zeal as he knew of Guthrie's doubts about her abilities. But she had held her own in the second Elsinore performance – this time on the castle ramparts, as scheduled – and even her worryingly small voice had proved equal to the challenges of open-air Shakespeare. Now, given their new domestic bliss and the "blessed relief" of gradually sharing their secret with the world, their work together at Denham could not have been happier.

But the film itself – an injudicious mix of love and mistaken identity – proved so dire that it would probably never have been released but for its stars' subsequent celebrity. Originally entitled *The First and the Last*, and directed with headmasterly rigour by a Basil Dean as short-tempered as ever, the script had been adapted by Graham Greene from a John Galsworthy story. Despite these lofty credentials, and the added bonus of Leslie Banks, the finished product was suppressed in the studio vaults out of sheer embarrassment. It was released only during the war when Olivier and Vivien were at their box-office zenith, in the wake of *Wuthering Heights*, *Rebecca* and *Gone with the Wind*. The couple happened to be in New York at the time and first saw this product of their early love in a seedy little downtown fleapit. It was so awful that they walked out after half an hour and could never thereafter bring themselves to see it right through.

"So I should think!" muttered a resentful Basil Dean, when the story reached him.[26] He recalled that during shooting Korda had, without explanation, scrapped an entire set from under him one day; only later did he discover that it was because of Olivier's and Vivien's visit to Elsinore, regarded by the studio as good publicity. Dean himself blamed the film's failure on the young lovers' "joyous awareness of each other", which took the form of "laughter and giggling on the set". Early on in the proceedings, he tells us, Olivier took him on one side to ask his advice: "Did I think he should run away with Vivien? I made him the only possible reply in the circumstances: 'Larry, you know jolly well, whatever I say, you'll go your own way in the end.' " The director had initially been surprised at Korda's nonchalance over the casting of Olivier, then struck by the firmness of his insistence on Vivien, despite her inexperience. "His ultimate purpose", Dean realized years later, "was to build Vivien into an international film star. It was not until long afterwards that I realized that both Galsworthy's story and myself had been pawns in this larger game."[27]

Even Greene, reviewing his own film in the *Spectator*, admitted defeat:

> Galsworthy's story was peculiarly unsuited for film adaptation, as its whole point lay in a double suicide (forbidden by the censor), a burned confession and an innocent man's conviction for murder (forbidden by the great public). For the rather dubious merits of the original, the adaptors have substituted incredible coincidences and banal situations.[28]

He laid the blame squarely on the capricious Korda: "I wish I could tell the extraordinary story that lies behind this shelved and resurrected picture, a story involving a theme-song, a bottle of whisky, and camels in Wales.... Meanwhile, let one guilty man, at any rate, stand in the dock, swearing never, never to do it again."

The filming of *Twenty-One Days* did at least bring one moment which nobody present would quickly forget. The final scene called for the lovers to take a river trip down the Thames from Tower Bridge to Southend. Olivier, Vivien, Ralph Richardson and their colleagues all climbed aboard the good ship *Golden Eagle*, only for it to pour with rain all day. As they beguiled the time with desultory conversation, the talk turned to MGM's much-publicized search for the right actress to play Scarlett O'Hara in their epic production of the new Margaret Mitchell novel, *Gone with the Wind*. Paulette Goddard, Bette Davis, Barbara Stanwyck, Miriam Hopkins and many other famous names were said to be in the running, though the producers might yet go for a complete unknown.

"You'd make a marvellous Rhett Butler, Larry," somebody said to Olivier, not altogether implausibly, for such Hollywood success as he had so far managed was based on the stiff-upper-moustache school of acting eventually essayed in the role by Clark Gable. Olivier laughed it off, while others put up such candidates as Robert Taylor, Gary Cooper, Errol Flynn and Cary Grant.

Vivien, who had said nothing and who had as yet to make her mark in any screen role, then silenced the group by drawing herself up on the rainswept deck, pulling her coat tighter around her shoulders, and declaring with sibylline sweetness: "Larry won't play Rhett Butler. But I shall play Scarlett O'Hara. You wait and see."[29]

CHAPTER 8

1937–9

Vivien was not to know it, but early in 1937 two of Selznick's talent scouts, Katharine Brown and Oscar Serlin, had already put her name forward for Scarlett on the strength of *Fire over England*. They had received a typically bleak reply from their boss: "I HAVE NO ENTHUSIASM FOR VIVIEN LEIGH. MAYBE I WILL HAVE BUT AS YET HAVE NEVER EVEN SEEN PHOTOGRAPH OF HER. WILL BE SEEING "FIRE OVER ENGLAND" SHORTLY, AT WHICH TIME WILL OF COURSE SEE LEIGH. . . ."[1]

The young lovers knew nothing of this that summer as they disappeared to Venice for a romantic breather to celebrate their new-found freedom. Olivier had bought Durham Cottage, a pretty seventeenth-century house in Christ Church Street, Chelsea, whose spiral staircase and deep-pile carpets they both loved, despite almost terminal damage caused to the drawing-room on Guy Fawkes' night by a home-made Ralph Richardson rocket. But Olivier feared that their idyllic *vita nuova* might founder on Vivien's high state of anxiety about her daughter Suzanne, whom she had felt obliged to leave with Leigh Holman. Hence the sudden vacation, from which they returned rested, optimistic and ever more in the throes of the most romantic of loves – but to the dispiriting news that neither of their partners was willing, as yet, to agree to a divorce. They were soon too busy to let it bother them.

While Korda loaned Vivien to MGM for *A Yank at Oxford* with Maureen O'Sullivan and Robert Taylor – which only heightened her anxieties by casting her as a flirtatious adulteress – Olivier knocked off a "quickie" comedy of manners notable as the screen debut in colour of Merle Oberon.

It was only her second appearance since the near-fatal car crash which had forced Korda to cancel shooting of *I, Claudius*, thus depriving the world of one of Charles Laughton's most remarkable performances. *The Divorce of Lady X*, a remake of London Films' 1933 production, *Counsel's Opinion*, is a pleasant enough tale of marital misunderstandings in which Olivier, according to *Film Weekly*, gave "his best screen performance yet". But it was Ralph Richardson who stole the picture with a deft comic performance that made Olivier's screen acting again look all too stagey.

In December, Olivier returned to the Old Vic for his second ambitious Shakespeare season. There were high hopes for his Macbeth, under the direction of the renowned French apostle of Stanislavsky, Michel Saint-Denis, who had recently imported the revolutionary naturalism of his Parisian *Compagnie des Quinze* to London. To Olivier, who had brought his own brand of realism to Shakespeare in Gielgud's *Romeo and Juliet*, the prospect of working with Saint-Denis was a heady one. "Find the truth *through* the verse," the Frenchman's oft-repeated *cri de coeur*, became a theatrical creed to the young actor whose verse-speaking as Romeo had been so pilloried. But the Old Vic company, like so many before and after them, were to find the old theatrical superstitions about "the Scottish play" uncannily vindicated.

The jinx was evident not just onstage, though Saint-Denis's elaborate attention to detail combined with the complexities of the Motley set to make rehearsals slip further and further behind schedule. Nor was it the car crash in which Saint-Denis was lucky to escape unscathed; nor the death of Lilian Baylis's beloved dog, run over before her eyes; nor the heavy cold which deprived Olivier of his voice on the eve of the first night. There was worse to come. The backstage chaos was such that, for the first time in the Old Vic's history, the opening had to be postponed. The condition of Lilian Baylis, already suffering heart flutters, caused the company even greater concern when she left for home, depressed and worried, at 3 a.m. Even so, she was back in next morning to spread the bad news of the postponement among her clients, via the press, and to sign the company's pay cheques.

Then, on the eve of the delayed first night, 25 November, came the news that Lilian Baylis had died. After three years of debilitating illness, a final heart attack had claimed her at the age of sixty-three. Characteristically, she had been ready for this as for all other eventualities, and had left written instructions that her death was not to disrupt the opening night. Before the performance the chairman of the Old Vic's governing body, Lord Lytton, came onstage to deliver an encomium to "this masterful woman of genius",[2] whose familiar seat stood poignantly empty in her stage-side box. Not until after the final curtain, however, on her instructions, was Olivier handed a note she had left him: "Welcome return to dear Laurence Olivier. May you be as happy in *Macbeth* as in *Hamlet* last season."

He was not. Saint-Denis's preoccupation with sheer stylized scale, at the expense of pace and passion, contrived to make the staging leaden-footed, if not ramshackle, and Olivier's false nose bigger than ever. Of his false gums, slanted eyes, raised cheekbones and yellow complexion, not to mention his luridly skin-tight gown, Vivien made the memorable observation: "You hear Macbeth's first line, then Larry's make-up comes on, then Banquo comes on, then Larry comes on."

Of the first-night critics, Trewin remarked that Olivier "appeared to be outlining a performance he would block in later". Dent waxed much more lyrical about Judith Anderson's Lady Macbeth, but Agate, of all people, was sufficiently enthused to go twice. Describing the whole performance as "a study in nerves", the great man defended Olivier against a spate of anonymous hate mail. "Why should a performance which interested me throughout and at times excited me greatly so fail with these others? Can it be that they were judging Mr Olivier's performance by some preconceived standard to which this actor's physical means, even if he were Garrick and Kean rolled into one, would still not let him conform?" As usual, the old curmudgeon then spoilt the effect by declaring that Olivier would play Macbeth "twice as well when he is twice as old".

Olivier has few happy memories of the production, beyond Andrew Cruickshank's "perfect" Banquo and the sound of Noël Coward's hysterical laughter from the stalls. Fifty years on, in his familiar self-deprecating vein, he shoulders the blame equally with Saint-Denis for a performance generally remembered as undistinguished. But the Old Vic archives show that the production broke box-office records, before a less successful West End transfer, and that many of the critics enthused – if not about the production, then about its star. "He has only to walk on stage to set it alight," trilled Lionel Hale, while *The Times* praised "his attack upon the part, his nervous intensity, his dignity of movement and swiftness of thought".

Many of the legion of *Macbeth* disaster stories concern sword-fighting injuries, and this production was no exception. As always, Olivier threw himself into the denouement with such gusto that each of his Macduffs lived in peril of his life. Apocryphal, alas, is the legend that a stagehand had to whisper each night to a hyped-up Macbeth: "Don't forget, Larry, you're supposed to *lose* this fight." All too gorily true, however, was the hand injury to the first Macduff, Ellis Irving, who had to be replaced by Roger Livesey. Undeterred, Olivier continued his attempts to rewrite Shakespeare's history each night by giving Livesey the fight of his life, so

131

much so that one evening Macduff's sword snapped and both watched its lethal steel blade fly out into the darkened auditorium. In vain they waited for a terminal gasp from a stricken audience member. Afterwards, a little old lady appeared backstage proudly clutching the offending weapon, which she asked Olivier to autograph.

While Gielgud packed them in with a wildly successful production of *The School for Scandal* – Olivier later described Gielgud's Joseph Surface as "the best light comic performance I've ever seen, or ever shall" – three weeks of mediocre business in the West End contrived to wipe out the whole month of *Macbeth* profits at the Old Vic. But the Vic's next production, a glossy *Midsummer Night's Dream* with decor by Oliver Messel, featuring Vivien Leigh as Titania to Robert Helpmann's Oberon, more than made amends. Another young actor who was to become a lifelong friend, John Mills, was ever grateful to Olivier for persuading Guthrie to cast him as Puck.

It was the first Shakespeare production attended by the young princesses, Elizabeth and Margaret, whose wide-eyed delight had Guthrie in thrall. More significant to Olivier, whose Macbeth had been attended by the Queen (now the Queen Mother), was the unspoken assumption that news of his liaison with Vivien had not yet reached the highest circles – or, if it had, that they had decided to turn a discreetly blind eye. It may be hard to imagine in the 1980s, but "living in sin" was a phrase still taken literally in pre-war England, and a rising young actor of unlimited ambition could well fear for the effect on his career. Already there had been the odd catcall from the gallery and a brick through the post labelled "For Olivier's folly". The throng of stage-door autograph-hunters, index as much of a dashing young actor's popularity as his vanity, had noticeably thinned.

Apart from her Titania, in which she was as enchanting as the production itself, Vivien had little work and contented herself with learning her trade from her mentor and lover, to her the greatest actor alive. She was to be found in the Old Vic stalls most evenings, and would share his delight in aping the mannerisms and speech patterns of friends and strangers alike. Despite the continuing difficulties with their spouses, they were blissfully happy. Life seemed to hold out infinite promise.

Olivier was now to follow his Macbeth with Iago to Ralph Richardson's Othello. Back in charge after the Saint-Denis débâcle, Guthrie had little trouble persuading him to pay a return visit to the oracular Ernest Jones, with whom they spent two long evenings in search of a Freudian key to what Coleridge called Iago's "motiveless malignity". Amid much psycho-analytical verbiage, Jones managed to persuade them that Iago was far from motiveless and that he was exercised by more than merely being passed over for promotion, or indeed any hint of sexual jealousy. The orthodox Freudian explanation of Iago's extreme behaviour was that he was subconsciously *in love with* his master, the Moor, an unrequited and thus unfulfilled homosexual longing which drove him to destroy both their lives. As Olivier summarized the Welsh seer's pronouncements:

> The clue to the play was not Iago's hatred of Othello, but his deep *affection* for him. His jealousy was not because he envied Othello's position, nor because he was in love with Desdemona, but because he himself possessed a subconscious affection for the Moor, the homosexual foundation of which he did not understand.

Though they swallowed the notion whole, both Olivier and Guthrie knew it was far too outrageous to try out on the urbane, down-to-earth and indeed happily heterosexual Richardson, who preferred to overlook the awkward fact, unmistakable in his own profession, that some human beings can feel sexual love for others of their own gender. "It's inescapable," said Guthrie excitedly, as they walked away from Dr Jones's home.[3] "On the unconscious plane, of course." "Yes," said a hesitant Olivier, "but I don't think we dare tell Ralphie." Richardson would never go along with anything which smacked to him of perversion. So they made a pact to implement Jones's theories without enlightening him. Othello would not have realized the true nature of Iago's angst, so why tell Richardson?

Their approach seemed vindicated one day at rehearsals when Olivier suddenly planted a lascivious kiss on Richardson's lips, causing his friend and partner nothing but acute embarrassment. "There, there now, dear fellow," the older man said gently, patting Olivier fondly on the head like a wayward child. "Come, come, dear boy, dear, good boy." But wily old Ralphie was not as innocent as Guthrie and Olivier assumed. Of course he could see that they were recreating their not altogether successful approach to last season's *Hamlet*, and that this new-fangled psychology rubbish was getting in the way of a straightforward, polished production, which left the text to do the work. The beauty of the play, the magnificence of its rhetoric, he told them, should be enough. "Leave me, I beg you, my monumental alabaster."

Undismayed, Olivier pressed on with his version of Iago right past the opening night. It was as if he and Richardson were in different productions, even different plays. Olivier still enjoys telling the story of how, when Othello fell to the ground in an epileptic fit, his Iago hurled himself down beside him and feigned a writhing orgasm – "terrifically daring, wasn't it?" Maybe; until Athene Seyler, whose views he much respected, came round to his dressing-room after a matinee and said how wonderful he'd been – except "I'm sure I have no idea what you were up to when you threw yourself on the ground beside Ralph."

So there were "no more shenanigans ... out it came" Olivier's Iago, "merely a roguish skylarker" to a mystified Dent, continued to play shamefully to the gallery, but otherwise mightily relieved Richardson by thereafter reverting to a typically malevolent underling, a more traditional mix of thwarted ambition and sheer racial prejudice. Olivier's own subsequent wartime experiences in the Royal Navy, amusingly enough, convinced him that the promotion issue *is* the key to Iago's hatred of Othello: "One has only to glance around a wardroom table and take note of the ageing, hard-bitten faces of those passed over."

Much as they had looked forward to their stage reunion, both Olivier and Richardson had to agree with Guthrie's verdict on the production: "A good row might have cleared the air. But everyone behaved too well. Each of us thought that by the next day the clouds of misunderstanding would lift and all would be well. Friendships remained unimpaired, but the production was a ghastly, boring hash."[4] Richardson was never really a classic Othello, anyway; much as he savoured the magnificence of the Moor's language, bravura roles were not his forte. Olivier's Iago, for the critics, who were of course as oblivious of his Freudian intentions as they had been with his Hamlet, was "too cheery", "too puckish".

But Agate spent most of his review burying poor Richardson. "I assure Mr Richardson that it is as painful for me to write this as it would be for him were he to read it," he wrote, merely dismissing Olivier as "a supersubtle dilettante ... as though a light tenor should be cast for the part of Mephistopheles". Richardson's biographer, Garry O'Connor, may be right in surmising that Olivier "was never going to allow any critic, and certainly not Agate, to dictate to him his limits",[5] but it is sad to see him suggesting that Richardson "meekly agreed" with Agate's devastating verdict that "Nature ... has unkindly refused him any tragic facilities whatever. His voice has not a tragic note in its whole gamut ... He cannot blaze. He saws away at his nether lip with the enthusiasm of a Queen's Hall fiddler or a maniac reducing a torso to its minimum."

As with Macbeth, Olivier was to make amends with an Othello which marked one of the many climaxes of his later career. The immediate compensation at the time was success in an unlikely Old Vic venture: a new play, amid the Shakespeare season, with a contemporary setting, James Bridie's *The King of Nowhere*. Olivier played the central figure of a baroque and bizarre intrigue: Vivaldi, a mentally unstable actor financed by a rich spinster into becoming a neo-Fascist political leader. In the energy of the wild derangement he brought to the role, as much as the nervous tension which was fast becoming his trade mark, Audrey

Williamson saw pre-echoes of his Lear eight years later. Trewin, too, saw "swooping flash and fury" (though he also suspected the piece might "come back to outlast many plays of the period").

But, in the era of Munich, it was Bridie's rather heavy-handed political satire which caught the attention of the critics, who seized the rare chance to devote their column inches to the issues of the day rather than another rehearsal of the participants' professional skills. A flurry of controversy did the box office no harm, however, and Olivier's proto-Arturo Ui (replaced by Robert Speaight for the Broadway transfer) made a fine and extravagant contrast to his forthcoming Coriolanus.

The climax of this second ambitious year at the Old Vic, *Coriolanus*, was by far Olivier's greatest classical success so far, largely thanks to the seasoned wisdom of his director, Lewis Casson, husband of his Volumnia, Sybil Thorndike. The first night, for Trewin, was "lightning-streaked. ... Olivier ('There is a world elsewhere') rose like flame on marble." Again he concentrated as much on the special effects as the characterization; his death fall, an acrobatic piece of gory somersaulting from on high to the footlights, is remembered and copied to this day. And, again, there was an especially powerful cry, a choking falsetto on "Oh mother, mother, what have you done?"

The critics, for the first time, were ashamed to be heard sniffing greatness. "Of a stature to come within the line of the great tradition," decreed Dent, declaring Olivier in this "most exacting of roles" a match for Kemble, Macready, Phelps, Irving and Benson. Agate too mentioned him in the same breath as Kean and Phelps: "The end is the grand organ of acting, with all the stops out." While complaining under his own name of Olivier's "clowning" and "excessive make-up", and that he "walked like an all-in wrestler", this perennial Janus used one of his often more honest pseudonyms to dub him "the nearest thing we have today to the heroic tradition". Speaight called it "Olivier's first incontestably great performance".

There survives from this production a backstage anecdote which over the years has lent substance to the carping of Olivier-haunters who have dismissed him as all technique and no substance. If we accept, however, that there can be no substance without technique, we should note first the verdict of the ever judicious Ivor Brown: "His voice has gained in volume, in reach and passion. It has notes of exquisite appeal, delicate finesse and such attack as makes the syllables shimmer like a sword's blade." Had Olivier really attained this technical maturity? Before her death, Sybil Thorndike recalled how it was competitiveness between her beloved husband and her beloved protégé which gave the production its edge:

135

Lewis made Larry get rid of some of his little tricks onstage and be more orthodox.... But they only argued in fun because they both liked a good argument.

On one occasion Lewis said, "You've got to do this speech all in one breath," and Larry said, "I bet you couldn't." But Lewis did, then said, "Now you do the same." And, of course, Larry could do it. After all, they used to have contests in breathing and Larry had a longer breath than anyone else, longer than anyone I ever knew. He could do the Matins exhortation "Dearly Beloved Brethren" twice through in one breath. Lewis could only do it one and a half times. I was so ashamed when he broke off and was beaten.[6]

The season ended on the eve of Olivier's thirty-first birthday. He had arrived at the Old Vic the previous year as an inexperienced Shakespearean with no feeling for verse. Now, six roles later, he had achieved recognition as a major classical actor, hailed for the poetry of his very presence. But this was his last appearance at the Old Vic before the war, and it would be another six years, thanks to a conspiracy of private and public events, before he would reappear on the London stage. He would return, however, with the bonus of a reputation as an international film star, a "great lover" as much offscreen as on.

This mixed return to the Old Vic arena had been played against an exhausting backdrop of domestic stress and strain, with Olivier and Vivien juggling their overwhelming love against the continuing pain of those they had abandoned. Another restorative vacation was called for, this time a long and sybaritic one, wandering through France for eight weeks in Vivien's ancient Ford V8 on a gastronomic tour mapped out for them by Charles Laughton, with whom she had been filming *St Martin's Lane*. Various theatrical friends, notably Gielgud and Ashcroft, were scattered around the Riviera that summer, and they were bouncing from one to the other when, in the first week of July, a cable arrived from Olivier's agent: "ARE YOU INTERESTED IN GOLDWYN IDEA FOR SEPTEMBER FIRST STOP VIVIEN YOURSELF AND OBERON IN WUTHERING HEIGHTS STOP ANSWER AS SOON AS POSSIBLE STOP".

They talked the prospect over for some hours before sending an ambiguous reply, suggesting that the idea be discussed further on their return to London. The immediate problems were several. First, Olivier's wariness of Hollywood since his bad experiences there; the Garbo rejection still haunted him even more than the misery of a contract system which yielded merely mediocre roles. Secondly, there was the awkward problem of which part Vivien was to play. If Merle Oberon, already a bigger screen name, was cast, it must be subsidiary – namely Isabella to her Cathy. Vivien would not even contemplate playing any role but Cathy. And Olivier, though he gradually realized what a major opportunity Heathcliff would be, was not prepared either to see his beloved in a secondary role, or to put up with the separation which her refusal would cause. So he proceeded with his plans to appear as Malvolio in a Saint-Denis *Twelfth Night*, which was designed to bring together an astonishing cast including Richardson, Edith Evans, Peggy Ashcroft, Michael Redgrave, Marius Goring and George Devine. (By the time it actually reached the stage, only Redgrave and Ashcroft had survived the 1939 thespian diaspora.)

These complexities dogged them for some time after their return, while Sam Goldwyn in Hollywood expressed disbelief that Olivier could turn down so plum a part. Goldwyn himself, if truth be known, had taken some persuading to go ahead with *Wuthering Heights*. Despite an unsolicited script by Ben Hecht and Charles MacArthur, he had left standing orders at the studio that he was not to be bothered with stories where the characters "appeared in period costumes and wrote with quill pens", or "plots where people die in the end".[7] Finally persuaded by Bette Davis that Emily Brontë had, in fact, written the most powerful love story yet available for filming, Goldwyn bought the script for William Wyler to direct with an all-British cast.

After screen-testing Charles Boyer and Douglas Fairbanks Jr for Heathcliff, Goldwyn had set his heart on Olivier. So now he cunningly let it be known that he was testing Robert Newton for the part, while sending Wyler on a visit to Durham Cottage.[8] The director soon realized that Olivier was clearly very keen to play the part, but would remain reluctant unless Vivien could co-star as Cathy. The couple took Wyler to a showing of Vivien's new film, *St Martin's Lane*, and he was genuinely impressed by her screen presence. But he was obliged to explain gently that the casting of Merle Oberon as Cathy – Goldwyn had thanked Bette Davis for the idea, then thrown her overboard – was irrevocable. Isabella, Wyler argued, was "a dream part" for a young actress making what amounted to her American screen debut.

As Vivien dug in her heels, Olivier at least had the consolation that Goldwyn and Wyler kept upping the ante: playing hard to get could prove lucrative. As he agonized over leaving a volatile Vivien behind, the issue was settled in his own head by a conversation with his alter ego, Ralph Richardson, with whom he was filming an aerial spy film called *Q Planes* for Korda. "Hollywood?" said Ralphie after a moment's thought. "Yes. Bit of fame. Good." ("Films", as Richardson subsequently put it to Michael Redgrave, "are where you sell what you've learned on the stage.") Then Vivien too, through the mists of her own disappointment, told him that he must go, sensing that professional self-sacrifice on his part might damage them much more than mere separation. Still believing, he argues to this day, that Vivien would have made a better Cathy than Oberon, and "blind with misery" at being parted from her, Olivier left London on 5 November, her twenty-fifth birthday, embarking on the *Normandie* for his fateful return to Hollywood.

Working with Wyler was to prove momentous. Olivier was still, by his own admission, "the bloodiest of fools" about film acting, regarding the screen as an inferior medium to the stage, requiring much the same skills, "only less so". It took constant harassment from Wyler not just to prove him wrong, but to open his eyes to the subtleties of celluloid performance. His co-star David Niven, who had suffered under Wyler in *Dodsworth* and had even risked breaking his contract to avoid playing the wimpish Edgar, had warned Olivier. But nothing had prepared him for quite such tyrannical direction.

It was not just his make-up which, as ever, needing toning down. It was his acting. But Wyler was not always the most articulate of directors about exactly what he wanted. He knew when something was wrong, but could prove infuriatingly unable to explain what would be right. Niven recalled that after one day's shooting, when Olivier had been required to play one small scene again and again, as many as thirty times, he finally cracked and yelled at Wyler: "Look, I've done it thirty times – I've done it *differently* thirty times. Just tell me, that's all. What the hell is it you want me to do?"

Wyler thought for "an age" before replying: "Just ... just be *better!*"[9]

To make matters worse, Olivier was having problems with his co-star Merle Oberon. Although they had worked quite happily together in *The Divorce of Lady X*, stardom seemed to have gone to her head, strengthening Olivier's belief that Vivien would have been better in the part. There had been yet another flurry of anticipation after his arrival, when an early Goldwyn–Oberon *contretemps* had again briefly raised, then dashed, Vivien's hopes of the part. But once the filming settled down, it became clear to Olivier that Goldwyn intended the movie primarily as a vehicle to make Oberon another lucrative star in the MGM firmament. So, like Niven, Flora Robson, Hugh Williams and others in the largely British cast, he had to suffer in silence.

His professional chivalry soon proved fragile. Olivier's tender love scenes with Oberon were, to say the least, difficult for an actor and actress feeling far from affectionate towards each other. But some sort of denouement was reached one day when she asked him publicly to "stop spitting at me" when delivering passionate dialogue only an inch or two from her face. Olivier reacted with an outburst so furious that both stars walked off the set and Wyler was forced to abandon the day's shooting. It seems that Olivier made some vituperative reference to Oberon's "pockmarked

(PREVIOUS PAGE) The newly wed Oliviers in a 1941 studio publicity photo

After a year in the RNVR (ABOVE) Sub Lt Olivier RN directs and stars in *Henry V*, 1943

1944–5: A triumphant return to the Old Vic as
Richard III (ABOVE), Sergius (ABOVE RIGHT),
Hotspur (BELOW) and Justice Shallow

Olivier's war ends with 'Oedipuff' (LEFT as
Oedipus, ABOVE as Mr Puff), and (BELOW)
a knighthood (outside Buckingham Palace
with Malcolm Sargent)

1947: The blond director and star of *Hamlet* knocks out a stunt man (ABOVE), contemplates a camera angle (RIGHT) and is knighted at thirty-nine, while squire of Notley Abbey

1949: Olivier and Vivien leave for an eventful tour of Australia (ABOVE LEFT), where they lead the Old Vic company in *The School for Scandal* (as the Teazles, ABOVE RIGHT) and *The Skin of our Teeth* (as Sabina and Antrobus, BELOW)

951–2: Vivien plays
Cleopatra to Olivier's
Antony (BELOW) and
Caesar (BOTTOM); these
triumphs in London and
New York are followed
by her disastrous trip
to Ceylon (RIGHT)

Success and failure onscreen: a dashing flop as Macheath in *The Beggar's Opera*, 1952, but a triumph as director and star of *Richard III*, 1954

face" – a minor disfigurement dating from a bout of smallpox in India as a child. It is a tribute to the director's instinctive art that none of their antagonism shows through in the finished product, with the exception of one scene in which Olivier was required to slap Oberon's face. For fear of overdoing it, so much did he relish the chance, he unleashed the gentlest of blows. It is the only really unconvincing moment in the now classic screen relationship of Heathcliff and Cathy.

But there were times when the whole experience seemed to Olivier positively surreal. Goldwyn had sent a camera crew to England to film the Yorkshire moors, then transformed some 500 acres of the San Fernando Valley, fifty miles outside Hollywood, into an instant replica: stripped of their natural vegetation, the Conejo Hills had been implanted with stone walls, crags and 15,000 tumbleweeds, on which Wyler's art department sprinkled purple-dyed sawdust to simulate heather, albeit four feet tall. A thousand genuine heather plants, specially flown in from Scotland – Goldwyn had to bribe the dubious import officials of the US Agriculture Department – had also been scattered around for the close-ups. Oberon slipped and sprained her ankle while running through the real heather for the climactic love scene; by the time she returned to the set a week later, the California sun had helped the heather grow as high as an elephant's eye – scarcely an authentic Yorkshire spectacle.

Heathcliff, meanwhile, had developed athlete's foot – one of those disorders which tend to provoke laughter more than sympathy, while in fact causing considerable discomfort. Most of Hollywood's leading men would have used it as a legitimate excuse for some time off. Not this cocksure and self-consciously professional young Englishman. No, the show must go on. But when Goldwyn visited the set one day, Olivier proved mortal enough to wish the great man to appreciate his heroism and limped elaborately past a conversation between producer and director, a cripple in search of a compliment. Far from sympathizing, Goldwyn called back the hobbling Heathcliff and said to Wyler (in a Teutonic voice which was to become one of Olivier's favourite impersonations): "Willy, look at this actor's face. He's the ugliest actor in pictures. He's dirty. His acting is stagey. He's hammy and he's awful. If he goes on playing the way he is, I'll have to close the picture – or he'll ruin me." Goldwyn then took Olivier off to his office and explained that "You don't have to act like Theda Bara or even Mary Garden in order to emphasize a point. Sincerity and credibility are more important than flailing your arms, spitting and thrashing around." As he talked, so legend has it, Goldwyn kept banging his head against the wall behind his desk, angrily repeating, "You see, I'm telling you this just like people talk. You understand me without my going through all those histrionics."[10]

Goldwyn later apologized; all he had been worried about, he said, was Olivier's over-elaborate make-up. And well he might. *Wuthering Heights* was to prove a huge box-office success and to create two major new screen stars. Both, in later years, acknowledged that the misery of the film's making had been more than worth it. Said Olivier:

> Looking back at it, I was snobbish about films. . . . He [Wyler] was a brute. He was tough. I'd do my damnedest in a really exacting and complicated scene. "That's lousy," he'd say, "we'll do it again." At first we fought. Then when we had hit each other till we were senseless, we became friends. Gradually I came to see that film was a different medium, and that if one treated it as such, and tried to learn it, humbly, and with an open mind, one could work in it. I saw that it could use the best that was going. It was for me a new medium, a new vernacular. It was Wyler who gave me the simple thought – if you do it right, you can do anything. And if he hadn't said that, I don't think I would have done *Henry V* five years later.

And Oberon:

> It is really interesting to look back and realize we were witnessing a great actor adapting his art from stage to screen, even though we all suffered a bit from the growing pains. I was essentially a screen actress, and though only twenty-two at the time, was treated like an old shoe. But the results of Larry's performance are now notable in the prouder annals of the history of motion pictures. The film itself (in spite of the old shoe) is honoured by being in the archives of the Library of Congress of the United States Government.[11]

Thirty years later, when he had long since mastered its subtleties, Olivier still believed film acting "more of a science than an art". At the time, when he had finished work on *Wuthering Heights* but not yet seen the results, the brash young purist was only marginally matured by the experience. "Acting for films", he told the *New York Times*, "is about as satisfying as looking at a Michelangelo fresco with a microscope. You may spot a few details which might otherwise be missed, but you also lose the whole, the main thing. It is impossible to get a full, free characterization before any eye which has as close a scrutiny as that of the camera. The sum total of the actor's work in a picture depends entirely upon the arbitrary manner in which the director puts together his mosaic." William Wyler, Olivier added in a sudden fit of becoming modesty, had earned his respect. "I hope he has made me, in this picture, a good film actor – which I am not."

During the filming of *Wuthering Heights* a miserable Olivier had written disconsolate letters to Vivien in London every day. Both regretted their decision to separate for the sake of their work, Olivier doubly so because of his difficulties with Oberon. And Vivien, apart from a brief appearance at the Gate Theatre in the title role of *Serena Blandish*, had the prospect of no work before Christmas. Smoking heavily, not sleeping well, she turned for solace to her parents, who, as Olivier had feared, tried to persuade her to return to her husband and daughter. She grew despondent enough to call John Gliddon one day, after re-reading *Gone with the Wind*: "You know the scene where Scarlett says how happy she is that her mother is dead and can't see what a bad girl she's become? Well, that's me."

After only three weeks apart she could bear the separation no longer and impulsively booked herself a passage to New York on the *Queen Mary*. She would have time for only five days in Hollywood before returning for a Christmas revival of *A Midsummer Night's Dream*, but the long journey seemed more than worth it. During the crossing, though her previous self-confidence about the part had now waned, she read *Gone with the Wind* yet again, dreaming of what might have been. When she arrived at Los Angeles airport – the fifteen-hour trip from New York, during which she practised Scarlett expressions in a mirror, had been her first flight – Olivier hid under a rug in the back of the studio car he had organized to meet her. Hollywood morality, he had to explain, as yet precluded any risk of their being photographed in a passionate reunion embrace.

He was ecstatic to have her with him. But the timing was even more fortunate than she could have known. Olivier had laid a plot involving his agent Myron Selznick, brother of David O., still in the throes of his search for Scarlett O'Hara. As part of Selznick's elaborate pre-publicity, American movie-goers, several million of them, had themselves voted for Clark Gable as Rhett Butler. Selznick had narrowed his Scarlett O'Hara shortlist down to Bette Davis (best available actress, but no physical similarity to Margaret Mitchell's heroine), Paulette Goddard (looks fine, but acting dubious), Jean Arthur (dark horse, unknown but fancied) and Joan Crawford (never in with a chance, just on the list to confuse everybody). When his investors began to lose patience, Selznick had been forced to commence shooting with Scarlett still uncast. Now he was getting desperate. At the time of Vivien's arrival in Hollywood, Selznick was filming the spectacular burning of Atlanta; pending his choice, he was shooting the distant progress of horse and buggy through the flames three times, using three different-looking Scarlett stand-ins.

It was by the still smouldering light of this enormous fire, on the Old Pathé lot at Culver City, that David O. Selznick first set eyes on Vivien Leigh. It had taken only one brief meeting for Myron to become an enthusiastic fellow conspirator, and he it was – as Olivier watched anxiously from a safe distance – who took Vivien up on to the director's rostrum, caught his brother's attention and said: "David, meet Scarlett O'Hara."[12]

With "her cheeks prettily flushed, her lips adorably parted, her green eyes dancing and shining with excitement in the firelight," said Olivier to himself, Selznick would not be able to resist her. He then witnessed what was to become a moment of cinematic legend:

> David peered very intently at Vivien, Myron made a vague gesture towards me. David threw a "Hello, Larry" into the air, roughly in my direction. Myron and I were left together, eye to eye and ho to hum. David had drawn Vivien a little way apart from the crowd and was fixing up an immediate test with her, promising to make every allowance for what would naturally be a very imperfect Southern accent.... I could hardly believe what was happening, but there it was.

The next day, 12 December, David O. Selznick wrote to his wife on the East Coast: "Shhhh: Vivien Leigh's the Scarlett dark horse, and looks damned good."[13] She was now on a shortlist of four, on which Joan Bennett had replaced Bette Davis, who had given up in disgust and gone off to make her Oscar-winning appearance in *Jezebel*. Selznick's indecision was now becoming less a promotional tease than a national joke. For two years the film had been hyped and, as far as the movie-going public knew, not a scene had been shot. Word was that Selznick was waiting for Shirley Temple to grow up. So the agony dragged on, as Vivien undertook countless screen tests in costumes which were, she joked, still warm from the other candidates.

Vivien could sense victory, but she was now due back in London for rehearsals for *A Midsummer Night's Dream*. As she and Olivier waited on tenterhooks in the Beverly Hills Hotel, they desperately cabled Guthrie for help; he responded sympathetically, finding a replacement Titania in Dorothy Hyson, a friend of Vivien's from drama school. Finally, on 21 December, came the last and decisive screen test, where the combination of Vivien's looks and her spiky celluloid sexuality seemed to meet the criteria of Selznick's director, George Cukor: "The girl I select must be possessed of the devil and charged with electricity." It was on Christmas Day, at a lavish Hollywood party, that Cukor took Vivien aside to tell her Scarlett was finally cast. She screwed up her face, expecting the worst, only to hear him go on: "I guess we're stuck with you."

So here were the beginnings of international stardom for Vivien too, though Selznick happily exploited her lack of renown by insisting on the maximum legal commitment, a seven-year contract, and offering the meagre sum of $20,000 for six months' work in the starring role of a mega-budget movie. But she was not going to turn him down. Vivien wanted the part so badly that she did not tell Olivier the terms, for fear of his wrath over the seven-year dimension, with all the separations which it would no doubt involve. Not until he escorted her to the lavish signing ceremony on Friday 13 January, a massive media event at which the long-settled casting of Leslie Howard and Olivia de Havilland was sim-ultaneously revealed, did Olivier learn what she had signed.

Neither history nor His Lordship have revealed what he said to Vivien that day, when safely out of earshot. All we know is that he sought an immediate confrontation with Selznick, storming into his office and announcing that they were to be married and could not tolerate a contract which would keep them apart so much.

"Larry," said Selznick, "do you remember when I was head of RKO and I wanted to star Jill Esmond in *A Bill of Divorcement?*"

"Yes."

"And you insisted that your wife give up the part and go back to England with you?"

"Yes."

"Larry, don't be a shit twice."[14]

Olivier was beaten. Whatever his true feelings about Vivien's sleight of hand, he wrote to her mother, Gertrude Hartley:

> It is difficult to make a decision to work apart, but I believe we were wise to make it, and that it will bid more for our ultimate happiness together to choose to work (even if we don't like it very much) at the expense of our temporary personal happiness.

Selznick, meanwhile, added to the strains on them both – once the contract was safely signed – by visiting their rented home to deliver a stern lecture on Hollywood morality. Their love affair, he argued, might be common knowledge in England, but it was not yet so in the United States. Even the studio's awareness of it had worried them enough to hesitate; hence the delay between Vivien's screen test and the confirmation that the part was hers. They were both, after all, still married to others, and there was a child on either side. The risk of a major scandal, which would ruin both their careers and cost the studio a fortune, had been weighed at board level. For their own sakes, if not just Selznick's, they must agree not to be seen showing any affection in public, and must be most careful about arriving or leaving a shared house or hotel room. To drive his point home, Selznick told them that he had privately made it worth Rhea Gable's while to give Clark a quiet, amicable divorce so that he could make an honest woman of Carole Lombard before filming commenced.

All this may have placed something of a damper on their ardour, but it was to prove largely irrelevant. By the time Vivien began filming on 26 January, Olivier had already left for New York, where he had agreed to appear opposite Katharine Cornell in a new play by Sam Behrman. This commitment, too, had been part of the lovers' schizophrenia about their work and their relationship. With *Wuthering Heights* in the can, regardless of Selznick's strictures, Olivier had no wish to take on the thankless role of Mr Vivien Leigh – seen, if only by Hollywood intimates, out walking the Pekingese while she chased after Selznick. Had her hopes been dashed, on the other hand, he would not have wanted his own to go down with them. Were American movie-goers to learn the truth about himself and Vivien, Olivier appeared to care more about the effect on his screen image than his screen career; with his brooding, macho Heathcliff soon to take their breath away, he was not about to accept offstage casting as puppy-dog to a paramour, especially a wide-eyed *ingénue* in search of her first big break.

So they were apart again, this time by *his* choice, and both too wrapped up in their work to die for want of each other. Vivien was very happy working with the sympathetic Cukor, who was bringing the very best out of her, and Olivier could sniff success ahead with Katharine Cornell. It took only three weeks of filming, however, for Selznick to decide that Cukor was not giving *Gone with the Wind* the grand panoramic sweep he had envisaged and to replace him with Victor Fleming, director of such contrasting successes as *Captains Courageous* and *The Wizard of Oz*. Vivien was distraught. Exhaustion, temperament and the pangs of separation threatened Selznick's whole enterprise enough for him to plead with Olivier, in Indianapolis with Cornell on their pre-Broadway run, to fly out – "if only for a day" – to soothe ruffled feathers. Miss Cornell proved duly understanding as Olivier missed the dress rehearsal.

Although they kept in daily contact by phone and letter, Vivien found her loneliness accentuated by the difficulties of the demanding role of Scarlett. While secretly visiting Cukor's home regularly – this good friend was still directing her Scarlett *in absentia* – she was reaching a point of no return with Fleming. Never without her battered copy of Margaret Mitchell, she would argue with him about fidelity to the Scarlett of the book until one day she flatly refused to play a particular scene his way. "Miss Leigh," replied the director, "you can stick that script up your royal British ass!" Fleming stalked off the set and could not be persuaded to return for four days. But his fate, too, was already sealed; within weeks the strain had proved too much, and he had suffered a nervous breakdown. Sam Wood, director of the Marx Brothers' *A Night at the Opera*, was brought in to replace him for the closing stages of shooting, but by now Selznick was virtually directing the film himself. He too had become ill with the strain, which was causing his own marriage to disintegrate. A close study of the whole epic story of the filming of *Gone with the Wind* suggests that Olivier and Vivien, for all their own anxieties, emerged from this carnival of emotional and professional chaos relatively unscathed.

Olivier was meanwhile scoring a significant success in Behrman's *No*

Time for Comedy, which he had consciously chosen as a good chance to re-establish his name on the New York billboards. The part of the volatile young playwright Gaylord Easterbrook proved, as he had suspected, a fine showcase for the full range of his talents. Though John Mason Brown thought him "too light" to play opposite Miss Cornell, he "acted ... with a virtuosity that seemed to have one hundred ways of saying what the author had in mind", said the influential Brooks Atkinson. "In his variety, change of mood and infectious personality, he is perfect for the part," declared *Commonweal*, typifying a critical response which went overboard with the simultaneous release of *Wuthering Heights*. Said the *New York Times*:

> Laurence Olivier's Heathcliff is the man. He has Heathcliff's broad lowering brow, his scowl, the churlishness, the wild tenderness, the bearing, speech and manner of the demon-possessed.... Olivier's Heathcliff is one of those once-in-a-lifetime things, a case of a player physically and emotionally ordained for a role ... he *is* Heathcliff, heaven-sent to Brontë and to Goldwyn.

Graham Greene was not so easily impressed. "Mr Olivier's nervous break-ing voice", he wrote, not unreasonably, in the *Spectator*, "belongs to balcon-ies and Verona and romantic love."[15] But the rest of the West was won. As *Time* magazine drily observed: "Mr Olivier boasts that he dislikes working for the movies, and only does it for money ... in which case his Heathcliff is an eloquent tribute to the efficacy of the profit motive."

All over the United States, from billboards heralding "The Greatest Love Story Ever Told", those beetle brows loomed down over the slogan "THE MARK OF HELL WAS IN HIS EYES". Suddenly Olivier was the major star of stage and screen – and the dashing, sought-after young sex symbol – he had always dreamed of becoming. He had combined *succès d'estime* on both sides of the Atlantic with mass public popularity, a hard trick to bring off, but the one for which he had consciously and carefully aimed. He sent a postcard to Ralph Richardson, then on the set of *The Four Feathers*, extolling the delights of American success and urging his friend to "come out and enjoy the climate and the absurd luxury of Hollywood". Richardson replied "firmly in the negative".[16]

Olivier himself was soon to discover, predictably enough, that success in America was not altogether to his liking. His generally sour mood, which grew from his distaste at becoming public property, his dislike of long stage runs and his separation from Vivien, was worsened by the news from England that his father had died. In his seventieth year, the Rev. Gerard Olivier had suffered a stroke. He had followed his son's rise to fame with great interest and not a little pride, fondly observing to friends that Laurence had made the best of his ecclesiastical upbringing. "Your

145

father wasn't a bad actor," he would say with a smirk to his son in later years.[17] Gerard was buried in the village churchyard of Addington, Buckinghamshire, his last parish. His famous son was, alas, unable to attend the funeral, as he was too busy in New York coping with his new-found celebrity.

After a week or two of being pursued every night from the stage door of the Ethel Barrymore Theater to the apartment he was sharing with some of the cast, besieged and clutched at by adoring fans, who even tore at his clothes for souvenirs, Olivier made the somewhat pompous public announcement that he was no longer prepared to sign autographs in the street. In an interview scarcely calculated to endear him to an American public out of whom he was doing very nicely, he declared: "As for auto-graph-hunters themselves, they want to see you, they want to touch you, but they are not very nice about it. In fact, they are dreadfully rude."

The tabloid press spoke up for an indignant American public, taking this presumptuous young Englishman to task for his rank bad manners. Olivier's response, after turning away many an interviewer, even when the opening of Q Planes required some promotion, was to adopt the bleak, world-weary mode he had tried once before in Manchester. It was another female reporter, this time for the World-Telegram, who mocked this particular act rather stylishly under the heading "LIFE AND LAURENCE OLIVIER ARE VERY DULL – BUT DEFINITELY".

Life is very dull for Laurence Olivier. Being a matinee idol is very dull. Having a couple of dozen adoring women waiting in the alley of the Ethel Barrymore Theater is very dull. Giving interviews is ditto, and playing opposite Katharine Cornell in the hit No Time for Comedy is very dull....

"Really I'm just a dull fellow," Mr Olivier repeated. "Really I am. I don't ever know what to say to you reporter fellows. I suppose it's because I don't have a viewpoint about anything. One should have viewpoints about things, I suppose, but I just don't. I just sit here and realize I am becoming more and more boring...."

Was he just pining for Vivien – marrying her being the one thing on his mind, and the one thing he could not mention to any reporter? Or was he merely adopting the pose he felt most stylish when required to respond to a new phenomenon, mass popularity? The second is true of his entire career, the first was true of the moment. As soon as he knew Vivien was within sight of finishing, he gave notice that he would have to leave the cast of No Time for Comedy. She was released, subject to retakes, to be in New York in time for his last performance, on 3 July. They spent a happy holiday weekend at Sneden's Landing with Cornell and friends, then embarked under false names on the Majestic for a month in Europe.

Another conspiracy was afoot. Their plan was to use the month at home to persuade both their partners to agree to divorces, so that their relationship could be sufficiently legitimized for them to co-star in Hitchcock's forthcoming film of Daphne du Maurier's *Rebecca*. With the success of *Wuthering Heights*, Olivier had already been cast as the brooding Maxim de Winter, though he did not know he had been Selznick's second choice to the more expensive William Powell. Again he shared Vivien's belief that only she would be right for the central role of de Winter's timid new bride.

But Selznick had, meanwhile, written to her friend John Hay Whitney:

> Vivien is still anxious to play in *Rebecca* for obvious reasons. She really thinks she could knock us dead in another test and the former test was unfair.... It is my personal feeling that she could never be right for the girl, but God knows it would solve a lot of problems if she was, and I have too much respect for her ability as an actress, too much consideration for my own peace of mind during the months of August and September when a certain young man is in these parts, and too much appreciation of how good it would be for her future with us if she were right to play Rebecca, to close the door on the possibility....
>
> I have therefore said that we would not close with anybody to play the role for a period of ten days from today, during which time she could if she wished make a test with Larry Olivier in New York....[18]

Vivien did just that, and it remains a curious celluloid document today, now that the scene in question – that torrid moment with Maxim in the clifftop summer-house beneath Manderley – is so familiar as played by Olivier with Joan Fontaine.

Having lived their recent lives insulated from the crisis in Europe, they were shocked by the London to which they returned: with air-raid shelters being dug, sandbags deployed and gas masks issued, it was a city nervously preparing for war. After delicate meetings with both their spouses, which in each case reached the conclusion that divorce could no longer be avoided, they slipped away for a fortnight's rest in France, then boarded the *Ile de France* for the return journey west, and on to Hollywood, taking Vivien's mother with them. Gertrude Hartley had now become reconciled to the affair; she liked and admired Olivier, reminding her daughter only that she had warned against so early and precipitate a marriage. Then she tactfully abandoned Vivien, who still regarded herself as a devout Catholic, to her prayers and her conscience.

The voyage was marked by the arrival, on 18 August 1939, of two lengthy cables from Selznick. From the time and care lavished on each, it was clear that he knew they spelt trouble. The text of Vivien's went:

DEAR VIVIEN: WE HAVE TRIED TO SELL OURSELVES RIGHT UP UNTIL TODAY TO CAST YOU IN "REBECCA", BUT I REGRET NECESSITY TELLING YOU WE ARE FINALLY CONVINCED YOU ARE AS WRONG FOR THE ROLE AS THE ROLE WOULD BE FOR YOU. YOU MUST REALIZE IT IS THIS SAME CARE, PATIENCE AND STUBBORNNESS ABOUT ACCURATE CASTING THAT RESULTED IN PUTTING YOU IN MOST TALKED-OF ROLE OF ALL TIME IN WHAT EVERYONE WHO HAS SEEN IT AGREES IS GREATEST PICTURE EVER MADE. IT WOULD HAVE BEEN VERY SIMPLE TO CAST BETTE DAVIS AS SCARLETT, THEREBY SATISFYING MILLIONS OF PEOPLE INCLUDING EVERYONE IN THE PROFESSION. IT WOULD BE MUCH SIMPLER TO CAST YOU, WHO ARE UNDER CONTRACT TO US, IN "REBECCA" LEAD, AND THEREBY HAVE SAVED US ALL A GREAT DEAL OF EXPENSE AND AGONY SEARCHING FOR RIGHT GIRL. AND EVEN THOUGH YOU MUST BE COMPLETELY WRONG CASTING, WE MIGHT STILL HAVE PUT YOU IN IT HAD WE THOUGHT IT WAS GOOD FOR YOU, REGARDLESS OF THE PICTURE. BUT I AM POSITIVE YOU WOULD BE BITTERLY CRITICIZED AND YOUR CAREER, WHICH IS NOW OFF TO SUCH A TREMENDOUS START WITH SCARLETT, MATERIALLY DAMAGED. ALTHOUGH HITCHCOCK FEELS EVEN MORE STRONGLY THAN I DO ON THIS QUESTION, I WAS STILL NOT SATISFIED AND THEREFORE RAN THE TESTS OF ALL THE CANDIDATES FOR ROBERT SHERWOOD, WHO IS WORKING ON SCRIPT, WITHOUT GIVING HIM ANY HINT OF OUR FEELINGS. HIS FIRST AND IMMEDIATE REACTION WAS HOW COMPLETELY WRONG YOU WERE FOR IT. STILL NOT SATISFIED I REPEATED THE PROCEDURE WITH GEORGE CUKOR, KNOWING HIS HIGH REGARD FOR YOU, AND GEORGE'S FIRST AND IMMEDIATE REACTION WAS IDENTICAL WITH SHERWOOD'S. AM HOPEFUL OF HAVING SOMETHING SOON FOR YOU THAT WE WILL BOTH BE HAPPY ABOUT, AND ALSO HOPEFUL YOU WILL RECOGNIZE THAT SAME CARE THAT HAS GONE INTO "WIND" AND "REBECCA" WILL GO INTO SELECTION AND PROMOTION OF YOUR FUTURE PICTURES, WHICH IS SOMETHING I HAVE NO HESITATION IN SAYING DOES NOT EXIST IN MANY STUDIOS. AFFECTIONATELY, DAVID.[19]

To Olivier, simultaneously, Selznick cabled:

DEAR LARRY: PLEASE SEE MY WIRE TO VIVIEN. I KNOW YOU MUST BE DISAPPOINTED, BUT VIVIEN'S ANXIETY TO PLAY ROLE HAS, IN MY OPINION, BEEN LARGELY IF NOT ENTIRELY DUE TO HER DESIRE TO DO A PICTURE WITH YOU, WHICH WAS BEST DEMONSTRATED BY HER COMPLETE DISINTEREST IN PART WHEN I FIRST MENTIONED IT TO HER AS POSSIBILITY AND UNTIL SHE KNEW YOU WERE PLAYING MAXIM. YOU WILL, AFTER ALL, BOTH BE WORKING HERE, SO I THINK HER EAGERNESS HAS BECOME EXAGGERATED AND NOT RATIONALIZED. BECAUSE OF MY PERSONAL AFFECTION FOR VIVIEN AND MY HIGH REGARD FOR YOU BOTH, AM HOPEFUL YOU WILL RECOGNIZE THAT MY JUDGEMENT HAS BEEN FAIRLY SOUND AND SUCCESSFUL IN THESE MATTERS FOR MANY YEARS. HOPEFUL WE WILL BE ABLE TO FIND SOMETHING FOR THE TWO OF YOU TO DO

TOGETHER FOR US AT SOME FUTURE DATE. SCRIPT IS COMING ALONG SPLENDIDLY, AND GLAD TO BE ABLE TO TELL YOU ROBERT SHERWOOD IS DOING FINAL DIALOGUE REWRITE. BELIEVE WE ARE ASSEMBLING EXCITING CAST INCLUDING JUDITH ANDERSON AS MRS DANVERS, GEORGE SANDERS AS FAVELL, REGINALD DENNY AS FRANK AND NIGEL BRUCE AS GILES. POSSIBLE MAY BE ABLE TO LET YOU HAVE DAY OR TWO IN NEW YORK IF YOU WANT IT AND IF YOU WILL CONTACT US BEFORE LEAVING FOR COAST. CORDIALLY, DAVID.[20]

They passed up the New York stopover to hurry straight back to the West Coast. The patriot in Olivier was beginning to feel a bit shifty. This was a time to be among friends.

CHAPTER 9

1939–41

O livier and Vivien spent the 1939 Labor Day holiday, the weekend
of 2–3 September, with Douglas Fairbanks Jr and his wife on a
chartered yacht bound for Catalina Island, sixty miles off the Los
Angeles coast. Others aboard for the weekend included Vivien's
mother (as chaperone), David Niven, Nigel Bruce, Robert Coote and their
families. This predominantly English gathering of thespians abroad had
been anxiously watching the news from Europe all week. Since the signing
of the German–Soviet Pact on 23 August, the news from Britain had
sounded increasingly pessimistic about the chances of averting war.

Early on the Sunday morning, they all gathered around the Fairbankses'
radio to hear the news that at 9 a.m. British time, nine hours ahead of
California time, Sir Nevile Henderson had delivered the British
Government's solemn ultimatum, demanding "satisfactory assurances"
and the withdrawal of German troops from Poland by 11 a.m. that day.
At the allotted hour, the tense voice of Neville Chamberlain had duly spelt
out the consequences. While the Hollywood exiles had slept in waterborne
luxury 8,000 miles away, their country had declared war on Germany.

Vivien wept and most of the men looked sombre. "We felt blighted right
through," Olivier recalled. "Careers, lives, hopes." Fairbanks broke open
champagne and proposed a toast to victory in an attempt to dispel the
holiday gloom. The toasts continued all day, until Niven went water-skiing
in his dinner-jacket and Olivier took off in the yacht's speedboat, careering
around the harbour with cries of doom to the other yachts moored there:
"You're finished, all of you; you're relics . . . that's what you are . . . *relics*."
He looked, said Fairbanks, "like some Cassandra in swimming shorts".[1]

It is not an episode of which Olivier is particularly proud. The harbour authorities took a dim view of this vulgar display, after receiving complaints from sundry rich and influential holidaymakers that a man bearing an uncanny resemblance to Ronald Colman was making a drunken spectacle of himself. Colman himself, also moored in the harbour that day, was duly astonished to hear from the yacht club secretary, over his ship-to-shore radio, that he must apologize for his insulting behaviour. Fairbanks had already taken the precaution of putting to sea, Olivier and Niven having collapsed back aboard, and the true culprit was never identified. "A shame," declared Olivier, rather limply, in later years, "for nothing could have been less typical of Ronnie's habitual dignity or exquisite manners."

As Britain braced itself for the Blitz, and the lights began to go out all over London's West End, Hollywood's British community found itself restless and uneasy. As Olivier noted: "It was a painful situation, and wretchedly embarrassing with the Americans who were, for once, our not very enthusiastic hosts. Many of them seemed far from certain whose side they were on."

With American policy still strictly non-interventionist, and Pearl Harbor more than two years away, the Hollywood Brits found themselves working uncomfortably alongside the film world's sizable community of German immigrants – directors, designers and actors – such as Olivier's co-star from his first Hollywood picture, Erich Von Stroheim. Charles Laughton, who had been badly gassed in the trenches of the First World War, had to return to work on *The Hunchback of Notre Dame* that week for the very German director William Dieterle. In the same cast was Cedric Hardwicke, the last British officer to leave France after the First World War; now Hardwicke applied to the British Consul in Los Angeles to resume his army commission, only to be told that at forty-six he was "unfit". Many more were too old to dash gallantly back to Blighty to sign on; those of the right age had movie commitments which they were reluctant to break. There was a patriotic case, they argued, for staying in Hollywood; of the 264 feature films shown in British cinemas in the twelve months before the Second World War, 172 had been made on the West Coast and only fifty in Britain. Had there been a headlong rush home of would-be heroes, as Olivier pointed out, "the public services would have to face an additional population of anything up to half a million extra mouths to feed and extra hands to find employment for".

The word from the British Embassy in Washington was to stay put for now. A delegation led by Hardwicke, ex-officio nabob of the Hollywood Raj, was told by the Ambassador, Lord Lothian, that they could best serve their country by getting on with their work – which meant "portraying the best of England to world audiences". In his memoirs, Hardwicke recalled the Ambassador's precise words:

> You are here in America on legitimate business. Yet what would Germany give to have such a corner as you actors have in the making of American pictures for the world market? And if Englishmen are to be portrayed in those pictures, how much better that real Englishmen act the parts rather than have them appear on the screen as portrayed by American actors with monocles or spats?[2]

Alas, the Ambassador was not a Hollywood casting director, or he would have realized that Hardwicke and others earned their livings largely as token, usually strip-cartoon Englishmen blundering around in American thrillers and love stories. Nor did it occur to him that the American film industry might be less than enthusiastic about producing propaganda films for a cause it had yet to espouse, set in a country it still regarded as peopled with Heathcliffs and Maxim de Winters. Lothian's instructions to the British exiles, moreover, went unpublicized at home, which led to unsavoury and often cruel attacks on what the tabloid press dubbed the "Gone with the Wind Up Brigade".

Some, such as Niven, simply defied Lothian's instructions. At thirty, a former regular army officer whose own father had been killed in the First World War, Niven took himself off with despatch. At first he told Sam Goldwyn that he had been called up and must leave immediately. But Goldwyn proved "as usual, smarter than I gave him credit for".[3] On checking with the Embassy in Washington, he discovered that no one outside the UK had yet been called up; indeed, they had been urged to continue working normally. Niven had long since resigned his commission and most likely would never have been called up anyway, but Goldwyn could not know this. So Niven resorted to subterfuge. After a discreet telephone call to his brother Max in England, he was able to show Goldwyn a cable reading "REPORT REGIMENTAL DEPOT IMMEDIATELY ADJUTANT". He was gone that week, the first Hollywood Brit to head for home, and within months he was serving in the Rifle Brigade.

Olivier, who was among the guests at a farewell party thrown for Niven by the ever-hospitable Fairbanks, looked on with apparent envy. But he allowed several factors to prevent him following his friend's lead. For a start, he was still filming Rebecca with Hitchcock, who was already the main target for virulent attacks back in Britain. There was the prospect of another meaty role in Pride and Prejudice. And it was the period of the so-called "phoney war", when hostilities had yet to commence in earnest and the painfully slow enlistment process had not yet reached men of his age. Furthermore, he was anxious to be married to Vivien before returning home, given the potential publicity surrounding their return, and his divorce from Jill was not due to become absolute until August 1940. Though Olivier was always to remain shifty about this prolonged delay, and was to suffer for it, his professional life for the moment proceeded regardless of events in Europe.

So the filming of *Rebecca* continued, with poor Joan Fontaine enduring – as had Merle Oberon in *Wuthering Heights* – Olivier's ill-disguised disappointment that his Vivien was not playing opposite him. Not a bad offstage chemistry, it might be argued, for the screen tension between the widowed Maxim de Winter and his nervous new bride. But it proved doubly cruel for Fontaine, given Hitchcock's penchant for establishing a sinister psychological mastery over his leading ladies; in this instance he did so by reminding her, whenever it suited him, that Olivier did not want her in the part. His point was cruelly proved on the nervous young Fontaine's twenty-second birthday, when an unusually churlish Olivier – along with other members of the cast, mostly fellow Brits who felt obliged to sympathize – failed to attend a studio party for her because, as Reginald Denny told her, they "couldn't be bothered". Olivier's churlishness expressed itself in a flurry of obscenities, until even Hitchcock one day remonstrated with him in front of his co-star. "Careful, Larry," said Hitch, "Joan is just a bride."

Olivier turned to her. "Oh, really? Who did you marry?"

"Brian Aherne," she replied sweetly.

Aherne was the man Olivier had beaten to the lead in Coward's production of *Theatre Royal*. "Couldn't you", he asked Fontaine, "have done better than that?"

Given the circumstances and the timing, it is a tribute to Hitchcock's directorial magic that *Rebecca* turned out to be the memorable, haunting document it is. Filming was unusually tortured those first few weeks, because of Hitchcock's own concern for his family in London, and indeed the anxiety of all the largely British cast about their country's fate. Olivier's dark, brooding quality, as yet his main screen asset, was perfect for the gloomily preoccupied de Winter. But this was not apparent at the time to Selznick. After seeing some early rushes, he was as worried as Goldwyn had been about Olivier's screen acting. In a letter to the director, who was endeavouring with some success to keep him off the set, Selznick wrote:

Dear Hitch,
Larry's silent action and reactions become slower as the dialogue becomes faster, each day. His pauses and spacing on the scene with the girl in which she tells him about the ball are the most ungodly slow and deliberate reactions I have ever seen. It is played as though he were deciding whether or not to run for President instead of whether or not to give a ball. ...
For God's sake speed up Larry not merely in these close-ups, but in the

rest of the picture on his reactions, which are apparently the way he plays on the stage, where it could be satisfactory. But while you are at it, you will have to keep your ears open to make sure that we know what the hell he's talking about, because he still has the tendency to speed up his words and to read them in such a way that an American audience can't understand them. ...[4]

Another memo from Selznick ten days later complained of Olivier's "habit of throwing away lines too much. ... I know that this is the modern style of acting, but it is also a modern style of losing points!"

But in Hitchcock, making his first American picture, even Selznick had met his match. When the grand showman suggested that the fire which destroys Manderley might spell out a giant, symbolic R in the sky, the director knew it would be much more effective to close in on the embroidered R on a bedroom pillow. He also knew how to get the best out of Olivier in close-up, given that the limited range of de Winter's emotions happily mirrored the actor's screen limitations. Olivier received his first Oscar nomination for the role, losing out to James Stewart (in *The Philadelphia Story*), though *Rebecca* won the 1940 Oscar for Best Picture – remarkably, Hitchcock's only film to do so. Hitchcock and Olivier were never to work together again. Several plans subsequently misfired: the following year Hal Wallis, boss of Warner Brothers, tried in vain to persuade Selznick to release Hitchcock to direct Olivier and Vivien in *The Constant Nymph*, and in 1941 Olivier made an unsuccessful bid for what became Cary Grant's role (again with Joan Fontaine) in *Suspicion*. But Hitchcock's biographer, Donald Spoto, argues that none of the director's male stars became intimates or even friends; Spoto includes Olivier's name on a list of such leading men as Michael Redgrave, Gregory Peck, Anthony Perkins, Rod Taylor, Sean Connery and Paul Newman, with whom Hitchcock "made no attempt to conceal his discomfort and even resentment ... because they appeared to possess what he lacked [in looks and sexual self-assurance]".[5]

A year before Olivier had "escorted" Vivien – still the role the studio insisted he publicly play in her private life – to Los Angeles to see her complete her professional fairy-tale by winning the Oscar for Best Actress for her Scarlett, one of an unprecedented eight awards for *Gone with the Wind*. But her remarkably rapid rise to a celluloid stardom more elevated than his had in no way affected their relationship. She was both realistic and honest enough to acknowledge him the superior actor, and their love was still fresh and powerful enough for them to ache to appear together. MGM's latest plans seemed to give them a double chance.

The studio believed Olivier perfect for the part of Mr Darcy in Jane Austen's *Pride and Prejudice*, to be co-scripted by Aldous Huxley – and this time even the director, Robert Z. Leonard, believed Vivien right for the role of Elizabeth Bennet. But the corporate view was that Vivien, still trapped in her Scarlett typecasting, and so too high-spirited for the demure Miss Bennet, should develop her screen persona in *Waterloo Bridge*, the torrid wartime tale of an ill-starred young dancer who turns prostitute when wrongly informed that her fiancé has been killed in action. If she could not be Miss Bennet, then Olivier would be equally perfect as the doomed dancer's doomed lover, who shares the meat of the film in flash-back. As the film had been planned as a vehicle for Vivien, the part had even been written with him in mind. Surely, this time, one of these projects would bring them together?

Again, it was not to be. MGM stuck to its corporate guns, the part opposite Vivien in *Waterloo Bridge* eventually went to Robert Taylor, and the role both regarded as hers in *Pride and Prejudice* to Greer Garson, the unknown Irish girl Olivier himself had "discovered" in *Golden Arrow*. But both had the consolation of considerable successes. For the third consecutive time, Hollywood had found a role which suited Olivier's emergent screen personality to perfection. *Time* magazine decreed that making the story of *Pride and Prejudice* "understandable to the US cinema addict of 1940 would have been impossible without the services of Laurence Olivier. From the moment when he, as Mr Darcy, walks into a ballroom in provincial Meryton with a memorable sneer, the picture is in."

They were, moreover, working on adjacent areas of the same studio lot. In between takes, and at their discreetly shared home on San Ysidro Drive, next door to Sylvia and Danny Kaye, they were planning a daring joint venture. If no one else would cast them opposite each other, they would have to do it themselves.

It was their friend George Cukor who came up with the idea of a stage version of *Romeo and Juliet*. What could beat the prospect of the star-crossed lovers being played by real-life lovers whose own romance had so far been conducted amid secrecy and intrigue? Olivier also saw the chance to capitalize on the money both had made out of their first successes at the box office, and to store up a little credit with New York audiences against the undoubtedly lean war years ahead. If they were to absent themselves from America awhile, there was no harm in leaving a trail of glory in their wake.

He flew out the Motley girls to work on the set and costumes, and decided not only to star and direct himself, but also to plot the lighting and even write the music. This was to be an Olivier–Leigh enterprise with a vengeance – to the tune of over $60,000, their entire joint savings. The auguries were so good that MGM matched their investment, and Vivien passed up a chance of more glory and money in a putative Selznick sequel to *Gone with the Wind*. Thanks partly to the British theatrical presence in the US, despite the war, casting went well: Alexander Knox for Friar Laurence; Carleton Hobbs as Capulet; Edmond O'Brien for Mercutio; Dame May Whitty as the Nurse and her husband Ben Webster as Montague, plus a young unknown, Cornel Wilde, as Tybalt. Vivien went to Dame May for voice coaching and worked hard to get on top of a part which she at first feared to be beyond her limited range. But Vivien's faith in her partner was such that she became convinced this production could make her stage reputation. It was soon clear, however, that even Olivier had bitten off more than he could chew.

So exhausted was he by the time of the first night in San Francisco that a spectacular piece of acrobatics he had designed for himself at the end of the balcony scene – leaping at the garden wall, hauling himself up and swinging elegantly over the other side – went embarrassingly wrong, leaving him dangling helplessly from the wall until the curtain eventually wound down. Vivien was palpably nervous. But the week-long engagement was sold out in advance and the critics were indulgent, pointing out that Miss Leigh's nerves only added to Juliet's youthful charms. Again in Chicago, where one reviewer dubbed the show "Jumpeo and Juliet", they played to enthusiastic capacity houses in the 4,000-seater Chicago Auditorium. The pre-publicity hype preceded them to New York, where huge advance bookings were recorded despite such tasteless slogans as "SEE REAL LOVERS MAKE LOVE IN PUBLIC", which were the beginning of their undoing, in an age when Americans did not approve of superstar lovers flaunting their unmarried status.

When the production itself turned out to be pretty dire, the prim East Coast critics turned on them with a vengeance. The theatre historian Bernard Grebanier and his party walked out after the first act, because of "artifice irritating beyond words [creating] the undesirable effect of a movie" and "the thin, shop-girl quality of Miss Leigh's voice". Brooks Atkinson recalled: "Olivier and Miss Leigh looked ravishing. But they had designed a production that crushed the performance. They had to play so far upstage that it seemed as if they were in another theatre, and that two strange actors were playing to some other audience." Shakespeare's casual "two hours traffic on the stage" lengthened to more than three. A gifted actor had "ingeniously designed his own destruction". Theatre history seems to pin the blame for the disaster squarely on Olivier's elaborate instructions to the designers, Motley. But its surviving members, Elizabeth Montgomery and Percy Harris, today believe that it was primarily because New Yorkers disapproved of Olivier "for openly living in sin – particularly in view of the choice of play – and for failing to return to England and fight".[6]

The overnight reviews were savage: "Laurence Olivier talked as if he were brushing his teeth" ... "plodding and uninspired" ... "explosive and incomprehensible" ... "the worst Romeo ever". Olivier confessed himself dumbstruck "that such things could be written about me or any human being; for sheer, savage, merciless cruelty I have never seen any judgements to approach those that faced me at breakfast in our New York hotel".

Leaving Vivien and his secretary sobbing, he went out to see what was happening at the Ziegfeld box office. As he turned the corner, he was astonished to discover enormous queues at that time of the morning, only to realize they were all advance ticket-holders demanding their money back. "Go ahead, give it to them," were his immediate orders, and he even moved among the crowd himself, distributing cash. The curiosity value of the whole enterprise was enough to keep the show running for four miserable weeks, during which Olivier, who was not enjoying himself at all, calculated that he sweated his way through the catcalls and humidity of the New York summer at a personal cost of some $5,000 a week. By the time the show closed, the couple had lost $96,000 – all their earnings, and more, from *Wuthering Heights, Gone with the Wind, Rebecca* and *Pride and Prejudice.*

They were living at Sneden's Landing, opposite Dobb's Ferry, in the luxurious old Hudson waterfront house Katharine Cornell had originally lent them for weekends. During *Romeo*'s death throes, they lived like impoverished hermits, even cancelling the crates of wine they had ordered for parties. Their one public excursion, more out of duty than enthusiasm, was to a ball at Radio City Music Hall organized by Noël Coward to raise money for the war effort. If they had grown reconciled to the failure of their *Romeo*, they were crushed by their host's greeting: "Darlings, how brave of you to come!"

It was time to go home. Both wished to flee their New York humiliation; but by now it was also June 1940, the "phoney war" was over and the news from Europe grew grimmer by the day. Belgium and The Netherlands were in German hands; France had all but fallen; and Britain itself seemed in imminent danger of invasion. From the stage-door telephone, during one of the last *Romeo* matinees, Olivier finally got through to London and his friend Duff Cooper, the new Minister of Information. Though over enlistment age he asked for a job, any job, even one working for Cooper, who promised to see what he could do. Olivier then precipitately announced that they were leaving for home, on the first ship available after the last performance of *Romeo and Juliet* on 8 June.

That same day, unknown to Olivier, the British Ambassador in Washington was arguing his case in secret cables to the Secretary of State for War in London. Hitherto unpublished, the text of Lord Lothian's message read, in part:

Noël Coward, who has just been to Hollywood, is strongly of the opinion that the continued presence of young British actors in this country at a time when heroic and tragic events are taking place in Europe, and some American actors are joining up for ambulance and other services, is creating a bad impression. ... I agree with Coward in thinking that it is a mistake for young men of military age with all the limelight on them ... not to go home to help in the present emergency. Even if they are not of great military value, they could probably be used for recreation and entertainment of the troops and civilians in these difficult days. ...[7]

It took more than a week for the Foreign Office to reply:

National Service Act does not apply to British residents in foreign countries and no official steps can be taken to recall these young men. If you think it desirable please take such unofficial steps as you can to persuade young British actors in the USA to return home and offer their services.

Lothian made no such unofficial approach to Olivier, whose optimism in announcing his departure had already proved premature. The only message he received from Washington instructed him, along with all other Britons over thirty-one, to stay in the US until further notice. A few days later he received a cable from Duff Cooper – "THINK BETTER WHERE YOU ARE STOP KORDA GOING THERE" – swiftly followed by a phone call from Alexander Korda: "Larry, do you know Lady Hamilton?"

The Lady Hamilton in question was far from being a fashionable society hostess, as Olivier at first thought. It took a cry from Korda of "For God's sake, Larry, the Battle of Trafalgar!" for Olivier to realize that he meant "Admiral Nelson's piece". Churchill himself had suggested to his friend Korda, who was a useful courier for discreet transatlantic messages, that he go to Hollywood and star Olivier and Vivien as Nelson and Lady Hamilton in a morale-boosting costume drama, stressing Britain's historic role as the scourge of all megalomaniac warmongers. By the time Korda arrived R. C. Sherriff, the author of *Journey's End*, had been signed up to work with Walter Reisch on a screenplay.

Korda had other motives in undertaking the project. Rumours had reached him that Olivier and Vivien were starting to show the strain of their exile, separation from their children and so spectacular a theatrical flop. Despite a few years living in what was aptly described as "the limelight of adultery", the cracks were beginning to show. Olivier was professionally morose, loathing the idea of returning to Hollywood with its band of absurdly professional Englishmen playing cricket in the sun while London burned. Vivien still loved him desperately, regarded him as a king among actors, as whose queen she longed to be crowned; but he, even before their marriage, was beginning to find the intensity of her attentions almost suffocating.

Soon after the closure of *Romeo and Juliet* Vivien received a call one night from John (Jack) Merivale, Gladys Cooper's stepson, a long-time acquaintance who had played Balthazar in the *Romeo* and was later to play a much larger role in Vivien's life. Merivale, who had drifted back into US summer stock, was worried when he heard Vivien's rather desperate voice urge him to "come over – now". Over he duly went to Sneden's Landing, to find the couple drowning themselves in lethally strong Martinis. After dinner Olivier sunk himself in a book and Vivien suggested a game of "Chinkers Chess", her pet name for Chinese Checkers. When Merivale won, after some gentle teasing, she threw a tantrum and accused him of cheating, screaming for Olivier to come and intervene. "Don't you try to come between us," she yelled at Merivale. "We've been together for years. Nobody's coming between us. Don't you try!" When Merivale looked over to Olivier, he still had his nose in his book and merely waved a weary arm towards what was obviously a familiar scene.

Korda, who was intensely fond of both Olivier and Vivien, had heard a growing collection of such stories and was keen to lend their lives some purpose. The Hamilton project, it seemed, would take everybody's minds off their problems for a while and give them all the feeling of surrogate war work in gratifying Churchill's whim. But when he arrived, Korda found Olivier and Vivien, whatever the state of play between them, both insensitive to the difficulties of the mission he had undertaken – largely for their benefit and at some personal cost.

Despite his Hungarian birth, so conspicuous a figure as Korda had been roundly criticized for leaving Britain at this juncture of the war, by a press and public ignorant of his understanding with Churchill. Two years later his significant contribution – measured in terms of twenty-eight transatlantic trips at a time when they were extremely hazardous – was recognized with a knighthood. Another, rather more back-handed compliment came in the shape of his presence on the Nazi blacklist. All Korda heard when he arrived in Hollywood in 1940, however, was Olivier's continuing wish to go home and Vivien's concern that Lady Hamilton was not the right role for her. But the wily producer quickly found their collective Achilles' heel. Making the movie, he told them, would not only be considered a contribution to the war effort. It would take only six weeks, and would bring in enough money to restabilize their finances, thus enabling them to evacuate their two young children to America for the duration.

That clinched it. Olivier was worried about Tarquin, who had been seriously ill with spinal meningitis, and Vivien was overjoyed at the prospect of a reunion with Suzanne, whose custody had now formally been granted to Leigh Holman. Sherriff and Reisch had barely begun work on the script, so they took off for a month's break, first with the Alexander Woollcotts in Vermont, then with Katharine Cornell on Martha's Vineyard, the fashionable island resort off the New England coast. Back in Hollywood, in a new home on Cedarbrook Drive, Olivier resumed a course of flying lessons he had begun over the Hudson during *Romeo and Juliet*, intended to prepare him for active service as a pilot. The only way to conquer his fear of flying, he had decided, was to learn how it is done. Vivien remained extremely nervous of his new hobby, not without reason, as this by no means natural airman managed to write off three aircraft before finally clocking up 200 hours' flying time and qualifying for his pilot's licence – to this day, one of his proudest offstage achievements. Olivier still, somewhat improbably, lists flying among his recreations in *Who's Who*.

Characteristically, he also used the experience as an alternative form of acting lesson. Learning to fly, he said years later,

> was very interesting, because your two enemies are tautness and ultra-relaxation, in anything you're trying to do, if it's cricket or any physical thing. And acting is largely a physical thing – it's to do with the senses of all sorts. It's the same equation you've got to find between tautness or over-relaxation, or between under-confidence and over-confidence. It's very difficult to find the right amount.
>
> The difficulty of acting, I've always thought, is finding the right humility towards the work and the right confidence to carry it out. With flying you have to learn a very exact, precise poise, between your feet being too heavy on the rudder, or your hand too heavy on the stick or too savage on the throttle. You learn a kind of very special poise. And that I've managed to bring into the acting – frightfully useful.[8]

Back in a Britain oblivious of his genuine agonies, the character attacks continued. The main targets were still Hitchcock and Gracie Fields, despite her travels entertaining troops and raising money for the war effort. Sir Seymour Hicks, an actor-manager of the old school who was now controller of the Entertainments National Service Association, better known as ENSA, declared that he "would deny these so-called Englishmen the right ever to set foot in this country again. I am thinking of starting a 'Roll of Dishonour' for film and theatrical runaways...." But public resentment of the "Gone with the Wind Up Brigade" reached a crescendo that August, in the shape of an article in the *Sunday Dispatch* by the film producer Michael Balcon, branding all the British actors and directors who had stayed in the United States "deserters": "In this country the public is being asked to make every possible sacrifice. These isolationists are being allowed to accumulate fortunes without sharing in any way the hardships their fellow Britons gladly endure for our cause. Are they the real war profiteers? I think they are."[9]

Hailing the likes of Robert Donat and Michael Redgrave, who were "touring great plays for nominal salaries, keeping the tradition of the theatre going, keeping the people happy, putting the British viewpoint to the world", Balcon went on to cast doubt on reports that the British Consul in Hollywood had told all Britons over thirty-one to stay put. "I find it hard to believe that any such suggestion was ever made."

This set the cat among the consular pigeons. The German Consul in Hollywood, whose main objective was to sabotage the making of British propaganda films, produced and distributed hundreds of copies of this and another tabloid article headlined "COME HOME, YOU SHIRKERS!" When the cry was taken up by J. B. Priestley in one of his influential radio broadcasts, it was time for the Ambassador himself to step in. In a cable to the Foreign Secretary, Lord Halifax, Lothian described both Priestley's broadcast and Balcon's article as "very undesirable ... [they] will do our cause no good".[10] He confirmed the issue of the order, reporting that it had largely been obeyed.

> It is therefore quite unfair to condemn older actors, who are simply obeying this ruling, as "deserters"....
>
> The maintenance of a powerful nucleus of older British actors is of great importance to our own interests, partly because they are continually champing the British cause in a very volatile community which would otherwise be left to the mercies of German propaganda, and because the production of films with a strong British tone is one of the best and subtlest forms of British propaganda. The only effect of broadcasts like this is quite unjustifiably to discredit British patriotism and British-produced films; neither do Americans like having British dirty linen washed for their benefit in public.

The British Consul in Los Angeles called in the British acting community to tell them to keep calm. There would be no sense in a stampede home. Perhaps the most effective way to silence their critics would be for each actor to put in writing an offer of his services and to hold himself in readiness against the day when the call might come.

Olivier then joined Cedric Hardwicke and Cary Grant in another delegation to the Ambassador in Washington, Lord Lothian. They endured a "nightmare" flight, through continuous thunder and lightning, during which Olivier slept and Grant sang; he was in love, he declared, with Barbara Hutton. Though born Archibald Leach in Bristol, Cary Grant was by now a thoroughgoing expatriate and far from anxious to return; when, over lunch, the Ambassador asked them their ages, Grant shattered the patriotic atmosphere by joking: "For years I've been stepping it down.

Now I'd better step it up." Lothian replied curtly: "The truth will do."[11] The Ambassador again urged them to return to Hollywood and resume their normal work, but suggested they form a liaison committee with the Consul to monitor developments. So they did, with most of the hard work undertaken by Hardwicke, Ronald Colman, Brian Aherne and, above all, the South African-born Basil Rathbone, who travelled the length and breadth of California raising money for Britain as president of the British War Relief Association (West Coast Branch).

Olivier, however, took little part. He had other, even more pressing, matters on his mind. It was some months now since their last visit to England had achieved its main object; on 29 January and 19 February, respectively, Jill and Leigh Holman had been granted decrees nisi after juicy hearings in the London divorce courts. Both Olivier and Vivien had been cited by name and the whole post-Elsinore episode made public. Now, six months later, in August 1940, both he and Vivien received the news that their divorces had been made absolute. At last they were free to marry.

Vivien had been informed of her decree absolute on 9 August. The very same day, without even mentioning the fact, she loosed off one of the highly affectionate, and no doubt very hurtful, letters she was still in the habit of showering upon her former husband:

> My Darling Leigh,
> Larry and I are to do a picture about Nelson and Lady Hamilton. I am extremely dubious about it. But now one does not plan a career much as it seems futile, and we are certainly only doing this for financial purposes which are useful in these days.[12]

Apart from the divorce, she made no mention of the plans being laid to evacuate the children, nor indeed did she inquire after Suzanne's well-being, beyond saying how "adorable" her daughter looked in the photographs Leigh had sent her.

Three weeks later, on 28 August, Olivier's divorce too became final. His plans were already laid, with the help of Ronald Colman and his wife Benita Hume (who, gratifying Olivier's wish for elaborate security, had herself already purchased a wedding ring). That morning they drove the 100 miles to Santa Barbara, whose county clerk, Colman had told them, was extremely discreet. Having registered with him, they would return after the three days required for the licence to become legally valid, to be married by a judge.

Obsessed with a melodramatic craving for secrecy, they held a small, early evening party on 30 August, with only the Colmans knowing the real reason behind it. Then, at mid-evening, they put through a call to

Olivier's friend Garson Kanin, who happened to be in the midst of a story conference with Katharine Hepburn. By Kanin's account, this was his big chance to work with his favourite screen star, and he was not pleased to be told by Olivier that he must come over at once, for reasons he could not reveal. Knowing he was being woefully unprofessional, Kanin excused himself to a mystified Hepburn on the grounds that it must be some sort of emergency.[13]

Kanin, at the time, was sharing a house with Olivier and Vivien ("It was too expensive for us as individuals, but we reasoned that if we pooled our resources, we could handle it"). Not until he arrived there, spoiling for a row if they did not have something important to tell him, was Kanin informed that they were to be married that night and that he had been chosen as best man. "Rather a good part, eh?" purred Olivier, convinced that nothing could be more important.

"Great. Thank you very much," said Kanin, still brooding about Hepburn. "And who's my partner? You know, maid of honour? Dame May Whitty?"

This was a suggestion which an alarmed Vivien took seriously. Kanin then decided that the best way to solve everyone's problems was to co-opt Katharine Hepburn as maid of honour, a notion which so delighted them all that they drove straight round to Hepburn's house, where she received them in her pyjamas. Though she had already been asleep, Hepburn entered into the spirit of things by tagging along with apparent delight. She would just need a shower first. "Didn't you have one before you went to bed?" asked Olivier, already worried about the time.

There followed a chapter of accidents which Kanin described as "a forerunner of the Theatre of the Absurd". After taking a wrong turning and losing their way, the bridal party finally arrived at the Colman residence an hour and a half late. "The most romantic and beautiful couple in the world, minutes from marriage," reports Kanin, "began to bicker." The judge, who had not been told the identity of the bride and groom, had been ready to leave after quarter of an hour, but had been persuaded to wait indefinitely by Colman's offer of a drink every ten minutes. By the first moment at which the ceremony could legally be performed, one minute past midnight, he was somewhat the worse for wear.

Vivien insisted on an alfresco ceremony, on a rose-covered terrace, which brought on Kanin's hay fever. Amid his uncontrollable sneezes, and the drunken judge's failure to take Vivien's vows or ask for the ring, Mr "Oliver" and Miss "Lay" were finally declared man and wife with only Kanin and Hepburn as witnesses. The Colmans had already gone on ahead to prepare the honeymoon yacht. The judge cried "Bingo!" and the deed was done. Vivien gave her new husband a topaz ring inscribed *"La fidélité ma guide"*, while the gold band Olivier slipped on her finger carried the rather more prosaic warning: "The last one you'll get, I hope."

Kanin and Hepburn drove the happy couple to a remote crossroads, where a car waited to take them to San Pedro Harbor and *Dragoon*, the yacht which the Colmans had offered to lend them for a brief honeymoon cruise to Catalina, despite Olivier's behaviour last time they had all been there. And so, after champagne and cake for four, away sailed the now institutionalized lovers towards their long-awaited *vita nuova*.

"Why, do you suppose, all the secrecy?" Kanin asked Hepburn as he drove her back home.

"Because it's fun," she replied. "Howard Hughes and I used to do it all the time. It's enjoyable, getting everyone into a tizzy with all that hush-hush. They're probably listening to the radio news right now, furious that no one has found out."

She was absolutely right. All through the next day, Olivier later told Kanin, he and Vivien remained glued to the radio, waiting with mounting disappointment for the breathless announcement that never came. It was as well that they could not flash forward three decades, by which time Olivier would bear feelings about this marriage so complex and ambivalent that he would get its date wrong in his memoirs.

That same month saw their two children, by coincidence, boarding the same ship, the *Cythia*, bound for Canada. Six-year-old Suzanne was in the care of Vivien's mother Gertrude, Leigh Holman having already been called up for active service. Four-year-old Tarquin was with his mother Jill, who was far from pleased to find Vivien's mother and child among her travelling companions. She went to some lengths to avoid meeting them, though the two children were at length introduced and rather awkwardly shook hands during lifeboat drill.

Jill had been suffering a recurrent nightmare about Vivien, in which she saw her about to be run down by a steamroller and had to jump on top of her to save her life. She was in a state of high anxiety when the ship docked at Toronto, planning to take the next train down to New York while Gertrude travelled on with Suzanne to Vancouver. But the newlywed Oliviers had flown to Canada to meet them, and a tense mass reunion ensued. Jill told Olivier about the legacies of Tarquin's illness: the boy was thin, pale and undersized, his co-ordination was poor and he was going to need expensive special treatment in New York. Gertrude fretted about Suzanne's welfare, deprived of both parents, and argued with Vivien about the suitability of the convent school in which she had been enrolled.

The Oliviers returned to Hollywood in rather low spirits, glad of the chance to drown their worries in work. *Lady Hamilton* – retitled *That*

Hamilton Woman in the US – was to be shot in a small, obscure studio in central Hollywood then called the General Services. Korda's talented brother Vincent had completed designs with what Olivier called "masterly regard to the all-important aspect of economy ... including miraculous model work – cunningly separated pieces of life-size ship for the close work on the *Victory*". In effect, the Battle of Trafalgar was to be refought in scale-model battleships, big enough for a technician to lie inside firing the guns and hoisting the sails, while another pushed the craft back and forth across a studio pond ruffled by a wind machine. Korda, who marshalled his battalions from a rowing-boat, kept close consultation about the line of battle with a British naval officer watching from the overhead gallery. The only problem that arose with this masterpiece of special-effect technology was that for one of his leading actors it turned out to be *too* lifelike; several of the love scenes had to be reshot more than Korda and his time schedule would have wished, as Vivien was frequently seasick.

Although Sherriff and Reisch had written the dialogue for only the first few scenes, Korda's meagre budget decreed that shooting begin without further delay. "From then on it was a desperate race to keep up with them," recalled Sherriff. "It was like writing a serial story with only a week between your pen and the next instalment to be published."[14]

Both Olivier and Vivien enjoyed the firm self-confidence of Korda's direction. Olivier still counts this one of his smoothest and most enjoyable experiences in a film studio, despite a reluctant decision to give Nelson little psychological depth, painting only the cardboard hero required by the times – so that over the years his performance has come to seem surprisingly wooden, encumbered as it was by extremely stagey make-up. But *Lady Hamilton*, which was to prove a surprise box-office success, very nearly had to be left unfinished. Shooting was almost complete when Korda realized, to his dismay, that the crash schedule had made him overlook one legally required formality: submitting the script to the Hays Office for approval. When the verdict came from Joseph Breen, the censor, it was devastating. "You cannot possibly make this picture," Breen told Korda and Sherriff.[15] It was not just a matter of changing one scene. The whole story was quite unacceptable. "Here is a man living in sin with another man's wife. His own wife is still alive, and her husband is alive, and she has a baby by him, yet neither of them shows the slightest remorse or even consciousness of wrongdoing. Impossible!"

In vain Korda protested that the film was more than half completed and practically a million dollars spent. If they had shown Breen the script before starting work, he told them, he could have saved them all that money. "The big trouble is that in your script you condone the offence. You glorify it, make it exciting and romantic. And you let them get away with it."

Sent away to find a solution, Sherriff saved the day by writing in a scene in which Nelson's wheelchair-bound clergyman father roundly condemns his son's immorality, despite the fact that he has returned to England a conquering hero. "What you are doing is wrong. It is an evil thing that all right-minded people will condemn. I beg you to see no more of this woman." A crestfallen Nelson replies: "I know. You are right in all you say. I realize it is a wicked, inexcusable thing to do, and I am ashamed at my weakness in surrendering to it."

If this totally invented scene, with no basis in historical fact, rescued the film from oblivion, others were to cause Korda further grief on Capitol Hill. The propaganda element in the script centred around two more wholly invented scenes, in one of which Hamilton explains the war to his simple-headed wife, stressing Britain's traditional role as the scourge of foreign imperialists; in the other Nelson denounces his seniors at the Admiralty for appearing ready to make peace with a tyrant like Napoleon, declaring that such men must be "destroyed, wiped out". The film became Exhibit A in a case brought by Senators Nye and Vandenberg before the Senate Foreign Relations Committee's hearings into the work of foreign agents in the United States. They accused Korda of running an espionage and propaganda centre for Britain on American soil, in contravention of a law requiring the registration of all foreign agents. Summoned to appear before the committee on 12 December 1941, he was about to break off work on another film when, on 7 December, fate intervened in the shape of the Japanese attack on Pearl Harbor. With America at war, the matter was forgotten.

By then *Lady Hamilton* had already become an international box-office success – not least in the Soviet Union, where it became the first non-Soviet film to go on general distribution and drew huge queues in a besieged Leningrad anxious for some escapist romance. Characteristically pleased with his own canniness, Churchill kept his own private print at Chartwell and treated guests to repeated private screenings. He even took the film with him aboard the *Prince of Wales* in August 1941, *en route* to the Atlantic Conference with President Roosevelt. One of the Prime Minister's party, Sir Alexander Cadogan, recorded in his diary:

> Film *Lady Hamilton* after dinner, excellent, P. M. seeing it for the fifth time and still deeply moved. At the close he addressed the company: "Gentlemen, I thought this film would interest you, showing great events similar to those in which you have just been taking part."[16]

In Emma Hamilton, thanks to Churchill, Korda had found the perfect vehicle for Vivien to capitalize on her success as Scarlett O'Hara – the role which had so far eluded David O. Selznick and his writers. The

Hungarian was well aware that he was reaping the interest on Selznick's huge and risky investment, as Selznick had been engaged in a long and sometimes heated exchange of letters and cables with Vivien on the delicate matter of her contract with him, which had lain dormant since *Waterloo Bridge*. The previous summer he had refused her permission to get involved in a New York stage production of *Marie Adelaide*, despite his confidence, "without fear of contradiction, that there is no film producer in America that is more lenient about his people doing plays than I am, or that is more kindly disposed towards excursions into the legitimate theatre". But he was "neither tolerant enough, nor stupidly quixotic enough, to permit our players' pictures to become a side issue".[17] After arguing the merits of a screen over a stage career, and reminding her how "generous" he had been over *Romeo and Juliet*, Selznick concluded: "Frankly, Vivien, I didn't expect to get another request so soon...."

The escalation of the war, and the Oliviers' eagerness to return home, had since disarmed Selznick's contractual wrath and forced him to suspend all further dissent for the duration. And now that *Lady Hamilton* was in the can, Olivier and Vivien at last really were on their way back to Britain. Olivier did not like the feeling that this would be his last professional engagement for an unpredictable length of time. Nevertheless, "almost as soon as Alex said 'Cut' on our last shot, we were off and away".

Not knowing when she would next be back in America, but sensing that she would not return without Olivier, Vivien flew to Vancouver to take an open-ended leave of Suzanne. The convent's Mother Superior took the opportunity to refuse to keep the child – for fear, she said, of kidnap threats. The little seven year old was thus transferred to a day school, which meant that Gertrude would have to stay and look after her, thus facing a prolonged separation from her husband Ernest. She had little choice but to agree, though she took the chance to make Vivien feel duly guilty about the effect of her own decisions on others' lives. As they parted, Vivien's gloom was deepened by news from Leigh that a German bomb had flattened Stanhope Street, the house they had once shared.

On 27 December the Oliviers boarded the American steamer *Excambion*, which had brought 400 passengers from Europe and was returning with just twenty-three. The advent of the U-boat was making transatlantic travel a hazardous business. One arriving passenger, the playwright Arthur Wimperis, gave them an eyewitness account of the sinking two months before of the passenger liner *City of Benares*, with the loss of 258 civilian lives, eighty-seven of them children. In theory the *Excambion* was neutral, but Olivier was none too heartened to learn that its captain, chief engineer and chief steward all bore German names. On New Year's Day, he and Vivien sat in nervous, outnumbered silence as the toasts included

"Deutschland uber Alles" and even *"Heil Hitler"*. Vivien, who spoke good German, became convinced from overheard snatches of conversation that they were in the hands of enemy agents. Both had nightmares involving their capture in mid-ocean by German submarine. It was a long, tense voyage – "the most apprehensive" he had ever known – to Lisbon, then the centre of Europe's massive spy network.

Air journeys to England had also become pretty hazardous, and the Oliviers were seeking to fly the very route on which three years later a civilian plane would be shot down in the Bay of Biscay, killing Leslie Howard, Vivien's *Gone with the Wind* co-star. It took three days for the British air attaché to wangle them aboard a nerve-racking, seven-hour flight to Bristol, the highlight of which was a fire in the cockpit. The Oliviers found themselves severely shaken by the scenes of devastation through which they drove into the heavily bombed city centre. They checked into a hotel which had just lost all its windows in an air raid, and into a room which had even lost its exterior wall. As they climbed into bed fully clothed, so cold and exhausted that Vivien kept even her gloves on, Hollywood seemed light years away. Next day it was almost a surprise to find Durham Cottage still standing.

CHAPTER 10

1941–4

I t is an intriguing footnote to the history of the Second World War that
while *Lady Hamilton* became one of Churchill's favourite diversions,
Hitler would apparently order screening after screening of *Fire over
England*. Before the war was over, the male star of both would make
his greatest contribution to the war effort by transforming Shakespeare's
Henry V into a rousingly patriotic cinema epic – and, in the process, become
the first director ever to commit Shakespeare effectively to film.

First, however, his swashbuckling as much as his patriotic instincts
demanded he make an attempt – as it turned out, a somewhat forlorn
one – to become a serviceman. At thirty-three Olivier was too old to dream
of glory as a fighter pilot; even his first attempt to join his friend Ralph
Richardson in the Fleet Air Arm was stymied when he failed a medical,
because of a tiny nerve defect in one inner ear. By mobilizing weighty
professional opinion in his favour he managed to get the verdict reversed,
and in mid-April 1941 finally climbed with Vivien into his beloved old
Invicta and drove down to Hampshire to enrol as Acting Sub-Lieutenant
(A) Olivier RN. His intrigues had worked; to his delight, he shared the
posting with Richardson. After three weeks' initiation at Lee-on-Solent,
he would be formally attached to HMS *Kestrel* at the naval air station at
Worthy Down, near Winchester.

The previous three months in London had been one long, rather desperate party, where by his own confession Olivier and sundry theatrical
chums had kept fear and depression at bay with "a liberal intake of
alcohol". He had killed ten days of the waiting time at Denham Studios,
putting in a brief guest appearance as a doomed airman, Johnnie the

Trapper, in a star-studded propaganda film called *49th Parallel*. Olivier joined such names as Eric Portman, Leslie Howard, Raymond Massey, Anton Walbrook and Elisabeth Bergner in agreeing to appear for half-pay. For all its brevity, his role gave him an opportunity to show off the range of his new-found celluloid skills, from gung-ho bravura to a poignantly slow death, so much so that on seeing the rushes Vivien declared this cameo his best screen performance to date. But the movie is now remembered, if at all, for making the screen name of Portman, hitherto better-known as a stage actor.

For all his occasional irritations with Vivien, Olivier now began to grow affectionately concerned for her. Since their return to England she seemed to be living on her nerves; always a cat lover, she now seemed almost manically devoted to a black stray she had taken in and christened Tissy. Thinking work would provide some sort of solution, he suggested she apply to join the Old Vic company and took her north to Burnley to see its director, his old friend and mentor Tyrone Guthrie. In the depressed and war-beaten North of England, however, theirs was very much the regal visitation of two glossy, newlywed international film stars, and the trip went badly wrong. Always a plain speaker, Guthrie was worried that Vivien would not be able to shed her star status and that the audience would "come for the wrong reasons". Besides, he told her bluntly, she was "not a good enough actress ... not on stage".[1] She had no alternative but to head back to London and set about proving him wrong. Olivier found a temporary solution by putting together a troop entertainment, which they toured with John Clements and the husband-and-wife team of Constance Cummings and Benn Levy. But an offer from the New York Theater Guild to play Shaw's Cleopatra opposite Cedric Hardwicke, which she felt obliged to turn down, only increased Vivien's frustration.

Privately, Olivier felt that Cleopatra was beyond her range. Trying to come up with something a little less ambitious, but still humouring her fascination with Shaw, he suggested the part of Jennifer Dubedat in *The Doctor's Dilemma*. Her response was lukewarm. Not only did she (with some justification) find the play rather depressing, but she had also heard that the director Gabriel Pascal was planning a film version of *Caesar and Cleopatra* and was determined to win herself the role. Inquiries were duly made, and Pascal expressed interest, but declared himself powerless because Shaw had casting approval over all his work. Sensing now that a success as Mrs Dubedat might be the way to Shaw's heart, Vivien allowed Olivier to persuade Hugh "Binkie" Beaumont, managing director of H. M. Tennent Ltd, to mount a production around her. Opposite Cyril Cusack, later replaced by John Gielgud, she scored a considerable critical and public success.

With London theatres still suffering regular onslaughts in the Blitz, Vivien spent six arduous months on tour before coming into the Haymarket. Those months were to take their toll of her physical health, so intent was she on travelling back and forth, on many a long, cold, late-night train journey, to spend as much time as she could with her husband. Back in the Hampshire countryside, reasonably reassured that she was more content with her lot, Olivier had meanwhile rented a comfortable furnished cottage and was living a none-too-demanding life. He and Richardson were both parachute officers, in charge of small units with the crucial task of repacking parachutes for reuse. "It surprised me", recalled Richardson after visiting Lieutenant Olivier's unit one day, "that he had, in so short a time, got such a hand of the work, but what surprised me more was the way he had with the workers ... as we went round he spoke to the Wrens and seamen and sometimes introduced me. He never made a mistake, and most were in overalls with no distinctions showing."[2]

Afterwards, Richardson found himself wondering cynically if Olivier had rehearsed it. Certainly he managed to wear his uniform with a dash:

> His natural perquisite of good looks went well with his uniform [which was] perfect: it looked as if it had been worn long on arduous service but had kept its cut. The gold wings on his sleeve had no distasteful glitter; only the shoes shone. The hair under his cap had a touch of debonair cheek, being perhaps a quarter of an inch longer than the dead correct. His manner was naval, it was quiet, alert, businesslike, with the air of there being a joke somewhere around....

With his gift for affectionate insight into his friend, Richardson also sensed that Olivier, like himself, was deeply bored. Often they would literally drown their sorrows together. One such night saw the two parachute officers calling on their friend Frank Duncan, who was appearing in *Night Must Fall* in Winchester. So much the worse for wear were they that both tried to climb onstage and join in the performance; they were gently dissuaded and led away.

Olivier's duties were otherwise little more than those of a glorified taxi-driver, flying trainee gunners on two-hour forays north, east or west – orders decreed that he never venture south, across the Channel – and delivering aircraft to other bases. He bought a BMW motor-bike to challenge Richardson's more daring four-cylinder New Imperial, and wheeled out the Invicta to pick up Vivien from Winchester Station at weekends. Instead of delight at finally being home, "doing his bit", all Vivien saw in Olivier's eyes was ineffable grief at the tedium of his new role and the banality of the company in which he found himself.

Years later, Olivier described just how miserable he had been in that

Hampshire ward-room. Miserable enough, he said, to turn into Iago, miserable enough to murder. He had

> wanted to kill men, wanted to do people down very much when I was in the service, and I think in every service they know that. It's a difficult life. I found the so-called ordinary people so terribly ordinary, so lacking in imagination, I'd hate them for it. They didn't understand each other's feelings at all. I thought when I joined "How marvellous, now I shall know real people, instead of this froth that I've been living amongst all my life." My God, give me the froth every time for real people. Real people are artists. Ordinary people aren't. They just exist in a kind of vacuum. Without any pity, feeling, imagination about each other's troubles or woes or sensitivities or sensibilities. Almost inhuman, I found the real people.[3]

He had managed, in one of his earliest forays, to wreck no fewer than three stationary aircraft in one kibosh landing. As at school, he found it hard to win acceptance among his peers; try as he might to be taken seriously as an intrepid airman, to his brother pilot-officers he always remained "that actor fellah", little better at playing a sub-lieutenant than Admiral Nelson. But above all this was scarcely active service, nor really his idea of a dashing part in the support of his beleaguered country. Feeling himself a bit of a fraud, and wondering whether he might not after all have made a more significant contribution by remaining an actor, Olivier applied for whatever operational work might be allotted to a competent Fleet Air Arm pilot of thirty-four. He was told that there might be a chance in a few months to fly unspecified missions in the ungainly old Walrus seaplanes, launched by catapult from the decks of aircraft carriers. Vivien was appalled by the very thought of it. But the Ministry of Information, to her evident relief, had other ideas.

Throughout this period Olivier had made himself available to Whitehall as a patriotic speechmaker and was all too often, to his commanding officer's growing annoyance, absent on rabble-rousing duties anywhere from women's institutes to major national venues. A stirringly sub-Shakespearean address would invariably be followed, in grandiloquent Churchillian vein, by "Once more unto the breach". A film clip which survives of one such performance, at a Royal Albert Hall rally organized by Basil Dean in January 1943 – to mark the twenty-fifth anniversary of the Red Army, then holding off the Germans – shows the uniformed Olivier in frenziedly histrionic form, looking for all the world as if he were intent on out-ranting the enemy leader. Lieutenant Olivier of the Fleet Air Arm ended the dedication with an impassioned exhortation to work and fight for victory:

We will go forward, heart, nerve and spirit steeled. We will attack! We will smite our foes! We will conquer! And in all our deeds, in this and in other lands, from this hour on our watchwords will be urgency, speed, courage: urgency in all our decisions, speed in the execution of all our plans, courage in face of all our enemies. And may God bless our cause!

Olivier had also narrated a number of short propaganda films, typified by one entitled *Build the Broken Walls*. Over shots of the rubble round St Paul's Cathedral, Olivier's most heroic voice issued an exhortation to rebuild England's walls, to send supplies to the troops at the front and "to work and save to prepare the home of freedom for their homecoming. Keep on saving! We have great things to do!"

Now he was summoned by Jack Beddington, the Information Ministry official in charge of showbiz propaganda work, and enlisted for two projects – one already in hand, one as yet but a gleam in Churchill's eye. First Olivier was to join the cast of *The Demi-Paradise*, an Anthony Asquith exercise designed to help the British people warm to their new Russian allies. Then he was to make a film of Shakespeare's *Henry V*.

An "intoxicating" brew of patriotic and artistic emotions stirred within him. In the interstices of hamming up a Russian accent as Ivan Dimitrievitch Kouznetsoff, a Soviet engineer coming to grips with dotty British eccentricities, Olivier began consultations for *Henry V* with Paul Sherriff and Carmen Dillon, art directors of *The Demi-Paradise*. The costume designer Roger Furse was also recruited, along with his wife Margaret, as were the scenic designer Roger Ramsdell and the brilliant lighting cameraman Robert Krasker, though he had never before worked in colour. Olivier called in the theatre critic Alan Dent to work with him on adapting Shakespeare's text, and commissioned music from "the most promising composer in England", William Walton.

So swiftly and thoroughly did Olivier assume total control of the project that it is now forgotten he was originally intended merely to be its leading actor. A BBC producer named Dallas Bower had first conceived the notion of a jingoistic film of *Henry V*, but had failed to raise the necessary finance from the Ministry of Information's film department, much more concerned at the time to produce cheap shorts on such themes as "Digging for Victory" and "Careless Talk Costs Lives". Bower had already adapted the play for both television and radio productions which never got off the ground. Then in May 1942 he had produced a short radio programme called "Into Battle", for which Olivier had been summoned from Worthy Down to perform Henry v's St Crispin's Day speech.

The project had rekindled Bower's enthusiasm. In 1936 he had been an associate producer on the ill-fated Paul Czinner *As You Like It*, which held such awful memories for Olivier that he had doubted Shakespeare could ever be filmed. If he were to try now, he said, he would insist on doing it on his own terms. The man who was to make this possible, the crucial link in the chain from the Ministry of Information to the frustrated sub-lieutenant, happened to have heard the Bower broadcast. He was an Italian immigrant called Filippo del Giudice, once a penniless refugee from Mussolini's Italy, now with Korda the twin mainstay of a foreign-run British film industry. Though at the end of the war del Giudice was to be gracelessly arrested as an enemy alien, he had already been responsible for so thoroughly patriotic a product as *In Which We Serve*, Noël Coward's version of Lord Mountbatten's heroics aboard HMS *Kelly*, which Coward co-directed with the young David Lean. Del Giudice's other wartime credits were to include such eminently British films as *This Happy Breed*, *Blithe Spirit* and *Odd Man Out*. Now, with Bower as associate producer, he set about liberating Olivier from bureaucratic restraints to make the most lavish of them all. While Bower scurried around Whitehall opening doors and cutting through red tape, del Giudice raised the finance and promised Olivier total artistic freedom.

This luxury, once it was his, gave Olivier a moment's pause. Was he really capable of pulling off so ambitious a project himself? It seemed only prudent to hire an experienced director, so he approached William Wyler of *Wuthering Heights*, fortunately stationed in England with the US Air Force. Wyler proved reluctant, saying he did not know Shakespeare well enough. "Never mind," said a desperate Olivier. "I know Shakespeare, you know film-making. Together we'll make a fine picture."[4] But Wyler remained unconvinced about the notion of representing contemporary British aspirations via the Battle of Agincourt, so Olivier turned to his friend Carol Reed, once his fellow spearcarrier, now himself an established director. "Thank you very much," said Reed, "but you'd be bottling yourself up in agony the whole time, so the one thing for you to do is to direct the bloody thing yourself." Only when Terence Young too turned him down, for the same reasons, was Olivier finally persuaded that the only way to get things done the way he wanted was to direct the film himself. By way of experienced support he hired Reginald Beck, then editing *The Demi-Paradise*, to direct those scenes where he himself was in front of the camera and offer technical advice with his all-seeing editor's eye.

Bower's persistence with the Ministry – and a casual friendship with the Minister himself, Brendan Bracken – helped Olivier assemble a much more distinguished cast than he might have expected in wartime. Michael Redgrave had turned down the role of the Dauphin, in the belief that Shakespeare could not be filmed, but Olivier had already enlisted the music-hall comedian Sir George Robey to play a Falstaff written in from

Henry IV. Now Leo Genn, Griffith Jones and Robert Newton (as what James Mason called a "wildly eccentric" Pistol) were among those released from their service duties.

Selznick, by contrast, refused to release Vivien from her contract to be, as he put it, "devalued" by playing the small part of the French princess Katharine. Olivier's first draft had already built up the part of Katharine especially for his wife; at first the Oliviers were inclined to argue, but del Giudice begged them not to anger Selznick, as Hollywood's co-operation was essential to the complex distribution deal he was setting up. Selznick's refusal, however, came as a blow, which was to lead to a long-standing grudge. The part went instead to an unknown young actress called Renee Asherson – only because, she modestly said in later years, she happened to fit the costumes already designed for Vivien Leigh.

Locations were more of a problem. Where in the Britain of 1943 could Olivier find an expanse of open countryside, uncluttered by pylons, the sky free of the vapour trails of Spitfires and Messerschmidts, on which to recreate an unspoilt fifteenth-century landscape and re-enact the Battle of Agincourt? And where could sufficient youthful manpower be recruited as extras to represent the English and French armies? They searched long and hard before Bower came up with the suddenly obvious answer: Eire. Neutral, nearby, at peace and blessed with the kind of "poetic" countryside Olivier required, the Irish Republic could also offer hundreds of men only too glad of the work; they were offered £3.50 per week plus free board and lodging, with a bonus of £1 a week for any man who brought his own horse. Olivier and Bower recruited some 700 men (and 150 horses) to represent the 90,000 troops estimated to have fought the battle. As their setting they finally chose Enniskerry, County Wicklow, the handsome country estate of Lord Powerscourt, barely an hour south of Dublin.

When he arrived in Ireland for shooting that May, Lieutenant Olivier found himself in command of a vast and unlikely mock army of farmworkers and policemen, taxi-drivers and even jockeys, camped around the estate in a motley collection of makeshift tents and huts. Playing himself into his dual role of director and star, he summoned his troops to gather near his caravan and rallied them with a rousing inaugural address worthy of Henry himself. It climaxed in a promise he was later to regret: "I may ask some of you to do things you may consider difficult, perhaps even dangerous. But I assure you I will ask none of you to do anything I am not willing to undertake myself."

This piece of rhetoric was to prove a rash hostage to fortune, as he was inevitably taken at his word. When explaining to a group of otherwise willing Irishmen how to jump out of a tree on to a "French" horseman galloping beneath, Olivier was naturally asked to demonstrate. In doing

175

so he fell heavily and sprained his ankle; ever mindful of his leadership role, however, he remained erect and strode off round a corner before doubling up in pain and calling for a doctor. His actors soon became accustomed to the sight of their leader hobbling around the set on crutches, or with either or both of his arms in a sling.

More often, however, he would ride among them in the shining armour and pudding-basin haircut of England's Harry, reappearing with a megaphone strapped around his neck to direct crowd scenes from horseback. For a novice director, his collaboration with Beck produced startling results. Olivier openly borrowed from his cinematic hero Eisenstein – notably the charge of the Teutonic knights in *Alexander Nevsky* – but proved more than capable of his own innovations, intercutting the resolutely still English bowmen with an exciting, steadily accelerating tracking shot as the serried ranks of French charged towards them in terrifying depth. It had taken ten days to drill the Irish soldiery in the ancient arts of bowmanship and galloping abreast, and to lay half a mile of single-track rail, for a mounted camera to film the French cavalry charge. There then followed a fortnight's frustrating delay because of rain before filming could finally begin on 9 June.

Six weeks later, on 22 July, it was all over, though not without incident. Some £80,000 of the film's £300,000 budget had been spent in Ireland on ten of its 137 minutes. Olivier had suffered one of the worst accidents of his injury-strewn career when a charging horse galloped straight into the camera through whose viewfinder he was setting up a shot; his mouth was cut clean through to the gum and he was streaming blood, but the director of *Henry V* seemed more worried about the condition of his new Technicolor camera – the only one then in the country – than of his leading actor's face. The scar can be seen on his upper lip, when moustache-free, to this day.

Del Giudice was, meanwhile, facing huge financial problems, with which he never troubled Olivier, once it became clear that the film's budget would rise way above initial expectations. The final figure came to £475,000, then the biggest sum ever spent on a British picture. Convinced that Olivier was making a masterpiece, the remarkable Italian told him not to worry. He went back to London and negotiated a deal with the flour millionaire-turned-movie mogul J. Arthur Rank, which involved surrendering control of his own production company, Two Cities Films. Del Giudice lost his hard-won commercial independence, but Olivier got his film. No wonder, when del Giudice came to initiate and finance his screen *Hamlet* as well, Olivier was to say of him – to Korda's evident discomfort – "I know of no one else in British films so kind, generous, imaginative and courageous."[5]

Apart from the six weeks in Ireland *Henry V* was made entirely at

Denham Studios, taking almost a year, from the summer of 1943 to the spring of 1944. Here it was that Olivier enacted the brainwave which had struck him in the back of a taxi shared with Anthony Asquith, known to his friends as "Puffin", during the latter stages of filming *The Demi-Paradise*. His problem was how to adapt Shakespeare's Chorus, who opens and closes the play, to the screen. The convention was familiar enough to regular theatre-goers, but Olivier's pledge was to deliver a version of Shakespeare sufficiently compelling to keep cinema-goers in their seats for over two hours. Purists would never forgive him, nor he himself, for simply discarding the Chorus. But how could this essentially theatrical device be presented without depriving his film of its vivid *reality*?

> Suddenly I saw the solution. I have always seen my films from the last shot backwards, and was trying out on Puffin the idea that the first time we saw the Chorus, who up to now would have been merely an off-screen commentator, would be for the last speech, when we would discover that we'd been in the Globe Playhouse all the time. I had no sooner said this to him than I saw immediately that the Globe Playhouse was to be the frame – with its actors employing a highly rhetorical method that would most felicitously set the central idea.[6]

Hence the film's unashamed, highly effective transition from stage to screen techniques, opening with a slow crane-shot over a vast model of Shakespeare's London and homing in on the Globe Theatre, where the performance is about to begin, before heading out into a naturalistic landscape. The device lent some logic to the speaking of blank verse in open countryside, while reassuring the theatre-goer that the Bard was being treated with due respect, and the cinema-goer that this was not merely the filmed version of a stage play. It even helped the budget by making use of some of the original Harfleur sets, on the point of being discarded as "too stagey".

His Irish army back on their farms, Olivier had a different problem in the hiring of extras at Denham. It was as well, del Giudice advised, not to ask where they came from, these youthful, able-bodied men prepared to bear swords and longbows rather than rifles and machine-guns. Many of them were English, American or Australian troops on the run from the military police, which lent a certain irony to the stirring speeches of war and glory, and "closing the wall with our English dead". A less patriotic band would have been hard to find. They were also devoutly unprofessional and caused Olivier moments of extreme annoyance which he had little option but to disguise. When it came to the famous tennis-balls scene, even the sacred text itself suffered. Upon delivering Henry's reply to the Dauphin's ambassador – "When we have matched our rackets to his balls" – Olivier was enraged to hear a gust of laughter amid the attendant extras. He had to reshoot it, changing the line to "these balls", with a conspicuous gesture towards the chest carrying them.

By April 1944 golfers on the nearby Denham links had become accustomed to pausing in mid-stroke for an armour-clad English king to ride by on his fine white steed as the final exteriors were shot. Now Olivier and Vivien were living nearby, he was able to take groups of friends riding on the *Henry V* horses at weekends; John Mills recalls how Olivier and David Niven were the only ones not to be thrown on the one Sunday he and his wife, Robert Helpmann, David Lean and Robert Donat (who would have played the Chorus if MGM had released him) went along for the ride.[7] Walton's music was yet to be recorded and Beck's months of editing lay ahead, but Olivier's extraordinary achievement was finally in the can.

He had not simply turned in a commandingly virile performance as a king symbolizing the grim necessities of war. That was taken almost for granted, when set alongside the feat of simultaneously producing and directing an epic of unprecedented scale amid the rigours and constraints of a real war. Some of his camera techniques were in their way as original as those of Orson Welles in his recent, multi-talented *Citizen Kane*. In his debut as a film director Olivier was shrewd enough to understand that with Shakespeare the verse, not the camera, should dictate moods, close-ups and climaxes.

After studying George Cukor's *Romeo and Juliet* – the Norma Shearer movie he had himself turned down – he consciously, for instance, pulled back at intense moments when Hollywood's instinct would have been to zoom in. Nor was he afraid to let the camera stand still for long periods of time. Still convinced that many West Coast "tricks" were merely expedients to conceal "bad acting and weak scripts", he clung to his conviction that a strong cast needed no such artificial aids. Closing in, he argued, made people "act smaller"; he would rather pull away and tell them to let rip. Wyler would have been horrified, but it worked.

The crowning touch was William Walton's music. Though Walton had written the score for Paul Czinner's film of *As You Like It*, in which he had played Orlando, Olivier did not know the name when Dallas Bower first suggested it to him. But working with Walton on *Henry V* was to forge one of the closest friendships of Olivier's life, as well as one of the most fruitful artistic collaborations. The director had definite ideas about the music he wanted, almost too definite for Walton's taste. One day Olivier suggested that the composer might care to use "a beautiful theme I've thought of: it goes dum de dum de dum". "Yes," replied Walton, "that *is* a lovely tune. It's out of Wagner's *Meistersinger*." The heroic effectiveness of Walton's score was due in part to his uncanny knack for underscoring the rhythms of Olivier's voice, as if it were another instrument in his orchestration. From the moment he first heard the Passacaglia on the Death of Falstaff, Olivier later told Walton's widow Susana, he suddenly realized that he had a great film on his hands. "The music was so moving and so exactly right."[8]

Henry V opened in London at the Carlton cinema, Haymarket, in November 1944. The reviews were muted. "In over-bright Technicolor, half an hour too long, at its worst it is vulgar and obscure, but at its best it is an indication of what could be done with Shakespeare on the screen," wrote Richard Winnington of the *News Chronicle*. Although "the most ambitious film of our time," said Ernest Betts in the *People*, "it is also the most difficult, annoying, beautiful, boring, exciting, wordy, baffling picture yet made. It has a sort of damnable excellence." After three weeks of slow business, word of mouth worked its magic and queues began to form. The Haymarket run was extended from one month to five, after which it transferred to the Marble Arch Pavilion for another six. An eleven-month London run: del Giudice predicted that the film would recoup its outlay in England alone.

But the response outside London, when *Henry V* went on general release in the spring of 1945, was less polite. War-weary Northerners, expecting some Hollywood magic for their hard-won admission fee, booed the film off the screen. Rank, who still stood to lose a fortune, appealed to British self-respect. "I refuse to believe that this picture won't appeal to the masses," he declared. "Anyone who affirms that underestimates the intelligence of the British people. I am certain that it will bring thousands of new patrons to the cinema."[9] And so it did. *Henry V* made film-going a more up-market activity than it had been hitherto; research in London and beyond showed that as many as fifty per cent of its patrons were not regular cinema-goers. Despite the withering dissent of Eric Bentley – who thought the film presented "a patronizing, picture-book account" of the play – many *soi-disant* intellectuals, hitherto convinced that film was an inferior medium capable of peddling only cheap romances and vulgar thrillers, began a lifetime of film-going with *Henry V*.

As did their children. By the summer many local authorities were paying for school outings to go and see it, provoking angry letters to newspapers from taxpayers suggesting that the Government take a rebate from the public money lining the pockets of the film-makers. But school matinees became the order of the day all over the country, the children delighted to get anything for nothing, and their teachers declaring that film had at last shown potential as an educational medium. There is no doubt that a generation of schoolchildren were helped to see Shakespeare through new, and more receptive, eyes.

There was inevitable criticism from the high-minded. Though Olivier had cut only 250 of the play's 1,675 lines, the film was "merely a colourful pageant". Olivier's script was too wordy, his approach too literary or theatrical; his performance too stagey and grandiloquent. The Globe Theatre sequence was "patronizing", with the actors "hamming in a way one hardly thinks Shakespeare would have tolerated". Conscious of his patriotic mission, Olivier had exaggerated the polarity in the play between the English and French courts; reviewing Richard Burton's *Henry V* at the Old Vic in 1955, Kenneth Tynan complained that the director Michael Benthall had been influenced by the Olivier film into making the French "fluttering mountebanks who pose no challenge to Harry".

But these were isolated voices amid a chorus of praise. By the time the film had its American premiere in Boston in April 1946 – once the US distributors had seen to the removal of such Shakespearean language as "damn" and "bastard" – its status as a classic was assured. Across two pages of *Time* magazine the respected critic James Agee declared it the herald of a new era of cinema, the "perfect marriage of great dramatic poetry with the greatest contemporary medium for expressing it". Olivier, declared Agee, had chosen to serve Shakespeare rather than compete with him.

It played to full houses in Boston for eight months and in New York for forty-six weeks, a record for a British film, proceeding to gross over a million dollars in only twenty American cities in its first year. The New York critics voted Olivier Best Actor of the Year and needed a second ballot to place Wyler's *The Best Years of our Lives* fractionally ahead of *Henry V* as Best Film. A lifetime of honorary degrees began for Olivier with a Master of Arts from Tufts University, and in March 1947 came the film industry's supreme accolade with a Special Academy Award to Olivier for producing, directing and starring in a film which had not only made movie history, but had massively enhanced the British film industry's status in the US. It was genuine gratitude, it seems, rather than false modesty, which saw him immediately hand over the Oscar to del Giudice, with the entirely accurate tribute that "Without you *Henry V* would never have been made."

By that time, three years after the film's completion, Olivier had consolidated his worldly glory enough to make such heady gestures. The immediate post-war and post-*Henry* years were to prove rich in achievement and acclaim; he was back scoring new triumphs with the Old Vic company even before the film's release assured his status as some sort of national hero. Said Kenneth Tynan:

Larry didn't realize it at first, because he was so close to it and so exhausted, but he had created what was perhaps the first true work of art that had ever been put on film. . . . With the brilliance and originality he showed in *Henry V*, he could have become one of the greatest film figures of all time – acting, directing, producing and so on. But by then he wanted nothing more than to get back to the stage.[10]

It was not quite as simple as that. In his contract for *Henry V* – as a *quid pro quo* for ensuring his artistic control, not to mention twenty per cent of the proceeds – Olivier had made an important concession. He had agreed to appear in no other films for at least eighteen months after *Henry*'s release and accepted an *ex gratia* payment of £15,000 by way of compensation. The deal guaranteed Rank and del Giudice the benefit of a temporary monopoly on their unlikely hot property; but to Olivier it was also a form of prescient self-discipline. If *Henry V* were any kind of success, he figured, the temptations to return to Hollywood, and fail to capitalize on his growing classical stature on the stage, would prove too great. If a rare moment of self-awareness, it was a typically shrewd piece of career planning.

Vivien, moreover, felt she had in some way lost touch with Olivier during the year he devoted to *Henry V*. As always, he had confided his doubts and fears to her, but less often in person than by phone or letter – as when he had persuaded her that six weeks entertaining the troops under the North African sun would restore her health. Virtually forgetting her disappointment at not being in the film, he proceeded to become so obsessed with it that she felt totally shut out. So Vivien made a decision which many other women have made in such circumstances, not always for the right reasons: she would have a baby. By the spring of 1944, when shooting was all but finished, she was able to tell Olivier that she was carrying his child.

Both were overjoyed. Olivier, guilty at the way he had become distanced from Tarquin, longed for another child, and Vivien above all longed to have Olivier's. But she was deep in professional commitments, and it was perhaps not the best time to embark on a pregnancy.

Shaw, who made it a rule never to see stage productions of his plays, had not seen Vivien's Jennifer in *The Doctor's Dilemma*. Once Pascal told him he wanted her for his screen Cleopatra, however, the great man agreed to receive her for tea at his London flat. Deploying all her feminine wiles, Vivien was careful not even to mention the part but managed to charm the flirtatious old playwright to the extent that he leant over and said mischievously: "You know, you ought to play Cleopatra!"

"Do you really think so?" she replied, summoning her most demurely innocent face. "Would I really be good enough?"

"You don't need to be an actress," declared Shaw. "The part is fool-proof!"[11]

And so it was that Vivien came to be cast opposite Claude Rains in Pascal's film of *Caesar and Cleopatra*. Shooting began on 12 July, hard on the heels of the Allied invasion of Normandy and of Vivien's discovery that she was pregnant. She had told her doctor, who advised against continuing to work, that she had never felt better or stronger. But progress was slow – the film was to become notorious as the most over-budget British picture yet made – and conditions more arduous than expected. Even by English standards the summer weather was cold and grey, which had Vivien swapping the electric fire of her dressing-room for bleak, windswept fields in which Pascal was attempting to evoke the blazing heat of Egypt. Only six weeks into the film she began shivering uncontrollably and was rushed to hospital. The baby was lost.

Vivien declined into an acute depression, made worse by the continuing rows with Selznick. Throughout the war he had kept up his own barrage of combative cables, trying to get his Scarlett O'Hara to honour her contract and return to Hollywood. Vivien had successfully pleaded that she could not possibly leave either her country or her husband at so difficult a time. But as the supremacy in Europe shifted, so her bargaining position became weaker.

She returned to the set of *Caesar and Cleopatra* after only a short period of recuperation from her miscarriage, but Pascal found she had changed dramatically.[12] There was a fierce intensity, a strange new passion in her acting. As he viewed the rushes of the last scene to be shot, the banquet at which Cleopatra orders the murder of Plotinus, the Frenchman noticed something in Vivien's eyes which, he said, "scared" him.

It was the summer of D-Day, and the Oliviers represented British aspirations of a sunlit and gloom-free peace. They were stylish, glamorous and in love; though both were past thirty, a youthful magic clung to them as they became the country's most sought-after couple. Any public appearance would draw huge crowds, and the popular papers were full of their exploits with an ever expanding circle of famous friends. In public and in private, Vivien kept up an air of bubbling gaiety which had everyone at her feet, everyone admiring, even envying this lustrous couple's celebrity and happiness. When alone with the Larry she still loved to the point of obsession, however, it was becoming a very different story.

Once Vivien's work on the film was finished, she went deeper and deeper into decline. However hard she tried, she knew she could never be Olivier's professional equal, which dealt a huge blow to her otherwise effervescent spirit. Few recognized it at the time, but she was also beginning to display the symptoms of serious mental illness. At first Olivier attributed her moods and tantrums to the loss of their child and the general bleakness of life in wartime Britain. Then one evening that summer, during dinner at home, Vivien suddenly rounded on him more brutally than ever before. For no apparent reason a pleasant, innocuous conversation turned ugly, until her verbal violence became physical and she collapsed into a sobbing heap at his feet.

When she recovered, Vivien could not remember anything about it. Filled with remorse, she tried to compensate in ways that might recreate the original passion which had so overwhelmed them both. But the spasms continued, and with them came a stream of abuse and wild physical violence which seemed to betray something more fundamental, some resentful rage which undercut the almost animal love they still, for all their more mundane spats, felt for each other.

Olivier was baffled. At these moments Vivien turned into a stranger, whom he was seemingly incapable of helping. It was the beginning of a long and tortured series of such attacks, to be diagnosed only some years later as manic depression. For every public triumph there was to be a private setback, for each new crest in their careers a trough in their life offstage.

CHAPTER 11

1944–5

W
ith his domestic life in discreet disarray and his professional life heading towards abeyance, Olivier was undergoing a rare loss of confidence when his next golden opportunity materialized, as so often, out of nowhere. He was to grasp it so eagerly and single-mindedly as to turn it into another stepping-stone to pre-eminence. But there was a note of anxiety, of that built-in self-doubt, in his remarks to the press about joining a triumvirate to run the Old Vic company: "I am a man who does what he is told. A year and a half ago I was told by the Government to make films. Now it is indicated that my place in the service is not, perhaps, as necessary as a place in the theatre."

There was also the usual note of self-aggrandizement in the suggestion that it was the Government, perhaps even the Prime Minister himself, who had prevailed upon the dashing Fleet Air Arm pilot to trade in his wings for a stick of make-up. This time it was not Churchill at all, but Ralph Richardson, who had issued not an order but an invitation. The Lords of the Admiralty may have had to approve Olivier's release from duty – "with a speediness and lack of reluctance", as he put it, "which was positively hurtful" – but that too was more of a formality than he made it seem.

The Old Vic company had been itinerant since 1941, when a Nazi bomb had flattened its Waterloo Road theatre. Under the direction of Tyrone Guthrie, it had based itself in the Yorkshire town of Barnsley and laid provincial roots which remain to this day in theatre-loving cities such as Bristol and Liverpool. But funds were running out, a weary Guthrie was hankering to step down, and by 1944 the governors thought a return to London timely, if not overdue.

At Guthrie's suggestion the board's chairman, Lord Lytton, invited Lieutenant-Commander Ralph Richardson to take charge. Too proud to request his own release from the services, Richardson accepted on condition that the board deal with the Sea Lords on his behalf. Equally modest about his own abilities, Richardson knew that his own name was not glamorous enough to draw the crowds back to the Old Vic. He needed "a real crowd-puller" and went after the only two available, Gielgud and Olivier.

Though he shared Richardson's dream of reviving this cherished old company, as a forerunner to some kind of National Theatre, Gielgud proved reluctant. Never much of a company man, he did not relish the prospect of competing with Olivier again. "It would be a disaster," he told Richardson. "You would have to spend your whole time as referee between Larry and me."[1] So Richardson turned to a more challenging, perhaps less manageable, friend in the shape of Lieutenant Olivier. He was able to present him with a *fait accompli* in the shape of a third partner, a former Michel Saint-Denis protégé called John Burrell, now a BBC drama producer. The outgoing Guthrie worried that Burrell, an unimposing man lamed by polio in childhood, would not have the strength of character to stand up to his more colourful colleagues in the triumvirate – that he would play Lepidus to their Antony and Octavius. But Burrell was to display hidden strengths and to become the linchpin holding together an alliance which might otherwise have been destroyed by Olivier's competitive instincts.

The three began to draw up plans at Denham, where Olivier was still putting the finishing touches to *Henry V*. With some trepidation they agreed to Richardson's proposal that they mount an ambitious programme – unprecedented in London this century – of keeping a repertoire of three plays in simultaneous production. A deceptively astute politician, Richardson maintained a pleasantly relaxed attitude to the project, taking Burrell's two young sons for rides in his Rolls-Royce while his partners talked brass tacks. So Olivier was slightly miffed to learn that one play, a star vehicle for Richardson, had already been chosen.

Richardson had first got to know Burrell when they worked together on Guthrie's radio production of Ibsen's *Peer Gynt*, in which he had played the title role. He had devoted a great deal of energy to the undertaking – one of the most substantial and successful of his own schizophrenic wartime schedule between the service and the theatre. And so he was keen, not unnaturally, to capitalize on his efforts by recreating his performance onstage. *Peer Gynt* was thus marked down as the first production ahead of the new company.

As they planned the rest, the new Vic leadership seemed to have inherited Lilian Baylis's rather patronizing obsession with bringing high culture to the masses. Olivier recalls

> the growing sense of dissatisfaction with the poor class of entertainment available. Those on leave from the services or other war work and even the civilian population were all members of a civilized community and justifiably felt they had the right to the sweets of emotional and intellectual uplift; and we three belonged to the lucky ones who were supposed to be able to do that for people.

It was a task he "embraced ... with a shamefully careless rapture".

He may have felt as guilty as ever about the prospect of enjoying himself, but he was also determined to re-establish his pre-war reputation as a classical actor destined for immortality. The early 1940s had seen him take on the lustre of a Hollywood screen idol, thanks to Heathcliff and Maxim de Winter. But it was six years since his triumph as the Old Vic's Coriolanus, and with *Henry V* still in the cutting-room he was anxious to remind the theatre-going public that there was no more powerful and versatile classical presence in the English-speaking theatre than Laurence Olivier's.

So the roles which fell to him in the first batch of productions were dismaying: the small but striking part of the Button Moulder to Richardson's Peer Gynt, and the humourless buffoon Sergius Saranoff – a part he hated – in Shaw's *Arms and the Man*. He and Richardson had agreed that they would alternate leading roles, so by way of compensation Olivier was to take on Richard III; but that too was a prospect he dreaded, as the part smacked so much of the predictable actor-manager tradition, and memories were still fresh of Donald Wolfit's powerful portrayal in just that vein. Add the doctor, Astrov, in *Uncle Vanya*, where Richardson was again to play the name part, and Olivier embarked on the enterprise with the feeling that he had drawn decidedly the shorter straw.

Richardson, he felt, had somehow outmanœuvred him. Would he really have to wait until the second season to win a role in which he could make a mark? His desperately competitive spirit brought Olivier so low that, by his own confession, he began to wonder if he should have stayed in the navy. But a talented company was quickly assembled, including Sybil Thorndike and Nicholas ("Beau") Hannen, two Old Vic veterans in Harcourt Williams and George Relph, and one promising leading lady in Joyce Redman. As they searched for another, Olivier felt obliged to take Richardson into his confidence about Vivien's increasingly neurotic condition; they could not risk adding her to their worries. So they consulted their old Birmingham "headmaster", Sir Barry Jackson, who invited them up to see his latest find, the young Margaret Leighton. Once she too was duly signed on, it was agreed that the fledgling group should stretch its wings tentatively in the North before settling into its new London home. So Burrell's production of *Arms and the Man* was scheduled to open at the Opera House, Manchester, in late August.

Over lunch at the Garrick Club, Richardson had had to use all his considerable charm to persuade Guthrie's Old Vic partner, Bronson Albery, to give the company a London base at the theatre he had inherited from his mother, the New in St Martin's Lane (now the Albery). Briefed by a perpetually gloomy Guthrie, Albery was unconvinced that the ambitious new repertory formula would work. "I've earned a good deal of money for the Old Vic in my time," he told Richardson, "but now you're going to lose it all." [2] Amid the latest wartime hazard – flying bombs – the company held their first rehearsals in an exhibition-room of the National Gallery, whose treasures had been evacuated for the duration to the caves of the Cheddar Gorge. The ominous sound heralding the approach of the V1s and V2s had most members of the company diving for cover, but Richardson and Olivier both displayed a nonchalant disdain for their own safety which endeared them to their colleagues. As did their own relaxed way with the actors they had hired; though awestruck at first, they soon found them the most approachable and friendly of bosses.

So company spirits were high when *Arms and the Man*, a highly topical comedy about soldiering, opened in Manchester. Morale was boosted even more when just one week of capacity houses proved enough to pay off the slimline production costs – a relief to the new management, in view of the Government's commitment to cover only half of any losses.

But Olivier's worst fears were realized when the Northern press – notably the one Manchester-based national paper, the (then) *Manchester Guardian* – were effusive in praise of Richardson's Bluntschli, but decidedly cool about his Sergius. He himself was aware that he had failed to invest the dreary fellow with much life. After the second performance, he remained moodily in his dressing-room, waiting for the arrival of Guthrie, who had not been able to make the first night. When Guthrie did not materialize, Olivier was all set to pack his bags. This was too much. Clearly even his mentor had thought little of his Sergius and was too embarrassed to come and say so. It did not cheer him much to bump into Guthrie and Richardson emerging from the Number One dressing-room – Thorndike's – in high spirits. As they set off for the hotel, Olivier hung a few despondent steps behind his ebullient colleagues.

At last Guthrie fell back to talk to him. "Liked your Sergius," he began, none too convincingly, and Olivier snorted resentfully, fully indicating how much he hated the role. Guthrie stopped and asked in astonishment: "What? ... Don't you *love* Sergius?"

Olivier cracked. "Love that stooge? That inconsiderable ..." He almost seemed ready to hit Guthrie. "God, Tony, if you weren't so tall – if I could reach you, I'd ..."

Guthrie's response, in Olivier's own words, "changed the course of my actor's thinking for the rest of my life". It is a remark now etched on the curriculum of all British drama schools and quoted at actors by directors the world over. Olivier can still describe the exact spot on the Manchester pavement, under a striped awning, where Tyrone Guthrie said to him simply: "Well, of course, if you can't love him, you'll never be any good in him, will you?" [3]

He took this "richest pearl of advice in my life" so much to heart that by the end of the Manchester run he loved Sergius with an intensity hitherto reserved for Vivien in her better moments. He loved Sergius, he recalls, "as I'd never loved anybody". He loved "his faults, his showing off, his absurdity, his bland doltishness". Vivien had been prepared for the worst when she travelled north to see the show at the end of that first week, but she came backstage "ecstatic". When he thought back to his first Old Vic season, and the help he had needed from Richardson in shedding his contempt for Henry v, Olivier realized that Guthrie's simple wisdom had completely altered his approach to his craft. It gave him "a new attitude, an attitude that had been completely lacking in me, up to that time, towards the entire work of acting".

The Old Vic company opened at the New Theatre on 31 August 1944, with Guthrie's production of *Peer Gynt*. After so long an absence from the London stage, Olivier was praised for showing due modesty, "in the true repertory tradition", by contenting himself with a brief appearance in the last act as the Button Moulder to Richardson's Peer. Richardson rightly won universal praise – this was always regarded as one of his greatest roles – while Sybil Thorndike, with her portrayal of Peer's mother, confirmed her position as the leading actress of the day.

But Olivier sensed, setting a pattern for other leading actors since – Nigel Hawthorne, for instance, to Derek Jacobi's Peer Gynt for the Royal Shakespeare Company in 1983 – that the sinister figure of the Button Moulder offers a chance to make a major impact in the ten minutes he is on the stage. The eeriness of the character, the hypnotic hold he establishes over the universal figure of Peer, have all the makings of one of the great cameo roles in theatrical literature. Olivier seized the chance to leave "an unearthly glow" behind him, in a powerful miniature of exquisite quality. His bent for naturalism still dominated his theatrical instincts; he made much of the practical, workaday manner of this homespun philosopher. But by moving, as Harcourt Williams recalled it, "on silent feet", he simultaneously conveyed the almost oracular force behind the character's every utterance. An ebullient Noël Coward, who went to the first night between lunch with Fred Astaire and dinner with Michael Redgrave, thought it a "tatty, artsy-crafty production" with Richardson "like a mad bull-terrier" and Olivier "wonderful – but only on for five minutes at the end".[4]

When *Arms and the Man* followed on 5 September, Olivier played Sergius for laughs, unashamedly and uproariously, earning notices utterly out of synch with those in Manchester. With his heel-clicking, moustache-twirling and self-parodying pillbox hat, Olivier wilfully abandoned Shaw's stage direction that Sergius have a "half-tragic, half-ironic air, the mysterious moodiness, the suggestion of a strange and terrible history that left nothing but undying remorse". But to the critics his performance was suddenly "a joyous travesty", "a museum of invention". Business boomed and company spirits soared. Even Olivier began to revise his views about the way his return to the West End had been stage-managed. His success in these lesser roles, however, only heightened public anticipation of his *real* return to centre-stage, and his own apprehension about the imminence of *Richard III* soon began to shatter the heady atmosphere, spreading gloom among his colleagues. Even Burrell, who was directing, seemed to lose his *joie de vivre* in rehearsals.

For the first time in his career Olivier had great trouble memorizing his lines. He laughed it off as "wartime rust", but the real reasons were clearly more deep-seated. As his anxieties grew almost pathological, he needed continual prompting even at the dress rehearsal, and was up till 4 a.m. on 12 September, the night before the opening, taking cues from Vivien and Garson Kanin in his London hotel room.

John Mills, then as now one of his intimate friends, was already dressing for the first night when Olivier phoned to ask him and his wife Mary to drop into his dressing-room before the performance. The Millses were alarmed; it was distinctly odd to be asked round *before* a performance, especially a first night. When they arrived, they were shocked to find Olivier in despondent mood. He told them:

> I just wanted you to know that you're about to see the worst bloody performance I've ever given. I haven't even been able to learn the blasted lines. I wanted to tell you because you're friends, and I don't want you to be too disappointed or embarrassed. Please tell any other friends out there that I'm sorry, but this is going to be an absolute disaster.[5]

By the end of the evening another friend, Noël Coward, was able to speak for all who had witnessed one of the most remarkable theatrical first nights of the century: "A tremendous evening. I think the greatest male performance I have seen in the theatre. Came out moved and highly exhilarated. He is far and away the greatest actor we have."

There are many theories about what happened that night. Did his "exercise in dark despair", as John Cottrell suggests, help Olivier "to enter the black, satanic mind of Gloucester"? Did his utter pessimism cause him to throw all caution to the winds and take the scale of risks which can midwife greatness? Or had he simply been misjudging himself throughout his preparations?

It seems most likely that Olivier's pessimism had him in utterly reckless mood. Cast members testify that he "did things that night he had never done in rehearsals". Mills even wondered whether Olivier had "played that scene in the dressing-room in order to get himself in the right mood". For the disaster Olivier predicted turned out to be the single most triumphant night of the many in his career. From the moment the dark, disfigured shape of his Richard shuffled menacingly downstage, scowling from behind a false nose prodigious even by his standards, he held his audience spellbound. As he sneered the opening lines which were later to become his hallmark, appropriated by this performance to be his alone, in perpetuity –

> "Now is the winter of our discontent
> Made glorious summer by this sun of York . . ."

– those privileged enough to be there knew that they were witnessing something very remarkable.

In that famous progress downstage towards the audience – conveying in its awkward, stumbling gait an impression of malignity incarnate before even a word had been spoken – lay Olivier's first real claim to greatness. All the years of technical development merged in this one moment; in the words of the *Daily Telegraph*'s representative that night, that same W. A. Darlington whose troublesome liver had led him to catch the schoolboy Olivier's Katharina:

All the complications of Richard's character – its cruelty, its ambition, its sardonic humour – seemed implicit in his expression and his walk, so that when at last he reached the front of the stage and began his speech, all that he had to say of his evil purpose seemed to us in the audience less like a revelation than a confirmation of something we had already been told.

This was "a return to acting in the grand manner, as our fathers had known it and as we had been allowed to catch a glimpse of from time to time". Wrote Trewin: "Play-goers, generations on, will be told how the actor, pallid, limping, with lank black hair and a long, peering nose, moved like a sable cloud into the opening soliloquy. . . ."

Olivier was careful to capitalize on this bold effect by milking his first soliloquy for even more than it was strictly worth. As had worked so well with the screenplay of *Henry V*, he had woven in a few lines from another play – in this case *Henry VI*, Act III, Scene 2 – allowing himself more chance at the outset to give the audience a taste of each of the many aspects of the Richard he was to unfold to them:

> "I can add colours to the chameleon;
> Change shapes with Proteus for advantages;
> And set the murderous Machiavel to school...."

Beyond the traditional satanic villain, all snarling lips and hollow laughter, he created an eerily attractive monster, who took such satisfaction in the cunning of his own diabolical scheming as to carry the audience with him. By plumbing the part for all its grim humour, and a dark, intense sexuality – but above all by taking the audience into his confidence, in effect making them fellow conspirators – Olivier's Richard achieved the rare feat of winning all watching hearts, so that his dramatic, convulsive death came almost as a disappointment.

His other unprecedented achievement was to play the two distinct sides of Richard, the inner mind and its outward persona, in powerful parallel – a technical juggling trick few other actors have ever been equipped to bring off. Trewin wrote in the *Observer*:

> Here indeed we have the double Gloucester, thinker and doer, mind and mask.... Other players have achieved the Red King, boar, cockatrice, bottled spider, and developed the part with a burning theatrical imagination; none in recent memory has made us so conscious of the usurper's intellect, made so plausible every move on the board from the great opening challenge to the last despair and death.

Recalling the production elsewhere, Trewin was still haunted by Olivier's "unholy magnetism".

Among those in the stalls was the seventeen-year-old Kenneth Tynan, about to go up to Oxford, who was then in the habit of composing reviews and sending them to James Agate on the *Sunday Times* in the hope of early recognition. "Olivier's Richard eats into the memory like acid into metal," he wrote (somewhat defensively, for his recollections of that night were clearly revised for publication thirty years later). But Tynan's unique appreciation of Olivier's qualities, and his eloquence in articulating them, are both clear in one astute observation about the daunting speed at which certain passages were taken:

> It is Olivier's trick to treat each speech as a kind of plastic mass, and not as a series of sentences whose import must be precisely communicated to the audience: the method is impressionistic. He will seize on one or two phrases in each paragraph which, properly inserted, will unlock its whole meaning; the rest he discards with exquisite idleness. To do this successfully, he needs

other people on the stage with him: to be ignored, stared past, or pushed aside during the lower reaches, and gripped and buttonholed when the wave rises to its crested climax. . . .[6]

Despite a tumultuous ovation, Olivier felt the need to drink himself towards oblivion – "I'd heard bravos many times before, and as a rule I don't take much notice of applause" – while awaiting overnight reviews which were to prove the making of him. "Moments bordering on genius" . . . "a masterpiece" . . . "the finest Richard III of our generation" . . . "the most riveting Richard in the history of the theatre". That afternoon, before the matinee, he went down to the stage early to sniff the atmosphere – and there it was, "like seaweed", the smell of success. "It was in the air . . . that people should come and see – *me*. It was the first time in my twenty-year-old career that I had ever felt anything like it."

No other English actor, as Robert Speaight wrote, could equal "the sheer pace and mounting excitement of his delivery, the still fire or sudden flash of temperament, the eye that holds you, the gymnastic grace". Olivier had made things difficult for other Richards; playing the part would henceforth be "like going in to bat after Bradman".[7] But Olivier had not merely colonized the part, so that every subsequent attempt at it would be measured against his. He had arrived at the plateau he craved. His Richard was the beginning of a series of Old Vic roles which would, within two years, place Gielgud squarely in his shadow and see off Donald Wolfit altogether. It was of this Old Vic season that Hermione Gingold was memorably moved to remark: "Olivier is a *tour de force*; Wolfit is forced to tour."[8]

Looking back, Burrell declared that "there was no question about it: we got Larry because Gielgud refused to come in".[9] So it was doubly moving when Gielgud, who had dominated Shakespearean acting for over fifteen years and who had given Olivier his first classical chance in that 1935 *Romeo and Juliet*, made a characteristically generous gesture to acknowledge the greatness of Olivier's Richard. Shortly before the performance one evening, while Olivier was making up in his dressing-room, a gift box arrived swathed in long-stemmed flowers. Inside it he found one of the most cherished relics of English theatrical history: the sword carried by Edmund Kean when he had played Richard III, which had in turn been handed on to Irving when he played the role in 1873. Gielgud had had it inscribed: "This sword, given him by his mother Kate Terry Gielgud, 1938, is given to Laurence Olivier by his friend John Gielgud in appreciation of his performance of Richard III at the New Theatre, 1944."

There had indeed been "a great deal of Irving in the performance . . .", as Agate declared in his *Sunday Times* review, "in the bite and devilry, the sardonic impudence, the superb emphases, the sheer malignity and horror of it". Olivier had consciously modelled his voice on Irving's, as he told John Mortimer in later years: "You have to use every sound in your voice for Hamlet. In *Richard III*, I only used three notes. I based it on imitations I'd heard people do of Irving."[10] As Agate immortalized it: "His high shimmering tenor has not the oak-cleaving quality; it is a wind that gets between your ribs."

When considering looks and deportment, he tried to think of the person he hated most, and came up with Jed Harris, the truculent director under whom he had suffered so grievously on Broadway in *The Green Bay Tree*. The reptilian nose, even bigger onstage than that immortalized in the subsequent film version, came from Harris, with a bit of Big Bad Wolf thrown in, as did other details of physiognomy: the warts on his face, the lank black hair which was blood-red by the time it sprawled across his twisted shoulders. He looked so chilling, recalled Harcourt Williams, that his fellow actors would give him a wide berth in the wings. And there was one other satanic external influence, then working his own brand of evil magic across the English Channel: Adolf Hitler. The sudden tantrums, the petulant outbursts of Olivier's Richard put many of the audience in mind of the enemy leader, and echoes of the mannerisms caricatured by Chaplin in *The Great Dictator* can be seen in Olivier's 1955 film version of the production.

At the age of thirty-seven, Olivier finally felt he had made it. By the end of that week, his self-confidence onstage was a remarkable contrast to his gloom before the first night. For the first time he knew what it was like – "an overwhelming, head-reeling feeling" – to hold an audience in thrall, to have them at his command. So much so that on occasion, he admits, he did not even bother with the laborious limp, on the assumption that they were too absorbed by what he was saying to notice. It is an actor's Valhalla to take to the stage assured of this scale of triumph – especially, perhaps, as a villain with the power to beguile, to tease and to astonish an audience. Success was heady. As always, Olivier wanted more.

But he would have to wait a while. When *Uncle Vanya* joined the New Theatre repertoire in the New Year, on 16 January, the response to his Astrov was lukewarm. He at least had the consolation that Richardson fared little better in the title role, his first attempt at Chekhov. Many critics and, indeed, some of the cast felt that the two leading actors would have done better to have swapped. Eric Bentley was to praise the way Olivier's Astrov buttoned his coat as "a perfect example of *Sachlichkeit*",[11] or the mastery of petty realistic detail; Trewin was to speak of his voice as "a darting, searching, twisting blade"; Agate, for once, waxed more positive than his colleagues, declaring Olivier's "a magnificently witty and feeling performance". But there was a consensus that the two leading

193

actors were merely coasting, in a play which did not inspire them to the Shakespearean heights they had just scaled. "Mr Olivier", wrote one critic, "would give us a magnificent ten minutes of the doctor, and then we could almost hear him say 'Passed to you, Ralph.' Whereupon Mr Richardson would give us a splendid ten minutes of Uncle Vanya." It may have been splendid, magnificent, but it was not up to the mighty, revelatory standards which had become their hallmark. John Mason Brown, one of Olivier's great champions, later made the point that his Astrov was an "entirely new creation", which had "no connection with either his Hotspur or his Shallow", whereas Richardson's Vanya was merely "a continuation, or rather a diminution of his Falstaff". For Richardson, who had felt miscast and "uncomfortable" as Richmond to Olivier's Richard, it was a disappointing end to that first year. But he was able to take sufficient satisfaction in their corporate achievement to put it behind him.

Even a downbeat ending could not dampen the huge popular success of the Old Vic company's first season back in business, under new management. It was not just that business had been good, their presence in the West End being taken as a signal that life in Britain was returning to pre-war normality. Said Guthrie:

> I think the enormous public interest is something more than just the attraction of two star names. The big scale of the scheme, the large company, live orchestra, *Peer Gynt*, Old Vic ... the whole set-up has captured the people's imagination, coming at the tail end of five years of war. [We have now] a certain momentum that carries things along with far less need to push and shove, on a scale that makes all our plans news....[12]

This Old Vic season, wrote Laurence Kitchin, could be taken as "a starting date for the modern English theatre".[13] The sheer excitement of their work, the virtuosity of Richardson's Peer and Olivier's Richard, the uniformly high quality of their ensemble playing – all heralded a new golden age of English theatre. This was not merely, even in retrospect, an undue response to the years of national hardship and cultural starvation. The upturn in the Allies' fortunes had happily coincided with the arrival at the height of his powers of one of the most powerful presences ever to grace the English stage. Given the bonus of his companionship – rare in the theatre – with Richardson, for all their unabashed competitiveness, the talented company's corporate leadership inspired an *esprit de corps* which made for sparkling work. Harcourt Williams fondly recalled the way Olivier and Richardson used to hold the curtain for each other at the end of every performance – a job normally reserved for the stage manager. Whoever was playing the leading role would make the curtain speech that night, with the other graciously playing second fiddle. "A matter of no great importance, perhaps," said wise old Williams, "but significant." [14]

But Olivier was not finished with 1945, which was to prove as much a personal *annus mirabilis* for him as for the history of his country. That autumn was to see him securely established as Britain's leading actor, with the release of *Henry V* to "beyond-wildest-dreams acclaim", establishing him "indisputably" as film director-actor-producer. And by then he had also scored his first major success as a stage director, for his first post-Richard project, before he and Richardson led the Old Vic on an end-of-season tour, was to direct Vivien in Thornton Wilder's *The Skin of our Teeth*.

Offstage as on the Oliviers remained a national phenomenon, drawing huge and adoring crowds at their every public outing, for all their continuing private travails. Vivien's insecurities had been little helped by Olivier's enormous success as Richard. She worshipped him all the more, but shrewdly sensed that he, in turn, worshipped greatness *per se* – a greatness she now more than ever felt the need to attempt to achieve herself, to retain his interest and affection. "Nothing he said or did", wrote Vivien's biographer, Anne Edwards, "convinced her that he loved her simply for herself." For if Guthrie's advice had helped Olivier's attitude to his work, it seemed to have had the opposite effect on his private life. Once Olivier started falling in love with his characters, he seemed simultaneously to start falling out of love with his wife.

"There was a certain irony in it," said their friend Cecil Beaton. "We often heard him talk about it, and it always struck me, though I said nothing to her, that he used it as a substitute for his flagging love for her. Of course, she never recognized it. Indeed, she was just as enthusiastic about the concept as Larry was, and kept telling everyone how brilliant an acting insight it was." [15]

When Vivien was sent a text of Thornton Wilder's new play, in which Tallulah Bankhead was triumphing in New York, she became obsessed with the notion that the part of Sabina – under Olivier's direction – might be the key to winning back his heart, both professionally and privately. Olivier shared her enthusiasm – Sabina was "a contemporary Cleopatra" – but agreed to it more as a passing project to take her mind off things and buy himself some respite from the incessant pressure she was placing on him. Besides, he was not unaware of the opportunity it offered himself and his own career to prove his versatility with success as a director.

David O. Selznick, of course, knew little of their marital problems. Throughout the war years they had continued to dodge cable after cable, and Vivien had managed to avoid returning to Hollywood. Selznick's patience had worn so thin that in 1942 he had even tried to co-opt Vivien's daughter Suzanne, then still in Canada, to play the young Jane in *Jane Eyre*, which would star Orson Welles. He had been paid a huge fee by Rank and Pascal for Vivien's appearance in *Caesar and Cleopatra*, but was still desperate to capitalize on his original bold investment. Now the war was all but over, Selznick made one last effort to bring his Scarlett O'Hara to heel. It was not to work – *Gone with the Wind* would prove the only picture Vivien ever made for Selznick – but it was to cause the Oliviers yet more harassment they could have done without. Over my dead body, was the gist of Selznick's response to Vivien's request for his contractual permission to appear in *The Skin of our Teeth*. The strength of his feelings is more than clear from an internal memo Selznick wrote on 19 February 1945 to his vice-president and general manager, formerly his legal counsel, Daniel T. O'Shea:

> There should be an entire review of our dealings with Vivien Leigh.
>
> We consented to her stage appearance in *Romeo and Juliet* because of her and Olivier's urgings, although this meant passing up having Scarlett O'Hara in other films. This endeavor seriously damaged her career and reviews were terrible. This is one reason why we are so fearful of another theatrical engagement prompted and participated in by Olivier, with possibility of further serious damage to our property.
>
> We heeded Leigh's urgings and pleas for a twelve-week leave of absence to go to England because we felt an Englishwoman should return to England during wartime and also because of her principal argument, which was that she might never see Olivier again, since he was planning on going into service. We made this gesture in good faith and at a loss to ourselves, as we did subsequent gestures leading to extensions and further leaves of absence....
>
> Olivier is no longer in service, and there is no reason why she should not return to America or at least make an attempt to do so; and it might be stressed that she has consistently refused to even consider any such attempt, although we have stood ready and still stand ready to make pictures with her that could have enormously beneficial effect on British–American relations, with a potential audience of between fifty and one hundred million people throughout the world by comparison with the small number any play could reach....[16]

Three days after the date of this memo, Selznick sought an injunction in the English courts preventing Vivien from appearing in the play. His counsel, Sir Walter Monckton, renowned as one of the leading lawyers in the abdication drama, described Selznick's "property" as "an exotic plant which must be exposed widely". Through hers, Vivien replied that if she did not act on the British stage, she could well be "drafted for work in a war factory". Though this was something of an exaggeration, Selznick lost the case.

So by VE Day in May, when Olivier and the Old Vic company were in Manchester, Vivien was not too far away in Blackpool on a pre-West End run of *The Skin of our Teeth*. The play, described by Wilder as "a comic-strip history of mankind", was rather too modern for Northern audiences, but delighted visitors from a nearby RAF station – among them at the VE Day matinee Jack Merivale, who decided to risk looking in on Vivien backstage. No mention was made of their last meeting, or the note on which it had ended. They simply swapped news – Merivale told her that, since he had last seen her, he had been married to and divorced from the actress Jan Sterling – and Vivien was all sunshine.

Next day the company moved on to London, where on 16 May the first night at the Phoenix was the glitziest social occasion London had seen for years. Olivier was on edge. His son Tarquin, now nearly nine, had just arrived home from his exile in Los Angeles and clearly found it difficult to regard this remote and famous man, whom he had not seen for almost six years, as his father. The double role of producer-director was one Olivier relished; that of famous husband he found rather less comfortable, as he had in the old *Gone with the Wind* days. Knowing Vivien's mental fragility, he was a hotbed of nerves in his stalls seat, as became all too clear to the entire audience after the interval. Ten minutes into the third act – the beginning of which he considered crucial to a proper understanding of the play – Olivier noticed the mighty Agate, doyen of the critical fraternity, returning late to his seat. His nervous anxieties got the better of his judgement and, in a moment of blind rage, Olivier strode across the aisle and struck the distinguished critic a clumsy blow across the shoulder, with a penetrating hiss of "You're late, blast you!"[17]

All the more credit to Agate, then, that his *Sunday Times* review (which made no mention of the incident) hailed Vivien's Sabina as "an enchanting piece of nonsense-cum-allure, half dabchick and half dragon-fly ... the best performance in this kind since Yvonne Printemps". It was one of a clutch of excellent notices, in which Wilder's play received due metropolitan understanding. Olivier's direction was credited with "inventiveness" and "ingenuity"; to the ever purple Trewin he was possessed of a "darting flame". But above all Vivien was accorded the triumph she so desperately craved: "startlingly good" ... "as sparkling as a diamond" ... "as volatile as quicksilver" ... "part gamine, part woman, a comedienne, an artist". Only Tynan, ominously signalling his intentions for the turbulent years ahead, voiced languid dissent: "She treats her lines as if she were going through a very fluent first reading, with little variation of pitch or tone, and puts important phrases in prodigiously inverted commas.... Miss Leigh is sweet; but when you have said that half a dozen times, you have said everything."[18]

A burst of higher spirits, however, did little for Vivien's physical health. Even before the play had opened, during its provincial tour, she had been alarmed to find herself coughing painfully and dramatically losing weight. As she bottled up her concerns, refusing to see a doctor, she found herself back on that emotional downward spiral, with exhilaration turning to exhaustion and tantrums after almost every performance. Accustomed to it all by now, Olivier allowed himself to be convinced that she was merely suffering a heavy cold. Reassured that her success in the play, and her commitment to it, would compensate for his absence, he set off as planned with Richardson and the Old Vic company on a six-week tour of the newly liberated areas of Europe.

After a four-week swing around the English provinces, which saw them in Manchester for VE Day, the Olivier–Richardson roadshow set off by troopship from Tilbury for a continental tour of powerfully mixed emotions. Under the auspices of ENSA (commanded by Olivier's old nemesis, Basil Dean), all sixty-six members of the troupe were granted the honorary rank of lieutenant and all required to wear uniform. Olivier and Richardson pinned wings over their breast pockets but agreed to differ in their choices of distinctive headgear, Richardson opting for a peaked cap, Olivier a beret. "Look at him," said Richardson of his friend in a photograph taken on that tour, as they sat side by side in a jeep, "look at poor Laurence, so *bored*." [19]

He may have grown weary of the repertoire, but the sights which unfolded before the travelling players were far from boring. Greeted rapturously by troops starved of any entertainment, many of whom had never been to the theatre in their lives, theirs was a triumphant progress from Antwerp to Ghent, from Brussels to Hamburg. In June, by particular invitation, they gave a special matinee of *Arms and the Man* at Belsen, for the British doctors and troops in charge of the 40,000 inmates still clinging to life and the 10,000 bodies rotting in open heaps around the camp. The three women members of the company went at their own request on a tour of the place before the evening performance, after which Sybil Thorndike wrote in her diary: "I shall never get over today – *never*." [20]

The tour ended in Paris, at the Comédie Française, where Olivier enjoyed the scale of wild, adulatory reception only the French can lay on. He understood their compliments even less than they had understood Shakespeare's text; but there was something wonderfully cross-cultural about it all, which in the heady aftermath of war had him delivering a curtain speech in well-rehearsed French, and kissing the stage with a declaration that he would now return this hallowed theatre to its rightful owners. Among those who saw his Richard in Paris, and admired it greatly, was the great theatrical designer Edward Gordon Craig, illegitimate son of Ellen Terry. Reminded again of his schooldays and the praise this *grande dame* had heaped upon him, Olivier had a strong sense that some external, almost supernatural, power was at work in his life and career, granting him the professional pre-eminence he craved, but making him pay for it with the turbulence of his private life.

Olivier did not know that, three weeks after his departure, Vivien had been told that she had developed tuberculosis; doctors had ordered her to drop out of *The Skin of our Teeth* immediately and take a long rest. Before reaching Paris he had received an alarming letter from her, with the unexplained phrase "Now that you know the worst...." He did not let it bother him too much, discovering only much later that it referred to her health, and that a previous letter spelling out the tubercular diagnosis had failed to reach him. But news of her condition now came with their friends Alfred Lunt and Lynn Fontanne, who had arrived in Paris directly from London to entertain American troops. Olivier could not return home for another three weeks, but he at least reassured himself that Vivien was out of *The Skin of our Teeth* and placed in the hands of diligent nurses.

The long downhill slope of his relationship with Vivien can really be measured from this moment, when the increasingly firm hold taken by her illness coincided with the dramatic upturn in his professional fortunes. There was no way, it is quite clear, that Olivier was going to let his wife's irritating inconsistency clutter his path to greatness. If he still felt strongly about her, it was because he now loved the idea of a publicly glamorous marriage more than the woman he happened to share it with. The fact that Vivien was still extraordinarily beautiful certainly helped; like all men, he was more than happy to be envied in his choice of partner. But his own admiration was now more aesthetic than sexual. Already, it seems, both were conscious that their passion had lost its sexual edge; all Olivier's considerable sexual energies were anyway, he believed, expended in his work. This would long continue to be the case, with ever more drastic results for their life together.

By the end of the war Vivien had become a problem to be kept at bay, an irritating source of diversions from his single-minded obsession with scaling every pinnacle his profession could offer him. His absorption in himself, and in the changing cast of characters he was to love enough to play well, left no room for her. If ever there was a moment to face up to a serious consideration of – let alone sympathy with – her emergent mental problems, this was it.

But his own account of this moment inadvertently, and thus all the more brutally, reveals how permanently he now decided to wrap Vivien in cotton-wool and place her on a back-shelf of his priorities. His memoirs have him arriving in Paris from a tour of *Titus Andronicus* behind the Iron

Curtain – a tour which, in fact, took place a dozen years later, in 1957, when he had already left Vivien for Joan Plowright. As he wrote that passage in the early 1980s, and recalled his heady triumph as Richard III at the Comédie Française – with lifelong friends like Ginette Spanier, head of Balmain, crowding adoringly into his dressing-room – it is starkly clear that in his mind, as in his memory, he had already left Vivien. Certainly, he was abandoning her to her fate.

The passage gives more energy to the "miraculous" design and "sublime" acoustics of certain continental theatres, more rage to the destruction of sundry "beloved" London ones, than to the poignant plight of the woman he had once adored. The way he tells it, he returned home merely to find her less ill than reported and took her off to Scotland for a fortnight to meditate upon the return of peace to Europe. Even the holiday is mentioned less for its restorative effects on Vivien than for the worrying risk of missing the first half of rehearsals for the next Old Vic season.

Olivier was to live out the lie for another decade yet, to share stage triumphs with Vivien, to wallow in his share of their joint public idolatry, but only because it was the course which least diverted his energies from his main preoccupation: Laurence Olivier, with whom he was a great deal more in love than anyone from Henry V to Scarlett O'Hara, from Sergius Saranoff to Vivien Leigh.

CHAPTER 12

1945–7

I f a sense of destiny presupposes a sense of history, Olivier already possessed both to a degree remarkable in one not yet forty. He had relished the company of the great men he had played, such as Nelson, and coveted that of the one he was soon to meet, Churchill. If he too was to achieve greatness, it was time to lend substance to his offstage persona, to offset the showbiz glitter with some show of the grandeur rapidly becoming his station. To an Englishman of such conservative values, only one status symbol could satisfy so deep-seated a yearning. His rise from a semi-detached in Dorking must be marked by his arrival in a country seat, preferably a stately home with historical associations.

It was two years since he had first set eyes on Notley Abbey, a twelfth-century manor-house at Long Crendon in Buckinghamshire, fifty miles north-west of London. When he and Vivien had visited the Abbey in 1944, shortly after he had completed *Henry V*, Olivier had defied all wartime logic by envisaging the glorious lifestyle of a gentleman-farmer, a country squire lording it over seventy-five acres endowed as an Augustinian settlement 800 years before. They had used a month's petrol ration just to make the daytrip. But Notley had been frequented by Henry viii and Cardinal Wolsey; it had been endowed by Henry v himself. It was *meant* to be his.

Vivien was bitterly opposed. It happened to be a cold, grey day when they first drove down Notley's broad avenue of a drive, through its over-grown pastures bordering the Thame, and beheld the huge, sprawling stone edifice long since sunk into decay. Relics of its former grandeur were evident in the mullioned tracery of the windows, the tall and elderly chimney stacks, the central tower added in the sixteenth century. But its rooms, all twenty-two of them, were huge and draughty, its yards of corridor grim and forbidding. Beyond the six-car garage and the four greenhouses, the refectory barn and the dingy farm manager's cottage lay the dilapidated remains of a farm once equipped to deal with six cows, twenty-four pigs and 400 chickens. The scale of the enterprise horrified her.

She enlisted such friends as David Niven to visit the place and try to talk Olivier out of it. The purchase price amounted to almost their entire joint savings. How could they afford to restore the crumbling fabric of the building, the overgrown wilderness of the garden, let alone decorate so many huge rooms? How would they deal with the primitive plumbing, the burst pipes, the total lack of heating, of any modern bathroom or kitchen facilities?

One room at a time, replied Olivier undeterred, and Vivien could see he was obsessed with the idea of casting himself in the role of feudal squire. It was a fantasy he was willing to come true, and she knew it would be counter-productive to argue further. Thus it was that Notley became theirs, and was for the next decade to be the outward and visible symbol of their glamour, their fame, their stature in their profession and the supposed happiness of their marriage.

Notley Abbey had been founded and built during the reign of Henry II by Walter Giffard, Earl of Buckingham, "in order that the souls of the King, his Queen Eleanor of Aquitaine, his own soul and those of all his own family might be prayed for in perpetuity". Still seeking his own peace with his maker, Olivier endearingly found this "a wonderfully simple way of bargaining with God". But he happily left Vivien the daunting task of turning the crumbling, ancient pile into a home. With the help of Lady (Sibyl) Colefax, a society hostess of the day skilled in the restoration of historic houses, she had just begun work when she went into *The Skin of our Teeth*. When she came out of it, ill and exhausted, with Olivier still abroad on the Old Vic tour, it was to the few habitable rooms at Notley that she retreated with her team of nurses. The alternative, she had been told, was a sanatorium – a dread word which to her spelt irretrievable mental illness. Neither her husband nor even her doctor knew it, but Vivien had already realized that her mental problems were worse than her physical ones. At Notley, she knew, with builders swarming all over the roof, Olivier would spend as much time with her as his London schedule would permit. For the more distanced he became, the greater her devotion to him grew.

But Olivier was not around much that spring, as he was by now caught up in his second Old Vic season, which was to begin with Richardson playing Falstaff in both parts of *Henry IV*. He himself had persuaded Richardson to tackle the mighty part of Sir John, which was to prove one of his greatest roles; when at first, however, Richardson was wary, complaining that the part was "rather long and difficult", Olivier told him: "Nonsense, all parts are difficult. Don't be so coy, don't be so silly. Just have a go at it." [1] As usual, he had an ulterior motive. Eager not to be outshone, Olivier saw the two parts of *Henry IV* as a chance to show off his own range and versatility from one night to the next. He would undertake the dashing role of Hotspur in Part I and the bumbling, eccentric country justice, Mr Shallow, in Part II. Then his turn in a leading role was to see him take on Sophocles's Oedipus.

Hotspur is scarcely a great role – "little more", in Agate's summary, "than a trumpet solo and, in the 'Pluck bright honour' speech, a coach-horn tootle". Olivier, of course, set about ways of making the role his, starting as always with the externals. He spent three hours each night working on make-up worthy of the lurid, carrot-red wig with which he would make this a Hotspur like none before him. That wig was to pass into theatrical folklore when he himself, re-entering after the interval, heard an audience member tell his companion, "Look, here comes old Ginger again!" [2] For the rest of his theatrical career, this became the standard text of the first-night good luck cables to Olivier from John Mills and other friends.

But his Hotspur rose above his obsession with mere appearances; sour, uncouth, fiery, it was a daring portrayal, best remembered for a piece of brilliantly distinctive invention, designed to give the authentic Olivier stamp to a role which can otherwise drown in merely virile heroics. Seizing on Lady Percy's reference to her husband's "speaking thick, which nature made his blemish", he gave Hotspur a stammer on all words beginning with the letter "w". The choice of this consonant – Agate called it "a stroke of genius" – was triumphantly explained in Hotspur's death scene, planned and staged almost as intricately as that of Olivier's Richard, in which he was able to milk every drop of pathos from his last line to his nemesis, Prince Hal:

HOTSPUR: "No, Percy, thou art dust and food for w-w-w ..."
HAL: "For worms, brave Percy. Fare thee well, great heart."

It was the climax of an elaborately dramatic departure from this world, in which the famous exit line, "Oh Harry, thou hast robbed me of my youth," would see Olivier stand stock still for several seconds, clutching at his throat to stem the liberal flow of blood oozing between his fingers, before collapsing in full and noisy armour down two steps to land heavily on his face and be heard no more. It is tempting to agree with the suggestion of Harcourt Williams that "on paper one would say an anti-climax, or perhaps a sure laugh".[3] But no, says Williams, "the whole thing held the audience spellbound", as Richardson's Falstaff then hauled him offstage by his heels, his head bumping unceremoniously along the floor.

Those returning the next evening would find the noble warrior quite unrecognizable beneath the shoulder-length white wig, straggling goatee beard and interminably long, thin false nose of the spindly, lecherous Justice Shallow. He was, to Agate, the perfect country justice, "peering through eyes purging thick amber and plumtree gum, tapering nose exploring chinlessness – the perfect jigsaw of old". It was Olivier's idea, naturally, that his Shallow should keep bees, a suggestion to which Richardson agreed with wary suspicion. He was wise to be cautious, for Olivier's Shallow, in his shrill, high-pitched voice, would shamelessly steal their four scenes together with outrageous invention, constantly slapping his face and sawing the air to deal with the troublesome swarm of bees intruding on the already lively dialogue. It was a masterpiece of comic invention, brazen enough to disarm even Richardson, who was enjoying sufficient praise for his "definitive" Falstaff to be content to surrender the stage for a few memorable moments to his ever competitive friend.

As if virtuoso versatility over consecutive evenings were not enough, Oliver now planned to "top myself" with a display of contrasting theatrical pyrotechnics in one outlandish double-bill, to be known to theatrical history as "Oedipuff". It was Guthrie who first suggested he look at the W.B. Yeats translation of Sophocles's *Oedipus Rex*, then a revolutionary text to a tradition steeped in Gilbert Murray. Olivier liked the Yeats, but felt that on its own this one shortish piece made for a "rather gloomy" evening. So he came up with the bright idea of coupling it with an utterly contrasting piece of froth, Sheridan's *The Critic*, in which the part of Mr Puff would give him the chance to show both extremes of his range within a span of four hours.

The ascetic Guthrie, already deep in preparations for his production of *Oedipus*, thought the notion "vulgar" (as he had, he told Olivier, the film of *Henry V*). He demanded a leadership meeting to argue his case that the double-bill was unthinkable. To Guthrie's mortification, Olivier not only refused to give way, but persuaded Michel Saint-Denis to take over *Oedipus*, having already invited Miles Malleson to direct *The Critic*. Although he had by now resigned from the staff of the Old Vic, Guthrie remained the prime mover behind the triumvirate and found it humiliating to have his views ignored and his productions hijacked. So he took himself off to New York in a huff, to direct a play appropriately entitled *He Who Gets Slapped*. It was the beginning of a feud which would have resounding consequences for them all.

New mountains of make-up were applied for both parts, Olivier's

Oedipus affecting a triangular Grecian nose with dark, streaming, kingly locks. It was an immensely powerful performance, moving from stark horror to affecting pathos as the doomed monarch gradually discovers that he has unwittingly murdered his father and married his mother. At the awesome moment when this dark truth dawns, Olivier uttered a cry so bloodcurdling, so haunting, that many who were there insist they can still hear it today. Reaching, as so often, for one devastating physical effect to form a centrepiece for the performance, he had been brooding on a discussion of the role with the Greek scholar Maurice Bowra. "Fated" was the single word they had agreed on for the attitude Oedipus brings onstage with him, and Olivier was looking for a sound which distilled that elusive concept. "Oh, Oh," was all the script offered, which he had already transformed to a sound nearer "Er" when he read in a magazine of the way ermine are trapped in the Arctic: the hunters put salt on the ice, the ermine licks it and its tongue freezes to the ice. It was from the unique torment of the trapped ermine that Olivier conjured his devastating Oedipus scream. To him, the technique justified his belief that "it is next to impossible to produce the effect of great suffering without the actor enduring some degree of it".[4]

The same actor who had left the stage as the self-blinded Oedipus, blood streaming copiously from the sockets of what were once his eyes, returned after a fifteen-minute interval as the foppish, periwigged Mr Puff, skipping around the stage with dandyish abandon, tossing up snuff and catching it in yet another comically grotesque nose. Even some of his Old Vic colleagues thought Olivier was too obviously showing off, demeaning the greatness of his tragic performance by a quick music-hall change into outrageously camp burlesque. Some critics, too, thought Sheridan's text quite witty enough without the exhausting array of stage business with which Olivier embellished it: Puff disappearing into the flies on a painted cloud and descending again, hanging desperately on to a theatre curtain, to gambol and somersault his way to the front of centre-stage amid a deafening ovation for his acrobatic daring.

Agate was so appalled – "Would Irving have followed Hamlet with Jingle?" – that he pretended to ignore the performance of *The Critic*, devoting his column to saying that he had admired Olivier's Oedipus, but somehow could not remember why: "I seem to remember a great cry, a swift flight, and a moving episode with some children of a compellingness to make me play with the notion of Mr Olivier as Great Actor. But something has wiped cry and flight and pathos from my mind...." The Sheridan comedy, he explained elsewhere, had "successfully dowsed whatever light I had seen the tragedy in". For his part, Olivier argued that "I could really sink myself deep into the Greek tragedy without reservation, secure in the anticipation of the joyous gaiety that was to follow it."

The interval metamorphosis involved a race against time to remove his blood-stained Grecian look and replace it, after a quick shower, with a round pink face, arched eyebrows and another long, pointed nose. During one such exercise, Olivier told Donald Sinden, there was a knock at the door and in came the actor George Curzon, then in rehearsals for *Peter Pan*, in which he was to "give" his Captain Hook.

"Ah," said Olivier, trying to keep to his breakneck fast-change schedule while his unhurried visitor helped himself to a drink. "I hope you're playing Mr Darling too. It's essential that the same actor should do both."

"Yes, I am, Larry," said Curzon, "but you've no idea how exhausting it is to play two parts in one evening." [5]

Richardson was playing a "Blake-like" Tiresias in *Oedipus* and the tiny part of Burleigh in *The Critic*. One evening the critic Harold Hobson, then writing a biography of Richardson, was taking advantage of his subject's relatively calm schedule to interview him in his dressing-room during a performance. On the in-house loudspeaker it was clear that the performance of *Oedipus* was nearing its end, when into Richardson's dressing-room suddenly burst Oedipus/Olivier, stage blood streaming down his face, apparently for a chat which the presence of an unexpected visitor pre-empted. The ensuing scene, which says a great deal about this rare and remarkable partnership, was well caught by Hobson:

> Richardson sat in a corner, puffing away at his pipe and talking quietly and calmly. Olivier burst in, a wild look on his face, peered at himself in the looking-glass, shrieked in a distraught voice "It's a rotten shame", and then, red paint pouring down from his eyes, groped his way along the wall to the door. A moment later there rang through the New Theatre Olivier's tremendous cry of horror and distress as the self-blinded Oedipus. These proceedings somewhat distracted me, but on Richardson they had no effect whatever. He just went on talking quietly, the apparent essence of an ordinary man. But, of course, only an extraordinary man could have contrived to behave ordinarily in such circumstances.[6]

Olivier's evident delight in his own *chutzpah* was dampened one matinee, when the technically daring routine of Mr Puff's ascent by cloud went dangerously wrong. The rope he clutched once aloft – so that the cloud could descend without him, as he transferred unseen to the stage curtain – had not been properly fastened. When it came away in his hands, he grabbed hold of a dangling piano wire and hung on desperately until rescued by panic-stricken stagehands, only narrowly avoiding a thirty-foot drop on to a sea of cut-ply battleships below. As it was, he was gently and humiliatingly lowered to the stage before the eyes of a puzzled audience.

What had been one of his favourite moments of derring-do thereafter became a frightening ordeal each night it was performed. His fears that it could go wrong again were confirmed during the play's New York run, when a rope-ladder involved in the routine broke loose and flung him painfully to the stage. The near-disaster began an unremitting series of nightmares, in which he fell from the flies of the theatre to the stage, or from the sky in a plane crash.

The virtuoso versatility of "Oedipuff", none the less, hard on the heels of Hotspur–Shallow, lifted Olivier's reputation to yet another plateau. He received standing ovations each night, and the street outside the New Theatre was thronged with adoring crowds chanting "We Want Larry." The critics became ecstatic, with Beverley Baxter of the *Evening Standard* left wondering "if anything is beyond his reach". Rather than being criticized for outlandish showmanship, Olivier was praised for his refusal to repeat himself, for the intensity of his fresh approach to each role. "His intelligence", wrote Baxter, "sheds radiance upon everything he touches."

Throughout this heady period Olivier was commuting each day from Buckinghamshire, where Vivien was making a steady physical recovery. Summer was at last coming to Notley. With Sibyl Colefax, Vivien was bringing the Abbey's great chambers to life, filling them with antiques and pictures, brocade and elaborate ornament, illuminated manuscripts and theatrical drawings. Tarquin Olivier, who spent some of that summer there, strikingly recalls an air of "exhausted sexuality about the place, regretful black rooks high out of reach, umbrella poplar trees silvering against the sky in unlabouring cascades".[7]

But Vivien's mental condition improved little. Throughout his heaviest season ever – the immense physical strain on him increased by the need to commute – Olivier still had to find a way of responding to his wife's intense, if less frequent, spells of hysteria. He could sense the worst when she became unusually agitated for a few days: her voice, her laughter, her nervous gestures all took on an obsessive edge. Above all her eyes could never settle. Once the objects of his worship, they would now find it hard to focus on him, on anyone or anything, darting hither and thither nervously. Soon would come an uncontrolled outburst of abuse and violence lasting hours, followed invariably by a long period of quiet, intense depression, then one of abject remorse. There no longer seemed to be any rational explanation for these episodes, not even alcohol, the smallest amounts of which had been known to provoke violent outbursts. As far as he could discern, Vivien had followed her doctor's orders, giving up both smoking and drinking throughout the prescribed nine-month rest period. To Olivier the situation began to seem hopeless.

By midsummer, when Notley's gardens bloomed under her care for the first time, Vivien was better than she had been for several years. Although the hard work she had put in to the Abbey had done little to help her condition, she realized she had now come to love the place perhaps even more than Olivier himself did. She had certainly spent more time there. By now she was well enough to want to tear herself away and be at his side as he and Richardson led the triumphant Old Vic company to New York, where they would present their most successful productions in six weeks of repertory at the Century Theater. This, of course, caused Olivier as much anxiety as relief. Although he still believed that he loved Vivien, he was not sure he could cope with her in New York as well as sustain his huge workload there. She, however, was adamant that she could not bear to be parted from him. The doctors, moreover, were predicting a nervous breakdown for *him* unless he eased up on his unremitting schedule. Vivien wanted to be there to look after him. It seemed wise not to try to dissuade her.

So they returned to New York in mixed spirits, having last left the place at such a low point five years before. The scale of the advance publicity for the Old Vic company held uneasy memories of *Romeo and Juliet*, as did that of the advance bookings at the box office. When the two parts of *Henry IV* opened the run, the critics too were in cautious mood, but "Oedipuff" disarmed them all. Olivier wallowed in a tide of superlatives. "This Oedipus", wrote John Mason Brown, "is one of those performances in which blood and electricity are somehow mixed. It pulls down lightning from the sky. It is as awesome, dwarfing and appalling as one of nature's angriest displays. Though thrilling, it never loses its majesty."[8] After analysing all five of Olivier's diverse roles in the season – Hotspur, Shallow, Astrov, Oedipus and Puff – Mason Brown was finally moved to use "that precious, dangerous, final adjective: 'great'". After spending two paragraphs explaining why he had been so reluctant to risk this hazardous word, he eloquently recalled the words of the essayist William Hazlitt in his theatre-going days: "I am not one of those who, when they see the sun breaking from behind a cloud, stop to ask others if it be the moon."

There was a lone dissenting voice in the shape of the high-minded American critic George Jean Nathan, who had been led to believe that what he was to see in the Old Vic company was English ensemble acting at its best. Sybil Thorndike – a notable Jocasta to Olivier's Oedipus – was the only member of the London cast not to make the visit to New York. But Nathan defiantly complained: "Unless I am sadly mistaken, what this Old Vic troupe amounts to is little more than two variably talented and honest Old Vic actors, Olivier and Richardson, surrounded by anything but a noteworthy group...." Though he adjudged Richardson's Falstaff the best male performance he had seen that year, Nathan declared Olivier's all-round contribution to the company "considerably more important".

Olivier had been there only a month when the New York drama critics voted him the best actor seen on Broadway in the 1945–6 season, against such opposition as the Lunts, Walter Huston, Raymond Massey and Oscar Homolka. On his arrival, a *New York Times* interview had reported him "in the pink of condition – tanned, rested, relaxed, eager for the fray". But by the end of the six-week run, he was drained. On top of his punishing nightly schedule – the climax of two years of virtually uninterrupted work – he had also taken on Sunday radio broadcasts to help pay the hotel bill.

Back at home, the bills were mounting inexorably. Olivier, who was earning only £100 a week at the Old Vic, had more than Notley to worry about. There were the growing medical costs for Vivien, who had been told she could not work for at least a year. There was the handsome allowance he paid to Jill Esmond[9] and Tarquin. There were his own considerable living expenses, given the style to which he was becoming accustomed. With *Henry V* about to ride to the rescue, he refused to panic. But then he never did worry too much about money. For almost a decade now he had been able to earn large quantities of it when necessary, and he was equally adept at spending it. While Vivien fretted, he remained irrationally optimistic. He had no intention of abandoning his Old Vic platform, whose professional rewards more than justified the financial sacrifice, for more lucrative pastures in Hollywood or elsewhere.

But the strain showed in the return of his recurrent nightmare, which refused to go away even when he actually *did* fall on the New York stage, tearing his Achilles' tendon. Next day the Oliviers flew nervously to Boston to collect his honorary degree at Tufts; when the ceremony overran, he sent Vivien ahead to the airport to see if she could persuade them to hold the plane. He arrived just as the pilot had refused to wait any longer and was taxiing for take-off. A distraught Olivier, fearing the effects of a solo flight on Vivien's condition, hobbled helplessly after it down the tarmac, shouting and gesticulating. When it took off without him, he publicly broke down and sobbed. To his own mortified embarrassment, he had to be helped back into the terminal to await the next flight to New York.

Two days after the season closed, the film of *Henry V* opened at the New York City Center, and Olivier wallowed in another chorus of praise. The satisfactions of professional success, as so often, outweighed private anxieties. But they also fed that competitive urge to move on, the restlessness which has always been the spur to so prolific a career. Within forty-eight hours he declared himself "bored" with resting his foot in their hotel room. There was also the small detail that they had simply run out of money. It was time to head for home and a month's holiday at Notley.

When they finally checked out of the St Regis, the Oliviers had exactly $17 and 40 cents between them.

He was physically exhausted and mentally drained, but the fates were not through with him yet. On 19 June, after he and Vivien had boarded a Pan Am Constellation Clipper for London with forty other passengers and ten crew, Olivier's nightmare almost came true. Soon after take-off Vivien screamed and rose from her seat; Olivier saw that one of the starboard engines had burst into flames. They could only watch helplessly as it fell away and the rest of the wing began to blaze. The plane was falling fast from 15,000 feet when the captain saw a small Connecticut airfield through a break in the clouds, only to discover that his under-carriage was jammed. He was forced to make a desperate crash landing, pancaking half a mile across the tarmac on the plane's belly before finally skidding to a halt, the wing still ablaze. Olivier's brief experience as a pilot was enough for him to know how lucky they were to have survived. "It was almost superhuman," he said of the pilot's feat, "such a brilliant piece of work that every passenger stood and cheered him."

The summer at Notley proved glorious, and both of them gradually returned to normality. While Olivier busied himself about his new role as gentleman-farmer, consulting with his farm managers about cattle and crops, Vivien found a new distraction from her anxieties in the role of society hostess, attending meticulously to every detail of weekend house parties which were to become legendary. The Richardsons and the Red-graves, the Millses and the Kordas, the Nivens and the Fairbankses, Coward and Beaton, Guthrie and Gielgud, Donat and Guinness – the names in the Notley guest-book formed a glittering audience for Olivier's stylish portrayal of a country squire. These metropolitan animals relished the pastoral hedonism of Notley, where the days were beguiled with tennis and croquet, picnics on the banks of the Thame, elegant teas in the drawing-room and lavish black-tie dinner parties in the mediæval ban-queting hall, followed by high-spirited party games well into the night.

The host, according to survivors of the period, would flit moodily in and out of the group activities, where he was happy to let Noël Coward, an ever closer friend of Vivien's, act as master of ceremonies. There was an air of constant vigilance about Olivier, a reluctance to let spirits soar too high. He was, of course, waiting for the combination of alcohol and lack of sleep to bring upon Vivien the major attack he dreaded. He was also brooding over his next big major enterprise at the New Theatre, where he was to direct himself in the title role of King Lear.

Always a bold choice for any actor, especially one under forty, Lear was doubly so in 1946 in view of the recent memory of Wolfit's success in the role – to Agate, "the greatest piece of Shakespearean acting I have seen".

Olivier's fortunes as Lear were to prove mixed, but he has since craved indulgence in view of the fact that he had never intended to play the part in the first place.

The triumvirate's planning meetings for each season, with Burrell in the chair, had become a tense battle of wits between the wily Richardson and the less subtly devious Olivier. Both were aware of the other's broad ambitions; there were roles, such as Falstaff and Richard III, which neither begrudged the other. But there were also roles both coveted, one of which was Cyrano de Bergerac. At the meeting to plan the 1946–7 season, their third in harness, it was Richardson's turn to choose first. Horrified to hear him nominate Cyrano, and knowing it was Richardson's ultimate dream to play Lear, Olivier claimed Lear for himself – to a barely perceptible frisson across the table. Burrell declared the meeting satisfactorily concluded, and the two leading actors set off for the pub together. "Okay, then, let's swap," said Olivier, confident Richardson would agree. "Certainly not, old boy," replied his partner, and that was that.

So Olivier, like it or not, was stuck with a part for which he was not really ready. His Lear, under his own direction, was a remarkable technical feat for one so young, but carried little of the depth a more seasoned actor can bring to the later scenes (which he shared with the young Alec Guinness as the Fool). Again his mercurial technique was to the fore, at the expense of a considered or sustained interpretation; it was a portrait, as Peter Brook later recalled when rehearsing Paul Scofield's Lear at Stratford, superficial enough to have been painted by Annigoni.[10] For once Olivier's fireworks had got out of hand, or perhaps out of their depth. "He was impersonating an elderly psychopath," wrote Laurence Kitchin, "but he was impersonating him out of the play."[11]

Most of the critics of the day, however, were by now so enamoured of the Olivier phenomenon that they were anxious to maintain the hail of superlatives. "If there is a better, more impressive Lear in human recollection," wrote Dent in the *News Chronicle*, "it is certainly not in my experience." And *The Times*: "Lately come to the plenitude of his powers, [he] plays the part with the magnificent ease which testifies that it is for him a completely solved problem." Noël Coward thought Olivier's Lear as good as his Richard III: "He is a superb actor, and I suspect the greatest I shall ever see."[12] In more ethereal mood, Jean-Louis Barrault praised Olivier for painting blood on his feet as Lear: "This realistic note enables the actor precisely not to play the realism of the situation, and liberates him poetically. In pushing realism to its extreme, poetry frees itself."[13]

It took the discerning courage of a Baxter, who had so unreservedly hailed his "Oedipuff", to declare Olivier's Lear "a brave but undoubted failure... King Lear floored him almost as completely as if he had been a

British heavyweight boxer." The young Tynan, already the most reliable judge of any Olivier performance, agreed: "He is our model Richard III and his Hotspur is unique, but he has no intrinsic majesty; he always fights shy of pathos; and he cannot play old men without letting his jaw sag and his eye wander archly in magpie fashion – in short, without becoming funny." Gielgud's recent Lear was held to have been more moving, more spiritual, with a greater intellectual grasp, if lacking the range and quick-silver mood-changes wrought by Olivier. None the less, Baxter summed up, "It is a matter of theatrical history that Mr John Gielgud has lost ground during the last three years before the tempestuous onslaught of Mr Laurence Olivier."

It was of Olivier's Lear that Agate delivered himself of a judgement astute enough to ring through the rest of the actor's career. Though complaining that he was not moved by it, he found the performance "brilliantly imagined and achieved". Agate was above all struck, as so many had been with Richard III, by the unexpected humour Olivier managed to mine within the wandering mind of the dying, deluded old king. "He keeps his sense of fun under control in his tragic parts, but I can see him controlling it," wrote Agate. This was the most hurtful possible criticism – the old taunt that the audience could see the wheels going round – but it was Agate's argument towards a deeper truth: "I have the conviction that Olivier is a comedian by instinct and a tragedian by art."

The *Daily Telegraph*'s W. A. Darlington made another telling point about the acting style of the day:

> Even the momentous performances by Olivier and Richardson in those never-to-be-forgotten Old Vic seasons, artistic successes on a grand scale though they were, had not much popular support. They packed the New Theatre, it is true – but only for limited seasons and as part of an extensive repertoire. The number of times that Olivier appeared as Richard III or Oedipus, or Richardson as Falstaff, must have been small by any standard, and negligible in view of the long runs enjoyed by less impressive revivals. The taste for bravura acting had finally, and possibly permanently, been lost by the rank and file of modern play-goers, and was now something to be cultivated by connoisseurs.

Olivier's public, happily oblivious of such niceties, loved it. All forty-eight performances were completely sold out, and he again emerged with the best of both the worlds he longed to conquer. He was a matinee idol, the role he had always craved, besieged at the stage door by shrieking autograph hunters; and he was a respected classical actor, already hailed as perhaps the greatest alive. When he took *Lear* to the UNESCO con-ference in Paris for a week that November, at the express request of the

Foreign Office, it amounted to a tacit acknowledgement from Whitehall that the Old Vic company was now regarded as an ex-officio National Theatre, with Olivier its figurehead. It was all the more galling, therefore, when the New Year Honours List for 1947 bestowed a knighthood, for services to the theatre, upon Ralph Richardson.

"I should have been the fucking knight!" Olivier was heard to complain in the wings as he brought *Lear* back to a rapt New Theatre.[14] His resentment ran remarkably deep. Fond as he was of Ralphie, "I've done every bit as much as he has, look how I've carried the flag abroad, New York, the American road, Hollywood pictures and an even fuller record in the classics; *and* there was a little film called *Henry V* . . . ." But Richardson's was an immensely popular honour among the company, who took to calling him "Sir-Rano" and clubbed together to have a brass plate inscribed and fixed to his dressing-room door. Olivier's mortification continued, for once ill-concealed, and his dresser was required to come to his defence in unconsciously prophetic terms amid the backstage backbiting: "My guv'nor would never accept a knighthood. He'd only take something bigger!"[15]

In a profession whose leaders are scarcely starved of awards and other forms of worldly recognition, titles still count for a great deal. Richardson had been the first to receive the accolade because he was the older man, he had been the original founder of the triumvirate and he was a particular favourite with the royal family (the then Queen, now the Queen Mother, had loved him in *Q Planes*). But they were so much a double-act that to knight one seemed almost like a deliberate slight to the other. The press, with no better mischief available, took up his cause. Could it be that Olivier, the son of a churchman, was the victim of ancient Establishment sniffiness towards divorcees? Would he now quit England, asked the American film critics, who had just voted him Best Actor of the Year, and seek his fortune across the Atlantic? Or was it true, as Harcourt Williams's backstage rumour had it, that he and Richardson had simply tossed for it?

All such speculation was ended only six months later, in the King's Birthday Honours List that May, when Olivier officially became Sir Laurence while still – just – in his thirties. To this day he remains by far the youngest actor ever to be knighted. It was, it seems, hypocrisy in high places over his divorce which had delayed the honour; when the formidable Sibyl Colefax took the matter up with the Chancellor of the Exchequer, Sir Stafford Cripps, he pointed out that "the chap has only been divorced three years, and you know the thinking in that regard". Lady Colefax replied that it was at least seven, and so Cripps undertook to see what he could do. Richardson himself, aided by J. Arthur Rank, had also been lobbying for the omission to be made good, for parity between Olivier and himself to be restored; now he was able to lend his old friend his black waistcoat for the investiture at Buckingham Palace.

Secure in his new eminence, Olivier could afford to be gracious. He wrote to Gielgud, offering embarrassed apologies that he had beaten him to the supreme theatrical accolade; then, with Richardson, he too began lobbying with the authorities to ensure that this omission would also be rectified. It was to take an absurdly long six years, supposedly because of his homosexuality, before Gielgud was finally knighted in the Coronation Honours List of 2 June 1953. Noël Coward, undisputed doyen of his profession at the time, and still unknighted for similar reasons, was another recipient of an Olivier letter, virtually seeking his permission to accept. Would Coward, Olivier wondered, be "hurt with me beyond repair if I just had not got what it took to turn it down"? Coward's response, of course, was gracious; though he had to wait even longer, until only three years before his death in 1973, for the accolade. Coward, in fact, remained rather less exercised about such matters than his protégé. In 1957, when Olivier proudly mentioned that he was to be made an honorary Doctor of Letters by Oxford University, Coward immediately replied, "Doctor of four letters, I presume?" [16]

Photographs of Olivier's visit to the Palace with Vivien to receive his knighthood from King George VI later that summer show his hair cropped and dyed blond, for by then he was filming *Hamlet* at Denham for del Giudice. The thinking behind the blond hair is revealing about Olivier's professional opinion of himself as he reached his fortieth birthday:

> In film work, my preference is for the job of director. I would have liked to have found an actor of sufficient standing to carry the role on whom I could have impressed my interpretation of the character of Hamlet without the actor resenting it. For myself, I feel that my style of acting is more suited to stronger character roles, such as Hotspur and Henry V, rather than to the lyrical, poetic role of Hamlet.
>
> In the end I thought it simpler to play Hamlet myself, but one reason why I dyed my hair was so as to avoid the possibility of Hamlet later being identified with me. I wanted audiences seeing the film to say, not "There is Laurence Olivier dressed like Hamlet" but "That is Hamlet." [17]

Olivier was also, as some critics were to point out, unusually old for the part, which had defeated several previous attempts to translate it from stage to screen. Seven years before, Leslie Howard had failed to find backing for his own *Hamlet*, in which he would have directed himself; and Hitchcock had failed to persuade anyone in Hollywood that he was serious about a modern-dress version starring Cary Grant. More recently, Gielgud had turned down several invitations from Hollywood to film *Hamlet*. He had walked out of the Leslie Howard–Norma Shearer *Romeo and Juliet* after ten minutes; and after seeing Max Reinhardt's film of *A Midsummer Night's Dream* he wrote to Peggy Ashcroft: "It's really like having an operation to see anything you really love, like this superb play, butchered in such an unspeakable way." [18]

Olivier, undeterred and besotted with the role of director, had first thought of filming *Hamlet* while he was still making *Henry V*. As the Old Vic triumphs had consolidated his stage reputation, del Giudice had remained an enthusiastic patron; a phone call from Zurich on New Year's Day 1947 confirmed that he had come up with the financial backing. The following month, trying to cheer an ailing Cecil Beaton when both were house-guests of the Duff Coopers in Paris, Olivier talked him through his conception of the film in a series of "schoolboy phrases" and "prep-school sounds" which astonished Beaton. "With arms flailing he emulated with a big 'whoosh' a great curtain falling down here – a pillar 'pffutting' down there – 'a hell of a lot of smoke and emptiness all over the place'." There were pops, bangs and a chorus of "corks being drawn, of internal combustion explosions, 'farts' and all sorts of other coarse noises.... 'A great blob here (bang! bangho!)' – 'A great cowpat here (bungho!)'." Beaton ruminated:

> It was a most gymnastic performance we were treated to. Larry's imitations have about them something of the original clown or, at least, the essential entertainer, who can be found in some remote music-hall or performing in the street outside a pub. This was the real Larry – the mummer, ale-drinking Thespian – not the rather overwhelmed and shy cipher with wrinkled forehead that goes out into society. [19]

From his sick-bed Beaton took a proxy role in Olivier's excited planning of the film's "abstract" look with the set designer Roger Furse. Also in Olivier's mind at the time was the next stage production he was planning for himself and Vivien, Sheridan's *The School for Scandal*, which they would take to Australia before a West End run. It soon became clear that Furse would still be too preoccupied with *Hamlet* to take on the design of the Sheridan; though Olivier made no secret about his first choice, Beaton was thrilled to be asked to take over both set and costumes. He hoped it might be the beginning of a lasting association with Britain's most illustrious theatrical partnership. So Beaton was delighted, as planning progressed, to become an Olivier intimate over working weekends at Notley, the recipient of the offstage confessions of the gentleman-farmer. Fresh from a session on drainage problems with his manager, the reflective, rural Olivier would confide his innermost professional thoughts to Beaton, who concluded in his diary one weekend that:

> It is rare to come across an actor whose self-assurance doesn't border on crass bumptiousness. Perhaps more by strength of character than natural ability he has succeeded even in developing his intellect. Now his problems are ones of how to sustain his success and how to save money for his old age. But the architecture of his professional life seems fairly solid.

By now Olivier had already arranged for Richardson and Burrell to carry on the Old Vic season without him. He took a quick break to direct Yolande Donlan and Hartley Power in *Born Yesterday*, the first stage play by his best man, Garson Kanin, whose first night at the Garrick drew further reassurance for his ambitions as a director. Then he took Vivien off for a month on the North Italian riviera, the first ten days of which were a vacation he had cunningly built into the planning phase of the film. Del Giudice, aware that the success of the project involved kid-glove treatment of Vivien, had booked the Oliviers a sumptuous five-room suite at the Miramare Hotel in Santa Margherita Ligure. Here, after their brief break, they were joined by the *Hamlet* team, most of them veterans of *Henry V*: set designer Furse and costume designer Carmen Dillon, technical adviser Reginald Beck and writer Alan Dent. To the rest of the *Hamlet* team left behind in England, the inner circle lucky enough to be head-quartered in Italy was known as "the O group".

Adaptation of the text was again the first hurdle: minimizing the damage done to Shakespeare as a four-and-a-half-hour play when reduced to a two-and-a-half-hour film. Olivier's goal was to make the story "easy to follow for people who are deterred by Shakespeare himself". Several characters made an abrupt exit; Cornelius and Voltimand, Reynaldo and the Second Gravedigger, and – most drastically, at Vivien's suggestion – Rosencrantz and Guildenstern were all dispensed with. Then out went Fortinbras, with the essentials of his closing speech given to Horatio. Great chunks of text, including such soliloquies as "Oh what a rogue and peasant slave am I", were reluctantly excised and other scenes moved. "To be or not to be" now came immediately after, rather than before, Hamlet's "Get thee to a nunnery" scene with Ophelia, to sow the seeds of Hamlet's apparent madness earlier and sharpen his motives for brooding upon self-slaughter. Justifying all this through verbose mists of guilt, Alan Dent wrote: "The film ... is, at root, a visual art. What we see is now, and I think always will be, more important than what we hear." [20]

Olivier's screen *Hamlet* was to discover the stunningly simple truth that Shakespeare's soliloquies might have been written for the cinema, which can solve all the old problems of staging them effectively by presenting them as "spoken thought" – the words heard from unmoving lips, as the character's face reflects his inner emotions. But even Olivier's own favourite soliloquy, "How all occasions do inform against me", is missing from the final cut of the film, causing great wonderment among the critical and academic fraternities. He was later to say he had to "tear my heart out" to cut the speech, making elaborate justification for its absence on the grounds that "it was dangerous to get discursive there, from a film put-together point of view". The sad but amusing truth, however, is that Olivier *did* film the speech, on horseback on the beach below his clifftop castle; but when he viewed the rushes, he saw to his dismay that the horse had closed his camera eye and looked ineffably bored throughout. There being no time in the schedule to reshoot it, the speech had to go. Recognizing the violence he had done to "the greatest of all plays", Olivier hoped the film would be regarded "as an 'Essay in Hamlet' and not as a film version of a necessarily abridged classic".

He opted for black-and-white photography, partly because he and Furse were conceiving the castle of Elsinore as a series of moody monochrome corridors, but more because of its greater ability than colour to make use of deep focus. If *Henry V* had been a series of missal illustrations, Olivier saw *Hamlet* as an engraving. For large ensemble scenes, lengthy takes and atmospheric long shots, deep focus seemed an especially invaluable tool in building a feeling of doom around the castle; it was essential to create a sense of space and variety even though the action of the play barely gets beyond the moat. In his role as deep-focus director, Olivier was to prove especially proud of what has been called "the longest-distance love scene ever shot", in which Ophelia is seen approaching Hamlet from a distance of over 150 feet, passing gradually through a series of arches, behind one of which hides her father.

William Walton was again commissioned to compose the score, while associate producer Anthony Bushell set about assembling a distinguished cast. Olivier had already snapped up his first choices for Claudius and Polonius, Basil Sydney and Felix Aylmer. Enchanted by his performance as the bowler-hatted Shell in *Odd Man Out*, Olivier had wanted the Irish character-actor F. J. McCormick for the gravedigger, but he had died while the O team were still in Italy; so Bushell instead signed on an equally popular English character-actor, Stanley Holloway, to take on his first Shakespearean role. Two young actors of great promise, Norman Wooland and Terence Morgan, were hired as Horatio and Laertes. Gertrude and Ophelia were the only parts still uncast when Olivier returned from Italy.

The Queen involved delicate problems; she had to be a powerful actress, old enough in appearance to be Hamlet's mother, yet attractive enough to have moved Claudius to kill his brother. Bushell negotiated with many leading actresses on both sides of the Atlantic before finally settling on a striking English girl called Eileen Herlie, thirteen years younger than her screen son. Ninety-four Ophelias were interviewed and thirty-three tested before Olivier finally signed his original choice, Jean Simmons, whom he had spotted in David Lean's *Great Expectations*. Simmons had never even seen a Shakespeare play, let alone performed in one, but Olivier sensed, as had Lean, that she had a natural screen presence which required only firm direction. The gamble was to pay off, which was just as well, for the condition for her release by Rank was stern: she would be available for only thirty days, before flying to Fiji for her next project.

That and Olivier's commitment to leading the Old Vic company on an Australian tour the following January made the filming schedule precariously tight. Work started at Denham in early May, under conditions of great secrecy. Olivier's "closed-doors" set irritated the press and, of course, the studio publicity department, but he was worried about the tight six-month schedule and happily aware that a cloak-and-dagger atmosphere would heighten public anticipation. The evidence of his actors is that life on the *Hamlet* set was good-humoured and professional, but less light-hearted than on *Henry V*. The new Sir Laurence – duly preoccupied in his triple role as producer, director and star – had also become a little aloof from his colleagues. He was courtesy itself to work with, but much less fun than when he was "one of the lads"; now they could feel the atmosphere stiffen whenever he was about.

They were not to know that Olivier's domestic life was on another downturn. Vivien had been working – filming *Anna Karenina* – but despite the reassuring presence of Ralph Richardson, it had been an extremely unhappy set, full of petty feuds among miserably miscast actors. Korda had wanted Olivier to play Vronsky, but his other commitments had forced him to withdraw. With Olivier to play against, Vivien's performance might have taken on more conviction. As it was the finished product disappointed her so much that she became obsessed with parallels between her own life and Karenina's, and plunged back into depression. It was most unlike Vivien to fail to join her own guests at a party after the premiere. Olivier's preoccupation with *Hamlet* gave him an excuse not to take too much notice, but the invisible rhythms of his life had become heavy again.

His mood was not helped by another accident: cracking his ankle while leaping on to the Elsinore battlements had him in crutches on the set for several weeks, and the shooting schedule was rearranged to bring forward the few scenes in which Hamlet did not figure. But he was fully recovered by the time they arrived at the play's final, climactic moment, which Olivier had kept to the end of the shooting schedule for reasons he now chose to reveal. On the characteristic premise that "it is not always easy to make something look dangerous without its actually being so", he was contemplating an act of bravado daring even by his standards.

Gertrude lies poisoned, Laertes stabbed with the poisoned rapier and Hamlet himself is mortally wounded by the time he finally avenges his father – killing Claudius with the famous cry of "The point envenomed too! Then, venom, to thy work." Olivier had decided to enact this from a great height – by jumping down on to Claudius, arms spread like an avenging angel, from a raised platform some fifteen feet above him. While planning the leap, he had borne in mind five possible outcomes: "I could kill myself; I could damage myself for life; I could hurt myself badly enough to make recovery a lengthy business; I could hurt myself only slightly; or I could get away with it without harm." Odds of four to one he was prepared to face.

Such bold realism excited everyone except the ageing Basil Sydney, who as Claudius was to bear the brunt of it; when he discovered that the moment would be shot from behind Claudius's back, he pleaded for a stand-in, perhaps even a stunt man, to be used in his place. So a professional double-act was duly hired, one an acrobat to help Olivier plan his jump, the second a strong-man named George Crawford to receive its impact. Planning was meticulous: Olivier had to ensure that his sword passed over Crawford's left shoulder, and that his own right eye avoided the king's dangerously encrusted crown. There could, for obvious reasons, be no rehearsal, and only one take. When it finally came to the big moment Bushell and Furse turned away, unable to watch. Olivier was in the air before he had reached the end of his line, and was amazed both to land in the right place and to find himself able to stand up, apparently intact. Then he heard groaning. It transpired that his full weight had caught Crawford right under the chin. The strong man was out cold, quite unconscious, and had lost two front teeth.

The scene, described by Olivier as "the only brave moment of my life", joined the lengthening list of great Olivier images when *Hamlet* was premiered at the Odeon, Leicester Square, on 10 May 1948, in the presence of almost the entire royal family. The King and Queen were there, with their daughters Elizabeth and Margaret, and Elizabeth's dashing new husband, Lieutenant Philip Mountbatten – but not Olivier, who sent his brother, sister and stepmother to represent him, as by then he was with the Old Vic in Australia. He was able to boast that he had kept to his production schedule (Miss Simmons had made it to Fiji on time) and his budget of £500,000. Although modest by today's standards, it represented a huge investment for J. Arthur Rank, who had again backed the film with del Giudice, at a time when his company had revealed a trading loss of £2 million over the previous six years. A businessman with little feel for

219

the artistic world in which he had sunk his fortune, Rank had backed *Hamlet* out of blind faith in Olivier, del Giudice and the *Henry V* balance sheets. When treated to a special preview, he had dismayed Olivier by seeming mightily bored; when the film ended, he said merely, "Thank you, Sir Laurence," and left.[21]

At an earlier production meeting Rank had asked for news from the closed set of *Hamlet*. One senior executive sought to reassure him by saying he had seen some rushes and they were "wonderful, Mr Rank. ... You wouldn't even know it was Shakespeare." A good many critics were to agree, notably the ever high-minded Eric Bentley, who called the film

> the very quintessence of dullness ... the film had no style: visually, it was simply grandiose in the academic manner. The Hamlet it gave us was an English gentleman with a public school education and a liking for his own handsome face. The only way Olivier indicates violent passion is by shouting.... The story was not told (they thought either that we knew it or that it doesn't matter); the situations were therefore simplified and attenuated, and the problem never had any serious existence.[22]

Olivier's Shakespeare films were "part of the horribly desecratory recent trend towards popularization-cum-prostitution of the Bard".

Prostitution or not, the popularization worked. *Hamlet* was an even more immediate commercial success than *Henry V*. Queues formed in Leicester Square, where it ran for six months, unaffected by a chorus of purists carping about the liberties taken with the text. When success in America followed – not to mention Australia, where Olivier had to go into hiding from over-enthusiastic fans – the superlatives were again in full flood. Even his old nemesis Sam Goldwyn (who, one imagines, would have taken some persuading to back the film) hailed Olivier as "the greatest living actor on stage and screen", and *Hamlet* as "without question the brightest spot on the drama of our day – perhaps of any day".

Over the years, however, Olivier's *Henry V* has worn better than his *Hamlet*. The broader visual canvas of the first film managed to absorb the staginess of some of the acting, as did the Globe Theatre framework, while the tighter frame of *Hamlet* if anything exaggerated it. The entire cast, except for Jean Simmons, were primarily stage actors; even Olivier himself, though more adept at miniaturizing for the camera, still prized a basically theatrical manner, especially in so theatrical a role. The film is above all so intensely stylized, again *à la* Eisenstein, that the great French director Jean Renoir was moved to complain that "the style confuses the issue".[23]

Even at the time, there were some dissenting voices. Homing in on Olivier's beloved deep-focus photography, John Mason Brown complained that at least forty precious minutes are squandered in travelogues up and down Mr Furse's palace. To sacrifice great language, to have innuendo dispensed with, and to lose key characters, speeches or scenes merely because so much time is wasted getting the actors from one part of the castle to another, is to be a Hamlet dislocated by being on location.[24]

Bernard Grebanier, in ironic mood, concurred: "In order to allow the camera to play lovingly with all that stonework at Elsinore, all those staircases, the raging sea, and especially, and oh so subtly!, Gertrude's bed, [Olivier] had to omit about a third of the play."[25] Olivier, he added acidly, had also absorbed Ernest Jones's Freudian interpretation of *Hamlet* "not wisely but too well".

Alan Wood, Rank's biographer, also pulled no punches:

> The normal use of focus in films dictates the attention of the eye to whatever point the director desires; with deep focus the eye is much more free (apart from the overriding compulsion of following movement) to study any part of the screen; just as a man in a theatre can look at any part of the stage, and study any of the actors on it. So the use of deep focus for *Hamlet* was, in a way, unfortunate.... It led me to the heretical opinion that Laurence Olivier is not a good screen actor.... For screen acting, in contrast to the theatre, the supreme virtue is naturalness. In *Hamlet* the audience was conscious throughout of Olivier's acting. ...[26]

But these were minority reports. As *Hamlet* scooped prizes at all the major film festivals, American newspaper verdicts ranged from "the greatest show on earth" (*The Star*) to "Hamlet puts Olivier at the top of his profession" (*New York Daily News*). It became the first foreign film to win Hollywood's Oscar for Best Picture and the first British film to scoop four Oscars – for Furse and Dillon, as well as Olivier for Best Actor (presented by Ethel Barrymore with a slight note of incredulity in her voice, as she considered Olivier's Hamlet inferior to that of her brother John). Olivier was especially touched at the end of a glorious year to be formally honoured by the nation of Denmark, invested as a Knight Commander of the Order of Danneborg.

Whatever the arguments about his performance, there can be no doubt that Olivier's imaginative energy, his insistence on detailed perfection and his constant questioning of established techniques led to the creation in these two films of works worthy of the name of masterpiece. His team of experienced professionals all paid public tribute to his remarkable leadership qualities, delving deep into their own areas of expertise, constantly questioning and challenging, always refusing to believe that the unprecedented or even the impossible could not be achieved. Said the most seasoned of them all, Reginald Beck: "One has often accepted a point of technique out of habit, rather than reasoning. But Larry would sweep away the dust of established prejudice with the impelling question 'Why?'"[27] And Alan Dent paid a florid public tribute to Olivier:

> Watching you in the studio, gaily or moodily at work – type of the true fastidious artist, ever and ever again stretching himself on the rack till perfection be found – I have often and often said to myself that this, unmistakably, is genius in action. For if that quality is not yours when you direct your own *Hamlet*, then I have never yet seen genius in an actor, director or man.[28]

No one summarized Olivier's achievement better than the great film critic of the day, James Agee, who had his reservations about Olivier's performance, about his approach as director and about the finished product. But he too paid due tribute to the sum of the parts, to an extraordinary achievement in both the short history of film and the long history of Shakespeare:

> A man who can do what Laurence Olivier is doing for Shakespeare – and for those who treasure or will yet learn to treasure Shakespeare – is certainly among the more valuable men in his time. In the strict sense, his films are not creative works of cinematic art: the essential art of living pictures is as overwhelmingly visual as the essential art of his visually charming pictures is verbal. But Olivier's films set up an equilateral triangle between the screen, the stage and literature. And between the screen, the stage and literature they establish an interplay, a shimmering splendour of the disciplined vitality which is an art.[29]

With his film in the can, and excited anticipation of its release on all sides, Olivier was riding the crest of a professional wave which had been gathering momentum for five remarkable years. Privately, too, despite what he saw as Vivien's mood-swings, he convinced himself that he was as content as he knew how to be. "From 1943 my fortunes seemed to be quite wondrous in their goodness, their completeness, their twofold richness. . . . I would boast to my close friends about this unblushingly and possibly with embarrassing frankness; it seemed ungrateful not to." Now, at the end of 1947, his contentment seemed "full to overbrimming. . . . I have everything, I would boast, so much more than anybody could deserve: the love of my life, more perfect than anyone could dream of; my career, after such laborious digging-in, yielding this fantastic harvest; a glorious house in the country; and two things I never asked for, a Rolls-Royce and a knighthood."

This last was not strictly true; even Olivier could admit that he had, in his way, petitioned for that knighthood. But he himself had also observed that "it is interesting how seldom life bestows equality of fortune in a man's public and his private life". And it was his closest friend Ralph Richardson who remarked to him, at various stages of his life and career, that he had "never known a fellow with such extremes of good and bad luck". In Olivier's fatalistic scheme of things, this meant that a surfeit of good luck had to be paid for with a strong dose of bad. At the end of this *annus mirabilis*, it seems, he himself could sense that the tide was about to turn.

CHAPTER 13

1947–8

By the end of 1947 the movement to form a National Theatre for Britain was fast gathering pace. A board had been set up under the chairmanship of Oliver Lyttelton, a member of Churchill's shadow cabinet, with the specific purpose of cajoling Attlee's Chancellor of the Exchequer, Sir Stafford Cripps, into funding a theatre to house a national repertory company. For the first time the notion of state subsidy of the arts had taken tangible form in the shape of an embryonic Arts Council. The Old Vic company, under the leadership of Olivier and Richardson, seemed the obvious pool of acting talent from which to form a company fit to institutionalize their art in the name of the nation.

Late in the year Olivier and Richardson represented their profession at a meeting with Lyttelton and his board, who had become anxious to discuss ways of getting the Old Vic more closely involved in its campaign. The discussion resulted in a twelve-year mandate to Olivier and Richardson to bring together a repertory company of actors capable of launching a British national theatre. As they strolled away for a drink afterwards, the two actors reminisced about Lilian Baylis, knowing how pleased she would have been to see her company finally acknowledged as the nucleus of the great National Theatre to come.

Then Richardson abruptly changed the mood with some highly prophetic thoughts:

> Of course you know, don't you, that all very splendid as it is, it'll be the end of us? It won't be our dear, friendly, semi-amateurish Old Vic any more. It'll be of government interest now, with some appointed intendant swell at

224

the top, not our sweet old friendly governors eating out of our hands and doing what we tell them. They're not going to stand for a couple of actors bossing the place around any more.... We shall be out, old cockie. But I still think we may have done the right thing.

Richardson's vision of the future, if not the National Theatre board's, was to come to pass sooner than either of them could expect. For the first time in five years these two great friends and partners were now about to go separate ways – Richardson to the richer pastures of Hollywood, Olivier to lead the company on a marathon adventure to the other end of the earth. In their minds, it was merely the end of the first phase of their stewardship of the Old Vic, which had proved far more successful than they had dared to imagine in 1943. Before parting, they reached an informal understanding that out of those next twelve years each would give six to the Old Vic, either separately or together. Both were as committed to the high life as to their art; and so to finance their commitment to the Old Vic, whose scant financial rewards neither saw any chance of improving, each would have to take substantial chunks of time off to make films. First chance to do so now fell to Richardson, while Olivier embarked on another project he saw as little less than a national duty.

"Why are you, the greatest actor in the world, taking a touring company to Australia of all places?" asked Sam Goldwyn, on hearing of Olivier's plans to lead the Old Vic company, plus Vivien, to Australia and New Zealand for ten months of 1948.[1] Scarcely renowned for its love of theatre – there was not one house in the entire sub-continent open year-round for live performance – Australia was also in anti-British mood. For an actor at the height of his powers and international acclaim it was hardly the most exciting, romantic or indeed useful venue to choose as a year-long showcase for his talents. Olivier's answer is not recorded in the detailed journal he kept in the early stages of what was to prove a most eventful episode. But it was Goldwyn's question, with its prophetic intimations of Antipodean angst, which would linger to haunt him.

The Australian tour was, in fact, the brainchild of one Sir Angus Gillan, head of the Dominions section of the British Council, following a visit he had made to Australia in the aftermath of the war. Sir Angus was concerned that the return of peace be celebrated in the Antipodes, and the anti-imperial sentiment softened, by the temporary export of the best entertainment Britain could offer. It would also serve as a symbol of British excellence to the Dominions, at a time when the break-up of Empire was threatening the prestige of the mother country. With Gillan's encouragement New Zealand's leading impresario, Dan O'Connor, visited London to see what could be arranged; he returned home with news of forthcoming visits from the Boyd Neel Dance Band, the Ballet Rambert –

and, best of all, the world-famous Old Vic company, led by the profession's most renowned and glamorous double-act, Sir Laurence Olivier and Vivien Leigh.

Behind the incongruity of the Oliviers, at the height of their lustrous fame and success, opting to leave it all behind for a year in the unglamorous Antipodes, lay the beginnings of an answer to Goldwyn's question. It was a chance for Olivier to try yet again to bolster his sagging relationship with Vivien, to restore some strength to their private partnership via their professional one. The more their love took on an institutionalized, public renown, the less it reflected any vestige of private truth. Olivier's huge capacity for adoration – both the giving and the receiving of it – had recently been devoted to his characters and his public respectively. Even he now saw that it was time to extend these courtesies to Vivien beyond the mere public display which had become a ritual in their lives. He still had romantic hopes that their grand passion could mature into a lasting bond. But even this aspiration, as always, was fatally founded on a much less romantic, career-minded notion: he could use the tour to build a new company for the Old Vic, and thus – his most cherished and secret dream – a nucleus of the first national theatre company to be formed in Britain. If the effort involved "a tumultuous welcome and an acceptable little package of dough", so much the better.

After a shaky winter, Vivien again seemed better. Her last major attack had coincided, curiously enough, with the announcement of Olivier's knighthood. Though she would now enjoy the distinction of being Lady Olivier, the honour simply meant he had again outshone her, and she took to expressing disdainful surprise that he had accepted it. At the time of his resentment of Richardson's knighthood, she had consoled Olivier with her strongly held belief that artists should not accept honours; that they would merely be compromised, even emasculated, by a metamorphosis into some kind of state-sanctioned, official performer. Now, to her horror, she saw how much Olivier's knighthood meant to him; it had transformed him more than ever into a consciously public personage, the private man more than ever subservient to the great national figure. Forty, moreover, seemed a tragically early age for this loss of innocence. Her husband's eyes, his most revealing assets in private as in public, no longer shone for her, except on public demand. They shone for himself, in the shape of the characters he played, and the legion of admirers who applauded and mobbed him wherever he went. All this merely made Vivien more petulant. When Cecil Beaton, enough of a traditionalist to mean it, stopped by on the set of *Anna Karenina* to congratulate her on becoming Lady Olivier, he was taken aback by the bleakness of her response: "I open the door. 'Oh, I'm so happy for you about the great news!' A face of fury is reflected in the mirror."[2]

Vivien's longest depression to date had lasted, on and off, right through the summer. Then the unusually cold end to 1947 caused renewed anxieties about her lung, soon solved by a family holiday in Cannes, at a villa lent them by Leigh Holman's brother. With Gertrude, Suzanne and Tarquin in tow, Vivien soon became her sparkling self again, and Olivier set his worries aside. He was especially touched to note the care she lavished on Tarquin, as she had at Notley that summer, little realizing that it was as much for his own benefit as his son's. He was still a distant and frightening figure to the boy, who longed desperately to find a way to express the love he felt for the father he also hero-worshipped; but the object of these filial affections seemed incapable of coping with them. As eleven-year-old Tarquin observed to his mother Jill on returning from one weekend at Notley: "Daddy seemed a little less frightened of me this time."

A party for "seventy intimate friends" marked the eve of the Oliviers' departure from their native shores. It was to be the longest period they had spent away since their marriage, and the first sustained period of being inseparably together, day and night. Vivien's sense of some doom, a premonition that this tour might mark the beginning of the end, proved infectious; as so often, Olivier responded to her mood. Next morning, St Valentine's Day, a throng of press and fans, not to mention the top-hatted station-master, gave the glittering couple and their forty-strong company a triumphant send-off from Euston, continued that afternoon in Liverpool, whence they set sail on the month-long voyage to Australia. A group of friends led north by their agent Cecil Tennant waved until long after the ss *Corinthic* had headed out across the Mersey sound, leaving both the Oliviers a feeling of being very alone.

They had few close friends in the company, apart from the husband-and-wife team of George Relph and Mercia Swinburne; most of the others were young protégés such as Peter Cushing and Terence Morgan. Although Olivier had encouraged them to bring their wives, finding backstage roles for those who were not actresses, he felt his leadership role too keenly to fraternize easily. "We are going to be a long time away," he told them, "in very close communication with each other, and we are all going to get miserable, and I want anybody with any kind of problems at all to please not bottle them up but bring them to us, and we'll try to sort them out."[3]

Beneath the considerable surface charm, perfectly genuine in its way, there now lay an assumption of superiority which could make his attempts at chumminess rather patronizing. Terence Morgan and his wife Georgina Jumel had even, somewhat embarrassingly, named their daughter Lyvia-Lee after the golden couple they so openly worshipped. There was also a clutch of young bachelors, notably Michael Redington and Dan Cunningham, who flocked adoringly around Vivien; to these less reverential members of the troupe their employers were known as "God and the Angel". That first evening the divine pair dined alone in their cabin – "Vivien not eating much," Olivier noted in his journal.⁴ Then he set off on a lone walk around deck in his duffle-coat, laden with premonitions of the trials ahead. "Poured bath, but went to bed without it. Read Logan Pearsall Smith's *English Aphorisms* for a while before turning out the light."

During the tour Vivien was to play Lady Teazle in *The School for Scandal*, Sabina in *The Skin of our Teeth* and Lady Anne in *Richard III*. She relished all three parts, Olivier knew, and she especially prized her first chance to act beside him onstage since their American *Romeo and Juliet* eight years before. Taking every precaution to avert another disaster, he had carefully selected roles well within her range and was ready to be scrupulous in humouring her every whim. But that night he already sensed that the trip would prove momentous, both personally and professionally. "It was in Australia", he would say to Vivien in later years, "that I lost you."

She cheered up visibly once they were at sea, creating quite a stir on the third evening of the voyage when at last she joined Olivier for dinner at the captain's table: "Vivien turned to me suddenly with an alarmingly wild look and said: 'Tonight I would like to play dominoes.'" Although he had promised the company a week's rest, Olivier's impatience soon got the better of him, and the next day he was negotiating rehearsal space with the purser, Mr Oliver (whose father happened to have been the captain of the *Titanic*). Soon he had imposed a rigid daily pattern: 10.30 to 12.45 rehearsing in the ship's dining saloon, which they then vacated so it could be rearranged for lunch, returning from 2.45 until teatime, when they moved to the Forward Lounge.

Olivier's log – more detailed, like so many, in its earlier entries – records the difficulties he experienced with Vivien in mastering the complexities of the Teazles' combative dialogue. He worried about Sheridan's stage directions – "it seems to me he indicates least movement where [the text] seems to require most" – and read Ibsen's *The Wild Duck* with a view to directing Vivien in it at the Old Vic the following season. *Richard III* rehearsals were also well under way by 1 March, when they arrived for a two-day stopover in Cape Town, the highlight of which was seeing their old friend Ivor Novello in his latest show, *Perchance to Dream*. "Vivien looking v. lovely in New Look black and white," noted her husband. "Lots of ripping applause from the publique on the way in."

Twelve days and 4,000 miles later the *Corinthic* finally docked at Perth, the starting-point of the tour. A freak heat-wave – for which they were sartorially, as in other ways, unprepared – added to the discomfort of their arrival, as they were jostled by press and fans hungry for a glimpse of glamour after the long austerity of the war years. Their last few hours at sea had seen huge junketings aboard the ship, blissfully unaware of the scale of the civic receptions ahead. "Woke at seven feeling worse than I remember since first evening of Irish whiskey with Roger and Dallas in Dublin 1943," wrote Olivier on the morning of 15 March, his first in Australia; "Vivien quite all right." After charming the necessary column inches out of an insatiable press corps, they were finally allowed to seek refuge at 16 Bellevue, the flat chosen by the advance party as their Perth base.

The theatre in which they were to launch the tour was a 2,280-seater cinema, the Capitol, specially converted for the occasion. It was immediately clear that there would be a shortage of dressing-rooms – only six available for some forty actors – so the Oliviers set a democratic example by settling for screened-off areas in the wings. He had nothing more than a chair and table sitting on a lone patch of carpet, while she dressed in a "cage" of wire netting and curtain which doubled as a quick-change area for other female members of the cast. Outside the queue for tickets stretched round several blocks, with hundreds of theatre-starved Australians ready to spend the night on the street before the box office opened; one woman was just complaining of the lack of buskers when she found much more exciting entertainment in the shape of the Oliviers themselves, come to visit their patient admirers.

As the first night approached Vivien lent a hand with the sewing and ironing of costumes – to the amazement of Australian trade unions as much as her fellow cast members – even though their daily routine amounted to an exhausting round of rehearsals, interviews and social events. It was quickly clear that they were more than mere celebrities; they soon took on the status of visiting royalty, as their tour became a dress rehearsal for that of King George VI and Queen Elizabeth scheduled for the following year. By night they were "eaten up" by mosquitoes as the heat-wave continued. Olivier's log constantly has him collapsing into bed utterly exhausted, but failing to sleep more than an hour or two as the insects – described by the company manager, Elsie Beyer, as "flying elephants" – got to work.

He was also suffering hot, sharp stabbing pains in his right foot, which had started during the voyage and were now worsened by the tight, buckled shoes designed by Cecil Beaton for his Sir Peter Teazle. "Foot v. painful," begins his entry for 20 March, the first night of The School for Scandal. "Audience very quiet and strangely disinclined to laugh. It became obvious during the evening that they could not hear. And we were really bashing over Sheridan's trifle like Hellzapoppin' with everything we knew and had...."

It was their first encounter with an audience unused to live theatre. Some were genuine theatre-lovers, starved of the real thing; others were the cream of society, intent on a high-visibility night out. Side by side in the front stalls were men in evening dress and others in open-neck shirts; many of the women wore their most expensive evening finery and glittering jewels. Expecting to see Olivier appear as himself, the majority had failed to recognize him under his latest cake of make-up, leaving his entrance painfully unapplauded, while the arrival onstage of the much more recognizable Vivien was hailed to the rafters. But there was, he recorded, "wonderful applause at the end", after which Olivier made one of his suavest curtain speeches – "Welcome to Old Vic ... first perf. of prod. in Perth ... added fillip being in cinema ... like reclaiming land from sea...." He even managed to mention a cricket victory that day by Western Australia before leading the entire cast in a rousing version of the national anthem. That night he recalled with gratitude some advice from Danny Kaye: "If you prepare every speech you are asked to make, you'll have a nervous breakdown. If you make enough lousy speeches – lovely! They'll stop asking you to make any more."[5]

The Perth schedule called for two weeks of the Sheridan, while the heavier sets for *Richard III* and *The Skin of our Teeth* went on ahead by sea to Adelaide. But rehearsals for the other two plays continued. On 22 March Olivier's foot was more painful than ever – "Run through Richard in afternoon with foot up" – but he had organized the installation of a voice amplification system in the Capitol. This involved apologies to the audience – "If we all went around with binoculars strapped to our eyes, soon forget to see etc." – but seemed to heighten their appreciation. 23 March was a typically civic and ceremonial day, the evening's performance being preceded by a Lord Mayor's reception in the morning – speeches required of both of them – and an afternoon lecture by Olivier at the university on "The Use of Poetry in Drama". "Delved mildly into uses of poetry, structural and practical, rhythmical and atmospherical...." At one point Vivien seized the microphone and, to his alarm, began a homily to the students on the advantages of marriage. He noted in his journal that in private she was making "the most damned awful fuss" about the pace of the tour, "but I think she's beginning to like it; anyway have tiny feeling she could not be discouraged even if that were necessary".

By the end of the Perth fortnight, Olivier's foot showed an unexpected improvement, so much so that he was able to perform the "little dance" he had choreographed for himself as Teazle, "instead of my comic would-be old man act which I was rather enjoying". Vivien was still not into the part as much as he would have liked: "loosening up, but she must bubble with delicious laughter both inner and audible". But still he thought the show "much better" and the audiences certainly loved it. Olivier himself was compelled, with suitably loquacious apologies, to call a halt to the prolonged ovation on the last night, for fear of missing the plane waiting to take them on to Adelaide. They left Perth with box-office proceeds of £15,000, needing a motor-cycle escort to the airport, where a huge, adoring crowd sang "Auld Lang Syne" until they finally took off at 1 a.m. Signing autographs to the last, the Oliviers had themselves been surprised by the intensity of the adulation offered them in Perth; during those two weeks they had received over 1,000 letters and been mobbed everywhere they went. But the residents of Bellevue, at first delighted to have such eminent neighbours, were glad to see them go. It was not only the late-night noise from the interminable post-theatre parties of which they complained; the Oliviers' domestic disagreements had apparently grown louder, more furious and more frequent. Their night-time bouts of mutual abuse could be heard right down the street.

After the seven-hour flight the company and its leaders arrived in Adelaide exhausted – the insomniac Vivien had awoken them all to see the glorious airborne sunrise – only to discover that the opening of *The Skin of our Teeth* had been brought forward a day. Though delighted with their venue, the "divine" 1,450-seat Theatre Royal, Olivier was worried about the schedule, and grew more so when none of the *Skin* lighting plot worked on the one day set aside for its rehearsal. Only when his lighting technician, Bill Bundy, discovered that the plans were back to front did everything at last begin to go smoothly. The first night on 12 April was a great personal success for Vivien, with Olivier noting: "V is wonderful – better than ever." The content of the play, however, caused outraged controversy in the columns of the Adelaide papers, which Olivier deftly deflected in his "longer and longer" curtain speeches: "A picture gallery must have its Rembrandts *and* its Henry Moores."

The Adelaide sojourn was punctuated by delightful tastes of the great Australian outdoors – Olivier's journal waxes lyrical about his first sight of a kangaroo – as well as an ever heavier civic burden. Governors and high commissioners were anxious to entertain them in the highest style, all the more encouraged to do so by the extraordinary public response to the Oliviers' presence. The fortnight's run had been sold out even before they arrived; the box office said they could have filled the house every night for ten weeks. Even the week's run of *The Skin of our Teeth* in Adelaide saw queues of over 1,000 people outside the theatre, many of whom had slept on the pavement overnight. One woman flew 2,000 miles from Darwin to seek a ticket, despite a critical response typified by: "Quite frankly, what the play was about or what was intended I have not the faintest conception. To say I was bored almost to tears would be to put it mildly." When Olivier opened in *Richard III*, the performance all Australia was clamouring to see, now with the added bonus of Vivien as Lady Anne, a crowd of 8,000 gathered simply to watch the audience enter the theatre. The stars, in the interests of self-preservation, had taken to slipping in and out of a back door.

Olivier had refined and altered the original Old Vic production in a number of ways, and was especially pleased by the new casting of George Relph as Buckingham and Peter Cushing as Clarence. But there were two innovations in the climactic fight scene that week which started as accidents, prompting such successful spontaneous effects that they became permanent. On the first night Olivier's sword broke at the hilt early in the battle; so many of the other actors leapt forward with replacements that the moment took life as an added token of Richard's authority, even in defeat. Then, apparently recalling a famous gesture of Edmund Kean's Richard, Olivier in his death throes unexpectedly threw his sword at Richmond, now played by Dan Cunningham.

There were those in the company who thought that this gesture, which also became a permanent feature of the production, really arose from less theatrical emotions. Cunningham had been paying a great deal of attention to Vivien. This was nothing unusual; at the height of her fame and beauty, she was often to be seen surrounded by a galaxy of young admirers. What was unusual, and made some of the Old Vic regulars uneasy, was the fact that Cunningham's feelings appeared to be returned.

As yet it was an innocent flirtation, though it alarmed the company and rallied them further behind Olivier, who seemed too busy to notice as he shouldered the considerable burden of his leadership role, both as an emissary for the homeland and a "father" to his troops. Their second weekend in Adelaide saw him host an almost too lavish party, all oysters and champagne, for the fifth wedding anniversary of Peter and Helen Cushing. Cast birthdays too were the subject of great celebrations. Everyone had been asked to let the Oliviers know their birth date in a rather arch rhyme – one couplet of which summed up how the celestial couple, scarcely the best of parents to their own children, now saw themselves:

> A lonely birthday is no joko,
> And we "Parentis" are "in loco" ...

Vivien's success as Sabina had seemed to cheer her, and their last few days in Adelaide were perhaps the happiest of the trip. For once she was Olivier's equal in the public regard – a status reinforced in private by his unhappiness with his own performance opposite her as Antrobus. "I wanted to play the part so much I hate disappointing myself in it," he recorded in his journal. The only other shadow over their farewell to

Adelaide, marked by an uproariously boozy visit to a vineyard, was the prospect of what lay ahead in Melbourne: an eight-week stay, performing all three plays in their travelling repertoire. If they had found it all rather hard work so far, they knew the worst was yet to come.

While the company travelled by train, the Oliviers decided to take a two-day drive to Melbourne, through countryside Vivien described in a letter to "Binkie" Beaumont as "so Dali-esque as to be incredible". They visited the remote house in which their friend Robert Helpmann had been born, where Olivier lamented that there were "never never no kangaroos". Instead he had to make do with "really wonderful pasture country, brown hills of dry grass cut by cypress windbreaks, always high mountains in the distance and always cream, dirty ochre and black dairy cattle in foreground". On their arrival in Melbourne that evening, 19 April, the contrast could not have been greater, as they were immediately swept into another, even more intense, round of press conferences and receptions.

Melbourne, if anywhere in Australia, was the post-war centre of residual anti-British feeling; its citizens, Olivier wrote to John Burrell, were "piss-elegant and nervously smug". Immediately there was some aggression from the huge press corps gathered to cover their arrival. A spate of questions jarred Olivier's patriotic instincts by beginning: "Now that Britain is finished. . . . " For "a wearing hour and a half" both worked hard – and successfully – to charm the baying pack into submission. "Vivien carried the wretched thing off with superlative charm," acknowledged her husband, so much so that one columnist present told her readers next morning: "Never, and I mean NEVER, in a long and somewhat disillusioning career, have I ever seen the men and women of the press fall so heavily, hook, line and sinker, for the charm of a couple they were all keyed up to resent."

But Olivier's quasi-ambassadorial status was beginning to get out of hand. By now he was being asked to inspect troops, even take salutes, and one Sunday afternoon he made an overtly political speech on the twin themes of monarchy and empire to an audience of 3,000 at an Empire youth rally in Melbourne Town Hall. Then on 24 April the couple were flown to Canberra to take part in the capital's Anzac Day celebrations. Their host for the day was no less than the Prime Minister, Ben Chifley, whom Olivier drily summed up as "amiable, very, if protected by an armour plating of political mysterioso". They lunched with the Governor-General, William McKell ("affable in manner, rather resembling a Peter Ustinov impersonation"), and took tea with most of Chifley's cabinet. That evening they had been invited to speak at a Food For Britain rally, and Olivier, warming to his new role, had decided to risk a defiant reply to the ubiquitous suggestions that his beloved homeland was done for. His self-confidence dimmed by his tiredness, he asked Chifley over tea to glance through the text of the speech he proposed to deliver. With "hooded" eyes, the Prime Minister demurred, muttering: "Oh, I would have thought just a few impromptu remarks. . . . "

Undeterred, Olivier stuck to his prepared speech that evening, before an audience of 6,000 people. Looking back now at the text of what he said, it is a graphic example not only of his Churchillian strain at its most virulent, but of the symbolic, quasi-royal role he had taken on in Australia. It is astonishing to hear a mere actor telling one of the Dominions, in front of its Prime Minister: "Britain is not finished. She is merely doing what she has done throughout history – starting again." Nor, he went on, was she looking for pity: "If one of your most loving relations in the Mother Country thought for a moment that any of your great kindnesses was provoked by pity, they would hope that not another food parcel, and not even a thought or a sigh, would come from Australia." Chifley was unamused. Despite a charming rendition of Shakespeare's Sonnet 116 by Vivien, whom Olivier described as looking "wonderful in pale lime green and a blood-red rose at her waist", the evening ended on an awkward note, and they learnt next day that radio coverage of his remarks had been cut short in the middle. Small wonder that the first Melbourne performance of *Richard III* two days later was "the flattest I have ever known", which left him "very depressed".

It was the last entry Olivier was to make in his Australian diary. From here on, "the strain, which was to mount steadily, was becoming too great to make it any pleasure to sit down at the end of a heavy day to record events". Both were so exhausted that they were becoming ill; to public indignation, Vivien had to let Georgina Jumel take over Sabina for a week, and Olivier himself cancelled four performances of *Richard III*. The company, too, were beginning to wilt on their treadmill. The only way to sustain them through the last six weeks in Melbourne was to rearrange the subsequent schedule to include a week's holiday in Tasmania, before moving on to Sydney and the most demanding sojourn of the entire tour.

But before they left Melbourne Olivier's status was enhanced yet further by the Australian premiere of his film of *Hamlet*, a print of which had been brought out by Cecil Tennant. Vivien, by now at loggerheads with the company manager, Elsie Beyer, was pleased to have Tennant around for moral support. The *Hamlet* premiere could not have come at a worse moment. Just as her self-confidence had been boosted by her success as Sabina, she was powerfully reminded yet again of Olivier's greater talent and versatility; for the first time, moreover, she had to sit with very mixed emotions through Jean Simmons's beguiling performance as Ophelia. And so began another downward curve.

Forcing the smiles with
Vivien, both onstage in
The Sleeping Prince, 1953,
and offstage as Britain's
theatre royals

The great 1955 Stratford
season: as Malvolio (ABOVE
LEFT), Macbeth (ABOVE) and
Titus Andronicus (with Vivien
as Lavinia)

Fun and games for charity, with Vivien and
Danny Kaye (ABOVE) in a *Night of a Hundred
Stars*; but for the master of disguise, even a
drag act (RIGHT) is a serious business

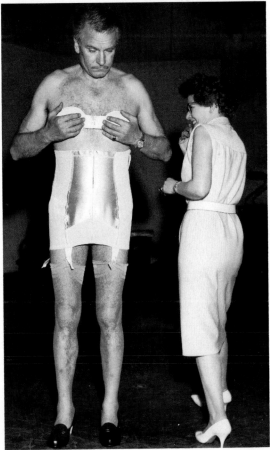

All smiles onscreen
(ABOVE) but tension off
(LEFT) directing and co-
starring with Marilyn
Monroe in *The Prince and
the Showgirl*, 1956

1957: *Vita nuova* onstage as Archie Rice in *The Entertainer* and off with Joan Plowright (as his daughter in the film)

1961: With his new wife, Joan Plowright, on Broadway, where she is winning awards in *A Taste of Honey* and he in *Becket*, at first in the title role (BELOW LEFT) with Anthony Quinn as Henry II, then as the King (BELOW RIGHT) with Arthur Kennedy as Becket

Two new theatres to run: Chichester, 1962 (ABOVE) and the National Theatre of Great Britain (BELOW), with architect Denys Lasdun

1963–4: Three early roles at the National Theatre: (LEFT) Astrov in *Uncle Vanya*, (BELOW LEFT) Othello and (BELOW) Solness in Ibsen's *The Master Builder*

Their love had become such public property that there was less and less time – and inclination – for it to grow in private. Olivier's remarks to his journal about Vivien in Australia are curiously impersonal. He writes always of the public beauty, the "enchanting" charmer, the "wonderful" actress. If this were deliberate objectivity, with a view to publication, it also bespoke the ever more impersonal nature of his feelings for her. He was tired of her unpredictability, her tantrums, her moods; she sensed a withdrawal on his part, a distancing of his real self from her as he sheltered behind his leadership role and his public standing. The knighthood became ever more of a barrier between them. The more Olivier grew exultant in its dignity, the more Vivien came to hate it and to insist on remaining plain Vivien Leigh. To her, Olivier's title was an uncomfortable symbol of the fact that he was now the property of his public, and happily so, rather than hers.

If this sometimes insecure man had derived self-confidence from her all these years, her reward now was to have her own steadily eroded. Olivier had drawn his colour from Vivien for so long that it had left her a pale shadow of the woman who had once overwhelmed him. Their love had become ritualistic; it was required of them. To him this was another role, an easy one to play, which added spice to his other professional rewards; to her it was simply not enough to live on with any degree of content or fulfilment. She sought refuge in a protective coterie of admiring young friends, Dan Cunningham high among them, which again left her little or no time alone with Olivier. The more they posed for the photographs required of great lovers, holding hands and looking adoringly into each other's eyes, the more each in their different way – she much more than he – knew that in truth their love was doomed.

For the strain which prevented Olivier continuing his journal went beyond his hideously taxing public and professional schedule. It served as a convenient camouflage when the document was published four years later in Felix Barker's semi-official biography of the Oliviers, the dustjacket of which described them as "two people sincerely dedicated to their art, to their profession and to each other". By then the marriage was under more strain than ever and would last only three more years. The seeds of the final decline – the reason Olivier would tell Vivien he "lost" her in Australia – were sown at just the moment the diary peters out. Clearly the Oliviers gave their biographer scant official detail of their first meeting with a young Australian actor called Peter Finch, with whom Vivien was to be desperately in love by the time the book was published.

It had, of course, been a delusion to hope that the stopover in Tasmania could be restorative. There was a week of the Sheridan in Hobart's charming little Theatre Royal; there was the reassuring presence of Cecil

Tennant, whom they both begged to stay on, largely to avoid being left alone together; and there was even a four-day break at Surfer's Paradise, though a large contingent of press and public somehow seemed to have got in on the secret. Four days off were enough for Olivier to recharge his batteries, despite the freezing weather, to cope with an arrival in Sydney more frenetic than ever, and the return to the role of a public couple whose private life had all but ceased to exist. They still had their irresistibly physical moments – a "Do Not Disturb" sign on their dressing-room door would send affectionately knowing nudges around the company – and the sheer strength of their emotions about each other caused all around them, even their close friends, still to believe in their great love. But in private it had long since begun to drown in its own myth.

"I suppose I had encouraged it, oh, quite innocently at first," lamented Olivier thirty years later, recalling the first time Peter Finch called on them backstage in Sydney. All over Australia they had heard praise of Finch's work; in a country with virtually no live theatre of its own he had won the Macquarie Award, an Australian radio "Oscar", twice running in 1946–7. Now he was winning further fame with the Century Theatre in Sydney, directing and starring in a series of classics he had boiled down to one hour for performance to office and factory workers in their lunch breaks.

Ever on the hunt for new talent – he had already auditioned the young Keith Michell, then teaching at the Adelaide Boys High School, and secured him a place at the Old Vic School in London – Olivier was eager to see Finch in action. So when he received an invitation from the Century Theatre's manager to see the twenty-four-year-old prodigy in the part of Argan in Molière's *Le Malade Imaginaire* (Olivier in his memoirs wrongly remembered it as *Tartuffe*), he was only too keen to fit it into their busiest civic schedule yet. Despite the packed hall and the uncomfortable seats, Olivier found himself watching "as brilliant a performance . . . in as expert a production as could be imagined". Though suspecting that Finch's "clever ballet-dancer wife . . . had something to do with it", he afterwards astonished the young Australian company with his enthusiasm and extended to Finch a momentous invitation to "look me up if you ever come to London".

Once the Olivier roadshow had settled in Sydney, they often sought escape from the "blue-rinse and brandy-clusters set" by letting Peter Finch take them to sundry low dives, where they could relax in the company of the only fellow actors they met in the entire sub-continent. By the time they left, Olivier's casual invitation to look him up had become a firm offer of a £100-a-week job. He had cabled Cecil Tennant, now managing director of the newly formed Laurence Olivier Productions Ltd, instructing him to put Finch under a three-year contract if he were to arrive in Britain before them. As things turned out, he would follow in their wake with almost indecent haste.

To add to his woes, Olivier was by now on crutches again. At the second Sydney performance of *Richard III*, a Saturday matinee, he overdid his whiplash attack on Cunningham's Richmond, slipped and fell in agony. Word went around town that he had broken his leg, but X-rays revealed a torn cartilage. He got through the evening performance on morphine, then found a solution to the rest of the run – he did not want to miss any more performances – by having the backstage team build him a period crutch. This soon proved an effective prop with which to rejuvenate a role which, he confided in a letter to Burrell, was beginning to stale. One junior company member who could testify to this was George Cooper, playing the minor role of Brackenbury; Olivier lashed out at him with the crutch one evening and broke it over his back. The audience, of course, loved it. The Olivier crutch quickly passed into Australian folklore; it became a favourite device for political cartoonists, and even a fashionable affectation among Sydney's smart young set. So *Richard* audiences knew it was an ingenious expedient to overcome a genuine injury, all of which served merely to add to the Olivier magic.

The man himself, for once, drew little comfort from the addition of this dimension to the Olivier phenomenon. In his fatalistic way, he believed it was all part of some conspiracy of the Furies; when things were going wrong, it was typical of his body to "jump on the bandwagon". Worn down by the performances, the speeches and the receptions, and by the strain of acting out his phoney public devotion to Vivien, he was in no shape to cope with the next thunderbolt to strike him, which now arrived from the direction he least expected.

It was on the morning of 15 July, a Thursday when he faced two performances of *Richard III*, that Olivier received a package from London containing a brief covering letter from Lord Esher, chairman of the Old Vic, and an internal memorandum notifying him in the most impersonal terms that the Board of Governors had decided to dispense with the services of Olivier, Richardson and Burrell as directors. It was five years since they had taken on the job and it was time for a change. "Time, in its tiresome way, has marched on since you have been away. . . . I am sorry to bother you with these things," wrote Esher by way of explaining the *Private and Confidential Memorandum on Future Administration* which amounted to Olivier's notice of dismissal.

"We fully realize", added Esher in a cursory gracenote, "the sacrifice you have made and the unceasing and exhausting work that the great position you have made for yourself entails." But the memo's four closely

237

typed pages merely summed up immediate plans for the Old Vic, hinted at its important role in the development of a National Theatre and argued that it could no longer be administered "by men, however able, who have other calls upon their time and talent". The triumvirate was to be replaced by a full-time administrator, answerable to his governmental paymasters and banned from acting or directing "save in very exceptional circumstances"; an artistic director, appointed annually, would work under his supervision. These arrangements were the beginning of the "corporate entity" necessary to a fledgling National Theatre, and appeared to render all artistic decisions subject to a Civil Service power of veto.

Olivier was so thunderstruck that at first "hysterical laughter" seemed the only response. The tone of Esher's letter, couched in "the brightest, jolliest terms", seemed "so ironical that ... laughter was a reflex action". Here he was 14,000 miles away, building up a new Old Vic company and earning the theatre some welcome revenue in the process, and he had been fired quite without warning. He felt, as he eventually wrote to Esher, "more than a little woeful ... apt to picture oneself as a pioneer disowned by his country in the middle of a very distant campaign". Sensing that a stiff upper lip would have its effect on so English a figure, he also added a rather pained report from the battlefield that he had been "at some pains" to train the new company "to the best of my ability", as "one has become accustomed to thinking of the Old Vic in terms of continuity".

But first he cabled Burrell: "OH ME I SEE THE DOWNFALL OF OUR HOUSE." Back in London, the third member of the triumvirate was fighting a losing battle to co-ordinate a counter-attack. It was no coincidence, as Burrell pointed out in cables to Olivier in Australia and Richardson in California, that the board had decided to act while their two leading men were as far away as they could be and prevented by commitments from making any dramatic flights home. "IMPORTANT WE REACT IN UNITED WAY", Burrell's cable urged his colleagues, "AND AVOID ATTEMPTS DRIVE WEDGES BETWEEN US WHILE SEPARATED." (Esher had not told Burrell that he was sending copies of the memorandum to Richardson and Olivier, with the inevitable result that Richardson at first thought Burrell had been in on the London plot. The truth, as he cabled desperately to both his partners, was that the memo had been prepared "in camera, without my knowledge".)

Burrell formally demanded that the board take no further action until Olivier and Richardson were back to speak for themselves – which would not be until November, another four months away. "It was indeed unfortunate", Esher blandly replied, "that two out of the three of the directors of the Old Vic Theatre Co. should have been out of the country at the time when these important matters came up for consideration." He agreed to delay final action, in the certain knowledge that his tactics had worked.

Separated, distracted and outmanoeuvred, each member of the triumvirate realized that there was no action they could take without making the matter public, which would enable the board to complain that confidences had been breached. They would be accused of conduct unworthy of their office and, no doubt, of sour grapes. The battle had been lost before they were even aware that there was one to be fought.

Richardson – who had received his copy of the memo in Hollywood, where he was filming *The Heiress* with Olivia de Havilland, Montgomery Clift and Miriam Hopkins – had deliberately allotted himself two years of film-making to subsidize a two-year return, in 1949, to the inadequately paid life of the Old Vic's joint leading actor. As a result of the twelve-year development plan, both actors had been planning their careers around long-term commitments to the Old Vic, while Burrell had been extremely busy in London, supervising the current season in their absence and planning several years ahead. Apart from the revivals of *The School for Scandal* and *Richard III* planned for 1949–50, Olivier was to have played Othello and the title role in James Bridie's *Lancelot*, with Richardson as Merlin. Burrell was also planning productions of *Dr Faustus* and *The Way of the World*; he had engaged Hugh Hunt, director of the Bristol Old Vic company, to direct *The Cherry Orchard* and Alec Guinness to direct *Twelfth Night*. None of the three had been given any intimation that their regime, still hailed on all sides as an artistic triumph, a milestone in the history of British theatre, was under bureaucratic threat.

But Tyrone Guthrie, still smarting from the *Oedipus* episode, had been at work in the wings. Later described by Burrell's wife Margaret as "the rogue elephant who kicked the whole thing down", Guthrie was also resentful (according to his biographer, James Forsyth) that their more conspicuous achievements had enabled Olivier and Richardson to beat him to the knighthood he felt he deserved quite as much.[6] More significantly the two star actors, according to Guthrie, had "tried, and failed, to have their cake and eat it". There were echoes of his point in the more recent controversies about the occasional forays into commercial theatre of Trevor Nunn and Sir Peter Hall, while directors of the Royal Shakespeare Company and the National Theatre respectively. Olivier and Richardson, in Guthrie's view, were absentee landlords, away making films, touring Australia and America, while remaining Old Vic actor-managers in name only. It did not subsequently help Olivier's case that, in his absence, the Old Vic "rump" carrying on in London had taken to calling themselves "Waiting for Larry".[7]

Standards were said to have declined in their absence, as Burrell took the entire burden of artistic and commercial management upon himself. The Old Vic, said J. C. Trewin, had become "pretty boring" in the absence of Olivier and Richardson;[8] wrote another critic, T. C. Worsley:

> Doubtless the dazzle of such performances as Olivier's Oedipus and Richard III and Richardson's Peer Gynt blinded us to weaknesses elsewhere. Now the twin stars have apparently withdrawn ... the second-rank lights have not proved bright enough to distract our attention from the plain fact that the Old Vic is just a very moderate stock company which displays all the constitutional weaknesses of repertory anywhere where money is not too plentiful.[9]

There was some truth in this; Richardson returned before Olivier, to find Cedric Hardwicke's Dr Faustus, a part he himself had handed on, "worryingly bad".[10] But Burrell had at least never complained of the burden bequeathed him by his more celebrated partners. On the contrary, he was outraged on their behalf. In a fit of righteous pique, he composed (but wisely never sent) a sour letter to Esher complaining of "Government of the Young and Eager by the Old and Ineffectual ... the tedium and frustration of fortnightly meetings with fumbling and amateurish Governors, to whom even good manners come grudgingly". He then threatened to take himself off to the United States, where "they know the mysteries of keeping the old men out of the way and giving the younger men a chance to get on with it".

Back in Sydney, a bitter Olivier was forced to keep this dark secret to himself, confiding his rage and anxiety only to Vivien. She had her own reasons, apart from her pride in him, for a share in his anger, for she had agreed to the financial sacrifice involved in this tour – which would benefit the British Council and the Old Vic much more than the Oliviers. He may have cannily ensured himself a percentage of box-office profits, while his company cheerfully laboured on starvation wages, but both Olivier and Vivien had foregone plans for various lucrative joint film ventures to undertake the Australian expedition. He had been invited to film *Cyrano de Bergerac* in Hollywood; *Othello*, possibly with Vivien as Desdemona, in Britain; a modern comedy, certainly with Vivien, also in Britain; and a life of Shakespeare, which he had been invited to star in and direct, with Vivien slated as Anne Hathaway. They could have been coining in excess of £3,000 a week – a fortune for the time – rather than their basic £60 a week Old Vic salaries. As if to hammer the point home, they donated their astronomic fee of £A5,000, for a radio broadcast about the highlights of their career, to the Food For Britain fund.

By the end of the long Sydney run, Vivien felt more isolated than ever, as Olivier brooded over the crisis beyond his control in London. For once others were beginning to notice their discontent. She was losing weight again, so much so that Olivier's chatty hairdresser at the Australia Hotel told him he thought Vivien looked consumptive. Doctors concerned about her fatigue diagnosed the possible onset of neurasthenia. The feelings aroused in her by Finch had revived all the restlessness of old, and she lost patience with the ever loyal fans at the stage door. When her public coldness excited newspaper comment, Olivier was driven to issue a statement declaring simply that "Miss Leigh is quite exhausted."

His own woes increased, meanwhile, as his knee gradually became more painful. Both of them were virtually on automatic pilot as the roadshow moved on to Brisbane, where they arrived to complaints that *Richard III* was not on the menu. Earlier in the tour both Oliviers would have gone to great lengths to appease public feeling; so numb were they now that Dan O'Connor was wheeled out to blind the audience with statistics about the cost of shifting scenery around the sub-continent and to tell Brisbane, in effect, that it should count itself lucky to see *The School for Scandal*. The audience, of course, loved it; but the reviewers sensed Olivier's fatigue and chose to complain of it. The inter-state jealousy which so bedevils Australia came to the fore as Brisbane's critical community protested that "not once, during the entire performance, did the virile dynamic assert himself". Vivien, meanwhile – "always the hornet, buzzing in and out of her husband's periwig" – appeared to suspend all critical judgement.

During the eleven-hour flight to New Zealand, which the Oliviers chose to make in solitary state aboard the cargo plane carrying the scenery, there was a sudden scare when Vivien became short of breath and almost passed out. The pilot swiftly descended to a lower altitude and she made it to Auckland with the aid of an oxygen mask. But all the signs were there: this tour had gone on too long for anyone's benefit. Its artificiality had become suffocating; the pace had taken its toll on the health of both of them; the notion of restoring the vitality to their partnership had turned sour; and Olivier was anxious to get back to London and join Richardson in taking up the cudgels against Esher.

With fifty performances in five cities lying ahead in New Zealand, Vivien began the final phase of the tour in an Auckland hospital. Olivier found it a convenient excuse to start cancelling public appearances and receptions – which, had their eager hosts had their way, would have been even more onerous than in Australia. As throughout the tour, all their movies were playing in local cinemas, adding to the tide of adulation on which they arrived. A week or so's rest, as the remainder of the company eased into New Zealand with just three matinees and three rehearsals, seemed to restore her spirits. But Vivien was scared: her Catholic superstitions had convinced her that a physical decline was but the prelude to a mental one. She made a determined effort, for her own sake as much as anyone else's, that the show – and not just the show onstage – must go on.

241

She had added incentives for recovery. Olivier had begun to see a silver lining in the Old Vic disaster. He had moulded this company, trained and field-marshalled it through all the trials and torments of the tour, until its *esprit de corps* was worthy of that of a regiment in prolonged battle. If it was not to be the nucleus of a new Old Vic company, then it could be that of a new commercial company launched by Laurence Olivier Productions. It could provide the infrastructure for himself and Vivien to become one of the great stage partnerships, rivals even to his own heroes Alfred Lunt and Lynn Fontanne. Vivien's range and technique had improved immeasurably during the tour; although her voice was still a little thin, and her impetuous manner more suited to comedy than dramatic or tragic material, he believed that under his tutelage she could prove a worthy foil for his own remaining stage ambitions. With Vivien at his side, he could launch a new era of actor-management.

As such heady and not unrealistic thoughts began to form, Cecil Tennant sent over the script of a new play by Tennessee Williams, *A Streetcar Named Desire*, already enjoying great success in New York. Olivier believed that the central role of Blanche, created on Broadway by Jessica Tandy, could prove the perfect vehicle for Vivien's return to the London stage. The Old Vic directors, mollified by the courtesy of his correspondence, had also agreed that the company he led could have the New Theatre for the coming season, with revivals of *Richard III* and *The School for Scandal*, plus the British premiere of Jean Anouilh's *Antigone*, directed by Olivier as a vehicle for Vivien's new maturity. Whatever their private future, Vivien sensed, a continued public alliance with Olivier could realize all her professional ambitions.

With remarkable rapidity, she was out of hospital and back on the charm circuit. Behind closed doors, she made every effort to give Olivier no cause for complaint. When they moved on from Auckland to Christchurch, she was as delighted as her public that an eager-beaver porter at the United Services Hotel leaked to the local papers an endearing little story about their illustrious guests. The Oliviers, on checking in, had been disappointed to find themselves allocated a room with two single beds; they insisted on being moved to one with a double bed. When Olivier confirmed the story with a coy blush – "Yes, that is what we are old-fashioned enough to prefer" – Christchurch, and Vivien, purred.

This facsimile of nuptial bliss was shattered, as far as the company was concerned, by an incident the following week during preparations for the first night of *The School for Scandal*. Garry O'Connor's exhaustive research into this year of the Oliviers' lives came up with witnesses for the backstage row which developed when the wardrobe department could not find Lady Teazle's red shoes. An imperious Vivien refused to wear any others, tearing into the overstretched wardrobe girls with a rage bordering on the hysterical. Enter Olivier, unaware that there were others within earshot, to tell Vivien she was late and must get onstage. Wearing bedroom slippers beneath her Lady Teazle costume, she refused to budge until her red shoes were found. "Put on any shoes and just get up there!" stormed her husband.

But still she refused, so he slapped her face and said: "Get up on that stage, you little bitch!" She slapped him back, saying: "Don't you dare hit me, you bastard." After a pause, he was then heard to say to her, in a quiet and carefully modulated voice, "Don't you dare to call me a bastard, because *we* all know who is one, don't *we*." Then he tapped her patron-izingly on the tip of that famous nose. At which Vivien started to cry, and he took her arm saying: "Come on, up on stage, I'll find some shoes for you."[11]

Exeunt both, to a new awareness of the savagery lying not far beneath the surface of what they had left. Word of their problems now spread around their Old Vic "children". Though life itself, especially the intermi-nable birthday parties, continued as if nothing had happened, it was growing increasingly difficult for the Oliviers to keep up their public act of wedded bliss. Fortunately, perhaps, physical problems compounded matters spiritual; Olivier's unhappy cartilage again made itself felt, and Vivien's run-down condition was confirmed as incipient neurasthenia. "You may not know it," Olivier told the ever attendant New Zealand press, "but you are talking to a couple of walking corpses."

It was in an uncomfortable trance that they proceeded via a rainsoaked week in Dunedin to Wellington, where the ss *Corinthic* – a sight so welcome as to take on the status of a mirage – waited in the harbour to take them home. Michael Redington, who could see the ship from the window of his digs, spoke for the entire company, parents and children, when he announced in a letter home that he would not let the *Corinthic* out of his sight. "If I see it creeping out one morning, I shall swim after it, no matter how cold the water is, or what state I am in!"

It was by now no surprise to Olivier to be asked to address the New Zealand Parliament, where he precipitated heated exchanges between the Maori minority and the ruling white majority in the course of what became a general debate on cultural issues. In an attempt to change the subject, the acting Prime Minister, Walter Nash, could not have known the extent to which he took his life in his hands on declaring that "when people look at Vivien Leigh they are inclined to forget her famous husband". But her famous husband rose, as always, to the occasion, with a response suave enough to make even Vivien, pale and quiet throughout the proceedings, look up: "I have become so accustomed to seeing faces falling about three

243

yards when I appear anywhere alone that I am for ever reminded of my wife's appeal. But I know how they feel. When I think of Vivien Leigh, I find it impossible to think of anything else."

By the final night of their Antipodean marathon, in Wellington on 9 October, Olivier's cartilage had firmly locked his leg straight. It was extremely painful, both on and off the stage. Though he managed the last few *Richard III* performances on morphine, dispensing with the climactic fight, it became clear that an operation could not wait, as he had hoped, until their return to London. He handed over his role as Teazle to Derrick Penley, an understudy's understudy; survived a highly emotional party in his honour; received a cable from the company wishing him "a successful opening in the other theatre"; and duly submitted to the knife at the Lewisham Private Hospital three days later. The surgeon who performed the operation told Olivier, after it was successfully concluded, that any further delay would certainly have entailed permanent disablement. He was to put no weight at all on the leg for at least the first two weeks of the voyage home.

Thus it was – Vivien having made the final, emotional curtain speech on his behalf – that Olivier's exit from Australasia was as stylishly stage-managed, and thereafter as legendary, as any of his entrances. Taken by ambulance to the quayside, strapped to a stretcher, he was hoisted aboard the *Corinthic* from the Wellington wharf by block-and-tackle, like a precious piece of cargo, and gently deposited on the deck outside his cabin, where he greeted his waiting wife with a cavalier "Good morning, Viv!" He obviously enjoyed the ride. It was, as he remembered it, "something that one literally dreams about . . . up, up and up I soared into the sky, smoothly floating over the side of the ship and gently down, as delicately as if upon an angel's wing".

They had travelled 30,000 miles, given 179 performances in front of more than 300,000 people, and grossed £226,318 at the box office, thus earning the British Council an undreamed-of profit of some £42,000 (of which the Oliviers themselves pocketed £5,000). On the voyage home, Olivier proudly told his travelling companions: "We are the first National Theatre company." Demob-happy, they all liberally boozed their way back to Blighty, despite the recumbent Olivier's insistence on a heavy schedule of rehearsals for the New Theatre season, due to begin only three weeks after their return. He was carried to and from the rehearsal room on his stretcher, and spent the evenings alone in his cabin, aware that his protégés were carousing to a somewhat desperate degree, and that Vivien's flirtation with Dan Cunningham was now an open secret of unacceptable proportions.

Olivier's is the only evidence that this relationship had by now, in the surreal atmosphere of the homeward voyages, become physical: "I really couldn't believe that it was justified that I should be so humiliated." Though aware that his company at the time was "dull in the extreme", he remonstrated with her, apparently to no avail. Other chroniclers of the marriage believe that the Vivien–Cunningham infatuation still remained just that, a device on her part to arouse Olivier to renewed ardour for her before they reached a point of no return. If this be true, it is certainly not the impression she made on her prostrate and helpless husband at the time.

The best she could manage was to listen to his complaints "very calmly and sweetly; she saw that she had been thoughtless and assured me that I wouldn't have cause for embarrassment any more". That, said Olivier long after her death, by when he had seen many another Dan Cunningham come and go, was "lovely – as far as it went ... but how far was that, I wondered?"

CHAPTER 14

1948–52

Olivier returned from Australia a changed man. Harcourt Williams, who had known him since his arrival at the Old Vic twelve years before, put it down to mid-life crisis: "His attitude to life was almost world-weary.... That's the most singular aspect of his character that I recall at the time: sobriety, and a tinge of sadness, resignation."[1]

Williams was not to know of the domestic strains on the fellow actor he so admired. But professionally, he was dismayed to note that "Larry had lost the basic need that propels every actor. He was leaning more and more towards directing and producing, because he no longer had the drive for attention." Shrewd as this judgement was about the shift in Olivier's ambitions – few performers, however high their self-imposed standards, manage to survive a surfeit of adulation – it necessarily overlooked his practical reasons for a change of direction. At the press conference which greeted his return, Olivier was obliged to deflect questions about the Old Vic management, avoid any hint of his still secret dismissal, and merely announce his plans for the imminent New Theatre season. He would play Richard again, Teazle opposite his wife in the Sheridan, and take the minor part of the Chorus while directing her as Antigone. But the role he really fancied now, though few could have guessed it that day, was that of impresario.

First, there was Esher to deal with. Before Olivier's return, Richardson had already begun to rally the company's spirits and steward a temporary improvement in standards with a sparkling production of *Twelfth Night* (with Harry Andrews as Orsino, Mark Dignam as Malvolio and a much happier Cedric Hardwicke as Sir Toby). But it was too late to put up any kind of a fight against the memorandum. Esher and his board were even unmoved by the fact that their share of the profits from Olivier's Australian tour had more than paid off the £8,000 overdraft bequeathed by the indifferent season without him. As they prepared for the fateful board meeting in early December, the triumvirate agreed that their best tactic, both individually and collectively, was to go quietly, displaying the dignity in which they found the governors wanting. "A fired butler", as Olivier bitterly put it, "does not complain of his master."

Soon after his return, however, and well before the meeting, Olivier was in for a shock. Summoned to Esher's London home, he was discreetly advised – in that coded way so beloved of the British Establishment – that the real idea was to unseat the triumvirate gracefully and then install him in sole charge. The proposal, which came as a complete surprise, Olivier genuinely considered outrageous. "I explained patiently that in my book partners as close as we had been just didn't do things like that to each other." Olivier swiftly bowed out, "only just avoiding falling over backwards down his elegant front steps". A desperate Esher quickly enlisted another board member, the respected economist Barbara Ward (later Baroness Jackson), to take Olivier to lunch and urge him to reconsider. However tempted he may have been, even he knew there was no way he could so flagrantly betray Richardson, his closest friend, or Burrell, a popular man among the company, without earning the degree of professional obloquy he would fully deserve. Now as later, in more complex theatrical politics, Olivier may have been capable of coldly self-interested calculation, but he was never a backstabber. The board's secret plan was never heard of again and, indeed, never revealed until Olivier chose to make it public in his memoirs more than thirty years later.

At the meeting formally convened to discuss the Esher memorandum, in early December, the disgruntled trio were summoned before the board one by one. Each emerged looking angrier than the last. Many a harsh word was spoken behind closed doors that day, though not one of them ever became public. When their "resignation" was announced next day, neither Olivier, Richardson nor Burrell would let himself be drawn into public comment. A noisy controversy nevertheless ensued, with critics dividing in a passionate debate on the board's competence, let alone that of the triumvirate, to run the Old Vic, and perhaps in time a National Theatre. All the arguments centred, naturally, around Olivier and Richardson, with poor Burrell left ever more isolated, like some loyal creature of these two giants who must now stifle grief at his own passing to mourn theirs.

The critic Cyril Ray spoke up for the board in an article in the *Spectator*:

"The Old Vic company is a repertory company, and the lesson every such company must learn ... is that the strength of a repertory company is not in stars but its general sense of purpose and direction."[2] This last season, in the absence of Olivier and Richardson, it had "patched away at the holes left in the top when what was needed was vigorous work on strengthening the foundations". Of Olivier specifically, he declared that "a great star should be an ornament to a national repertory company, not the keystone of its arch". In the *New Statesman* Basil Dean, one of the candidates for the new post of artistic director, had the gall to suggest that the artistic triumphs of these two "supremely good actors", reviving British theatre single-handedly after the ravages of war, had "only helped to confuse the picture and delay the day of reckoning for those who sought to give the Old Vic the authority and status of a national theatre as it were overnight".

Surprisingly, the only notable to leap to the defence of the still silent protagonists was the theatre impresario Stephen Mitchell. In a letter to the *Daily Telegraph* Mitchell argued that the board should be pleading with Olivier and Richardson to stay, rather than summarily "dropping" them. Noting the new Arts Council subsidy of £30,000, he asked: "If Olivier and Richardson did wonders without that sum, what could they not have done with it?"

Mitchell denounced the board as incompetent to run Britain's "most important" theatrical enterprise. "It is disturbing that people so little qualified should be so responsible for our highest artistic endeavours and be given so much money to play around with in an industry in which they have neither trained nor laboured." In a merely abusive response, in which he did "not propose to go fully into the main reasons" for the changes, Esher defended the traditional "English system of government ... based on the principle that independent and intelligent minds, free from both profit and prejudice, should control public enterprise." Mitchell's failure to understand this, he said, showed "a lamentable ignorance of how things are run in this country".

How Olivier and Richardson lamented the death of Lord Lytton, the chairman of the board who had first appointed them and given them the free rein which had resulted in one of the most glorious periods of English theatrical history. There had been one short-lived successor, Lord Hambledon, before the chairmanship had gone to the coldly ambitious Esher, who had latched on to Guthrie as an ally in his ambitions to beat Lyttelton to the credit for the formation of a national theatre. There were other board members who had doubted the wisdom of an actor running a national company, but few with the temerity to question the triumvirate's remarkable achievements. Their only consolation was that the public debate caused considerable embarrassment to Esher and his board at a time when the National Theatre Bill was under debate in Parliament and when the Arts Council, whose relationship with the proposed National Theatre was the basis for the new management structure of the Old Vic, was still going through its birth pangs.

For all his efforts to maintain a dignified public silence, Olivier's outrage was only barely contained when Esher, as part of the "resignation" package, blandly invited him and Richardson to lead the Old Vic's contribution to the forthcoming Festival of Britain in 1951. So that was what they wanted, as Olivier put it to Burrell and Richardson: to fire them and then have them back when it suited them, or when the Old Vic needed a bit of a boost. Esher was guilty of the crime of which Guthrie had accused them: wanting to have his cake and eat it. Olivier would plan a Festival special of his own spectacular enough to exact a stylish revenge.

It was eventually one of the conspirators, Llewellyn Rees, drama director of the Arts Council, who took over as the first administrator of the newly constituted Old Vic, with Hugh Hunt of the Bristol Old Vic as artistic director. Together they were to see a new company into the rebuilt Waterloo Road theatre in 1950 – and control restored to none other than Tyrone Guthrie the following year – but the Old Vic's reputation had suffered damage from which it would take years to recover. So sensitive was the new regime to comparisons with the old that, as Garry O'Connor discovered when researching his biography of Richardson, all the files relating to the triumvirate's stewardship of the Old Vic were destroyed.

Small wonder that even Harold Hobson, one of Britain's most influential drama critics throughout the post-war period, was still puzzled four decades later by the "inexplicable" firing of this immensely successful regime by apparently resentful and incompetent bureaucrats. The exciting momentum forged in British theatre as a whole, he argued, was immediately lost, "for great things had been expected to flow from the united work of these actors, had it been allowed to continue".[3] Ironically enough, in view of Esher's stated ambitions, the establishment of a National Theatre was delayed for many years as a direct result of their dismissal. "No one has ever clearly understood this extraordinary action," said Hobson in 1984, "the men chiefly concerned, Olivier and Richardson, least of all."

For Olivier, however, as 1949 began, there was no time to brood. The New Theatre season was upon him even as the row continued to simmer. He had become determined to go out in style, proving the merits of the triumvirate's case for all to see and painting Esher and his board as the bureaucratic philistines he believed them to be. So it was gratifying, if somewhat inconvenient, that word of Australia's Olivier-worship had reached Britain, where their adoring public were determined not to be outdone by their Antipodean cousins. After merely the dress rehearsal of *The School for Scandal*, the couple needed police assistance to get through the stage-door crowds to their car. Three hundred people slept on the pavement in St Martin's Lane in the hope of first-night tickets, despite Olivier arriving to tell them that it wasn't worth it. And the opening night, on 20 January 1949, was one of the most glittering the West End had ever seen.

Apart from the reputation which preceded the production, it was of course the Oliviers' debut together on the London stage. They had made three films together and acted on the same stage at Elsinore, on Broadway and in Australia; but even they were rather surprised to have got this far without appearing together in the West End. "For the first time together in London," ran the publicity, "the greatest actor in the world and his wife, one of the loveliest of women...." Whatever the state of their marriage, the couple still had a professional pretext for touching displays of affection. As *le tout Londres* took its seats out front, diamonds glinting beneath the house lights, Olivier crossed the stage to Vivien's dressing-room and, to mark the occasion, presented her with an elegant drawing of a lady of the period, accompanied by a bottle of her favourite perfume; she, in turn, gave him a pair of eighteenth-century cufflinks of garnets, rubies and emeralds.

In an *Evening Standard* preview, Beverley Baxter cheekily quoted the old theatrical adage that "the only way a producer can make an actress great is to marry her". Next day he was eating his words. Vivien's performance was "exquisite"; this was "a production ... that will be ineffaceable from one's memory" and "make bores of us all when we attain our anecdotage". His colleague Harold Conway also found her Lady Teazle "exquisite to behold, beautifully modulating devilment into contrition by the merest flicker of her eyes, the subtlest inflection of the voice". The critical consensus harped more on Vivien's appearance than her performance, but the production was an enormous public success. The first night saw the Oliviers take six curtain-calls.

Looking back, Harold Hobson suggested that Olivier had "stood aside" to allow all attention to be concentrated on the "exquisitely fragile beauty" of Vivien's Lady Teazle. The truth is that he had grown somewhat weary of the role; though it was new to London, he had played it exhaustively in Australia and New Zealand. Now the only way he could rekindle his interest was to make Teazle progressively younger, thus prompting protests that he had distorted Sheridan's intentions – that "instead of December wedded with April", as Baxter put it, "we have early June married to late October". Olivier's Sir Peter, "in his youth, could never have made a leg, nor quizzed a beauty", complained Hobson. Olivier was unmoved. He now sought acclaim more as a director than as an actor, and he was relieved that the critics had treated Vivien gently. He still believed that her voice was too shrill, and she knew it; Lady Teazle, though logged as a personal success, was never one of her favourite parts. With her husband's patient guidance and support, she was already much more intent on rising to the challenge of Anouilh's *Antigone*.

One member of the team unable to share in the general elation was the Oliviers' long-standing friend Cecil Beaton, whose lavish sets and costumes, such a feature of the Australian tour, had been recreated in even more sumptuous style for the London run. Newspaper clippings from Australia had whetted Beaton's appetite to see his own designs onstage for the first time; but now a long-arranged photographic assignment in the United States prevented him from joining in the preparations for the New Theatre opening. He called Olivier from New York after the first night, to be told that "In my curtain speech your name, Cecil, won the loudest applause." Beaton was thus puzzled and astonished to be told by the film producer Anatole de Grunwald: "What have you done to the Oliviers? My God, are they gunning for you!" Nothing else had prepared him for the shock in store when he returned to London and made haste to the New Theatre, in the company of an equally expectant John Gielgud.

The two friends dined so happily before the show that they were too late to visit the Oliviers before the curtain. Both, however, spent the evening in raptures, Beaton at the skill with which Olivier's set builders and wardrobe staff had brought his designs to life, Gielgud at what he considered a "magical" evening in the theatre. They agreed to take separate backstage paths afterwards, "Johnny G" beating a path to Olivier's dressing-room while Beaton went to pay court on Vivien. He expected "the usual backstage superlatives, the 'darlings', the hugs and the kisses". Instead he was treated to "a view of Vivien's back; she did not turn round to greet me".[4] Beaton launched into "a hollow flow of flattery, filled with green room jargon", but his reward was to see Vivien's "eyes of steel" staring only at herself as she "rubbed a slime of dirty old cream, a blending of rouge, eyeblack and white foundation over her face. Not one word did she say about my contribution to the evening. She broached no other subject and answered any question with a monosyllable. Somehow, after a short while, I managed to extract myself from the room. Phew!"

His hopes of a better reception from her husband were disappointed. Beaton found himself forced to wait in embarrassed silence as Olivier ignored him, blithely continuing a conversation with some ecclesiastical relation, whom he did not trouble to introduce. Even when at last alone with his old friend, the avalanche of praise Beaton heaped on the production and their performances won the stoniest of responses. A terrible silence finally descended, Olivier chatting with his dresser, until Gielgud returned to take Beaton off into the night. Other than his unavoidable failure to see his designs from drawing-board to stage – which he himself had much regretted at the time – Beaton was never allowed to know what heinous crime he had committed. Squeamish about rows, he never even asked; unforgiving and unforgetting by nature, he went to his grave ignorant and resentful.

Beaton would have us believe that after his humiliation that night he never saw or spoke to either of the Oliviers again. As of that January evening in 1949, according to his diary, "they were both out of my life for ever". It was as if those uproarious evenings under Duff Cooper's roof in Paris, the tenderly affectionate weekends with Larry and Viv at Notley, the hours of excited discussion and planning at Durham Cottage had never happened. But it is by his own subsequent evidence that we know that Beaton in fact went to some lengths, almost desperately so, to remain in touch with the Oliviers. In March 1949 Beaton sat in the front row of the New Theatre for *Richard III*, deliberately offending Olivier by failing to go backstage afterwards. In April 1950 he lunched with both Oliviers and afterwards wrote to Greta Garbo: "I didn't like her. Oh dear no, she has lost her looks, very fat in the face."

Although he had overreacted in his private record of that night backstage, Beaton still could not understand why relations remained so strained. His sin, it seems, was to have handed over the designs for *The School for Scandal* to his assistant, Martin Battersby, who found Vivien very difficult to deal with. There was a particularly vexed episode over some mother-of-pearl buttons, of which Battersby reported to Beaton: "A hard glint came into Miss Leigh's eye, a hard tone in her voice and a very hard line in her jaw." Beaton's own self-estimation appears also to have offended the Oliviers, neither of whom were accustomed to professional partners who regarded themselves as equal stars in the theatrical firmament. The bulk of Beaton's own ego is evident in another letter to Garbo later in 1950: "I should be very jealous if you had even met the Oliviers. They aren't real friends of mine, though they may now pretend to be." That the Oliviers of 1950 would pretend to be friends of anyone was, to them, laughable; it was others who pretended to be friends of theirs. There were to be further professional contacts between the two men, all of which came to naught, but Olivier could never forgive this egocentric dandy for regarding himself as his equal. Though misty-eyed in his memoirs about the "rich jewel" of friendship and the many treasured ones which had so enriched his life, Olivier somehow managed to chronicle his entire career without once mentioning the name of Cecil Beaton.[5]

With *The School for Scandal* securely established, *Richard III* was next to rejoin the repertoire, on 26 January, four years since it had first astonished London. All the superlatives were again on parade – Baxter merely expressed his "humble gratitude" – but this time there was the added attraction of Vivien as Lady Anne. It was another part she had come to feel unworthy of her growing abilities, but she garnered openly surprised praise for the development of her range and the *gravitas* she brought to the seduction scene. She displayed, in one verdict, "a force of manner and voice unlike anything she has done before ... an impressive performance and a brilliant contrast to her Dresden china Lady Teazle".

For all Olivier's public support, he still could not quite hide from Vivien his private doubts about her potential as a dramatic actress in heavier roles. For once, it seems, he may have been underestimating her, his judgement clouded by the anxieties she was still causing him in their offstage lives. *Antigone* proved a personal triumph for both of them – a breakthrough in critical recognition for Vivien and a fillip for Olivier's growing stature as a director. She held the eye from the moment the curtain went up – a solitary, star-crossed figure, seated cross-legged at the back of the stage as Olivier, in evening dress in his role as the Chorus, outlined the doom ahead of her. The long, hard hours which both had invested in Vivien's performance, especially her voice, were acknowledged by the discriminating Ivor Brown of the *Observer*, to whom she had developed "a new and strong vocal range, a fanatical force of character, and the calm intensity of the unshakable devotee. It is a most notable achievement and surpasses expectation."

Vivien had persisted in her determination to risk *Antigone* despite Olivier's initial hesitation. By the time it opened she was driven by a need to convince her husband, as much as anyone else, of the full extent of her powers. Olivier himself passed up the leading male role of Creon, casting George Relph in his place, not because he was also directing, nor because of the simultaneous demands of Teazle and Richard, but to avoid the slightest chance of distracting attention from Vivien. If this were to be her debut as a leading actress of real substance, he would spare no effort in helping her succeed. With each month that passed, she was giving him greater cause to value their professional if not their private partnership.

It was early that spring that Vivien casually let slip a remark that, according to Olivier, set him reeling. It came "like a bolt from the blue" when, after lunch, in the small winter-garden of a porch at Durham Cottage, Vivien told him she no longer loved him.

The lucid emphasis he gives to the moment in his memoirs is more than mere over-acting. However hollow their private reality had become, Olivier still bore a deluded belief in "the Oliviers", both on and off the stage. His superstitious guilt would not permit him to admit defeat, however clearly it stared him in the face. That is why Vivien's sudden candour made him feel, so he would have us believe thirty years later, as if "the central force of my life, my heart in fact, had been removed.... It had always been inconceivable that this great, this glorious passion could ever not exist, like a crowned head after the execution." Vivien, he tells us, was surprised by the strength of his reaction. Perhaps, since they no longer found much but work to talk about, she had simply assumed that he too had recognized this unspoken truth, even assumed it was mutual. Perhaps she had made the mistake of thinking his head and heart as realistic as hers. Seeing him looking "stricken", she gently began to elucidate. As he remembers it, she said: "There's no one else or anything like that ... I mean I still love you but in a different way, sort of, well, like a brother."

Like a brother! "Ho hum", was his response to that, though he was pleased to note in the following weeks, as he struggled to come to terms with his humiliation, that "occasional acts of incest were not discouraged". It did not cross his mind, as friends suggested, to "kick her out" rather than suffer in silence for the sake of appearances. Still harping on his knighthood, even at a moment like this, still mindful more of his public standing than his private sensibilities, Olivier "just could not bring myself to offer people such crude disillusionment". No; he would, as she suggested, carry on as if nothing had changed. He supposed he "would learn to endure this coldly strange life, so long as I never looked to be happy again". In this unfamiliar darkness there would still be "the lantern of my work, though its flame seemed all but burnt out". He would have to find other means of inspiration, now that "this one's throne was empty".

Lurking behind Vivien's revelation was the arrival of Peter Finch as a regular fixture in their lives. He and his wife Tamara had reached London on 17 November, just six days after the *Corinthic* had docked at Tilbury, and were soon among the regulars at the Durham Cottage soirées and the Notley weekends. Under the auspices of Laurence Olivier Productions Ltd, Finch had opened to warm notices as Ernest Piaste, the Viennese lover, opposite Edith Evans in James Bridie's *Daphne Laureola* on 23 March 1949. For this, his first independent enterprise since the announcement of his resignation from the Old Vic, Olivier took Wyndham's Theatre, whose stage door was handily back-to-back with that of the New. It was unprecedented in the 350-year annals of the London stage, wrote Hobson in the *Sunday Times*, for "a world-famous actor, appearing himself in one theatre, to present a world-famous actress in a rival attraction at a theatre only a few yards away". It was quite a week for Olivier: on the Monday his film of *Hamlet* received the Venice International Film Festival Prize for Best Foreign Film; Wednesday saw this triumphant opening; and Friday brought news of *Hamlet*'s Hollywood Oscars for Best Performance by an Actor and Best Picture.

Despite his growing suspicions about Finch and Vivien, Olivier had taken a strong liking to the younger man, in whom he saw a great deal of himself; when Finch and his wife had their first child, Anita, he happily agreed to be her godfather. If he later believed that he had in some way "encouraged" Vivien's affair with Finch, without quite understanding why, it may be because he wanted his wife to be reminded, through the younger man, of the Olivier with whom she had first fallen in love. He may also have felt that surrogate excitement, not uncommon among self-confident married men, in another man's enjoyment of his wife. As long as the liaison remained discreet, it could even prove useful to his colder, more calculating self in keeping Vivien on an even keel.

Vivien needed all the reserves she could muster as professional life proceeded regardless, and the Oliviers warily squared up to their most challenging joint enterprise yet. Olivier's initial hesitation over *A Streetcar Named Desire* was not, this time, over Vivien's capacity to play the tormented Blanche Dubois, a very different Southern belle from Scarlett O'Hara. Olivier was worried, as befitted the new public stature he so prized, about the play's "respectability". Post-war London was so starved of realistic contemporary drama that even *Antigone*, Anouilh's version of Sophocles's ancient Greek tragedy, had seemed rather daring. What would it make of Tennessee Williams's strong dose of steamy American realism, which saw the heroine raped by her bestial brother-in-law, driven to the point of suicide and finally removed to an asylum?

Friends such as Michel Saint-Denis and George Devine told Olivier to steel his nerves. The play was a conventional tragedy in form; if that meant "a brutal kick in the stomach for the audience", why should it disturb them more than watching Lear go mad or Oedipus blind himself? It was the most substantial piece yet produced by an important contemporary playwright. If he funked bringing it to London, he would be guilty of "dangerously warped judgement" – more bluntly, in their view, he would be "selling out" for fear of offending his new-found friends in the Establishment.

Shrewd in both the soliciting and accepting of advice, however much it contradicted his own initial instincts, Olivier did not need much more persuading. If a clincher were required, however, *Streetcar* was causing a sensation, not least at the box office, on Broadway. Any lingering fears that he might be stripped of his knighthood were staunched when the leading impresario of the day, his friend "Binkie" Beaumont, eagerly agreed to a managerial partnership, licking his lips at the good old-fashioned combination of a celestial leading lady, a star director and a proven hit of a play. As soon as the Old Vic season ended in June – when Olivier was able to savour his bequest of £60,000 in box-office takings to the men who had fired him – rehearsals for *Streetcar* began.

For Olivier, it turned out to be his "most painful undertaking yet". The American producer, Irene Selznick (ex-wife of David O.), came to London to represent Tennessee Williams's interests and soon got involved in many an argument with Olivier about changes he had made to the script. She also showered Vivien with advice about how to play Blanche, citing the several American versions she had by now supervised; Vivien, not surprisingly, had her own ideas. Worst of all, for Olivier, was the shadow of Elia Kazan, who had directed the original Broadway production and whose prompt book had been passed on to him. Try as he might, Olivier could not resist scanning it to see how Kazan had dealt with various scenes; by the time his own version came to the stage, he felt he had adopted so many ideas that pride compelled him to add a credit line – "After the American production" – to his own name as director.

At Notley one weekend that summer, as Vivien was learning the role, one of the few critics who had become a friend, Alan Dent, offered her an intriguing *aperçu*: "I have found that although actors can play any part and shake it off, actresses cannot."[6] Oh, you are impossible, was the gist of Vivien's light-hearted reply. But her friends were worried. The part of Blanche was huge and exceptionally demanding by any standards, let alone those of an actress whose physical strength had already proved vulnerable. Not only was Vivien onstage for two very strenuous hours, but each performance required her to crumble towards the most harrowing mental breakdown. What, worried those in the know, might be the cumulative effect on Vivien's own fragile state of mind?

Extra police were on duty outside the Aldwych Theatre for the opening on 12 October 1949. A crowd of 100 people burst past the box office and tried to storm the gallery doors; more than seventy were ejected. Hair dyed blonde, her face reflecting Blanche's long ordeal, Vivien gave a performance of great intensity in a play which struck its audience dumb; she ended the evening taking fourteen curtain-calls, with Olivier declining demands that he too take a bow. "I've never known a night like it," said the stage-doorkeeper, as huge crowds bayed for the Oliviers afterwards.[7] They slipped away, for once, without signing autographs or much acknowledging the cheers. Vivien was drained, as she was to be every night for eight months after performing the role of which she was to say in later years: "It tipped me over into madness."[8]

Harold Hobson was deeply affected by the closing scene, in which Blanche finally succumbs to madness: "This is an affecting performance, casting out pity with terror." But most critics were too busy denouncing the play to bother with considered verdicts on Olivier's direction or Vivien's performance; one wrote that he felt as if he had "crawled through a garbage heap". American drama was still regarded in Britain as brash and crude; British playwrights had yet to espouse the brand of naturalism Tennessee Williams had pioneered in *The Glass Menagerie*, and British audiences were as yet unfamiliar with the Method school of acting, which had midwifed the American production.

Noël Coward thought Vivien "magnificent". Not so Kenneth Tynan, out on his usual limb. Tynan disapproved of Olivier's dismissal of Method, citing his staging as "a good illustration of the way in which a good play can be scarred by unsympathetic and clumsy direction".[9] He argued passionately that Vivien and her leading man, Bonar Colleano, were miscast; British actors were still too well-bred to emote effectively on this scale. The Oliviers, he taunted, had really chosen the play as "A Vehicle Named Vivien". But the public debate about the play drowned out such niceties.

Olivier's production had proved expensive; it would take a year of full houses, he calculated, merely to recoup its £10,000 budget. So Laurence Olivier Productions, for the purposes of *Streetcar*, had become a non-profit-distributing registered charity; to avoid paying entertainments tax, the management argued that this was a "partly educational play". Snorted one Tory MP during a heated House of Commons debate on *Streetcar*: "The play is only educational to those ignorant of the facts of life." It was denounced in Parliament as "low and repugnant", and condemned as "salacious and pornographic" by the Public Morality Council; Vivien's public grew dismayed that she had appeared in so "sooty" a role. *The Times* declared that the play's purpose was "to reveal a prostitute's past in her present", incensing Vivien, who rightly pointed out that there was nothing in the text to support this view of Blanche's past. The key to the character's sense of guilt lay in references to her broken marriage to a homosexual; as the Lord Chamberlain's Office had removed this word, even this implication, the point had become rather lost. But Blanche was no prostitute, present or past; she was a solitary, unloved woman, aware that her beauty was fading, fighting for her last slender hope of respectability.

Vivien clung desperately to her belief in the part and the play, even though Blanche's descent into madness left her shaking in her dressing-room after every performance. In time she was vindicated by Warner Brothers, who cast her as Blanche in the screen version, which was to be the making of Marlon Brando as Stanley Kowalski and to win Vivien her second Oscar. Tennessee Williams himself would later say that Vivien brought to the role of Blanche "everything that I intended, and much that

I had never dreamed of".[10] As he watched her long, hard-won success in the part, Olivier sensed that Vivien had at last found the perfect role in which to prove herself as an actress – to herself, to him and to anyone willing to take the play seriously. But at what cost?

After leaving the Old Vic that summer, Olivier was taking a six-month break from acting to pursue his latest ambition: to "open his own shop". A few hits might finance his dream of adding his name to the theatre's proud roll-call of actor-managers. Encouraged by the success of *Daphne Laureola*, which ran at Wyndham's for nearly a year, he took a chance on Anouilh's new play *Romeo et Jeanette*, which he had admired in Paris; convinced that "French into English doesn't go", he commissioned Donagh MacDonagh to transplant the story to Ireland, and retitled it *Fading Mansions*. But French into Irish proved no more successful. Despite an effective production by Anthony Bushell, designs by Roger Furse and a fine central performance by the young Siobhan McKenna, Olivier was forced to close it after only two weeks.

Consolation was on hand in the shape of *Venus Observed*, an ambitious new play Olivier had commissioned from Christopher Fry. It was already cast and rehearsal dates set, as he flew to New York for twenty-four hours to read the preamble to the United Nations' first anniversary celebration at Carnegie Hall. When he told Alfred Lunt how proud he was that a British actor had been selected for this honour, Lunt teased him: "And not too bad for Laurence Olivier, eh?"

On his return it was announced that Alexander Korda's London Films had bought a substantial shareholding in Laurence Olivier Productions. After losing money on *Anna Karenina* and *An Ideal Husband*, Korda thought it made "financial sense" to be involved with "the two outstanding figures of the British theatre". So he joined Tennant, Bushell and Furse, along with Olivier's solicitor and stockbroker, on the board of LOP (as it came to be known). Olivier had shown no hesitation in stealing two trusty backstage friends from the Old Vic, Lovat Fraser and David Kentish, as general manager and general stage director; he had already hired a director of music in Herbert Menges, whom he had known since *Bird in Hand* over twenty years before. All he needed was a theatre of his own; and, as luck would have it, one with special associations for him just happened to become available.

On 14 November 1949, Olivier was proudly able to reveal that his production company had taken a four-year lease on the St James's, a plush early Victorian theatre famous as the fiefdom of the actor-manager Sir George Alexander in the 1890s. Here Alexander had staged the premieres of Oscar Wilde's plays *The Importance of Being Earnest* and *Lady Windermere's Fan*. It was also in this theatre that Olivier had first met Sir Gerald du

Maurier. The dawn of a new decade would be marked by that of Olivier's reign as an actor-manager, which would begin on 18 January 1950, with his own production of *Venus Observed*.

He had first approached Fry from Australia, in that fit of creative activity which had followed the letter from Esher. It was Olivier's own bold suggestion that Fry essay a play in verse, with parts for himself, Vivien, George Relph and other members of the company he was building. But Fry had taken longer than either he or Olivier had hoped to finish the play; at one point he received a small parcel from Olivier containing a typewriter ribbon, an eraser and a brush to clean the keys, with a note saying: "Let me know if there is anything else you need, won't you? I'm not making you nervous, am I? I do hope I'm not making you nervous. My prayers and affections are with you and for you. L." By the time Fry had finished, Vivien was committed to the long run of *Streetcar*. Olivier himself would play the Duke of Altair, but Vivien was replaced as Perpetua by Heather Stannard, whom they discovered on a talent-spotting excursion to Windsor Rep. Olivier also recruited Rachel Kempson, Brenda de Banzie and the young Denholm Elliott. Determined that the St James's would open with a bang, he lavished a large, rather unrealistic budget on the production. At his insistence, for example, all the male members of the cast went to Savile Row for their suits and had their shoes made to measure, while all the females were regularly visited in their dressing-rooms by a hairdresser.

The play itself, when delivered, proved somewhat eccentric. Set in an observatory during an eclipse of the sun, it has the astrologer-Duke (Olivier) trying to decide which of his former loves to marry; his reveries are interrupted by the arrival of a young girl, who subsequently shoots an apple out of his grasp, suggesting it symbolizes her freedom. In the end, after a long symposium in a garden temple, she goes off with the Duke's son.

The strains of presenting, directing and starring were briefly evident on the first night, when an unplanned move by Brenda de Banzie caused Olivier to "dry" – to forget his lines; he improvised so expertly that few noticed, but the nasty moment spoilt his enjoyment of what should have been a great occasion. He had the consolation that *Venus* proved popular enough, with both critics and public, to enjoy a better-than-average run of seven months. One first-night critic thought that "only one in ten seemed to understand what it was all about",[11] but the credit for success at the box office seems due more to Fry than to his new patron. Since his successes with *A Phoenix Too Frequent* and *The Lady's Not For Burning*, there had been something of a vogue for Fry's work, which led an unlikely post-war revival in verse drama (not to last long, except in Louis MacNeice's radio work).

Neither Olivier's production nor his performance won much enthusiasm. As the handsome, womanizing Duke, thought J. C. Trewin, he bore a striking resemblance to his forerunner at the St James's, Sir George Alexander. Olivier was, of course, enough of a draw to guarantee six months at the box office in almost anything. But T. C. Worsley spoke for the majority when he described the production as "a real mess". Olivier's part, he wrote, called for nothing but an easy command and a negligent air: "Sir Laurence supplies them both."

With professional excitements blotting out private anxieties, Olivier now advised Peter Finch not to travel to New York with Edith Evans and the *Daphne Laureola* company. It would be better for his career, he argued, to take on a new part in London. He cast him opposite his close friend John Mills, just voted Britain's most popular film actor, in a new play by Bridget Boland called *The Damascus Blade*, which he would direct himself. The results were so dire that they were forced to close the show even before it reached London – a double disappointment to Mills, as this turned out to be the only time he worked with Olivier.[12] The blame was placed squarely on Miss Boland, though neither Olivier, Mills nor Finch could ever fathom exactly why the play did not work.

Daphne Laureola had packed them in for almost a year, but the expensive success of *Venus* and the two flops had more than mopped up the proceeds. The Oliviers decided it was time to head back to Hollywood, always a convenient way to refill their emptying coffers. But Olivier's decision to accept the leading role of George Hurstwood in the screen version of Theodore Dreiser's *Sister Carrie*, opposite Jennifer Jones (the new Mrs David O. Selznick), was in truth more for Vivien's benefit than his own. Nine months in the stage version of *Streetcar* had taken its toll; with prophetic self-knowledge, she was reluctant to go through it all again for the screen. It is doubtful that Vivien would have accepted the part if *Carrie* had not enabled Olivier to go with her. While she went on ahead to commune with Kazan, Olivier dashed off a quick production of a new Denis Cannan comedy, *Captain Carvallo*, which gave Finch his first starring role on the London stage.

The problems Finch represented in their lives were left behind with the man himself as the Oliviers closed ranks against the alien environment of the West Coast, where each felt the need of the other's moral support. It was ten years since they had last worked there, and now they returned – if only for five months – with vastly enhanced international reputations, not to mention the fairy-tale glamour of a title. Hollywood, it quickly transpired, was in wide-eyed awe of the Oliviers. Vivien's producer, Charles K. Feldman, had thoughtfully rented them the same Coldwater Canyon home in which they had lived while making *Lady Hamilton*. Here they exploited their new grandeur in showy interviews. When the *New York Times* came to call, suggesting that they were here for the money, both audibly protested too much. No, they were here for their art – Olivier quoting Shelley, and Vivien Shaw, to prove it.[13] Meanwhile they acted out the ritual lives Hollywood required of such distinguished visitors if they wished to be accepted into the community. Danny Kaye, who had become a weekend regular at Notley, returned their hospitality by throwing a huge, all-night party in their honour, memorable as the beginning of two lastingly close friendships: for Olivier and Spencer Tracy, and for them both with Humphrey Bogart and his new wife Lauren Bacall.

Olivier's director on *Carrie* was again William Wyler, who noticed with amusement how much his leading man's respect for the art of film-making had grown since the days of *Wuthering Heights*. The director of *Henry V* and *Hamlet* kept a predatory eye on Wyler's methods of working, and badgered his technicians with detailed inquiries about the latest movie equipment and techniques. On Korda's advice Olivier had recently set up his own production company, specifically for the filming of Shakespeare, and *Richard III* was already in his sights. For the demanding part, meanwhile, of Hurstwood, who sacrifices his suburban respectability for love, he grew a dapper moustache and went on a severe diet to lose weight for the closing scenes, which called for him to end his days in emaciated poverty. Olivier turned in a meticulous performance – "the truest and best portrayal on film of an American by an Englishman", in Wyler's view[14] – but rightly predicted that the film, which ends with his suicide, was too dark and depressing to catch the popular taste.

Vivien's adventures on the set of *Streetcar* attracted much more publicity than Olivier's on *Carrie*. All Hollywood was agog to hear about the professional chemistry between Vivien and Brando. They got off to an awkward start when, over lunch in Jack L. Warner's private dining-room, Brando asked her why she always wore such pungent scent.

"Because I like to smell nice," said Vivien sweetly. "Don't you?"

"Me?" replied Brando. "I just wash. In fact, I don't even get in the tub. I just throw a gob of spit in the air and run under it."[15]

Unshocked, Vivien giggled, then laughed even more when Brando treated her to his cruel impersonation of Olivier's Agincourt speech from *Henry V*. At the subsequent press conference she upstaged even his boorishness by memorably informing the press, who thought they should address her as Lady Olivier, that "Her Ladyship is fucking bored with formality." Thereafter the chemistry between Vivien and Brando was all Kazan could have wished. By the second week of filming, when Vivien had finally let go of her stage version of Blanche, they were, said the director, "two highly charged people exploding off each other". She gave

261

a very powerful performance, but paid a high psychological price. There was a metaphor for Vivien's own subsequent life in the famous moment when Karl Malden thrusts a light in Blanche's face, to expose her to reality, and she pulls away, terrified, saying, "I don't want the light – I want magic." Vivien had "nothing but her own talent to protect her," wrote her most recent biographer, Alexander Walker, "and she fed into it, like a resourceful tributary, the instinctual feelings of her own drama.... The psychic wear and tear she suffered did not show on the screen: it was to erupt later in notes of delirium and despair which echoed the very text of the madness she had embodied so brilliantly."[16]

The journey home, which they chose to make the "long way round", two of five passengers in a tiny French freighter carrying apples, sardines and cotton, highlighted the poignant schizophrenia which now characterized the Oliviers' marriage. While working simultaneously, if not together, their separate and joint vanities fed by admirers, they were each other's prop and mainstay – their own greatest fans, themselves in love with the seductive idea of the Oliviers, the most stylish showbiz couple the world had yet seen. In Hollywood, wrote Olivier in his memoirs, "our love, which amounted to our religion, was still triumphant ... confident in an eternal future". And yet in the very next paragraph, even before he has reached the Panama Canal, he is contemplating suicide.

The romantic decision to return home slowly had swiftly turned into "a dismal failure". Left alone with only their own and each other's company, they quickly and brutally realized how little was truly left between them. "The stark reality plunged us both into deep depression ... we had never before been made to face the extent to which our lives together had been supported and bolstered up by the companionship of our friends and the glitter of our position." Again he took to lone walks around the deck each evening; this time he found himself leaning over the ship's rail and staring moodily into the foam beneath. Olivier managed to restrain himself from cutting short his glorious career. But the news which greeted his return to London did not prove much of a tonic.

On their first night back at Durham Cottage, 18 November, they paid a "courtesy visit" to the new St James's production which had opened in their absence, *Top of the Ladder*, again starring John Mills, and written and produced by Tyrone Guthrie. It says much for Olivier's willingness to forgive and forget – if not for his artistic judgement – that he was willing to finance so prominent a platform for his old sparring-partner, now assumed by the theatre world to be his main rival for the directorship of the putative National Theatre. Even Guthrie's own admiring biographer and friend, the playwright James Forsyth, grants that "it says something for Olivier and friendship (even allowing for his sense of showmanship) that he went against considerable opposition in his production office about doing it at all". But Guthrie had only himself to blame for its failure. Despite John Mills's pleas that he trim his three-hour epic, or at least test it on a provincial run, the play opened at the St James's to reviews proving Mills's point: "It is a tragedy that Sir Laurence wasn't there to protect Mr Mills by cutting away some of the boredom that surrounded him."

Top of the Ladder was doomed even before Olivier saw it, and closed two weeks later. There was no truth in the dark suggestions that Olivier had expensively furnished Guthrie with enough rope to hang himself. He had liked the play (first recommended to him by Mills's wife Mary, herself a playwright), thought the production "masterly" and Mills's performance in the very demanding lead "quite superb"; but the St James's was anyway in no position to afford such self-indulgence. *Captain Carvallo* had enjoyed a long run after being transferred to the Garrick, but Laurence Olivier Productions was now in desperate need of a commercial hit. A gambler to the last, Olivier boldly imported Gian Carlo Menotti's new opera *The Consul*, a somewhat dour contemporary saga about red tape behind the Iron Curtain. The risk doubled when the St James's proved too small to house the scale of orchestra required, and he had to take the Cambridge Theatre. It was a typically daring move by Olivier, but again he had misjudged his audience. Despite its *succès d'estime* in New York, *The Consul* proved alien enough to British tastes to last only seven weeks. Olivier, who looked back on the enterprise as "an honourable failure", estimated his losses at £10,000.

Another expensive mistake would "sink" him. As a theatrical manager, wrote T. C. Worsley, Olivier displayed "many of the same qualities that we enjoy in his acting. He is bold, adventurous, daring; he doesn't play for safety.... " But the instincts behind his choice of plays were always theatrical, never ideological; he would decide to present a piece on the basis of one or two good lines or moments, looking simply for strong parts for his company, occasionally for himself and Vivien – though they did not hog the show like other actor-managers, appearing in only a handful of their own productions. But the early 1950s was anyway a lean time to start out as a theatrical impresario. Few new plays of much interest were being written; post-war Britain wanted nothing more demanding than anodyne escapism, the most popular dramatist of the day being Terence Rattigan, whose tortured middle-class dramas were the nearest British theatre was prepared to tiptoe towards realism. Even Noël Coward had lost his way; he found it a "surprising and salutary jolt" when the Oliviers rejected his new play *Home and Colonial* on the grounds that it was "old-fashioned Noël Coward" and would do his reputation great harm; "I have a strange feeling", Coward wrote in his diary, "that they are right."[17]

Olivier was commendably on the lookout for new material – he had little difficulty turning down Basil Dean's offer to star in a revival of *Hassan* – but it seems to have been a condition of the times that so few of the playwrights lucky enough to have won Olivier's patronage were to make any lasting impression. These early years of the decade appear, in retrospect, to have been the calm before the storm that would break at the Royal Court in 1956, when the economic upturn encouraged Britons to look life in the face again.

Throughout these trying commercial times at the St James's, whose finances were indistinguishable from the Oliviers' own, life at Notley Abbey proceeded in apparently oblivious style. Every Saturday night, after the curtain, there was a procession of great showbiz names from theatres all over London to Durham Cottage, where drinks and sandwiches would be served before the ninety-minute drive out of town. As the convoy drew near, the lights of Notley would beckon them through the darkness like those of Manderley. Guests would arrive to find flowers everywhere, a fire blazing in every room and their hostess – if not always their host – eager to party all night. Notley anecdotes abounded: the night Ralph Richardson put his foot through the ceiling, the night another of his home-made firework displays nearly started a blaze *really* worthy of Manderley.

Peter Ustinov visited Notley only once, but came away with a vivid impression: "Vivien sat like a cat on the sofa and said very little and seemed to dominate [Larry] by not saying anything. Every time he looked at her he would start becoming more buoyant and more aggressive." When Ustinov retired for the night he was prevented from sleeping by a slight pressure on his feet, "as though somebody had left a copy of *Life* magazine on the bed". On further investigation, he discovered that the bed had been made the wrong way up, and the weight was due to an enormous monogram with the initials L. O. and V. L. intertwined. "Once I knew what it was, I could put up with it."[18]

Guests would return entranced by Vivien's attention to detail and the remarkable stamina of one so physically frail. She may have gone to the lengths of choosing appropriate books for their bedsides, but they were to get precious little time to read them as she insisted on dancing, charades and mutual impersonations until dawn. Often, Olivier would long since have excited his weary guests' envy by excusing himself and slipping quietly off to bed; by day, as Noël Coward and Danny Kaye did their party pieces at the piano, he could be seen through the window deeply preoccupied in some therapeutic tree pruning. Peter Finch was only one of many Notley guests, though a not disinterested one, who sensed that Olivier would have preferred to have spent rather more of his precious time alone there. As yet, however, these visitors underestimated how much it meant to him to see Vivien contentedly sink her own preoccupations into the role of glittering chatelaine.

It was fine to joke about Hollywood subsidizing the British theatre, but not if Notley had to be sold as a result of the St James's continued losses. This became a distinct possibility when the combination of good times at Notley and bad at the St James's quickly consumed the proceeds of *Carrie* and *Streetcar*. Olivier's need for a hit, moreover, had become as much professional as financial; in his failure to prove himself as a manager, he had also enjoyed no personal success in a role since leaving the Old Vic. Esher's *schadenfreude* was almost tangible. The opportunity to solve all these problems in one dramatic stroke grew, as he had foreseen two years before, from the need to come up with some outstanding spectacular for the 1951 Festival of Britain. Already his friends and rivals were announcing their own plans: Gielgud was to play Leontes in *The Winter's Tale*, directed by the rising Peter Brook; Alec Guinness would be directing himself as Hamlet; at the Old Vic, in the absence of Olivier and Richardson, Guthrie was hosting Donald Wolfit's Tamburlaine; at Stratford, Anthony Quayle and Michael Redgrave were together mounting a complete cycle of Shakespeare's history plays. Determined to outshine them all, Olivier had up his sleeve an idea so ambitious that even he had thought it worth long and careful reflection.

The evenings in Hollywood, as he and Vivien rested from the work and the parties, had been spent discussing whether they might really dare to couple Shakespeare's *Antony and Cleopatra* with Shaw's *Caesar and Cleopatra*, themselves playing both title roles on alternate nights. It had been Roger Furse's idea, and it had visibly frightened Vivien, despite her having played Shaw's heroine on screen. But circumstances now compelled them to attempt it.

Wisely resisting the superhuman temptation to direct as well, Olivier hired Michael Benthall for both productions, with a strong cast led by Robert Helpmann, Wilfrid Hyde White and Harry Andrews. The announcement of this bold double-act had created the excited anticipation Olivier had hoped for. But the risks were dire. Shakespeare, as Herbert Farjeon put it, "might almost have written the part of the two lovers for the express purpose of ruining histrionic reputations".[19] Michael Redgrave, who was to play Antony at Stratford two years later, found it "a part that calls on all the strength one possesses and tests out every weakness".[20] The more cerebral Redgrave, always rather dismissive of Olivier's work, did not think him "notably successful" in the role; in his memoirs, and his authorized biography by Richard Findlater, Redgrave virtually mocked Olivier's request for advice from the Shakespearean Professor John Dover Wilson: "How much of Antony's nobility should I show – and how?"

Pinned in the back of a taxi to Durham Cottage, Dover Wilson poured forth learning couched, on the contrary, in the most practical and useful terms; where Maurice Bowra had summed up Oedipus in the one word "fated", Dover Wilson urged Olivier to concentrate on Antony's "nobility". Vivien, awestruck by the undertaking, rested content with making herself more so by reading A. C. Bradley's intimidating essay on Cleopatra.

This time she learnt the part while cruising on Alexander Korda's yacht. The Oliviers' old friend, now their business partner too, was one of the few privy to the state of their marriage. He worried that the strain of playing a romantic role onstage opposite Olivier might bring upon Vivien another major attack; his young nephew Michael, also on the cruise, noticed how close an eye Korda kept on her drinking.[21] But the trip was a great success, restoring Vivien's spirits after Blanche and rebuilding her strength for the marathon ahead. Aware since the filming of *Lady Hamilton* of Vivien's tendency to be seasick, Korda was touched by her refusal to let any queasiness show, out of consideration for his feelings as her host, while being tirelessly graceful to all around her. Vivien, he told Michael, was "the only person in the world who would be charming while she was throwing up".

Most of Olivier's energies during rehearsals were again directed more towards Vivien's performance than his own, constantly persuading her that Cleopatra – probably the most exacting female role in all Shakespeare – was no more complex to play than Blanche Dubois. He shrewdly decided to open with the Shaw, in which she felt at home, in the hope that the second-night audience – all the critics and first-nighters back in the same seats – would be in receptive mood for the Shakespeare.

The trick – if trick were needed – worked. *Caesar and Cleopatra* was so well received that a supportive buzz went through the stalls even before the curtain rose on *Antony*. That night Vivien, to Olivier as much as to herself, finally proved her true stature. "A LASS UNPARALLELED" was the headline over Ivor Brown's glowing review in the *Observer* that Sunday. She had arrived, but at some cost to her husband. Offsetting the chorus of praise for Vivien was a distinct descant that Olivier was below his best in the twin productions. It took the fearless eloquence of Kenneth Tynan to explain why, launching a critical theme which was always to enrage both Oliviers. Calling Vivien "a minor actress", Tynan suggested that Olivier was "acting down", in a deliberate attempt to help his wife look a better Shakespearean actress than was truly the case. "Miss Leigh's limitations", wrote Tynan at his most memorable (though as yet merely "auditioning" for the London *Evening Standard*), "have wider repercussions than those of most actresses. Sir Laurence with that curious chivalry which sometimes blights the progress of every great actor gives me the impression that he subdues his blow-lamp ebullience to match her." Olivier had "climbed down" to "meet her half-way", proving that "a cat can do more than look at a king; she can hypnotize him".

Tynan himself, at the time, still hankered after a career on the stage. That week he granted a rash hostage to fortune by appearing as the First Player in Guinness's *Hamlet*. Declaring it "the worst *Hamlet* I have ever seen", Beverley Baxter singled out Tynan's performance as "quite dreadful ... [he] would not get a chance in a village hall unless he were related to the vicar". In the same article Baxter put Tynan yet more firmly in his place by declaring that Vivien Leigh had at last

> achieved a position entirely her own. ... She is apart from her sisters, an actress who achieves her highest womanhood in the theatre. Once she was addicted to irritable vocal mannerisms, but as Shakespeare's Cleopatra she speaks low notes of such diamond-pointed beauty that even the critic can only say: "This is a woman who not only enslaved Mark Antony but could only enslave a man of his quality."

The double-act had scored its greatest success. The combination of these two performers in these two plays, separated by 300 years, "would have made any season in any decade", wrote Trewin. At the pinnacle of their already considerable success on home ground, the Oliviers that summer enjoyed what has been called their "royal" period. His forty-fourth birthday in May was marked by a dinner hosted in his honour by Churchill, with whom he had become a favourite. As for Vivien: "By Jove," Churchill would say, "she's a clinker!" The great man had seen Olivier's Richard, during which the actor could hear him, from the stage, speaking the lines in unison with him; now he came to see *Caesar* and *Antony* – booking, as was his custom, three seats: one for himself, one for his daughter Mary, and one for his hat and coat.

The Oliviers' private tensions remained cleverly hidden from the world. During these months they gave a series of interviews to the rising critic Felix Barker – initially for a newspaper series which, at a time of continuing paper rationing, to Barker's own amazement as much as his colleagues' resentment, ran daily for five weeks on the leader page of the London *Evening News*. As the series grew into a book at Olivier's suggestion, Barker spent hours with them both – in their dressing-rooms, on tour and at Durham Cottage. He drove with Olivier in his new Bentley (which broke down) to visit his brother Dickie; he was at home with Vivien when Olivier and Coward returned, in scathing mood, from the premiere of Chaplin's *Limelight*. Not once, however, though almost part of the family, was Barker allowed to sense that anything might be amiss between them. Only very late in the day, when Vivien looked up from the proofs and said to Olivier,

"Do you really think this is wise?", did Barker wonder about the rosy portrait he had painted. It would be over thirty years before his publisher, the Oliviers' friend Hamish ("Jamie") Hamilton, would tell Barker what Olivier said to him while approving the jacket photograph of an apparently radiantly happy couple: "Would it help sales, Jamie, if we got a divorce?"

But for now the show went on. Olivier took a day off to personify the first cinema audience in history in a three-minute appearance as a policeman roped in off the street to see Robert Donat's new invention in *The Magic Box*. He did not speak – merely widened his eyes in wonder as Donat's image flickered on to a makeshift screen – but the juxtaposition between the two actors, Donat trying so hard, Olivier effortlessly effective, was poignant. In 1947 James Bridie had written to Donat: "Your next play must be *Hamlet*. You must do it in style and as a direct challenge to Larry, who is the only English actor who comes within miles of you. He is ahead on points now because he knows what you are after and can make up his bloody mind. That is why you should go all out for a knockout." Four years later, Olivier was still winning on points.

For him, the summer of 1951 was the beginning of other, more public distinctions – the acknowledged doyen of his profession, at forty-four, Olivier was fast becoming a member of the British Establishment. July saw him officiate at the opening of the new gardens built around Sir Henry Irving's statue, declaring: "He died two years before I was born, and yet I am as conscious of him as if I had served as a member of his company." As a member of the Joint Council of the National Theatre, he was a host at the ceremony which saw the then Queen lay a foundation-stone in what turned out to be the wrong place. (It was later moved to make way, appropriately enough, for the Queen Elizabeth Hall.)

They were heady days: the titled gentleman-farmer was now hobnobbing with prime ministers and princes. But America beckoned. Given a large company, lavish sets, and thus a maximum profit of some £40 a week, even six hard months of capacity business was not enough to set the St James's balance sheets to rights. Olivier endearingly calculated that, on those figures, the two *Cleopatras* would have to run for fifteen years to pay their way. But Cecil Tennant had meanwhile negotiated another six months on Broadway at a potential weekly gross of $58,000. So November saw Cleopatra, her consort and their company boarding the *Mauretania*, accompanied by her barge, her Sphinx and twenty-five tons of scenery, bound for Billy Rose's Ziegfeld Theater – the scene, by chilling coincidence, of the Oliviers' disastrous 1940 *Romeo and Juliet*. This time the omens were better; advance bookings already exceeded $320,000.

The only danger to their pre-eminence as the sensation of the New York season was Billy Rose himself. This astute showman, well aware of the

Oliviers' drawing power, rightly anticipated that the first night would be a spectacular public occasion even by Broadway standards. Among those in attendance were Cole Porter, Richard Rodgers, Danny Kaye, John Steinbeck, Ethel Merman, Tyrone Power and the Lunts. Largely thanks to Rose's largesse, these were merely some of the *gliterati* out in unprecedented strength to witness his own arrival at his theatre with his mistress on his arm – a deliberate attempt to force a divorce out of his second wife, Eleanor Holm, a sometime Olympic swimming champion who had subsequently found screen stardom as Tarzan's Jane.

Luckily the glorious scandal which ensued – swiftly dubbed "the War of the Roses" by newspapers anxious to ignore the Korean War and Eisenhower's run for the presidency – failed to dim the impact made by the Oliviers. The critics were sufficiently seduced to erase all memory of the couple's last appearance on the Broadway stage. Olivier gave a clutch of suave interviews, praising the discrimination of American audiences, to scotch other memories of other interviews, and their success was complete. The reviews were like a ticker-tape parade. *Antony and Cleopatra*, declared the *New York Times*, was the best production of this or any other Shakespeare play for twenty-five years; everything about it was "glowing or crackling with vitality". The news from London, moreover, was also good: Orson Welles's production of himself as Othello – with Finch as Iago – was doing good business at the St James's, despite a withering review from Tynan, who had Welles showing "the courage of his restrictions".

But it was early in the New York run of the Cleopatras that Wilfrid Hyde White noticed Vivien "shivering with weakness" while waiting in the wings.[22] Olivier himself had been struck, even before they left England, by a slight but significant change in her attitude to him; more and more she would lay her head on his shoulder, "like a slightly frightened daughter", and plead with him to put his arms round her. At the time he rather liked this new development; if she was reaching out for him, needing his comfort and protection, it endowed him with a new, asexual, almost fatherly role which neutralized the memory of past storms. Still unaware of the real depth of her psychological problems, he had put it down to anxiety about the New York opening. By the time this had passed successfully, but the mood had not, he noticed other causes for anxiety.

In the huge apartment lent them by Gertrude Lawrence, Olivier would more and more often return to find Vivien perched on a corner of the bed, wringing her hands and sobbing inconsolably. There was no apparent explanation; at first he put it down to their punishing social schedule, then to the bleak colours in which the apartment was furnished. But it persisted to the point where he felt obliged, with great reluctance, to seek psychiatric help. The very idea plunged Vivien into deeper depression, and the first appointment proved so traumatic for both of them, even though nothing very helpful was said, that Olivier did not have the heart to insist on more. She seemed able to disguise her condition from everyone but him, which briefly encouraged Olivier to think she was recovering.

He felt confident enough to leave Vivien alone by day, while he mounted a Broadway production of *Venus Observed*, with Rex Harrison taking over Olivier's own role opposite his wife Lilli Palmer. But by the time the *Cleopatra* run ended in April, and he took Vivien off to Blue Harbour, Noël Coward's Jamaican hideaway, for a rest, Olivier believed her to be back on the edge of a full-scale nervous breakdown. As Olivier remembered it, Coward remarked: "Nonsense. If anybody's having a nervous breakdown, you are." In his diaries, however, Coward expressed real concern: "I am worried about Vivien, who is terribly overtired and suffering from nervous exhaustion. . . . I love her and can't bear to think of her being unhappy inside."

For all the hype, "Two on the Nile" proved a commercial failure on Broadway. They needed to fill the Ziegfeld for sixty-five performances of each play to maximize their gross; but whole rows were empty by the end of the run. Olivier's management company just broke even, though of course he and Vivien were able to bank their handsome salaries. The only man to do really well out of the enterprise was Billy Rose – who, apart from getting rid of his wife, clocked up $100,000 in fees for leasing his theatre. 23 April 1952 saw the Oliviers only too happy to be home again, driving down to Notley as soon as they could. Perversely resistant to American psychiatric advice, Olivier again thought he detected signs of improvement in Vivien. The phrase "manic depression" had been mentioned in New York, but he had failed to take in its meaning. All too soon he had good cause to inquire further and coin his own, heartfelt, textbook definition: "A possibly permanent cyclical to-and-fro between the depths of depression and wild, uncontrollable mania." These changes of mood, he was led to believe, followed no particular pattern; but the more regular they became, the more likely the patient was to progress to another condition whose name was unfamiliar to him, and with which he was at first impatient: schizophrenia, a condition little understood and regarded as incurable.

The doctors had tried to explain, but he had been unwilling to listen. It was pretty much his own fault, he later admitted, that he was "quite unprepared" for what lay in store.

CHAPTER 15

1952-5

For most of his life Olivier's private and public fortunes had been interdependent: a downturn in one had invariably, often miraculously, been offset by an upturn in the other. Even with Vivien he had now managed to reach an unspoken accommodation, allowing them to drown their private miseries in their joint public successes – or, more rarely, to laugh off public adversity by counting their domestic blessings. For once, as the dawn of 1953 saw Britain rejoicing in a glorious new Elizabethan era, he seemed to have run out of steam on both fronts. At the height of his international fame, apparently luxuriating in a heroic stature granted few actors before him, Olivier had reached rock-bottom.

Looking back, he was to describe the 1950s as the decade in which fate took hold of him and shook him "like a rat". Again the ghost of his father's religion had returned to haunt him: was this the price he must pay for *too much* success? Someone up there had hitherto smiled on him more than he deserved. Now it was time for destiny to exact its revenge on the unbeliever.

As his life with Vivien began another downward spiral – soon to gather a momentum from which, this time, there would be no recovery – Olivier found little to console him in the immediate prospects for his professional life. His stewardship of the St James's was scarcely proving triumphant; although he had won high-minded praise for importing the best in foreign theatre, notably the work of Jean-Louis Barrault and his wife Madeleine Renaud, he could not yet add real distinction as an actor-manager to his lengthening list of laurels. Even his "beloved" Sybil Thorndike, though he could not know it at the time, was becoming disillusioned; in a letter to her son, John Casson, she wrote: "*Where* are our Picassos – our Matisses or Nashes – our equivalents in the Theatre? The leaders like John G. and Larry don't seem to do anything *new.* ..."[1]

The immediate future offered Olivier little hope of swift improvement. He had always enjoyed surprising his public, but now it was dismay rather than disbelief which greeted the news that he was to play Macheath in a film of John Gay's *The Beggar's Opera*. Was financial adversity, wondered the critics, at last forcing Britain's greatest theatrical figure to compromise his standards? If they sniffed at material so unworthy of him, they were slack-jawed at the announcement which soon followed. As his contribution to Coronation Year, Sir Laurence Olivier would be playing the Grand Duke of Carpathia in *The Sleeping Prince*, a comedy which even its author, Terence Rattigan, described as "a very slight piece". Just as his faithful public expected Olivier, in his mid-forties, to sink his teeth into another mighty Shakespearean role, it appeared that he preferred to let them decay in candy-floss.

At first, Olivier's mood was defiant. Rising to new challenges, entering new fields, was at the heart of the versatility he craved, the unpredictability he treasured. When the acclaimed young director Peter Brook had first approached him about *The Beggar's Opera*, during the London run of the Cleopatras, Olivier was intrigued. Never averse to adding new strings to his bow, Olivier grew childishly excited at the thought of being able to call himself a singer – even, perhaps, a musician. While in New York for the Cleopatras he took voice coaching with Mary Martin's teacher, Helen Cahoon, and made a recording of several of Macheath's songs which he sent over to Brook and Sir Arthur Bliss, who was arranging the score. When Bliss replied that his voice was not only "pleasant" but "musician-like", Olivier's joy was unconfined.

His spirits were still high when shooting began at Shepperton that summer, after he had taken a short break with Vivien to reassure himself that she seemed all right. The omens were good: apart from Brook and Bliss, the team assembled by the producer, Herbert Wilcox, was the best that British film money could buy. Denis Cannan had written a sparkling screenplay; Christopher Fry was on hand to embellish it; Brook's partner Georges Wakhevitch had designed sets and costumes both authentic and stylish; and the excellent cast included Stanley Holloway, George Devine, Hugh Griffith, Daphne Anderson and the young Dorothy Tutin. The cinema hits of the day were such American musicals as *Annie Get Your Gun*; this could be the chance to prove that Britain too, despite its dismal track record, could produce a hit musical. So enthused was Olivier that he agreed to Wilcox's suggestion that he become co-producer, which proved his first mistake. It is never easy for a director's leading man also to be his producer, on hand to question his every move. When it is the first film of a self-confident young stage director with innovative ideas, the chemistry can turn sour very quickly.

By September the arguments between director and producer/leading man had grown so fierce that the set was in crisis. Relations between them were not helped by the fact that Olivier knew Brook would have preferred Richard Burton as Macheath; while he was striving for cinematic realism, Olivier was acting a dashing gallant straight out of some Restoration comedy. But Brook was also behind schedule and had already exceeded his £250,000 budget. "Peter", recalled Wilcox, "enjoyed a superiority complex that shone from his young blue eyes like highly polished brass buttons, insolently surveying and cocking a snook at the conventional; whereas long experience embracing success and failure had mellowed any suggestion of superiority Larry or I may have nursed in our early professional days." [2]

Olivier worked harder than ever, devoting his lunch breaks to more voice coaching and dispensing with the services of a double for the hair-raising sequences on horseback; he rode one horse so hard that it died of a heart attack beneath him. Then came his own Waterloo: on the sixth take of a gymnastic feat in which he leapt on to a gaming table in mid-swordfight, Olivier fell heavily and tore a calf muscle. It put him out of the film for three weeks.

Wilcox manfully resisted his investors' demands that he change either star or director – which meant, in this case, director – and urged Olivier to let Brook have his head, or the film would never be finished. Though Olivier swallowed his pride and did so, for the sake of an enterprise in which he had a sizable professional and financial interest, he had already realized his second fundamental mistake. Of all the cast, only he and Holloway (as fine a singer as actor) were using their own singing voices; those of every other character were being dubbed by professional singers. Not only would Olivier's "acceptable" light baritone suddenly appear woefully inadequate; but the uneasy mix would upset the equilibrium of an otherwise stylish product.

How right he was. For all his dandyish swashbuckling, *The Beggar's Opera* turned out to be a personal flop of embarrassing proportions – the worst, he hoped, that he would ever "disenjoy". "Olivier's failure in the realm of musical comedy", wrote Eric Bentley, "would have mattered no more than his failure in the realm of musicianship, had it not been redoubled by a failure in the realm of reality. His highwayman is not only no singer, he is no musical comedian, he is no highwayman." [3] Pauline Kael was a lone, dissenting voice: "His Macheath is a brilliant caricature of the romantic bandit...his exuberance – his joy in

273

the role – leaps through the whole production."[4] But the only real gain Olivier made from the film was a small Corot given him by Wilcox as a memento. He was to work with Brook again on the stage; but Brook's career in films suffered a major setback. "You know," the director said later, "when you flop to the tune of quarter of a million pounds, you have to do penance until the people concerned forget you or die off." [5]

As *Carrie* was also released to muted reviews, Olivier had notched up two box-office flops in succession. He had enjoyed no unqualified success onstage for four years, nor onscreen for six, and could see no immediate prospect of either. He retreated in gloom to Notley, for which he now felt a love so obsessive that it filled him with guilt. He considered it "inhuman, immoral to love a thing more than people, work, intellect, art, my dead, my friends". He felt like "an eccentric who, having had the love of my life extracted like a rotten tooth, turns all his affections to his dog, or some collecting hobby".

So even the consolations of Notley were decidedly mixed. There were, of course, reminders everywhere of the absent Vivien, then filming in Ceylon, which set off other nagging doubts in Olivier's own freewheeling psyche. They were crystallized one weekend by Alexander Korda, joking about "some ancient contractual tie" between himself and Vivien which she had again chosen to overlook. "Forgive me, dear Larry, but I nearly had to laugh when I asked her who was to be her leading man and she said 'Peter Finch' in that incredibly off-handed way. I mean, really! It was the only truly bad performance I've ever seen her give!"

Olivier did not need to be told. The idea for *Elephant Walk*, the torrid tale of an affair between a teaplanter's wife and his plantation manager, had come from a Hollywood producer friend, Irving Asher, as a vehicle for both the Oliviers. But Vivien's sudden enthusiasm for it, or so thought her husband, dated from the moment she realized his commitments to *The Beggar's Opera* and the St James's would rule him out. He anyway thought the script undistinguished and was doubtful about the wisdom of her taking her fragile health to Ceylon at the height of its humid monsoon season. It was when she told him, with the utmost nonchalance, that Finch would be his replacement that "the penny dropped, and it dropped with the knell of a high-pitched chapel bell".

With sinking heart, Olivier had seen them off from Heathrow. He recalled Finch "making a gallant effort to look the assuringly protective friend", and Vivien, "with a little smile of infinite sweetness", blowing him a sad little kiss. Less than three weeks later, he was in Paris booking the Comédie Française for a short St James's season when Asher telephoned from Ceylon in a state bordering on panic. Vivien was not herself. She was behaving haughtily, unreasonably, without a vestige of her usual professional discipline. She was making filming impossible. Could Larry possibly come out and reason with her? Anxious to see "the state of the union" for himself, but in the least optimistic of moods, he headed straight out from Paris airport.

The mission proved, as he had expected, futile. After an interminable journey he was surprised to be met at the airport by Vivien, whom he had vaguely expected to be in front of a camera somewhere. When she suggested a drink and he gently demurred, saying he did not want to worry Asher with any further delays, she burst into a furious tirade which lasted all the way to Kandy. There it quickly became apparent that she and Finch were now lovers. Vivien's maid told Olivier that they spent every night lying together in the open, on the hillsides, beneath the stars.

Finch, to give him his due, was doing his best to keep Vivien to her daily shooting schedule. His hold over her was probably, at the time, greater than Olivier's, but neither man could exert much beneficial influence. Vivien's husband knew her well enough to see that she had at last given way to the overwhelming love he had watched building up for so long; he himself had seen her in just that condition nearly two decades before. Olivier felt helpless and humiliated. After only three days in Ceylon he took his leave – wishing Asher luck and telling him he would need it – and embarked on the epic journey back home. He was due in *The Beggar's Opera* editing studios on the Monday morning.

As soon as he was no longer needed, Olivier sought sanctuary at the "magical" home of William Walton and his wife on the Italian island of Ischia. He arrived to find a cable from Cecil Tennant in London, telling him not to bother to unpack. He should get the first boat back to Naples – where his friend Peter Moore, Italian director of London Film Productions, would meet him with details – and then be ready to come straight back home. Vivien, by now in the studios in Hollywood, had suffered a nervous breakdown.

Peter Finch's biographer, Elaine Dundy (then Mrs Kenneth Tynan), suggests that Olivier subsequently blamed Finch for Vivien's breakdown. In Ceylon, according to Olivier's own evidence, he could not find it in his heart to blame Finch: "Was he not doing what I had done to her first husband seventeen years before?" He even found himself mildly impressed by the actor's efforts to get Vivien back to work. But her behaviour on location, it transpired, had only worsened after his visit. She had been coldly unco-operative with *Elephant Walk*'s director, William Dieterle, who was distraught about the woodenness of her performance. Dieterle and her other co-star, Dana Andrews, had been patient with Vivien's many tantrums. But the climax came when she spent an entire day taking and retaking a difficult scene which called for her to emote with a snake wrapped round her neck. By the time the director was satisfied, she was understandably exhausted; but Finch, like Gabriel Pascal before him, noticed something more than exhaustion in her eyes. It was the last week of their work in Ceylon, and Vivien had already shown signs of strange disorientation, calling Finch "Larry" in front of embarrassed bystanders. She had told him she had been hallucinating. Now she began to recite chunks of Blanche's dialogue from *Streetcar* and then broke down into fits of uncontrollable, violent sobbing.

At Finch's urging, Olivier was not notified of this latest attack. The location work was finished; if she could be got back to Los Angeles, where she could be placed in capable medical hands, it might all pass. Director and producer were only too happy to go along with the plan: a huge investment hung on Vivien's swift recovery. Her fear of flying did not bode well for the daunting, seventy-two-hour flight to California; soon after take-off she became hysterical, trying to tear off her clothes and screaming that she wanted to throw herself out of the aircraft. Heavily sedated, she made it to California with a vigilant Finch at her side.

Here there had been a brief recovery, marked by a chatty interview with Louella Parsons to reassure the Hollywood rumour mill that all was well. That afternoon, tired by the effort of showing a brave face to Parsons, Vivien needed some Dutch courage to return to the set. Then she could not remember her lines, took another drink and again collapsed in a sobbing heap. Abuse was hurled at anyone – Asher, Dieterle, even Finch – who offered help. Through Vivien's slammed dressing-room door, they heard Blanche Dubois's southern twang declaiming the famous lines she too had used to keep the world at bay: "Get out of here quick, before I start screaming Fire." Then, just "Fire! Fire! Fire!"

Finch decided to call in David Niven, one of the Oliviers' oldest and closest friends. Niven rushed straight over. After he had closed her door behind him, there ensued a long period of calm before he emerged with Vivien's frail figure on his arm. "Get hold of Larry," Niven whispered, as he led Vivien away. The set went quiet as actors, directors and technicians realized that Vivien had slumped into a trance. She said nothing. Her eyes were dead.

After their overnight flight from London, Olivier and Tennant had been met at Idlewild airport by Danny Kaye, who passed on these grim details while seeing them into Manhattan for a night's rest. Next morning it was on to Los Angeles, where Niven's news was worse. John Buckmaster, the very man who had squired Vivien to the Savoy on the night she first met Olivier, had taken up residence with her in the house provided by the studio. Hearing of "strange goings-on", Niven and another old friend, Stewart Granger, had called by one day to find Vivien cavorting naked on a balustrade at the head of the staircase. They promptly ejected Buckmaster, who had clearly been taking unashamed advantage of Vivien's condition. But she had soon sought out others.

Feeling distanced and bereft, Olivier decided to lodge with Niven, waiting until the next day to call on Vivien at her own home, as if at a stranger's. He found her on a balcony, staring into space, her eyes utterly unmoved by the sight of him. "I'm in love," was all she told him, in an awestruck voice. "I'm in love with ... Peter Finch." And where the hell, wondered Olivier – not knowing that Finch's wife had by now arrived in Hollywood – was he?

Now, for the first time, he resented Finch with a vengeance, believing he could have taken better care of Vivien. Whatever his own public memories of the episode, Olivier privately blamed Finch ever after for Vivien's breakdown and was capable of cursing the man's name long after his death in 1977. At the time, although he hated Hollywood, Finch immediately accepted another film contract there, to avoid all risk of seeing the Oliviers back in London. He would not disappear from their lives for long, but the next time he saw Vivien she would be a deeply changed woman. Before Ceylon and Hollywood, he had had the good fortune to have known Vivien at her best. "Of all the women I loved," said Finch many years later, "only Vivien had the mind, style and wit to match her beauty."[6]

Paramount proved more understanding than the couple had any right to expect, agreeing that Olivier must get Vivien back home as quickly as possible, and hiring twenty-one-year-old Elizabeth Taylor to take over her role in the film. Vivien was heavily sedated and carried aboard a New York flight by stretcher, Olivier and Cecil Tennant standing guard. "Careful with those flash bulbs. She's a very sick woman," Olivier snapped at photographers, before taking an emotional leave of Niven. At New York they were again met by Danny Kaye, whose reunion with Olivier grew so intense that Vivien – by now able to smile sweetly at the photographers – had a jealous relapse.[7] Her sedation having worn off, she noisily refused to board the flight to London. Kaye made himself scarce, but still she struggled. So Olivier had to arrange for them to be driven across the tarmac to the aircraft steps, where before astonished passengers and crew he and Tennant physically dragged Vivien out of the limousine and on to the plane.

Olivier had now reached his lowest ebb. It was agony to have excited photographers recording Vivien's worst moments yet, as she screamed and resisted, punched and kicked him all the way into the aircraft. Once aboard, he could not bear to look at her until the nurses had sedated her yet again, and she had slipped into a heavy sleep. He refused to believe their glorious passion, their dazzling partnership could end this way. His heavy thoughts made more emotional by liberal amounts of whisky, he brooded his way through the long flight home, as his wife slept. Once at Heathrow, BOAC allowed them to remain aboard the plane for half an hour after the other passengers had left. Olivier helped Vivien compose herself and hide her drawn, haggard features beneath some heavy make-up, before she limped slowly down the steps, a frail, forlorn figure, still dazed from the drugs, leaning heavily on her husband's arm.

She was taken straight to a private room at the Netherne Hospital, near Coulsdon in Surrey, noted for its treatment of nervous conditions. She would immediately be put "under" for three days, Olivier was told, and remain in isolation for three weeks. There was nothing more he could do for the present. Visiting was not encouraged. The best help he could give his wife would be to get a good rest himself.

In some despair, wondering whether Vivien would ever again be out of an institution, Olivier retreated to Notley. But even here there was no peace; besieged by reporters and photographers, he decided next day to fly straight back to the Waltons in Ischia. When the world's press even caught up with him there, his hosts selflessly suggested fleeing to the mainland for a few days. So Olivier left the Waltons' house hidden under a rug on the floor of their Bentley, and the trio enjoyed a quieter few days motoring around southern Italy, as the London papers reported him "on the verge of collapse". The *Daily Mail* quoted "friends" saying Olivier was trying to recuperate from "utter physical strain and spiritual depression verging on a nervous breakdown". He looked "horrible – ashen, drawn, and with a quiver about the mouth". Olivier and the Waltons arrived back in Ischia to another telegram summoning him back home.

Vivien's condition could no longer be kept from the world, let alone their friends. Noël Coward's diary for 28 March 1953 records:

> We are all terribly sad about Vivien. She is in a mental home and has been asleep for a week. She had apparently really gone over the edge, poor thing. Larry, wisely, has gone away to Italy. This is just as well for she has turned against him. It is a tragic story and my heart aches for both of them.

Coward, unlike Olivier, had been thoughtful enough to arrange for flowers, perfume, toilet water and make-up to be waiting beside Vivien's bed, to cheer her when she awoke. On 12 April he received a phone call from a Miss Hartley, not realizing who it was until he heard Vivien's voice. "It was a heart-breaking conversation. She started off in floods of tears and then made a gallant effort to be gay and ordinary, but the strain showed through and she didn't make sense every now and then."

Olivier returned from Italy to find Vivien a calmer, but drastically changed woman. She was no longer, he realized with a fierce shock, "the same girl that I had fallen in love with". After consulting with her doctors, who warned him that a complete cure would never be likely, he sadly attributed the personality changes he noticed in Vivien to the course of electric-shock treatment she was undergoing. He knew her feelings towards him had changed, as long as four years ago, but he had never believed the same could happen to him. Now, for the first time in this long ordeal, he realized he in turn was falling out of love with her. This strangely calm, at times zombie-like creature was not his beloved Vivien. Cruellest of all: if she showed signs of gaiety, her familiar quality of old – well, that, said the doctors, was the time to get worried, probably to bring her back in for further shock treatment.

On 22 April Coward went to visit her in University College Hospital and was relieved to find her "calm and normal and really very sweet. She solemnly promised to be good in future and not carry on like a mad adolescent of the Twenties. ..." That evening Olivier poured his heart out to Coward for the first time, giving him a graphic account of the last few years of their married life. "A curiously depressing saga," Coward found it, though he too clearly failed to understand the nature of her illness: "Attractive and enchanting women can certainly wreak havoc when they put their silly minds to it. I am sorry for him and for her. They both have so much and are so lacking in common sense."

Later that week Olivier was finally allowed to take Vivien back to Notley, where she was to have three months' complete rest. In the pallor of her convalescence she looked more beautiful than ever, arousing in Olivier feelings of the most concerned tenderness. She seemed anxious to get back into the swing of things, and they gradually began to appear together in public again: a dinner party here, a first night there. Told that it was merely a recurrence of her old lung trouble which had deprived them of her for so long, Vivien's fans grew reassured. So did the Oliviers' friends. In July the couple went to see Coward as King Magnus in Shaw's *The Apple Cart* and dined with him afterwards: "Vivien looked papery and rather frail but there was no sign of there ever having been a mental breakdown. She was calm and sweet and gay and with no tension. I do hope that she will remain so."

Olivier felt encouraged. Vivien herself now said that only work could speed a full recovery, and he felt tempted to agree. Could he dare, after all, to include her in his Coronation Year plans? With Gielgud directing *Richard II* (with Paul Scofield), and Wolfit mounting an Oedipus cycle, Olivier knew he would look very trivial by comparison in *The Sleeping Prince*, unless it could be presented as a light-hearted husband-and-wife double-act. Besides, there were rich pickings to be had from the American tourists who would crowd into London for the Coronation. He consulted Vivien's doctors, who declared it a considerable risk, but one probably worth taking. When the news was announced, at Rattigan's Ascot Week party, Vivien deflected the press's anxious inquiries with all her old charm: "I did some hard thinking while I was ill. ... I stared myself in the face and mapped out a new way of living. I shall work just as hard, but rest harder too. It's early to bed from now on." Olivier had another reason to beam proudly that week: he had been chosen as narrator of the official, eighty-minute film of the new Queen's Coronation.

Terence Rattigan wrote *The Sleeping Prince* as "a little nonsense for a great occasion". His diplomat father had been an official host at the Coronation of King George v in 1911, the year of his birth, so he decided to write his tribute to George v's grand-daughter around that occasion; it would be a present to his mother, as consolation for the fact that his own imminent arrival had prevented her attending. His scenario was deliberately outrageous: the Grand Duke of Carpathia, in London for the Coronation, would seek a night of shame with an American chorus girl in the midst of his ceremonial duties. But the chorus girl would take his empty blandishments seriously and assume that he intended to make her his Grand Duchess. Knowing it was a slight piece, which he did not wish the critics to take as a worthy successor to his last play, *The Deep Blue Sea*, Rattigan had hoped for a short run, a small-scale production and an unknown cast.

In mid-February, however, when the play was half-written, the phone rang at Rattigan's Sunningdale home shortly after midnight. It was Olivier: "I hear you're writing a play for the Coronation that might suit Vivien and me." Rattigan claimed that at first he demurred: "No, it'll be a disaster. We'll all end up in the Tower!" Some confusion surrounds the ensuing events. Rattigan has left conflicting versions of whether he really tried to dissuade the Oliviers, fearing it would give his piece of froth undue weight – or whether, as seems more likely, he went to some lengths to encourage them to grace it with their presence. Whatever the state of Rattigan's *amour propre*, it seems to have been Olivier himself who made the running, hoping for the commercial success which both he and his production company needed. So it was a relief to both of them that the intervention of Vivien's illness postponed any chance of a first night well past the Coronation, in June, when comparisons with other, more substantial fare would have been at their height. Rehearsals did not begin until September, for a provincial run before a grand London opening at the Phoenix Theatre on 5 November – Vivien's fortieth birthday.

Rattigan's concern now was that both the Oliviers were miscast. How could Vivien Leigh, "one of nature's Grand Duchesses if ever I saw one", impersonate a chorus girl "thrilled to her Brooklynese death at the prospect of meeting a real Grand Duke in the flesh"? How could Olivier, who could even make *Richard III* a sexually attractive figure, make the Grand Duke the repulsive "Prince Uncharming" he wanted him to be? Rattigan never changed his opinion about the miscasting of Vivien. But he was immensely impressed by the chance to see Olivier's working methods at close quarters:

> Over the weeks, he built his performance slowly and with immense application from a mass of tiny details, some discarded, some retained. "Are you going to say it like that, Larry?" Vivien would ask. "I don't know yet," Larry would reply: "Let's go on". . . . Sometimes he would break her up into helpless giggles. "Is it as funny as that?" he would ask anxiously. Vivien, unable to reply, would nod, wiping her eyes. "Terry, what do you think?" In paroxysms of laughter myself, I would say: "Yes, marvellous." Then he might consider, frowning: "No, I think it's too much. It's out." And out it would be for no discernible reason except that we had both laughed too much and *we* weren't the audience. His instinct for such things is superb, and he was almost certainly right.[8]

Any lingering doubts about the casting of Olivier were resolved an hour before the dress rehearsal in Manchester, when Rattigan visited his dressing-room to be confronted by "a rather dull-looking little man, with an anaemic complexion, a thin, prissy, humourless mouth, hair parted in the middle and plastered repulsively downwards over his ears, and a sad-looking monocle glued over his right eye". It was only, Rattigan claimed, when he noticed his Edwardian evening dress, with an obscure Order around his neck, that he recognized Olivier – "my own, true, living, breathing, Sleeping Prince".

In his absorbing account of the rehearsal period, Rattigan tells how he had expected his "flimsy little confection to be burst asunder by the vastness of [Olivier's] talent", only to find that "it was in fact held firmly in shape by his quietly magisterial performance which, while remaining resolutely faithful to his author's frivolous intentions, succeeded in adding to the part those dimensions that one looks for from great acting". But he too thought that, even in so light a piece, Olivier again chose to lower his own performance to boost Vivien's.

During the first-night interval Rattigan went backstage to tell Olivier he thought the reception "pretty good". But Olivier shook his head. "I don't think so. I don't think so at all. I don't think Vivien's going over as well as she should be." Thereafter Rattigan noticed that Olivier lowered his own performance even more, giving the distinct impression out front that he was "below par". Both audiences and critics agreed. The Oliviers' presence was enough to ensure a run of 274 performances in thirty-five weeks, which could have been many more if their commitments had allowed. Not for the first or the last time, public estimation of the Oliviers was quite out of step with that of the critics. The London *Evening Standard's* Milton Shulman summed up for his fraternity when he wrote: "It seems a pity in these spare times that so much talent should have gone into so little. . . . The Rattigan frolic has not enhanced Olivier's reputation, except as a devoted husband."

During the nine-month run Olivier had kept as busy as ever. He had recorded a series of twenty-six thirty-minute radio dramas for an American network, NBC, under the title "Sir Laurence Olivier presents . . .", for which he had garnered such actors as Richardson, Redgrave and Orson Welles. He had produced two West End plays, *Waiting for Gillian* at the St James's and *Meet a Body* at the Duke of York's. One of several gala nights at the London Palladium, in aid of the Actors' Orphanage, had seen him don drag for a "Triplets" act with Vivien and Danny Kaye; he also performed a stylish soft-shoe-shuffle with Jack Buchanan (another new talent he was to develop for a much wider public before very long). He had played the tiny part of the Porter in a BBC radio production of Shakespeare's *Henry VIII*, made to mark Sybil Thorndike's fiftieth year on the stage. But the winter of 1954 was to be devoted to a project he had long been planning, and which was to be by far his most substantial achievement in the first half of the 1950s: the filming of *Richard III*.

Again Olivier was to direct, against his own initial instincts. When Korda first asked him to film his renowned *Richard*, he felt he had used so much energy and so many of his cinematic ideas on *Henry V* and *Hamlet* that he did not feel confident of bringing sufficient originality to another Shakespeare film. Carol Reed, his friend since early stage days, now Britain's leading film director, was one of the friends urging him to place his *Richard* on permanent record. Was Reed not the man to direct it? No, said Reed firmly. Besides, Korda was adamant that the box-office pull of Olivier's Shakespeare films depended to some extent on his now mythic double-act of starring and directing. Saddled again with being his own source of inspiration, Olivier also felt the need to bring new ideas to a portrayal which had grown "ham fat". He withdrew from the world for a fortnight to master the part anew, trimming down extravagant stage effects and finding a whole range of new small-scale gestures and inflections which would convert his Richard into a genuinely cinematic performance, rather than merely a filmed record of his stage portrayal.

Anthony Bushell, meanwhile, had been asked by Olivier to scout out locations for the filming of the Battle of Bosworth – the end of the play, but the first section to be filmed, while there was still some chance of decent weather. Together, with endearing optimism, Bushell and Olivier had travelled to the site of Bosworth Field itself, in Leicestershire, only to find that the Industrial Revolution had intersected it with a railway and a canal. Bushell then thought of Spain, today a commonplace location for Hollywood epics and Westerns, then virgin territory for film-makers. With the help of the Spanish military, he eventually found around the Escorial a stretch of open countryside green enough to pass muster. Bosworth was to be refought in Technicolor on a bull farm outside Madrid.

Shooting began in September. Compared with the filming of Agincourt in Ireland eleven years before, Bosworth in Spain looked like plain sailing. Olivier was now an experienced director, and he had assembled the most accomplished crew. Apart from Bushell, now a fully fledged director in his own right, there were several other old loyalists from *Henry V* and *Hamlet*: Roger Furse as designer, Carmen Dillon as art director, Alan Dent to help with text editing and William Walton to compose the score. Muir Matheson, who conducted it, recalled that this time Olivier asked Walton for "less austere" music than that he had written for *Henry V* and *Hamlet*. "One day during rehearsals the orchestra leader called my attention to the instruction Walton had written at the top of the music: '*con prosciutto, agnello y confitura di fragioli*'. It was Walton's way of getting back at Olivier." [9]

He had an expert new cameraman in Otto Heller and a truly remarkable cast. Three actors could boast a part in each of Olivier's three Shakespeare films: Esmond Knight, John Laurie and Russell Thorndike. But now Olivier also assembled four theatrical knights – himself, Richardson (Buckingham), Gielgud (Clarence) and Cedric Hardwicke (Edward IV) to lead a company including Andrew Cruickshank, Stanley Baker, Alec Clunes, Timothy Bateson and Patrick Troughton; Pamela Brown, Helen Hayes and Claire Bloom.

This time the editing process with Alan Dent was even more complex than with *Hamlet*. The plot was, if anything, less familiar to film-goers, containing so many historical figures that there was the danger of confusion. So minor characters were liberally dispensed with, including, to the horror of purists, the proudly vengeful Queen Margaret. Whole scenes rather than speeches were cut, on Olivier's thesis that "If you are going to cut a Shakespeare play, there is only one thing to do – lift out scenes. If you cut the lines down merely to keep all the characters in, you end up with a mass of short ends." Olivier's self-confidence is evident in the number of his own words he wrote into Shakespeare: the famous opening speech, "Now is the winter of our discontent . . .", is in fact an amalgam which lurches back and forth from *Henry VI Part III* to Olivier – "[Here she comes], lamenting her lost love" – to *Richard* itself and back to *Henry VI*. In a later scene he delighted the theatrical profession by conferring immortality on Colley Cibber's interpolation: "Off with his head; so much for Buckingham!" It has been used in many a production since.

The Coronation of Edward IV was lifted from *Henry VI Part III* to help clarify the historical background and the crown used as a unifying motif, a visual aid to place the complexities of the plot in a clear context. Edward IV's crown is the opening image of the film, its glitter emphasized by some shimmering Walton *arpeggios*, and the closing image, snatched from Richard's head to roll through the mud at Bosworth and lodge ignominiously in a bush.

But perhaps the most effective single innovation, born partly out of necessity, was Olivier's decision to play his seduction scene with Lady Anne (Claire Bloom) over the coffin of her husband Edward, whom he "stabb'd in my angry mood at Tewkesbury" (more of Olivier's own pastiche Shakespeare), rather than that of her father-in-law, Henry VI, as in the play. The device naturally rendered Richard's designs upon her all the more outrageous: "Was ever woman in this humour woo'd, Was ever woman in this humour won?" And it gave added spice to her capitulation, which he sealed with a darkly lascivious kiss. Claire Bloom, who had hero-worshipped Olivier since his Old Vic days, smilingly says she had no difficulty in making so unlikely a surrender look convincing.

It was the battle scene with which Olivier had most trouble. This time he had the luxury of 500 extras – mostly Spaniards, who spoke no English – to make look like 60,000 troops. But the pains he had taken over Agincourt were still fresh in his mind: "Somehow, I couldn't find another battle in me." In the intervening years Hollywood had shot countless mediæval battle scenes; the only way to compete, he decided, was not to try. He would shoot Bosworth as if it were a tapestry, a delicate visual counterpoint to the domestic interiors which comprised most of the action leading up to it. To compensate, the fighting would be as savagely realistic as Richard's villainy in the rest of the film. He would die – as he had onstage by the end of the four-year performance cycle – in an elaborate, long-drawn-out agony, his deformed hand finally holding his sword aloft, letting it slip through ninety degrees in his dying fingers, so that it finally took on the appearance of an avenging crucifix.

"A horse, a horse, my kingdom for a horse!", the first climax of that very scene have, of course, for some unfathomable reason, become the most famous words in the play. To point them up, as a gesture to the cinema-going millions, Olivier devised an especially dramatic sequence showing Richard deprived of his steed and forced to face his doom on foot. It called for Richard to gallop at full tilt towards the camera, only to have his horse shot from beneath him at precisely the point they came into close-up. Master archer George Brown, reputedly able to hit a sixpence at fifty yards, rehearsed and rehearsed the dramatic moment until the director was satisfied. Olivier's own armour was all too visibly made of rubber, so the shot had to be deadly accurate. The flank of his horse, beneath its conventional regalia, was protected by plated steel, covered by hardboard and cork, into which the arrow would appear to have found its mark. Even the horse had been trained to perfection in its own, uncharacteristic task: to role over and act dead.

The great take came. Olivier urged his mount up the hill towards the elevated camera position with especial vigour. In so doing, he edged his left leg a shade further forward than it had been during rehearsals. George Brown let rip, and the arrow found its mark – inch perfect – via Olivier's calf. Cast and crew froze as Olivier sat there, speechless and motionless, blood pouring from his wound. When Bushell ran over, Olivier said simply: "Did we get that in the can?" Reassured that his suffering had not been in vain, Olivier then embarked on an earnest discussion of how best to exploit the accident in the interests of cinematic realism. Not until he was satisfied did he finally wince with pain and say: "Okay, then, will you please get me off this horse and find a doctor?"[10]

As Olivier's luck would have it, the injured leg was his left, the one with which his Richard limped. There was no need for too much similitude when filming shifted to Shepperton, where he completed the film – 160 minutes of it, comprising 165 scenes involving seventy actors and hundreds of extras – in a miraculous seventeen weeks, compared with six months for *Hamlet* and over a year for *Henry V*. By now Olivier knew his trade – and the part – so well that the meticulously detailed shooting script was committed to celluloid without a single hitch.

The remarkable power of Olivier's stage performance was, unusually, recreated to almost the same degree onscreen because of one central insight. The conspiratorial glee with which his Richard had taken the theatre audience into his confidence could now be transferred even more effectively to the camera. More even than in his *Hamlet*, Olivier exploited the camera's potential for solving the problems of staging the Shakespearean soliloquy – by regarding it, with confidence, as an essentially cinematic device. Above all, Olivier had the self-confidence to believe that Richard could become a truly cinematic figure, an epic-scale villain of the kind movie audiences have loved to hate from Citizen Kane to Count Dracula.

From the famous opening scene, immediately following Edward's Coronation, Olivier's Richard positively makes love to the camera, confides in it, cajoles it to follow him through to the throne-room, even looking as if he might put his arm around it and hug this strange, mechanical confidant in exultation at his own deviousness. The flexibility of Vista-Vision allowed him to retreat from the camera for moments of high-decibel rage or petulance without losing the intimate hold upon his audience already established in close-up. Film buffs will also note the green ring at the top right of the screen towards the end of this scene, indicating to the projectionist that it was time to change the reel. VistaVision allowed only five-minute reels, instead of the usual ten, which Olivier also managed to turn to his advantage: his apprehension at getting through this crucial speech before the reel ended, he decided in retrospect, added an extra edge to his performance.

He was highly pleased with the results: "Who knows," he said in 1986, "in a hundred years time, it may be a cult cassette." [11] The moment where Richard turns on Buckingham – "I am not in the giving vein today" – is still, to Olivier, "one of cinema's chilliest moments". But he did bear one shrewd regret, with which many would concur. As in the stage version, he felt his friend Richardson was not "oily" enough as Buckingham; he would have preferred Orson Welles.

Another of his regrets was Korda's enterprise in negotiating a deal, then unprecedented, whereby the American premiere of *Richard III* was a one-off showing on television rather than in the cinema. The $500,000 fee made a handsome dent in the costs of a film which was to take many years to pay its way. But the small screen could not cope with the subtleties of Olivier's beloved VistaVision effects; even worse, the fact that most American televisions were then still black-and-white made a mockery of Roger Furse's "marvellous Technicolor palette". And Olivier's artistic temperament was then unprepared for commercial breaks. Although the sponsors, General Motors, generously bought time for an American academic to deliver a brief lecture on the play, it still amounted to an advert for an automobile, which apparently boasted "more power than all the horses in *Richard III*".

Olivier's passing cloud, as so often, had a remarkable silver lining. When his film of *Richard III* was screened coast-to-coast on the afternoon of Sunday, 11 March 1956, on 146 NBC stations in forty-five states, the estimated audience was 62.5 million. Not only was this the largest number ever to watch any daytime television show (excluding sports broadcasts) anywhere in the world: It was calculated that more people saw Olivier's Richard that one night than had seen the play in the theatres of England since it was first performed in 1592.

CHAPTER 16

1955

"For ten years now, Laurence Olivier has done nothing that has added an inch to his stature. Once he had a reputation; now he has only fame." [1] Thus spake the *Daily Express* theatre critic, John Barber, in mid-1955. Olivier felt confident that the release of *Richard III* would bring a long overdue shower of those superlatives he had come to take for granted in the post-war years. But he would have to wait until December before critics and audiences could judge his mightily self-confident achievement. Thus far the 1950s had seen Olivier, in the biting judgement of another critic, "coasting".

Few knew the extent of his troubles with Vivien, but even Olivier could not blame her long cycle of illness for the rapid decline in his own prestige. His self-conscious quest for novelty and innovation in his work had become a conceit which he could now ill afford. He was in his late forties, supposedly at the height of his powers, frequently described as the world's greatest classical actor, yet he had not played one of the mighty Shakespearean roles since his *Lear* in 1946. The London *Evening Standard* tauntingly mentioned "the shadow behind him", referring to the growing stature of Michael Redgrave, and suggested it was time Olivier got down to "some serious acting" again. So in the summer of 1954, before spending the winter filming *Richard III*, he had eagerly accepted an invitation from Glen Byam Shaw, a guest at Notley one weekend, to take on Macbeth and Titus Andronicus at Stratford-upon-Avon the following season.

Olivier had not, though he did not know it, been Byam Shaw's first choice. His luck had struck again, in an uncanny echo of the 1935 *Romeo and Juliet* in which Gielgud had given him his first chance to shine in

Shakespeare. Now the chance to restore his classical reputation came –
just as had that opportunity to make it – through being second choice to
a reluctant Robert Donat. Twenty years earlier Donat had turned down
Gielgud because he was planning his own production; now he was forced
to turn down Byam Shaw because of illness. Before the year was out Olivier
would be reading the lesson at the tragically premature funeral of Donat,
a man to whom he had good private cause to be grateful.

Olivier's memoirs recall the 1955 season as Byam Shaw's tenth as
director of the Shakespeare Memorial Theatre, though in fact it was his
third as joint director with Anthony Quayle. Stratford, then stronger on
romance than prestige to the discriminating theatre-goer, had benefited
immensely from another inexplicably foolish decision by the governors of
the Old Vic, who had got nothing right since their decision to dispense
with Olivier and Richardson. In 1951 they had closed down the Old Vic
Theatre Centre and School, started by the triumvirate four years before
under the joint directorship of Byam Shaw, Michel Saint-Denis and George
Devine. Quayle seized the chance to snap up both Byam Shaw and Devine,
hoping that together they might form a Stratford triumvirate to rival the
one that had revived the Old Vic.

Quayle's visionary hopes were not entirely to be realized, but for a while
at least he had the services of two of the most talented directors of the
day.[2] 1953 saw Byam Shaw running Stratford in Quayle's absence, as he
led the company in Olivier's footsteps on a tour of Australia, but by 1955
Devine had left to found the English Stage Company at the Royal Court.
Quayle's three-year plan to develop a young troupe of unknowns into a
strong, cohesive repertory company had brought a lukewarm response to
the 1954 Stratford season, moving him to complain that "all the press are
interested in are stars". So it was with mixed emotions that he was proved
right when news of Olivier's plans leaked. The end of the 1954 season was
totally eclipsed by a surge of interest in the next. "The 1955 season was to
mark the zenith of the Memorial [Theatre]'s prestige during the Fifties,"
wrote Sally Beauman, historian of the Royal Shakespeare Company, "as
if Olivier, by agreeing to appear there, had set the seal on the theatre's
success." If the press were disenchanted with Olivier, his public still
remained faithful. Before the box office was even open for the season's first
booking period, 500,000 applications were received for the 80,000 seats
available. Hundreds camped outside the theatre – in vain – while telephone
bookings were abandoned when the local exchange was jammed by more
than 400 calls an hour.

Olivier was delighted that his old friend "Glennie" would be directing
his Macbeth and that the eternal *wunderkind* Peter Brook – his celluloid
shortcomings forgiven for his innovative brilliance in the theatre – would

be staging *Titus*. The critics awaited with bated breath Olivier's return to their version of orthodoxy. It was not his fault – in fact he relished the chance for a little more antique clowning – but it was to prove unfortunate, to say the least, that the Stratford season was to open not with one of the two mighty roles, but with a Gielgud production of *Twelfth Night*, in which Olivier would play Malvolio to Vivien's Viola.

Since the run of *The Sleeping Prince*, which had weakened her physically, Vivien had spent most of her time at Notley in a state of high anxiety. A fear of permanent mental instability haunted her; whenever she felt an attack coming on, she would summon her mother to help her through. Only Gertrude Hartley and Olivier ever saw this other Vivien during the long, dark winter that he spent filming *Richard III*. Much of the time the huge house rattled at weekends, deprived of the ritualistic merriment of their guests. But as soon as she recovered Vivien would signal the fact by metamorphosing into the gay and gracious hostess, wreathed in charm and smiles, giving the world the impression that her illness was conquered. Olivier, who knew better, had now found his own solution to these sudden shifts of gear. He had become all but self-sufficient, distanced enough from Vivien not to be hurt by her rages.

So the couple now lived virtually separate lives, even at Notley, each inviting their own set of weekend guests, each absorbed in their own preoccupations. Left alone to themselves, they got along best in silence; attempts at conversation too often provoked a row, proving how little they had left to say to each other. What they did have in common, despite their unhappiness, was a reluctance to lose the joint public eminence they had achieved, a mutual unwillingness to admit total defeat. It was clear that their marriage could never again be an idyll; but there was still the tempting illusion, which both refused to relinquish, that Vivien's illness could have been some sort of bad dream. If they could not recreate passion, they could at least develop a *modus vivendi*, a dependence on one another which would see them both through. The key to this – the only key which had thus far seemed to fit – was to find Vivien congenial work.

There was method in this apparent madness. Apart from the nightmare of *Elephant Walk*, work had indeed proved therapeutic to Vivien, even when illness appeared to be threatening. For she was a very clinical actress. Once she had worked out the way she would play a part – the voice, the moves, the gestures, the effects – she never varied them from night to night. "What she did on stage", as Anne Edwards put it, "was done by rote, allowing her to park her psyche in the wings to be collected after the last curtain." This may have pointed to her limitations as an actress, but it also pointed towards a solution to her problems. Olivier, though he hated to admit the first of these truths, was only too keen on the second.

Could the same be true on a film set? It seemed less likely, as any director worth his fee would want to create a sense of immediacy by digging deep into his performer's reserves. When Korda offered Vivien the part of Hester Collier in the film version of Rattigan's *The Deep Blue Sea*, the omens seemed wrong. The scenario, according to Rattigan, concerned "an affinity between a man and a woman who are mutually destructive to each other"[3] – scarcely the kind of part likely to sidetrack Vivien from her own private realities. But she wanted to work, and Korda was willing to take the risk. As irony would have it, the weakness of the film proved the saving of Vivien. The complete absence of sexual chemistry between her and the actor chosen to play her lover, Kenneth More (who had created the part onstage), made for the least spontaneous, most contrived performance of her celluloid career. She *could* park her psyche in her dressing-room and pick it up after the day's work. It made for a lousy film, but a happier Vivien.

The experience encouraged Olivier to believe that Vivien could cope with Lady Macbeth and Lavinia in *Titus* – both roles so demanding, so harrowing, in content as much as scale, that it seems in retrospect highly irresponsible of him even to have contemplated the idea. Would a loving husband, oblivious to his own personal ambitions, really have wanted the Vivien of 1955 to risk playing Lady Macbeth's madness scene? As for *Titus*: its plot is so horrific, almost laughably so, that the play had never before been performed at Stratford, the home of Shakespeare production. Lavinia is ravished on her husband's corpse, has both her hands hacked off, her tongue cut out and must then emote dumbly through three more blood-stained acts before she is murdered by her own father. This was not an obvious role for any actress at her best in light comedy, let alone one with psychological problems of her own.

But the die was cast, and Vivien with it. She still harboured ambitions of establishing herself as a classical actress; she also hoped that working with Olivier again might help restore that curious, surrogate love they still, occasionally, seemed able to rekindle.

Viola in *Twelfth Night* looked set to prove a gentler prelude to the demands ahead. When even this went wrong, long before it reached the stage, the blame was placed squarely upon the director. John Gielgud had not worked with Olivier in the theatre since that 1935 *Romeo and Juliet* which had so altered their respective careers. He had remained a giant of the English stage, retaining the most discerning of followings, but he had long since seen Olivier carry off the all-rounder's crown. The two men were as friendly as fierce professional rivalry can permit; Gielgud had been a regular, if somewhat reserved, Notley weekender, and he had been pleased to oblige his colleague by undertaking Clarence's "one or two short scenes" in the film of *Richard III*. But to expect, as Glen Byam Shaw evidently did, that Olivier would take direction from Gielgud, was to court disaster.

Olivier's own meticulous technique as director has always astonished his fellow actors; scores have testified to their wonderment at the detailed planning in the prompt-book he brought to the first rehearsal and the ruthless precision with which he carried through his own initial ideas. Gielgud as director was always much more spontaneous, much more prepared to change his mind. Some actors like this in a director. Others, including Olivier, most definitely do not.

Olivier, of course, arrived in Stratford with his own detailed pre-conception of Malvolio. He would reinvent the part, quite simply, by eschewing the prissy, self-satisfied buffoon of theatrical tradition, turning him into an equally pretentious, but more worldly and thus more appealing figure. To the very first rehearsal he brought with him his familiar range of exotic make-up and comic invention. Olivier's Malvolio would be a social-climbing parvenu, with crinkly hair, permanently raised eyebrows and yet another long pointed nose, this time with a rounded tip; he would affect a deliciously dainty walk, a superior nasal whine and a self-parodying speech defect ("Some have gweatness thwust upon them").

Olivier must have known that Gielgud would not take too kindly to all this. He himself would never have permitted any actor to bring so complete a conception to any play *he* was directing. At first they agreed to disagree – "peaceful co-operation", says Olivier, "was possible" – but this *entente* clearly did not remain *cordiale* for very long. Olivier's account of what followed is brutal:

> [Gielgud] still had the disconcerting habit of changing moves at every single rehearsal; of course a director has the right to change his mind, but after almost four weeks and with the opening night looming closer, I began to be nervous that the occasion would be a shambles.... At the rate [we] were going, our first performance would have been more like a game of Blind Man's Buff than anything else.

He went behind Gielgud's back to Byam Shaw, finally persuading him to get Gielgud to leave the set. This humiliating request was made in front of the entire cast. "I'm afraid he was a bit hurt by the suggestion that he quit his own rehearsals," Olivier recalled, "but for the sake of avoiding a disaster I had to be firm and insist."

Olivier took over, maintaining to this day that he made "not a single change" in Gielgud's production, merely instilling some discipline into the cast. "I wouldn't quite put it that way," Gielgud tactfully told the author.[4] His recollection, while gently self-deprecating, amounts to a firm return of service:

Somehow the production did not work, I do not know why.... [Vivien] was torn between what I was trying to make her do and what Olivier thought she should do, while Olivier was set on playing Malvolio in his own particular, rather extravagant way. He was extremely moving at the end, but he played the earlier scenes like a Jewish hairdresser, with a lisp and an extraordinary accent, and he insisted on falling backwards off a bench in the garden scene, though I begged him not to do it.... He was inclined to be obstinate. But then Malvolio is a very difficult part....[5]

Luckily, perhaps, the first night coincided with a newspaper strike, so it was three weeks before Olivier's efforts, not to mention Gielgud's, were greeted with a polite but rather half-hearted response. Olivier's Malvolio was "a diverting exercise but hardly the substance of Sir L's vocation". It was "eccentric". Only Ivor Brown "came away with the feeling that I had now met a Shakespearean character whom I had never seen before; now how often does that happen?" To Olivier's irritation, Vivien's performance was virtually overlooked; *The Times* added insult to injury by saying merely that she was "lovely to look at".

It is to Olivier's credit that, for all his stature, he has never been one to pretend that notices are of no account to him. On this occasion, by his own confession, two critics *really* got under his skin; and he took some delight, thirty years later, in hitting back. The first was Kenneth Tynan, who had recently graduated from the *Spectator* to the *Observer* seat formerly graced by two of Olivier's favourites, St John Ervine and Ivor Brown. Olivier's retrospective rage had the young upstart "flicking a duster over his clothes and sleeking down his hair to mount the stairs to this rickety throne". His crime, on this occasion, was to have accused Vivien's Viola of "dazzling monotony" [6] – to Olivier, a "blatantly prejudiced" judgement. It was to be the first shot fired in one of the great long-running theatrical engagements of our time, which was to mature, unlikely though it then seemed, into one of the great theatrical partnerships.

The other critic to arouse Malvolio's ire was the *Daily Express's* John Barber, "hireling" of Olivier's detested Lord Beaverbrook – who "was reputed to have instructed his entertainments writers: 'Make a star or break a star, I'm not interested in anything in between.'" It was no wonder this crusty old Beaverbrook legend rang true to the Olivier of the mid-1950s, for Barber chose this moment to unleash a tabloid tirade under the headline "HAVE THE OLIVIERS LIVED ON TOO LITTLE FOR TOO LONG?"

I hate that phrase "The Oliviers". It kow-tows to the most fashionable couple in show business. The titled lions of Mayfair salons. The pair royalty knows as Larry-and-Viv. Now look beyond the gloss. Olivier was a great actor. But since his gleaming, viperish Richard III, his fiery Hamlet, he has lost his way. Now, at forty-eight, he is an ageing matinee idol, desperately fighting to win back his old reputation. To young people, he is a name that attaches to no outstanding achievement. She is a great beauty – still, at forty-two. As an actress, excellent in a dainty waspish way that seldom touches the heart. It is time we saw them both as they really are.

Thanks, perhaps, to Barber and Beaverbrook, the British theatre *was* now at last to see the Oliviers at their very best – even, to some extent, as they really were. "You must be married to play the Macbeths," Sybil Thorndike had told them, and they found they could indeed draw on the darker recesses of their own recent pasts to bring the murderous couple to savagely realistic life.

It was eighteen years since Olivier had first essayed the role of Macbeth. Remembering that Agate had then said he would play it twice as well when he was twice as old, he no longer felt that need for the elaborate make-up Vivien had once mocked. At last he found the confidence to rely on inner more than outer resources to conjure up a Macbeth which once again defied theatrical tradition, but this time most memorably. Again there were the "big moments" he could never resist, but in this performance, as in the Old Vic years, they lingered powerfully in the theatrical memory: his gymnastic leap on to the table in the banquet scene and the convulsive gestures with which he tried to thrust away Banquo's ghost. These were miraculous effects which, as Tynan put it, "few other actors would have risked". With an understatement which boded well for his performance, Olivier himself called Macbeth "the sort of man who makes you feel a little uncomfortable"; the one "external" asset he had reached for was the voice: "I've tried to simulate an edgier, more resolute voice than I've really got."

The whole performance, meticulously conceived, planned and executed, was an overdue but thoroughly worthy addition to the line of Olivier's mighty partnership with Shakespeare. It amounted, in terms of originality and insight, to an alternative form of literary criticism. This was Shakespeare reappraised quite as much as in a new book by Bradley or essay by Dover Wilson.

But it needed a Tynan, then also reaching the height of his powers, to wield his rare gift for putting the actor's insights into words. The critic took on a role tantamount to Olivier's amanuensis – a kind of literary executor who brought each performance to life on the page, at the same time setting each new interpretation in its historical context, both theatrical and literary. The extraordinary empathy Tynan felt towards Olivier – the Platonic ideal, assuredly, of the actor he would himself like to have been – has left us some of the most perceptive and eloquent eyewitness accounts of great acting we possess. Thanks to Tynan, one suspects, Olivier himself was fully able to understand for the first time the insights towards which his stage intuition had led him.

Olivier's 1955 Macbeth at Stratford saw this unique conjunction of talents at its most telling. Tynan sweepingly began:

Nobody has ever succeeded as Macbeth, and the answer is not far to seek. Instead of growing as the play proceeds, the hero shrinks; complex and many-levelled to begin with, he ends up a cornered thug, lacking even a death scene with which to regain lost stature. Most Macbeths, mindful of this, let off their big guns as soon as possible, and have usually shot their bolt by the time the dagger speech is out.[7]

The remarkable quality of Olivier's Macbeth was that it instinctively reversed this process. If Shakespeare, being an actor himself, was a playwright who wrote parts as much as plays, at times like this he found a true interpreter in Olivier. It was the instincts of his craft, rather than his intellect, which prompted Olivier to pace his Macbeth so that it began low-key. "Taking up his stance," in Richard Findlater's description, "with arms folded, he *waits* ... he radiates a kind of brooding sinister energy, a dazzling darkness ... one glimpses the black abysses of the general's mind, the pre-history of life at Dunsinane." The unwonted quiet of Olivier's first appearance, in comparatively little make-up, led one critic to dub it "restraint run amok".

This Macbeth, to take up Tynan's theme, was paralysed with guilt before the curtain rose, "having killed Duncan time and again in his mind". In the dagger speech, for instance, far from recoiling in the stock theatrical horror, he greeted the blade "with sad familiarity". It was "a fixture in the crooked furniture of his brain". Once the murder was accomplished – the point at which, for most Macbeths, the play's climax passes – Olivier's anguish progressively *grew* with his frustration at being cheated of its reward: not the crown itself, but the serenity that should go with wearing it securely. There was "true agony", wrote Tynan, in Olivier's cry of "I had else been perfect". And, at the end, "I 'gin to be a-weary of the sun" held "the very ecstasy of despair, the actor swaying with grief, his voice rising like hair on the crest of a trapped animal". The cumulative effect of the performance was so affecting that *exeunt omnes* seemed "a poor end for such a giant warrior. We wanted to see how he would die; and it was not he but Shakespeare who let us down."

That opening evening, Tynan concluded, Olivier "shook hands with greatness". Robert Speaight agreed, adding only that they had met before. Trewin and Darlington both called it "the best Macbeth of our time". Hobson said there was no actor in the world to approach Olivier. "There is no actor of our time", wrote Ivor Brown, "who can put more into the turn of an eye or the curl of a lip.... A new thing was being shown to me. I was seeing, of course, a great one in a series of notable performances. But, more than that, I was meeting Macbeth."

Olivier, for his part, said that he hoped his Macbeth was "the kind of man whose arm you would not take as he crossed the street".[8] At last he could again afford such jaunty self-mockery: his career was back on track. For the first time in his career, extraordinarily enough, he was being praised without qualification as a Shakespearean. It mattered little to Olivier that Byam Shaw's production had been indifferently received, and Roger Furse's sets derided. His performance had received all the more praise for transcending its surroundings. But he was now about to learn, perhaps for the first time, how much a great production can lend added lustre to the mightiest of performances. Even Stratford itself admitted that its own inadequate resources were somehow transcended by the remarkably powerful cohesion of director, company and leading actor in *Titus Andronicus*. If *Macbeth* was a popular and critical success, almost entirely because of Olivier's performance, *Titus Andronicus* was a triumph.

The contrast with Byam Shaw's restrained, under-produced *Macbeth* could not have been greater. Shaw had decided to "go easy on the ketchup", which had lent greater force to Olivier's stark realism. Brook, on the other hand, had little option with so gory a play but to give carnage free rein. The text calls for thirteen murders, two mutilations and one rape, and ends with a cannibal banquet at which Tamora, Queen of the Goths, is served a pie containing the flesh and bones of her two murdered sons. Before the run was out, the Stratford bar was to report record interval takings, as shattered theatre-goers called for double upon double. The St John's Ambulance Brigade dealt with fainting audience members at an average rate of three per night, their record toll for one performance being twenty. The para-medics' nightly rush hour came when an offstage sound-effects man scrunched some bone while Olivier's Titus surrendered his left hand to the axe, a ransom for his sons' lives.

Originally invited to direct *Macbeth*, Brook had refused – surprisingly, for so austerely cerebral a man – because of the Scottish play's reputation for ill-luck. The only Shakespeare play he wanted to direct, he told Quayle and Byam Shaw, was *Titus*. The Stratford directorate was thrown into disarray. Because of its outlandishly bloodthirsty plot and some unworthy textual passages, the play was the only one in the folio never to have been performed at Stratford. The history of Shakespeare scholarship was littered with claims that it was beneath the Bard; scholars including Dr Johnson had attributed the blame elsewhere. Though *Titus* was apparently popular in Shakespeare's own day, the one previous revival this century – itself only the third in 200 years – had ended in disaster at the Old Vic in 1923, when audiences had laughed it off the stage. T. S. Eliot had called *Titus* "one of the stupidest and most uninspiring plays ever written, a play in which it is incredible that Shakespeare had any hand at all" (for so discerning a writer, an unfortunate choice of metaphor).

But it was typical of Brook to be inspired by such apparently unpromising material. He saw *Titus*, he said, "not as *grand guignol*, but as an austere and grim Roman tragedy, horrifying indeed, but with real primitive strength, achieving at times even a barbaric dignity".[9] Brook had recently enjoyed great success with a revival of another rarely performed curiosity, Otway's *Venice Preserved*; and it was this which persuaded Quayle, Byam Shaw – and, most importantly, the Oliviers – to let him have his way. Once their agreement was secured, Brook spent eight months "through-composing": apart from meticulously planning his production, adapting the text and pruning its grosser excesses, he designed the sets and costumes himself and even wrote the incidental music. If this production marked the beginnings of "director's theatre" – and Brook's preparations were closely watched by another young director making his Stratford debut that season, Peter Hall – the term could not yet be taken to mean that the actors were reduced to mere puppets.

Brook's solution to the play's extravagances was most clearly expressed in his set – a huge, dark, sombre open space, dimly lit by shadowy, smoke-filled torchlight, occasionally defined by giant pillars which dwarfed the actors. As the death-count mounted, the whole arena was gradually bathed in a blood-red light, as if the play's universe were suffused with gore. This bold effect dispensed with the need for anything approaching stage blood; after the removal of Lavinia's hands, for instance, she returned to the scene with red streamers flowing from her wrists. The cumulative effect was to play remorselessly on the audience's nerve endings and on their capacity to endure the suffering before them. "*Titus Andronicus*", Brook later wrote, was above all "a *show*; it descended in an unbroken line from the work of Komisarjevsky.... It was the totality – the sound, the visual interpretation, everything interlocking that made it happen." [10] His work on *Titus* clearly prefigured Brook's intense later interest in the "Theatre of Cruelty", climaxed by his *Marat/Sade* for the Royal Shakespeare Company in 1964.

In 1955, his production of this unlikely vehicle for the Oliviers' talents was immediately hailed as a landmark in post-war British theatre. Brook's own brilliance for once received its due attention; but it provided the ultimate showcase for Olivier's talents, which were hailed as never before. His Titus was a general risen from the ranks, a "leathery old campaigner, vinegar-pickled in misfortune, riven in battle and gnarled and weather-beaten after a seeming lifetime bivouacked in the open". Again Olivier relied less on external artifice than on his two greatest built-in assets, his voice and his eyes, to squeeze almost unbearable pathos out of a role in which no actor before him had managed to rise above the banal. Tynan declared:

This is a performance which ushers us into the presence of one who is, pound for pound, the greatest actor alive. . . .

As usual, he raises one's hair with the risks he takes; Titus enters, not as a beaming hero, but as a battered veteran, stubborn and shambling, long past caring about the people's cheers. A hundred campaigns have tanned his heart to leather, and from the cracking of that heart there issues a terrible music, not untinged by madness. One hears great cries, which, like all this actor's best effects, seem to have been dredged up from an ocean-bed of fatigue. One recognized, though one had never heard it before, the noise made in its last extremity by the cornered human soul.[11]

The performance was "an unforgettable concerto of grief". If Olivier students knew from his Hotspur and his Richard III that he could explode, they now knew that he could suffer as well. All the grand, supposedly unplayable parts could now be his: Skelton's Magnificence, Ibsen's Brand, Goethe's Faust – "anything," concluded Tynan, "so long as we can see those lion eyes search for solace, that great jaw drop". Findlater, equally moved, described the moment when Olivier's Titus was given the news of his sons' murder and thus of the betrayal of his own sacrifice: "He leans against a pillar, head tilted back, and his face is a tragic, unforgettable mask of grinning whiteness. . . . 'Now this is the time to storm, why art thou still?' says his brother. And Titus answers with a gentle laugh. . . ."

Robert Speaight, writing in 1973, still considered this "perhaps the greatest Shakespearean production of our time" and Titus "arguably Olivier's greatest performance".[12] Between them, Brook and Olivier had lifted the play "to altitudes not yet within Shakespeare's reach". Trewin joined Tynan in discerning the umbilical link drawn by director and actor between Titus and Lear; Brook had even given them a clue by having some "wanton boys" pull the wings off dead flies.

Restraint had so become Olivier that season that his use of silence was as potent as his extraordinary command of sound. After the axe had removed Titus's hand, wrote Philip Hope-Wallace of the *Guardian*, Olivier momentarily froze and "for an eternity of seconds withheld his howl of pain". *The Times* seemed to write in hushed tones when it hailed "one of the great things of his career". Only Bernard Levin, of the *Daily Mail*, shattered his fellow critics' measured mood with his own raucous brand of superlatives; this was a performance "not so much on the heroic scale as on a new scale entirely, the greatness of which has smashed all our measuring-rods and pressure-gauges to extremes".

One of the first-nighters testified that "the curtain-call that August evening brought the longest, loudest cheer in Stratford memory. One heard people, normally decorous, shouting at the pitch of their voices, hardly knowing that they did so, and denying it afterwards; a critic said it should

297

have been a scene at a Cup Final."

Olivier's triumph was qualified, offstage, only by the uncomfortable fact that Vivien had not fared so well. Where his Malvolio had simply drowned out her Viola, his Macbeth and Titus had made her performances seem shallow and puny. Olivier himself believes, to this day, that her Lady Macbeth was the best he has ever seen; few of the critics agreed. Beaverbrook's John Barber was at his cheapest, calling it "the most monumental piece of miscasting since Arthur Askey played Shakespeare", and Tynan was even more hurtful: "Miss Vivien Leigh's Lady Macbeth is more niminy-piminy than thundery-blundery, more viper than anaconda, but still competent in its small way." For her Lavinia, however, Tynan reserved one of the most stylishly damning lines even he was ever to come up with: "As Lavinia, Vivien Leigh receives the news that she is about to be ravished on her husband's corpse with little more than the mild annoyance of one who would have preferred foam rubber. Otherwise, the minor parts are played up to the hilt." [13]

For once, Olivier "felt bound to agree" with Tynan. Vivien's condition had deteriorated so sharply since the beginning of the *Titus* rehearsals that she had never even begun to master the part. She seemed content to give the impression that it was beyond her – out of her sense of irresponsibility, thought Olivier, "like a spoilt woman a bit bored with things" – and Brook thought it best to leave well alone. With the exception of this production, Olivier has always staunchly championed Vivien as an actress capable of great range and power. Any suggestion that he "acted down" to make her look better has always been rejected with an imperious snort. But the great debate seems to have been conclusively settled that season at Stratford, though it rages in certain circles to this day: Vivien was never a great classical actress, certainly not within base camp of the peaks reached by her husband. There was no denying her charm at light comedy. She obviously did have a capacity to convey a particularly fragile brand of feminine suffering: the agony of the fading beauty, the misery of a fallen woman haunted by her past, the affecting decline of a once beautiful woman into a future which holds little but delusion and madness. These, of course, were the qualities not just of Sabina and Blanche Dubois, but of Vivien herself. They had become more so as the 1955 season progressed.

The *Macbeth* cast were merely the first among the Stratford company that season to see that the Oliviers' marital bliss fell rather short of its publicity. From early in rehearsals they argued publicly, if at a rather tetchy level, which as the run progressed ironically brought greater strength to both their performances; the Macbeths, too, have their disagreements. The long summer seasons create a small-town community atmosphere among Stratford companies, all lodged in the area for the duration, and it was not long before everyone knew that Peter Finch was hanging around Vivien. They were often seen walking hand in hand. Finch was even said to be a regular weekender at Notley Abbey, which the Oliviers used as their Stratford base. Olivier himself seemed inclined just to shrug his shoulders, but it was clear that he was disguising a deeper pain.

For Olivier, giving his all in titanic nightly performances, it was handy to have Finch around to relieve him of the strain of Vivien and her problems. The deeper she got into Lady Macbeth, the more disturbed the offstage Vivien became, and the more she relied on Finch for support. After Ceylon and Hollywood, he was one of the few from whom she need no longer hide the true extent of her problems – which were not helped at all by having to give her rote performances night after night in the wake of such patronizing reviews. Finch, indeed, was among the weekend guests at Notley on the Sunday morning when Tynan's *Observer* bombshell dropped. While Olivier "shook hands with greatness" for the best part of a thousand words, Vivien was "quite competent" for one short, dismissive sentence. In later years Olivier was to tell Tynan that his attacks on Vivien that season had caused "at least one" of her nervous breakdowns. But his retrospective rage at Tynan on Vivien's behalf rings very hollow. His response at the time, charmed that this sharp young man should seem so discerning about him, was to invite Tynan to join the Notley regulars and expect Vivien to treat him with the same grace as any other guest – which, of course, she did. The turmoil inside her simply raged the more.

Before seeing *Macbeth*, Noël Coward too shared Vivien's agony at her reviews: "Their ignorance and cruel, common personal abusiveness make me sick. . . . Much the same as I usually get from the mean, envious little sods." [14] One Saturday that August Coward went to see for himself and found Vivien "quite remarkable". Returning to Notley with the Oliviers afterwards, he was horrified to find Vivien "on the verge of another breakdown". Olivier was "distraught and deeply unhappy". Two weekends later, Coward went to see *Titus Andronicus*, in which even he had to admit Vivien was "frankly not very good. . . . She looked lovely throughout, regardless of ravishment and her tongue being cut out and her hands cut off. Her clothes and hair-do were impeccable and her face remained untouched by tragedy." At Notley afterwards Vivien was "in a vile temper and perfectly idiotic". Olivier was "bowed down with grief and despair".

Coward's naïve view was that Olivier had brought it all on himself. "If Larry had turned sharply on Vivien years ago and given her a good clip in the chops, he would have been spared a mint of trouble. The seat of all this misery is our old friend, feminine ego." This intemperate verdict chillingly reveals how little Vivien's mental illness was understood at the time, even by the most sympathetic of friends and sophisticated of society. On Coward's previous visit, Olivier had again poured out his heart to him, describing in detail the build-up to this latest relapse: Vivien had been sleeping less than ever, picking petty scenes and inviting ridiculous numbers of people to Notley, where their life together had become "hideous". Coward, nevertheless, reached the conclusion that Vivien was, and always had been, "thoroughly spoiled" by Olivier. "This, coupled with incipient TB and an inner certainty that she can never be as good an artist as Larry, however much she tries, has bubbled up in her and driven her on to the borderline." Fond as he was of Vivien, and as sorry as he felt for her, Coward would have "liked to give her a good belting, although now I fear it might push her over the edge, and be far, far too late".

He was nearer the mark when he described the Oliviers as trapped by their public acclaim, "scrabbling about in the cold ashes of a physical passion that burnt itself out years ago". The problems between them were now swiftly being exacerbated by Olivier's failure to satisfy Vivien sexually. One of the side-effects of Vivien's incipient tuberculosis, so he told Coward, was that she needed "more and more sexual satisfaction". But Olivier, as he has himself confessed, was unable to provide it. In his memoirs he is almost too candid on the subject, several times confessing to a lifelong problem with premature ejaculation. More to the point, one of the great qualities of his most powerful acting was its sexual energy. Whenever playing one of the huge roles, he invariably had little left for the boudoir. "You can't", in his own words, "be more than one kind of athlete at a time." Defensively, he added that he had heard much the same about "the most magnificent of specimens of boxers, wrestlers and champions in almost every branch of athletic sport"; they too proved a disappointment "upon the removal of that revered jockstrap". But the real problem, to Olivier, was that Vivien had never herself been a predominantly physical actress and so simply did not understand.

If she found solace in Finch, Olivier too indulged in casual affairs during this publicly triumphant but privately wretched Stratford season. Though this was the only time in his life he fell into the habit of regular dalliance, it would continue through the next two years, until he fell in love again. He later recalled these passing passions with the mistiest of eyes: these "tender venturings into the blessed unction of sex" had been acts of kindness, laced with "some love, warm understanding, and ... no doubt, with pity. Gradually, they clawed loose the last of my fingers still clinging to the flickering torch I had carried for Vivien – as I had believed for ever."

CHAPTER 17

1955–6

I f Olivier was going to fall in love with someone else, he thought it
might as well be Marilyn Monroe. The theatrical world did not
quite know how to react when it was announced that the reborn
Shakespearean was now to co-star with the Siren of the age, the most
voluptuous sex symbol since the term was invented, in a film version of
The Sleeping Prince. But the man himself did. He was going to fall for her
"most shatteringly".

This outlandish partnership – soon dubbed "the Knight and the Garter"
by a feverishly excited Fleet Street – could not have come at a worse time
for Vivien. There had been relief all round when the Stratford season
ended; Olivier hid his inner turmoil behind his tireless charm, right up to
a last-night curtain speech in which he thanked every last member of the
Stratford staff – more than a hundred of them – by name, from memory.
But Vivien had reached her lowest ebb yet, obsessed that she had let
Olivier down. She should have crafted a subtler Viola to counterpoint his
ingenious Malvolio, Vivien thought, a less hysterical Lady Macbeth, a
more affecting Lavinia. To have done so, she knew, would have involved
plumbing dangerous depths within herself, reaching down into areas best
left alone. What dark forces might she have unleashed? But the consequences of her failure to take the risk haunted Vivien. When she went to
see Gielgud's *King Lear* that autumn, she sat and wept throughout.

Life at Notley had now become so unreal that Peter Finch moved in.
By this stage Olivier was content to tolerate a demeaning *ménage à trois*
simply because it meant he could get on with his work. With Korda's
encouragement he was planning a film of his *Macbeth*; Monroe's production

company, incredibly, was nibbling at Rattigan about *The Sleeping Prince*; the St James's was still in the doldrums. So preoccupied did Olivier become that he did not even notice, one afternoon that autumn, when Vivien packed a suitcase and ran away with Finch – until the couple returned only a few hours later. They had boldly boarded a train to London – apparently planning to escape somewhere, anywhere – but a combination of claustrophobia, guilt and panic had soon moved Vivien to pull the emergency cord and stop the train. When the couple slunk sheepishly back to Notley, Olivier could afford some hollow laughter at Finch's expense. Now he, too, could see what Vivien could do to a chap. Her husband's weary response to the episode was simply to sigh and summon her mother. By now Olivier could read Vivien, if not handle her. Gertrude arrived just in time to see her daughter succumb to hysteria and collapse.

Leaving his wife and her problems to her lover and her mother, Olivier piked off to Scotland with Roger Furse to scout out locations for *Macbeth*, which he felt sure could set a consummate seal on his achievement in the filming of Shakespeare – perhaps, he now began to think, his best chance of a place with posterity. It was December 1955 and *Richard III* had at last been premiered, in the presence of the Queen and her husband – though Olivier was miffed that Grace Kelly and Cary Grant, in Hitchcock's *To Catch a Thief*, beat him to the supreme annual accolade of the Royal Film Performance. On both sides of the Atlantic the reviews of *Richard III* had been ecstatic; the critic of the London *News Chronicle*, Paul Dehn, had even found himself moved to tears of gratitude "for having been born at a time when such talent co-existed". *Richard III* swept the board at the British Film Academy Awards and earned Olivier another Hollywood nomination for Best Actor (though this time the Oscar went to a Siamese rather than an English king, in the shape of Yul Brynner).

The omens for *Macbeth* seemed to Olivier as promising as had those of the three witches to Macbeth. By now he had even located their blasted heath. He would take great Scottish actors to Scotland – John Laurie again, Andrew Cruickshank and others – and make a *director*'s picture. Britain's emerging pre-eminence at special effects, to reach its zenith in the era of James Bond and *Star Wars*, was all set to create him a terrifying supernatural world of batwool and lizard legs, dragon scales and baboon blood. For the first time, he would be able to cast Vivien in one of his films. It could, he still wistfully believed, be the saving of her.

But the Scottish play would not relinquish its monopoly on misfortune, even when transferred to the silver screen. For the first and only time in his life, Olivier was engaged in characteristically meticulous preparation for a project which was never to materialize. There were to be many subsequent explanations, primarily that movie economics had Hollywood on the defensive, forcing it to use only its most "bankable" stars – a category in which, given their recent track record, neither of the Oliviers figured. But Olivier's cherished masterpiece really died in the small hours of 23 January 1956, when in a London hospital sixty-two-year-old Sir Alexander Korda peacefully breathed his last. With Korda gone, there was no one left in film-making who believed in the commercial viability of an Olivier *Macbeth*.

Korda's death also deprived Vivien of one of her closest and most supportive friends. The same was true of course, of Olivier; but to lose his *Macbeth* into the bargain seemed too much to bear. Vivien's problems he had no time for. He refused to believe that no one but Korda was prepared to put up the money for his glorious movie. In time he would approach the Rothschild family, even the New York "clothing trade", for finances. All he was looking for was £400,000 – less than the final cost of any of his other three Shakespeare films. Even when Sam Spiegel did put up £260,000, Olivier could find no one, not even J. Arthur Rank, to come up with the other £140,000. It made Olivier realize, to an extent he never had hitherto, how crucial Korda's support had been to his career. His tribute at his partner's cremation was one of the most moving of the many such addresses he has given. It was the only occasion on which the great Shakespearean risked concluding with the obvious, but this time heartfelt, salute from Hamlet to his dead father: "Take him for all in all, I shall not look on his like again."

Korda's death had spelt out the most chastening of lessons for Olivier. He could no longer take even his fame, let alone his reputation, for granted in the cruelly money-conscious world of film-making. In these recent troubled months, when he seemed to have exhausted all currently available theatrical possibilities, and indeed wearied of the draining effort required by nightly stage magnificence, Olivier had been tempted to devote his future to film, that most seductive and lucrative corner of the actor's market-place. "One may be daring, bold and resolute, even a bloody dreamer," he later said bitterly, lamenting his stillborn *Macbeth*, "but one cannot laugh to scorn the money men."[1] When in time others filmed the same play, financed on the bankability of their very different talents, he did not trouble to conceal his resentment. "Posterity", he complained, had been "dispossessed of another version of the Scottish play to compare with Orson Welles's or Roman Polanski's".

It was because he considered Macbeth such a difficult part – having mastered it so convincingly at Stratford, he could afford to – that Olivier was intent on having more fun as director than as actor. The shooting script which he prepared, this time without assistance, provides a tantalizing glimpse of what might have been. In Olivier's hands, Shakespeare's

303

great tragedy turns into an essentially visual text, prepared with a taste and discretion which would surprise many of Olivier's literary detractors. The document, a copy of which is now a prized collector's item, is the most eloquent tribute to Olivier's capacities both as film-maker and instinctual Shakespeare scholar.[2] Determined that his celluloid Macbeth would outshine his Henry, Hamlet or Richard, his vision of the film's conclusion shows that Olivier was ready to set yet another precedent by playing his death scene underwater:

> Shooting down again towards the bottom of the [gravel] pit, the reflections of two horsemen are seen to appear at the edge of the pit and gaze down. There is a slight movement underneath the water. CUTTING CLOSE: The face of the dying Macbeth slowly breaks through the water, a man for a brief instant alive in death. As he stares towards the top of the pit, we see in his expression again the realization of the completing point of fortune's whim. With a last stare of piercing anguish, he falls back submerged in the water, whose ever-reddening colour obscures him.

If *Macbeth* was not to be, Marilyn Monroe now appeared *ex machina* as incongruously ample consolation. When Noël Coward heard who Olivier's new co-star was to be, he said simply, "*Il faut vivre.*" The knight dutifully flew the Atlantic to pay homage to the garter; the deal, after all, made Monroe not only his co-star but his boss. The production company Monroe had formed with her stills photographer, Milton Greene, had quietly bought the rights to Rattigan's play before Olivier knew anything about it. Even Rattigan had been astonished by the sudden sequence of events caused by Hollywood's interest in his little Coronation present to his mother.

The playwright had first been summoned to Hollywood by a phone call from William Wyler: "Terry, we'd like you to come over here to discuss making a film of your play *The Sleeping Prince*. We're planning to star Marilyn Monroe. Laurence Olivier would probably take the part he played in the theatre. When could you fly here to have a word about all this?"[3] Rattigan, who suspected (rightly, as it turned out) that Olivier had no idea his name was being used, and who still was not at all sure that he wanted such attention drawn to his "little nonsense", was most reluctant to go. A keen amateur golfer, he agreed only when he realized that the trip could become an all-expenses-paid visit to the Ryder Cup at Palm Springs.

During the ten-hour stopover in New York, Rattigan had been approached by an excited stewardess with the news that Monroe would like him to join her downtown, at the Barberry Room, for a cocktail. "I imagine that to most people that news would have been electrifying, but it wasn't to me," said the happily homosexual Rattigan, who had heard of Monroe – just – but never seen any of her films.[4] He was kept waiting for an hour – the bare minimum, as Olivier was to discover – before an entourage swept in. Somewhere deep within it, behind dark glasses, was the lady herself. Rattigan's biographer, Michael Darlow, takes up the story:

> She bought him a stiff cocktail, his fourth, and after the formalities got down to business. This was made difficult by the fact that Monroe's quiet, shy manner meant he only understood about every third word she said, while she appeared to understand nothing at all that he said. However, he grasped the central points – if no definite offer materialized from Wyler's company, she would buy the rights. The terms she was talking were in multiples of hundreds of thousands of dollars rather than tens of thousands. She was prepared to write out a contract on the bar table there and then.
>
> She had by now removed her dark glasses. She gazed straight into Rattigan's eyes and asked with that distinctive quality of knowing innocence: "Do you think there's a chance that Sir Larry would do it with me?" Rattigan felt unable to say anything other than that he was sure he would. Indeed, he went so far as to assure her that he would leave no stone unturned to see that he did.[5]

Rattigan went on to Hollywood, saw Wyler and the Ryder Cup, then Wyler's producers, but no definite offer was forthcoming. (Though neither he nor Olivier knew it, Paramount was talking to Noël Coward about making the play into a musical, with Coward in the leading role.) On the way back through New York Rattigan phoned Monroe and told her the rights were hers. Her production company swiftly invited Olivier not just to co-star, but to direct.

In February 1956 Rattigan flew back with Olivier and Cecil Tennant to set up the unholy alliance of Thespis and Aphrodite – "the most exciting combination", said the director Joshua Logan, "since black and white". For two hours Milton Greene dispensed liberal cocktails at Monroe's Sutton Place apartment, so Olivier was "a little the worse for wear" by the time he boldly shouted through his hostess's door that it was time for her to put in an appearance. Monroe made an entrance worthy of the occasion, looking stunning in a very simple dress and virtually no make-up: "I'm sorry, I just didn't know what to wear. Should I be casual or formal? I went twice through my entire wardrobe, but everything I tried on wasn't kinda right." Olivier was immediately at her feet. After tying up the contract next morning and taking her to lunch at the 21 Club, he was utterly besotted. "*What* was going to happen? She was so adorable, so witty, such incredible fun and more physically attractive than anyone I could have imagined, apart from herself on the screen."

Next day they gave a joint press conference in the Terrace Room of the Plaza Hotel, where a chain-smoking Olivier had to field ever more inane questions for the statutory interval before Monroe made another tardy but spectacular entrance, wearing a black velvet sheath which plunged dramatically at both front and back. Olivier declared:

> Marilyn is a brilliant comedienne, which means to me she is a very fine actress. She has the extremely cunning gift of being able to suggest one minute that she is the naughtiest little thing, and the next minute that she is beautifully dumb and innocent. The effect on the audience is that they are gently titillated to a sense of excitement in not knowing which is which.

Yes, he added in answer to the inevitable question, he did think she could play Shakespeare. Monroe purred, the photographers moved in and – surprise, surprise – the spaghetti-thin shoulder-strap of her gown chose just that moment to give way. Flashbulbs popped in ecstasy as Olivier and a semi-*déshabillé* Monroe backed, giggling, against the wall. Olivier seemed as excited about it all as the press corps. "No more leg pictures, fellas!" he cried. "From now on she is too ethereal." It was perhaps just as well that Monroe was then being very publicly squired by the playwright Arthur Miller.

While in New York Olivier lunched with a testy Cecil Beaton, still smarting from his treatment after *The School for Scandal*. After much huffing and puffing he asked Beaton to design Monroe's costumes for the film. Beaton had hated the play in London, was wary of getting involved with Olivier again, but adored Monroe and indeed the pre-First World War period. Showing less enthusiasm than Olivier had expected, Beaton did not commit himself. Next day he told his agent to ask for "the highest fee that any designer in the history of entertainment has ever been given".[6] Beaton never heard another word from Olivier – "not even a thank-you for the lunch".

Back in London, the first highlight of the summer was another *Night of a Hundred Stars* at the London Palladium, in which the Oliviers did a "Top Hat" song-and-dance routine with John Mills, before Bob Hope cut in for a waltz with Olivier. As the new president of the Actors' Orphanage, in succession to Noël Coward, Olivier had himself organized the event, which also featured Jack Benny and Tyrone Power.

The following month, on 14 July, a honeymoon couple flew into London, to the most ecstatic welcome accorded anyone all year. Mr and Mrs Arthur Miller, whose two-week-old marriage was still the sensation of the United States' gossip columns, arrived at Heathrow with twenty-seven items of luggage, three of which were his. Miller remembered Olivier "near to giggling with excitement". An impromptu press conference – the biggest,

Miller was told, in British history – turned into a frenzied carnival of chaos, which followed Monroe all the way to Parkside House, the eleven-bedroom Surrey mansion she had rented from Lord Moore, the publisher of the *Financial Times*. A more orderly press conference followed at the Savoy next day – Olivier had pleaded for punctuality, so she was only an hour late – but the British press could not get enough of Monroe. They hunted her in packs, everywhere she went, sharing the delights she conveyed in letters home of her first visit to Britain:

> Compared to California, England seems tiny and quaint with its toy trains chugging through the English countryside.... I am dying to walk bareheaded in the rain. I want to eat real roast beef and Yorkshire pudding as I believe only the English can cook it. I want to buy a tweed suit that fits me – I have never worn a tailored suit in my life. I want to ride a bicycle, and I'd like someone to explain the jokes in *Punch* – they don't seem funny to me.[7]

The fun lasted two weeks, which Olivier had declared a holiday "so that we should all feel at home with each other". Even he was surprised by how swiftly this would prove impossible.

On the first day scheduled for shooting, Monroe arrived at Pinewood Studios with an entourage including her own make-up man and hairdresser, a cook and secretary, two publicists and several bodyguards – not to mention Milton Greene, who immediately queried Olivier about the security arrangements on the set: "You never know, there may be a sex-mad carpenter at work." Also on hand, to Olivier's deep dismay, was Monroe's "drama coach", Paula Strasberg – wife of Lee Strasberg, high priest of the Method school of acting. To Olivier the very names of Method and Strasberg were anathema; to Monroe they were sacred. She had recently undergone Method training to "broaden" her acting skills, and had even played Aristophanes's Lysistrata with Strasberg's company. Paula, it seemed, "always came along" wherever Monroe went. Her presence was essential. It was also going to add to a burden greater than Olivier had borne on any of his epic Shakespeare films. In Miller's account of what followed, "Olivier was soon prepared to murder Paula outright, and from time to time I would not have minded joining him."[8]

Rattigan, adapting his own play for the screen, had found Monroe surprisingly pliable. When she wanted to change a "Gosh!" to a "Golly!", he refused. "Oh well," she replied, "I'll think 'Golly!' and say 'Gosh!'" (Rattigan later told the Queen that Monroe was "a shy exhibitionist – a Garbo who likes to be photographed".) In this amiable atmosphere the first few weeks went reasonably smoothly, apart from Monroe's intense nervousness on set. She was clearly in awe of the abilities of Olivier, who began to have the greatest difficulty extracting the performance he required of her. Few of the cast had ever seen an actress require so many takes to get the tiniest scene right, though they had to admit that the finished product was magical. What seemed appallingly wooden and awkward on the set would emerge as utterly deft and delicate in the rushes. Olivier, more and more exasperated, could not understand why he himself had begun to look wooden by comparison.

There was one very short scene, set in Westminster Abbey, which required Monroe simply to look up and appear moved. Told by Paula Strasberg that music would help, Olivier played a tape of the "Air on a G String" continually for some twenty-five takes without success. "Look," he finally asked Monroe, "how can I help you? I don't know what more I can say. I thought you loved the 'Air on a G String'?"

"Yeah," came the reply, "but I think I could do it better if you played 'Danny Boy'."

A scene in which Monroe was required to nibble some caviar, while the Duke ignores her, took two days, thirty-four takes and twenty jars of $8 caviar to get right. She simply could not summon up the expression of innocent delight Olivier had asked for. Paula Strasberg finally managed it by telling her charge to "think of cold sausages, Coca-Cola and Frankie Sinatra".

After a tolerably punctual beginning, Monroe then began to arrive a little bit later each day, until whole mornings went by with the rest of the cast idling helplessly around the set. One morning the redoubtable Sybil Thorndike, playing the Grand Duchess, was kept waiting for hours in her very heavy robes when Monroe failed to turn up for the shooting of the Coronation scene. When she finally arrived, Olivier's suggestion that she apologize to Dame Sybil saw Monroe flounce off the set in a huff. Half an hour later she returned, with a mumbled apology, to which Dame Sybil grandly replied: "Not at all, my dear. I'm sure we're all very glad to see you – now that you are *here*." For all the exasperation she caused, Monroe was always able to charm her way out of it. One morning Olivier finally cracked, railing at her: "Why can't you get here on time, for fuck's sake?" "Oh," said Monroe, wide-eyed, "do you have that word here in England, too?"

On another occasion Olivier told Monroe to "act sexy". She looked coldly at him for a long time before replying, "Larry, I don't have to act sexy. I *am* sexy." There ensued, said the cameraman, Jack Cardiff, "a terrible row".[9] Paula Strasberg intervened: "I never tell her how to say a line. You don't have to teach her to be sexy. She *is* sexy. You don't have to teach her how to be American. She *is* American." Cardiff later summed up:

It was the most dreadful experience of [Olivier's] life. He had greatness. And all that greatness went up against a stone wall when he was working with Marilyn. It was two personalities which didn't get on because she wouldn't listen to him. She doubted his wisdom about how to play the part. She wanted to play it the way she felt and the way her coach had told her.

Olivier found it impossible to take Dame Sybil's advice to relax: "She's an intuitive actress. . . . That little girl is the only one here who knows how to act before a camera." According to Miller, he took completely the wrong approach to directing Monroe, given "an arch tongue too quick with the cutting joke, an irritating mechanistic attitude in positioning her and imposing his preconceived notions upon her". Soon, as her husband remembered it, Monroe verged on the belief that Olivier had agreed to work with her "only because he needed the money her presence would bring in".

But again he was shouldering the triple burden of producer, director and leading actor, only this time without Korda or del Giudice to worry about the logistics – not least the expensive time wasted by Monroe's unpredictability. The plain fact was that his chief source of grief, in his view, was also his employer. She was paying the bills. He could only exert his most diplomatic skills, and grin and bear it.

There was, according to Alexander Korda's nephew Michael, another source of tension between them. When Korda asked his friend Milton Greene about the rumoured "problems" between Olivier and Monroe, Greene at first tried to shrug it off. It was just that "Olivier has problems with the close-ups".

"Why?" asked Korda. "I would have thought a close-up with Marilyn Monroe would be stimulating, even for Larry."

"He says she doesn't wash enough. He says she has, um, BO."

"Oh. Did he tell anyone?"

"Yes, he told Marilyn. That's the problem."[10]

Vivien had gritted her teeth and mustered a tense smile during the welcoming ceremonies and the leering publicity which had ensued. "No, Marilyn will *not* be staying with us," she had told reporters. "She will weekend with us sometimes at Notley Abbey ... but Miss Monroe desires vacant possession of her own little bit of England. . . ." According to Olivier Vivien had caused no trouble at all over surrendering to another actress, let alone this one, the part which she had created; Vivien later claimed she had suggested Monroe for the part, after seeing her in *How To Marry a Millionaire*. But she had already come up with her own way of keeping Monroe at bay. Not long before Monroe's arrival, and soon after she had returned to the West End in Noël Coward's new comedy, *South Sea Bubble* (a revised version of *Home and Colonial*), Lady Olivier announced that she had delightedly discovered, at the age of forty-two, that she was pregnant.

She wanted the child, Vivien told friends, "for Larry's sake". He adored children, which were the only ingredient missing from their blissful marriage. Such pretence by now rang too hollow. Vivien was stung by rumours that she had invented the pregnancy to distract attention from the Larry-and-Marilyn show. Why had she waited until she was four months pregnant to make the announcement? And how come she still looked so slim? Noël Coward, irritated that she was leaving his hit play at such short notice, confided to his diary: "I shall be hopping mad if, as I suspect, the whole thing comes to nothing."[11] On Saturday 12 August, four months before the baby was due, Vivien dropped out of *South Sea Bubble* and retired to Notley. Next day she felt unwell. By the time the doctors arrived, she had suffered another miscarriage.

Olivier's brother Dickie had now moved into a cottage at Notley and was managing the estate. That same day, by a cruel irony, his wife Hester gave birth to a baby girl only a few hundred yards from where Vivien lay sobbing. But both she and Olivier knew this latest collapse was more mental than physical. He now firmly accepted the diagnosis that his wife was more than just a manic depressive; she was clinically schizophrenic. Her old lung trouble had mercifully remained dormant, but the tuberculosis apparently exacerbated her manic symptoms. As Olivier struggled to get Monroe's performance in the can and the lady herself on the first plane home, Vivien embarked on her worst winter yet.

The attacks were coming more frequently and with greater ferocity. Vivien underwent more electric-shock treatment, but it merely contained rather than cured. Her collapses now led to bouts of nymphomania and she would take to the streets in search of "rough trade". The dangers of scandal were all too obvious. She took to carrying around with her a report from Dr Arthur Conachy, the physician she trusted most, not least because he was one of the few to resist the diagnosis of schizophrenia, arguing that Vivien was no more than manically depressive. In case she should undergo an attack – and its consequences – beyond his range, Dr Conachy had written that after each such seizure his patient

> develops a marked increase in libido and indiscriminate sexual activity. These illustrations of her symptoms, particularly her overt sexuality, loss of judgement and persistent overdrive make me feel, from the social and publicity consequences that derive from this, that her manic phase is much more understandable than the depressed phase.... The one undesirable factor in this pattern is her tendency to take considerable and regular amounts of alcohol, particularly in moments of stress. She refuses to modify this, but is in no sense an alcoholic.[12]

In tax exile in Jamaica, Noël Coward received the news of Vivien's miscarriage in none-too-sympathetic, I-told-you-so mood: "The hysterical, disorganized silliness of the whole thing infuriates me.... It is not very bright, if pregnant, to dance about at the Palladium with Larry and Johnny Mills, and go to parties while playing an arduous part eight times a week." A miscarriage was "about as inevitable as anything could be.... A smash success is destroyed, she is wretched and on her way round the bend again, Larry is wretched, a large number of people, including me, are inconvenienced, and all for nothing...."

The Oliviers had not behaved as the "loving friends" Coward thought them to be. He believed, with some justice, that *South Sea Bubble* had been a "lifesaver" for Vivien, "if only they had had the sense to see it.... It gave her a glamorous success on her own, away from Larry's perpetual shadow, and she should have played it for at least six months...." Now Coward was "sick to death of them both.... I've been bored and involved with their domestic problems for years and done all I could to help, and as they haven't even troubled to write to me they can bloody well get on with it."

Vivien went off to recuperate in Italy with Rex Harrison and Lilli Palmer, leaving Olivier to concentrate his energies on Monroe. By this time even Miller had defected back to New York, ostensibly to visit his sick daughter. But he was having as hard a time from the British press – "lumbered by English upmanship, he secretly respects Sir Laurence too much" – as from his wife about his failure to support her in her battles with Olivier. Some Monroe biographers even date the breakdown of the Monroe–Miller relationship from these tense Pinewood days, only a month after they had married. The staff of Parkside House gleefully testified that the newlyweds had separate bedrooms. Monroe's New York psychiatrist, Dr Marianne Kris, had to be flown over half-way through the shooting schedule.

All the film's cast, including Thorndike, Richard Wattis, Esmond Knight and Paul Hardwick, have testified to the immense grace which Olivier displayed under pressure. Billy Wilder was the only director ever to agree to work with Marilyn Monroe a second time: "It behooves the Screen Directors Guild to award me a purple heart." Rumours had stretched from Pinewood to Hollywood; Olivier received a letter from Wilder saying that directing Monroe had been like "working with Hitler". Joshua Logan, who had directed her in *Bus Stop*, sent more reassuring news: shooting would be "pure, unmitigated hell", but the results would be "a pleasant surprise".

Olivier earned the displeasure of the press by declaring the set closed. It was the only way to keep the picture on schedule, and mask from the world the deep rift between himself and his co-star. The delays, tantrums and retakes continued to the bitter end; by November, to everyone's astonishment, including his own, an exhausted Olivier had managed to bring the picture in a few days ahead of schedule. There was even time, despite himself, to offer Monroe the chance for a few retakes. He hated the new title foisted on the film by Monroe's American backers, *The Prince and the Showgirl*, moaning that it sounded "like an old Betty Grable musical". But it eventually opened to golden reviews and won Monroe her only acting award, Italy's David di Donatello statuette. Her performance, for all the anguish which went into it, looked as irresistibly fresh and natural as anything she ever did. Over the years Olivier grew uneasily aware that she had made him look stagey, though an impromptu screening at the home of some Hollywood friends in the early 1980s pleasantly surprised him.

Five years and only three films after *The Prince and the Showgirl*, Monroe was dead at thirty-six, eaten alive by her own rampant celebrity. "She was the victim of ballyhoo and sensation," said Olivier, "exploited beyond anyone's means." At the time, he was only too happy to see the back of her, gritting his teeth through the "charade" of waving her off for the cameras at Heathrow. Vivien and Arthur Miller again played stalwart supporting roles. But Olivier's own performance, kissing and hugging Monroe, grinning, saying how much he looked forward to seeing her again – "Working with her?" "Well, who knows?" – was one of the least convincing he ever turned in.

As Mrs Miller flew out of his life, Olivier already had a notion of the next, outlandish step he and his career might take. In a way, he had Monroe to thank for the role which would set the undisputed seal on his greatness. He never wanted to see her again, but he had extracted his usual slice of unexpected good fortune from the agonies of keeping her happy all those weeks.

During his time in England Arthur Miller had naturally expressed an interest in visiting the London theatre and respectfully asked Olivier to recommend the best in contemporary English drama. There's nothing worth seeing, Olivier had told him, still smarting from his stewardship of the St James's – *"niente"*. But what about this new play at the Royal Court, Miller had asked – the one exciting such controversy, by this new playwright the newspapers were calling an "angry young man"? Oh no, said Olivier, you don't want to bother with that; "I've seen it. It stinks.... Besides, it's a travesty on England, a lot of bitter rattling on..."[13]

Miller persisted, largely because he liked the title, and Olivier decided at the last minute to take the chance to pay a second visit to John Osborne's

Look Back in Anger. In the interval Miller told Olivier he thought the angry young man had something. The play was marvellous: angry, yes, but stirringly so, eloquent, new. It reminded him of Clifford Odets at his most lyrically bitter. There were "a lot of hanging threads, but who cared? It had real life, a rare achievement." Olivier was intrigued. If Arthur Miller thought this Osborne fellow was okay, maybe he should too.

Olivier may have proved himself a born leader, but he has always had as great a capacity to be led. Built into his marvellous readiness for risk, very much to the fore in the sequence of events begun that evening, is the discriminating opportunist's eye for the main chance. Seeing George Devine across the crush bar, Olivier asked if Osborne was "in" tonight. No, he was not. Well, get him in by the end of the show, said Olivier. Tell him Arthur Miller's here and likes his play.

After the curtain, an excited young Osborne duly presented himself for Miller's congratulations. The two playwrights chatted for a while, then Olivier seized the chance to draw Osborne to one side. Miller listened with astonishment as Olivier asked this "young guy with a shock of uncombed hair and a look on his face of having awakened twenty minutes earlier": "Er, you're not writing anything which might have the littlest opportunity for ... well ... me, are you?"

So Laurence Olivier would always have one reason to be grateful to Marilyn Monroe. It was thanks to her, and her remarkable choice of husband, that he first met Archie Rice.

313

CHAPTER 18

1956–8

Late in 1956, nearly twenty-two years since he had first set eyes on the "wondrous, unimagined beauty" of Vivien Leigh in *The Mask of Virtue*, Laurence Olivier felt similar feelings coursing through him as he rather dutifully attended a Royal Court production of William Wycherley's *The Country Wife*.

Olivier was still trying to establish some sort of presence at the Royal Court, whence George Devine's English Stage Company was sending shock waves through the moribund British theatre. Playing Margery Pinchwife that night was a forceful young actress called Joan Plowright, one of Devine's cockiest *enfants terribles*, who eyed Olivier askance when he went backstage to congratulate the "young people". To her, Olivier represented everything that was wrong with the profession she had recently joined: he was titled, pleased with himself, resting on his laurels and now he was being patronizing. As more and more of "George's children" filed into Devine's office to meet the great man, Olivier found he had eyes only for this brassy girl from Lincolnshire. By the end of the evening, the "very name of Joan Plowright was enough to make me think thoughts of love".

He had to get in on this act. "Do you really think", Olivier asked Devine, *devant les enfants*, "that young Osborne might be serious about a play for me?" The toast of Sloane Square, folk-hero to Miss Plowright and her peers, Osborne had apparently begun writing the successor to *Look Back in Anger*. It would be one of the most eagerly awaited second plays in theatrical memory. In fact he was working on the first act of a piece about a broken-down, third-rate music-hall comedian, a man living in a past which had never really amounted to much, and whose present was hidden behind a pair of utterly dead eyes. Archie Rice was to be a metaphor for the state of post-Suez Britain.

Olivier was off to New York to scout out new material for the St James's, but Devine promised to airmail whatever Osborne had to offer. Ten days later the first act of *The Entertainer* arrived. Olivier cancelled an engagement for that evening, read the typescript and immediately telephoned Devine to say that on the strength of the first act alone he would take the part: "I could be run over and killed at the beginning of Act 2 for all I cared."

Olivier was desperate to do something "different". Acutely depressed by Vivien's decline, and the disappearance of any pretence that the Oliviers still had a professional future, he was again in profoundly bleak mood about his career as well. He expressed his feelings about this low period very candidly in a contribution to a volume published in 1981, to mark the silver jubilee of the English Stage Company:

> I had reached a stage in my life that I was getting profoundly sick of – not just tired – sick. Consequently the public were, likely enough, beginning to agree with me.... I was going mad, desperately searching for something suddenly fresh and thrillingly exciting. What I felt to be my image was boring me to death.
>
> I really felt that death might be quite exciting, compared with the purgatorial, amorphous *Nothing* that was my existence. And now, suddenly, this miracle was happening....[1]

He began to feel the existence of a new self, a "vitally changed, entirely unfamiliar *me*". That all this showed the worst side of him was so much the better: it felt "something like a confession, a welcome and beneficial expulsion of filth". In the opportunity afforded him by Archie Rice he sensed "a great sea-change, transforming me into something strange. I felt, in fact, that I was starting a new life." And so he was, in more ways than he could yet realize.

John Osborne has slightly spoilt the story by revealing that Olivier had at first wanted to play Billie Rice, Archie's father. "When I finished the play, he changed his mind. Just as well – for both of us."[2] Early in 1957 Osborne and the director, Tony Richardson, escorted Olivier around London's few remaining music-halls to soak up the atmosphere. "The music-hall is dying, and with it a significant part of England," wrote Osborne in a brief preface to *The Entertainer*. "This was truly a folk art.... Not only has this technique its own traditions, its own convention and symbol, its own mystique, it cuts right across the restrictions of the so-called naturalistic stage. Its contact is immediate, vital and direct."[3] When Olivier visited Collins's Music-Hall in Islington and chatted backstage afterwards to the chorus girls, the management were excited enough to put up a plaque (lost when it closed down, to make way for a haulage company, the following year). He had soon found the externals he needed – check suit, bow tie, white socks, grey bowler – to build one of his most memorable creations.

But the part appealed to something deeper in Olivier than merely outlandish impersonation. All his life he had played with the joke that he might have been born Larry *Oliver* – a third-rate stand-up comic as whom he had convulsed many a Notley soiree. He told the *Daily Mail* at the time:

> I feel I can play this Archie Rice quite intuitively. There must have been something of Archie in me all along. It's what I might so easily have become ... because I'm always thinking that I've never had the opportunity to make people laugh as much as I would have liked. I'd like to make them *die* with laughter. There is to me a tremendous attraction in being a general entertainer and bridging the lines of demarcation in the theatre.

Olivier had met countless Archie Rices in his early days on the road for Birmingham Rep. The theatrical digs in which he had begun his career were the last resting-places of these forlorn, gin-stained figures, hammering out remorseless one-liners to mask their desperate feelings of failure, hiding a poignant awareness of their own limitations behind a leer and hard-line professionalism. It was Olivier's capacity to catch both ends of the spectrum, switching from a gleefully tacky comic routine to moments of the most wrenching pathos, which made his portrait so powerful. He opted for puffy cheeks and an accent of edgily phoney refinement. He perfected the too-hearty laugh, the gurgling relish in the cheap, smutty, none-too-funny jokes. The rest – the *real* Archie, consumed with suffering of a heroic order – he had mastered elsewhere. But above all he expressed his respect for Archie – for all the Archies he himself might have been, had he been less talented – by conveying the man's angry intelligence. The moments of acutely disgusted self-analysis, to which Osborne gave some of his finest writing, were among the most powerful of an evening both hugely entertaining and considerably disturbing.

Osborne, who later became a close friend of Olivier's, sensed the core of his kinship with Archie:

> I suspect that Olivier has a feeling sometimes that he is a deeply hollow man. That doesn't mean that he *is* a hollow man, but he knows what it's like to feel hollow. And that's why – or it's one of the reasons – he was so good as Archie Rice. Olivier understands that kind of character and his feelings of inadequacy, of being fifth-rate. All comics are ready to duck even when they appear to be aggressively confident, perhaps even more so then. Olivier knows the ready-to-duck mentality.[4]

Tony Richardson, on a more practical level, added with equal shrewdness: "Undoubtedly he's a great comic actor.... He's a very active man and comedy involves action, whereas tragedy needs passivity and he's not very good at that."[5]

As with *Richard III*, the sheer theatrical excitement of Olivier's performance as Archie Rice was inevitably missing from the subsequent film (despite its X certificate). But the movie version does preserve very effectively the most chilling moment in the play, when Archie brags to his daughter that "nothing matters" because he is "dead behind the eyes". As Olivier leers forward at the camera, his eyes are indeed dead, devastatingly so. Then Archie hears the news that his son has been killed at Suez and there is the most remarkable transformation. "The man's agony shows naked," wrote an appeased John Barber of this moment onstage. "Before your eyes you see how a body crumbles as the heart cracks within." From Olivier's mouth came a series of moans and mumbles which gradually grew into pained but discernible song; Archie was singing the blues. In that moment, wrote Tynan, Olivier achieved "a miracle".

Olivier was very nervous before rehearsals of *The Entertainer*, sensing that he had taken on a risk of make-or-break proportions, with only himself to rely on. Both writer and director, though highly talented, were of too little experience to lend much support. But the first run-through was enough to reassure Olivier that a new kind of triumph was in the offing. In the initial limited season of four weeks at the Royal Court, the sheer virtuosity of his performance tended to crowd out the play, already the object of some controversy. *The Times*, for instance, speaking for its constituency, said that were Archie less expertly played, "the part would fall all over the place in the last quarter of an hour". When the production was revived later in the year, for a longer run at the Palace Theatre, the performance and play merged more effectively, benefiting from a more thoughtful response to Osborne's polemic from critics and audiences alike.

For Olivier the risk had more than paid off. Neither of his great contemporaries, Gielgud or Richardson, would have dared set foot on the stage of the Royal Court in the late 1950s. The place was full of four-letter words and brazen challenges to the world of the Establishment to which they – and Olivier – belonged. The script of *The Entertainer* was replete with attacks on the government of the day, the Suez invasion, even the royal family; Britannia, in Archie's seaside stage show, *Rock'n Roll New'd Look*, was naked from the helmet down. So desperate was Olivier to reach another plateau of versatility, that he did not, as with *Streetcar*, worry himself about his title and his public respectability. There had been a boardroom row at the Royal Court over Osborne's text, which might never have reached the stage had not one of Devine's council, Lord

Harewood, intervened with the chairman, Neville Blond. ("You must be barmy to turn down the play, with Olivier wanting to act in it," Blond's wife Elaine had told the poet-dramatist Ronald Duncan, who was leading the opposition.)[6] But this time Olivier did not get involved. At last the esteem in which he was now secure had freed him to be simply an actor.

William Gaskill, who succeeded Devine as director of the English Stage Company, argues that all Olivier's qualities as an actor combined to be seen at their best in his portrayal of Archie Rice: "Larry had a complete understanding of the role. In an odd way he knew it was about him."[7] At a memorial evening for Devine ten years later, the leering face of Archie Rice – "that peculiar mask" – suddenly confronted Gaskill, and from behind it Olivier's voice said: "This is really me, isn't it?" It *was* him, thought Gaskill, absolutely him. "That kind of heartless clown's mask is very much part of Larry Olivier. I don't mean that he's cold and unemotional, but at the same time I think it's sentimental to expect him, because he is an outstanding actor, to be a man of great feeling and depth. Not many actors are."[8]

It is now generally held that in Archie Rice Olivier achieved his greatest stage performance outside Shakespeare. Olivier's "masterly" Archie, as Richard Findlater later put it, "was acting *about* acting, its shams and realities; it was the personification of a dying theatre and (less certainly) a dying society; but it was also the incarnation of one man's suffering and despair, none the less overwhelming in its theatrical truth because the man was a third-rate comic rather than a Shakespearean king."[9] Olivier himself remained profoundly grateful to Osborne: "For so long I hadn't been able to bring anything out of my bag of tricks that was going to be a surprise to anyone, and this changed it. It made me feel like a modern actor again."

Olivier's mere presence at the Royal Court had also lent respectability to the "new wave" of British drama Devine's company was fostering. The text of *Look Back in Anger* had originally been received in response to an advertisement seeking new material in *The Stage*. When Olivier had first shown an interest in the part, most of his friends had tried to talk him out of it. "I must say", said Osborne, "that I formed the opinion that most of his friends at the time were very stupid people – frankly, little more than third-rate sycophants." But Olivier's commitment to the *nouvelle vague* braved even the wrath of this cherished coterie. Now, despite them, his presence in an Osborne cast had given the brutally realistic working-class drama of the day a valuable boost by lending his name and support to one of its founding fathers. A new movement was afoot in the English theatre. The revolutionary work of Joan Littlewood's Theatre Workshop at Stratford East, followed by the young Peter Hall's innovative seasons at the Arts Theatre, now combined with Devine's Royal Court to give

British youth a theatrical voice for the first time since the war. Olivier's appearance on one of these stages "was the Establishment's first bow to 'the angries'", wrote Tynan. "It meant they had officially arrived."[10] Somewhat cynically, Tynan added that Olivier had asked Osborne for a part "presumably on the principle of joining what you can't lick". In truth it was not quite that simple.

Olivier's opportunism helped him know a good – and different – thing when he saw it. But his bout of professional self-disgust, his latest suggestion that death would have seemed a merciful release, was more to do with matters domestic. In this Arthur Miller had again proved a salutary visitor. During his ordeal at Pinewood with Monroe, Olivier had himself come to the conclusion that she was "schizoid". Gradually he realized that Miller had problems very similar to his own. A stable character like himself, an artist of some eminence, he was married to a creature whose fame and beauty combined to make her self-doubting, neurotic and, to say the least, difficult to live with.

For years, according to Tynan, Olivier had been in a quandary about Vivien: "Each time she'd have a breakdown, he'd say, 'Okay, that's it, this time I'm leaving.' But then she'd bounce back and he'd say, 'Wait a minute, perhaps I was too hasty.' "[11] He had reached a crippling cycle of indecision, producing an emotional paralysis – in Tynan's words, "an inability to act on his own needs. He wanted to get out, but he knew that if he did he'd be consumed by guilt for abandoning this helpless creature." Now he sensed the same dilemma in Miller, even so early in his marriage. The two men, though never intimate friends, did pool their problems to some extent; and Olivier began to see that Miller was being destroyed by his sufferance of Monroe. He was "confused, paralysed, and he couldn't work, he couldn't do the things he needed to, he couldn't concentrate". Feeling pity for Miller, Olivier suddenly understood that people must feel a similar pity for him. The thought concentrated his mind enormously. "He resolved, once and for all, to get hold of his life and change it. He realized, he said, that he was about to be fifty, and he didn't want to live the rest of his life in that personal purgatory he found himself in."

Soon after Olivier had agreed to play Archie Rice, Devine conceived the dangerous notion that Vivien might play Phoebe, his dowdy, shrill, long-suffering wife. He had even, to Olivier's horror, discussed it with her; they had been friends since Devine took over from Olivier as Antrobus to Vivien's Sabina in *The Skin of our Teeth*. Vivien grew excited. Oblivious to the effect of her own drinking on her once lovely features, she even suggested that she could wear a rubber mask, as she had when playing the aged Emma Hamilton. Yes, she told Devine, she was enthusiastic – "if it's all right with Larry".[12]

It was not. Olivier had only just extricated himself from a lucrative Hollywood offer to film Rattigan's *Separate Tables* because of Vivien, even though the deal would have fulfilled a long-standing (and mutual) wish to play opposite Spencer Tracy. There were complex contractual problems involving Burt Lancaster, who owned the rights; but the real reason Olivier pulled out was his dread of working with Vivien. It was a dire admission, but he was resolved. He had not settled for £50 a week at the Royal Court, instead of a $300,000 movie contract, only to be saddled with her again.

The Oliviers had recently sold Durham Cottage, so it was to their suite at the Connaught Hotel that Osborne and Richardson came for the awkward task of discussing Vivien's suitability for the role of Phoebe. Olivier put his case as tactfully as he could: she was "too beautiful to play the part effectively", he said with apparent regret. When Vivien mentioned her notion of the rubber mask, he laughed it to scorn. He had tried to handle a delicate matter with sensitivity. But the evening was to prove another watershed. In Vivien's mind he had made it clear that he was no longer prepared to go to great lengths to work with her. He had made it pretty clear that he did not much want to work with her at all.

She scarcely troubled to conceal her resentment. Vivien insisted on coming to rehearsals of *The Entertainer*, making Olivier as nervous as Richardson and Osborne. When she began to interfere with Richardson's direction, he was forced to appeal to Devine, who on the morning of the dress rehearsal reluctantly banned her from the theatre. Back at Notley she went berserk. Olivier returned to find that his wife had gone on a rampage worthy of a thousand movie scenes – smashing lamps, vases, precious ornaments, mementoes. The possessions so prized by this very materialistic woman were the first things she turned on in moments of despair. No wonder Olivier's first night as Archie Rice was a multiple trauma for him. Conscious that his spiritual pain was showing, he told visitors to his dressing-room that he was suffering from gout – adding the double-edged, apparently self-deprecating afterthought: "psychosomatic, no doubt".

As soon as the run was over he and Vivien were pre-contracted, ironically enough, to work together again; in the wake of his mighty success at Stratford, he had some time ago agreed to a European tour of *Titus Andronicus*.[13] So the original company reconvened that May to head off to Paris by train – at Olivier's insistence, so fearful was he of what flying might do to Vivien. Their itinerary would take them on to Venice, Belgrade, Zagreb, Vienna and Warsaw before a short run back in London at the Stoll Theatre.

The decision to travel by train proved disastrous. Even on the way to Paris – where Olivier celebrated his fiftieth birthday watching Vivien join him as a member of the *Légion d'honneur* – it became clear that the unusually hot weather would aggravate her sense of claustrophobia. The Stratford company, mindful of the scenes they had witnessed the summer before, grew anxious. By Belgrade, Vivien was back on her roller-coaster: she was smoking and drinking to excess, and launching random attacks on fellow members of the cast. To central Europe she was still Scarlett O'Hara, mobbed wherever she went, which only made her more tense. On the twenty-two-hour train journey from Vienna to Warsaw, in ninety-degree heat, she paced the train's corridor restlessly, then began to run up and down it, shouting abuse and inanities. When Olivier tried to restrain her, she threw a make-up case at him and smashed the window. He retired, defeated, to the next carriage, leaving protective members of the company to calm her. In Warsaw he sought medical help for Vivien, who survived the rest of the tour and the journey home under sedation.

Back in London, on the opening night at the Stoll, the strain showed in Olivier's performance. He kept up a spirited façade, giving his curtain speech in seven different languages and joking that in Belgrade he and his wife had metamorphosed into Ser Lorens Olivije and Vivijan Li. But Tynan, his greatest advocate, noticed that "he was well below par. His voice seemed constipated, a crafty squawk instead of a terrible bellow; he rushed and gabbled...."[14] Ignorant as yet of Olivier's real problems, Tynan glibly suggested that "our greatest actor" was "betraying all the signs of an over-tired actor who is addressing a foreign audience and counting on their inability to understand what he is saying".

As if he did not have enough to contend with, Olivier had also returned home to the news that the St James's was under threat of demolition. Just when his production company had managed to present a lucratively successful show at the New Theatre, *Summer of the Seventeenth Doll*, Parliament was debating the destruction of his professional home to make way for an office block. For once in his life, Olivier was so tired and low that he could not muster the energy to put up much of a fight. He asked Dorothy Tutin (to whom he had become very close when she played his daughter in *The Entertainer*) to represent him in leading a protest on Downing Street; "I'm not", he told the press, "very good at this sort of thing." Besides, he knew in his heart that the theatre was a lost cause: bombed in the war, it now had an unsafe roof and had been declared a fire hazard. With a seating capacity of only 800, there seemed little likelihood of a fairy godfather coming up with the £250,000 needed to save the St James's.

Vivien, however, decided to throw all her fragile energy into the fight. At first, she led a forlorn protest march from the theatre to St Martin's-in-the-Fields; Alan Dent carried a sandwich board as Vivien clanged a handbell at the head of a threadbare thespian procession. This failure merely roused her, two days later, to a more dramatic form of protest. On 22 July, during the final House of Lords debate which might have sealed the St James's fate, she staged a solo demonstration in the Strangers Gallery, interrupting the speeches with a cry of "My Lords! I wish to protest against St James's Theatre being demolished." Vivien did not, as theatrical legend now has it, throw a kipper at their noble lordships. But the serried ranks of peers were mortified at this flagrant breach of protocol – by a conspicuous public figure, moreover, the wife of a knight. In vain did the Gentleman Usher of the Black Rod, Sir Brian Horrocks, try to lead Lady Olivier out discreetly. So distraught did she become that he was obliged to summon attendants and have her forcibly ejected.

An hour later Vivien was at the Stoll, preparing to take to the stage as Lavinia. Besieged by reporters, she mixed defiance with charm as she told them: "If the St James's Theatre goes, I go too. I will quit the English stage and this country. I really mean it." Enter her husband, dressed as Titus, to plant a kiss on her cheek for the benefit of the cameras and announce that he thought it was "a very sweet and gallant thing" that she had done. Next day Olivier entered the lists himself, with the rather more orthodox weapon of a letter to *The Times*. But in private even Equity now agreed with him that the St James's was a hopeless cause. Vivien kept lobbying as if her life depended on it: Churchill charmingly offered a donation of £500, with a cautionary letter saying that "as a parliamentarian I cannot approve of your disorderly methods". Olivier joked that he was going to change his name to Mr Pankhurst. But by 27 July the Oliviers were hosting a champagne party to bid their theatre farewell.

Their turbulent seven-year tenancy of the St James's was marked by a marble slab, bearing both their heads in profile, in the lobby of the building which replaced it. The end of their dreams of making theatrical history there coincided, as it happened, with the last performance the Oliviers were to give together, on stage or screen. When the final curtain came down on *Titus Andronicus* on 4 August 1957, it was also falling on their professional partnership. Its private counterpart still had one painful, long-drawn-out act to run.

Hitherto they had managed to keep the state of their marriage a closely guarded secret among their most intimate friends and a number of fellow actors who were too fond of them both to noise the ugly facts abroad. All that was now to change, thanks to a Labour MP who decided to extract some political mileage from the Oliviers' decision to take separate holidays that summer. The story had surfaced in the gossip columns because their plans entailed turning down President Tito of Yugoslavia, who had invited them to join him at his summer residence near Dubrovnik.

With Vivien's health still delicate, they had amicably decided it best for her to go to Italy with Leigh Holman, her first husband, and their daughter Suzanne. Vivien had always remained close to Leigh, a man of the most placid nature, who had never shown any resentment of the way she had treated him. Perhaps because he was the only man in her life who constituted no threat of any kind, he had proved on frequent visits to Notley that he was the only person whose company was guaranteed to keep her stable, to ensure she remained on the straight and narrow. Olivier, meanwhile, was glad of the chance to take his son Tarquin to Scotland, where they would combine the pleasures of motoring, painting and the continuing, optimistic search for *Macbeth* locations. With his son approaching his twenty-first birthday, Olivier felt the need to make the first conscious effort of his life to forge a bond with him. Olivier's contact with Tarquin's mother had been minimal all these years; but the two were about to get together to give Tarquin a big twenty-first party at Notley, while Vivien was safely away on the Continent.

To the Oliviers, as they later told the newspapers, these arrangements were "a civilized and adult way to behave". Besides, how they chose to organize their family affairs was no one's business but their own. Mrs Jean Mann, a fiery Scottish mother-of-five who sat on the Labour benches of the House of Commons, did not agree. Addressing the National Conference of Social Work in Edinburgh, not far from Olivier's idyll with Tarquin, she forced her way on to the next day's front pages by denouncing the Oliviers' vacation plans:

> There is a woman who has taken the House of Lords by storm, and now she has gone off on holiday with her first husband. Her second husband is on holiday elsewhere. I do not know of any protest about it. It would seem you can pack your first husband up – that is what our young people will be telling us – and you can go on holiday with him now and again. You might even be able to spend weekends with the first and the middle of the week with the second. It is a terrible example for people who occupy high places in life to place before our young children today. Where is the flood of indignation?

The self-righteous Mrs Mann that day made the Olivier marriage fair game for the tabloid newspapers. For the first time in all these long years, Olivier and Vivien now found the state of their union the subject of extensive rumour, gossip and discussion in the national press. From Italy Vivien responded angrily to suggestions that divorce was in the offing: "There is absolutely no question of divorce. My first husband and I are still good friends, and there is no earthly reason why I should not see him. Larry and I are still very much in love." Run to ground in Scotland,

Olivier said merely: "I have no comment on something that does not exist." Press speculation about their marriage was a price of fame they had been lucky not to have paid earlier. Now the rumours of break-up and divorce would continue for the three more years it would take them to come true. That summer both Oliviers managed to rise above it, continuing to enact the world's greatest lovers when out and about together. But it all added to the strain of living their uncomfortable lie.

Olivier's holiday with Tarquin, moreover, did not turn out to be the success either had hoped. His need to reach out to his son was another condition of the increasing gulf between him and Vivien, who had taken infinitely greater pains than Olivier himself to befriend Tarquin. Now she was surrendering this role, too, which prompted Olivier to fill the breach. He had still not abandoned all hope of *Macbeth*; a little location-scouting amid the fishing and painting would be doubly appropriate, as the Scottish play is one in which Shakespeare gives a dashing mention to the Tarquin after whom Olivier had named his son.

The trip was supposed to be the beginning of a beautiful, if somewhat overdue, friendship. But it was almost exactly twenty years since Olivier had walked out on Jill Esmond. Tarquin, then ten months old, was now an Oxford undergraduate. The gulf had become too wide to bridge. Father was proud of his son's achievements; though undistinguished (and somewhat unhappy) at Eton, Tarquin was now stroking the Christ Church eight, which had just won the Head of the River. The holiday passed amiably enough for father and son, but the ice refused to yield. Neither could relax in the other's company. Olivier, still riddled with guilt about both mother and son, imagined that Tarquin could not yet understand or forgive. His mind, moreover, was on other things, as so often. As he put it in his memoirs: "And so to business matters, for which in *my* book private matters, no matter how precious, must always give way."

As always, Olivier sought relief from his private griefs in professional triumphs. Still he scouted around for *Macbeth* finance, on both sides of the Atlantic. All he secured in the process was a contract to star opposite Burt Lancaster and Kirk Douglas in a film of Shaw's *The Devil's Disciple*. So while girding his loins for another stint as Archie Rice – a West End run, a provincial tour and a Broadway transfer – he also took to wielding them in extra-marital directions. One of these liaisons, with a well-known actress who has always kept his secret, even led him to propose marriage; her mother gently but firmly intervened. In retrospect Olivier was grateful to his putative mother-in-law for saving them both from a dreadful mistake.

At the time he believed himself very much in love and decided one evening to make a clean breast of it to Vivien. By now they were renting the Waltons' London house, in Lowndes Place, though Olivier quietly took a furnished room in a nearby mews as "an escape-hatch". Here it was that Vivien asked him one evening if he was in love with someone else – and, for the first time in the long cycle of mutual deception, he admitted that he was. That night she was sympathetic, even managing to say "How marvellous for you – and for her." But it needed only a couple of days for the inevitable reaction to sink in. Vivien took off on what Olivier called "a sky-high phase of scaring proportions", which "fed itself" by the determination to allow him no sleep. One night that week, when he finally drifted off, she began slapping him around the eyes with a wet face-cloth. At his wits' end, Olivier ran from the bedroom and locked himself in Walton's study, only to find her beating on the door and screaming at him hysterically. "She was obviously prepared to keep it up all night."

Something in his brain snapped – his own phrase – and for once, weary of months of vacillation, Olivier gave as good as he got. In an "all-possessing rage" he threw open the door, grabbed Vivien's wrist, dragged her down the passsage and bodily hurled her across the bedroom. She struck her left eyebrow on the corner of her marble bedside table, opening up a wound frighteningly close to her temple. Realizing with horror that "each of us was quite capable of murdering each other", he left at once. After reaching the safety of his "escape-hatch", Olivier reflected on the long years he had been forced to cope with Vivien's disease. By now, his whole nature was "in revolt against further voluntary torture". He had several times suggested a formal separation, but Vivien had always resisted, and he had not had the heart to leave. But now, Olivier decided, "the break must be made".

Next morning he went round to see how she was, to find John Mills's wife Mary dressing the wound and comforting Vivien, who looked at him with "horrified reproach". Both knew it was the end. From this point on, the Oliviers were no more. They would keep up a public pretence for a while yet, but the heavy schedule ahead of Olivier in the next three years would keep him away from Vivien anyway. By unspoken mutual consent, without ever admitting to each other that it had happened, they slipped into separate lives.

The rumour mills were active again that December, when Olivier took a back seat to Vivien and Leigh Holman at Suzanne's wedding to a young insurance broker, Robin Farrington. Photographers gleefully caught him hanging back on the steps of the church with other guests, and then waving good-bye as Vivien drove off with Leigh. The *Daily Express*'s William Hickey column quoted Olivier as saying it was an "awkward situation" in which "I feel like the uninvited guest", but in truth he was not troubled. His life, though the world would not know for some time yet, was already heading in another direction.

If John Osborne's script had given Olivier the chance he had been seeking to rejuvenate his career, the cast changes in the revival of *The Entertainer* now offered him the chance to find a new private happiness he considered long overdue. Twenty-two years his junior, Joan Plowright was young enough to be Olivier's daughter, precisely the role she played at the Palace Theatre, taking over the part of Jean Rice from Dorothy Tutin. By the time the show took to the road, after eight weeks at the Palace, they were already deeply in love. Though she too was married – to the actor Roger Gage – there followed a "euphoric" progress through Glasgow, Edinburgh and Oxford to the Brighton Hippodrome – the scene of Olivier's first professional stage entrance, flat on his face, over thirty years before. Those three days in Brighton were blissful enough to resolve them to find a home there four years later, by which time their first child was on the way.

The Entertainer's continuing success meant a return to the Palace before heading for Broadway, but Joan already had other New York commitments. So there was a temporary parting of the ways – Geraldine McEwan took over as Jean – before a joyous reunion in Boston, where Joan rejoined the cast in time for the twelve-week Broadway run at the Royale. Their relationship, in Olivier's own words, "brought a new kind of headiness in its rapture – nothing exotic, rather a strangely natural kinship, and more powerful than anything I could remember". But when they returned to London he still could not quite muster the strength of his own convictions. Like so many men in similar circumstances, Olivier embarked on a coming-and-going period, with which Joan Plowright simply had to put up.

He would meet her for secret trysts in a Walpole Street bedsitter lent them by George Devine, one of the few friends privy to their secret. But Vivien, despite it all, still had a considerable hold over him. As Olivier came and went, so did Peter Finch and sundry other young men. A steady erosion had set in, but still he could not quite let go. On the advice of friends, he even suggested to Vivien that they try having another child: this time, it was she who did not think this too bright an idea. When he confided to Noël Coward "that he really couldn't face living with Vivien any more", Coward was surprised; he shrewdly suspected that neither of them was "willing to face the contumely and publicity of a divorce".[15] Wracked by his indecision, Olivier felt helpless. Professional commitments would anyway keep him apart from Joan for the rest of 1958. Not knowing what the future held, they resigned themselves for the present to separate lives.

Joan went off for a Spanish holiday with her husband, who had conveniently been away for some months filming in India. Soon after she left, her name was linked with Olivier's in a newspaper gossip column for the first time – as one of several women with whom he was apparently involved, another of whom was said to be Susan Strasberg, the actress daughter of Paula, possibly the woman he disliked most in the world.[16] It was so laughable that even Vivien shrugged it off to the press, quoting him as saying "Well, at least there's safety in numbers!", and adding her statutory "People have been saying for seventeen years that Larry and I would part. We love each other. We have a happy married life."

Olivier himself had disappeared back to America, where his first commitment was to Burt Lancaster, his boss as well as his co-star in *The Devil's Disciple*. Still smarting about the movie moguls' refusal to finance his *Macbeth*, Olivier found himself resenting the fact that a lesser actor like Lancaster could so easily double as producer and actor on a big-budget epic to be partly filmed – just to rub salt in his wounds – in England.

The part of General Burgoyne was a plum, in which he should easily have been able to outshine Lancaster's Pastor Anderson and Kirk Douglas's Richard Dudgeon. But Olivier was not himself. The strains of the last six months – "the heart-wrenchings, the guilt, the longing, the romantic joy and the tortured conscience" – had taken their toll. For the first time in his professional life Olivier lost touch with his craft: "I just couldn't seem to handle the normal problems of acting any more." Worse, he kept calling people by the wrong names. Even Lancaster, the boss, he would address as Kirk. "Burt," Lancaster would point out coldly. By way of apology, Olivier explained that he thought he might be having a nervous breakdown. When co-producer Harold Hecht tried to sympathize, suggesting that he "put more Mr Puff into your General Burgoyne", Olivier simply collapsed in hysterical laughter. At the end of his screen career, he still could not remember having had "such a miserable a time in a job". He thought himself awful in the film and avoided seeing it.

The critics, when it was released a year later, did not agree. The consensus was that Olivier had "stolen" the picture from Lancaster and Douglas, in what was generally perceived as some sort of heavyweight celluloid contest. In a fit of patriotic zeal, the London *Evening Standard* gave the film a front-page review under the headline "THE GREATEST ACTOR IN THE WORLD", declaring: "It is a film to see. Just because Laurence Olivier gives the performance of his life. And because, in his superb self-confidence he dared to take the third lead."[17] Olivier made Lancaster and Douglas look like "stupid oafs who have wandered back from a Western into the world of the American War of Independence".

His misery on *The Devil's Disciple* set gave Olivier the adrenalin to make one desperate last attempt to find a backer for *Macbeth*. By now almost paranoid about the refusal of both the American and British film world to finance him, he began to suspect a plot against him. Throughout the haggling over his *Devil's Disciple* contract, Olivier had worn his Macbeth beard in readiness, confident that the money would be forthcoming. But Lancaster and his co-producers had nevertheless continued to issue complacent statements to the effect that he would not come up with the cash for his own enterprise, would be free to join theirs and would finish up shaving.

Now came a new flurry of excitement when the American billionaire Huntington Hartford offered to put up the finance for *Macbeth*; but Hartford was insisting on a rather awkward *quid pro quo*. He wanted Olivier to stage and star in his own adaptation of Charlotte Brontë's *Jane Eyre* – an offer both Errol Flynn and Eric Portman had found impossible to refuse in the United States, making wealthy fools of themselves in the process. Olivier knew that even for a reward so close to his heart he could not stoop so low. Now he finally had to face the fact that after *The Beggar's Opera*, *Carrie* and *The Prince and the Showgirl*, his own box-office credit was lower than that of the likes of Burt Lancaster. British film-goers cruelly confirmed this for him in a fan magazine poll: a majority said they would no longer queue to see a Laurence Olivier movie. With Wardour Street looking for quick profits from low-cost films, and Rank moaning about the new seven per cent bank rate, Olivier finally decided to admit defeat. "I think", he said forlornly, "it's the only time I've ever given up on anything."

It is very much in character that his failure to film *Macbeth* now made him turn instead to another medium. If the world of films had abandoned all interest in quality, deeming him a less valuable asset than Burt Lancaster, then he would try the brave new world of television. Established stage actors were still wary of the medium. Few, as Donald Wolfit put it, were prepared "to risk in one evening reputations built up over the years in the West End".[18] Already Olivier himself had fought shy of television, earning himself some brickbats for refusing to allow one of his *Nights of a Hundred Stars* to be televised, despite the offer of a £4,000 donation to the Actors' Orphanage. "They tell me", he said loftily, "the TV audience is not particularly noted for taking things in." Still unsure of the dangers, Olivier restricted himself at first to two tentative toes in the water, one on each side of the Atlantic. His one main incentive, apart from handsome fees, was the pleasure of notching up another "first"; he would be the first to tiptoe, if not quite rush in, where Gielgud and Richardson, Redgrave and Guinness were still afraid to tread.

Before long Olivier would display an embarrassing lack of televisual expertise by joining the board of Ulster Television, only to resign within a year upon discovering that they could only receive, and not initiate, network programmes. Meanwhile he proved himself enough of a television rookie by choosing the wrong part for his small-screen debut: the impossibly long, turgid and dark title role in Ibsen's *John Gabriel Borkman*, directed by a then novice, Caspar Wrede. Though an appropriate challenge to his stature, it was also the kind of period costume role which even in those early television days was likely to prove a huge turn-off. Anticipation of Olivier's television debut was immense: when Associated Television screened it on Britain's ITV network on 19 November 1958, the *Daily Express* – not a paper noted for its interest in classical drama – hired no fewer than five different writers to deliver judgement. Critical verdicts on Olivier himself ranged from "stagey" and "remote" to "faultless" and "compelling". Clearly he would take time, as he had in films, to realize that television acting requires its own brand of small-scale subtlety. But the verdict of the audience was an unqualified disaster: ATV's private ratings showed *John Gabriel Borkman* to be their biggest flop of the year. The seventy-minute transmission, according to the official report, "had a big audience at the beginning, which fell off half-way through";[19] subsequent figures showed they had switched over *en masse* to an old feature film, *They Live By Night*, on the BBC.

Olivier's Borkman, according to *The Times*, "displayed a series of characteristics rather than a continuous character; there was nothing arbitrary in the playing, but it tended to be episodic".[20] All he himself would say was that television needed "a great deal of concentration" and that three weeks' rehearsal had not been enough. Next time he would know better. So saying, he flew to New York to take part in a television version of Somerset Maugham's novel about Gauguin, *The Moon and Sixpence*. Hardly had rehearsals begun when he was summoned home by the news that his brother Dickie had died at Notley, at the age of only fifty-four. Dickie had been ill for over a year, but it was a mere five months since leukaemia had been diagnosed. For several years Dickie had been happily managing his brother's seventy-acre farm, and they had grown as close as they had been in childhood. Only the previous summer, they had enjoyed a Spanish holiday together. After a moving burial at sea, in accordance with his brother's wishes, Olivier escorted Dickie's widow Hester, their sister Sybille and Vivien back to Notley. To avoid any awkwardness, he spent the night in his brother's cottage, Notley Mead.

Earlier that autumn, between finishing *John Gabriel Borkman* and leaving for New York, Olivier had written to Vivien from France, where he had taken himself for a solo, contemplative break. He had spelt out the realities of their situation and again pleaded for a legal separation. In his own mind, he felt it the only way he could formalize arrangements with Vivien sufficiently to concentrate on his growing need for Joan. But when he took Vivien out for dinner in London shortly before her birthday, it was clear that she was still reluctant to let go completely. She was much better physically. There had been fewer fits of violent mania of late, and even

329

her depressions had grown containable enough for her to resume her career. That year she had appeared with considerable success as Paola in *Duel of Angels*, Christopher Fry's adaptation of Giraudoux's *Pour Lucrèce*. Olivier himself believed the part had confirmed her as "an actress of the first rank, richly developed in all the strengths – bearing, composure, vocal power, technique and magnetism".

Both hating the increasing newspaper gossip about their marriage, these perennial self-deceivers launched into a series of extravagant gestures to show the world that there was life in the Oliviers yet. Some recent theatrical investments, notably a stake in the long-running *Roar Like a Dove*, enabled Olivier to present Vivien with a £7,000 Rolls-Royce for her forty-fifth birthday, 5 November, which they marked with a lavish show-business party at a London night-club. The 150 guests included Lauren Bacall, Douglas Fairbanks, Beatrice Lillie, Alec Guinness, Jack Hawkins, Emlyn Williams and Richard Burton; as they arrived Vivien presented each of the men with a red carnation, Olivier the women with a miniature red rose. Though she had recently, with mixed feelings, become a grand-mother, Vivien showed the world her bravest and gayest face, striving to counter the rumours that her days as Lady Olivier were numbered. For the sake of his own *amour propre*, Olivier for now went along with the sham.

But lies had become second nature. Over dinner that evening only three weeks before, Olivier had told Vivien that, although he wanted his freedom, there was no one else in his life. Vivien had heard rumours about Joan Plowright and raised them directly, but Olivier disavowed his beloved. Though husband and wife had scarcely seen each other for some months, she too denied disloyalty. The evening had ended inconsequentially.

The day after Dickie's funeral, Olivier headed for a busy day in London before returning to New York. He spent the evening with Joan, lamenting the fact that they must now face six months apart; after *The Moon and Sixpence*, he was due in Hollywood for *Spartacus*. Later that night he received a rather wild phone call from Vivien. It sounded like she was at a party. She was calling, she told him, to tell him she had fallen in love – with Jack Merivale, their old friend from 1941, who had recently taken over as her stage husband in *Duel of Angels*.

Thought a wary Olivier: "Time will tell." Mentally, however, both of them would date this as the moment they really parted. Again, nothing specific was said. But now, at last, it really was over. Before fleeing back to New York, Olivier paused only to tell an interiewer that "little of significance" had happened to him in 1958.

1967–71: Defying illness
and stage fright at the
National Theatre as
Edgar in Strindberg's
The Dance of Death, 1967
(ABOVE LEFT); Shylock,
1970 (ABOVE); and
James Tyrone in Eugene
O'Neill's *Long Day's
Journey into Night*, 1971

Three worlds, three roles: on the big screen in *Sleuth*, 1972 (TOP); on the small screen as Big Daddy in *Cat on a Hot Tin Roof*, 1976; and in the House of Lords as the theatre's first peer, 1970

At seventy, putting a brave face on debilitating illness (LEFT), there is at last time to take the children to school in Brighton

1966–81: A gallery of screen cameos as The Mahdi in *Khartoum* (ABOVE), the Russian prime minister in *Nicholas and Alexandra* (RIGHT), Sir John French in *Oh! What a Lovely War* (OPPOSITE RIGHT), Mr Creakle in *David Copperfield* (FAR RIGHT), the Duke of Wellington in *Lady Caroline Lamb* (BELOW), Dr Christian Szell in *Marathon Man* (BELOW RIGHT), Julius in *A Little Romance* (OPPOSITE LEFT), General Douglas MacArthur in *Inchon* (CENTRE RIGHT) and Zeus in *Clash of the Titans*

(ABOVE) 1981: Theatrical history is made as Sir Ralph Richardson (left), Sir Laurence Olivier (centre) and Sir John Gielgud (right) play their only scene together in Tony Palmer's epic film of *Wagner*, starring Richard Burton; (LEFT) Lord and Lady Olivier attend Richardson's memorial service at Westminster Abbey, 1983

1981–2: Three last great television roles as Lord Marchmain in *Brideshead Revisited* (RIGHT), Clifford Mortimer in *A Voyage round my Father* (BELOW), and King Lear

1987: (ABOVE) The only one to ignore the camera, Lord Olivier celebrates his eightieth birthday with his wife and children: (left to right) Tamsin, Richard and Julie-Kate. On the wall is a portrait of Olivier as Romeo, fifty-two years before. (LEFT) At eighty, Olivier can still pull off his lifelong disappearing trick, complete with Cheshire Cat smile

PART THREE

"Some Have Greatness Thrust Upon Them"

"A man's gifts are not a property; they are a duty."

Henrik Ibsen

CHAPTER 19

1958–62

L aurence Olivier once compiled a list of injuries sustained in the
course of duty. It included:

1 broken ankle
2 torn cartilages (1 perforce yielding to surgery)
2 broken calf muscles
3 ruptured Achilles' tendons
Untold slashes including a full thrust razor-edged sword wound in the breast
Landing from considerable height, scrotum first, upon acrobat's knee
Hanging by hand to piano wire 40 feet up for some minutes (hours?) on
account of unmoored rope
Hurled to the stage from 30 feet due to faultily moored rope ladder
Impalement on jagged ply cut-outs
Broken foot bone by standing preoccupied in camera track
Broken face by horse galloping into camera while looking through viewfinder
Near broken neck diving into net (while fighting celluloid Spanish Armada)
Several shrewd throws from horses including one over beast's head into lake
Water on elbow
Water pretty well everywhere
Near electrocution through scimitar entering studio dimmer "while backing
away from unwelcome interview".[1]

Actors up against Olivier in stage fights lived in dread of his ferocious
intensity, not to mention his expert swordsmanship; he has fond memories
of Ralph Richardson, in mid-duel, saying *sotto voce*: "Steady now, old
boy.... Easy, fellow.... You've got two [performances] today, don't
forget." Olivier also admits to "quite a few pretended injuries while it was

really gout". Both his hands are today misshapen as a direct result of the number of stage falls he has taken, or failed to take.

Olivier himself believes that the single-minded commitment he has always brought to his work is a direct result of his upbringing. He and another churchman's son, Ingmar Bergman, once listed the consequences of a childhood steeped in religion: a guilt complex, an ingrained sense of service and a compulsive need to work. To Olivier, says Joan Plowright, "the theatre is his form of Church – a temple to man's knowledge of man, a place where people gather together and somebody talks to them and they are moved".

But Olivier's ferocious work-rate has also been a condition of his need to escape from himself and from reality. Richard Burton once told Olivier that he thought acting was woman's work. "I don't know why I go on with this bloody nonsense," said Burton. "You don't know?" replied Olivier. "If we didn't do it, we'd go mad."

Many an actor believes it is only his craft which prevents him slipping into madness. Actors are notoriously insecure creatures, desperately in need of attention or affection or both, only too happy to escape their own worldly woes by slipping into another identity. Olivier himself has said how much the chance to become a Macbeth, a Malvolio, an Archie Rice by night eased the personal nightmare he endured throughout the late 1950s.

"If I wasn't an actor," he said to Joan Plowright, "I think I'd have gone mad." In her view, it was the only way he could find a release for "that immense energy". In his own, the constant proximity to some form of madness added an extra tension to his performance: "You have to have some extra voltage there, some extra temperament to reach certain heights. Art is a little bit larger than life – it's an exaltation of life – and I think you probably need a little touch of madness." To Olivier, the donning of tights, make-up, doublet and hose has always seemed "hardly the preoccupation of an adult". He once said: "I don't enjoy acting, but I can't live without it. I'm like a sort of carthorse with a collar round its neck: if you take it off, it starts whinnying for it."

In early 1958, the world was too much with him. Olivier chose to flee it by drowning himself in work, at a pace which exhausted those around him. Jessica Tandy had never seen anything like it:

> No other actor I have known could display such incredible stamina, maintain such high standards under that amazing degree of pressure. He shot for sixteen hours on the first day, slept for about five hours, shot for twenty hours on the second day, slept for two or three hours on the set – there was no time to go back to his hotel – and then shot another gruelling eighteen hours on the third day, as actors with less responsibility fell apart all around him.[2]

Back in New York after his brother's funeral Olivier had told Noël Coward of "several more ghastly scenes with Vivien" during his brief visit to England.[3] Through his impatience with their eternal ups and downs, Coward now felt real sympathy for his old friend and protégé; everything seemed to be "so downbeat" with him. "I think he rather self-indulges this, but I am sure he is genuinely lonely and unhappy." Significantly, Olivier still did not confide in even so close a confidant about Joan. Missing her sorely, he threw himself back into his work on *The Moon and Sixpence* with the intensity that had astonished Tandy and her husband Hume Cronyn. They were but two of the "actors with less responsibility", the others including Judith Anderson, Cyril Cusack, Geraldine Fitzgerald and Denholm Elliot. Tandy was familiar with the Olivier work ethic, from his pre-war Old Vic season, but this bordered on the hysterical.

His mind spinning, Olivier was thankful of the exhausting hours – dictated not so much by the producer, David Susskind, as by his own enforced trip home. With shooting due to begin on 20 December and to be finished in three days, there was time for only two weeks of rehearsal. So Olivier rather disavowed his own good intentions about television when, despite pressure of this degree, he turned in another highly praised performance. The ninety-minute colour production proved so expensive – his fee alone was $100,000 – that a long search for sponsors delayed its screening for ten months. But Olivier, after his false start, had clearly taken to the new medium with all the technical subtlety now at his command. As Charles Strickland, Maugham's Gauguin-like hero, said the *New York Herald Tribune*, he proved "a towering craftsman" with "a brilliance and magnetism unmatched in the annals of television". This was "the closest thing to dramatic perfection ever known on television, and the most inspired work to come from the television architects to date". *Life* magazine thought "the image of a man gone to ruin was made a little easier for Olivier to enact by the punishing pace of the TV sessions". But the *New York Times* declared it "a towering accomplishment", for which Olivier won the Emmy award for the best individual television performance of the year.

By then he had long since moved on to Hollywood, for the first time since *Carrie* eight years before. *Spartacus* was to be filmed on such a scale that Olivier had agreed to a six-month commitment. The carrot successfully dangled before him was a fee of $250,000, despite the cruel irony of accepting a supporting role in a middle-grade $10 million epic after failing to raise even $1 million for his own *Macbeth*. All the film's stars – Olivier, Peter Ustinov, Charles Laughton, Tony Curtis, Jean Simmons – later learnt that they had been sent different scripts in advance by their co-star and producer, Kirk Douglas, in which their own part had been written up to tempt them to climb aboard the *Spartacus* bandwagon. When they began to foregather in Hollywood, their roles somehow seemed to have shrunk. But Olivier, cannily enough, managed to arrive a week before anyone else. By the time the others turned up, recalled Ustinov, "he had already inspired a yet newer version of the script in which his role had grown somewhat in importance".[4]

The original director, Anthony Mann, was swiftly fired in favour of the virtually unknown Stanley Kubrick; and not many of the cast knew that the scriptwriter, one Sam Jackson, was in fact Dalton Trumbo, forced into anonymity by Hollywood's Communist witch-hunt. He, in turn, had fallen out with the original book's author, Howard Fast, but Trumbo produced some of his most effective scenes for Olivier's patrician Roman general – even though he was required to deliver such lines as "Will you have some squab?" to Jean Simmons. The text abounded with other anachronisms and banalities – at one point the Christian slaves all cry "Yippee" – prompting one critic to remark that he had not laughed so much since the Marx Brothers. But Olivier relished playing the film's villain, Marcus Crassus; his most melodramatic, eye-rolling vein of acting – again false-nosed – suited Kirk Douglas's style and often managed to lift a scene above its surroundings.

Olivier surprised Douglas by suggesting effeminacy and self-doubt in the haughty Roman leader – qualities the producer himself had not perceived. Perhaps the best scene in the film has Olivier suggestively telling a slave about his sexual preferences, tugging lasciviously on his necklace the while. Douglas also remembered being astonished, much later in the film, by the way Olivier chose to deliver the line "Never have I faced a battle with such confidence":

> Incredibly, he took that line and made it mean the exact opposite. He started off with a great firmness and ended hesitantly – "Never have I faced a battle with such ... confidence" – and in one line he had transformed complete self-assurance to complete insecurity. Extraordinary.[5]

Douglas, though he had recently worked with Olivier on *The Devil's Disciple*, was very much in awe of his employee, and further astonished that he could behave like a mere mortal:

> I was just dumbfounded by his simplicity and humility. He was the easiest actor to work with that I have ever known. I remember asking him for a piece of advice, and he gave it so modestly and with such humility. I am quick to offer advice, or criticism, but here was Larry, with his tremendous background, being so reticent about making suggestions. . . .[6]

The marathon filming of *Spartacus* became a project akin to painting the Forth Bridge: it was a seemingly unending task. After the first twelve months of shooting, Simmons remembers receiving a magnum of champagne from Kirk Douglas, with a note hoping the second year would be as happy as the first. But the film is remembered by most participants primarily for the fierce competitiveness between Charles Laughton, conscious of having "sold out" to Hollywood, and Olivier, there to make a not-so-quick killing. Olivier, as Ustinov put it, "was the Vestal Virgin to Laughton's Hollywood whore".[7] Laughton would sit morosely around the set "waiting to have his feelings hurt ... feasting his eyes on the work of great painters as he emerged dripping from his pool of contemplation", while "Larry fretted at arithmetic and tried to pick holes in the bills of the supermarket".

When Olivier gave him some hints on the acoustics at Stratford, where he was shortly to play King Lear, Laughton was deeply suspicious, convinced that Olivier was out to sabotage his performance. When it came to filming their climactic confrontation in the Senate, the rivalry grew so fierce that shooting broke down. Laughton, required to ask some penetrating questions of Olivier's Roman leader, did so with masterful nonchalance, shooting sidelong glances at his colleagues in the Senate rather than fixing Olivier in the eye. Then came the reverse shots, in which Olivier had to play his half of the scene; after a few attempts, he found it impossible to do so now that Laughton's beady eye was directly challenging him. Finally Olivier was forced to ask him to leave. Laughton's unfilmed exit from the Senate, remembers Ustinov, was much better than anything in the film: "A sort of outsize mannequin from Swan and Edgar's dowagers' department, walking out with tremendous dignity and suffering." Once Laughton had gone, Olivier played out his scene perfectly, speaking his lines to thin air.

British exchange controls had Olivier living on a shoestring in Hollywood, counting every penny while the contented tax exile Laughton floated, whale-like, in his pool and purred over his Old Masters. Years later Richard Burton had something to say about this:

> If you're going to make rubbish, be the best rubbish in it. I keep telling Larry Olivier that. It's no good playing a minor role in an epic like *Spartacus*.... Larry had a dressing-room half the size of Tony Curtis's on that film. Well, that's ridiculous. You've got to swank in Hollywood. When I go there I demand two Cadillacs and the best dressing-room. I'm not worth it, of course, but it impresses them.[8]

Olivier's unwonted solitude during the making of *Spartacus*, and the pain of his long, enforced separation from Joan, were both alleviated by the fact that his old friend Roger Furse was the film's costume designer. He moved into an apartment on Sunset Boulevard with Furse and his wife for the duration. Also in the same building at the time was another old British friend, Max Adrian, who became something of a Father Confessor to Olivier, who "was lonely and needed company".[9] Adrian got into the habit of cooking him an evening meal, after which Olivier would pour out the story of his sufferings with Vivien. To spare them both any chance of embarrassment, Adrian began charging his friend $2 per meal, presenting him with a weekly bill on Saturdays: "It turned out to be a very good idea because it freed him of any feeling of obligation, so he was able to relax and he often stayed on after dinner chatting and talking out his troubles."

In his daily letters to Joan from Hollywood – telephone calls were expensively rare treats in those days – Olivier had discussed the possibility of "violent tragedy" when Vivien learned of their love. Indeed, while he was away, Vivien had told Noël Coward that she was "in despair" about his having left her. The previous December, she and Coward had rowed over his failure to offer her the title role in his new play *Look After Lulu*, an adaptation of Feydeau's *Occupe-toi d'Amélie*; an impatient Coward declared her "barmy" and himself "bored" with it all, "in no mood to cope with the carry-on". On 8 February, however, he found in a long, quiet session with Vivien that "she was very pathetic and perfectly sane and sweet"; he concluded that "the shock of Larry packing up and going may have done her a power of good".

Coward believed that Olivier would return to Vivien; she sadly doubted it. But by May she was "counting the days until Larry's return" the following month, "refus[ing] to believe that he really intends to leave her for ever". She met Olivier off his plane at Heathrow on 5 June, but the very next day he was due in Stratford to begin *Coriolanus* rehearsals. He had neither time nor inclination to talk of their future. The one subject he did raise, to her dismay, was the notion of selling Notley. Over this past year, so much of which she had spent alone there, Notley had taken on greater significance to Vivien. Yet it was already a shadow of its former self: there were no more of those weekend parties, and most of the time there was no Olivier. This Stratford season, he now told her, he would be living in a hotel. If his heart was no longer in their home, Vivien knew the real reason why. She had no choice but to agree.

The 1959 season at Stratford saw the last of its "starry" line-ups before the take-over of "director's theatre" in the shape of Peter Hall, who was to direct Olivier as his second Roman general of the year. Other notables appearing to mark the theatre's centenary, and Glen Byam Shaw's departure, included Laughton (as Lear and Bottom), Paul Robeson (as Othello to Sam Wanamaker's Iago) and Edith Evans (as Volumnia to Olivier's Coriolanus); the younger members of the company included Vanessa

Redgrave, Albert Finney and Ian Holm. They made a great baseball team under Wanamaker's enthusiastic leadership;[10] Olivier valued the exercise on top of his already intensive training schedule. But so top-heavy a company made for a season of some artistic chaos – described by Tynan as "an all-star benefit show run in doublet and hose, lacking either unity or purpose". In the midst of the maelstrom, however, there was no doubting the pre-eminent production of the season, largely thanks to its outstanding central performance.

Olivier arrived for rehearsals that June thinking he knew all about Coriolanus, whom he had played in traditional vein for Lewis Casson at the Old Vic twenty-one years before. Hall vividly remembers the difficulty he had persuading his eminent charge *not* to cut every line referring to the character's pride, arrogance and mock modesty – all traits now, perhaps, rather close to home.[11] Olivier would listen "eyebrows down, some suspicion on the face, trying to find the catches". But the twenty-eight-year-old Hall was to prove the first in a line of younger directors brazen enough to challenge Olivier's preconceptions and express a little weariness with some of his more familiar mannerisms; ever eager for perfection, the great man managed to accept their suggestions and their boldness with good grace.

The key to the huge success of both performance and production was Hall's insistence on the aspects of Caius Marcius which Olivier would otherwise have discarded. On greeting his mother, for instance, Olivier's Coriolanus displayed immodest complacency in his recent victories, which he then instinctively played down in his dealings with the Senate: "Nobody, I think, lacking knowledge of English public school *mores*," wrote an ecstatic Laurence Kitchin, "could have hit exactly this note of sulky pride, a result of the man of action's narcissism held back by the necessity to belittle success in the presence of social equals."[12]

With this performance, Olivier finally put paid to a perennial myth about his limitations – the suggestion that his art as an actor was confined only to such qualities as the range of his voice, his innate virility, his humour and emotional power. "Great as these are," wrote Kitchin, his Coriolanus showed them to be "controlled by interpretative intelligence of a very high order". The kind of liberties he took with the text, which reinterpreted the play even for a scholar of Kitchin's standing, "ought to be Olivier's exclusive privilege". He milked the text for unaccustomed laughs, but with perfect justification:

> I mention it only to rebut the fallacy that Olivier is a privileged *id*. The man had brought his intellect to bear on this role.... When he chose to draw a loud laugh from Hercules in parting with his mother, I did not flinch. Let him enjoy himself; he had earned the right.

It was the vindication Olivier had always craved. Although his interpretative intellect was entirely intuitive – needing, in Kitchin as in Tynan, another mind of a different discipline to rationalize, record and evaluate its insights – his effects were receiving their due from an intellectual of the order Olivier had always rather feared, on a level he has always believed beyond his own grasp. "This", Kitchin concluded, "was great acting, to hold a day-tripper from Birmingham as tightly as it held American lecturers homesick for the printed page and a bout of close analysis."

Olivier had begun his Coriolanus by delivering "You common cry of curs!" with a rolling of the head and a charge of concentrated emotion chilling enough to move Kitchin to the memorable feeling that he was watching "one man lynching a crowd". By the end of his titanic performance, Olivier's response to the famous taunt of "Boy" was equally devastating: "The audience quivered at the sound of Olivier's voice like Avon swans at a sudden crack of thunder." Then he contrived a death which has passed into theatrical history: pierced by a dozen spears, he hurled himself vertically down from the twelve-foot-high Tarpeian platform, trusting two soldiers to catch his ankles at the last minute, so that he dangled there momentously (looking deliberately reminiscent of the dead Mussolini) during Aufidius's closing speech – which, as a result of the sheer power of Olivier's coda, had the effect on the audience of "a well-earned tranquillizing drug". Twenty-five years later, when the same director, Peter Hall, was staging Ian McKellen's Coriolanus in the Olivier auditorium at the National Theatre, the cast crowded round for an awe-struck look at his 1959 prompt book, as if the sight of his notes might charm them like some theatrical talisman.[13]

The Times, recalling that its review of his earlier Coriolanus had sniffed intimations of greatness, now declared that Olivier played the part "just as well as it can be played". Tynan, anticipating Kitchin, praised the "sheer intuitive intelligence" of the performance:

> Olivier understands that Coriolanus is not an aristocrat; he is a professional soldier; a *Junker*, if you like, reminiscent in many ways of General de Gaulle – a rejected military saviour who returns, after a long and bodeful silence, with an army at his back.

Then he grew very excited, even by his standards:

> This ... is all-round Olivier. We have the wagging head, the soaring index finger, and the sly, roaming eyes of one of the world's cleverest comic. actors, plus the desperate, exhausted moans of one of the world's masters of pathos. ... The voice is soft steel that can chill and cut, or melt and scorch. ...
> It sounds, distinct and barbaric, across the valley of many centuries, like a horn calling to the hunt, or the neigh of a battle-maddened charger.[14]

That roll of the head which Olivier affected before launching into each performance was, amusingly enough, a tension-relaxing exercise recommended by Elsie Fogerty to her students. It was no surprise, during his run in this particularly draining part, that he chose to make use of it. For his offstage schedule was even more demanding. While playing Shakespeare's tragic hero several times a week, Olivier was also commuting to Morecambe, Lancashire, where with Joan (whose part was built up for the screen version) he was filming *The Entertainer* for Tony Richardson. Olivier hired an ambulance for the summer, so he could sleep in the back while commuting. Archie Rice by day and Coriolanus by night: it was a metamorphosis wrenching enough to test the hardiest of spirits.

One evening that September, when Olivier declared himself "tired out" after spending the entire day filming Archie's subsequently famous tap dance, Richardson asked him, in the director's immortal phrase, for "just one more take". "Snap", as Olivier put it, went the old cartilage, which had held good for the decade since it was hoisted in plaster aboard the ss *Corinthic* in Wellington. In the next day's two performances of *Coriolanus*, the lead was taken over by his "baby" of an understudy, Albert Finney. "Well, it's much less tiring than First Citizen," Finney joked to Olivier when he resurfaced. Later, he paid his mentor due tribute, as only a "shadow" player can:

> What one did learn from it is how a great actor can take the kind of peaks and valleys of a performance, the ups and downs of a character as written, and push them even further apart. He makes the climaxes higher, and he makes the depths of it lower, than you feel is possible in the text.[15]

By the end of November, Olivier had bid exhausted but fond farewells to both Coriolanus and Archie Rice. He turned down the part of Caesar to Elizabeth Taylor's Cleopatra – to the delight and enrichment of his friend Rex Harrison, who inherited it – and disappeared with Joan for a secret holiday in France. All the arrangements had to be made huggermugger; mention of Joan by name was forbidden even in telephone calls from George Devine to Michel Saint-Denis, asking advice about hideaway hotels for "Larry *et un tel*", while Olivier insisted on a rental car with anonymous local licence plates. As the lovers beguiled the time on the Seine, not far from Paris, Vivien went to stay with Noël Coward at Les Avants, his home in Switzerland. Christmas Day guests included the William Holdens, the Alec Guinnesses and a posse of English pressmen intent on asking Lady Olivier where her husband was. Coward, though finding her devastation "genuine, sad and almost irritating", charmed them into submission, while upstairs Vivien sobbed out her misery to his secretary, Cole Lesley.

341

By now Olivier was back in New York, to direct Charlton Heston and Rosemary Harris in *The Tumbler*, a new verse play by his old friend Benn Levy. The torrid tale of an English country girl whose lover turns out to be her stepfather, suspected of murdering her father, it proved another misjudgement. When the show closed after just five performances, neither Levy nor Olivier could explain what made them believe that Americans would crowd to the Helen Hayes Theater to see a drama of such distinctively English sensibilities.[16] Heston himself remembers the play as a "no-hoper". He would never have gone near it, let alone turned down a film with Marilyn Monroe to do so, had it not been for the chance to work with Olivier. Heston recalls with admiration Olivier's "inspiring professionalism". In the midst of his marital agonies, as the play refused to yield to his directorial skills, he was never less than "utterly committed, both to the project and his performers. I learnt a great deal from him, for which I have always been grateful. *The Tumbler* may have been a disaster for everyone else, but I've never regretted for one moment the experience of working onstage for Olivier." Heston especially remembers one of Olivier's memorable theatrical *dicta*: "Sometimes the gods inspire a performance, and then the actor can do no wrong, but the actor must also prepare a performance for the night the gods do not attend."[17]

Laurence Olivier Productions, meanwhile, was not faring much better. A life in which "hope is constantly at odds with better judgement" is how Olivier once described the lot of the theatrical manager: "He knows that if he finds one great play in a lifetime, he will be lucky," he told his biographer Felix Barker, then theatre critic of the *Evening News*, "but for eight plays out of ten, he is simply taking a gamble with something he knows is not of the best."[18] In London his company had recently presented several more flops, including *One More River* and *The Shifting Heart*, but they hurt much less than a failure in which he was personally involved as director. This latest New York débâcle was prompting a spate of easy newspaper cavils, wondering if "Sir Larry" had "lost his touch", when he landed a vigorous counter-punch. Olivier, it was announced, would return to the London stage in another utterly unlikely vehicle, Eugene Ionesco's *Rhinoceros* – to be staged at the still controversial Royal Court.

A surreal melodrama in which the entire cast gradually turn into beasts of the jungle, *Rhinoceros* can be read as an allegory of Ionesco's early life in Romania, where all his friends gradually became Nazis; it also confronts such psychological themes as group behaviour and tribalism. For Olivier the central part of Berenger satisfied his perennial craving for risk, as well as his professional desire to be associated with the best of contemporary theatre. As always, however, the risk was carefully calculated: *Rhinoceros* may have been his first venture into the utterly *avant-garde*, but it had already proved a spectacular box-office success for Jean-Louis Barrault and his company at the Odéon in Paris. Olivier added to his own box-office appeal in London (where his stage performances were now being described as "all too rare") by asking Orson Welles to direct. With Vivien and Jack Merivale safely across the Atlantic in the Broadway run of *Duel of Angels*, he also managed to persuade the backers to give the part of Daisy to Joan Plowright (who had scored a success as a cabin boy in Welles's 1955 stage version of *Moby Dick*).

Welles was to look back on *Rhinoceros* as "a black moment". Olivier's invitation was timely: the failure of the stage version of *Chimes at Midnight* in Dublin had forced a disappointed Welles to cancel plans to bring it to London; the opportunity to direct Olivier there, however, was ample consolation. But his determination to outshine Barrault, which had him designing the set, Anglicizing the text and even considerably restructuring it, also soon had Welles out of sympathy with the play and abandoning his plans to join the cast himself. "It's a terrible play," he said. "I *hate* it. But I wanted to do it for Larry."[19]

Such touching devotion was not, as Welles tells the story, returned. Olivier, Welles revealed towards the end of his life, "behaved terribly". Always, to Welles, a "sinister" figure, who did "strange things", Olivier apparently took all his directions "like a perfect soldier – and I gave him some wonderful things to do, I must say". He never argued, in private or in public. But he was meanwhile taking the rest of the cast aside, one by one, and telling them that Welles was misdirecting them. "Instead of making it hard for me to direct *him*, he made it almost impossible for me to direct the *cast*. He got them off in little groups and had little quiet rehearsals having nothing to do with me."

Olivier was apparently playing the same game with which he had humiliated John Gielgud in the Stratford *Twelfth Night* six years before. Welles, as his biographer Barbara Leaming points out, was also an actor "not averse to taking over another man's production and directing it himself" – but, unsurprisingly, he did not care for it too much when someone else did the same to him. This time even he had been out-manœuvred.

Four days before the opening, exactly as with Gielgud, Olivier asked Welles to stay away, to give the cast a chance to perfect a co-ordinated performance. "He told me to stay home and I *did*. I was so sick and humiliated about it that you can't imagine." Welles had to attend the dress rehearsal, strictly in his capacity as lighting designer, but he could not bear to visit the production again, feeling that it had been "wrested away" from him in rehearsal. Even when the West End transfer brought intriguing cast changes – Maggie Smith took over from Joan – Welles could not bring himself to rehearse them. He went to his grave believing that the cast thought very badly of him, on the grounds that he "simply wasn't interested". But the truth was that he felt so humiliated he didn't know *how* to come back: "All those actors thought that I was unthinkably cavalier, but I just didn't have the *guts*! *He*'s the leader of the English stage, *he*'s playing the leading role and directing it all the time. What was *I* going to do?" Asked why he thought Olivier would treat him thus, Welles replied: "He *had* to destroy me in some way. He did it to John G.... He doesn't want anybody else up there. He's like Chaplin, you know. He's a real fighting star."

Blissfully unaware of all this, theatre-goers bought out the Royal Court run as soon as the box office opened. Welles remembered the opening being overshadowed by that of Harold Pinter's *The Caretaker*, and the excited discovery of a major new British playwright; but the record shows that the *Rhinoceros* first-nighters hailed another night of Olivier magic. Though Tynan, believing him "not so much miscast as undercast", lamented "the waste of [Olivier's] time", other critics such as Bernard Levin were again searching for phrases adequate to his box of theatrical tricks: "He can do things that in anyone else would be trickery and quackery, but that in him are refined into the quintessence of the character he is playing." An *Observer* profile of Olivier that Sunday ranked his performance "among the most perfect of his career".[20] It was not, in the ordinary sense, a triumph: the range was deliberately limited, and those who waited for theatrical pyrotechnics would wait in vain. But it was "a performance that dramatic students will see as often as they can, the first time in sheer admiration and thereafter with their notebooks on their knees".

During the six-week run of *Rhinoceros* at the Royal Court, before its transfer to the Strand Theatre, Joan Plowright abruptly dropped out of the cast. The reason, though she and Olivier made clumsy attempts to disguise it, was that the couple's guilty secret had suddenly and dramatically become public. The formal announcement that they hoped to marry "as soon as they can obtain divorces from their respective partners" had been forced by circumstances which took Olivier totally by surprise.

In mid-May he had written to Vivien in New York, telling her at last that he and Joan were "very much in love". After much soul-searching, he was asking his wife of nearly twenty years to release him from their "obviously untenable relationship".[21] Olivier had not known what kind of reply to expect, but he had assumed it would at least arrive by mail. So it was to his surprise and dismay that on 22 May, his fifty-third birthday, he was awoken by a telephone call from a newspaper telling him that his wife had issued a statement from Broadway's Helen Hayes Theater – via, of all people, her dresser: "Lady Olivier wishes to say that Sir Laurence has asked for a divorce in order to marry Miss Joan Plowright. She will naturally do whatever he wishes."

Olivier was horrified. A letter from Vivien would have enabled them to work out the necessary steps with decent discretion. But the phrasing of her announcement not only named Joan as co-respondent – embarrassing enough in itself, given that she was still married to Gage. It was worse than that: under the framing of the divorce laws at the time, Vivien's publicly announced attitude could easily have been construed as "collusion", which would have proved a legal bar to divorce. Olivier had several theatrical friends whose partners had wilfully made such announcements specifically to prevent their errant partner remarrying. When he looked out of the window on to Eaton Square, Olivier saw that the entire street was crowded with reporters and photographers. Cameras were there to relay live pictures of his firmly closed front door to the television news bulletins. While trying to work out the consequences of Vivien's statement – which she later told Merivale she did not remember making – he sent his secretary down to read out a heartfelt message, apologizing that the waiting pressmen had been so "inconvenienced" and saying he had "no comment at all. I need time to think." To his press officer, Virginia Fairweather, he gave the simple instruction: "Do your best not to let them persecute Joanie or Viv. If anyone is going to come out of this looking a shit, let it be me."[22]

By telephone he persuaded George Devine that Joan must be dropped from the cast of *Rhinoceros* at once; when a surprised Devine asked why, the magisterial Olivier, pompously aware of his public standing, replied testily that he did not want her pelted from the stalls with rotten fruit. Her part as Daisy was taken over by her understudy, Monica Evans, that very night; and a week later, in a statement issued through the Scunthorpe newspaper edited by her father, Joan pleaded doctor's orders and an attack of gastro-enteritis for her disappearance from *Rhinoceros*.

The same day brought news from New York that an enterprising American film producer named George Jessel had high hopes of co-starring Olivier as Abraham Lincoln and Vivien as his wife in *Mary Todd, Kentucky Belle*, "a story of turbulent quarrelling between two temperamental people".[23] Vivien, it seemed, had told Jessel she had "strong hopes" that Olivier would like the idea. Even more forlornly, she had asked Jessel to "give him my love" when he approached Olivier. But a fortnight later, when she flew to London for twenty-four hours in the hope of discussing a reconciliation, Olivier refused even to see her. When he told her as much by telephone, Vivien felt moved to apprise the *Daily Sketch* of the matter – and of the fact that she had that morning taken a "sentimental" trip to Notley Abbey. Through her steadfast friend Robert Helpmann, who had made the trip with her, she equally helplessly informed the *Daily Mail* that she hoped to see her husband in *Rhinoceros* before her return next day – "but that did not necessarily mean she would meet him". And so Vivien flew empty-handed back to New York and out of a relieved Olivier's life.

It is from this moment that Olivier dates his "change of life" – the beginning of a new era, now nearly thirty years old, which has seen him privately contented and publicly ever more triumphant. "From the last half of 1960 onwards life took on a pattern which, if it were not for my unbelieving gratefulness, might read like a steady crescendo of happiness and success...." Joan Plowright was to bless Olivier with a third life to follow his second – a life in which he became a family man, properly, for the first time, the founder-director of Britain's National Theatre, a peer of the realm, and a thoroughly fulfilled man for the first time in his turbulent existence. At an age when many men are beginning to edge towards the downhill slope, Olivier embarked on a new phase of his career, which for most would amount to a career – a life – in itself.

It began in heady self-indulgence in France, where August saw Olivier and Joan heading south from Paris for ten days in the Loire. Then both were off to the States: Joan to open *A Taste of Honey* in Los Angeles, Olivier to play the title role in Anouilh's *Becket*, directed by Peter Glenville, with Anthony Quinn as Henry ɪɪ. Her production moved to the Lyceum Theater, New York, on 4 October; his opened at the St James's Theater the next day.

Both Olivier and Quinn, for different reasons, had turned down lucrative film contracts for the chance of opening the new Anouilh in America. Olivier wanted to be near Joan; Peter Glenville had also flattered him into accepting the title role, instead of the more obvious part of the King: "My dear Larry, if you played the King, who on earth would I get to play the Archbishop?"[24] Quinn's motives were less ethereal: "He's the greatest!" If he counted the cost of the films he had turned down to act with Olivier, *Becket* would amount to a $250,000 acting lesson. "And at that price he'd better damn well give me one."

Olivier would have been more naturally cast in the flashier part of Henry than the grave, contemplative Becket, but Quinn was a strange choice for either role. Inevitably he tried to compete, and inevitably he lost. It was Olivier's "clarion tone" of a voice of which Quinn was most in awe; early in rehearsals his attempts to match it had totally deprived him of his own, to the extent that he called in a psychiatrist to help him understand the hopelessness of the rivalry he was involved in, and thus get his voice back. By his own account, the only way Quinn could even relate to Olivier was to treat him as Henry treated Becket – a risky piece of Method-ology which led to somewhat strained relations between them.

According to Peter Glenville, "Tony had a great desire to strike up a close relationship with Larry, but Larry didn't encourage it."[25] The story has been told that when Quinn asked Olivier where he got his marvellous voice, the great man told him that in Brighton, where he had been living, he walked about the beach declaiming Shakespeare with his mouth full of pebbles, like the Greek orator Demosthenes; Quinn was so impressed by this that he immediately sent to California for pebbles and walked about Broadway with a mouthful, almost choking himself as he rehearsed his lines. The anecdote has now, alas, officially been declared apocryphal (by Glenville), but the fact that it received such wide credence speaks for the awe in which Quinn held Olivier.

Quinn has since been generous in his excited recollections of the partnership, even though it cannot be counted one of the great stage duos of modern times. Most memorably, Quinn passed on another piece of wisdom imparted by Olivier during rehearsals: "You American actors are all like football players. You wait until you have the truth in your arms before you start running with the ball. We English start running when the curtain goes up and hope the truth will catch up with us."[26]

Olivier's Becket was described as "elegant and articulate", Quinn's Henry as "slurring, uncouth and arrogant". The play itself received a lukewarm reception, but both central performances won excited praise – with Olivier, on the opening night, taking no fewer than seventeen curtain-calls. In the critical view he had won the easy contest with Quinn, his Becket showing "admirable scope" while Quinn's Henry, after a stirring first scene, could only "duplicate his effects" for the rest of the evening. But *Becket* was a box-office smash and ran for almost six months – Olivier's longest stint on the Broadway stage. The opening coincided with the American premieres of *Spartacus* and *The Entertainer*, making it a stirring week for them both when Joan received rave reviews in *A Taste of Honey*. In time it was to win her that year's Tony award for the best performance by an actress; *Becket* won the award for best play, while Olivier lost out in the best actor stakes to Zero Mostel for his performance in, of all things, *Rhinoceros*. (In an interview with *Newsweek*, Mostel claimed Olivier had refused to join him in the production "because I wasn't a big enough star". This most generous of men resented Olivier thereafter.)[27]

After a six-week tour *Becket* reopened on Broadway without Quinn, who had a movie commitment, and with a dramatic cast change – which had been kept secret from Quinn and which he deeply resented.[28] Olivier returned to even greater triumph as Henry, with Arthur Kennedy replacing him as the turbulent priest. Much more suited to the part of the King, Olivier also brought to it a major reinterpretation; as Tynan put it, "the actor implied what the character never suspected, namely, that his attachment to Becket was homosexual". It was impossible to take your eyes off Olivier, wrote the *New York Times*, "as he makes Henry change from a gay, roistering king during the first half to a bitterly frustrated, temper-ridden man during the second". He had, according to the *Herald Tribune*, given Henry a new tragic stature: "If only Olivier's Henry could have played against Olivier's Becket!" The switch, given the new version of the part, was an act of the utmost *braggadocio*, which soon had Quinn seething on location in Italy. "Against Quinn's clod-like vigour," ran another review, "Olivier's Henry has an easy swagger, a skipping verve." When Quinn read it in Rome, he felt "quite sick.... I'd never have left if I'd known he was going to do that. Never!" His agonies were compounded at the following year's Tony awards, when Olivier *did* pick up the Best Actor trophy for his performance as Henry.

Two days after *Becket* had first opened, Olivier and Joan, instinctive Democrats both, had shared the excitement of John F. Kennedy's narrow election to the White House. It was not long before Frank Sinatra invited Olivier to take part in Kennedy's inaugural gala, which he was organizing. With a singular lack of tact, Sinatra initially asked Olivier to declaim a passage from John Bright arguing the merits of republics over monarchies; the English knight politely declined, preferring, he said, to put together a few remarks of his own, welcoming the new President to office on behalf of his transatlantic cousins. At the post-gala party at Paul Young's restaurant, Olivier fell into conversation with the new President's father, Joseph Kennedy, whose controversial views while wartime Ambassador to the Court of St James's he had most certainly not forgotten. Already uneasy with the former Ambassador, Olivier was positively outraged when he slapped his son on the back and introduced him as "Mr" Olivier. "Sir Laurence," the President immediately corrected his father, with a deadly glance, and proceeded to thank and flatter him for his speech, "which I understand you wrote yourself". Olivier subsequently declared President Kennedy "a smart cookie indeed".

Six weeks before, on 2 December, Vivien had wept in the Divorce Court as she was awarded her decree nisi from Olivier, on the grounds of his adultery with Joan. Roger Gage, himself already intent on remarrying, gave evidence to back up that of a private detective, who testified that he had "found Miss Plowright and Sir Laurence in nightclothes" in a flat in Ovington Square, Chelsea, the previous June. Tears streamed down Vivien's cheeks throughout her brief appearance in the dock.[29]

In twenty-eight squalid minutes both marriages were ended. It was twenty years and four months since the judge had cried "Bingo!" in Santa Barbara.

CHAPTER 20

1962–3

"I wouldn't mind her so much, my dear, if she didn't *smell* so," was Vivien's verdict to friends on her husband's new choice of partner.[1] Joan Plowright suited Olivier, but she was a controversial choice among those who cared about him. "Rather a hard little lump, I think," said one.[2] "A *very* tough cookie," said another.[3] "A nice enough girl," was Noël Coward's view, "and a good enough actress, but I do wish Larry wouldn't marry her."[4]

He did, of course, as soon as he could. Two weeks after their divorce decrees had become absolute, fifty-three-year-old Sir Laurence Olivier and twenty-nine-year-old Joan Plowright became man and wife in a two-minute ceremony above a drug-store at Wilton, Connecticut, on 17 March, St Patrick's Day, 1961. For a fortnight Olivier's sense of drama, not to mention his self-esteem, had deemed it necessary to lull the press into a false sense of security with an elaborate series of fake post-theatre arrangements, which would see the furtive lovers going into separate friends' Manhattan front doors each night and straight out the back into each other's arms. The wedding too was conducted hugger-mugger, fifty miles north of New York, with the discreet help of their US lawyer, Arnold Weissberger, and Hume Cronyn's tame cab driver, Louie Cooper;[5] that night Richard Burton hosted a celebration party for a handful of guests allowed in on the secret. Olivier's attitude to it all was highly reminiscent of his wedding to Vivien twenty years before: the ceremony itself conducted amid great secrecy, with a lady judge touchingly innocent of his renown, then immense pride at the announcement in *The Times* the next day. His pleasure in concealing his third marriage from the press could be capped, it seems, only by his delight at the promptness with which they reported it.

Over the previous few months Olivier had felt it necessary for his own peace of mind to unburden himself of Vivien in the most formal of ways, making an official handover of this fragile package – complete with detailed instructions on care and maintenance – to Jack Merivale. During her lightning visit to London the previous June, he had called Merivale in New York to say she had told him they were in love: "Any chance of a union, old boy?"[6] To his dismay Merivale, who had just been subjected to one of Vivien's depressive rages, replied strongly in the negative. By the time she returned to New York, however, after a visit to Dr Conachy, Vivien was back on an upswing, and Merivale back at her feet; by August 1960 he had written Olivier a long, secret letter spelling out his feelings for Vivien and his sense of commitment to her. A delighted Olivier replied immediately, confiding that he had "broken down and sobbed, with relief and gratitude, on receipt of the news". He was "very happy", he said, "for everybody". Olivier wrote of Vivien's illness at some length, advising Merivale how to recognize the advance warnings of an attack. Wishing everybody well, her husband concluded, à la Coriolanus, that he now felt free to proceed with his own life elsewhere.

The ensuing months, as the divorce machinery creaked into action, had luckily allowed Olivier little time to indulge his huge capacity for guilt. When Vivien turned up in New York, while filming *The Roman Spring of Mrs Stone*, he stunned her by agreeing to meet only if it were in a public place and with Joan present. An awkward pre-theatre dinner duly took place at Sardi's, which he had deliberately chosen because its noise level would prevent any delicate turn in the conversation. The tense trio managed a little small talk before Olivier reached across the table for Joan's hand and held it tenderly as he told his former wife that they planned to marry in a few days. The news visibly devastated Vivien. Although very happy with Jack Merivale, she still worshipped Olivier, still regarded him as the mainstay of her adult life. Less than an hour after they had sat down, Olivier and Joan were seeing Vivien into a taxi and out of both their lives. They had not told her the other news which had so preoccupied them both of late – which was a kindness, for the thought of sharing Olivier's next project with him would have filled Vivien with impossible longings.

Apart from the nightly demands of *Becket*, and the weighing of sundry offers of American television work by day, he and Joan had found themselves mulling over news from England which appeared to them to be some sort of divine sanction upon their union. Two months before, in mid-January 1961, Olivier had received a letter from a Sussex optician hitherto unknown to him, offering one of the few theatrical opportunities he still coveted: a purpose-built theatre of his own, with his own company to recruit and lead. The fact that it would be in Chichester, conveniently down the road from the house which he and Joan had just bought in Brighton's Royal Crescent, made the offer seem almost magically attractive. It was the only wedding present which could possibly be calculated to excite the actor-director with everything.

It was at Tyrone Guthrie's suggestion that Leslie Evershed-Martin, a former mayor of Chichester, had steeled himself to write to Olivier – little expecting a response, let alone an acceptance.[7] For Evershed-Martin, it was the realization of a most unlikely dream dating from 4 January 1959, when he had watched *Monitor*, the BBC TV arts programme on which Guthrie was being interviewed about his work at the Shakespeare theatre built in Stratford, Ontario, to the open-stage design he had conceived during Olivier's improvised *Hamlet* at Elsinore in 1937. The programme sung the praises of a prominent local citizen, Tom Paterson, who had worked long and hard to build Guthrie his beloved thrust stage, in a community with little attachment to the theatre beyond the fact that it happened to have been named after Shakespeare's birthplace. It struck Evershed-Martin that Canada's Stratford was a town much the same size as his own Chichester, itself without a theatre since 1847 – a fact its inhabitants did not seem to mind too much. Unlike Stratford, however, where people now thought nothing of driving a few hundred miles to see the only good theatre within reach, Chichester was a mere thirty miles from Brighton, only sixty from London. Stratford, Ontario, had built its theatre in its civic park; Chichester too had a park, Oaklands, with space to spare. Evershed-Martin, himself a keen theatre-goer, and the founder twenty-five years before of an amateur group called the Chichester Players, began to hatch an audacious plot.

He wrote to the programme's presenter, Huw Wheldon, who put him in touch with Guthrie. Ever anxious to midwife the birth of any new theatre, especially one of a design so close to his heart, Guthrie steered Evershed-Martin through the early planning stages. Both were gratified to see half the £100,000 building costs raised within a year, at which point Guthrie warned that the entire enterprise would most likely be an expensive disaster unless a big name could be tempted aboard as founder-director. Why not approach Olivier in New York? His career had reached some sort of crossroads, as indeed had his private life; he was about to remarry and was anxious to settle in Sussex. "You never know. It might be worth a try."

The previous summer, Olivier had been among thousands on a mailing list to have received the preliminary brochure about the proposed Chichester Theatre. He remembered reading it with sympathetic interest because he had used the bells of Chichester Cathedral for the Coronation scene in his film of *Richard III* (having discovered, typically enough, that they were the only cathedral bells in England "congruent with the period"). For all their ups and downs over the years, Guthrie had read his sometime protégé well: when Olivier received Evershed-Martin's letter in New York that January, he was indeed in a mood to take stock. He was well into his fifties, embarking on a domestic *vita nuova* and weary of camping on either coast of the United States to make a living he regarded as indecently handsome. He and Joan had agreed that both wanted children as soon as possible – another reason to crave a settled life in his beloved England. He had recently seen two theatres pulled down around his ears: the St James's and the Stoll, whose last production had been his *Titus Andronicus*; with his familiar flair for self-dramatization, he had consequently begun to believe that his presence in any London theatre "would only be enviable to a member of the IRA". And his failure to raise the money for the film of *Macbeth* still smarted: "Apart from creating my own films, I had known no joy in all my life's work equal to that of forming a new theatre group."[8]

Olivier was intrigued, but he took a month to reply to Evershed-Martin, asking him to talk details to his London agent, Cecil Tennant. The exchanges which subsequently flowed across the Atlantic catered to his every whim, from complete artistic freedom in choice of plays and players to the positioning of the theatre switchboard. By 3 March, the day his divorce from Vivien became absolute, Olivier already knew it was likely that Joan was carrying his child. That day he wrote a letter of acceptance to Evershed-Martin, whom he had yet to meet, with the cavalier postscript that he would accept a salary of £3,000 per annum rather than the £5,000 on offer. He and Joan were both going to enter into the spirit of the Chichester enterprise as if their new lives depended on it.

As his triumphant reappearance in *Becket* drew towards its conclusion, David Susskind tempted him to spend a final exhausting week in New York taping a television performance as Graham Greene's Mexican "whisky priest" in *The Power and the Glory*, with Julie Harris, George C. Scott and Cyril Cusack, under the direction of Marc Daniels. By the last of the seven days allotted for shooting Olivier had developed an eye infection, thanks to his insistence on wearing contact lenses to make his hazel eyes dark enough for Mexican authenticity. He was so tired that he quite uncharacteristically forgot a line that last day; young Patty Duke afterwards won his thankful praise for an ad lib which steered him back on course. By the end of the twenty-four-hour session, kept going by coffee and cold compresses, Olivier was so exhausted that he had to be lifted on to the burro which carried him through the final jungle sequence.[9] Though he again thrived sufficiently on the pressure to turn in a memorable performance, he still considered it inferior to Paul Scofield's in the same role on the London stage five years before. Scofield's priest had "floored" him: "I think it was the best performance I remember seeing.... I went to see one matinee and went again the next matinee – and I don't often go to see things more than once. He was wonderful."

Early June saw him collapse aboard the *Queen Elizabeth* for a restorative voyage home. A possible sighting of what Olivier termed "Joan's bulge" had drawn the *paparazzi* across the Channel to Le Havre, lest the Oliviers flee before the liner docked at Southampton; again it was Cecil Tennant to the rescue, spiriting her away, unphotographed, while Olivier dealt with all journalistic inquiries. So intent were they on keeping Joan's pregnancy to themselves that it was three weeks before they dared venture out of their Brighton hotel – their home for six months while 4 Royal Crescent was suitably gentrified – to inspect Mr Evershed-Martin and his Chichester site. After satisfying himself that his chairman was suitably "aldermanic", Olivier found himself confronted by a large mudpatch, distinguished only by six drainpipe-like objects sticking into the air. They marked the corners of the hexagonal building which, within a year, would supposedly house 1,360 theatre-goers on three sides of a dramatically raked thrust stage.

His then press aide, Virginia Fairweather, remembered Olivier looking at this huge, muckridden hole in the ground "with love and awe, much as one of the Pharaohs might have regarded the sands in the desert when the pyramids were built".[10] He was sceptical about the time schedule but, in his own words, "well and truly stuck with it". Eagerly he sank himself into his multifarious plans, attending board meetings, liaising with the architects, reading plays "from Webster to Wodehouse", recruiting a company. He enthused about the theatre to Lord Harewood in the first edition of ITV's arts programme, *Tempo* – "as King Lear said, 'I will do such things – what they are yet I know not – but they shall be the terrors of the earth'" – and donated his £500 fee to the building fund. His commitment to Chichester was total: among the work he turned down to sustain it was Sam Spiegel's offer of a choice between Lord Allenby and King Feisal in David Lean's film of *Lawrence of Arabia*, which was to prove the making of Peter O'Toole. In the months that followed Olivier took only one week off from Chichester, to record a large chunk of the Old Testament, before Joan gave birth to their first child on 3 December; unusually for the time, Olivier was present as his son – named Richard after his brother – was born in a Hove nursing home. Tarquin Olivier was among the godparents when the boy was christened six months later in Chichester Cathedral, by which time Joan was pregnant again, despite the fact that her husband had cast her in leading roles in two of his three inaugural productions.

A week after Richard's birth, having seen Joan into Royal Crescent and the safe hands of housekeeper, cook and nurse, Olivier repaired to Ireland to collar a decent fee for playing Graham Weir, the tormented schoolmaster in Peter Glenville's film *Term of Trial*. Some of his friends believed that Joan's influence was already at work in his acceptance of the unlikely part of the meek, downtrodden Weir – the kind of character in vogue in those days of British cinematic naturalism – opposite Simone Signoret. Playing the flirtatious schoolgirl who falls in love with him was a coy newcomer called Sarah Miles, making her film debut (as was Terence Stamp, as the school bully). Glenville's own adaptation of James Barlow's novel appeared to capitalize on the recent success of *The Blackboard Jungle*, with a touch of *Lolita* for good measure. As with *Carrie*, however, Olivier's sombre, lip-pursing mode lent his character more depth than perhaps the script warranted; the film was only a modest success, and Olivier below his best while attempting to portray a nondescript, unheroic figure. In the film's climactic trial scene, where Olivier's schoolmaster is falsely accused by Miles of raping her, he suddenly explodes into a typically powerful fury, quite out of character with the subdued, henpecked figure he has sketched hitherto. "No matter how patiently and skilfully Olivier plays the role," wrote the *New York Times*, "with all of his skill at portraying discomfort and down-at-heel wistfulness, he cannot quite make this fellow absorbing – or even real." Wrongly, for once, Tynan believed Olivier undertook "common man" roles only out of a sense of duty; but this time he put his finger on why they always went wrong: "That outside emotional candour cannot help breaking through. The actor impatiently bursts the seams of the role, and the common man becomes extraordinary." Olivier, as the *Daily Express* put it, "can play a king – but he cannot play a mouse".

Though far from the most interesting of Olivier's few failures, *Term of Trial* provides a good illustration of why his talents are not best served by the cinema – why an Olivier performance can so often disappoint on screen. To Tynan, it was "partly because the reticence of movie acting is awkward for him, but mostly because his performances need to be seen as flowing, consecutive wholes, not chopped up into long-shots and close-ups and spread over months of shooting".[11] Even the film's director, Peter Glenville, who had of course just worked with him onstage in *Becket*, declared Olivier "a natural theatre actor, rather than a natural cinema actor.... A great actor wants to act, which he has more freedom to do on the stage. He doesn't want to worry about mechanical things, as he has to do in the film studios."[12] One reason the climactic courtroom scene seemed so at odds with the rest of his characterization was that Glenville chose to disregard camera angles or close-ups and give Olivier his head; it was filmed in one uninterrupted take, as if in the theatre – and one take, with this actor giving his all, was enough.

Joan and their baby had joined him in Ireland on 12 January for the last six weeks of shooting, during which they rented the handsome country house of the local judge. Here Olivier received a stream of Chichester visitors as plans developed for the first season, due to open within six months. Among them was his old friend and colleague Roger Furse, whom he had hired to design John Ford's *The Broken Heart*, one of the unlikely triptych of plays he had selected for his inaugural festival; the others were Chekhov's *Uncle Vanya* and, to open the new theatre, *The Chances*, an obscure piece which Olivier had unearthed in the British Museum and is believed by theatrical history to have been adapted in 1666 by George Villiers, 2nd Duke of Buckingham, from Beaumont and Fletcher. Chichester's artistic director, who had managed to assemble a most distinguished inaugural company, would direct all three plays himself and appear in two.

Though the eccentricity of his choice of repertoire was to earn him untimely criticism, Olivier himself has explained that he saw these three plays as offering him "three entirely different styles with which to show off the amenities of this particular theatre", boasting as it did Britain's first "arena" stage – itself, like the theatre, hexagonal in shape, surrounded by the audience on three sides. *The Chances* used "no sets at all beyond that designed more or less for permanency by the architect"; *The Broken Heart* was as "scenically ambitious as it could well be without impinging upon the lines of sight"; and *Uncle Vanya* "utterly realistic". The designer Sean Kenny was to change his mind about too naturalistic an approach to *Uncle Vanya*, but Olivier's rationale for the repertoire remained. Unduly conscious of his lack of a university education, he had gone to enormous lengths to choose a repertoire which was tried and tested, but fresh: of the two Jacobean plays, *The Chances* had not been produced since a Drury Lane revival in 1808, and *The Broken Heart* since 1904. *Uncle Vanya* was his act of defiance; it was impossible, said the sceptics, for so naturalistic a drama to work on so unnatural a stage, where actors accustomed to holding an audience with their eyes must speak with their backs to at least half of them.

At five minutes to seven on Tuesday, 5 July 1962, a tape recording of Olivier's most unctuous voice boomed through the loudspeakers rigged around Oaklands Park to urge the Chichester Festival Theatre's first audience – chosen by ballot from thousands of applicants – to take their seats. The evening was suitably festive, with the Duke of Buckingham's *jeu d'esprit* providing a celebratory opening, but the general high spirits were soon dashed by a wave of politely muted critical dismay. Infected by the sense of occasion, the critics would forgive Olivier so flimsy a first course; but they would expect some red meat from *The Broken Heart*. They were even, for now, prepared to forgive the fact that the company, however distinguished, seemed rather *old*.

By the Queen's visit to the theatre on 31 July, conveniently during Goodwood Week, both theatre and company had been hailed to their concrete rafters and Olivier's choice of plays damned to beneath the maple stage. *The Chances*, despite a stylish cast including Joan, Rosemary Harris, John Neville, Keith Michell and Robert Lang, was said to be an "enjoyable Jacobean romp"; but Olivier, as director, was declared – even by such friendly spirits as Harold Hobson – to have failed to make full use of the revolutionary "peninsular" stage at his disposal. *The Broken Heart*, which opened four days later, with Neville and Michell joined by Fay Compton, Joan Greenwood, Andre Morell and Olivier himself as the obsessively jealous Bassanes, was an unqualified disaster. Leading the critical assault was Kenneth Tynan, who wrote a subsequently famous "Open Letter to an Open Stager" in the *Observer*:

> Dear Sir Laurence,
> I have now seen all but one of the inaugural productions you have directed
> for the Chichester Festival Theatre, and I have to report a general feeling
> that all is not well with your dashing hexagonal playhouse. When you
> opened your season with *The Chances*, a flimsy Jacobean prank by Beaumont
> and Fletcher, one shrugged and wrote it off as caprice; but when *The Broken
> Heart*, a far more challenging piece, likewise fails to kindle one's reflexes, it
> is time to stop shrugging and start worrying. Something has clearly gone
> wrong: but how? Who put the hex on the hexagon? Does the fault lie in the
> play, in the theatre, or in you, its artistic director...?
> Within a fortnight you will have directed three plays and appeared in two
> leading parts. It is too much....[13]

Tynan's tirade centred on harsh technical criticism of Olivier's direction and use of the theatre, even of his acting. It might not have mattered so much had Chichester's opening night not been marked by an embarrassing newspaper leak which, to Olivier's chagrin, began to undermine all his work at Chichester. The critics had arrived from London that first night clutching evening papers which announced that Sir Laurence Olivier was tipped to be the first director of Britain's National Theatre.

It was true, of course – he had been agonizing over the invitation for some months – but he had hoped that the news would not get out until that inaugural Chichester season was established. Suddenly it looked as if he had been using worthy little Chichester as a dry run for higher things. Worse, from Olivier's personal point of view, all his work there would be measured against the very different standards of a National Theatre in the making. As he put it, at his most casuistic, twenty years later:

It was the worst luck imaginable.... An announcement of that sort was bound to provoke comments of the most harsh, snide and merciless kind: is one to think that a man who makes this sort of choice/error of judgement/wild statement/childish mistake ... is *really* to be considered the best choice for the director of the National Theatre of Great Britain? Gone is the hope of charitable welcome. Once more it is gritting-of-the-teeth time.

This retrospective bitterness was aimed directly, if posthumously, at Tynan, whose open letter was read with mounting rage by its addressee and his wife in bed that Sunday morning. According to one in the room with them, Olivier turned to Joan and said: "Darling, in my most silky, throwaway tone I would suggest that I employ Mr Tynan at the National. In the time-honoured phrase: 'If you can't beat 'em, join 'em.' And at least he would not be able to write notices about the theatre again."[14]

According to Olivier, however, Tynan's enrolment on the National Theatre staff was entirely Joan's idea. That October, on receiving a letter from the critic applying – "with the coolest sauce" – for the job of literary manager, Olivier turned to Joan with poison pen poised and asked, "How shall we slaughter the little bastard?", to which she replied thoughtfully: "You know, you might do worse...." Coming from him, she argued, Tynan's appointment would show that Olivier was not too set in his theatrical ways. "We may have our own reasons for hating this fellow, but if you could bring yourself to have him ... everyone would be surprised and relieved that you were able to forget the past and turn up such a trick. They would look at you with a new eye; all the younger generation would rejoice." Olivier reproduced his wife's speech in meticulous and lengthy detail in his memoirs to illustrate the "leavening value" of Joan's advice to him over the years. But the most likely explanation for the appointment remains Tynan's own typically candid, if inelegant, version: "I expect they would rather have me on the inside pissing out than on the outside pissing in."

All that, however, lay three months in the future as Tynan arrived in pink evening dress for the first night of Olivier's production of *Uncle Vanya* on 16 July, the day after his open letter had appeared. Seeing him approaching across the lawns, Tynan's fellow critics left Virginia Fairweather's office to meet him, drinks in hand, and raised their glasses in a chorus of boos and raspberries, to which Tynan responded with a sweeping bow. The spectacle delighted Fairweather, who rushed to tell Olivier. But the news did little to cheer him: he and his cast had become convinced that *Uncle Vanya* was going to provide their critical arch-enemy with more cannon fodder. Never in his career, he tells us, not even before the curtain rose on *Richard III*, had he faced a first night with a greater certainty of failure – despite having assembled a magnificent cast including his patrons of old, eighty-year-old Dame Sybil Thorndike and her eighty-seven-year-old husband Lewis Casson, Fay Compton, Joan Greenwood, and Michael Redgrave as Vanya, Joan as Sonya and himself again playing the doctor, Astrov. The direness of the dress rehearsal had left them all apprehensive, largely thanks to the nervous fumblings of the young girl in charge of the crucial sound-effects tape; during the final run-through a guitar played where there should have been a peal of thunder, and where the guitar should have played, a dog barked. Back in her dressing-room Joan, pregnant beneath Sonya's tightly-laced stays, collapsed in an untypical fit of sobbing.

The dress rehearsal had belied Olivier's initially high hopes for the production. When his august company had met for the first read-through in a drill hall behind Sloane Square, he had whispered to Michael Redgrave, "I know you think there's no such thing as a definitive performance, but *this*...".[15] Olivier's first-night apprehensions, however, as with those backstage stories which are part of the *Richard III* legend, form a characteristic prelude to the unveiling of one of the great productions of its generation; *Uncle Vanya* was to stay in the Chichester and National Theatre repertoires for three sold-out years. Even Tynan, though still unconvinced by the effectiveness of the Chichester stage, hailed two "superlative" performances: Olivier's Astrov, "a visionary maimed by self-knowledge and dwindled into a middle-aged *roué*", and Redgrave's Vanya, "torn between self-assertion and self-deception, and taking the stage in a tottering, pigeon-toed stride that boldly amalgamates both". Joan Plowright's emotional coda as Sonya, spelling out a defiant avowal of faith in the future, "drained every tear-duct in the house". Never before or since has there been a cast so suited to Chekhov's great work, each playing a character his or her own age, each an individualist of supreme talent with the self-disciplined professionalism to blend into a tight-knit ensemble. As time went on, Olivier told Evershed-Martin that they had "woven themselves into such a fantasy that they were held together by gossamer threads".

Olivier and Redgrave had not worked together since the Old Vic *Hamlet* of 1937. One of Olivier's curtain speeches that year had announced that during that night's performance Laertes's wife had given birth to a daughter – "destined, no doubt, to become a great actress"; twenty-five years later Vanessa Redgrave, who married Tony Richardson during these *Uncle Vanya* rehearsals, was indeed beginning to carve out a substantial name for herself. Though the two actors had since gone separate professional ways – perhaps because Redgrave, who had turned down the part of the Dauphin in the film of *Henry V*, was occasionally billed as Olivier's leading rival – he and his wife, Rachel Kempson, had been regular Notley weekenders.

As preparations for *Uncle Vanya* advanced, Redgrave swallowed all his previous, rather high-minded reservations about Olivier's talents, finding him a "constructive, concise and considerate" director. Yes, his swift and merciless tongue was capable of unwarranted cruelty: there was the day, for example, on which he had crushed Joan, in front of the entire cast: "Darling, you're like a little girl from Scunthorpe doing an audition for RADA." He had then proceeded to irritate Redgrave deeply: "Very good, Michael, but loud echoes of Sir John, very loud echoes." Such outbursts, however, were the exception rather than the rule. More than aware how vulnerable are the sensibilities of the rehearsing actor, Olivier prided himself on showing a tireless concern for every detail of the lives of those working with him. When Redgrave missed an *Uncle Vanya* rehearsal to attend his daughter's wedding, which was a top-secret affair, he lied to Olivier that he had a grumbling appendix; that weekend Redgrave received a telegram from his director saying he should have a colonic irrigation, for which he had fixed him an appointment in Harley Street. A week later, too absorbed in his work to have told Olivier the real reason for his disappearance, Redgrave received another telegram: "You naughty boy. You didn't keep the Harley Street appointment. You are still un-irrigated."

Now, as *Uncle Vanya* established itself as the hit of the Chichester season, Olivier took Redgrave in on his secret that the production would form the centrepiece of the inaugural season of Britain's National Theatre, whose first company they would lead together. An "overjoyed" Redgrave, "proud of my work and proud of Larry's company", later looked back on these seasons at Chichester as among the happiest of his career. Nor was it only the cast, like so many countless others he had worked with, but all the Chichester staff, no matter how humble, who testified to Olivier's constant attention to their every need. Only once, when Evershed-Martin tried to oppose Olivier's decision to revive *Uncle Vanya* in the second season, did his hasty tongue cause permanent damage to a relationship; Olivier shouted angrily that the theatre was not being run solely for its founder's benefit. "He had a cruel streak," says Evershed-Martin, "but he always apologized the next day."[16] Sybil Thorndike, who had known Olivier and his family for so long, believed that he had inherited this ability to endear himself to all manner of people, however high or low their station, from his father: "To be a parson, you must have no side, no scholarly superiority," said Dame Sybil. "You need the common touch. Larry learnt that from his father."[17]

The common touch he may have had offstage – during National Theatre days Jonathan Miller, quoting *Henry V*, dubbed Olivier's ministrations "a little touch of Harry in the night"[18] – but he was still unable to find it in performance. *Term of Trial* had just opened to lukewarm reviews, with Alexander Walker of the *Evening Standard* summing up the consensus that Olivier was miscast: "If there is one role that Sir Laurence Olivier cannot play well, it is that of the little man.... I beg him to refuse any more [such] roles." Defiant as ever, and determined to defeat this one critical reservation about his talents, Olivier immediately chose just such another part as his one theatrical detour *en route* from Chichester to the National. He would return briefly to the West End stage as Fred Midway, the cocky, *petit bourgeois* Birmingham insurance salesman in *Semi-Detached*, the first stage play by a teacher-turned-writer named David Turner, then a script-writer for BBC radio's long-running saga of country folk, *The Archers*. Rather than use his usual zest to caricature the wily, put-upon, suburban Midway – as his director, Tony Richardson, wanted – Olivier insisted on authentic restraint, lest he make Fred too appealing a figure, as love-hateable as Archie Rice. He had seen a commuter on the Brighton train who gave him an almost Chekhovian vision of Midway; it was a vision which he could not shed, despite the worried urgings of Richardson, other members of the cast and even Joan. Richardson found Olivier "very depressed" at the time:

> He knew himself it wasn't working, but somehow he couldn't break out of the misconception. It was very odd and unusual for him. He seemed to be buried under a false image and he hadn't the energy, or the will, to free himself.... I think he had too much on his plate. He was involved in extensive preparations for the National Theatre: he was over-extended and fatigued.[19]

Semi-Detached had proved one of the biggest box-office hits in the history of the Belgrade Theatre, Coventry, where Leonard Rossiter created the leading role (which he later played in New York). But the play failed dismally in London, largely because, in John Russell Taylor's shrewd analysis, it was "about suburbans, by a suburban, for suburbans. Turner himself lives in a semi-detached, and admits that he is the sort of man who, like Fred Midway, would put down a red front drive just to annoy the neighbours."[20] It made sense, therefore, that the play should succeed in suburban Coventry, but could not mean much to "anyone who does not know the semi-detached world intimately, as unfortunately few London theatre-goers do (or, worse, will admit to knowing)". Russell Taylor was not alone in suspecting that Olivier himself did not fully grasp that Turner's work was neither pro- nor anti-suburban life, merely a sympathetic and naturalistic account of the way it is lived. For many, perhaps, it was too much so, too *uncomfortably* true to life; Tynan later told Olivier he believed the play had failed because "It is a comedy which fulfils a perfectly proper purpose, that of making the audience hate themselves. You can't expect them to thank you for that."

Olivier had spent so much time perfecting Fred's Midlands accent – which ended up somewhere on the trunk road from Nottingham to Birmingham – that his strangled strivings towards authenticity swamped the rest of his performance. Few other members of the cast, which included Eileen Atkins and Mona Washbourne, had bothered much about a Midlands accent, believing that it would make them hard to understand and that Olivier would anyway "tone it down a bit" once the production reached the stage. Far from it: when John Osborne visited his Brighton home, he found Olivier surrounded by yards of tape recordings of Midlands dialects, which he was practising in the bathroom mirror: "He lavished tremendous care on it – literal-minded care – but in the end it didn't matter. He missed any poetry that might have been there by concentrating too much on the technical aspects ... [the part] needed a smaller talent than Olivier's."[21] His obsession with such detail even saw him make a special trip to Birmingham to buy the clothes he would wear as Fred, which in the meantime he wore all day every day, to "get the feel of them" and give them a "lived-in look". Touring the Midlands with Tony Richardson, Olivier one day decided to try out his accent on a Nottingham tobacconist; the shopkeeper looked at Olivier oddly for a moment, then asked Richardson: "Which part of America is your friend from, sir?"[22]

As if the voice and clothes were not enough, Olivier donned *two* wigs for his metamorphosis into the virtually bald Midway: one a shiny bald pate, the next a highly unattractive dome with a few straggles of lank, greasy hair trailing from it. Add a drooping moustache and Virginia Fairweather, who visited him backstage, thought he looked "revolting". When she told him so, a hurt Olivier confided that he had modelled his looks on those of his father-in-law, William Plowright, the Scunthorpe newspaper editor.[23]

After an opening night at a Saville Theatre half-empty because of a dense London fog, critical opinion sharply divided even over the accent; J. C. Trewin thought it "a masterpiece", while Philip Hope-Wallace of the *Guardian* called it "a terrible amalgam" that "rang completely false". Olivier was already miserable in the role, to which he would be committed for sixteen weeks; himself a recent father, he was particularly upset to feel across the footlights the rejection of the many children brought by their equally disappointed parents to see a rare London stage appearance by this great actor, of whom they obviously expected classical heroics. By the time the two-week closure notices went up, his misery had brought on another psychosomatic case of gout. He felt he had let down both cast and author; but worst of all, in his capacity as impresario, he had inadvertently besmirched the virgin reputation of the National. "If this is the kind of play the director of the National Theatre thinks worth putting on," wrote Bernard Levin in the *Daily Mail*, "I can only say that it were better that the Foundation Stone be hanged about his neck, and he be cast into the uttermost depths of the sea."

Whatever the merits of the play, Olivier thought it depressingly typical of the Levins of the critical world, in their remorseless quest for wordy hyperbole, to expect a National Theatre to eschew such contemporary experimentation. Surely one of the functions of a National Theatre, as well as reinterpreting the classics, would be to provide a showcase for young British playwrights? As he retreated to Brighton for Christmas – his second Chichester season planned and his second child by Joan imminent – Olivier brooded over the crucial appointments which would shape not just the early character of the National, but its success or failure.

His sense of responsibility was lonely and awesome. There was candour, as much as familiarly pompous self-grandeur, in the Churchillian vein he had adopted when his appointment had been formally confirmed that August: "I shall strive my utmost to lay the foundations of a National Theatre that will finally justify its long wait for existence, and be a source of pride to my profession and to the country as a whole."

It was precisely 115 years since the modern movement to found a National Theatre had begun in earnest. Had Olivier not existed – and it would have been difficult to invent him – it is quite possible those efforts would have continued for another century or more. All the vicissitudes of his career, all the energy and imagination he had expended, all the brainpower, all the make-up, the tragedies as much as the triumphs, the calculated risks and the complacent certitudes merged in this moment. He was the only man who could possibly have taken on what most thought an impossible task. As now he climbed to the bridge of a ship still without a hull, Olivier was well aware that he was on a hiding to nothing. "Hopes for the National Theatre?" he shrugged. "Who has hopes? I shall just put on my thickest suit of armour and stand there for all to see."[24]

CHAPTER 21

1963-4

"To avoid any coyness and nonsense, let me say at once that I would not accept the job of director of the National Theatre."[1] It was not Olivier but Tyrone Guthrie who chose to make this blunt announcement on the BBC radio programme *The Brains Trust* in the summer of 1956. Guthrie had not even been offered the job; he was speaking in response to rumours that he would be. But his purpose was also to rule out Olivier, the grapevine's other leading candidate. Whenever it came to Olivier, Guthrie's fervent idealism always seemed to be sharpened by a personal edge: "There are plenty of old duffers around who would jump at the chance. But I don't think that the National Theatre would work with an old duffer at the head of it. It needs young blood."

The other spur for Guthrie's remarks was a much-publicized gesture by Kenneth Tynan and his *Observer* colleague Richard Findlater. The two critics had donned funereal frock-coats and top hats with tassels to stage a protest beside the foundation-stone laid by Queen Elizabeth five years before on Friday, 13 July 1951. Already moved since the Queen had laid it, the stone now stood in absurd isolation on the south bank of the Thames – an embarrassing symbol of the lack of any progress towards the establishment of a National Theatre company, let alone a building to house it. To Tynan and Findlater, as well as Peter Hall, Peter Brook and other young theatrical meteors of the day, the fault lay with the old duffers on the various official committees formed to lobby the Government into action.

Guthrie had anyway decided the job would be impossible. Whoever was appointed the National's first director would find himself torn limb from limb by the conflicting demands of the Establishment for tradition and classicism, and of the powerful emergent "new wave" for experiment and innovation. The National's founder-director, in Guthrie's view, would have to be someone "of an almost heroic stature: infinitely patient (to deal with committees), of an unassailable theatrical reputation (to attract the support of the political establishment) but also sufficiently flexible to absorb the ideas and styles of the new generation".[2] He would have to be, in the words of the historian of the National Theatre, John Elsom, "a theatrical Hercules, who could carry like Atlas a world of responsibility, as well as cleaning out the Augean stables of commercialism".[3] Nowhere in the theatrical profession of the day, amid the ranks either of old duffers or young whizz-kids, did any one figure combining all these qualities stand out as pre-eminent.

There was one man, however, who fell into neither category, yet seemed to possess the right credentials. As Olivier himself put it, "I don't think I'm really the right man for the job, but I can't think of anyone better." At the time the issue first arose, in the mid-1950s, his stage career was passing through the doldrums, thanks to his difficulties with Vivien as much as his personal loss of direction. Olivier, like Guthrie, had hated the theatrical landmark of the era, *Look Back in Anger*; unlike Guthrie, however, he had put his ear to the ground and realized that this was a bandwagon worth boarding. With *The Entertainer* and *Rhinoceros*, not to mention the plethora of contemporary plays his production company had presented, many of them at a considerable loss, Olivier had proved his ability to adapt to theatrical change. With his classical reputation indeed unassailable, he alone was a figure possessing both sufficient stature and the right track record to prove a sturdy enough bridge between the old and the new. He would soon embrace the "angry" new generation enthusiastically enough to marry into it; already, in his chameleon-like way, he had even begun to adopt its mannerisms, dressing in the casual fashions of a man half his age and moving among the Royal Court coterie with an acclimatized nonchalance which owed much to his performing skills. In time Guthrie himself was to concede that Olivier was "the right figurehead"[4] for the National Theatre's inception (though even that came as a preamble to a call for his "abdication"[5]).

It was early in 1957, at a weekend party at Notley, that Olivier had first been sounded out about the directorship by Lord Chandos, the recently ennobled Oliver Lyttelton, former Conservative cabinet minister and now chairman of the joint council of the various groups working towards the establishment of a National Theatre. Olivier was wary: at the time there was no immediate prospect of a National Theatre to run, and the tangled, interminable history of recent attempts to raise the necessary money went back even beyond the date of his birth. As long ago as 1848 a London publisher, Effingham Wilson, had become the first figure in modern times to propose the notion of a national theatre for Britain; even such luminaries as Matthew Arnold, Henry Irving and, in Olivier's own lifetime, Harley Granville-Barker and George Bernard Shaw had got nowhere. "The subject is not exhausted," declared Shaw, "but we are."[6] Olivier had lived through the failure of the Old Vic's attempts to have itself declared Britain's ex-officio National Theatre. But the prospect remained close to his heart, and he agreed to become a trustee. All this really meant at the time was that his influential voice and considerable energies would join those of many another notable, both political and theatrical, in the continuing struggles ahead.

Nearly nine years had passed since the post-war Labour Government had finally seen through the National Theatre Act, thereby promising £1 million towards a suitable building, but a Conservative Government was now refusing to implement it – refusing, in other words, to deliver the promised money. Lord Esher, Olivier's old sparring partner from 1948, was still active in the fray; in 1960 Esher and Chandos found a powerful new ally when their fellow peer, Lord Cottesloe, was appointed chairman of the Arts Council. By now the putative building costs had risen to £2.3 million, but Cottesloe led a powerful theatrical lobby, including Olivier, in warmly recommending the project to the Chancellor of the Exchequer, Selwyn Lloyd. It took six months for the Treasury even to make a response, which, when at last it came, remained in the negative. On 21 March 1961, a week after the announcement of Olivier's appointment at Chichester, the Chancellor told the House of Commons that the Government had decided not to release the money for the building of a National Theatre. Instead, it would offer the Arts Council an extra £450,000 to help various regional theatres around Britain.

The main company specified was that based at the Shakespeare Memorial Theatre, Stratford-upon-Avon, which that day received its royal charter and became the Royal Shakespeare Theatre – in effect, a *de facto* national theatre. It was the climax of long, tortured discussions about an alliance between the National and Stratford, and a major tactical victory for the latter in the shape of its chairman, Sir Fordham Flower, and its artistic director, Peter Hall.

Stratford's triumph, though years in the Machiavellian making, turned out to be short-lived. Selwyn Lloyd's news prompted uproar. It was an insult to the Queen Mother, raged Chandos in the House of Lords, that the foundation-stone she had laid while Queen was treated with such high-handed philistinism; the London County Council, led by Sir Isaac Hayward, also protested that it was the Government's responsibility to see that "the site on the South Bank which the LCC has reserved for nearly ten years is not sterilized indefinitely and lost to other cultural purposes". By October 1960 the joint council had published a memorandum to the Government proposing the absorption of Stratford into a wider concept of a National Theatre – a notion supposedly cooked up at a secret meeting at Notley Abbey on 10 April 1959, Olivier's last day there.

Peter Hall remembers the meeting taking place amid tea chests awaiting the removal men; Olivier had given him a pot of jasmine.[7] But Hall and Flower, the Stratford representatives at Notley that day, subsequently denied reaching any such understanding with the National team of Olivier, Chandos and Esher. The undeclared war continued with Olivier, the utterly unofficial director-designate of a still non-existent National Theatre, losing sleep as the empire-building Hall found the Royal Shakespeare Company a London base at the Aldwych Theatre. The previous year, while preparing for *Coriolanus*, Olivier had asked Hall over lunch: "I'm going to have a go at making the National ... will you join me as my Number Two?" To which Hall had replied: "I'm very flattered, Larry. I'd love to ... but I'm going to make my own as Number One."[8]

Given the emergent personal rivalry between Olivier and Hall, and Stratford's jealous pride in its new status, the joint council's memorandum was a non-starter. But it usefully brought the National Theatre's perpetual non-appearance back on to the public agenda. Their re-election safely secured, the Labour-led LCC returned to Selwyn Lloyd with a new plan drawing Sadler's Wells opera and ballet company into their South Bank proposal, which cleverly made it seem much more attractive. Now the Treasury could see its arts subsidies being streamlined towards three main companies: the Old Vic (which would form the nucleus of the National), Stratford and Sadler's Wells. On 21 July 1961, the Chancellor boldly announced the Government's support for the LCC plan – with the miserly proviso that it would not provide a penny more than the £1 million originally promised by its predecessors thirteen years before.

It seemed like victory at last – until dissenting voices were heard, predictably enough, from Stratford. Arnold Goodman, the lawyer advising the joint council, returned from a summit there with the news that the Stratford board had wanted to know who would be "in charge". When Goodman had suggested that the National Theatre's first director might well be Laurence Olivier, there seemed to be "an immediate diminution of interest".[9] Hero-worship for Hall was such that no one at Stratford, not even a board anxious to maintain its subsidy, was prepared to see him become Olivier's number two. It took another nine months for Stratford to pull out, thus putting an apparent kibosh on the entire scheme. The National Theatre looked to have foundered again – this time, it appeared, over the *amour propre* of thirty-year-old Peter Hall (who has always believed that Goodman, as chairman of the Arts Council, subsequently "victimized" Stratford in the annual subsidy round).

Chandos immediately embarked on an urgent mission of damage containment. By unilaterally revising the global subsidy, marginally in the National's favour, he managed to persuade the Government that Stratford's withdrawal was not terminal; even better, he took the opportunity to remove Sadler's Wells from the equation and restore the National to a separate entity in its own right. Stratford could not complain; by protesting about its reduced subsidy, it would only draw attention to the fact that its bank account was £100,000 in surplus, thus undermining Hall's master plan: to spend that surplus lavishly enough to establish a labyrinthine palace of such excellence that no government, however philistine, could allow it to go under. It is pretty much the basis on which the subsidized theatre has been run in Britain ever since.

So July 1962 saw Selwyn Lloyd giving the go-ahead to the revised National Theatre plans. A start would be made the following year at the Old Vic, pending the construction of a suitable theatre on a 1.2 acre site across Waterloo Bridge from the existing South Bank concert halls. At last Olivier could be formally approached to become its founder-director, answerable only to a board chaired by his old friend Chandos. Realistic though he now was about the huge political complexities of the task, Olivier never seriously considered refusing. It was the logical climax to his career – the ultimate job in recent theatrical history, in which every disparate strand of his versatile career could be merged to best advantage. Actor and director, impresario and administrator, team-leader and rallier of troops: all the roles in which he had ever cast himself combined in this mighty challenge, as heroic a part as any in the classical repertoire.

Chichester would indeed have to rest content with being a mere springboard to greater things; more than he realized, perhaps, its vignettes had been but a taste of the larger-scale demands to come. The many offstage roles in which Chichester had cast him were now to become positively Shakespearean in scale: the great man climbing a precarious ladder for the topping-out ceremony; joking charmingly with the hard-hat workers; braving interminable fund-raising events and mind-numbing board meetings to achieve his artistic goals; jollying his way through countless dealings with the press; grinning obsequiously as a procession of royalty disrupted his rehearsal schedule; charming bureaucracy's Keystone Cops into submission (notably the Chichester fire authorities as they attempted to cancel the opening night because of the absence of a safety curtain, indeed of *any* curtain); trickiest of all, beguiling distinguished, capable and unknown actors into working for rather less than their usual commercial rates.

It may have taken 115 years to win government approval for a National

Theatre, but Olivier had been given only one to act on it. Suddenly, things started to move fast. Once the Chancellor's approval was made public in July, and Olivier's appointment in August, it was quickly settled that the Old Vic company's last season as such would end in June 1963, its golden jubilee year, and that the National Theatre's inaugural production would open there on 5 August. While instigating a complete overhaul of the building, interviewing architects fit to design a new one and defending his corner in an ever more acrimonious subsidy war with the RSC, Olivier set about choosing his key lieutenants. His first instinct was to turn to his close friend George Devine, whose work in making the Royal Court the focal point of contemporary English drama distilled at least half Olivier's own aspirations for the National. Devine, though free with cautionary advice about the running of subsidized theatres, was reluctant to abandon his power-base, or to function as anyone's second-in-command; but he happily agreed to direct Samuel Beckett's *Play* during the National's first season.

Devine was also remarkably generous about the fact that Olivier promptly turned instead to his own two chief lieutenants, the two younger men who (with Tony Richardson) had helped the English Stage Company earn the Royal Court its rejuvenated reputation: John Dexter and William Gaskill. Though Gaskill at first played "hard to get", wary of being able to do things his way in so institutionalized a theatre, both he and Dexter soon signed on as associate directors, thanks to the urgings of Devine as much as Olivier. Olivier repaid the favour with the announcement that the National would "co-operate in certain activities", such as the training of young actors and the commissioning of plays, with the English Stage Company; the joint committee established never met again, but the gesture enabled Devine's Royal Court to "flash the credentials of a major state institution".[10]

Olivier had Dexter in harness right away with an invitation to direct Shaw's *Saint Joan* in Chichester's second season, a role in which he had cast Joan "by public demand" following her performance in *Uncle Vanya*. Stuart Burge was hired to direct John Arden's new play, *The Workhouse Donkey*, and *Uncle Vanya* was revived to even more ecstatic reviews: it was now "more perfectly and exactly modulated than one would have thought possible" ... "the admitted master achievement of British twentieth-century theatre".

Only the birth of his first daughter, Tamsin, on 10 January gave Olivier momentary and "rapturous" pause in his almost obsessive schedule. By now he was on a demanding daily treadmill which he would endure for ten years: boarding the Brighton Belle for London each morning, running the National Theatre from behind his desk all day and, more often than not, performing by night. "A man of perennially youthful outlook," observed the *Sunday Times* critic, J. W. Lambert, Olivier "was called upon not merely to act on the stage but to impersonate in real life, if metaphorically, one of those circus performers who ride, while themselves turning somersaults and the like, several horses simultaneously".[11] Always proud of his physical fitness, he stepped up his daily sessions at a London gymnasium, aware of the demands he was making of his constitution. At fifty-six Olivier was embarking on a schedule which would have daunted men half his age; he had been persuaded, moreover, to mark the first season by undertaking one of the most demanding of all roles, Othello. So on New Year's Day, 1963, for the first and only time in his life, he gave up drinking. For a man who could drink a great deal without becoming too much the worse for wear, Olivier had for years relied heavily on the solace of the bottle, from neat whisky to vintage champagne, to sustain his enormous workload. A year on the wagon – well, until Christmas, anyway – was to afford him especial pride in his powers of self-discipline.

Before moving to its notorious offices in prefabricated huts opposite the Old Vic, the National Theatre's administrative headquarters were initially in Hamilton Place, W1. Here Olivier sat in the autumn of 1962, wracking his brains for "some trumpet call of an idea for an opening", when in walked Peter O'Toole to announce that he intended to play Hamlet in the West End for a short season the following year. Would Olivier direct? No, said Olivier, he regretted that he had commitments elsewhere. But if O'Toole would settle for the Old Vic rather than the West End, then, yes, he would direct his *Hamlet* as the inaugural production of the new National Theatre. August was already looking a bit optimistic, so how about October? Olivier and O'Toole, who had taken the precaution of bringing his agent, happily shook hands on the deal.

O'Toole's mission that day had rather less noble origins than Olivier realized. He and Richard Burton had just been filming *Becket* – Olivier having turned down both their leading roles – and had concocted a bet during a champagne-fuelled three-day break. Their genial rivalry on the set must now continue, they pledged, on the stage: they would set out to play the same role, simultaneously, on opposite sides of the Atlantic. A coin was tossed over directors; Burton won and demanded Gielgud, leaving O'Toole to seek out Olivier. "We flipped the coin again", recalled O'Toole, "and I got London, a fact that we duly celebrated. Then Richard had to do his Hamlet in New York" – which in time Burton duly did, under Gielgud's direction – "and we toasted that."[12]

Whatever the truth of this *braggadocio* – O'Toole was later to claim that it was Olivier who had first approached *him* – Olivier was delighted to have landed such a big name for so obviously appropriate an opening play. But Dexter and Gaskill were "disappointingly unimpressed". So the National was to be a vehicle for stars, rather than a homogeneous, adaptable, versatile company of equals like the Berliner Ensemble? Olivier's problems were already beginning. His own personal model was more the Moscow Arts Theatre, then at the height of its renown for all-round excellence in a distinctive house style. He took the view, he told his young cohorts, that a few big names would be needed to launch the theatre, but thereafter he very much hoped to build just such a company as they envisaged.

It was because of this exchange, though they were not to know of it, that a number of Olivier's oldest and closest colleagues felt slighted during the genesis of the National. Though Redgrave had been recruited, there was as yet no such invitation to Gielgud or Richardson. In his sixtieth year Gielgud began to think that his career as a leading actor, if not as a director, might be over;[13] in fact, he was soon to work at Olivier's National, though Richardson would have to wait ten years, until the next regime. Old Olivier loyalists such as Esmond Knight, John Laurie and Norman Wooland, all veterans of the Old Vic and his Shakespeare films, were among many who eagerly offered their services, only to receive a polite but firm refusal. "It was so hurtful", said Knight, "that I wished I had never asked him in the first place. It was a bit like the king in *Henry V* casting aside all his old chums, Falstaff and co."[14] The young bloods around Olivier, soon to be joined by Tynan, were acting as a corrective – with hindsight, a healthy one – to some of his natural instincts. Much as he revelled in his task, Olivier was never good at turning away friends.

So Olivier recruited the "renowned", and his associates those "to be renowned" (most of whom, thanks to the long-suffering Devine, also came from the Royal Court). These were the rather worrying categories under which Olivier listed the leading members of the fifty-strong company hired for the National's opening season. The first group, the stars, included Michael Redgrave, Max Adrian, Colin Blakely, Tom Courtenay, Cyril Cusack, Maggie Smith, Rosemary Harris, Joyce Redman and Billie Whitelaw, not to mention the director and his wife; among those of whom he intended to *make* stars were Frank Finlay, Derek Jacobi, Robert Stephens, Michael Gambon, John Stride, Louise Purnell and Lynn Redgrave. Stephen Arlen of Sadler's Wells was brought over as administrative director, to ease Olivier's workload; and, once he had been persuaded to accept the title of "literary manager", rather than the Brechtian-sounding *dramaturg* he had proposed for himself, the unlikely figure of Kenneth Peacock Tynan was soon to be found institutionalized at Olivier's shoulder.

The illegitimate son of a prosperous Midlands businessman, Tynan had clawed his way to pink-suited prominence via Oxford, a failed career in the theatre and Fleet Street. By his early death in 1980 he had more than fulfilled the goal he set himself when a young "Birmingham bastard": "to become an apostle of international hedonism, and to do that without ever having owned anything other than books and a typewriter". The most eloquent of Olivier's admirers, he had also been among the most damning when disappointed, as by the film of *Hamlet* ("metronomically monotonous ... technically pedantic, aurally elephantine"[15]). But if Olivier had bought Tynan's silence – in effect, taken him hostage – he had also hired the reading and intellect he had always felt himself to lack.

During the next ten years Tynan believed himself to be Olivier's conscience, while in fact functioning – and at times malfunctioning – as his brain. Though not unaware of his own intuitive intelligence about matters theatrical, Olivier's self-doubt had again brought out his capacity to be led. Tynan's widow and biographer, Kathleen, not unnaturally claims for her husband more credit than is really his due for the success of the Olivier years at the National.[16] But her detailed account of his relationship with Olivier – one of the most extraordinary of recent theatrical history – shows above all how staunchly Olivier always stood by his headstrong lieutenant, even against his own better judgement, when dragged into deep political waters.

It was a phrase of Tynan's which formed the centrepiece of Olivier's cautious "statement of intent", delivered at his first press conference on 6 August 1963. Britain's National Theatre, he announced, would aim to present "a spectrum of world drama" and to develop a company which in time would become – his own phrase, this time – "the finest in the world". Tynan's spectrum was indeed more than adequately reflected in the initial repertoire of ten plays, also announced that day. The classics were represented by three of the heftiest available, *Hamlet*, *Othello* (Olivier's gesture to Shakespeare's quatercentenary) and Ibsen's *The Master Builder*; Restoration romps were promised with Farquhar's *The Recruiting Officer*; modern European drama was acknowledged in the shape of Max Frisch's *Andorra*, ancient Greek tragedy in Sophocles's *Philoctetes* and the *avant-garde* in Beckett's *Play*. A neglected minor comedy classic, *Hobson's Choice*, was designed to allay any public fears of too much solemnity, and two established hits from Chichester, *Uncle Vanya* and *St Joan*, to allay the management's fears of box-office disaster. Besides, what "judicious mix" would be complete in the mid-1960s without the statutory "one Chekhov, one Shaw"?

Like most major creative enterprises, the National Theatre at the Old Vic was born out of a frenzy of chaos. Its gestation period saw Olivier supervising drastic changes to the theatre, in which he seemed to take an almost sado-masochistic pleasure. "God, how I hate this place," he said on first revisiting its familiar stage, startling those around him into realizing just how powerfully the Esher snub of 1948 had cauterized his happier memories of Old Vic triumphs before and after the war. Not only did he deem the ten-year-old decorations insufficiently grand for the theatre's new role, but Olivier set about rebuilding the stage with a (perhaps literal) vengeance. Sean Kenny, who was designing the inaugural *Hamlet*, was commissioned to construct a large new revolving stage, or "revolve" (which, in time, proved so unreliable that the company rechristened it the "revolt"). Olivier meanwhile had the first two rows of the stalls removed and a new forestage extended way out beyond the proscenium arch, in open defiance of the Old Vic's excellent acoustic, which was traditionally appreciated by downstage actors for bouncing their voices back towards them off the rear wall. "Yes," he cheerfully told Melvyn Bragg twenty years later, "I *ruined* the place."[17]

Rehearsals took place amid a bedlam of mess and noise. Max Adrian, Polonius in the O'Toole *Hamlet*, remembered beginning work while "the whole place was still littered with rubble and mortar, and there was a bloody enormous hole in one wall which allowed the wind to blow straight in from Waterloo Road. It was frightfully uncomfortable and chaotic."[18] Kenny's set proved so complex and elaborate that Adrian told his fellow Irishman: "I suppose this is your revenge on the English." There were moments when he believed the theatre would never open – and that if it did, the inaugural production was sure to be a catastrophe. The only available consolation was the insouciance of O'Toole, blissfully immune to the gravity of the enterprise, blithely indulging in practical jokes such as filling the dressing-room showers with ice. "The star dressing-room", said Adrian, "became a sort of oasis of relaxation while he was there."

Before the opening night on 22 October, however, even O'Toole was to be found wandering around nervously in his habitual red dressing-gown, his hair dyed a pristine blond. O'Toole worshipped Olivier – "I mean, he's done it: he's sat on the top of Everest and waved down at the Sherpas"[19] – and now he was to follow in his hallowed footsteps on the same hallowed stage where his director had triumphed in the same hallowed role. The prospect had at last sobered even so notoriously cocksure a performer. Apart from one sole rehearsal, after which Olivier (according to O'Toole) told the company, "Ladies and Gentlemen, for the first time in living memory we have today seen the real Hamlet," O'Toole felt he had not lived up to his director's expectations. Technically, he was simply unable to deliver the goods.

Despite O'Toole's protests, moreover, Olivier was insisting on preserving the full uncut text, lasting four and a half hours, to be performed six nights and two matinees a week. Rehearsals had been tense. The two men had failed to establish the rapport both half-expected, partly because of O'Toole's sense of inferiority, but mostly because he refused to be seduced by the Olivier charm or kowtow to the Olivier myth: "At first glance I could see through him, and he could see through me, and he knew that I knew that he knew." But he had to admit that Olivier was "the most persuasive bastard ever to draw breath". Apart from losing the argument over cuts, O'Toole had wanted to play Hamlet with a beard because, as he put it: "Why should I be the only man in Elsinore with a razor blade?"[20] Three weeks later, however, "there I am on the stage clean-shaven in a Peter Pan suit with my hair dyed white. Such is the power of Olivier."

Olivier thought it appropriate to save all the inaugural junketing for the move into the new building, so the National Theatre's opening night at the Old Vic was a curiously muted affair. No royalty attended; the senior dignitary present, appropriately enough, was the Chancellor, Selwyn Lloyd, come to see whether he had got his money's worth. Gentlemen were not encouraged to wear evening dress; because of its sheer length, the performance began in daylight, at 6.30. There were the usual last-minute backstage panics – Sean Kenny's trapdoor, crucial to the graveyard scene, stayed firmly shut until the eleventh hour – but the production ran through without too many hitches. Even the "revolt" worked. Over the next few days the critical reaction, though lukewarm, was not as bad as a nervous Olivier had feared.

There was a natural reluctance among the critical fraternity to pan the National in its opening week, but only the ever generous, wide-eyed Harold Hobson of the *Sunday Times* spoke in the hushed tones of one who had glimpsed greatness: "The manly, richly spoken Hamlet of Mr O'Toole matches Sir Laurence's conception", which was apparently "to give us a *Hamlet* which will assault the emotions by the sheer force of its acting rather than by its curious titillation of the intellect." *The Times*, disdaining to mince words, spoke more for the consensus: the "tired and routine performance" appeared to have been mounted only "as a means of exhibiting a number of big names in the most famous and popular work in the classical repertory". O'Toole was "ordinary".

Only Michael Redgrave's villainous Claudius won universal praise, though he too had been apprehensive. In rehearsal Olivier had raged at him: "When you came on as Macbeth, it was as if you were saying, 'Fuck you, I *am* Macbeth.' As Claudius you are *dim*."[21] But Olivier was relieved: the National was in business, and its arrival had been unreservedly welcomed *per se*. If the opening production could have been better, well, the reviews could have been worse. As the run wore on O'Toole lived up to his cavalier reputation, sniggering over his dying speech and wandering back from the wings with his glasses still on. He did not enjoy playing "the

Moody One" and made no complaint when Olivier decided to take *Hamlet* off after only twenty-seven performances. Later O'Toole was to be found garrulously biting the hand that had fed him: he had agreed to play "his melancholy nibs" only because "I was flattered out of my trousers to be invited". But he did not think Olivier ought to be running the National Theatre; he did not have "much to contribute" as a director and should stick to acting: "He belongs in the stable, as head stallion."

There were to be others ready to join this particular chorus, without its being led by supposed friends and admirers. As yet, however, Olivier and the National were entitled to a honeymoon period, and the arrival of the two proven successes from Chichester, *Uncle Vanya* and *St Joan*, maintained the solid start. But the second original production, William Gaskill's version of *The Recruiting Officer*, did far more to establish a distinctive corporate identity. It saw Olivier conspicuously playing the company man by settling for a lesser role, that of the preeningly self-important Captain Brazen, and even swallowing his self-esteem sufficiently to take part, with what appeared to be enthusiasm, in Gaskill's improvisation sessions.

Gaskill, then thirty-three, may have been overdoing the *enfant terrible* bit – a deliberate gesture to start as he meant to go on – but behind techniques which he knew were anathema to Olivier lay a fundamental seriousness of purpose. Impressed by Brecht's adaptation of Farquhar's play, *Trumpets and Drums*, which the Berliner Ensemble had brought to London seven years before, he was anxious to avoid the familiar English approach to Restoration comedy, all foppish flourishes of the hat, elaborate bows, arch vowel sounds and antique gallantry. Intent on using the text as a naturalistic social document, presenting the verities of life in an early eighteenth-century garrison town – stressing, above all, the contemporary power structure through the social and civic pecking order – Gaskill began the first cast meeting with an earnest discussion of social and political issues of the day, including "who owns whom". Fortunately, perhaps, Olivier's managerial duties caused him to miss the first few sessions; but Max Adrian, the only other "old school" actor in the cast, struggled to conceal his dismay, as the director called for some improvisation "to establish the sequence of emotions in the actors' minds".[22] In the first exercise Gaskill required his actors to pass an imaginary object from hand to hand, transforming its identity by means of mime. Then he challenged them to use a chair for anything other than sitting on it; one rode it like a horse, another made love to it, a third combed his hair with it.

On they went until, on Day Four, Olivier arrived. Tynan, present at all rehearsals to compile a "logbook" he later published, expected the worst. But Olivier's other preoccupations had left him no time to prepare the part; arriving for once with no preconceptions – "all at sea," as Gaskill remembers it – he entered into the improvisation exercises with zest and inventiveness. Almost too much so: he was soon inventing speeches and gestures for Brazen which were perfectly in character, but carried the scene through to a conclusion totally different from that of the text. Thus, concluded Tynan, Olivier had implicitly proved the value of improvisation, by discovering "aspects of the character overlooked or (for dramatic reasons) suppressed by the author". As the writer watched closely, he saw Gaskill's techniques helping Olivier transform his reading of Brazen from being too foppish and perky – "a sort of Mr Puff in uniform" – to the right tone of boorishness and sleazy vulgarity, until his lines took on "the elephantine loquacity of the pub bore". Gaskill was as delighted that the great man bowed to his techniques as he was with the results, but he nevertheless believed it was all an act, *pour encourager les autres*: "I don't think he enjoyed himself at all. In fact I think he hated it."[23]

If this were true (as it surely was) Olivier's agonies were worth it. *The Recruiting Officer* had not been seen in London for twenty years; its rediscovery as a lively comedy and a challenging social document was hailed as "exactly the kind of work for which the National Theatre had been established".[24] Gaskill's production proved the National's first major home-grown success, establishing Maggie Smith, Robert Stephens and Colin Blakely as leading lights of the company, and Olivier as the company man *par excellence*, content to play a demure second fiddle to his protégés. It was a close-run thing: Brazen had at times reminded Olivier of his Sergius Saranoff, and he had to be talked out of dusting down an ancient piece of business from that twenty-year-old performance – clicking his heels so repeatedly and officiously that eventually the spurs became entangled. He settled instead for outrageously padded calves, a short-sighted squint and – to the technical admiration of actors who dared not accuse him of scene-stealing – a muscular twitch in his left cheek.

The one show-stopping scene Olivier could not resist was encapsulated for posterity by *The Times*: as "an irrepressible pockmarked vulgarian", he was "seen characteristically in dialogue with a lady during which his gaze travels down from her face until he is addressing his compliments vertically into her bosom". While Bernard Levin told his readers he had laughed himself "into a bad attack of bronchitis", Milton Shulman of the *Evening Standard* more helpfully characterized Olivier's Brazen as "the essence of every doltish, bravura, self-important officer that ever wore uniform". To the American critic Harold Clurman, the performance was "a masterpiece" to be set beside Olivier's Shallow and Puff:

> He plays a small part in a manner so absolutely right and original that it
> lingers emblematically as the obtuse, mendacious, boastful, good-natured,
> thoroughly self-satisfied (satisfied with the fun of cheating, fighting, guzzling,

375

wenching) petty officer who is as much at ease in the army as a pig in a trough.[25]

To an excited Tynan, a Restoration masterpiece had been reclaimed, "stripped of the veneer of camp that custom prescribes for plays of its period". Company morale, at first tentative, now soared – proof to Tynan that Gaskill's production had gone a long way towards fulfilling their mutual aspiration for the National: a working atmosphere emulating that of the Berliner Ensemble, to which he now escorted a wary Olivier on an official visit. Ever open to Tynan's intellectual leadership, Olivier proved over lunch in the Berliner canteen that he had got the point: "This isn't just a theatre," he said, "it's a way of life."[26]

Within days of his arrival in the Waterloo Road Nissen huts, Tynan had embarked on what he regarded as little less than a national duty: the persuading of Olivier to undertake the only major Shakespeare role he had so far, by his own confession, funked: Othello. Tynan tried to present the idea as a *fait accompli*, rightly suspecting that he would be hitting a raw nerve. Years of shouldering the mightiest Shakespearean parts had convinced Olivier that they were "cannibals":

> You give them all you've got and the author says to you: "You've given all you've got? Good. Now, more. Good. Now, more. More, damn you. More, more! *More! More!*" Until your heart and guts and brain are pulp and the part feeds on you, eating you. Acting great parts devours you. It's a danger-ous game.[27]

And Othello was the most dangerous of them all. The part was a "monstrous, monstrous burden" for any actor. "I think Shakespeare and Richard Burbage got drunk together one night and Burbage said, 'I can play anything you write, anything at all.' And Shakespeare said, 'Right, I'll fix you, boy!' And then he wrote *Othello*." Olivier pointed out to Tynan that no English actor this century had succeeded in the part; the play really belonged to Iago, who could make the Moor look "a credulous idiot". Olivier was guiltily reminded of his own exotically Freudian Iago, which had so undermined Ralph Richardson's Othello in this same theatre a quarter of a century before. "If I take it on," he told Tynan, "I don't want a witty, Machiavellian Iago. I want a solid, honest-to-God NCO."[28] The notion suited John Dexter, who was eager to direct what he believed could be Olivier's greatest performance. And just the right NCO was available from the junior ranks of the company: Frank Finlay, whose only previous Shakespearean experience was a brief appearance from the waist up as the gravedigger in the O'Toole *Hamlet*.

For a while Olivier still hesitated, though Tynan suspected that it may all have been more offstage acting: "It was not easy to persuade him to play Othello. At least, he made it seem difficult; perhaps, deep in his personal labyrinth, where the minotaur of his talent lurks, he had already decided and merely wanted to be coaxed." Tynan's gambit was to tackle the issue head on: "You've done all the others. People will wonder why you're ducking this one." Still Olivier protested that he was not right for the part: "I haven't got the voice, Ken," he kept saying. "Othello has to have a dark, black, violet, velvet *bass* voice." Tynan mentioned the problem to Orson Welles, who agreed: "Larry's a natural tenor, and Othello's a natural baritone." All it took was for Tynan to voice Welles's doubts to Olivier himself; he was fixed for a moment by what O'Toole had called "that grey-eyed miopic stare that can turn you to stone", and the next thing everyone knew was that the boss, after forty years in the business, was taking voice coaching. Day by day, through the plywood walls of the temporary offices, Tynan heard a throbbing, growling noise which grew ever lower and lower. With the help of Barry Smith, a voice teacher at RADA, Olivier spent six months deepening the pitch of his voice by an entire octave.

The effect at the first read-through was "shattering". Into what is normally a relaxed, get-to-know-you session, at which the actors mumble their way amiably through the text, Olivier "tossed a hand grenade". Even Tynan's jaw dropped as Olivier, "seated, bespectacled and lounge-suited, fell on the text like a tiger ... a fantastic, full-volume display that scorched one's ears, serving final notice on everyone present that the hero, storm-centre and focal point of this tragedy was the man named in the title". This was not the urbane, civilized Othello of theatrical tradition, but "a triumphant black despot, aflame with unadmitted self-regard", who even at that reading managed the impossible trick which was to make Olivier's Othello, for all the controversy which came to surround it, so memorable: "So far from letting Iago manipulate him, he seemed to manipulate Iago, treating him as a kind of court jester. Such contumely cried out for deflation."

The windows shook at the sound of Olivier's voice, and Tynan's scalp tingled: "A natural force had entered the room." As the cast sat "pole-axed", Tynan pondered the scale of the risk Olivier appeared to be taking this time. Might not the "knockdown arrogance" of this interpretation be too close for comfort to comedy? By cutting the hero down to size, dispensing with his intrinsic majesty, was not Olivier doing to Othello precisely what he had deplored about Paul Scofield's *King Lear* (directed by Peter Brook), which he had witheringly taken to calling "*Mr* Lear"? Then came "Farewell the plumed troop" – to Tynan, the chronicler of the *corrida*, "like the dying moan of a fighting bull" – and all reservations vanished.

We were learning what it meant to be faced with a great classical actor in full spate – one whose vocal range was so immense that by a single new inflexion he could point the way to a whole new interpretation. Every speech, for Olivier, is like a mass of marble at which the sculptor chips away until its essential force and meaning are revealed. No matter how ignoble the character he plays, the result is always noble as a work of art.

Olivier, having got the voice right, now decided what he wanted to look like. His lifelong obsession with make-up reached its apogee, as he told Dexter he thought the modern trend towards "coffee-coloured compromise" was a "cop-out . . . as if the Moor could not be thought a truly *noble* Moor if he was too black, and in too great a contrast to the noble whites". This, surely, was a "shocking case of pure snobbery". Anxious as ever to stun, to astonish, Olivier's Othello would overlook the genetic difference between a Moor and a negro; he would be black with a vengeance, black as night, jet-black as the text could justify. Did it not refer to his "thick lips", his "sooty bosom"? Did he himself not say: "Haply for I am black," etc.? The man was a *negro*: he would look and talk and walk like a negro – yes, a contemporary negro, of the kind now commonplace (if only recently) on the streets of London. Across Waterloo Bridge, on the edge of the black ghettoes developing in the south of the capital, Olivier began to gift-wrap the most risqué of 400th birthday presents for his beloved Bard.

Olivier took two and a half hours each night to transform himself into Othello, and an hour afterwards to re-emerge. He started by covering his body from head to toe with a coat of dark stain, over which went a layer of greasy black make-up, which he and his dresser then polished vigorously with a chiffon cloth, to achieve a shiny finish – as if his body were the toecap of a giant army boot, due on the sovereign's parade. The palms of his hands, the soles of his feet, his specially thickened lips and even his tongue were then dyed with incarnadine; a course of drops added a penetrating sheen to the whites of his eyes; he even varnished his fingernails to give them a pallid blue lustre. The wig was of crinkly, matted curls, flecked with grey at the temples, and the final touch was a thin, surly-looking moustache. Most backstage anecdotes about this production concern people of either gender walking in on a naked Olivier, of various hues between Brighton white and Caribbean black, because it all had to dry before he could don Othello's pristine white robe.

Then came the walk: a gently rolling, loose-limbed gait, swaying from the hips on naked feet, prowling around the stage with the easy, flowing movements of a giant cat. His first appearance each evening, idly toying with a red rose, his mouth smiling the most complacent of smiles, falling open to reveal a blood-red tongue, drew gasps even before his unwontedly deep, dark voice froze the theatre back into stunned silence. As Olivier stood with his feet wide apart, trunk leaning gently forwards, emphasizing his words with the palms of his hands, his arms so languid that they might have been on ball-bearings, there was a sense of theatrical history, of legend-making in the air.

"By heaven knows what witchcraft", wrote Herbert Kretzmer of the *Daily Express*, Olivier had "managed to capture the very essence of what it must mean to be born with a dark skin.... It is a performance full of grace, terror and insolence. I shall dream of its mysteries for years to come." Harold Hobson, too, believed that "the power, passion, verisimilitude and pathos of Sir Laurence's performance are things which will be spoken of with wonder for a long time to come." Philip Hope-Wallace of the *Guardian* found that "the inventiveness of it, the sheer variety and range of the actor's art ... made it an experience in the theatre altogether unforgettable by anyone who saw it". Only Alan Brien of the *Sunday Telegraph* dissented, in a vivid minority report still remembered by those who thought that this time Olivier – the "Creole" Othello – had gone too far:

> There is a kind of bad acting of which only a great actor is capable. I find Sir Laurence Olivier's Othello the most prodigious and perverse example of this in a decade.... Sir Laurence is elaborately at ease, graceful and suave, more like a seducer than a cuckold. But as the jealousy is transfused into his blood, the white man shows through more obviously. He begins to double and treble his vowels, to stretch his consonants, to stagger and shake, even to vomit, near the frontiers of self-parody. His hips oscillate, his palms rotate, his voice skids and slides so that the Othello music takes on a Beatle beat.

The physical disintegration was, in fact, deliberate. As he prepared for the physical demands of the role, jogging along the Brighton seafront and intensifying his daily workouts at the gym, Olivier realized precisely why actors had always found Othello so mountainous a challenge. The part reaches so many climaxes, most of them (the epileptic fit, for instance) as taxing physically as vocally, that it drains the performer long before the climactic final scene. At the age of fifty-seven, the only way Olivier could pace himself through its rigours was to let go of the immense physical discipline he imposed on himself in the early scenes. As Iago's poison did its work, this Othello would go to pieces bodily as much as emotionally. Olivier did not spare the audience with his final collapse, tearing the crucifix from around his neck, and wailing hopelessly to the pagan gods from which baptism had supposedly delivered him – returning, on "O the pity of it, Iago," to the atavism of his true, ancestral past. For a hero whose tragic flaws had been so vividly drawn, the spectator felt less sympathy than awe. Here, as Olivier finally pulled off a mercurial, almost magic-trick suicide, was a death to inspire pity and terror rather than tears.

It was but one aspect of the production which sparked a debate lasting to this day. Given so towering a central performance, and the ego of the actor giving it, did Iago really have to become so doltish a lump as poor Frank Finlay was obliged to portray? Olivier's Othello, "endeavouring to escape reality" and pathetic in his self-dramatization, owed a good deal to T. S. Eliot's essay on the play. But the programme notes also quoted F. R. Leavis,[29] mentor of the Cambridge generation then beginning to hold intellectual sway, to the effect that Iago was "not much more than a piece of dramatic mechanism" – less a character in his own right than the physical embodiment of an aspect of Othello's own mind. Tynan had persuaded Dexter to read Leavis's essay on *Othello* – his argument that Iago was "subordinate and merely ancillary" amounted in terms of academic warfare to a blunt refutation of Coleridge and A. C. Bradley – and Dexter had passed it on to Olivier. Both had swallowed it wholesale. It is certainly one function of Iago to behave as Othello's *alter ego*; but, as *The Times* commented, "to erect it into the whole truth amounts to mutilation. Iago is not merely on the level of a tempter in a miracle play...." Left to his own devices, Finlay's Iago became an unconvincing, inconsistent rogue, his crime more than ever out of proportion to his grievance. Only when dealing directly with Othello – thanks also to the fact that Olivier was always at his best when in close tactile contact with another actor or actress – did Finlay really come into his own. In the latter stages of the play, as Olivier's Othello began to disintegrate, Finlay's Iago clung about his neck – "almost", as one critic put it, "with the embrace of a succubus", pouring poison into his ear "in tones of satanic lullaby".

Olivier's stunningly vivid negro also drew the play, more directly than was entirely comfortable, into the embattled contemporary arena of race relations. It was not just that Olivier's Moor belonged more to the Caribbean than to Cyprus. That Iago was portrayed as "thick-headed" was, to Hobson, John Dexter's way of proving Arnold Toynbee's recent dictum that "everywhere there is a revolt against the ideals and the faith of the white races".[30] In the 1960s, Hobson reluctantly accepted, it would have been "unrealistic" to expect Iago, a motiveless persecutor of a black man, to be portrayed as a person of high, if malicious, intelligence. But above all it was Olivier who, with the curl of his lip, the rhythmic movements of his body, the roll of his staring eyes, the uneasy mixture of arrogance and inferiority, transformed *Othello* into an urgent "world-drama" as much as a harrowing case-history of individual betrayal.

The textual argument tended to drown in controversy over Olivier's negro – an astonishing technical achievement, it was agreed, but at what price to the text? If Olivier was too much the sophisticated negro, too little the noble Moor, Shakespeare, as J. W. Lambert argued, would surely have cared little for the distinction: "But he would surely have delighted in the portrait of an alienated man, fighting against his own people, a black among whites, a soldier among civilians, a middle-aged professional with an upper-class wife." In Shakespeare, said Olivier himself,

> I always try to reassure the audience initially that they are not going to see some grotesque, outsized dimension of something which they can't understand or sympathize with. If you have succeeded in the initial moments, either by a very strong stamp of characterization so they recognize you as a real guy, or by a quiet approach, then I think there's no end to where you can lead them in size of acting a little later in the evening. God knows, you have to be enormously big as Othello. It has to be big stuff.[31]

Displaying a canny sense of his times, moreover, he added with a wistful regret: "I don't know: it may be that this is a time which refuses to look greatness full in the face. Perhaps it will tolerate it only with an oblique look...."[32]

As the argument raged, Olivier's *amour propre* was not helped by the excited loquacity of Sammy Davis Jr, who revealed on a David Frost television show (seen, to Olivier's relief, only in America) that Larry – "I'm now close enough to him and his wife Joan to call him that" – had sat in the wings of London's Prince of Wales Theatre "at least four or five times a week" to study his song-and-dance routine. The devastating opening to Olivier's performance, when he brushed Iago's cheek lightly with his red rose, was modelled, it transpired, on the way Davis played with the microphone ("a kind of arabesque in the air") at the opening of *his* performance. Davis also helped Olivier with sundry bodily rhythms and movements; he jumped up on the Frost show, indicating the upper half of his torso as he described Olivier's entrance: "He walks out and goes ... like *this* ... I'm so *complimented*!"[33]

Laurence Kitchin took it upon himself to restore Olivier's dignity, defending both his "vulgarizing" of Othello ("the mood of the Sixties is anti-heroic enough to enjoy the sight of Iago cutting the rhetorical warrior down to size") and placing the performance in its historical context. Kitchin, like Tynan, had developed a unique appreciation of Olivier's gifts. His own gift, however, was broader than Tynan's in seeing past technical excellence to social relevance. Kitchin was the first to see in Olivier "an actor unusually responsive to climates of history outside the theatre".[34] Before the Second World War his *Henry V* had anticipated the patriotic response to Churchill's oratory; his post-war *Hamlet* had caught a European mood of imprisonment and defeat. His *Titus* had predicted an *avant-garde* vogue for cruelty, and post-Suez he had become "the new

Thersites, Archie Rice". His reading of Othello was thus, perhaps, "inevitable" amid the racial convulsions of the 1960s. The emotional idiom Olivier had chosen showed certain affinities with "the Hip sensibility", as most memorably chronicled by Norman Mailer in *The White Negro*:

> There is a depth of desperation to the condition which enables one to remain in life only by enjoying death, but their reward is the knowledge that what is happening at each instant of the electric present is good or bad for them, good or bad for their cause, their love, their action, their need.

Olivier's *Othello* had been playing for six months before the Italian director Franco Zeffirelli saw it: "I had been told that this was the last flourish of romantic acting. It's nothing of the sort. It's an anthology of everything that has been discovered about acting in the last three centuries."[35] *Othello* was also to prove the penultimate Shakespearean tragic hero Olivier played onstage. The physical disintegration of Othello was the beginning of the end of Olivier's own good health; after each performance he felt "useless in the office next day – as if I'd been run over by a bus".[36] All too soon he was to pay cruelly for the unblemished physical strength he had enjoyed over the years, to watch the remarkable stamina he had prized and cossetted ebb away. But for now there was the consolation that the pulling power of his *Othello* transcended the rare theatrical sight of queues stretching round the block outside the Old Vic; soon the ticket touts were selling not tickets, because there were none, but places in the queue for returns. Even the Queen's brother-in-law, Lord Snowdon, was forced to stand through a matinee. Olivier was fulfilling what he saw, he said, as the prime duty of the director of the National Theatre: "Getting bums on seats."

With so celebrated a *coup de théâtre*, the National was establishing itself as a force in the land even faster than Olivier had hoped. Now the foundations were laid, he began a rapid expansion of the repertoire. For the company, and for the backstage staff, life in the Waterloo Road did indeed become a Berliner-style "way of life" – and a very taxing one, as Olivier realized his ambitions to change the programme not just every night, but between matinee and evening performances. Six different plays could thus be presented in three days, even if it meant Maggie Smith commuting from Chichester by helicopter – a notion Olivier borrowed for his Desdemona from the example of some royal visitors.

Still Tyrone Guthrie chose to carp. Olivier, he said, had been "the right figurehead" for the National's inception and was doing a fine job; but it was "not the job he does best".[37] Apparently oblivious to the renown of Olivier's Othello, Guthrie protested that "much of what he is at present doing could be done equally well by several other people, none of whom could play Othello, Macbeth, Lear, Faustus and a dozen other great parts which, at present, he has no time to think about". Olivier was growing no younger. "I suppose it is idle to wish it, but I'd like him to be less celebrated, less distinguished, less important and more free. I want to see him abdicate. I want to see a sign that advertises: 'Throne vacant – will suit hard-working, honest, methodical monarch.'"

Olivier, nothing if not hard-working, honest and methodical, had no intention of outstaying his welcome. While presiding over the birth of the National Theatre at the Old Vic in October 1963, he had privately put a five-year limit on his directorship. That would take him past his sixtieth birthday, and to the moment where he could see his growing infant safely installed in its shiny new concrete playground on the South Bank. Within a month of the opening his building committee had chosen an architect "sympathetic to our needs":[38] Denys Lasdun's appointment had been announced on 22 November 1963, the day of President Kennedy's assassination. After the performance of *Uncle Vanya* that evening, Olivier stepped forward to suggest to the audience that applause was not appropriate; cast and theatre-goers alike stood in silence for two minutes before, on his instructions, "The Star Spangled Banner" was solemnly unfurled over the Old Vic sound system.

Emotional as he was over the death of "a favourite, glamorous young uncle", the date was in time to prove a black anniversary for Olivier too. The building of the new National Theatre was to take not five but thirteen harrowing years, by the end of which he would already have made his final exit, a pale and exhausted figure, emaciated by illness, convinced that he had been shabbily treated by an ungrateful world.

CHAPTER 22

1964–7

Ⅰ n the *Coriolanus* summer of 1959, after Notley Abbey had been sold
to a Canadian businessman, Olivier took to driving up to Stratford
with his old friend Harry Andrews. Lost in his thoughts one day, he
mused aloud: "Well, Harry, my baronial period is over. I wonder
what comes next?"[1]

The answer was to prove his Regency period. Olivier's draining role in
launching the National Theatre was played against a backdrop of domestic
tranquillity in Royal Crescent, Brighton, where for the first time in his life
he was becoming a settled family man. He and Joan also purchased a 300-
year-old farmhouse not far away at Horsebridge Green, near Steyning,
West Sussex, for quiet family weekends very different from those at Notley.
All visitors to Royal Crescent were proudly introduced to two-year-old
Richard and one-year-old Tamsin. "I know of nothing more beautiful",
Olivier told Harold Hobson, "than to set off from home in the morning
in a taxi and to look back and see your young held to a window and being
made to wave to you. It's sentimental and corny, but it's better than
poetry, better than genius, better than money."[2]

On the day of Hobson's visit, as often at the time, Olivier was in nostalgic
mood. He showed the critic around his little theatrical *musée*: here was the
earliest known stage wig, worn by Garrick as Abel Drugger; here was the
dagger with which Irving had killed himself as Othello; here a lace collar
which had been Edmund Kean's: "Oh, the sense of the past!" With misty
eyes Olivier talked of his mother and the terrible sense of loss which had
haunted him since her death. "I think I've been looking for her ever since.
Perhaps with Joanie I have found her again."

John Osborne, one of the first to abolish them on stage, had recently suggested to Olivier that "there aren't any third acts in life any more, either". Olivier had found it an uncomfortable truth:

> Life used to be full of third acts, bringing everything nicely to a comforting close, with a satisfying solution. But life isn't like that any longer. There is no solution. You can't send people back to their homes any more with their problems solved. If you did solve their problems, they just wouldn't believe it.

In his own life, however, as in the theatre, the nostalgic in Olivier still believed in happy endings. And his own third act was just beginning.

The National's autumn season relied almost too heavily on his own prestige, as he shouldered two, sometimes three *Othellos* a week and took over the part of Solness in Ibsen's *The Master Builder* from Redgrave. The company's other theatrical knight, now a close enough friend to have become Tamsin's godfather, had contributed much to the success of the National's first season, with his Claudius in *Hamlet* and his (less successful) Hobson in *Hobson's Choice*. But for reasons he could not at the time understand, Redgrave had been miserable as Solness, the part he had most wanted and had felt most equal to his talents. After trouble mastering the lines, he found himself trembling each time he crossed Waterloo Bridge in order to play Ibsen; not for another decade was Redgrave to realize that this was the onset of Parkinson's Disease, which was to shadow his last twenty years.

Given *Othello* as well as his daytime duties, Olivier was reluctant to take over another major role, but there was no other candidate of sufficient stature available as an avowedly "obstinate" Redgrave insisted on leaving. Apart from a growing unease with himself – "I had the feeling that the rest of the company were whispering about me"[3] – Redgrave was intent on launching his own mini-Chichester, the Yvonne Arnaud Theatre in Guildford, Surrey.

Redgrave could never bring himself to see Olivier's Solness, not least because all the critics, to a man, said how much better it was. Olivier, wrote Ronald Bryden, Tynan's successor on the *Observer*, made it seem a totally different play: "His is no Nietzschean hero, as Redgrave's was. Olivier's builder exists socially, in a social play. . . . This is why I preferred it."[4] Olivier's Solness had the neat, oily grey hair and dapper little walk of his Hurstwood in *Carrie*; it was the noisy sniffs, the bending of the middle-aged ear to listen, the constant play of eyes and drumming of fingers, and then the sudden stillnesses, which made it so distinctively an Olivier performance. To Ronald Hayman, he made Solness "far more of a petty bourgeois; he was more convincingly selfish".

As Hilde Wangel, Maggie Smith was also enhancing her stature in *The*

Master Builder, belying her reputation as a light comedienne. But she too, with Desdemona and three other roles in the repertoire, was feeling the strain. So Olivier persuaded Joan to join him in the renovation of *The Master Builder*, taking over Hilde for his own first night on 29 October 1964. That week saw the only cloud pass over their private world that year, as Joan suffered a miscarriage on the eve of the opening. During a runthrough, she suddenly collapsed. Summoned to London in the middle of that night, when Joan began to experience savage pain, their Brighton doctor declared the baby lost and had her rushed to an operating theatre. There was no question, to Olivier's dismay, of her making the first night; but her understudy, Jeanne Hepple, coped admirably. Joan was back onstage only three days later, but it was clear that the frantic pace of life around Olivier was beginning to tell on them all.

For Solness now began to prove some sort of Waterloo for Olivier as well as Redgrave. There had been trouble with Edith Evans on the provincial tour of *Hay Fever*, directed by Coward himself; Olivier had nearly had to face the uncomfortable task of firing this beloved old *grande dame*, who was having trouble remembering her lines, and even remembering to put on her false eyelashes ("I decided", she explained to Olivier after one dire performance in Manchester, "that I didn't want to think of it as a *performance*"). Now, at the National, he was in the Number One dressing-room Dame Edith had used, as had Redgrave before her – both of whom had managed to find their way thence to the stage, only to belie all their years of professionalism, and their lofty status in their trade, by forgetting their lines. Worse than that, in Evans's case, thought Olivier, she "hadn't got a grip of her part". So when he too, mindful of his pique at these two distinguished failures, now began to forget his lines, he at first blamed it, superstitiously, on the dressing-room.

It could have been anything. Guilt still riddled him about Vivien, although with Jack Merivale's support she was managing to carry on with her career, despite a considerable worsening in her mental condition. Joan's miscarriage had upset him mightily; conscious of her desire for more children, he became possessed by an irrational fear that he might be too old to sire them. As ever, he was working too hard; and the strains of acting the ever jolly team leader, as gracious to tea lady as to superstar, had taken their toll. Olivier was playing so many offstage roles that for the first time in his long career he could not keep going onstage. At the age of fifty-seven, at the height of his powers, distinction and achievement, Olivier developed stage fright.

The symptoms were horrifying. As the disease spread to his Othello, he could only apologize to the rest of the cast for his unprofessionalism and ask them not to look him in the eye. It was the worst thing, he knew, that one actor could ask of another; but he also knew that the slightest eye contact with any of them would undo him. For more than five years, in five new and closely scrutinized stage roles, Olivier was to dread every performance. As the fear of acting grew, he attributed it to guilt about the happiness he had found with Joan.

Publicly, Olivier remained every inch the self-confident, almost heroic figure, fast becoming a national institution. He was the natural choice to narrate Independent Television's coverage of Churchill's state funeral that January, a task in which he took an inordinate, highly emotional pride. By the summer, after directing a well-received production of Arthur Miller's *The Crucible*, he considered the National securely enough established to absent himself by day for the first time to make a quick – if unlikely – film. The part of Inspector Newhouse in Otto Preminger's *Bunny Lake Is Missing*, a London-based psychodrama adapted by John and Penelope Mortimer from an Evelyn Piper novel, would certainly restore his depleted bank balance; perhaps it would also ease his growing torment onstage, to be back in a world where lines could be learnt scene by scene. It had been Olivier's great delight to consolidate a Noël Coward revival in Britain by inviting him to direct *Hay Fever* for the National that spring; the telegrams they exchanged during the planning stages were couched in terms of such mutual love that Joan joked: "If one of these is intercepted, you will both be arrested."[5] Now the two friends were acting together again, for the first time since *Private Lives* in 1930, and hugely entertaining both themselves and their fellow cast members on location in Hampstead. No one much liked the tyrannical Preminger, the butt of many a Coward joke; and one of the younger members of the cast gratefully remembers Olivier, though plagued by gout throughout the filming, intervening on his behalf: "I say, old boy, I do wish you wouldn't scream at the children."[6]

While Coward camped around as Carol Lynley's lecherous old landlord, an exotic aesthete who collected whips and de Sade memorabilia, Olivier merely strolled through the part of the thoughtful but mundane police inspector, out to prove that a missing girl is a figment of her American mother's imagination. Again the viewer is constantly aware of Olivier suppressing his own natural dynamism to make a fairly ordinary man believable; this time Alexander Walker, the critic who had begged him to play no more such roles, declared that "only a great actor can make himself this small. It is a rare sight." While the American critics expressed muted disappointment, the patriotic London *Sunday Express* remained loyal to Britain's leading actor. "With his towering technique of wit and timing," wrote Michael Thornton, "[Olivier] makes this inspector one of the most beguiling policemen in the history of criminology." But the film's most memorable moment seems to have come off camera, when Noël

Coward crept up behind one of the leading actors to express his immortal opinion of the young man's future in films: "Keir Dullea, gone tomorrow."

"All posterity will want to know is how he played," Ronald Bryden had written in the *Observer* of Olivier's Othello.[7] "Before it exhausts him, a film should be made. It couldn't tell the whole truth, but it might save something the unborn should know." Now, in July 1965, Olivier reluctantly set about it. A "filmed record" of the Chichester *Uncle Vanya* had already been made the previous year, directed by Stuart Burge – in his own words, "the only person around, I suppose, who knew about quick TV".[8] To adapt *Uncle Vanya* for a two-dimensional medium, Burge had asked for three weeks' rehearsal and a month in the studio; in the throes of the National's birth pangs, "I got one rehearsal – *one* – and five days in the studio." The result, though intended only as a literal television record of the production, was so "rough-edged" that Olivier permitted it to be shown only in the United States. "I don't think", said Burge, "he liked it very much."

But Burge was chosen again for *Othello* – this time, he believes, "because Olivier was in a hurry, and I was probably the only person who could have done it, as he wanted, in three weeks". Burge was fortunate indeed to have the services of the legendary lighting cameraman Geoffrey Unsworth, who could work "in several different directions at once". This meant that only one take of each scene, even the major ones, was required of Olivier; Unsworth was then able to edit them into close-up, long shot and deep focus – "even cutting in the middle of a word, which had never been done before".

Writing in the *Observer*, John Mortimer declared of the result that Olivier's Othello "must now be counted among the world's great film performances" (although Burge himself never much liked the portrayal and suspected that "it probably resulted from Larry having watched a West Indian with a headache"). Sensing the greatness of the performance, critics on both sides of the Atlantic were generous about the unashamed attempt to do little more than record it for posterity: "Now at last", wrote Pauline Kael in the *New Yorker*, "this impossible play almost makes sense." Anyone seeing the film, said *Variety*, could "stake a claim to having witnessed one of the great performances of our time". Though scarcely considered a film by some critics, *Othello* brought Olivier his seventh Oscar nomination as Best Actor (won that year by Lee Marvin for *Cat Ballou*); there were also nominations for three of his supporting cast, Frank Finlay, Maggie Smith and Joyce Redman (Emilia). Thanks to Olivier, Shakespeare achieved an ironic contemporary relevance in South Africa as the film was banned for five years because of its depiction of "love across the racial lines".

As soon as he completed *Othello* Olivier was struck down by a virus infection, the third time in eighteen months that National Theatre plans had had to be altered because of its director's health. He missed the early rehearsals for Peter Wood's new production of Congreve's *Love for Love*, in which he was to play Tattle, the "half-witted beau, vain of his amours". But he was sufficiently recovered by 6 September to don a British Airways uniform and cap, and act the steward at the aircraft door to welcome his sixty-five actors and technicians aboard a scheduled flight to Russia. The National Theatre's first overseas tour was taking *Othello*, *Hobson's Choice* and *Love for Love* to Moscow, where they were to become the first foreign company to act within the Kremlin walls, at the 1,400-seat Kremlevsky Theatre (built for Stalin thirty years before, but opened to the public only after his death).

Familiar with the celluloid Olivier from *Lady Hamilton* on, Russians literally fought for the chance to see the man they had long regarded from a distance as the world's greatest actor. Heavy-duty police had to control the crowds in Red Square as Olivier – who had once played a Russian in *The Demi-Paradise*, but had never before visited the country – arrived at the Kremlin wearing a cloth cap, conspicuously the fellow worker much more than the renowned actor-manager. Equal to every offstage role which presented itself, he took to calling everyone "comrade" – also the word by which he chose to address the audience during his first curtain speech, as flowers hailed down on him during a ten-minute ovation for his *Othello* (lengthened in his memoirs to thirty-five). In a further gracious tribute to his hosts – who, he could tell, knew their Shakespeare in either language – Olivier then touchingly led the cast in the local custom of applauding themselves.

It proved rather more rash to expect Soviet eyes and ears to take in the Congreve – the first time a British company had ever premiered a production abroad. What were they to make of John Stride's Valentine, "fallen under his father's displeasure"? Even Miles Malleson, as the illiterate old Foresight, was hard pressed to milk any laughs from the seventeenth-century text, despite the dubious benefit of simultaneous translation echoing around the theatre. Olivier's luck, as the theatre world had come to call it, decreed this time that his best piece of business came with Tattle's harum-scarum escape through a window, falling flat on his face in a piece of stage slapstick which needed no translation. The contrast with his Othello the night before brought the audience rushing down the aisle again, gathering ten deep at the front of the theatre to shower him and his colleagues with adoring bouquets. Of the lucky English critics present J. W. Lambert confessed to feeling "nothing but unstinted pride", while Felix Barker was moved to use of Olivier the understatement of Othello on himself: "I have done the state some service. . . ."

Back in London, via more performances in West Berlin, it was the

National's second anniversary, a time to take stock. Of the twenty plays presented in Olivier's first two years, only three had proved box-office flops – the minimum necessary, it might be thought, to a national institution presenting "a spectrum of world drama". Highlights, some of them tried out first at Chichester, had included Peter Shaffer's *The Royal Hunt of the Sun*, and the wonderfully spiky partnership of Robert Stephens and Maggie Smith as Benedick and Beatrice in Franco Zeffirelli's production of *Much Ado About Nothing*. Artistic standards were high; box-office returns could have been doubled, given the scrum for tickets in a theatre seating only 879 people; yet Olivier and his team were criticized for financial mismanagement. The complaints were double-edged: there was carping that visiting dignitaries could not get in, that complimentary seats were "like gold-dust", that even company members and National Theatre staff were made to pay for tickets for friends and family; yet the National Theatre was running at a deficit. In a public debate from which Olivier was conspicuous by his absence, his administrator Stephen Arlen made the intriguing confession that the National had originally "budgeted for failure": that over-safe decisions had been made in the expectation that there would be more box-office flops than successes.

In point of fact it was Olivier's *Othello* which had thrown Arlen's planning out of kilter. Applications for tickets arrived literally by the sackload – and "half a sack would fill the theatre". Members of the Old Vic–Sadler's Wells Society, the hard core of the subscribing audience, complained that even they could not obtain tickets, which they anyway considered overpriced. All other productions averaged a more than satisfactory eighty-six per cent capacity; and there was no way Olivier's health could stand extra *Othello* performances. That production would have to be discounted, in budgetary terms, as a box-office freak, which must not be allowed to overshadow the solid consistency of the theatre's other work.

A look at the accounts of Olivier's first two years in charge does indeed show a deficit which, in a nation now accustomed to theatre and opera houses fighting a constant battle to increase inadequate state subsidies, falls far short of disastrous:

PRE-OPENING EXPENDITURE (to 22 October 1963)[9]

	£
Refurbishing Old Vic	93,578
Formation expenses (legal, etc.)	14,511
Part repayment of loans	9,169
	117,258
Less loan	40,000
	77,258

FIRST SEASON (October 1963–April 1964)

Expenditure (incl. opening deficit)	268,500
Income: Box-Office receipts	115,000
Treasury/Arts Council grants	130,000
Arts Council touring grant	1,000
	246,000
Deficit	22,500

SECOND SEASON (April 1964–April 1965)

Expenditure	580,500
Income: Box-Office receipts	284,000
Treasury/Arts Council grants	130,000
LCC grant	40,000
Arts Council touring grant	10,000
	464,000
Deficit	116,500
Total overall deficit	139,000

Given the huge expense of Olivier's original alterations to the theatre, the operating budget was in fact only some £45,000 in deficit for those first two years – by today's standards, a mere bagatelle. Olivier himself may have had little to do with the day-by-day budgeting, but he kept a careful eye on economies – too much so for some of his staff. "This is going to cost someone their job," said a jaded actor fingering the lavish *The Recruiting Officer* set – yet design budgets, ranging from £7,500 to £16,000 a production, were very much on a par with those of the RSC at Stratford. A statistical survey of audiences, moreover, spelt out by Tynan in a speech to the Royal Society of Arts, revealed that thirty-five per cent of the National Theatre-goers were either "teaching or being taught", so that the theatre was fulfilling the educational role seen by so many as the only possible justification for its state subsidy.[10] Twenty-four per cent, to Tynan's champagne-Marxist delight, consisted of "clerical or other white-collar workers"; while only point three of one per cent, to his dismay, could be called "manual workers".

On his return from the Soviet visit, Olivier was worn out. Even he was beginning to worry about his health; early in the run of *Othello* he had suffered a bout of 'flu which had "shaken me like a dog shakes a rat". It was time to give up responsibility for Chichester, which for two years he had anyway been running in name only, as a junior outpost of the National. Now he persuaded Evershed-Martin and his board that the actor John

Clements, his friend and next-door neighbour in Royal Cresent, was the ideal man to take over. Olivier meanwhile planned himself a light year for 1966, directing only one production, Sean O'Casey's *Juno and the Paycock*, and undertaking no new stage roles. If disappearing to play major film parts would thus appear dereliction of duty, there was nothing, he decided, to stop him accepting the occasional supporting role. So that autumn saw him begin two decades of lucrative cameo appearances with an exotic portrayal of The Mahdi, the fanatical Arab religious leader, in Basil Dearden's epic film of *Khartoum*. There were days that December when Olivier found himself playing one breed of black man by day and another by night. The Mahdi's elaborate make-up, which took three hours each morning at Pinewood, proved typical Olivier perfectionism right down to the V-shaped gap in his front teeth. On one side of the Atlantic *The Times* thought the results absurd, giving Charlton Heston's General Gordon the chance to show Olivier "whose shadow has more substance on the silver screen"; on the other, however, *Time* magazine found Olivier's Mahdi "a small masterpiece of single-minded religious insanity – the lambent black eyes never blinking, the measured voice conjuring up holy terrors from his private heart of darkness".

The reflective calm of early 1966 was shattered by the death of George Devine, a man both Oliviers loved beyond mere "theatrespeak". Patron of momentous events in both their careers and confidential midwife to their marriage, Devine had been like another brother to Olivier, a second father to Joan. This universally popular man was, moreover, generally considered to have worked himself to death, which renewed Olivier's determination to take things a little more easily. For most of the year he prided himself on working "office hours", his daily commuting schedule disrupted only by more performances of *Othello*, demand for which showed no signs of abating. On the production went into 1967, the fourth year of its life, with the strain increasingly beginning to tell. If 1966 had proved, by Olivier's standards, an oasis of relative calm, both domestic and professional, the following year would see him pay for it with a vengeance. Nineteen sixty-seven was soon to have him quoting *Hamlet*: "When troubles come, they come not single spies but in battalions."

The year began promisingly enough, with the happy news that Joan was pregnant again and the discovery of a startling new stage challenge for Olivier. This time he insisted that his wife cut down her performance schedule, while in the same breath stepping up his own. In Strindberg's *The Dance of Death* Olivier professed to have found a part to prove that Geraldine McEwan, like Maggie Smith, was more than just a deft comedienne. But in the role of her tormented husband Edgar, Olivier had found himself a new stage identity which many would later prefer to

Archie Rice as his finest creation outside Shakespeare. Edgar is a snarling, embittered army captain, passed over – memories of Iago and Olivier's own wardroom resentments – for promotion. He and his wife Alice live out a lop-sided love-hate marriage: "ten per cent love", as Olivier put it, "and ninety per cent hate". The approach of their silver wedding anniversary becomes a chance to reopen the accumulated wounds of the years and reach a condition approaching total war. With his severe Prussian crew-cut, military moustache and mercilessly hard-set jaw, Olivier's Edgar was chilling in its intensity – by turns devious and vain, pompous and insinuating, brutally cruel and nakedly evil.

Edgar's crumbling belief in himself gave Olivier a chance to lurch from mood to mood with superb technical control. Most remarkable was his capacity to convey that the captain's rage, phased to grow with his drinking, was subconsciously directed at himself as much as his wife and her cowering brother, Kurt. "The man's spiritual meanness seemed to glitter from every glance, to rasp in every word," wrote J. W. Lambert.[11] There were the usual set-piece highlights: a momentarily endearing, precise little mazurka and a climactic, humiliated collapse to the floor, amid the pathetic whimpers of the real, spiritually crushed Edgar, which had Harold Hobson declaring: "Even Sir Laurence has never done anything more exciting." Again, the performance was later preserved for posterity on film.

One night that summer Olivier returned to Brighton at midnight, from an Edgar performance, to find that Joan had been rushed to the local nursing home for an emergency Caesarian section. A tiny four-pound waif emerged, apparently starved of nutrients and oxygen for six weeks, and for several days the lives of both mother and daughter were in danger. But the oddly-named Julie-Kate ("Julia" because of the Caesarian, abbreviated and hyphenated to the already chosen "Katharine") showed as much will to survive as her "tough cookie" of a mother, and Olivier breathed again. The arrival of his third child, just past his sixtieth birthday, was soon followed by that of his first grandchild, Tristan, son of Tarquin (now working as a Commonwealth development officer on a Tanzanian sugar plantation). The curious phases of Olivier's moon were soon to be marked by a death as momentous as these births. But 1967 first chose to subject him to a long and agonizing trial by ordeal.

Whatever the state of the National Theatre's finances, its artistic management structure had hitherto proved highly effective, in a relaxed, almost amateurish sort of way. For the first two years the inner circle of Olivier, Tynan, Gaskill and Dexter had enjoyed comfortable enough relations with Chandos and his board. They had to suffer in silence only once, when they were talked out of Tynan's plan to present Wedekind's

Spring Awakening, an uncompromising study of teenage sexuality which (though written in 1891) would have been most unlikely to get past the Lord Chamberlain, then still Britain's theatrical censor. Tynan's plan was to present the play with the cuts demanded by the censor, as a cunning ploy in his long-running campaign to abolish His Lordship's archaic hold over the British theatre. The board, not unreasonably, argued that the National should be above such censorship. Little internal blood was spilt, and the battle to dispense with the Lord Chamberlain was won anyway in 1968; *Spring Awakening* duly joined the National Theatre repertoire six years later.

But an uncomfortable precedent, revolving around the board's power and willingness to intervene in artistic decisions, had been set. As Tynan hailed Peter Brook's controversial production of *US* for the Royal Shakespeare Company, in which an actress suggested that napalm be dropped on Hampstead to bring home the realities of the Vietnam war to the British, he began to argue that the National should tackle similar themes. In an internal note to Olivier, he wrote:

> I'm worried. Nothing really specific: just the general feeling that we're losing our lead, that we're no longer making the running, that what the NT does has become a matter of public acceptance rather than public excitement. At a time when – as I Cassandra-like keep saying – audiences even for *good* theatre are dwindling all over Europe, we are doing nothing to remind them that theatre is an independent force at the heart of a country's life – a sleeping tiger that can and should be roused whenever the national (or international) conscience needs nudging.[12]

Already Tynan had commissioned "workshop" scripts about the General Strike and the Cuban missile crisis. "One of the functions of a National Theatre", he argued in a newspaper interview, "should be to create a place where the gigantic historical issues, such as the Greeks and Shakespeare understood them, could be raised." Yes, but could a National Theatre, directly funded by the Government, present productions overtly critical of that Government? Up to a point, was the consensus. Said Chandos to the *Sunday Times*:

> The board should give the artistic director the greatest independence possible – and, I repeat, possible – in a modern society. This cannot be absolute because certain questions arise which bring other considerations into play. Now suppose you had a satire of the present Government [which happened to be Labour] – well, only a board can decided if it's harmlessly amusing ... or concerted propaganda to win a few Conservative votes.

It was in this uneasy atmosphere, with Tynan seeming to be seeking a head-on collision, that Olivier's happy management family began to break up. For two years this curious quartet had co-operated effectively enough, with Olivier, the oldest by twenty years, so much the father figure to his ageing whizz kids that he actually took to referring to them as his "boys", and they to him as "Dad". "Olivier ran the place as a college of cardinals," said his eventual successor, Sir Peter Hall, "with himself, I suppose, as Pope."[13] But Devine's death gave Gaskill the chance he had been seeking to leave – returning to the Royal Court to take over the English Stage Company – because of his personal aversion to Tynan and his increasing hold over Olivier. At one management meeting Tynan had begun to argue that the theatre needed more "stars"; Gaskill angrily retorted that he believed quite the opposite: "I can understand that you have to rely on Ken's advice about the choice of plays," he told Olivier in front of Tynan, "but I don't think in any circumstances he should be allowed to dictate the choice of actors." The exchange grew so heated that Olivier abruptly left the room. After half an hour he reappeared, to tell Gaskill: "I have to tell you that I must have Ken involved in all these discussions." Exit Gaskill: "It was at this point that I knew it was no good going on. I couldn't work in that kind of set-up."

Olivier put a brave face on Gaskill's departure: "The Lord gave and the Lord has taken away." But only six months later, in March 1967, Dexter too had a watershed row with Olivier, this time over his cherished plans to direct an all-male production of *As You Like It*; inspired by an essay by Jan Kott about the effect of boy actors on the play's sexuality, Dexter had spent more than a year planning the production. It was already in rehearsal when Olivier "seemed to get cold feet".[14] He apparently thought Dexter was "indulging himself in a drag show". Whatever the hidden pressures on Olivier – who subsequently permitted Clifford Williams to go ahead with an all-male production, which proved a great success – the episode gave Dexter the excuse he was seeking to head for richer pastures elsewhere. He had anyway been anxious for some time to capitalize on his reputation to earn more than his £50-a-week salary at the National and to make himself an international name; he later became director of productions at New York's Metropolitan Opera.

Dexter's departure was not as acrimonious as Gaskill's – both, in fact, were to return as freelances to direct more National productions – but it put an end to the happy days of the founding fathers. It also drew attention to Olivier's instinctively autocratic style as director. Though all things to all men most of the time, his own distinction led him at difficult moments to assume a superiority over his right-hand men which they came to resent.

Now Tynan felt that he and Olivier were a dynamic duo to rival the post-war Old Vic triumvirate. He was also freer to steer his biddable employer towards bolder realms. The former critic had worked hard on his transformation to literary manager, compiling a list of 400 plays suitable for the repertoire of the National Theatre, and evangelizing about the need for a judicious mixture of "showbiz" (which had come to characterize the National) and "high art" (still the preserve of the RSC). By the National's fourth year Olivier had come to lean on Tynan as "more than a literary manager – rather an early-warning system, a promoter of bright ideas and a spokesman".[15] Aptly described as a "C. B. Cochran of serious theatre", Tynan had in turn come to think of himself as the National's *éminence grise*. Only recently he had passed into the history of the Swinging Sixties by becoming the first person to use the word "fuck" on television. Now, more than ever, it seemed likely to be only a matter of time before Tynan's deep-seated need to *épater les bourgeois* would rock the steady, dignified progress of Olivier's ship of state.

Early in 1967 Tynan proposed that Britain's National Theatre present *Soldiers*, a new play by the overtly political German dramatist Rolf Hoch-huth, who took the blanket bombing of Dresden as the basis for a tract about the rights of innocent civilians. In the course of his argument he branded Churchill a war criminal, arguing that he had knowingly been a party to the assassination of the Polish wartime leader, General Sikorksi, in 1943. This was strong stuff by anyone's standards, let alone those of a British National Theatre, and the board would not hear of it. To Tynan's protests that it was the most "*imposing*" new script he had ever read, Chandos, who had of course been a member of Churchill's war cabinet, replied: "The play is a grotesque calumny on a great statesman."

Summoned before the board on 25 April, Tynan was challenged to produce historical evidence to support Hochhuth's case. But he was on weak ground; Hochhuth himself had said the relevant documents were locked away in a Swiss bank vault, where they would remain unseen for another fifty years. Asked for supporting testimony from historians of the period, Tynan cited Hugh Trevor-Roper (now Lord Dacre), Professor of History at Oxford, as having "an open mind"; Trevor-Roper replied that he had told Tynan that Hochhuth's idea was "absurd", with "neither evidence nor probability to support it". The day ended with the board formally overruling Olivier and forbidding production of the play. "Some of the characters," it said in a statement, "in particular Sir Winston Churchill and Lord Cherwell, are grossly maligned.... The board unanimously considered that the play was unsuitable for production at the National Theatre." Olivier publicly declared himself "unhappy" and Tynan remained defiant: "I am not sure that the statement put out by the board does not constitute a libel of the play." Both, according to the press, were considering resignation.

"I serve the National Theatre", Tynan proudly proclaimed, "not the National Theatre board." Now he lobbied MPs to promote support in the Commons, to which Chandos responded with more newspaper interviews:

> If we put on this play, some poor Italian gentleman might say, "Ha ha, so that's what went on in England during the war." If somebody chooses to put it on at some theatre club in Hampstead, that's a different matter.... I'd die for free speech, but remember the foreigners.

The middle ground, which Olivier was having understandable difficulty articulating, was best expressed by one of the more thoughtful members of the embattled National Theatre board, Hugh Willatt, also secretary general of the Arts Council: "It is essential for the lay board to recognize that the theatre must be run by professionals ... but as more and more theatres are partly supported by public money, the governors become trustees of the public interest. The problem has not yet been solved."[16]

The *Soldiers* débâcle, which was to rumble on for a while yet, showed Olivier at both his best and his worst. The memory of it pains him to this day; in his memoirs he could not bring himself to speak of it, dealing with its labyrinthine complexities by printing some of the written exchanges, without comment, in a twenty-four-page appendix. Privately he believed it a weak play (as did most literary authorities), and that Tynan was being "naïve" in promoting so public and symbolic a row over it. Publicly he stood solidly beside Tynan against the board, as much for reasons of personal solidarity as for the principle of protecting his artistic control as director. "My choice when I joined the National Theatre", Olivier wrote in a letter to *The Times*, "was cloudy but simple. Do we have a National Theatre with a *faute de mieux* ambivalent contract between its director and its board, or do we not have a National Theatre at all? I decided to plump for the former."

At the height of the brouhaha, Chandos had revealed his resentment of Tynan in the midst of a frank acknowledgement that the National Theatre must consider the sensibilities of its paymasters: "Getting a National Theatre has been forty years' work. I wouldn't like Tynan to ruin it in two weeks." Not content with victory, Chandos was now trying to force Tynan's resignation. Tynan, in turn, was publicly manipulating Olivier: "If Larry does throw in his hand, I shall clearly do the same." But Olivier was not going to let this squalid little nightmare undo what he saw as the climax of his life's work. He had no intention of resigning. An over-excited Tynan had miscalculated, lost the battle and undermined his own position. He saw to it that *Soldiers* subsequently received a commercial production in the West End, which served only to prove its severe limitations both as a play and as a historical document.

Tynan's status at the National was never the same again. Within a few months he was tacitly admitting this by resuming outside journalism and embarking on independent work as a producer, already planning the components of an outrageous, on-the-rebound revue which would eventually emerge as *Oh, Calcutta!* It would be two years before he returned to the National from a six-month sabbatical to discover that his title had been downgraded to "literary consultant", and that Olivier's friend Derek Granger had arrived from London Weekend Television to share the same billing. Even then he held his ground until Olivier's successor, Sir Peter Hall, made it a condition of his acceptance that Tynan must go. *Soldiers* had proved a Pyrrhic battleground, even in defeat.

Twenty years on the saga still remains a source of theatrical debate and gossip, centring around Olivier's seemingly inexplicable support for a play which, apart from anything else, demeaned his own personal hero, Churchill. Why was he going to such lengths to champion Tynan? Were they having a homosexual affair? There are many in their circle who will tell you, to this day, that this was the case. Olivier has admitted to homosexual experience and has been unwontedly demure in his public statements about Tynan and *Soldiers*. For now the last word must go to Tynan's widow, Kathleen, who has boldly (if cryptically) tackled the rumours head on:

> Ken felt that Olivier would be bound to avoid anything involved with an intimate relationship. Olivier, in turn, felt that Ken was responsible for the distance between them, and would have liked their relationship to be warmer. He believed that "Ken had an absolute dread of any hint of homosexuality. I greeted him tremendously warmly, I remember, and I found him very reserved, as if to say 'Keep your place, just in case you think I'm a sucker.'" Wrong though Olivier was on this score, Ken was obtuse in understanding that Olivier, on occasion, needed his hand held, and that it was inhuman to act solely as the keeper of the flame.[17]

By mid-1967 events were taking their toll. For once Olivier looked as ill as he felt. Onstage he put as much energy as ever into every performance, be it Othello or Edgar, while offstage he could no longer keep up the façade. Colleagues and friends alike were alarmed by how pale and drawn his face had become, and how frequently it was contorted with pain. During his dispiriting bout of 'flu two years before, he had characteristically left his sick-bed for a run along the Brighton front, intent on keeping his muscles in shape – only to collapse helpless, unable to move, and await rescue from a friendly passer-by. For two years Olivier had been feeling his age more than he admitted. Now he could disguise his discomfort no longer. Hospitalized again in June 1967, because of "a pain in my innards which grew ever sharper and less possible to dismiss", he allowed it to be made public that he was being treated for cancer – a neoplasm (or tumour) of the prostate gland, which, though discovered at an early stage, had proved malignant. The board of the National announced that Olivier would not be appearing on its stage for the rest of that season, while privately wondering if he ever would act again. The feeling backstage at the National, in the words of its historians, was that "that marvellous vigour, the flow of life which had helped so much to bring the National into existence, and had sustained it, the very soul and energy of the place, was suddenly threatened".

His doctors gave Olivier a choice: a straightforward, conventional operation to remove the tumour, and hope for the best, or a new, lengthy and enervating treatment known as hyperbarbic oxygen radiotherapy. This, he was told by its inventor, Dr Churchill Davidson, would involve several weeks of regular hospital visits, three times a week, to be isolated in a torpedo-shaped, hermetically sealed chamber and "bombarded" with X-rays. With Gaskill and Dexter as yet unreplaced, and Tynan for the moment emasculated, Olivier was anxious to minimize his absence from the tiller. He opted for the treatment, attending St Thomas's Hospital as an out-patient while continuing the rehearsals already in progress for his production of Chekhov's *The Three Sisters*, with Joan as Masha, due to open on 3 July. The stamina and determination he chose to display during this appalling period bordered on the heroic. At first he continued playing Edgar, gearing his cancer treatment around the days he was scheduled to perform. Then came another collapse; and on Joan's orders, the part was taken over by his understudy, Anthony Hopkins.

Olivier, said Joan, regarded cancer as "his due. . . . It was something that had been meted out to him. It just came a bit before he expected it." The treatments were "scarifying": Olivier's fascination with all matters technical recalled two huge containers, the shape of "inverted artichokes", revolving around him in his metal coffin, which was fitted with a small square of glass above the eyes to reduce the sense of claustrophobia. It was from this living death that he escaped briefly on the afternoon of Sunday 30 June for the dress rehearsal of *The Three Sisters*. By the time he returned to St Thomas's he had developed pneumonia and was told that he would not be allowed out of the hospital again. After the first night, on the Wednesday, Joan brought two other members of the cast, Robert Stephens and Louise Purnell, to his bedside, along with a bottle of champagne to celebrate a triumphant opening. Four days later, on the Saturday, still swooning from the debilitating treatment, he received an 8 a.m. call from Jack Merivale to tell him that Vivien had died during the night.

Olivier immediately rose from his hospital bed, temporarily discharged himself and went straight round to Eaton Square. Suspecting the presence of press photographers, he slipped in by a secret side entrance in the basement. In the flat which had witnessed the last days of his marriage to Vivien he found Merivale waiting, sensitive enough to Olivier's feelings to escort him to the bedroom door and close it behind him, leaving him alone with his thoughts.

Olivier noticed that Vivien's favourite photograph of him remained, as ever, beside what had once been their bed. Yet in the six years since he had married Joan, Vivien had managed to enjoy a final professional flourish, for all the increasing rigours of her illness. In 1961 she had led the Old Vic company, ironically enough, on another tour of Australia and New Zealand; two years later she had won a Tony award in a Broadway musical, *Tovarich*. In the midst of further electric-shock treatment she had filmed *Ship of Fools* for Stanley Kramer and attempted a return to the West End stage in what proved to be a bad choice, the title role of Paul Osborn's *La Contessa*, which had folded before it ever reached London. But only the previous year, despite more frequent collapses and worsening tuberculosis, she had scored a last stage triumph opposite Gielgud, and under his direction, in a New York production of Chekhov's *Ivanov*. In recent weeks, despite her illness, she had been preparing for the London premiere of Edward Albee's *A Delicate Balance*. Vivien, Olivier believed, had finally "come into her own" as an actress of the first rank, but he guiltily suspected that she had needed to escape from his shadow to do so.

Privately she had enjoyed the consoling love of Merivale, who had weathered the many storms of her declining years with great patience and devotion. But he, too, had his own career to pursue and was often away. She had replaced the rural delights of Notley with a Queen Anne house in Sussex called Tickerage Mill, found for her by Dirk Bogarde, where weekend regulars loyal to the last had included Coward, Gielgud, Rattigan and Rex Harrison (with *his* new wife, Rachel Roberts). Tarquin Olivier, too, had remained very close to the woman who had so befriended him, and it was at Tickerage one day that she confessed to him: "Leigh taught me how to live, your father how to love and Jack how to be alone."[18]

She had remained in distant touch with Olivier, taking in his Chichester Astrov (twice) and his Old Vic Othello. He had never ousted her from her directorship of Laurence Olivier Productions, and they had met irregularly, and rather stiffly, at its board meetings. During one of Vivien's West End appearances, Olivier had paid a surprise visit backstage one evening. Cast members in her dressing-room were as thrilled as Vivien to see her distinguished ex-husband arrive smiling and bearing a single red carnation in a smart florist's package. They all then watched in stunned silence as Olivier removed the cellophane, snapped the stem of the flower and deposited the detritus on the floor, before elaborately placing the flower in his own button-hole, turning on his heel and leaving.

Never able to accept Joan as a "worthy" successor, Vivien went to her grave refusing to accept that it was her illness which had finally forced Olivier to abandon her. Mementoes of their life together still adorned her bedroom, at Tickerage as at Eaton Square, long after she had started sharing it with Merivale. Looking at them now, Olivier felt consumed with guilt, and has remained so ever since:

> It has always been impossible for me not to believe that I was somehow the cause of Vivien's disturbances, that they were due to some fault in me, in spite of assurances to the contrary from every one of the many psychiatrists with which our situation had made it necessary for me to come into contact. . . .

"Enough to drive a fellow barmy, isn't it?" he added, in a tasteless afterthought, almost as tasteless as his observations about the stain he saw on the floor beside the bed which still contained Vivien's corpse. Cross-examination of Merivale that morning led Olivier to suppose that it was seeing this stain, and getting out of bed to deal with it, which had precipitated Vivien's death. Not at all; Merivale had naturally cleared up, as best he could, the residue of Vivien's death throes. But Olivier would not be deflected from his final, tragic irony: "What a cruel stroke of fate to deliver that particular little death-blow to one as scrupulously dainty in all such matters as was she." Not much of an epitaph, from a man who still confesses, twenty years later, that this was the love of his life.

Though Joan had long since provided the stability Olivier craved, she had never matched Vivien's magic. With Joan he had never competed on the stage, largely because she had so swiftly mastered him off it; with Vivien there had been constant, corrosive tension, both private and professional. When first they met, Olivier and Vivien had been sucked into a passion bred of mutual need. Neither, perhaps, would have been attracted to the other, "had both been unmarried and available", as Garry O'Connor put it, "but both found themselves at a stage when they needed to tap greater resources of feeling".[19] Olivier's final instinct with Vivien, however, which saw him through the wrench of leaving her, was mere self-preservation: "You can reach a point where it's like a life raft that can hold only so many. You cast away the hand grasping it. You let it go. You do not take it on board because otherwise it's both of you. Two instead of one. . . . Then you go on living and there you are, with it, knowing what has happened, remembering its details. Yet what else is there to do?"[20]

Vivien was only fifty-three when she died. Looking for the last time at "that beautiful dead face", Olivier stood and "prayed for forgiveness for all the evils that had sprung up between us". Then, leaving Merivale to organize the funeral, he returned to his own sick-bed as furtively as he had left it.

CHAPTER 23

1967–73

It was another death-bed scene which haunted Joan. Eighteen months before, as George Devine lay dying in St George's Hospital, she had been one of the devoted friends who had maintained a daily vigil at his bedside. Old before his time, half paralysed, a shrivelled shadow of his former self, Devine had beckoned her behind his screen one last time and whispered: "It's done for me and I'm not sure if it's worth it. Don't let it happen to him. Get him out before it does."[1]

If it was his inspirational work at the Royal Court which had killed Devine, Olivier had twice the responsibility in an organization twice as large. He was also, by nature, twice as determined. There was no keeping Olivier out of action for long. "How", as the critic John Elsom put it, "do you stop Sisyphus half-way up the hill?"

The cancer treatment appeared to be working, but it had aged and weakened Olivier alarmingly. Undeterred, he went ahead with plans to lead a six-week National Theatre tour of Canada that autumn, in defiance of his doctors, who told Joan they could not answer for the consequences. The one concession Olivier would make to mortality was to cancel the scheduled performances of *Othello*; after five years, this mighty portrait would now be seen no more. Secretly, Olivier was relieved: "With all the preparation it had become like a sort of pontifical midnight mass, which became so sacred it was awful. Putting on make-up, playing and taking off make-up was a seven-hour job, a dreadful punishment.... It had become an obsession."[2] His friend "Binkie" Beaumont, a valued ally on the National Theatre board, reassured Olivier that it was a greater compliment to his Canadian hosts to export his more recent success, Edgar in *The Dance of Death*.

The play's title took on grim overtones with another death, as it were, in the family. On the way home from Vivien's funeral, their long-standing friend and agent Cecil Tennant was killed instantly when his car veered off the road into a tree. "Oh, Boy," Olivier was heard to say, using one of his favourite nicknames for Vivien, "what have we done?" To Virginia Fairweather, when she offered her condolences by telephone, he murmured: "Do you know, my darling, I'm no longer afraid of dying. I shan't be lonely. All my friends are up there."[3]

After the National's summer break, Olivier returned from a family holiday in Switzerland looking as if he had never been ill. An arduous autumn lay ahead; the National's management had large gaps waiting to be filled, and Olivier was due to appear in all three of the plays they were taking to Canada. Apart from Edgar and Tattle, he had decided to "have a little fun" in the cameo part of the butler, Etienne Pulcheux, in *A Flea in her Ear*, a Feydeau farce adapted by John Mortimer.

The doctors had told Olivier that his cancer treatment could cause depression, especially if he were left too much alone, so he arranged for Joan to fly out to join the company in Montreal. His brush with cancer, he said, had made him count his blessings:

> It has changed my values a lot. Certain things I just won't tolerate any more – like being separated from my family. I won't accept that again. When you are my age and you have a young family, you must make the most of it – and during that time of illness they became extra precious to me.[4]

Of the disease itself, he added: "I said to myself, 'I will beat you, you bastard,' and I think I have." A month later, in February 1968, he found out – the hard way – that this was so. During a performance of *The Dance of Death* in Edinburgh, Olivier was suddenly assailed by what he took to be stomach cramps. Next morning he woke up with agonizing pain throughout his abdomen. A Scottish doctor diagnosed acute appendicitis, recommending immediate surgery, but Olivier pleaded to be allowed to fly to London, to St Thomas's, so that he could convalesce nearer his work. By the time he went under the knife, his appendix was on the brink of explosion. The surgeon who removed it, Ken Shuttleworth, took the opportunity to open his abdomen and was able to inform his patient that all trace of the cancer had gone. The news was more than sufficient consolation for the inevitable bout of pneumonia which ensued.

In his pocket on that uncomfortable flight back from Edinburgh Olivier had carried a momentous letter which was now giving him some pause. The Prime Minister, Harold Wilson, had invited him to accept a life peerage, the first ever offered to an actor. Though Wilson was, at the time, rather given to a strong showbusiness element in his honours lists, it was a singularly striking tribute to the status Olivier had achieved in his profession, both on the stage and off it, that the notion of "Lord Larry" was entirely credible. His pioneering work at the National – which, by universal agreement, would probably never have been founded without him – had raised him above the rank of outstanding performer to elder statesman of the artistic community. His vanity was naturally tickled, but Olivier hesitated. A knighthood he considered dashing and gallant, a peerage merely "stuck-up". The ever down-to-earth Joan agreed. Both thought it would, in fact, damage his continuing professional career to be so elevated above his fellow actors. In a fiercely jealous profession, his eminence had for years caused other actors to treat him with an awe he found awkward to handle; this could make whole-hearted teamwork impossible. The Prime Minister received a polite but firm – and utterly discreet – refusal. The Oliviers, so they say, "proceeded to forget about it".

Meanwhile, there was another boost to Olivier's morale as he recuperated in hospital that month. He received "the best news of my professional life", when the Government at last approved the provision of £7.4 million for the building of the new National Theatre, to be divided between the state and the LCC's successor body, the Greater London Council. The announcement had been so long in coming that Olivier cautiously added that he would "not be opening the champagne yet". He had lived through so many bureaucratic delays in the formation of a National Theatre, let alone the building of one, that he would now believe nothing until he saw – literally – concrete evidence. As the year dragged by without so much as a sod being dug, Olivier began to wonder if he would live to see his company installed in its own building, let alone to act in it.

By now Olivier had managed to lure Gielgud to the National, to play Seneca's Oedipus and Molière's Orgon (in *Tartuffe*), but this latest illness forced him to abandon his hopes of directing the Seneca himself. Casting around for the right replacement, Olivier was persuaded that the doom-laden Roman author ("Seneca cannot be too heavy," as Polonius puts it) had much in common with the Shakespeare of *Titus Andronicus*; Gielgud's Oedipus would be a natural vehicle for tempting Peter Brook to the Waterloo Road. Although recently on record as saying "The Greeks and Romans embody everything I detest,"[5] Brook agreed out of "homage for Gielgud", on the condition that the English version Olivier had planned to use, by David A. Turner, be developed into a verse translation by Ted Hughes. Striving to express the "miraculously powerful" inner core of the play, Brook opted to eliminate all unnecessary physical movement in favour of an emphasis on sound. Cast and chorus were made to listen to tape-recordings of the chants of primitive tribes and Tibetan monks; eerie *musique concrète* was commissioned from Richard Peaslee; the terrifying atmosphere of doom Brook contrived was to be sharpened by actors both onstage and around the auditorium lending a chorus of grunts, drones, hums and whispered hisses to the unfolding action.

The opening approached amid an atmosphere of great tension. As his gesture to the Greek concept of *katharsis*, the purifying effect of watching tragedy, Brook had planned a spectacular end to the performance, in which the house lights came up and the cast joined the audience in a wild, orgiastic dance to a jazzed-up version of "God Save The Queen". This Olivier could not countenance. He admired Brook enormously and was impressed by the awesome power of his production, but now he felt that Brook was becoming "clever-clever". Earlier that month Olivier had boldly given courtroom evidence in support of the English Stage Company, prosecuted for presenting Edward Bond's *Saved* – in which a baby is stoned to death in its pram – without the Lord Chamberlain's licence. He had been hailed as a champion of the liberal arts, an indispensable leading light of the campaign to abolish the Lord Chamberlain's powers of theatrical censorship (to be won later that year). But this was too much. Olivier's patriotic instincts, as Brook well knew, were mightily offended by the idea of abusing the National Anthem, and he dreaded to think what the board would have to say. For a while there was deadlock; only when Olivier promised, to Brook's cruel amusement, that the National Anthem would never again be played at the end of any National Theatre performance while he was director, did Brook agree to go away and think of something else.

Cruelly duped, as he came to believe, Olivier was astonished by what unfolded before him at the end of the dress rehearsal. As Gielgud's noble, self-blinded Oedipus was led offstage, he was replaced at its centre by a tall, cylindrical object draped in a white sheet. Now, as the final chorus trailed away, this was unveiled to reveal a giant golden phallus, ten feet high, its tip shaped so suggestively that there could be no mistaking what it was. Olivier, Tynan and Brook were up all night arguing about it. Brook refused to budge, hurled an ashtray at Olivier (which only narrowly missed him) and stalked out. Not until the afternoon of the first night did Olivier, deserted by Tynan, finally concede defeat. As a giant golden penis was unveiled before it in portentous silence, the first-night audience found itself totally non-plussed. "We were left", wrote a bemused J. C. Trewin, "wondering whether it was all over."[6]

In later performances, after the notorious unveiling, cast did move among audience, inviting them to join their dance around the phallus to the strains of "Yes, we have no bananas". There were perfectly respectable historical grounds for it all, as the pro-Brook camp pointed out, in the Ancient Greek tradition of purging the tragic experience in a frenzied fertility dance. But Olivier was miserable. He had been tricked, humiliated and defeated: "Peter had dealt a shrewder blow to my *amour propre* than he could have known." Like a defeated boxer, he said ten years later, he would remember this as the punch that began his undoing.

In April 1969 he made a flying visit to New York to receive a "special" Antoinette Perry Award – a Tony – to honour the work of the National Theatre of Great Britain. Struggling as ever to distinguish his own prestige from the corporate identity of the company, Olivier was genuinely embarrassed by the extravagance of the introduction he received from the presenter, Arthur Miller, who brought him onstage as "a man whose name has been spoken with undiminished admiration for several decades now, wherever in the world theatre exists. A romantic movie star, a sublime comedian, to many he is the greatest Shakespearean actor of our age. In a time of rockets that light up the theatrical sky and vanish in the night, this is a planet." It seemed doubly inappropriate, after such celestial praise, that Olivier had to grab the award, murmur a few words of thanks, speed to a waiting car and fly back to London that same night for an emergency operation for piles.

Looking back he declared 1969 a bad year, "as one might describe a disappointing wine". It began with that dispiriting haemorrhoidectomy and continued with the publication of a gossipy "intimate memoir" by his former press officer, Virginia Fairweather. As he approached sixty-two Olivier's illnesses had turned his hair grey, and he seemed to be losing some of his enthusiasm for his job. His burden at the National, since the departure of Gaskill and Dexter, was now eased as the director Frank Dunlop came aboard as associate director, to which rank the actor Robert Stephens was also promoted. But Olivier still felt like a lonely one-man-band. As he became swamped in interminable meetings about the design, construction and funding of the new theatre, he seemed for the first time to have lost his appetite for acting, even directing. Six years since it was founded, his empire was still run from the cramped and scruffy Nissen huts in the Waterloo Road, once so romantically pioneering, now merely depressing. "Look down that corridor," he said to one visitor, pausing outside his office. "That is my most unfavourite view. You should hear what overseas visitors say about the place. They cannot believe that this is the brainbox of Britain's National Theatre."[7]

Peter Shaffer had written *The Battle of Shrivings* as a vehicle for Olivier and Gielgud to be reunited on the stage for the first time since the 1935 *Romeo and Juliet*. But Olivier was in no mood for that, either. His huge administrative burden weighed too heavily upon him. Beyond concern for his health, friends and observers were beginning to wonder if he were wasting what could be the final performing years of his rare talent. Olivier's tacit understanding with the National Theatre board had always been that he should be director for five years or until the theatre was built, whichever was the longer. It had already been six years and now looked like being at least ten. Was it perhaps time to pack in the back-breaking bureaucracy and concentrate on acting? "I do get dreadfully tired at times, but I remain addicted to the idea of really getting the National launched as an actors' theatre," he told an interviewer. "I wouldn't go on with this job if I thought I was losing my nerve or anything, if I thought I was losing the confidence of the public."[8]

The parts Olivier took on that year – "just to keep my hand in" – were modest and, for him, unremarkable. As A. B. Raham, the sly solicitor in Somerset Maugham's *Home and Beauty*, he even felt the need to list himself in the programme under the traditional theatrical pseudonym of "Walter Plinge". His continuing stage fright and his unwonted loss of faith in his physical staying power had combined to bring Olivier's habitual self-assurance to its lowest ebb. He felt more at home as Chebutikin, the mischievous old doctor in *The Three Sisters*, where he had the companionship of Joan's Masha to see him through. But even his enthusiasm for directing now seemed to be on the wane. Having chosen Natalia Ginzburg's play *The Advertisement* as a showcase for Joan's technical maturity, he shared its direction with Donald McKechnie; the one production he undertook on his own that year, *Love's Labour's Lost*, was accounted undistinguished. Despite the *Oedipus* débâcle, he managed to persuade Gielgud to stay on at the National for the Molière, in the safer hands of Tyrone Guthrie, but could only look on with helpless resignation as the result was (in the verdict even of Guthrie's admiring biographer, James Forsyth) "inept". There was little enthusiasm, either, for Guthrie's production of Ben Jonson's *Volpone*, despite a spirited Colin Blakely in the title role. Even a director as inventive as Clifford Williams (on loan from the RSC) could not bring Shaw's monumental *Back To Methuselah* to life. Audiences began to dwindle, and Olivier openly confessed that the film he directed of *The Three Sisters*, another of those only half-satisfying studio records of the stage performance, was "absolutely and entirely" to help swell the theatre's coffers. Its annual public subsidy of £330,000 had stood still for three years, during which costs had risen alarmingly. As the first cement-mixer at last appeared beside Waterloo Bridge, the National seemed to be heading into artistic crisis, which could all too quickly turn financial.

Olivier's uncharacteristic mood lasted into early 1970, despite his delight in the award of a CBE to Joan in the New Year's honours list. When he led the company for the first time to the United States that January, for a six-week run in Los Angeles, he surprised American journalists with his world-weariness:

> It does seem sometimes that acting is hardly the occupation for an adult. False noses, lots of make-up and gum on my face. I can't stand it any more. I hope I'll never do another West End play.... I don't know of any elderly actors who enjoy acting very much. One is too conscientious to enjoy it. But without it I would die, I suppose.

Intimations of mortality very much to the fore, there were two Shakespearean parts Olivier still felt he must take on before he *did* die. He had already announced that he would be playing Lear, but had no real immediate intention of doing so: "I'm terribly inclined to do that every time I've got nothing better to announce." *The Merchant of Venice* he had always found an "unpleasant" play, while knowing he would one day have to square up to Shylock. Tynan had recently rearoused his interest with the rediscovery of an Agate article hostile to the play, but neither of them could think of the right director. Then Tynan came up with an intriguing thought: what about Jonathan Miller, Cambridge *wunderkind*-turned-polymath, who was now combining a career as a stage director with his continuing work in medicine? "Brilliant," thought Olivier: Miller's "undoubted genius" had shone through so brightly in the Cambridge Footlights and in the revue *Beyond the Fringe* that "it was completely clear to me that a touch like his would be ideal for the conception". As the production took shape, with Joan cast as Portia, Olivier could enthuse about Miller in the plural: "He excited us beyond measure by the limitless variety, the originality and the fascinating colour in the expression of his ideas. He was the only man; we were thrilled by him and remain so."

This gushing testimonial may have been partly due to the fact that Miller, like Brook and Hall before him, was a director young and brash enough to stand up to a great man by now rather set in his great ways. For months, according to Joan, Olivier had been practising a range of voices in front of the bathroom mirror; now he appeared at the first dress rehearsal with a huge hook nose, obviously based on George Arliss's famous film portrayal of Disraeli, as well *as* a goatee beard, a curled forelock and a massively protruding upper lip, beneath which flailed away a proud new set of jutting teeth. "Please," begged Miller, "*please* can we do away with some of these extravagances? The nose, first: do you really want to look like every Jewish caricature there's ever been, George Arliss included? Then perhaps the beard...?"

"Certainly, dear boy, certainly; we must do nothing to offend our beloved Hebrew brethren!" replied Olivier, oblivious to the fact that

Miller himself, though far from orthodox, was born a Jew. "Many of them", Olivier blundered on, "are, of course, my best friends...."[9] These embarrassments over, Miller and Olivier found themselves wholly in sympathy about the thrust of their production: that Shylock, though not the most attractive of men, was morally far superior to the Christians portrayed by Shakespeare – a bunch of "vile, heartless, money-grubbing monsters" who should be made, after the Jew's final, humiliated exit, to feel "thoroughly ashamed of themselves". They agreed to set the play in the neo-Baroque Venice of the 1880s – an era, as Olivier put it, "redolent of successful merchandise".

Olivier had always felt *The Merchant of Venice* a bit of a "school play". So he was firmly behind Miller's determination to make this production as wringingly naturalistic as possible. Apart from the exaggerated lines of the mouth, he donned a top hat over his skullcap and ensured that his clothes otherwise reflected the pseudo-gentility of the social *arriviste*: the pin-striped City trousers a little too baggy, the frock-coat rather worn, the stiff collar a little frayed. The effect was capped by an insinuating, oily new voice, which dropped its final g's at moments of stress. Finally, a typical piece of Miller ingenuity during rehearsals brought the indispensable piece of business which would prove the making of the performance. Shylock's gleeful *schadenfreude* at the loss of Antonio's ships reminded the director of Hitler's notorious skip of triumph at the signing of the armistice in the Forest of Compiègne; Miller suggested that Olivier might essay a little dance of glee. So delighted was Olivier with this notion that he was thereafter only too pleased to comply when his forward young director suggested that "we had all seen one or two of his other mannerisms and gestures perhaps once too often before". Said Sir Laurence: "Of course, my dear boy: out they must go."

The "high intellectual power" and "sheer interpretative originality" of his performance led the *Guardian*'s Michael Billington to declare Olivier's Shylock "the finest of its generation". Billington liked the harshness of the portrait, rightly speculating that had Olivier tackled Shylock in the post-war New Theatre seasons, "following hard on pogroms and persecutions", he would inevitably have shown the Jew in "a mellower, more sympathetic light". But Billington was alone in his virtually unqualified praise; most critics felt uncomfortable with the "grotesquery" of Olivier's Shylock. There were some extraordinary moments: Olivier's various cries of pain, outrage and humiliation were, even to such a hard-boiled modernist as Charles Marowitz, writing in the New York *Village Voice*, "paralysing" in their poignancy. But even that longest-serving loyalist, Harold Hobson of the *Sunday Times*, was for once disappointed: "Dancing with glee at Antonio's misfortunes, coming to court to cut off the pound of flesh with a briefcase more prominent than a knife, and after sentence apparently falling downstairs offstage, Sir Laurence will not be remembered for his Shylock. Or if he is, he will be singularly unlucky."

Olivier too dissented from his Shylock in later years, needlessly swayed, it would seem, by the critical consensus – but the role marked the beginning of a renaissance in his fortunes, both on and off the stage. His huge personal following, ignoring the reserved reviews, returned to their old places in queues such as had not been seen outside the Old Vic since his Othello. By his sixty-third birthday that May, moreover, Olivier's popular success as Shylock had helped him at last conquer his stage fright. Before the first night he had asked Joan for tranquillizers, or he would "walk out of that stage door and get on the first bus that comes".[10] In the first few performances, he had again had to ask fellow actors to avoid looking him in the eye; thankful to have got through the first night at all, he then began to feel the old confidence surging back. It was time to enjoy his stature again, rather than fear it. This personal nightmare had lasted five-and-a-half years, from October 1964 to May 1970; its disappearance prompted Olivier to reflect: "Now I could feel free to retire from stage acting, if I wished and if funds allowed, without the personal trauma of knowing for the rest of my life that it was fear and not choice that had driven me from my personal metier." It was to take another three years for illness to make that decision for him.

In the meantime, the state was again anxious to recognize that Olivier had done it some service. It was two years since Harold Wilson had first offered him a life peerage; now the offer was renewed, with the politically powerful injection of some strong-arm persuasion from their mutual lawyer and friend Lord Goodman, chairman of the Arts Council. Sir Laurence and Lady Olivier found themselves invited to dinner at Downing Street, where Joan's neighbour, a veteran of such occasions, looked around the table and murmured to her: "Hmmm, forty. That means everyone is here for some definite reason. I wonder if you know why you are here?" They soon did, when Wilson took Olivier's elbow and said: "Look, I'm serious about this thing, you know." The Prime Minister then turned to Joan and continued: "You will see that he does it, won't you?"

Goodman's blandishments had at first fallen on stony ground. Already showered with theatrical awards and honorary degrees, Olivier had asked about other honours: a few more strings of letters after his name, perhaps, rather than so lofty a rank in front of it. Still fearing its effect on his relations with other actors, he also clung to a romantic vision of himself as a player of the "rogue and vagabond" school, a Kean rather than an Irving, a jobbing actor rather than an artist licensed and approved by the state. But Goodman had argued that other honours were merely self-indulgent ribbons and "kickshaws". He and Wilson had both urged upon Olivier the value of the chance to represent his professional constituency in the House of Lords, where he could express weighty views in public debate on behalf of the entire world of the liberal arts. Olivier was persuaded – though still, it seems, reluctantly – that it should be his duty rather than his pleasure to accept.

So the Queen's Birthday Honours List of 13 June 1970 finally announced the first ennoblement of an actor in the history of his profession. The new Baron Olivier modestly insisted via that morning's newspapers that he would still prefer to be addressed as Sir Laurence, or Sir Larry, while his wife joked that she would have to change the name on all the household accounts. Eight-year-old Richard Olivier, now suddenly The Hon. Richard, was reported to be more excited about the award of an OBE to the England goalkeeper Gordon Banks. "It shows", said his father, "a remarkably sound sense of values in the boy." In a circular letter to all members of National Theatre staff that day, Olivier solemnly announced that the first person to address him as "Your Lordship" would be fired on the spot.

"I accepted the title", he declared, "out of a sense of duty.... I shall speak in the Lords on any cause on which I can speak with authority." But the former Sir Larry was not entirely comfortable beneath his heavy ermine mantle. "The feudal days of this country are over, after all. A peerage seems to suggest a division which I don't like between myself and any other actor and the man in the street." Besides, it was the British way to mock anything strange or unusual: "An actor is a sitting duck in any case, but an actor who is a lord is a duck flying straight towards you, a figure of fun." His Lordship gloomily supposed he would "get used to the derision". Privately, that same day, he wrote to the Minister for the Arts, Baroness Lee (the former Jenny Lee, widow of Aneurin Bevan): "Joanie and I were much troubled by the idea of my accepting a peerage for quite a time, but now I think we can probably face up to it, and only hope to God we can do something of good by it."[11]

In the same Honours List Dame Sybil Thorndike was made a Companion of Honour; in an exchange of telegrams, Olivier told his oldest friend and patroness: "I can't imagine the Queen having a nicer companion."[12] In time Gielgud too would become a CH, traditionally the highest honour conferred on the British artist. But in breaking that rule, wrote Michael Billington, Olivier's unprecedented peerage symbolized the elevation of the actor in modern times to the role of "sage and prophet".

Some prophecies, however sage, do not come true. One of the first announcements to be made by Baron Olivier of Brighton, as he chose to be styled, was that he would shortly be undertaking the role of Mr Nathan

Detroit in a National Theatre production of the Damon Runyan-inspired musical *Guys and Dolls*. In the role of "good old reliable Nathan", host of "the oldest established, permanent, floating crap game in New York", he would be directed by Garson Kanin, the Broadway producer who had been best man at his wedding to Vivien.

Barely a month later, on 1 August, Olivier was back in hospital. Pleurisy, on top of another attack of bronchial pneumonia, had led this time to the discovery of a "whopping great" thrombosis in his right leg, from "mid-thigh up to the vena cava" – an after-effect, apparently, of his cancer treatment, which would haunt him for years yet. It began, in his mind, as another temporary setback, but his doctors persuaded him that he should not return to the stage for three or four months. Robert Lang took over as Shylock in *The Merchant of Venice*, which was enjoying a lucrative West End transfer at the Cambridge Theatre.

By the time he emerged from hospital in September, Olivier was weaker than he had hoped or expected. With his right leg twenty pounds heavier than his left, he was forced to announce that he would not return to the stage for a good twelve months. Never again would he play Shylock – "I really did not make much of a hit in it, anyway." For *Guys and Dolls*, scheduled to open that December, it was back to the National's drawing-board.

With the administration severely weakened by his absences, as Frank Dunlop began to concentrate on the development of the Young Vic, Olivier now proposed that Joan – an informal member, throughout the National's history, of its senior councils – should be officially upgraded to associate director. Uncertain of his own physical future, he had hatched the idea of grooming her as his successor. Lord Chandos, sensing what was afoot, disagreed strongly and openly. Others felt merely embarrassed at Olivier's uxorious empire-building, but Chandos, a friend since before the National's formation, had the unenviable task of trying to talk him out of it. Relations between them deteriorated rapidly. By November Olivier told Lord Goodman, a member of the National Theatre board, that he could not work with Chandos any more. His resignation was on the table. Goodman, ably supported by Baroness Lee, devoted an entire evening of his renowned diplomacy to talking Olivier out of anything so precipitate. "Larry says he can't work with Oliver Chandos any more," said the wily lawyer when Lee arrived to join their discussions. "Well," said the Minister for the Arts, "no one will blame him for that." A disarmed Olivier found himself "stroked and patted", and persuaded simply to "carry on as usual".

Behind the scenes, unknown to Olivier, Machiavellian wheels quickly began to grind. Chandos was to chair only one more National Theatre board meeting, after which he said to Olivier: "Well, it seems they've decided to get rid of me." Olivier had been sounded out about the notion of the financier Sir Max Rayne (now Lord Rayne) as an ally in his continuing struggle to get the new theatre built. But it was a surprise to him as much as anyone else when Rayne sat in the chairman's place at the next board meeting. Although his own relations with Chandos had soured, it was an abrupt and unworthy end to the mighty role played by the former Oliver Lyttelton in the establishment of the National Theatre. His contribution was at least to be commemorated, after his death, by the naming of one of the three auditoria of the new National Theatre in his honour.

By December Olivier felt well enough to revise his performance schedule for the following year. He would after all be returning to the stage as Shylock, the role he had said he would never play again, on 23 April, the anniversary of Shakespeare's birth (always a date of great romantic significance to Olivier, who had ensured in every year of its life so far that the National Theatre of Great Britain was performing the Bard on his birthday). Olivier would thus be acting onstage again only seven, rather than twelve, months after his last discharge from hospital.

There was method behind this apparent madness, greeted by critics with concern as Olivier admitted: "I get puffed – too puffed to do an emotional scene or a long speech. Also, in the theatre an actor needs that little something extra – adrenalin, perhaps, or heart – and just for the moment I haven't got it any more." The ever profligate Olivier had accepted another of the lucrative cameo roles which the film world was now increasingly bringing his way. His habitual guilt again uppermost, Olivier had calculated that as director of the National Theatre, and thus an employee of the British taxpayer as well as a peer of the realm, he could not in all conscience reappear before American film cameras only three months after his illness, while still delaying his return to the British stage for twelve.

Amid all the vicissitudes of the last few years, he had managed to tuck in four small but exquisite cameo performances onscreen; now he was off to Madrid, beard and all, to be the crowning glory of Sam Spiegel's latest epic, *Nicholas and Alexandra*. Given the unpredictable gap between the making of a film and its release in Britain, the likelihood is that no one would even have noticed. But there was good cause both for the guilt and its consequences: the Olivier bank balance was again in need of a boost.

It was for that same reason, while recovering from the early cancer treatments in 1967, that he had disappeared to Rome for three weeks to play the Russian premier, Kamenev, in *The Shoes of the Fisherman*, supporting his old sparring-partner from the New York *Becket*, Anthony Quinn, as a highly unlikely Russian Pope. The film was generally accounted so awful that it was not released in Britain until 1972, when one English critic said: "Olivier strolls through the part, but I suppose it pays the rent." As director of the National Theatre, the experience gave him pause. Olivier then agreed to speak the prologue and epilogue to his friend Zeffirelli's film of *Romeo and Juliet* (starring Leonard Whiting and Olivia Hussey) only on condition that neither his face be seen nor his name appear on the credits. In fact he enjoyed himself so much during the recording that he also dubbed the English voice of the Italian actor (Antonio Pierfederici) playing Montague.

That same year, still weak from his radiation treatment, Olivier turned in one of the most memorable four-minute appearances in movie history as a cartoon comic version of the bandy-legged, buffoonish Chief of the Imperial General Staff, Field Marshal Sir John French, mazurka-ing his way through Richard Attenborough's film of *Oh! What a Lovely War* (the anti-war satire first produced onstage by Joan Littlewood in 1964). Olivier agreed to take the part for £100 a day, knowing that his presence alone would give a friend and fellow actor the chance to direct. First approached before his cancer treatment, Olivier had subsequently telephoned Attenborough from his sick-bed: "Look, I don't know what I'm going to be allowed to do. I don't know whether I'm going back into the repertory. I don't know whether I'll be able to do movies. But I said I would appear in it and appear in it I will, even if it's only for three-quarters of an hour on a Sunday afternoon, walking along Brighton front."

The use of Olivier's name, apart from clinching things with his backers, also enabled Attenborough to recruit an all-star cast – including Gielgud, Richardson, Redgrave and Mills – for his directorial debut. Attenborough affectionately remembers how Olivier, during his first day on the set, stopped in mid-rehearsal and said, "Darling boy, that was just dreadful. I do apologize. I don't understand quite what you're after, so just give me some direction and I'll do it." This was said very loudly – Olivier's way of showing the whole crew that Attenborough was the boss and that even the great Laurence Olivier recognized the fact. "Without his help on that film, in all sorts of ways, I would never have gone on to make a career as a director," said Attenborough in 1985, shortly after picking up his clutch of Oscars for *Gandhi*.[13]

Then, amid Shylock, Edgar and more illness, Olivier's patriotic instincts had led him to accept £20,000 to play Sir Hugh Dowding, head of RAF Fighter Command, in Guy Hamilton's *Battle of Britain*. It was a fraction of his usual fee – three years before *Khartoum* had earned him £250,000 for eight days' work – but it was worth it as he proved the hard core of an otherwise unmemorable movie, conveying the introverted sang-froid of one of the war's unsung heroes. On a visit to the studios the habitually unemotional Dowding, then eighty-six, wept as he watched Olivier re-enact his famous confrontation with Churchill: "Our young men will just have to shoot down their young men at the rate of five to one." Olivier next relished the contrast in Delbert Mann's film of *David Copperfield*, which "came alive", in the view of the *New York Times*, only during his brief, snarling appearance as the sadistic Mr Creakle, headmaster of Salem School. He and a peg-legged Attenborough as his assistant, Mr Tungay, made "a perfect Dickensian double-act"[14] who "would have brought down the house closing the bill at the New Cross Empire".[15]

Now he was to make a similar impact in an equally fleeting screen appearance in *Nicholas and Alexandra*. Again Olivier's name had been used to attract an all-star cast; scarcely recognizable as the bearded Russian Prime Minister, Count Witte, he was said to be the only player to "pierce the pantomime by inventing details of performance that trick us into feeling for a moment". Even in dull and undistinguished films such as this, Olivier's meticulous attention to detail, and his now long experience in the minutiae of film acting, unfailingly raised him above his surroundings. The same was true of *Lady Caroline Lamb*, where another brief appearance, this time as the Duke of Wellington, sent a charge of electricity through a rambling historical romance. However fleeting, Olivier's "witty and rounded characterization", to one critic, was "worth the price of admission in itself".[16]

The clutch of cameos had begun to cause comment among the more restive members of the National Theatre board. Anxious not to appear an absentee landlord, Olivier quickly announced plans to direct Giraudoux's *Amphitryon 38* in the New Year, as well as to reappear as Shylock. During his long absence from its stage, the National Theatre company had been boosted by the arrival of Paul Scofield as an associate director, to appear in three plays. But 1970–71 turned into a desultory season. Scofield, not a company man, never settled in and left after only two of his three roles. From the doldrums the theatre began to sail into storms; that summer saw a spate of angry press attacks, typified by the headline "PANNED, PAMPERED AND HALF-EMPTY".[17] Tynan's influence on Olivier in the choice of plays came under fire. The National, its critics argued, was "afraid of presenting the obvious", so obsessed had it become with "curiosities" more suited to experimental theatres. The ensemble playing had grown weak, as the theatre had failed to attract actors of sufficient stature. Above all, it was showing a deficit of £100,000, despite increases in its grants the previous year to a total of £380,000 of public money.

The National had already taken the New Theatre for the summer, hoping to swell its revenue by doubling its output. But Tynan and Olivier again miscalculated in their choices, presenting obscure plays performed by actors unknown outside Britain, and thus failing to attract the tourist trade vital to the success of the venture. The season had to be prematurely abandoned and emergency funds begged from the Arts Council.

For the first time, Olivier's position seemed seriously threatened. Eight years since his appointment, there was still no foreseeable date for the move to the new theatre. Now it was openly rumoured that Peter Hall, whose expansion of the Royal Shakespeare Company had proved highly successful, both commercially and artistically, would soon be replacing him. Tynan, whose "highbrow" choice of plays was blamed for the failure of the New season, took it upon himself to leap to Olivier's defence. Arguing that a £50,000 loss for 1970–71 was "hardly catastrophic", he insisted:

> Our track record over the past eight years is better than that of any West End management. We have had seven really great years and now we have had a bad year. I am only surprised that the slump didn't come sooner. There is nothing wrong with the National Theatre that a couple of hits will not put right.

Olivier had to accept that his own drawing-power was still an indispensable element of the National's success. No longer, therefore, could he resist Tynan's long-standing pleas that he crown his classical career outside Shakespeare by playing the marathon part of the ageing actor James Tyrone in Eugene O'Neill's *Long Day's Journey into Night*. "Not because we want to, Kenny," he told Tynan, "but because we've *got* to." For several years Olivier had resisted the idea because he felt a fundamental reluctance to act an actor – especially an actor like Tyrone, whom it was hard not to portray as "a stereotype: vain, florid, flamboyant, affected and more than a trifle absurd". Olivier had seen Frederic March's legendary Tyrone in the original New York production of 1956 and remembered thinking that the part was not for him, containing as it did "every single trap". There were times, as he now began to discover, when the phrase "You were born to play this part" could seem cruelly double-edged.

Olivier's subsequent triumph in the role was to help prove Tynan right on both counts. Olivier *was* born to play Tyrone; and all the National *had* needed was a couple of box-office successes. When the West End success of *Long Day's Journey into Night* was swiftly followed by Michael Blakemore's revival of *The Front Page*, Jonathan Miller's ingenious *The School for Scandal* and a new play by Tom Stoppard, *Jumpers*, the panic had proved unnecessary. For the cost of one *Guys and Dolls*, the company had mounted four small-cast, one-set productions, all of them praised and lucrative. Within the year the National's £100,000 deficit had been turned into a £50,000 surplus, to the relief of its director, who had "never felt quite happy about the idea of billing the Government for one's failures". The National

Theatre was back on track – hailed, in the one compliment Olivier had always craved, as the finest stage company in the world.

His apprehensions about playing Tyrone quickly melted away in rehearsal. Strongly supported by Constance Cummings, Denis Quilley and Ronald Pickup, Olivier was surprised by how easily the enormous part "seeped in" as he learnt it behind his newspaper on the commuter train to and from Brighton. Under the highly sympathetic direction of Michael Blakemore, the cast became "as harmonious", in Quilley's description, "as a string quartet".[18]

The Australian-born Blakemore had been a spear-carrier to Olivier's Stratford Coriolanus and Titus in 1959, but since he turned director the two had had their disagreements. Olivier had resisted Tynan's pleas that the National present *A Day in the Death of Joe Egg*, the moving and autobiographical study of a family with an autistic child by Peter Nichols, with whom Blakemore had formed a professional partnership. When Blakemore did direct Nichols's next play, *The National Health*, for the National, there were a few hiccups. Olivier threw out a character overtly modelled on his friend Lord Goodman and never really liked the play; it took a semi-public argument between him and Blakemore for it to receive more evening than afternoon performances, thus coming into its own as a major artistic and commercial success. But once Blakemore had become an associate director of the National, he and Miller had come to replace Gaskill and Dexter as Olivier's "boys". In *Long Day's Journey into Night* Blakemore was shrewd enough to see that Olivier did not really require overt direction:

> I left him pretty much alone when he had the stage to himself and only really directed him in the group scenes. He had a tendency, I felt, to walk around too much on the stage, and I wish I had been sterner about that. But the interesting thing, in retrospect, is that Olivier's Tyrone was better at the beginning of the run, before he had *refined* his performance, before he got in the habit of pointing up the Big Moments. In fact, it was at its very best, I think, before he had learnt the lines, when he was just muttering experimentally through the part.[19]

Physically, Olivier was below par throughout most of the seven-week rehearsal period; at the end of each session he would have to head for his desk and a backlog of paperwork, then transform himself into Shylock in the evening. It was as well, therefore, that Blakemore urged him to rein in his Tyrone during the first three acts, giving the other three "room to act", before reaching his own explosive climax in the fourth.

O'Neill's old warhorse made for an especially hypnotic performance, even by Olivier's standards, as he set out to portray the kind of actor he had spent his whole life trying not to become. There was an overwhelming aura of defeat about his Tyrone from the very opening, after which it proceeded to burst into carefully phased explosions of life. Here was a great actor employing a vanished acting style to portray a great actor *manqué*, managing to convey the impression that this ruined ex-matinee idol had once had the makings of an American Kean. As Olivier crooned "We are such stuff as dreams are made on", in the vein of a rather hammy actor-manager of the period, he was attempting (wrote Michael Billington in the *Guardian*) "the hardest technical feat of all". He pulled it off "to perfection".

It was fitting that what would prove Olivier's last major role onstage drew some of the most ecstatic – and deserved – superlatives of his career. This, said Billington, was "a massive performance, moving from an initial nervy jocularity to a throttled red-brick despair at his wife's relapse to a thrilling, soul-baring intensity in his cups". And Irving Wardle in *The Times* wrote: "All the components of the man are there simultaneously – the tight-wad, the old pro, the distracted husband, the ragged Irish boy." There was "the sense not only that O'Neill is showing off the different sides of the character, but that Olivier is consciously manipulating them for his advantage".

The set-pieces were there, as usual: this time a nimble leap down from a table, backwards, after changing a light bulb, and an agonizing moment when Tyrone, realizing that his wife has again taken to morphine, buries his head in her bosom with a great wail of despair. It was, for Benedict Nightingale of the *New Statesman*, "one of those moments, rare in the theatre, when you feel you have intruded deeply into somebody's privacy; and the sight is so painful and your own presumption is so great that you just have to look away".

Constance Cummings, who received high praise as Tyrone's drug-addicted wife, believes she could never have managed it without Olivier, her close friend since the 1930s: "Acting with the greatest actor of the day, in one of his greatest roles, obviously raised my performance – rather like playing tennis against someone better than yourself raises your game."[20] Pickup and Quilley were both awestruck by Olivier's lead. "Unlike other actors, who are dangerous to work with," said Quilley, "Olivier maintains a dependable framework, so you don't get lost."[21] But that framework could vary excitingly:

> One night, at the moment where I rage at him for sending my brother to a cheap sanatorium, the audience gasped louder than usual at my character's audacity. Olivier noticed this and sat back, let his eyes fill with tears, then waited fully fifteen seconds before saying, "You liar," in a way that was totally different from usual. I will never forget how he *seized* that moment and milked it for all it was worth.

When Quilley took his wife Stella to Olivier's dressing-room after the first night, "the boss" was too tired to get up from his chair. During the run of *Long Day's Journey into Night*, Olivier would often fall asleep in the wings between scenes. The strain of his workload was beginning to tell more visibly. His maiden speech in the Lords that July was an embarrassment – so florid as to be at times incomprehensible. It ended:

> I believe in the theatre. I believe in it as the first glamourizer of thought. It restores dramatic dynamics and their relationships to life size. I believe that in a great city, or even in a small city or a village, a great theatre is the outward and visible sign of an inward and probable culture. I believe in the Common Market, in the Concorde, in Foulness [then the potential site for London's third airport] and in the Brighton Belle. I believe in any thing that keeps our domains, not wider still and wider, but higher still and higher in the expectancy and rose of quality and probity.[22]

As he sat down to the approving grunts of his fellow peers, Lord Olivier was unaware that Sir Max Rayne was sufficiently concerned about him to be sounding out a possible successor. Olivier was not to know for another nine months – a fact for which he never forgave Rayne – that the National Theatre's new chairman had recently invited Peter Hall to think about taking over.

Hall had handed over the Royal Shakespeare Company to Trevor Nunn four years before and accepted an appointment as co-director of the Royal Opera House, Covent Garden, with Sir Colin Davis. But the summer of 1971 saw Hall pull out of the Covent Garden job just as he was due to take it up. "It was nobody's fault but my own," he said. "I had not been right to accept it.... I had miscalculated the possibilities."[23] Soon after he was invited to lunch at Lord Goodman's flat, where Rayne told him that Olivier's health was "very uncertain" and that "there was a feeling that he was finding it difficult to continue as director". Rayne went on that Olivier had "indicated, though vaguely, that he was thinking of stepping down". Would Hall, he asked, consider succeeding him?

The sequence of events begun by Rayne that day has become the source of much misunderstanding and resentment, some of which lingers to this day. Hall insists that his immediate response was that he would be happy to enter into discussions only if Olivier really intended to resign and were himself involved in those discussions. He was asked to do and say nothing for the time being because the situation was "unclear.... Olivier was saying he was going one day and thinking of staying the next." That is how things were left, says Hall, for the next nine months.

That same summer Olivier's morale reached another low ebb with the unilateral cancellation by the board of his beloved *Guys and Dolls*. The musical arrangements and designs had been ready; Geraldine McEwan (Miss Adelaide), Robert Lang (Nicely-Nicely Johnson) and Dennis Quilley (Sky Masterson) had been taking singing and dancing lessons; the production was all but ready for take-off. "I'd love to have played Adelaide to his Nathan Detroit," said Geraldine McEwan, one of the few rehearsal eyewitnesses to Olivier's Detroit-in-the-making. "It was so sort of tired and casual and laid-back. Oh, I don't know, it was very shrugged off, the way he played it. He would have been wonderful." Olivier could never bring himself to see the subsequent National Theatre version (a huge success staged by the eventual third director of the National, Richard Eyre). He remained too bitter about another supposed conspiracy, which seems to have been hatched only in his battle-scarred imagination. Olivier believed then, and still does, that the cancellation was an act of "treachery" on the part of his supposed friend "Binkie" Beaumont, who was said to have argued for a more overtly commercial musical like *Oklahoma!*. But in truth it was Olivier's own ill-health which had forced the issue, against a background of continuing cost reductions. In his diary that day, 21 June 1971, a gloomy National Theatre director secretly recorded: "Gs & Ds cancelled after twice laid on – decided not to stay much longer – 9th year."

During the next six months, in the apparent belief that the succession was in his gift, Olivier became something of an unguided missile. He was determined that the National should continue to be run by an actor rather than a director. If it could not be Joan – as even he now accepted – then who else? Richard Attenborough and Richard Burton were among those to whom he said: "I want you to succeed me."[24] But it was not until 2 February 1972 that Olivier formally told Rayne that he was thinking of phasing himself out. On that occasion, he proposed Michael Blakemore as his heir – an actor-turned-director, popular with the company and provenly successful. It was a clever compromise, but Rayne immediately made it clear that he did not consider Blakemore a figure of "sufficient stature". A week later they met again and discussed Olivier's alternative suggestion of a "regency council" to include, among others, Joan and Tynan. Then, six weeks later, on Friday 24 March, Rayne informed Olivier of the board's decision that he was to be replaced by Peter Hall.

Once Hall had been formally offered the job, he had begun to discuss terms. It was at this stage that he consulted his agent and friend Laurence Evans, who was also Olivier's agent and friend. When Hall told him over lunch that he had been "offered the National", Evans found himself in a difficult ethical position. He was appalled that Olivier knew nothing of the secret negotiations and immediately telephoned Beaumont with the ultimatum: "If you don't tell Larry within the next ten days, I will."[25]

Rayne's news came to Olivier as "a bit of a shock. . . . I had expected to be consulted and had, indeed, requested to be; after ten years' hard labour one might feel it was almost an obligatory courtesy." He bore no hard feelings, he says, towards Hall, who apologized that he had been sworn to secrecy. They met for four hours on the Monday morning, when Hall formed the impression that Olivier was "clearly upset" and his feelings "very ambiguous". One day he wanted to retire; the next day he did not. "Larry still has heroic energy, but he strays from the subject, forgets names, muddles up attitudes. You have the impression of a great and splendid animal constantly being deflected by the fight with some stronger power."[26]

Over the following agonized weeks, as Rayne and his board felt they were leaning over backwards to indulge his *amour propre*, Olivier himself became increasingly bitter about their failure to consult him in the choice of Hall. To friends he began to talk of it as a "betrayal" – a word he still uses to this day. At the time, a series of very awkward meetings resulted in an agreement that his present contract, due to expire in July 1973, would be extended until the move to the South Bank at the end (as then hoped) of that year.[27] Hall would come aboard in the summer for a six-month "transition" period. Rayne, meanwhile, pressed Olivier to remain an associate director of the National and accept the title of President for Life.

By 12 April the news had inevitably leaked. Olivier called a meeting of the company in the Old Vic rehearsal rooms and assured them that there was no truth in rumours that he would be leaving before they moved to the new theatre. Next day the board issued a statement in his support, but in less than a week Hall's appointment was formally announced. At a Windsor Castle reception for the Queen of The Netherlands that evening, Olivier bumped into Attenborough, who recalls: "I've never seen him so shattered. He gave me no details of his betrayal by the board, nor has he ever since. All he said that night was: 'I just hope I don't run into one of those buggers.' "[28]

Olivier had recently contracted to narrate *A World at War*, the marathon ITV series then being produced for London Weekend Television by Jeremy Isaacs (later to become the founder-controller of Channel 4 and general director of the Royal Opera House, Covent Garden). Isaacs thought he had hired "the greatest living actor" to voice-over his remarkable documentary series, but when a weary Olivier arrived to dub the first episode, *The Fall of France*, he was horrified. "He did it appallingly badly. I very rarely lose sleep, but I lost a lot that night."[29] Olivier was so tired that he was almost inaudible. "When I played it back to him next day, he agreed it was awful and offered to do it again." The next thing Isaacs knew, Olivier was trying to get out of the contract. "His agent came to see me and said, 'Why don't you try telling him how wonderful he is?' I felt shocked, but I tried it, and it seemed to work."

The twenty-six episodes took eighteen weeks to dub, but the finished product had Olivier speaking with authority and clarity. "He has a great voice," said Isaacs, "which can do fantastic virtuoso things. He desperately wanted the prose more purple-y, and we steadfastly refused to make it so. But he worked amazingly hard and would rather redo lines innumerable times than permit a mediocre take to go through." In the end Olivier's name as much as his voice was the commercial making of the series. "What we paid him was worth it to us many times over in terms of his pull, especially in the United States, where the series was advertised with his name and picture prominently displayed."

As the building of the new National Theatre continued to drag further and further behind schedule, there was soon no hope of moving in before early 1975. Peter Hall's diary records an interminable catalogue of inconsistency on Olivier's part. The associate directors' meetings became a battleground in which an unpredictable Olivier would either assert his lingering authority or bow obsequiously to Hall's long-term plans. Still it remained unclear quite when he would leave, and whether he would really let Hall run the place after he had. After many changes of heart and mind, it was eventually agreed, at Olivier's own wish, that Hall should join him as an equal co-director of the National Theatre – his name would even appear first, in strict alphabetical order, on the new notepaper – in April 1973.

Olivier announced the news himself, burying Hall's new role beneath the sombre fact of his own resignation, at a tense news conference on 13 March. Approaching his sixty-sixth birthday, and seated beside a successor a quarter of a century younger, Olivier in his dark suit and club tie was described as looking "very much the businessman, but not one about to retire". May saw him climb to the roof of the new building for its "topping-out" ceremony; Olivier's genial flourish of a symbolic trowel, to smooth the last corner of exterior cement, belied the continuing emptiness of the shell beneath. By 31 October Hall was at last able to enter in his diary: "Tomorrow I ascend the throne."

Olivier's reign as absolute monarch had lasted just over ten years. He had not, contrary to some subsequent reports, hogged the show while director of the National Theatre. Of the seventy-nine productions mounted in his regime (roughly half of which could be counted critical and box-office successes, compared with a ratio of about one in twelve in the commercial theatre), Olivier had acted in eleven and directed only eight. "It's not that I did it all," he said when the new National Theatre opened without him, "but perhaps without me it wouldn't be there." Olivier has made it quite clear, however, that he would not wish posterity to regard

423

Denys Lasdun's South Bank edifice as his monument. He would prefer to be remembered as an actor.

His last night as director of the National Theatre saw Olivier open in the small part of Antonio, the dotty old grandfather in Eduardo de Filippo's *Saturday, Sunday, Monday*. Persuaded by Tynan of the charms of de Filippo's work, Olivier had persuaded Zeffirelli to direct this most "Chekhovian" of his fellow Italian's plays, really as a vehicle for Joan. He had then persuaded Hall to transfer it to the West End, thus earning them all a handsome bonus to their meagre National Theatre salaries.

Before his resignation was announced, Olivier and Joan had agonized for some time over the choice of the final role he would play for the National Theatre. There was a temptation to choose something symbolic – again there was a public demand for his Lear – to set the final seal on this climactic period of his life's work in the theatre. But it was Joan who confirmed his own instinct to go for the unexpected: "If you do something as predictable as Lear, I really don't think I shall ever speak to you again. Do something modern, for heaven's sake." It so happened that Dexter, now back in the fold, had been trying for some time to interest Olivier in the part of an ageing Trotskyite politician, John Tagg, in *The Party*, a heavy political tract by the left-wing dramatist Trevor Griffiths. It was not the leading role, but it was a powerful and controversial one, said to be based on the then leader of the Workers' Revolutionary Party, Gerry Healy. It climaxed, moreover, in a virtuoso soliloquy lasting fully twenty minutes (which was to take Olivier four months to learn). He had been further attracted to the role by the challenge of mastering a Glaswegian accent for the first time in his career.

Proud that he was ending his days at the Old Vic by giving a young contemporary a showcase, Olivier was delighted when Harold Hobson found in Griffiths's work a *gravitas* "worthy of Bernard Shaw". After a three-month run in the repertoire it closed on Thursday, 21 March 1974. At the end of the performance, as Olivier took his umpteenth bow, Peter Hall materialized beside him onstage. "What the hell are *you* doing here?" hissed Olivier, before realizing that Hall proposed to mark the occasion of his farewell performance with a presentation and a speech. The new director voiced his delight that his predecessor's work for the National Theatre would continue the following month, when Olivier would be directing his wife in J. B. Priestley's *Eden End*. Olivier then knelt down and kissed the stage.

Hall had laid on a party of bigwigs upstairs, but neither Olivier nor the rest of the cast bothered to go. Instead there developed an impromptu knees-up backstage, at which Olivier was on his most relaxed and beguiling form, tripping through some Archie Rice routines with Denis Quilley at the piano. Gradually the happy throng grew tinged with sadness, as the suspicion grew that they might have just witnessed Olivier's last performance for the National Theatre, his last at the Old Vic.

It was, in fact, to prove his last performance on any stage anywhere. That night, unknown to himself or anyone else, Laurence Olivier had trodden the boards for the last time.

CHAPTER 24

1973–83

E arly in *Saturday Night Fever*, the major box-office movie of 1978, one of John Travolta's would-be dance partners is trying to impress him over a desultory hamburger. She works, she tells him, as receptionist in a Manhattan theatrical agency. He is unimpressed. She meets famous people all the time. He remains unimpressed.

"Hey," she squeals, "you know who came in the office today?"

Travolta, without looking up from his hamburger, asks, "Who?"

"Laurence Olivier."

"Who?"

"Laurence *O-liv-i-er!*"

"Who's that?"

"Who's Laurence Olivier? You don't know who he is? He's just the greatest actor in the whole world, that's who. Oh, *come on.* You know, the guy on television, the one who did the Polaroid commercials."

"Oh yeah, him. He's good. Maybe he could get you a free camera?"

To the consternation of his global following, Olivier appears to have spent his twilight years bequeathing posterity ample evidence that he was a rather hammy B-movie actor unashamed of accepting any role, however unworthy, if the money was right. How come Olivier, of all people, is known to the generation taking over his profession as the guy who did the camera ads?

Not until his sixties did Baron Olivier, for the first time in his life, discover the delights of becoming a family man. After two failed marriages and an obsessively busy career, he was a grandfather before he gave himself time to savour the joys of fatherhood. They opened up a new and softer side of an always sentimental man, a man now craving respite from increasingly public pressures.

As his bouts of illness continued, Olivier increasingly felt he must make provision for his children. Though always a high earner, he had also been a big spender; he had enjoyed a life of such profligate style that money had somehow never accumulated. But he also had a compulsion to keep working; work, he would say, was the only thing which could keep him alive. March 1973 saw the theatre lights of Shaftesbury Avenue darkened to mark the passing of two of his oldest friends, Noël Coward and "Binkie" Beaumont; since Vivien's death six years before, Michel Saint-Denis, Stephen Arlen, Lord Chandos and Max Adrian were among many others close to Olivier whose deaths had begun to turn his life into a procession of memorial services. He was determined that it was not going to happen to him for a good while yet. The fifteen years between his departure from the National and his eightieth birthday in 1987 were to bear eloquent witness to Olivier's boundless lust for life.

They were also to see a remarkable Indian summer in the working life of a "jobbing actor" now confined by declining health to what he witheringly called "the mechanical media". Those first few cameo film roles in his last years at the National Theatre, though they had literally taken only a few days each, proved the dawn of yet another Olivier career, cornering a market in television and movie parts – some more worthy than others – in which to take a little lucrative exercise each year. "I think you've become one of the stately homes of England," Tynan told him. "You're hired for those two-week cameo-performances to give the film some class – the way they hire the exterior of a castle in Scotland." Somewhat stung by the remark, for all its flattering truth that he was fast becoming some sort of national institution, Olivier now found the perfect rebuttal. Before giving way to the inevitable, and dedicating himself to the fine art of stealing pictures with the briefest of appearances, he was determined to accomplish one last major screen role. Not since *The Prince and the Showgirl* nearly twenty years before had Olivier played the leading role in a film; not since leaving Hollywood in 1941 had he had an undisputed success in one, outside the classics. Now in his last year as director of the National Theatre, along came the perfect opportunity in the screen version of ·*Sleuth*, a hit West End whodunnit by Peter Shaffer's competitive twin brother Anthony. On the rebound from the news of Hall's appointment, Olivier asked the board's permission for a fourteen-week leave of absence.

Sleuth's sleight of hand began with the opening credits. Although six actors were listed (one of them, Margo Channing, being the character played by Bette Davis in *All About Eve*), it was really a two-man film. Michael Caine, though an established star since he was twenty-nine, was awed to find himself co-starring with Olivier. Only Caine's availability had won him the part against such competition as Alan Bates and Albert Finney, on a list of acceptable co-stars Olivier had compiled at the request of the director, Joseph L. Mankiewicz. And yet if anyone was *not* going to be awed – was, in fact, going to give Olivier, *mano a mano*, the professional fight of his life – it was the confident Cockney born Maurice Micklewhite: "With Olivier, I can't lose. If I'm not as good as he is, nobody will be surprised. If I give him a run for his money, people will say, 'Fancy Michael Caine doing *that*!' "

Caine, who had never met Olivier, was wondering how to address a co-star who happened to be a peer of the realm, when a week before filming he received a handwritten note:

Dear Mr Caine,
It suddenly occurred to me you might be wondering how to address me, as I have a title. I think the first time we meet we should introduce ourselves by our own titles, so you would be Mr Caine and I would be Lord Olivier. One minute after that, I shall call you Michael and you will call me Larry, and that's how I hope it will remain for ever.[1]

And so it did, though the competition on the set at Pinewood was as fierce as that between the two characters they were playing: Andrew Wyke (Olivier), a famous writer of detective novels, who discovers that his young neighbour Milo Tindle (Caine) is having an affair with his wife (supposedly played by Margo Channing, though she never appears in the film, it being no coincidence that Mankiewicz also directed *All About Eve*). Intent on revenge, Wyke manœuvres Tindle into playing an elaborate and deadly game.

"Out of nowhere", said Caine, "came this whirlwind." Though priding himself that he was in better movie fettle than Olivier, Caine learnt what it was to be up against an actor of such vast accumulated experience.

Once you start acting with him you'd better watch out, because he is completely and utterly merciless.... It's like you're sitting there, and suddenly there's this tornado of acting comes straight at you. And you go "Jesus Christ, what am I going to do with this?", and you just stand there dumbfounded, and you just look at him, and you just see him standing there, and they say "Cut", and then you just see this look in his eyes, which is sort of manic, and you say "Oh, Christ, I hope he doesn't do that again today. I can't take two of those!"

At such moments Caine felt like "a pavement artist – throw a couple of pennies down – whereas Larry is a bit like Leonardo da Vinci saying,

'We'll now do the Mona Lisa again for you in case you didn't see it the first time.'"

The theatrical character of Wyke gave Olivier the chance to indulge in a whole range of wild impersonations, from Fu Manchu via a Western sheriff to a Cockney charlady; he would threaten to steal scenes from Caine even with his back turned, whether fixing a snack of caviar or chalking a snooker cue. In *Sleuth* Olivier was able to demonstrate his mastery of this once "anaemic" medium with a bewilderingly virtuoso sequence of moods: now waspish and aggressive, now sulky and defensive, he displayed a mercurial energy which belied his real physical state. Once he had glued on an arrogant little moustache, which Caine would see lying on his dressing-room table "like a caterpillar" between takes, Olivier *turned into* Wyke in a way Caine had never before encountered in a film actor. But Caine managed to give almost as good as he got; it was an intense experience, which forged an unlikely friendship. "I've had trees from him", says Caine, "and flowers, beautiful orchids when my baby was born."

Sleuth was important to both of them. It enhanced Caine's stature immensely and re-established Olivier, after his long absence running the National, as a leading film actor. Both won rave reviews and both were nominated for that year's Oscar for Best Actor, surely the only time the entire cast of a film has been. They lost out to Marlon Brando in *The Godfather* – this was the year Brando chose not to turn up to collect his prize – but Wyke won Olivier the next best thing, the New York film critics' Best Actor award.

During the filming of *Sleuth* Olivier found himself astonished not only that Caine had demanded a television in his dressing-room, but that he was able to watch Wimbledon between takes, rather than going over his lines for the next scene. When not watching Evonne Goolagong, or drinking each other under the table (strictly in the evenings, once the day's work was done), the two talked about money. Says Caine:

> I told him to stay in movies and make a packet.... I said, "All you've got out of it all is a Lordship. I've got several million dollars." He said, "Do you really think so? Do you think I should make pictures and earn a lot of money?" I said, "Of course you should, go out and do it, they can't take the Lordship away from you...." I planted the seeds of avarice in him.

Before he left the National, Olivier tucked in a quick film record of his Shylock, again directed by Jonathan Miller, for television and posterity. But once he was a free agent, Olivier used the daunting scale of Britain's private education fees as an excuse to act (if that is the right word) on Michael Caine's advice. As Joan returned to Chichester for the season, he paused at Pinewood for six weeks to film *Love Among the Ruins*, with his old friends Katharine Hepburn and George Cukor, for American television. The part of Sir Arthur Granville-Jones, the elderly barrister who re-encounters the love of his youth, afforded him an easy chance for some winsome wistfulness. Then, greedy and unashamed, he plunged into that $1 million Polaroid commercial.

Guilt, as always, guided Olivier's hand. He had in his time turned down so many commercials that he knew he must now have his excuses ready – for his own benefit as much as anyone else's. Before accepting the commission, Olivier went to great lengths to assure himself of the product's quality and reliability; it was a "remarkably clever camera" invented by "that brilliant engineer, Dr [Edwin] Land". After making the commercial, moreover, he felt reluctantly compelled to exclude the British Isles from seeing or hearing him recommend a product he felt free to plug regularly all over the United States and Europe. While these countries would surely sympathize with "a fellow who needed a buck", his fellow countrymen appeared to believe that "people who like to think of themselves as artists . . . seem to cheapen themselves by advertising some commodity". Had not Sir Alec Guinness, after all, reputedly turned down a similarly astronomical sum for the simple task of saying the five words "Guinness is good for you"?

"Commercial? What commercial?" Olivier was to ask in later years, a faintly discernible twinkle in his eye, when asked in Britain about the Polaroid advertisement. Those privileged enough to see it in the United States were treated to a typically suave performance, filmed while he was on holiday in France. Apparently in his dressing-room, Olivier greeted the viewer: "You are about to see a magnificent performance." Wielding the camera, he continued: "The cast of characters: a simple bowl of fruit and Polaroid's new SX-70. Just touch the button" – he did so – "and it hands you a picture. Minutes later" – cut to evidence to prove it – "you have a finished photograph of dazzling beauty." The deed was done. Olivier's name, at his own request, did not appear on the screen to identify him. It was assumed that all Americans (apart, perhaps, from John Travolta) would know who he was. As a Polaroid executive put it: "We couldn't really have him stand there and say, 'Hi! I'm Laurence Olivier!'"

The British "Oscar" Olivier had received for *Oh! What A Lovely War* came in handy in June 1973, when he disturbed an intruder on returning home from a three-week summer break at Steyning. Suitcase in one hand, drink in the other, he was brutally coshed as he entered his library. Seizing the statuette in self-defence, he bellowed in his best epic-heroic vein: "You come back here and stand your ground, Sir." But the burglar (their second in three months) was too fast for him. In the kitchen the rest of the Olivier family took a few minutes to register his cries for help. "Wasn't that Daddy shouting?'' Joan asked the children. "Oh no, Mummy," said ten-year-old Tamsin, "*Hamlet*'s on the telly tonight and you know how he roars and screams in that." Badly bleeding about the face, Olivier needed urgent hospital treatment; the following year, after discomfort in one eye, he discovered that the blow had permanently damaged his sight and was prescribed a course of eyedrops which he is still obliged to use daily. "That", as he puts it bitterly, "is the charming little visiting-card our uninvited young guest left with me."

After directing Joan in *Eden End*, Olivier had no immediate plans for the first time in his professional life. Supposedly embarking on a year's sabbatical, he took his family on a prolonged summer break as the guests of Zeffirelli at his encampment near Positano: "I must get to know my children. I am a besotted father, but I have not been doing my bit." Diving from the Italian rocks one day, Olivier saw – almost too late – one of those children swimming by beneath him. Somehow he managed to swerve in mid-air, missing the child but jarring his back painfully. As the vacation wore on, the pain persisted, then began to spread through his neck and shoulders, arms and hips.

Back home, Olivier's osteopath attributed it all to the mid-air swerve. But new and curious symptoms soon began to follow: a dryness of the skin, a swelling of the face, a deadening of the whites of the eyes, a soreness around the edges of the fingernails. After vain visits to doctors, dentists, oculists and skin specialists, Olivier was examined by a Sussex consultant, Dr Joanna Sheldon, who diagnosed a rare and potentially serious complaint called dermato-poly-myocitis, inflammation of the skin and muscles. He must prepare himself for at least six months in the Royal Sussex Hospital.

Olivier abandoned the one project he had on the stocks: a production of Verdi's *Macbeth* for the Metropolitan Opera, New York – a missed opportunity much lamented thereafter, combining as it did his lifelong love of music with his vast theatrical expertise. But he had quickly succumbed to a devastating side-effect of his initial course of steroids. It drove him "out of my mind. . . . It was an appalling feeling, as if there was something right through my face and head turning at a steady pace round and round, about on a level with my right eye from front to back, churning like a wheel."

Once the dosage was reduced, the hallucinations mercifully vanished. But Olivier was in very poor shape. He gradually lost the use of every muscle in his body; at one point even the bell for the nurse was beyond the strength of his thumb. With tubes "everywhere", he received a procession of distinguished visitors – come, as they all believed, to bid him farewell. "He looked awful," said Sir John Mills. "I was sure he was going to die. I was convinced he thought so himself, because he asked me and my wife about ourselves – something he never usually did."[2] Sir Richard Attenborough, too, assumed that he would never see Olivier again. When Ralph Richardson came to call, said Olivier, "he contrived to treat me with such ultra-calm, as if nothing in the least was out of the ordinary, that I was confirmed in my suspicion that my condition was critical in the extreme".

After eight weeks' flirtation with his Maker, however, Olivier astonished his doctors, his family and his friends by recovering sufficiently to begin a course of physiotherapy. Drained of all strength, unable to lift either arm or leg, he had to relearn every basic physical movement one by one, even breathing, talking and voice projection – almost as if he had been reborn within an elderly adult frame. It was weeks before he was able to stand, but sheer determination soon had him entertaining hospital staff with knee-bends and balancing acts on either leg. On Christmas Day he was allowed a brief visit home; by February 1975, after six months in hospital, he was finally discharged – only to contract every ailment available, from colds and 'flu via the extraction of a wisdom tooth to a quinsy on the back of his tongue, which swelled up against his soft palate "so that again I thought I was in for the definitely not-to-be-chosen death by asphyxiation".

He was beginning to feel his way back into the world, pottering about the Brighton seafront, reflecting upon a habitual phrase of Tyrone Guthrie's – he had been "spared" – when the offer of a return to work came from his long-time friend and supporter, the film director John Schlesinger. Although he was a member of Hall's new regime at the National Theatre, along with the playwright Harold Pinter and the designer John Bury, Schlesinger had long been on mutually respectful nodding terms with Olivier. Now he sent him a copy of William Goldman's screenplay of his own novel, *Marathon Man*, the menacing saga of Dr Christian Szell, a fugitive Nazi who emerges from hiding in South America to retrieve a hoard of diamonds in New York, the legacy of his wartime concentration camp victims. Olivier was excited by the part, which centred around Szell's persecution and hideous torture-by-dentistry of the one civilian getting in his way, Babe Levy, to be played by Dustin Hoffman.

After Olivier's initial expression of interest, a delighted Schlesinger invited him to his London home to discuss the project. But when he answered his front door, the director was utterly cast down. Olivier still seemed very ill. While keen to play the part he looked very tired, complaining that only one side of his face was working, and refusing the elaborate meal Schlesinger had prepared. Over a meagre bowl of soup Olivier enthused about the script, but Schlesinger remained guarded.

Would Olivier, to put it bluntly, pass the medical demanded by the studio for insurance purposes?[3]

To his own amazement as much as anyone else's, he did. But Olivier, accustomed to working from strength, was not at home within a lamentably weakened frame. He accepted a warm-up role before *Marathon Man* – "just for the practice" – and proved his fitness by effortlessly stealing *The Seven Per Cent Solution* from its supposed stars Nicol Williamson (Sherlock Holmes) and Robert Duvall (Dr Watson). As Nicholas Meyer's highly original version of Holmes's arch-enemy, Moriarty, whom he presented as a doddering, timid old mathematics professor, Olivier's outrageously witty performance proved in a few brief moments onscreen that his illness had eroded none of his technical sorcery. "The ace in this poorly shuffled deck" was, for *Time* magazine, "no surprise, Laurence Olivier. He has not often done comedy onscreen, but his extravagantly funny Moriarty is a creation of wit and invention."

When he arrived in New York, nevertheless, to make his first film in America for sixteen years, Olivier was still very frail. His hands were bandaged to conceal the swelling and disfigured skin which were the legacy of his last, emaciating illness. No one on the set of *Marathon Man* dared to suggest that it was time to have his head shaved – which the script and the part demanded – until he mentioned it himself. But he was robust enough, it seemed, to risk a joke against the Method School. When Hoffman arrived on the set, announcing that he had not slept for two days and nights to "get into" his drawn and dishevelled role, Olivier said: "My dear boy, you look awful. Why don't you try *acting*?" Then occurred an episode which has passed into contemporary Hollywood folklore.

Olivier and Hoffman, under Schlesinger's supervision, were still at the rehearsal stages of the film's climactic scene, where Hoffman's character, with a gun to Olivier's ribs, forces him into Central Park to extract his final revenge. The actual filming was weeks away, but Hoffman, intent on Method-style verisimilitude, was keen to improvise. When Olivier at first politely demurred, Hoffman brashly insisted. After a glance at Schlesinger as referee, Olivier had to muster all his professionalism to agree to something he neither believed in nor felt up to. "Okay, get going," said Hoffman, and they began to walk around the rehearsal hall.

Olivier attempted an ad-lib, but it simply was not his style. Could someone, he asked, give him his lines? "Don't worry," cried Hoffman, "you're doing great, just say anything, come on, we're getting somewhere." On they walked and walked, until Olivier's ankles began to swell. Further onward they walked, as Schlesinger watched in tense silence – all too aware that it was Hoffman he must humour, his brash and expensive star, much more than the sick, suffering, but consummately professional first lord of the English theatre. On they walked and ad-libbed until Olivier's ankles visibly bulged. "Part of it", says Goldman, who watched helpless, "was Hoffman's need to put himself on at least an equal footing with this sick old man." As Olivier refused to admit defeat, an exhilarated Hoffman drove him to the point of collapse. The spectacle pained everyone in the room and quickly became a talking-point in the industry. "It was disgusting," said Charlton Heston, then president of the Academy of Motion Picture Arts and Sciences, one of many actors appalled by Hoffman's behaviour. The strength of Heston's remarks to the author reflect the film world's feelings about Hoffman's "arrogance" towards Olivier: "It was obscene, revolting. I and some others might accept direction from Hoffman, but not Larry Olivier. Hoffman had no business telling Olivier how to do his job."[4]

Olivier himself was less concerned with Hoffman than with Charles Laughton. Fifteen years before, during their rivalry on *Spartacus*, Laughton had told him: "If you really want to do the heavies, do them well. They will pay you much more than if you make them sympathetic." It was good advice to the man who had made Richard III almost lovable. Olivier had mixed feelings about playing so unremittingly monstrous and sadistic a character as this Nazi dentist: "The best villains, I think, are the ones that are amusing. I really don't mind what I play, but this villain is really horrific. They tell me that's the fashion."

He seized the opportunity with all the considerable relish still at his command. Though filmed against enormous physical odds, Olivier's Szell has now become one of the cult movie portraits of recent years, mentioned in hushed tones even by the many who have never been able to watch the scene where he drills into one of Hoffman's dental nerves. Sick as he was throughout filming, walking with difficulty, visibly stumbling in a scene where he is pursued through the streets of Manhattan, Olivier demonstrated, for *Newsweek*, that "a great actor is the sculptor of his self, turning his body into a sign, a symbol and a force that jolts us into a higher consciousness". To another American film writer this was "one of the great screen performances of all time".[5] A monster "worthy of appearance in our own nightmares", he was "a giant presence – totally the man he plays, nothing of the actor – in a perfectly calibrated, cosmic performance that illustrates the banality of evil".

Marathon Man won Olivier yet another Oscar nomination, his ninth, though his first in the category of Supporting Actor; this time he lost out, ironically enough, to another Hoffman co-star, Jason Robards (for his portrayal of Benjamin Bradlee, editor of the *Washington Post*, in the Watergate movie *All the President's Men*). Olivier's pleasure at being back in the saddle, though it had sapped his energies more than he admitted, led him straight on to a powerful cameo for his old friends Zeffirelli and Lord (Lew) Grade in the television epic *Jesus of Nazareth*. The capacity of film and programme makers to devise a short appearance powerful enough to tempt Olivier, yet important enough to their production to make their huge investment worthwhile, was becoming amazing. Though the obvious attraction to him, as his stamina diminished, was a large amount of money for a few days' work, his lifetime's accumulated expertise made every fleeting glimpse memorable. As Nicodemus lamenting the sight of the crucified Christ (Robert Powell), Olivier spoke barely a hundred words at the end of a six-and-a-half-hour epic, but still he managed to hog the reviews, still he could reassure himself that he had done nothing to harm his stature or reputation. After one more such film appearance – another favour for Attenborough – he was to embark on a series of mistaken artistic decisions. Was it any coincidence, asked Olivier loyalists, that they followed the pain of watching Peter Hall open the National Theatre, the monolith on the south bank of the Thames which had so haunted his last fifteen years?

A Bridge Too Far was another of those latter-day epics which boasted Olivier as the lodestar of a glittering firmament which could never have been assembled without his presence. As the cream of American screen acting joined forces with their British counterparts to re-enact the disaster of Arnhem, Olivier's brief arrival in their midst as a heroic Dutch doctor seemed to inspire them all. It was Attenborough at his most ambitious, thinking and filming on the grand scale, but for once nearly all of these proud international superstars managed to disappear beneath the identity of the courageous men and women they were playing. Robert Redford, Ryan O'Neill, James Caan and Elliott Gould from the US; Dirk Bogarde, Michael Caine, Sean Connery, Anthony Hopkins and Edward Fox from the UK; Hardy Kruger, Maximilian Schell and Liv Ullmann from elsewhere in Europe: all combined, under Attenborough's grand design, to confound critical cynicism by producing a huge celluloid canvas for once generally agreed to be worthy of its subject.

Olivier's Dr Spaander, tirelessly helping Ullmann treat the wounded and wandering through the rubble of the devastated, innocent Dutch village, provided the film with its unspoken moral coda. Only his magisterial restraint could convey the doctor's simple dignity, an implicit rebuke to the absurdity of warfare. "Larry was a god to me, and still is," said an unashamedly emotional Attenborough, recalling Olivier's arrival on location: "He turned up in an old blue suit and battered old shoes, which he announced he was going to wear during filming. 'I've been gardening in these shoes for a month,' he declared gleefully, 'and all for you, Dickie. Well, this fellow's a country doctor, isn't he?'"[6]

In December 1976 Peter Hall took Jenny, his seventeen-year-old daughter by his first wife, Leslie Caron, to see *Marathon Man*. Jenny found the sense of menace so overwhelming that she wanted to leave after twenty minutes. But they stuck it out; Hall found the theatricality of Olivier's "demon king" a welcome *leitmotif* amid the chilling reality of the other performances. It was exactly a year since the film had been made, and Hall was amazed to see Olivier sustaining so powerful a performance, however "theatrical". Only a few months before he had left to make it, on 1 August 1975, Hall had been shocked by his condition when they met at Roebuck House, Victoria, where Olivier then had an apartment. "The scale of him seems to have been pressed, reduced," Hall noted in his diary. "The strong physical presence seems to have gone."[7] Olivier told Hall of his muscular illness: how he could not keep even his eyelids open, how he had had to learn every basic bodily function anew. Even now, as he told of his fears when crossing the road, the famous voice was abnormally high-pitched, almost shrill.

The meeting amounted to something of a *rapprochement*. They had not worked together since Olivier's production of *Eden End*, after which Hall had presented him with a silver replica of the auditorium to be named after him in the new National Theatre. But since Hall's take-over of the National, Olivier had used his associate directorship to become something of a thorn in his successor's side. Hall still bore immense admiration for Olivier and sympathized with his reluctance to surrender the theatre he had created. But Olivier's inconsistencies, the failure to turn up to functions, the policy disagreements at associates' meetings had all tried Hall's patience. Olivier had gleefully played devil's advocate in the protracted but vain agonies over whether Hall's National should merge with Nunn's RSC. He had made several promises he had failed to keep, and even refused a request from the Harold Wilsons that he accompany them to the National's *The Front Page*. Hall was privately relieved when Olivier confirmed that morning that he would be retiring as an associate when his contract expired that autumn. "But", said Hall, "you must somehow take part in the opening of the new theatre next year."

Since 1972 they had been discussing Prospero and Lear. Olivier had hesitated so long over the former that Hall eventually directed Gielgud in the role. But Lear had remained off limits to other actors; it was Olivier's whenever he decided he wanted it. Now it became clear, for the first time, that Olivier had realized he would never act onstage again. The energy just was not there any more. It was a poignant moment when he told Hall: "I know there would be disappointment if I didn't act in the new theatre, but I would sooner that than have people disappointed if I did."

Hall urged him to accept the presidency, and they parted on a promise that Olivier would think about it. One day that October Olivier appeared unexpectedly in Hall's office; he had asked Denys Lasdun to give him a tour of the new building. "It must have taken great courage on Larry's part", said Hall, "to come and see everybody after a year, his appearance so different, feeling so frail, and being the man outside this wonderful place that he had created." But it was not long before Olivier was again giving Hall a difficult time.

In February 1976, Olivier was embarrassingly conspicuous by his absence from the National's last night at the Old Vic, even though it consisted of a tribute to his beloved Lilian Baylis. By May, he had upset both Gielgud and Richardson, then appearing at the National together in Pinter's *No Man's Land*, by going backstage to tell them he could not hear a word either said and had fallen asleep; Hall, of course, bore the brunt of Gielgud's wounded protests. Peter Shaffer then told Hall that Olivier had been rubbishing him over dinner in New York. So it came as no surprise two months later when Olivier declined to speak the prologue to Hall's production of *Tamburlaine*, to mark the opening of the 1,160-seat Olivier Theatre – the largest of the new National's three auditoria and the last to be ready.

The official opening of the new National Theatre of Great Britain by the Queen was now set for 25 October 1976. With two months to go, Olivier was still dismissing Hall's enthusiasm for *Tamburlaine* (which eventually went ahead with Albert Finney in the title role). Outlandishly, Olivier suggested a ball instead of a play for the royal evening, with a dance orchestra on the stage. Or, if there had to be live theatre, why not revivals of single acts from some of the productions of *his* regime? So saying, Hall noted, Olivier "left to catch a train to Manchester, and we all ruefully surveyed an impossible situation". Though Olivier had agreed to open the new Royal Exchange Theatre in Manchester, he was moodily refusing to come to the first performance on 4 October in the theatre named after him, acting cruel only to be kind: "No, no, Peter, it's *your* evening – yours and the actors." Throughout that month he kept Hall on tenterhooks about the big royal night. As the papers, having got wind of it all, were saying, the opening of the Olivier Theatre without Olivier would be a somewhat extreme example of *Hamlet* without the Prince.

The first performance in the Olivier Theatre did, indeed, take place in its namesake's absence, but even Hall thought there was little chance that Olivier would fail his monarch. It was eventually agreed that Olivier would give a speech from the stage. By 21 October, four days before the Queen's visit, Hall was relieved to hear that, unknown to him, Olivier had been coming in between 8 and 8.30 each morning to rehearse his lines in the unfamiliar auditorium. With the assistance of his young friend Gawn

Grainger, an actor-writer to whom Olivier had taken in his last days as director, he was secretly pinpointing the precise position which exists on every stage – known in theatrical parlance as "the spot" – from which an actor can be heard all over the auditorium without raising his voice. Olivier and Grainger mischievously agreed to keep the precise location of "the spot" to themselves.

Come the evening itself, Hall noted that Olivier was "much in evidence, but not particularly warm to me". By June of the following year Olivier had written to Lord Rayne saying that he wished to resign his one lingering role as "consultant director"; he was "fed up with being asked what was going on at the National Theatre when he was not involved at all". It had long been inevitable, thought Hall, who a week later was hurt but not surprised when there was no message of congratulations from Olivier on his knighthood. The Oliviers, in fact, had been "deafeningly silent".

Somehow, Olivier's lingering resentment of the board's failure to consult him had been transferred personally to his successor – though Hall, by his own lights, had behaved with impeccable courtesy and patience throughout a very difficult period. But there were many aspects of the new National which Olivier would continue to resent for years. On one of his infrequent visits, he bumped into Michael Caine in the foyer. "Do you get in the Olivier theatre free?" asked Caine. "No, I fucking well pay for the tickets like anyone else," Olivier replied. He seemed, said Caine, "quite pissed off about it".

Miserable not to have led the company into the new theatre, piqued that it was run by directors rather than actors, depressed by his illnesses yet anxious to keep working, Olivier had even thought of forming his own rival company. Joan Plowright had approached Jonathan Miller, who had long since resigned from the Hall regime, to join them in running it (a fact which duly reached the ears of a despairing Hall). While Olivier was still in hospital in late 1975, however, his brother-in-law David Plowright, then Controller of Programmes (now managing director) of Granada Television in Manchester, had come up with an even better idea. At Olivier's Sussex bedside Plowright offered him the chance to choose six of the best plays of the century and to produce them for television, directing and/or acting in as many as he cared to. It was a gesture as thoughtful as ingenious from Joan's brother, and gave Olivier the extra spur he needed to speed his recovery. By the time he was discharged he was narrowing down his choice, and from June 1976 to July 1977, as his involvement with the National Theatre wound down, it turned out to be the ideal way of returning gently to work.

"He rose to the idea as a new challenge, requiring every ounce of energy and concentration that he could muster," recalls Derek Granger, who was co-opted by Granada to share the burden of production with him.[8] A former critic and literary editor, Granger had worked for years in Granada's play department and had been Olivier's choice to share the job of literary consultant with Tynan at the National. Now, as Olivier convalesced in the garden at Steyning, they sat with the great plays of the twentieth century scattered on the grass around them. An enthusiastic convert to Pinter, Olivier eagerly seized on *The Collection* with one eye on a part for himself; he was also anxious to reintroduce James Bridie's *Daphne Laureola* to a contemporary audience, having produced it for Dame Edith Evans (and Peter Finch) nearly thirty years before. John Osborne, Somerset Maugham, Tennessee Williams and Arthur Miller were also discussed between therapeutic laps of the new swimming-pool. Granger watched fascinated as the project brought Olivier back to life before his eyes. The only other obsession to which it occasionally took second place was the new Steyning garden, which Olivier had designed himself. "Inch perfect," as he still proudly boasts, though the plans were drawn while he was 3,000 miles away in New York, it contained every herb mentioned in Shakespeare. Olivier made a point of mastering the Latin names of every flower and shrub he planted. Ever nostalgic for Notley, he also did much of the topiary himself, including one hedge in the shape of the Three Sisters. Those summer evenings at Steyning, to Granger, were indeed heavily redolent of Chekhov.

By the autumn the choice had been finalized: *The Collection, Daphne Laureola* and two other familiar personal favourites, *A Streetcar Named Desire* and *Saturday, Sunday, Monday*, would be joined by Stanley Houghton's *Hindle Wakes* (a narrow victor, from the "Manchester School", over *Hobson's Choice*) and one other American play, Paul Osborn's *Morning's At Seven*. Before filming *Marathon Man*, Olivier charmed the tycoons of America's NBC network into a large financial contribution as co-producers, and the project was set. He made no objection when NBC requested Tennessee Williams's *Cat on a Hot Tin Roof* rather than his *Streetcar*, partly because it was less familiar, mainly because it contained a marvellous part for Olivier in Big Daddy. But he was less pleased by their rejection of the obscure *Morning's At Seven*, not least because he was lining up a cast including Jack Lemmon, Walter Matthau, Henry Fonda, Katharine Hepburn, Myrna Loy and himself. The expressionless faces of the ratings men prevailed even over Olivier's most sullen *Richard III* glare of resentment.

Back in Manchester after *Marathon Man*, Olivier seemed to have forgotten his illness. Granada had offered him "total supervision", and that was precisely what he chose to exercise, poring over design plans, scouring Manchester and London for locations, even composing the theme music of the series, designing the credit sequences and climbing to the top of a derelict office block for a long, cold wait to ensure that the main titles were set against a mud-red Northern sunset. For more than a year, he gradually returned to an Olivier as vigorous as ever, lost in a blur of auditioning, cutting, editing, dubbing, directing and acting. Olivier personally edited each text down to small-screen scale by reading all the parts aloud – "the best way to discover the boring bits" – and himself selected every actor and actress, however junior.

For the first play to go into production, Pinter's *The Collection*, he had recruited Alan Bates, Helen Mirren and Malcolm McDowell. Under the direction of Michael Apted, Olivier himself would play the ageing, effeminate couturier Harry Kane. Helen Mirren remembers:

> I'm not easily overawed, but if anyone had the potential to frighten me, it was Olivier. But he was wonderful. Within hours we were simply colleagues, fast becoming friends. I even plucked up the nerve to tell him I thought he was overdoing it in one scene, getting a bit hammy; far from chewing me out, as I half expected, he immediately thanked me, said he thought I was absolutely right, and toned it down.[9]

Pinter's precisely drawn piece has much in common with a musical chamber work, and the four performed it like a finely-tuned quartet. Kane, to Granger, became one of Olivier's "finest and most haunting later performances". To *Variety*, Olivier's stamp of authority was "as usual, sharp and compelling. But not overwhelming, which is one of the actor's virtues." This could not be said of the interview he gave to America's *TV Guide*, in which he chose to hype the opening presentation of his series with some forgivable overstatement: "I think it's the most beautiful bit of work I've ever had anything to do with. And I don't think I've ever been so happy in any job before."[10]

The American film actress Natalie Wood was then "astonished and delighted" to be invited, with her husband Robert Wagner, to join Olivier in the leading roles of *Cat on a Hot Tin Roof*, Williams's steamy saga of lust and sexual perversity in the Old South, under the direction of Robert Moore. In the roles originated onstage twenty years earlier by Barbara Bel Geddes, Ben Gazzara and Burl Ives (who joined Elizabeth Taylor and Paul Newman in the 1958 film version), they made perhaps the most effective trio yet. Wood watched breathless as Olivier wound up "like a baseball pitcher"[11] for Big Daddy's big speech about "getting a choice woman", then smothering her in diamonds and mink. Still filming *A Bridge Too Far* in Holland, Olivier arrived back in Manchester to play Big Daddy's birthday row with Big Mamma with volcanic energy, despite complaining that he was not feeling well and was short of sleep. "In the third act," said Natalie Wood, "when Maggie tells him she has Brick's baby in her body, he played it differently every time. Once he just looked at me. And looked and looked. It went on so long I began to feel faint." Maureen Stapleton later told her: "One thing, honey, when you've been looked at by Olivier, you know you've been looked at!"

Daphne Laureola was easy meat after these two heavies, with Joan in Edith Evans's role as the eccentric Lady Pitts, and Olivier scrupulously supportive as her aged husband. Then it was back to the heavy emotional backdrop of the American Midwest, as Joanne Woodward came over to share the enormous burdens of William Inge's *Come Back Little Sheba* under the direction of Silvio Narizzano. Woodward was outstanding as the crumbling Lola, a part which might have been written for Vivien Leigh, mourning as she did both her lost youth and her beloved dog Sheba. Metamorphosing into another large-scale American dinosaur, Olivier played Doc, the small-town chiropractor slowly losing a lifelong battle with alcoholism. He himself then directed *Hindle Wakes* and recreated his hat-destroying old grandfather, Antonio, in *Saturday, Sunday, Monday*. And so the series ended, Osborne's *A Patriot for Me* having slipped through the NBC net. When the first three were screened on both sides of the Atlantic in December 1976–January 1977, the *Los Angeles Times* declared Olivier's productions "the best reason yet to own a television set". Against extraordinary physical odds, said Granger, Olivier had made an "unforgettable contribution" to the history of television drama.

In the five years after being given up for dead in the Royal Sussex Hospital, Olivier was to act in a total of twenty large- or small-screen films. This did not seem at all likely during 1977, which saw him back in hospital again, thanks to another after-effect of his cancer treatment ten years before; this time the ureter belonging to his left kidney developed a double loop, which had become caught up in a small fibrous mass of tissue still "floating around" from that old treatment. He had to undergo more surgery, the most serious yet. But he had already managed, since the Granada series, to tuck in two more film roles – substantial ones, too, though they soon had his admirers wondering if the lure of megabucks was beginning to warp his judgement.

The Betsy, Harold Robbins's soap opera of family intrigue in the dynastic Bethlehem Motor Corporation, saw Olivier enjoy himself hugely as the founding father, Loren Hardeman Sr ("Number One"), in a product that was never going to win too many Oscars. Jack Kroll of *Newsweek* rechristened it "The Larry", wondering what on earth – apart from "a zillion dollars, one hopes" – had possessed Olivier to slum it like this. "In the crystalline winter of his glorious career, Olivier reaches new heights as horny old Hardeman, humping a chambermaid furiously right before your boggled eyes.''[12] But Kroll also sensed the sheer showmanship which had attracted Olivier to the role: "See Olivier chew out his homosexual son. Watch him try, at the age of eighty-six, to put the make on a juicy broad.... Watch him show the suffering cast how to kid a ridiculous script without losing your integrity.''

When *The Betsy* was released in Britain, Gielgud permitted himself a rare giggle at Olivier's expense over lunch at the Garrick with Peter Hall. He himself was enjoying acclaim for his fine performance in Alan Resnais's *Providence*, which was even more satisfying because of Larry's "odd" notices for *The Betsy*. The film's director, Daniel Petrie, defensively insists that he had turned down the script three times before hearing that Olivier had agreed to be in it: "What can you say when you're asked to work with *him*?"[13] Countless stars were soon on the phone begging Petrie for parts at minimum studio pay – *anything* to act with Olivier. It was to become a familiar Hollywood spectacle, as Olivier seemed to shed all discrimination in the pursuit of – his own words – "filthy lucre".[14] The man himself remained unrepentant:

> Thank God for the movies. I can no longer be a stage actor, because I don't feel I've got the power ... the physical attributes that are absolutely necessary to be a very good, powerful, meaningful actor. So we have the movies, and I get a fortune for doing it, which is absolutely what I'm after because I've always overspent in my life and now I'd better get on with it.... They criticize me in the papers. "Why's he doing such muck?" I'll tell you why ... to pay for three children in school, for a family and their future. So what should I do? Write to the critics and ask them to support us? Would that satisfy them?[15]

For a while yet, critics and audiences alike indulged him. Though at times bordering on caricature, he was rather touching as Ezra Lieberman, the Nazi-hunter (based on Simon Wiesenthal) who pursues Gregory Peck's Josef Mengele in *The Boys from Brazil*. Olivier's health was known to be waning again; Peck recalled that he even had difficulty shaking hands. The fight between them at the film's climax was as painful for Olivier as for the crew filming it. Wrestling with Peck on the floor, after being attacked by a pack of savage dogs, Olivier was obviously, said one of the producers, in "holy agony". But Lieberman earned him his eleventh Oscar nomination – his tenth for acting, breaking the record set by Spencer Tracy. This time the vote went to Jon Voight for his Vietnam war veteran in *Coming Home*; but Hollywood's 1978 Oscar jury atoned by honouring Olivier with a "Lifetime Achievement" award.

Olivier now began to wear even his loyalists' indulgence thin – as a lovable old rogue in George Roy Hill's *A Little Romance*, a lurid Professor van Helsing in John Badham's *Dracula* and the hammy old cantor-father of Neil Diamond's *The Jazz Singer*. Even the director of *Dracula*, John Badham, was surprised at Olivier's presence in his unambitious frolic; he understood why when he offered Olivier a day off to go home to Brighton: "No thanks, John, Brighton is death."[16] But Richard Fleischer, who directed him in *The Jazz Singer*, "got no sense in his attitude or concentration that he was in it only for the money".[17] Fleischer was not to know that even Olivier had said "God forgive me!" of his performance as "Al Jolson's father".[18] But the relentless pursuit to keep working and accumulating movie millions was soon to lead to Olivier's most demeaning appearances yet. A veil is best drawn over his be-haloed Zeus in *Clash of the Titans*; and another was anyway drawn, like it or not, over his portrayal of General MacArthur in Terence Young's *Inchon*, a film generally accounted so bad that it was never released in Britain. American critical verdicts ranged from "stupefyingly incompetent" (*Los Angeles Herald Examiner*) to "the worst movie ever made, a turkey the size of Godzilla" (*Newsweek*). On this occasion Olivier was drawing his megabucks from the coffers of the subsequently imprisoned Rev. Sun Myung Moon.

He undertook his last work in the theatre in New York early in 1980, as four of his recent movies played outside on Broadway. Directing Joan and Frank Finlay in their friend Eduardo de Filippo's *Filumena* was simply, he said, "a labour of love". Later that year there was a unique moment in the history of British theatre when its three leading knights, Olivier, Richardson and Gielgud, played a scene together for the first time. It was also, sadly, to be the last, for their brief appearance as three wily old courtiers in Tony Palmer's epic, twelve-hour television life of *Wagner* was the last scene Richardson was ever to play. The unique privilege of having these three grand old men as his supporting cast went to Richard Burton – an Olivier *manqué*, surely, but also perhaps, the kind of figure Olivier himself might just have become, settling for glamour at the expense of greatness, had it not been for that second-hand *Romeo and Juliet* invitation from Gielgud nearly fifty years before.

From March 1980, an unwonted new occupation – writing – had otherwise taken precedence. After many refusals, Olivier had at last been persuaded by the publisher Lord (George) Weidenfeld to write his memoirs. He had always had an inordinate dread of doing so, but an even greater dread of biographies written by others. In 1978 the London *Daily Mail* had alarmed and infuriated him by publishing a series of interviews by an American journalist who had talked to him on a movie set without revealing that he had a tape-recorder concealed about his person. When revealed to a voyeuristic tabloid world, the candour of Olivier's supposedly private remarks, especially about his relationship with Vivien, persuaded him that it was time to take matters into his own hands. (He had also disappointed Tynan by refusing to co-operate on a biography: "I owe Ken a lot," he told the American writer Gore Vidal, "but I don't owe him my life.")[19] Weidenfeld laid on a ghost-writer, Mark Amory, who for many months struggled to reproduce his master's voice; but his master changed his mind, dispensed with his services and sat down to write the whole thing himself.

This, alas, was why the book, published in 1982, did him such a disservice. The awkward, gushingly stagey prose combined with too much candour here, too little there, to embarrass his friends and bemuse his public. Olivier had further compounded the felony by being unable to resist settling a few old scores, notably with the National Theatre board, so that the book's serialization in the *Sunday Telegraph* led to a clutch of angry letters lamenting that Olivier's memory had played him false. Lord Rayne, by now the National Theatre's chairman for twelve years, recalled a letter from Olivier in 1972 saying, "how lovely it would be if nobody ever made a fuss about anything, and how very much he resented 'these stirrer-uppers' ". Now, said Rayne, after reading Olivier's account of their dealings, he "recalled those sentiments with nostalgia".[20] The reviews were heavily sarcastic, even about a figure now regarded in his native Britain with little short of reverence.

In 1981 Olivier's stature as a national treasure, officially scheduled for immortality, was confirmed with the award of the Order of Merit, the highest civilian honour in the sovereign's gift. Only narrowly did it please him more than British Rail's request for his permission to give his name to a locomotive, in the company of Sir Francis Drake, William Shakespeare, Robert Burns and Sir Winston Churchill. The theatre's second peer, Lord (Bernard) Miles, founder of the Mermaid Theatre, was unable to contain his envy: "Now that *was* fame."[21] In a letter to Olivier, Miles wrote: "Quite honestly, and to be brutally frank, I don't mind if they make you a Duke – and bloody well deserved too – so long as I can have an engine named after me. Even a little shunter would do. That's where the true honours lie – in the goods yard."[22]

The memoirs, for all their eccentricity, sold well enough to justify Olivier's huge advance. But his public did not look to him as a writer, especially when he could turn in such spellbinding television performances as the two crotchety old curmudgeons he allowed to interrupt his labours at the typewriter: Lord Marchmain in Granada's adaptation of Evelyn Waugh's *Brideshead Revisited*, and Clifford Mortimer in his son John's autobiographical play, *A Voyage round my Father*, exquisitely directed for Thames by Alvin Rakoff. This last, especially, was Olivier at the summit of his powers: however enfeebled his seventy-five-year-old body, a lifetime of spiritual and technical wisdom went into the deeply affecting portrait of an opinionated old lawyer approaching death, still pretending to himself and his family that he had not long since gone blind.

It more than compensated for the performances which Olivier historians would have preferred to consign to the cutting-room floor, several of which were yet to come. In recent years it has been his close friend, manager and agent, Laurence Evans, who has borne the delicate responsibility of balancing Olivier's reputation against his appetite for work and money. "People say to me, 'Why do you let him do such rubbish? You're doing him no good at all in the eyes of posterity.' All I can say to them is: 'You should see the things I've managed to *stop* him doing.' "[23]

As for posterity: a young friend of Olivier's later years asked him how it would feel to *know* that his name would go down in theatrical history – that, thanks to the camera, his work as an artist would be admired for centuries to come. "It is just as cold in Westminster Abbey as it is in the village churchyard," replied Olivier. "I don't want to die."[24]

CHAPTER 25

1983-7

*"We that are young shall never
see so much, nor live so long."*

Granada Television studios, Manchester, 1983: an elderly, painfully frail but visibly reverend figure, clad all in white, pure white hair trailing down his back, needed help to pick his way across a twisted seaweed of cables, beneath a canopy of booms, towards a polystyrene Stonehenge. There he rested against a pillar, panting, as a horizontal, also pristine white, maiden was lowered on wires into his presence.

The irony of Shakespeare's *King Lear* is that actors of the dying, deluded monarch's advanced age cannot themselves play the part onstage, as the text requires them to enter for the final, climactic death scene carrying the corpse of Lear's daughter, Cordelia. Thanks to the sorcery of television Laurence Olivier was able, at seventy-five, to do what no actor before him has done since the part was written: to play Lear when he himself was old, weak, perhaps a little deluded and, yes, possibly even dying.

Like Lear, too, Olivier in his way had abdicated: a once heroic stage actor, he had now sub-divided his kingdom into films and television. He had decided to undertake one of the most taxing of all roles at seventy-five because, he said, "I've never heard of a good play about Methuselah."[1] After cheating death for twenty years, Olivier's radiant physical presence had gone. The strong masculine face behind so many contemporary theatrical icons was now a thin, pale, emaciated mask. But still it bore an ethereal beauty, a deathly pallid, skin-and-bone version of its sometime Hollywood handsomeness. Still, though bowed and fragile, this wizened version of a once mighty animal exuded an almost frightening energy, a menacing sense of danger. He was like a tightly wound steel spring that might snap free at any moment. On the *King Lear* set there was an awesome expectation, as there always has been, that any minute now, quite without warning, anything could happen.

Cordelia, hanging prone from the heavens, whispered to the old man that she felt like a slice of cheese lying on a grater. He smiled affectionately, then placed his arms beneath her with a look of almost amused concentration, gradually bringing his frame to erect attention, so that soon, by imperceptible degrees, he gave the ever more distinct impression of actually bearing her weight. The wires seemed simply to disappear. A hush descended, then actors and technicians suppressed a gasp as suddenly a huge charge of electricity seemed to go through the old man. As if possessed he actually lifted Cordelia – the wires went limp – and stumbled forward, directing his eyes like arrows towards the heavens, with a cry of "Howl ..." (hushed and tense, in open-mouthed anguish), "Howl ..." (louder, part scream, part sob), "Howl ..." – this last an icy falsetto, the final gasp of a trapped animal, dying into a whisper full of pain and fury: "Oh, you are men of stone. Had I your tongues and eyes, I'd use them so that heaven's vault should crack...."

Now he was on the floor, bent over Cordelia's corpse, holding a feather to her nose. "I know when one is dead and when one lives...." There followed a pause, at first seemingly meant, then gently giving way to agonized embarrassment, as the old man looked up helplessly, desperately, and seemed to come out of a trance. His eyes wandered. The silent spectators almost expected him to ask "Where am I?" But his expression turned to self-disgust and he said merely, "Help!" Those watching had a strong impression that it was Lear, not Olivier, who had forgotten his lines.

Dorothy Tutin, who was at hand as Lear's daughter Goneril, said:

> Normally an actor has two tracks running – the character you are playing, and a tiny track recording what you are doing and telling you what comes next. When a great actor is *very* good, the role is taking over. He is allowing something to happen through him.... So when Larry dries, he has gone completely out of himself and then suddenly he comes to....

Given his line, Olivier–Lear finished his speech in another, last charge of high-voltage crescendo, then lay dead across Cordelia. The director called "Cut"; there was a spattering of awed applause; and the old man struggled to move. Kent, in the shape of Colin Blakely, an old friend and companion, was on his knees beside "Sir", about to congratulate him, when he realized that the man who a moment ago lifted Cordelia could not now command his aged frame upright. "Silly old fool," murmured

447

Olivier, no longer Lear, his features twisted in pain, "I can't even get up." Gently, Blakely helped him to his feet and half-carried him across the floor to a resting-place. "Bloody legs," muttered Olivier and slumped in Lear's throne.

Five years later, Blakely was to die before Olivier, who had meanwhile tackled another half-dozen television roles, a handful of film cameos, and shrugged off the premature obituaries which marked eightieth-birthday celebrations on a scale little short of canonization. Even at eighty – even, he knows, after his death – Olivier can be seen on the London stage in the form of a hologram, his three-dimensional features and disembodied, stereophonic voice booming the inanities of Akash, the all-seeing, omniscient, if slightly wobbly, presiding genius of the space-age musical *Time*, whose changing stars are pop singers born long after Olivier had already lived several lifetimes.

But this television Lear was Olivier's last real farewell. "You know," he said on the set, "when you get to my age, you *are* Lear, in every nerve of your body.... Here I am, at the very end of myself, in both age and experience." The power and clarity of his performance, especially in the madness amid the storm, beguiled even the younger critics who had never warmed to the bravura tradition. "He *was* every inch a king," wrote one such, Robert Cushman of the *Observer*. "Leo McKern as Gloucester shuffled towards him with the duty that a very fine actor pays to a great one. Their duet was, literally, breathtaking." Cushman confessed to weeping at *King Lear* for the first time in his theatre-going life:

> It was the scene on Dover cliffs with the blind Gloucester that awoke [Olivier] to magnificence. His mind almost visibly wandered, but each cruel paradox it seized on ("Handy-Dandy, which is the justice, which is the thief?") was brilliantly lucid. He would begin small ("Behold yon simp'ring dame") and would never rant at a climax, but by the time he reached it ("There's damnation"), you, like Gloucester, were seeing with his eyes.[2]

Ten years before, at the height of the Watergate scandal, Olivier had politely declined an invitation from President Nixon to be feted at a Washington dinner. Now, in April 1983, he was pleased to attend a special screening of his *King Lear* at the White House as the guest of President Reagan, who also had tears in his eyes as he turned to Olivier and said: "After that, I don't think I'll call myself an actor any more."

Friends and followers came to wish that Olivier had made this performance his last. The three working years left to him saw Olivier's compulsion to keep going drag him back down to unworthy depths. There was admiration for the man's determination, praise for his sheer guts and sympathy for his touching belief that he must keep working to stay alive.

But his two other television appearances in 1983, opposite Jackie Gleason in *Mr Halpern and Mr Johnson* and Angela Lansbury in *A Talent for Murder*, were best described as courageous. It was uncomfortable to see an Olivier performance restricted rather than driven by his physical prowess, to hear him stumble over his lines, to see gestures and to hear inflexions which had by now become predictable.

In the right part, his increasing frailty could be turned to advantage – as, for instance, in his portrayal of the crusty old painter, Henry Breasley, in John Mortimer's adaptation of John Fowles's short story, *The Ebony Tower*. Sharing the credits with two aspiring actresses more than half a century younger, Greta Scacchi and the punk, crimson-haired pop singer Toyah Wilcox, Olivier was visibly enjoying himself again (especially, it might be said, while presiding over a nude sunbathing scene). There was an element of mischief in both the part and the portrayal which worthily echoed the Olivier of stronger, healthier days; there was a magisterial rage about the dying character which was in harmony with that of the actor. But there was no such chemistry at work in either of Olivier's next two brief appearances – routine, money-grubbing cameos as Gaius in an American television version of *The Last Days of Pompeii*, and as a painfully wizened Admiral Hood, presiding over the fate of Anthony Hopkins's Captain Bligh in the latest remake of *Mutiny on the Bounty*.

As these were appearing the following year, Olivier defied his annual bout of pneumonia to enact the head of the British Secret Service, Sir Gerald Scaith, in Terence Young's *The Jigsaw Man*, which again brought him together with Michael Caine. Olivier collapsed during filming, while on location on the Thames Embankment, so that his efforts seemed doubly futile when the picture proved disappointing enough to disappear without trace. By September 1984, weakened by a kidney complaint, Olivier was in Berlin for ten days, making what proved to be his last film appearance. As irony would have it, heavy beetle brows were required for his portrayal of Rudolf Hess in Peter Hunt's *Wild Geese II*; after all his efforts to be rid of them in his youth, bushy false eyebrows were now the centre-piece of his fifty-seventh and last big-screen disguise. Olivier's own emaciated face, pinched cheeks and sunken eyes needed little further artistry to lend his looks a chilling likeness to those of Hess. An hour or two's shooting each day was all that he could manage, and then only thanks to the constant vigilance of a team of nurses. But his Hess was above all a visual perform- ance, re-enacting "snatched" newspaper photographs of the eternal pris- oner of Spandau (the unwitting object, in the film, of a rescue attempt by mercenaries). For several weeks the following year, when the film was released to predictable box-office success, Olivier's disturbingly gaunt features peered down from posters on the front of a hundred London buses, like some gloomy mobile monument to his vanished powers.

There were to be just two last gasps for television. After exuding aged majesty as King William III in a rambling epic about *Peter the Great*, seventy-nine-year-old Laurence Olivier ended his acting career, appropriately enough, with an endearing little song and dance as an Archie Rice-like music-hall comedian. Harry Burrard, in J. B. Priestley's *Lost Empires*, was to prove Olivier's last role. It came exactly seventy years since his first stage appearance as Brutus in the All Saints' production of *Julius Caesar*.

On Olivier's eightieth birthday in May 1987 came a formal announcement that he would never act again. Seemingly indestructible for so long, Olivier had finally, as he himself most reluctantly admitted, "run out of steam". Sir Laurence, the only peer of the realm to prefer to be addressed by his lesser title, might still allow the occasional camera to be pointed at him while he read favourite verse or extracts from the Bible. But even the television cameo roles which had so prolonged his working life were now beyond him. As for films: the blunt and unseemly truth, a poignant end to so majestic a career, was that no one would insure him any more. As with Olivier's much lamented film of *Macbeth*, the money men had had the last word. There was now no insurance company prepared to indemnify movie producers against the chance of Olivier dying in the midst of a multi-million dollar epic; and there was no producer prepared to take the risk.

Weaker than ever, but in good heart, Olivier accepted only one of the countless invitations to celebrate his octogenarian status with friends and followers. The evening of 31 May 1987, nine days after his birthday, saw an illustrious gathering fill the National Theatre's Olivier auditorium for a special entertainment mounted in his honour. From the front row a fragile and bearded Olivier watched with his family as his place in theatrical history was spelt out by a parade of leading British actors: Alec McCowen paid his tribute as Richard Burbage, followed by Edward Petherbridge as David Garrick, Ben Kingsley as Edmund Kean and Anthony Sher as Henry Irving. There was a surprise appearance by Dame Peggy Ashcroft as Lilian Baylis, and some gentle self-mockery from Sir Peter Hall as Shakespeare. Though the text was light-hearted – Geraldine McEwan and Frank Finlay sang "Dry Bones" to Olivier's list of his stage and screen injuries[3] – the atmosphere remained rather solemn. As the evening ended in a prolonged standing ovation, the halting old man in the front row had clearly enjoyed himself. Even a graceful wave to the cheering auditorium looked to be an effort. But when Joan and his nurse gently took his arm, to lead him away, Olivier would not be persuaded. He knew that this was likely to be the last ovation which he would ever receive from any audience in any theatre. He could not bring himself to let go.

After fireworks over the Thames, the champagne flowed until 1 a.m., when Olivier finally climbed into the car to return to Sussex. The following Sunday evening, to widespread dismay, he permitted his former self to be travestied on British television. In a thin, fragile voice, Olivier read poems billed as his own choice, though it was painfully clear that he had never seen most of them before. As the texts were gently explained to the old man by an awkward interlocutor, then handed over for recital, Olivier seemed rather to be performing the last of Shakespeare's Seven Ages of Man, "second childishness and mere oblivion". All that remained of Olivier's former glory were his eyes, those eyes which once could penetrate to the back of the balcony – eyes that could still, for the camera, flash, rage, weep, even go blind in close-up, as in the devastating opening to *A Voyage round my Father*. Olivier once said that he would rather lose his voice or his arms than his eyes. "If I haven't got [my lines] twenty times better than I need to, really, there'll be something in the eye which will say, 'What's coming next?' I don't want one twitch of any muscle anywhere that I don't intend." But even the eyes, that night, had to flicker through bi-focal lenses.

When his closest friend Ralph Richardson died in 1983, at the age of seventy-nine, Olivier told a friend: "I know what old Ralphie did. He just turned his head to the wall."[4] Giving up like that was something Olivier himself could never contemplate. Still, when his strength permits, he will swim a few naked lengths of his Sussex pool, in which half a mile per day sustained him through his seventies. The ample Sussex cottage – deliberately hard to find, a mile down an unmade road – has become a fastness from which, even now, he can ring his agent's office like an anxious young hopeful, to inquire: "Anything on offer today?"[5] But the ability to learn lines has gone – his last two parts were played from giant cue-cards, which he hated – and so has some of his awareness. Today, Olivier tends to remember a moment, a speech, a performance from forty years ago more clearly than he can remember this morning. To see this giant spirit cramped within a failing frame grieves the diminishing handful of intimate friends whose visits he still welcomes.

Just occasionally, the old stamina can resurface. After a kidney operation in 1984, Olivier insisted on proving his convalescent powers by drinking one hospital visitor under the bed. In the late summer of 1987, in California for his son Richard's wedding, he tumbled down the stairs of the Malibu beach-house he had rented with Joan; but the following month saw him insisting on his regular visit to William Walton's widow in Ischia. As Richard Olivier begins to make himself a name as a stage director, his father dutifully tries to attend all his first nights. When all three of their children embarked on theatrical careers, Olivier and his wife were at first alarmed that they should choose so unreliable a profession; now he is delighted, he says, to have been "spared" long enough to see them all overcoming early setbacks – and the monstrous burden of their surname – to sense the beginnings of success.

Olivier has now been married to Joan Plowright longer than he was to Jill Esmond and Vivien Leigh combined. While maintaining her own distinguished stage career, Joan has sustained him through the physical trials of his last two decades, and provided him with the reassuring insulation of family life to an extent which he had never before enjoyed. The marriage has had its difficulties – visitors have noted, in recent years, how Olivier seems more than ever haunted by the ghost of Vivien – but they have managed to keep them to themselves. For the stability of his old age, for the loving care which has enabled him to keep working, Olivier has publicly expressed his "wonderment, as well as deep, loving, inexpressible gratitude, for ever" to Joan.

Standing beside a Spanish pool a few years ago, about to embark on his daily naked swim, Olivier caught his friend Gawn Grainger staring wide-eyed at the elaborate network of operation scars on his long-suffering torso. "Ah, yes," cried the old actor vaingloriously, "this is the body they used to worship. They all fell for me in my day."[6] Nostalgia may remain a source of sustenance, but nothing will stop Olivier raging against the dying of the light. Asked recently to whom he would be handing on the sword used by Kean as Richard III, presented to him so long ago by Gielgud, he replied quite simply: "No one. It's mine."[7]

If the Olivier story is that of an actor who has spent his life auditioning to be himself, and who somehow seems less than the sum of his parts, it is only as an elderly, revered but decaying national institution that he has finally felt quite miscast. As long ago as 1973, after laying the foundation-stone of an extension to the Belgrade Theatre, Coventry, he found himself appalled upon reading the inscription: "This stone was laid by Sir Laurence Olivier, the first director of the National Theatre." "Suddenly," he said, "I felt dead. Absolutely finished.... I can't bear this institution talk. People say, well, after all, you are a legend. Jesus ... it's like being a ghost."[8]

Contrary to the last, he has nevertheless announced his own preferred choice of epitaph: "He was funny." The phrase with which Archie Rice's daughter defends her father, for all his failings, it might serve for those who have always considered Olivier an actor of primarily comic gifts. But it seems a trifle inadequate for a tragedian who, in his heyday, recalled Coleridge's description of Edmund Kean: "To see him act was like reading Shakespeare by flashes of lightning."

Olivier's great contemporaries, says Peter Ustinov, "could only have been what they are, whereas Larry could have been a notable ambassador, a considerable minister, a redoubtable cleric". Ustinov concludes with what must surely be a far more fitting epitaph for Laurence Olivier: "At his worst, he would have acted the parts more ably than they are usually lived."[9]

At best, perhaps, he has spent his life acting the role of Laurence Olivier more ably than anyone else could have lived it.

Chronology

In this chronology of Olivier's career, films are listed, where possible, under the year in which they were made rather than that in which they were released.

1907 Born 22 May, Dorking, Surrey

1917 First public stage appearance: BRUTUS in All Saints' production of *Julius Caesar*

1918 MARIA in All Saints' production of *Twelfth Night*
Family moves to Letchworth

1922 KATHARINA in school production of *The Taming of the Shrew* (revived at old Shakespeare Theatre, Stratford-upon-Avon)

1923 PUCK in school production of *A Midsummer Night's Dream*

1924 Central School of Speech Training and Dramatic Art
ASM/understudy for Algernon Blackwood and Violet Pearn's *Through the Crack*, Letchworth
LENNOX in Letchworth *Macbeth*; prod. Norman V. Norman
First appearance on London stage: THE SULIOT OFFICER in Law's *Byron*; dir. by and starring Henry Oscar; Century Theatre, London

1925 MASTER SNARE and THOMAS OF CLARENCE, *Henry IV, Part II* with Edmund Willard, Alfred Clark, Horace Sequeira; dir. L. E. Berman; Regent Theatre, London
ARMAND ST CYR in Frank's *The Unfailing Instinct* and
POLICEMAN in Ridley's *The Ghost Train* with Ruby Miller; Century Theatre, London
Number of parts including FLAVIUS in *Julius Caesar* with Lena Ashwell Players; based at Century Theatre, London
Walk-on parts and ASM in Shakespeare's *Henry VIII* with Sybil Thorndike, Lewis Casson; Empire Theatre, London

1926 SERVANT and ASM in Shelley's *The Cenci* with Sybil Thorndike, Lewis Casson, Jack Hawkins; Empire Theatre, London
Joins Birmingham Repertory Company:
A MINSTREL in Ghéon's *The Marvellous History of Saint Bernard* with Robert Harris; Birmingham Rep production at Kingsway Theatre, London
Minor part in Davies's *The Barber and the Cow* with Cedric Hardwicke, Ralph Richardson; Birmingham Rep at Clacton
On Birmingham Rep tour as RICHARD CROAKER in Phillpotts's *The Farmer's Wife*

1927 Bigger parts at Birmingham Rep:
GUY SYDNEY in Phillpotts's *Something To Talk About*
MAT SIMON in Synge's *The Well of the Saints*
TOM HARDCASTLE in Whittaker's *The Third Finger*
PETER MANNOCH in McClymond's *The Mannoch Family*
Walk-on part in Ghéon's *The Comedian*
Title role in Chekhov's *Uncle Vanya*
PAROLLES in *All's Well That Ends Well*
YOUNG MAN in Mayor's *The Pleasure Garden*
TONY LUMPKIN in Goldsmith's *She Stoops to Conquer*
ENSIGN BLADES in Barrie's *Quality Street*
GERALD ARNWOOD in Drinkwater's *Bird in Hand*
MERVYN JONES in Farjeon and Horsnell's *Advertising April*

JACK BARTHWICK in Galsworthy's *The Silver Box*
YOUNG AMERICAN in Rice's *The Adding Machine*
BEN HAWLEY in Dean's *Aren't Women Wonderful?*
MR MILFORD in Holcroft's *The Road to Ruin*

1928 Birmingham Rep at Royal Court Theatre, London:
YOUNG AMERICAN, *The Adding Machine*
MALCOLM in *Macbeth*
MARTELLUS in Shaw's *Back to Methuselah*
HAROLD in Tennyson's *Harold*
THE LORD in *The Taming of the Shrew*
GERALD ARNWOOD in *Bird in Hand*, with Jill Esmond; prod. Barry Jackson; dir. John Drinkwater; Royalty Theatre, London
GRAHAM BIRLEY in John's *The Dark Path*; dir. Evan John; Royalty Theatre, London
CAPTAIN HENRY STANHOPE in Sherriff's *Journey's End* with Maurice Evans, Melville Cooper, George Zucco; dir. James Whale; Apollo, London

1929 Title role in Dean and Mann's *Beau Geste* with Madeleine Carroll, Marie Lohr, Edmund Willard, Jack Hawkins; dir. Basil Dean; His Majesty's, London
PRINCE PO in Klabund and Laver's *The Circle of Chalk* with Anna May Wong; dir. Basil Dean; New Theatre, London
RICHARD PARISH in Barry's *Paris Bound* with Herbert Marshall, Edna Best; Lyric Theatre, London

JOHN HARDY in Wilbur's *The Stranger Within* with Olga Lindo, Roland Culver; Garrick Theatre, London

HUGH BROMILOW in Vosper's *Murder on the Second Floor* with Phyllis Konstam, O. B. Clarence, Viola Lyel; Eltinge Theater, New York

JERRY WARRENDER in Harvey's *The Last Enemy* with Athene Seyler, O. B. Clarence, Nicholas Hannen, Frank Lawton; dir. Tom Walls; Fortune Theatre, London

RALPH in van Druten's *After All* with Elissa Landi, Cathleen Nesbitt; Arts Theatre, London

Films
PETER BILLE in *The Temporary Widow* (US title: *Murder for Sale*) (Germany: UFA/Wardour) with Felix Aylmer, Lilian Harvey, Athole Stewart; prod. Erich Pommer; dir. Gustav Ucicky

THE MAN in *Too Many Crooks* (GB: Fox) with Dorothy Boyd, Bromley Davenport, Mina Burnett, Arthur Stratton, Ellen Pollock; prod. and dir. George King

1930 Marries Jill Esmond
VICTOR PRYNNE in Coward's *Private Lives* with Noël Coward, Gertrude Lawrence, Adrianne Allen; dir. Noël Coward; Phoenix Theatre, London

Film
STRAKER in *Potiphar's Wife* (US title: *Her Strange Desire*) (GB: British International Pictures/First National Pathe) with Nora Swinburne, Guy

Newall, Norman McKinnell, Elsa Lanchester; dir. Maurice Elvey

1931 VICTOR PRYNNE in *Private Lives* with Noël Coward, Gertrude Lawrence and Jill Esmond; Times Square Theater, New York
Arrives in Hollywood

Films
LIEUTENANT NICHOLLS in *Friends and Lovers* (US: RKO) with Erich Von Stroheim, Lily Damita, Adolphe Menjou; dir. Victor Schertzinger

JULIAN ROLPHE in *The Yellow Passport* (US title: *The Yellow Ticket*) (US: Fox) with Elissa Landi, Lionel Barrymore, Walter Byron, Boris Karloff; dir. Raoul Walsh

1932 *Films*
NICK ALLEN in *Westward Passage* (US: RKO) with Ann Harding, Juliette Compton, Zasu Pitts, Bonita Granville; dir. Robert Milton

NICHOLAS RANDALL in *Perfect Understanding* (GB: United Artists) with Gloria Swanson, John Halliday, Nora Swinburne, Nigel Playfair, Genevieve Tobin; dir. Cyril Gardner

CLIVE in *No Funny Business* (US title: *The Professional Co-Respondents*) (GB: United Artists) with Gertrude Lawrence, Jill Esmond, Gibb McLaughlin, Edmond Breon, Muriel Aked; dir. John Stafford and Victor Hanbury

1933 STEVEN BERINGER in Winter's *Rats of Norway* with Raymond

456

Massey, Gladys Cooper;
Playhouse Theatre, London
Screen test for *Queen Christina*
with Greto Garbo
JULIAN DULCIMER in Shairp's
The Green Bay Tree with James
Dale, Leo G. Carroll and Jill
Esmond; dir. Jed Harris; Cort
Theater, New York
Records extracts from the *Old
Testament* on set of twelve discs
(Mercury Records, US; Philips,
GB); prod. Douglas Fairbanks
Jr

1934 RICHARD KURT in Behrman's
Biography with Ina Claire,
Reginald Tate, Joan
Wyndham, Frank Cellier, Sam
Livesey; dir. Noël Coward;
Globe Theatre, London
BOTHWELL in Daviot's *Queen of
Scots* with George Howe, Glen
Byam Shaw, Campbell Gullan,
Gwen Frangcon-Davies; dir.
John Gielgud; New Theatre,
London
TONY CAVENDISH in Ferber
and Kauffman's *Theatre Royal*
with Marie Tempest, Madge
Titheradge, Mary Merrall; dir.
Noël Coward; Lyric Theatre,
London

1935 PETER HAMMOND in Winter's
Ringmaster with Dame May
Whitty, Colin Keith-Johnston,
Nigel Patrick, Cathleen
Nesbitt, Dorothy Hyson, Jill
Esmond; dir. Raymond Massey;
Shaftesbury Theatre, London
Directs and plays RICHARD
HARBEN in Thompson and
Cunard's *Golden Arrow* with
Greer Garson, Helen Hayes
and Cecil Parker; Whitehall
Theatre, London

ROMEO in *Romeo and Juliet* with
Peggy Ashcroft, Edith Evans,
John Gielgud; dir. Gielgud;
New Theatre, London
MERCUTIO in same production,
with Gielgud as Romeo

Films
VINCENT LUNARDI in *Conquest
of the Air* (GB: London
Films/United Artists) with
Henry Victor, John Turnbull,
Hay Petrie, Margaretta Scott,
Franklyn Dyall; prod. Donald
Taylor (for Korda); dir.
Alexander Shaw, John Monk
Saunders (released 1940)
IGNATOFF in *Moscow Nights* (US
title: *I Stand Condemned*) (GB:
London Films-Capital) with
Athene Seyler, Harry Baur,
Penelope Dudley Ward; prod.
Alexander Korda, Alexis
Granowski, Max Schach; dir.
Anthony Asquith

1936 Co-directs (with Ralph
Richardson) and plays ROBERT
PATCH in Priestley's *Bees on the
Boat-Deck* with Ralph
Richardson, Raymond
Huntley, Kay Hammond and
John Laurie; Lyric Theatre,
London

Films
ORLANDO in *As You Like It* (GB:
Inter-Allied/Twentieth Century
Fox) with Elisabeth Bergner,
Henry Ainley, Felix Aylmer,
Leon Quartermaine, Sophie
Stewart, Mackenzie Ward,
John Laurie; music by William
Walton; prod. and dir. Paul
Czinner

457

MICHAEL INGOLBY in *Fire over England* (GB: Pendennis/United Artists) with Vivien Leigh, Flora Robson, Raymond Massey, Leslie Banks, Robert Newton, James Mason; prod. Erich Pommer; dir. William K. Howard

1937 Old Vic Theatre, London:
Title role in *Hamlet* with Michael Redgrave, Cherry Cottrell, Dorothy Dix, Francis L. Sullivan, George Howe, Alec Guinness; dir. Tyrone Guthrie

SIR TOBY BELCH in *Twelfth Night* with Jessica Tandy, Alec Guinness, Jill Esmond, Marius Goring; dir. Tyrone Guthrie

Title role in *Henry V* with Ivy St Helier, Thomas Owen-Jones, Lawrence Baskcomb; dir. Tyrone Guthrie

Title role in *Hamlet* with Vivien Leigh, Anthony Quayle, John Abbott, Leo Genn; dir. Tyrone Guthrie; Kronborg Castle, Elsinore, Denmark

Title role in *Macbeth* with Judith Anderson, Ellis Irving, Andrew Cruickshank; dir. Michel Saint-Denis

Films

LOGAN in *The Divorce of Lady X* (GB: London-Denham Films/United Artists) with Merle Oberon, Ralph Richardson, Binnie Barnes; prod. Alexander Korda; dir. Tim Whelan

LARRY DURANT in *Twenty-One Days* (US title: *The First and the Last*) (GB: London-Denham Films/Columbia) with Vivien Leigh, Leslie Banks, Francis L.

Sullivan, Hay Petrie, Robert Newton; screenplay by Graham Greene, from story by John Galsworthy; prod. Alexander Korda; dir. Basil Dean

1938 Old Vic:
IAGO in *Othello* with Ralph Richardson, Curigwen Lewis; dir. Tyrone Guthrie

VIVALDI in Bridie's *The King of Nowhere* with Marda Vanne; dir. Tyrone Guthrie

Title role in *Coriolanus* with Sybil Thorndike; dir. Lewis Casson

1939 GAYLORD EASTERBROOK in Behrman's *No Time for Comedy* with Katharine Cornell, Margalo Gillmore, John Williams, Robert Flemyng; dir. Guthrie McLintic; Ethel Barrymore Theater, New York

Films

TONY MCVANE in *Q Planes* (US title: *Clouds Over Europe*) (GB: Harefield-London Films/Columbia) with Ralph Richardson, Valerie Hobson, George Curzon, George Merritt; prod. Alexander Korda and Irving Ashcroft; dir. Tim Whelan

HEATHCLIFF in *Wuthering Heights* (US: Samuel Goldwyn/United Artists) with Merle Oberon, David Niven, Flora Robson, Donald Crisp, Hugh Williams, Geraldine Fitzgerald, Leo G. Carroll; screenplay by Ben Hecht, Charles MacArthur; prod. Samuel Goldwyn; dir. William Wyler; *nominated for US Academy Award: Best Actor*

MAXIM DE WINTER in *Rebecca*

(US: Selznick/United Artists) with Joan Fontaine, George Sanders, Judith Anderson, Nigel Bruce, C. Aubrey Smith, Gladys Cooper, Reginald Denny, Florence Bates; prod. David O. Selznick; dir. Alfred Hitchcock; *nominated for US Academy Award: Best Actor*
Father dies

1940 Marriage to Jill Esmond dissolved
Marries Vivien Leigh
Directs and plays ROMEO in *Romeo and Juliet* with Vivien Leigh, Dame May Whitty, Edmond O'Brien, Cornel Wilde, Alexander Knox; 51st Street Theater, New York

Films
DARCY in *Pride and Prejudice* (US: MGM) with Greer Garson, Mary Boland, Edna Mae Oliver, Maureen O'Sullivan, Ann Rutherford, Heather Angel, Marsha Hunt, Edmund Gwen; screenplay by Aldous Huxley and Jane Murfin; prod. Hunt Stromberg; dir. Robert Z. Leonard

1941 *Films*
NELSON in *Lady Hamilton* (US title: *That Hamilton Woman*) (GB: Korda/United Artists) with Vivien Leigh, Gladys Cooper, Sara Allgood, Henry Wilcox, Heather Angel; screenplay by Walter Reisch and R. C. Sherriff; prod. and dir. Alexander Korda
JOHNNIE THE TRAPPER in *49th Parallel* (US title: *The Invaders*) (GB: Otrus Films/General) with Finlay Currie, Glynis Johns,

Leslie Howard, Raymond Massey; prod. and dir. Michael Powell
Reads commentary of *Words for Battle*, eight-minute "call to arms" produced by Crown Film Unit; prod. Ian Dalrymple; dir. Humphrey Jennings
Lieutenant (A) in Royal Naval Volunteer Reserve

1942 RNVR

1943 *Film*
IVAN DIMITRIEVITCH KOUZNETSOFF in *The Demi-Paradise* (US title: *Adventure for Two*) (GB: Two Cities/General) with Penelope Dudley Ward, Margaret Rutherford, Felix Aylmer, Leslie Henson; prod. and screenplay by Anatole de Grunwald; dir. Anthony Asquith

1943–4 *Film*
Produces, directs and plays title role in *Henry V* (GB: Two Cities/Rank) with Renee Asherson, Robert Newton, Leslie Banks, Ivy St Helier, Leo Genn, Felix Aylmer; music by William Walton; *Honorary Academy Award for "outstanding achievement as actor, director and producer in bringing* Henry V *to the screen"*

1944 Appointed co-director with Ralph Richardson and John Burrell of Old Vic Theatre, London
BUTTON MOULDER in Ibsen's *Peer Gynt* with Ralph Richardson, Sybil Thorndike, Nicholas Hannen; dir. Tyrone Guthrie (also Paris and New York)

459

SERGIUS SARANOFF in Shaw's *Arms and the Man* with Ralph Richardson, Sybil Thorndike, Nicholas Hannen, Margaret Leighton; dir. John Burrell (also Paris and New York)

Title role in *Richard III* with Harcourt Williams, George Relph, Joyce Redman; dir. John Burrell (also Paris and New York)

ASTROV in Chekhov's *Uncle Vanya* with Ralph Richardson, Harcourt Williams; dir. John Burrell

1945 Directs Wilder's *The Skin of our Teeth* with Vivien Leigh, Cecil Parker, Joan Young, Terence Morgan; Phoenix Theatre, London

Old Vic tour of UK, Belgium, Holland, Germany and France with *Arms and the Man*, *Peer Gynt* and *Richard III*

1945–6 Old Vic company at the New Theatre, London:

HOTSPUR in *Henry IV, Part I* with Ralph Richardson, Margaret Leighton; dir. John Burrell

JUSTICE SHALLOW in *Henry IV, Part II* with Ralph Richardson, Nicholas Hannen, Joyce Redman; dir. John Burrell

Double-bill: Title role in Sophocles's *Oedipus Rex* (trans. W. B. Yeats) and MR PUFF in Sheridan's *The Critic*; dir. Michel Saint-Denis and Miles Malleson

1946 HOTSPUR, SHALLOW, OEDIPUS, PUFF, ASTROV: Century Theater, New York

Directs and plays title role in *King Lear* with Pamela Brown,

Margaret Leighton, Joyce Redman, Alec Guinness, Nicholas Hannen, George Relph; Old Vic production at New Theatre, London

1947 Receives knighthood for "services to stage and films"

Directs Kanin's *Born Yesterday* with Yolande Donlan, Hartley Power; Garrick Theatre, London

Founds Laurence Olivier Productions Ltd (LOP Ltd)

Film

Produces, directs and plays title role in *Hamlet* (GB: Two Cities/Rank) with Jean Simmons, Basil Sydney, Eileen Herlie, Norman Wooland, Felix Aylmer, Terence Morgan, Peter Cushing, Stanley Holloway; music by William Walton; *wins US Academy Awards for Best Actor and Best Film; nominated for Best Director*

1948 Leads Old Vic tour of Australia and New Zealand:

Title role in *Richard III*

Directs and plays SIR PETER TEAZLE in Sheridan's *The School for Scandal* with Vivien Leigh

Directs and plays MR ANTROBUS in *The Skin of our Teeth* with Vivien Leigh

1949 Old Vic company at the New Theatre, London:

Directs and plays SIR PETER TEAZLE in *The School for Scandal* with Vivien Leigh, Mercia Swinburne, George Relph, Terence Morgan, Peter Cushing

Title role in *Richard III*, with Vivien Leigh, Peter Cushing,

George Relph, Terence Morgan; dir. John Burrell
Directs and plays CHORUS in Anouilh's *Antigone* with Vivien Leigh, George Relph
Directs Chekhov's *The Proposal* with Peter Cushing, Derrick Penley, Peggy Simpson
Directs Williams's *A Streetcar Named Desire* with Vivien Leigh, Bonar Colleano, Bernard Braden, Renee Asherson; Aldwych Theatre, London
Takes lease of St James's Theatre, London, for four years

1950 Directs and plays DUKE OF ALTAIR in Fry's *Venus Observed* with Heather Stannard, Denholm Elliott, Valerie Taylor, George Relph, Rachel Kempson, Brenda de Banzie; St James's
Directs Cannan's *Captain Carvallo* with Peter Finch, Richard Goolden, James Donald; St James's

Film
GEORGE HURSTWOOD in *Carrie* (US: Paramount) with Jennifer Jones, Miriam Hopkins, Eddie Albert, Basil Ruysadel; prod. and dir. William Wyler (released 1952)

1951 Festival of Britain productions at the St James's, later transferred to Ziegfeld Theater, New York:
CAESAR in Shaw's *Caesar and Cleopatra* with Vivien Leigh, Robert Helpmann, Wilfrid Hyde White, Harry Andrews, Norman Wooland, Maxine Audley, Jill Bennett; dir. Michael Benthall

ANTONY in *Antony and Cleopatra* with Vivien Leigh and same company; also dir. Michael Benthall

Film
PC 49 in *The Magic Box* (GB: Festival Films/British Lion) with huge all-star cast headed by Robert Donat; prod. Ronald Neame; dir. John Boulting

1952 Directs *Venus Observed* at New Century Theater, New York
CAESAR in *Caesar and Cleopatra* and ANTONY in *Antony and Cleopatra*; Ziegfeld Theater, New York

Film
Co-produces and plays MACHEATH in John Gay's *The Beggar's Opera* (GB: Imperadio/British Lion) with Dorothy Tutin, Stanley Holloway, George Devine, Mary Clare, Hugh Griffith, Daphne Anderson, Athene Seyler; co-prod. Herbert Wilcox; dir. Peter Brook

1953 Directs and plays GRAND DUKE OF CARPATHIA in Rattigan's *The Sleeping Prince* with Vivien Leigh, Martita Hunt, Richard Wattis, Jeremy Spenser; Phoenix, London

Film
Narrates *A Queen Is Crowned* (GB: Rank), a documentary on the Coronation of Elizabeth II; written by Christopher Fry; prod. Castleton Knight

1954 *Film*
Produces, directs and plays title role in *Richard III* (GB: LOP/London Films/Big Ben

Films) with Claire Bloom, Ralph Richardson, John Gielgud, Cedric Hardwicke, Stanley Baker, Alec Clunes; music by Sir William Walton; *nominated for US Academy Award: Best Actor*

1955 Shakespeare Memorial Theatre, Stratford-upon-Avon: MALVOLIO in *Twelfth Night* with Vivien Leigh, Angela Baddeley, Alan Webb, Keith Michell, Michael Denison; dir. John Gielgud
Title role in *Macbeth* with Vivien Leigh, Keith Michell; dir. Glen Byam Shaw
Title role in *Titus Andronicus* with Vivien Leigh, Anthony Quayle, Michael Denison, Alan Webb, Maxine Audley, Lee Montague; dir. Peter Brook

1956 *Film*
Produces, directs and plays title role in *The Prince and the Showgirl* (GB: Warner Bros) with Marilyn Monroe, Sybil Thorndike, Richard Wattis, Paul Hardwick, Jeremy Spenser, Esmond Knight

1957 ARCHIE RICE in Osborne's *The Entertainer* with George Relph, Brenda de Banzie, Dorothy Tutin, Richard Pasco, Aubrey Dexter, Stanley Meadows; dir. Tony Richardson; Royal Court Theatre, London
Title role in *Titus Andronicus*: the Peter Brook production in Paris, Venice, Belgrade, Zagreb, Vienna, Warsaw, then to Stoll Theatre, London
ARCHIE RICE in *The Entertainer*: the Richardson production, now with Joan Plowright,

Robert Stephens, Albert Chevalier; Palace Theatre, London

1958 ARCHIE RICE in *The Entertainer*; Royale Theater, New York

Film
GENERAL BURGOYNE in *The Devil's Disciple* (GB: Hecht-Hill-Lancaster Films/United Artists) with Burt Lancaster, Kirk Douglas, Janette Scott, Eva LeGallienne, Harry Andrews; prod. Harold Hecht; dir. Guy Hamilton

Television
Title role in Ibsen's *John Gabriel Borkman* (GB: Associated TV) with Irene Worth, Pamela Brown, Maxine Audley, George Relph, Anthony Valentine, Anne Castaldini; dir. Caspar Wrede
CHARLES STRICKLAND in Maugham's *The Moon and Sixpence* (US: NBC TV) with Judith Anderson, Hume Cronyn, Denholm Elliott, Cyril Cusack, Jessica Tandy, Geraldine Fitzgerald; dir. David Susskind; *US Emmy award for Best TV Actor*
Brother Dickie dies

1959 Title role in *Coriolanus* with Edith Evans, Harry Andrews, Robert Hardy, Paul Hardwick, Peter Woodthorpe, Mary Ure, Vanessa Redgrave; dir. Peter Hall; Stratford-upon-Avon

Films
MARCUS CRASSUS in *Spartacus* (US: Universal-International) with Kirk Douglas, Jean Simmons, Charles Laughton,

Peter Ustinov, Tony Curtis, Herbert Lom; screenplay by Dalton Trumbo; prod. Edward Lewis; dir. Stanley Kubrick
ARCHIE RICE in *The Entertainer* (GB: Woodfall) with Joan Plowright, Brenda de Banzie, Alan Bates, Roger Livesey, Albert Finney, Shirley Anne Field; prod. Harry Saltzman; dir. Tony Richardson; *nominated for US Academy Award: Best Actor*

1960 Directs Levy's *The Tumbler* with Charlton Heston, Rosemary Harris, Martha Scott; Helen Hayes Theater, New York
BERENGER in Ionesco's *Rhinoceros* with Joan Plowright, Peter Sallis, Alan Webb, Miles Malleson; dir. Orson Welles; Royal Court Theatre, London
BERENGER in *Rhinoceros* with Maggie Smith replacing Joan Plowright; Strand Theatre, London
Title role in Anouilh's *Becket* with Anthony Quinn; dir. Peter Glenville; St James's Theater, New York
Marriage to Vivien Leigh dissolved

1961 Marries Joan Plowright
Takes over Henry II in Peter Glenville's production of *Becket* with Arthur Kennedy as Becket; Hudson Theater, New York

Television
THE PRIEST in Graham Greene's *The Power and the Glory* (US: Paramount TV) with Julie Harris, George C. Scott, Roddy McDowell, Keenan Wynn, Cyril Cusack; prod. David Susskind; dir. Marc Daniels

Appointed first director of Chichester Festival Theatre

1962 Chichester Festival Theatre: Directs Villiers's *The Chances* with Joan Plowright, Keith Michell, John Neville
Directs and plays PROLOGUE and BASSANES in Ford's *The Broken Heart* with Keith Michell, John Neville, Joan Greenwood
Directs and plays ASTROV in *Uncle Vanya* with Michael Redgrave, Joan Plowright, Joan Greenwood, Sybil Thorndike
FRED MIDWAY in David Turner's *Semi-Detached* with Mona Washbourne, James Bolam, Eileen Atkins; dir. Tony Richardson; Saville Theatre, London
Appointed first director of the National Theatre

Film
GRAHAM WEIR in *Terms of Trial* (GB: Romulus/Warner Bros) with Simone Signoret, Sarah Miles, Roland Culver, Hugh Griffith, Terence Stamp; prod. James Woolf; dir. Peter Glenville

1963 ASTROV in revival of his production of *Uncle Vanya*; Chichester
National Theatre opens at the Old Vic, London
Directs *Hamlet* with Peter O'Toole, Michael Redgrave, Rosemary Harris, Max Adrian, Diana Wynyard
ASTROV in his own Chichester production of *Uncle Vanya*, revived at the NT
CAPTAIN BRAZEN in Farquhar's *The Recruiting Officer*

with Robert Stephens, Maggie Smith, Colin Blakely, Max Adrian, Derek Jacobi; dir. William Gaskill

Film
ASTROV in *Uncle Vanya* (GB: BHE Productions) with Michael Redgrave in title role of film version of Olivier's Chichester/NT production; dir. Stuart Burge

1964 Title role in *Othello* with Maggie Smith, Frank Finlay, Derek Jacobi; dir. John Dexter; NT and Chichester
HALVARD SOLNESS in Ibsen's *The Master Builder* with Maggie Smith (succeeded by Joan Plowright), Celia Johnson; dir. Peter Wood; NT

1965 NT tour to Moscow and Berlin: Title role in *Othello* (with Billie Whitelaw as Desdemona)
TATTLE in Congreve's *Love for Love* with Albert Finney, Miles Malleson, John Stride; dir. Peter Wood; NT, Moscow and London

Film
INSPECTOR NEWHOUSE in *Bunny Lake is Missing* (US: Columbia) with Keir Dullea, Carol Lynley, Noël Coward, Anna Massey; prod. and dir. Otto Preminger
Title role in *Othello* (BG: BHE Productions) with Maggie Smith, Frank Finlay and original cast in film version of NT production; prod. Anthony Havelock-Allen and John Brabourne; dir. Stuart Burge; *nominated for US Academy Award: Best Actor*

1966 Directs O'Casey's *Juno and the Paycock*; NT

Film
THE MAHDI in *Khartoum* (US: United Artists) with Charlton Heston, Richard Johnson, Ralph Richardson; prod. Julian Blaustein; dir. Basil Dearden

1967 EDGAR in Strindberg's *The Dance of Death* with Geraldine McEwan, Robert Stephens; dir. Glen Byam Shaw; NT
Directs Chekhov's *The Three Sisters* with Joan Plowright, Louise Purnell, Jeanne Watts; NT
NT tour of Canada (Expo 67):
TATTLE in *Love for Love*
EDGAR in *The Dance of Death*
ETIENNE PULCHEUX in Feydeau's *A Flea in her Ear*; dir. Jacques Charon

1968 Co-directs (with Donald McKechnie) Ginzburg's *The Advertisement* with Joan Plowright; NT
Directs *Love's Labour's Lost* with Joan Plowright, Jeremy Brett, Ronald Pickup, Derek Jacobi; NT

Films
KAMENEV in *The Shoes of the Fisherman* (US: MGM) with Anthony Quinn, Oscar Werner, Leo McKern, David Janssen, Barbara Jefford, John Gielgud, Vittorio de Sica; prod. George Englund; dir. Michael Anderson
Speaks prologue and epilogue in *Romeo and Juliet* (Verona/De Laurentis) with Leonard Whiting and Olivia Hussey in

the title roles; dir. Franco
Zeffirelli
FIELD MARSHALL SIR JOHN
FRENCH in *Oh! What a Lovely
War* (Paramount) with John
Gielgud, Ralph Richardson,
Michael Redgrave, John Mills,
Kenneth More, Ian Holm;
prod. Brian Duffy and Richard
Attenborough; dir. Richard
Attenborough
EDGAR in *The Dance of Death*
(GB: BHE) with original cast in
film version of NT production;
prod. John Brabourne; dir.
David Giles

1969 A.B. RAHAM in Maugham's
Home and Beauty with Geraldine
McEwan, Hazel Hughes, Jane
Lapotaire; dir. Frank Dunlop;
NT
EDGAR in *The Dance of Death*;
NT revival
Takes over part of CHEBUTIKIN
in own NT production of *The
Three Sisters*; NT and Los
Angeles

Films
AIR CHIEF MARSHAL SIR HUGH
DOWDING in *Battle of Britain*
(GB: Spitfire/United Artists)
with Trevor Howard, Ralph
Richardson, Michael Caine,
Robert Shaw, Harry Andrews,
Kenneth More, Susannah York;
prod. Harry Saltzman and S.
Benjamin Fisz; dir. Guy
Hamilton
MR CREAKLE in *David Copperfield*
(GB: Omnibus/Fox) with
Robin Phillips, Edith Evans,
Michael Redgrave, Emlyn
Williams, Wendy Hiller, Susan
Hampshire, Sinead Cusack;
prod. Frederick H. Brogger; dir.

Delbert Mann
Directs and plays CHEBUTIKIN
in *The Three Sisters* (GB:
Clore/British Lion) with
original cast in film version of
NT production; prod. John
Goldstone

Television
HOST/NARRATOR in *Male of the
Species* (US: NBC TV) with
Sean Connery, Michael Caine,
Paul Scofield, Anna Calder-
Marshall; written by Alun
Owen; prod. Cecil Clarke; dir.
Charles Jarrott

1970 Leads NT company tour to Los
Angeles with *The Three Sisters*
and *The Beaux Stratagem*
Created Life Peer in Birthday
Honours List
SHYLOCK in *The Merchant of
Venice* with Joan Plowright,
Anthony Nicholls, Jeremy
Brett; dir. Jonathan Miller; NT

1971 Directs Giraudoux's *Amphitryon
38* with Christopher Plummer,
Geraldine McEwan; NT
production at New Theatre,
London
JAMES TYRONE in O'Neill's
Long Day's Journey into Night
with Constance Cummings,
Denis Quilley, Ronald Pickup;
dir. Michael Blakemore; NT
production at New Theatre

Films
COUNT WITTE in *Nicholas and
Alexandra* (Columbia) with
Michael Jayston and Janet
Suzman in title roles, Michael
Redgrave, Harry Andrews,
Tom Baker; prod. Sam Spiegel
and Franklin J. Schaffner; dir.
Franklin J. Schaffner

DUKE OF WELLINGTON in *Lady Caroline Lamb* (Anglo-EMI) with Sarah Miles in title role, Jon Finch, Richard Chamberlain, John Mills, Ralph Richardson, Margaret Leighton, Michael Wilding, Pamela Brown; prod. Fernando Ghia; dir. and screenplay by Robert Bolt

1972 JAMES TYRONE in NT *Long Day's Journey into Night*; Old Vic

Films
ANDREW WYKE in *Sleuth* (US: Palomar) with Michael Caine; prod. Edgar J. Scherick; dir. Joseph L. Mankiewicz; *nominated for US Academy Award: Best Actor*

Television
JAMES TYRONE in *Long Day's Journey into Night* (ATV) with original cast in film version of Michael Blakemore's NT production; dir. Peter Wood; *US Emmy award as Best TV Actor*

1973 Resigns as director of National Theatre
ANTONIO in Eduardo de Filippo's *Saturday, Sunday, Monday* (adapted by Keith Waterhouse and Willis Hall) with Joan Plowright, Frank Finlay, Denis Quilley, Anna Carteret; dir. Franco Zeffirelli; NT
JOHN TAGG in Trevor Griffiths's *The Party* with Frank Finlay, Ronald Pickup, Denis Quilley, Anna Carteret; dir. John Dexter; NT; *last stage appearance*

Television
SHYLOCK in *The Merchant of Venice* (ATV) with original cast

in film version of NT production; dir. Jonathan Miller
NARRATOR of *The World at War* (UK: Thames Television): a history of the Second World War in twenty-six sixty-minute episodes produced by Jeremy Isaacs
SIR ARTHUR GRANVILLE-JONES in *Love Among the Ruins* (US) with Katharine Hepburn, Colin Blakely, Joan Sims; dir. George Cukor; *US Emmy award for Best TV Actor*

1974 Directs J. B. Priestley's *Eden End* with Joan Plowright, Leslie Sands, Michael Jayston; NT

1976 *Films*
PROFESSOR MORIARTY in *The Seven Per Cent Solution* (US: Universal) with Nicol Williamson, Robert Duvall, Alan Arkin, Vanessa Redgrave; prod. and dir. Herbert Ross
DR CHRISTIAN SZELL in *Marathon Man* (US: Paramount/CIC) with Dustin Hoffman, Roy Scheider, William Devane, Martha Keller; prod. Robert Evans and Sidney Beckerman; dir. John Schlesinger; *nominated for US Academy Award: Best Supporting Actor*
DR SPAANDER in *A Bridge Too Far* (US: United Artists) with Dirk Bogarde, James Caan, Michael Caine, Sean Connery, Edward Fox, Elliott Gould, Gene Hackman, Anthony Hopkins, Ryan O'Neill, Robert Redford, Maximilian Schell, Liv Ullmann; prod. Joseph E.

Levine; dir. Richard Attenborough

NICODEMUS in *Jesus of Nazareth* (RAI/ITC) with Robert Powell in title role, Cyril Cusack, Peter Ustinov, Rod Steiger, Olivia Hussey; written by Anthony Burgess; prod. Dyson Lovell; dir. Franco Zeffirelli

Television

Co-produces (with Derek Granger) and plays HARRY KANE in Pinter's *The Collection* (UK: Granada TV) with Alan Bates, Malcolm McDowell, Helen Mirren; dir. Michael Apted

Co-produces (with Derek Granger) and plays BIG DADDY in Williams's *Cat on a Hot Tin Roof* (UK: Granada TV) with Natalie Wood, Robert Wagner, Maureen Stapleton, Jack Hedley; dir. Robert Moore

Co-produces and co-directs (with June Howson) Houghton's *Hindle Wakes* (UK: Granada TV) with Donald Pleasance, Rosemary Leach, Jack Hedley, Pat Heywood, Rosalind Ayres, Roy Dotrice

1977 *Television*

Co-produces (with Derek Granger) and plays DOC DELANEY in Inge's *Come Back Little Sheba* (UK: Granada) with Joanne Woodward, Patience Collier, Carrie Fisher, Nicholas Campbell; dir. Silvio Narizzano

Co-produces (with Derek Granger) and plays SIR JOSEPH PITTS in *Daphne Laureola* (UK: Granada TV) with Joan Plowright

Co-produces (with Derek Granger) and plays ANTONIO in de Filippo's *Saturday, Sunday, Monday* with Joan Plowright

1978 *Films*

LOREN HARDEMAN SR in *The Betsy* (US: United Artists) with Robert Duvall, Katharine Ross, Tommy Lee Jones, Lesley-Anne Down; prod. Robert R. Weston; dir. Daniel Petrie

EZRA LIEBERMAN in *The Boys from Brazil* (Grade/ITC/Twentieth Century Fox) with Gregory Peck, James Mason, Lilli Palmer, Rosemary Harris, Denholm Elliott; prod. Stanley O'Toole and Martin Richards; dir. Franklin J. Schaffner

Special US Academy Award to Laurence Olivier for "the full body of his work, the unique achievements of his entire career and his lifetime of contribution to the art of film"

1979 *Films*

JULIUS in *A Little Romance* (Warner Bros) with Thelonius Bernard, Diane Lane, Arthur Hill, Sally Kellerman, Arlene Francis, Broderick Crawford; prod. Yves Rousset-Rouard; dir. George Roy Hill

PROFESSOR VAN HELSING in *Dracula* (Universal) with Frank Langella in title role, Donald Pleasance, Kate Nelligan, Jan Francis; prod. Walter Mirisch and John Badham; dir. John Badham

1980 Directs de Filippo's *Filumena* with Joan Plowright, Frank Finlay; St James's Theater, New York

Films

MACARTHUR in *Inchon* (US: One Way) with Jacqueline Bisset, Ben Gazzara, Omar Sharif, Toshiro Mifune; prod. Rev. Moon and Mitsuharu Ishi; dir. Terence Young (unreleased in the UK as of 1987)

CANTOR RABINOVITCH in *The Jazz Singer* (EMI/Associated Films) with Neil Diamond, Lucy Arnaz, Catlin Adams, Franklyn Ajye; prod. Jerry Leider; dir. Richard Fleischer

1981 *Film*

ZEUS in *Clash of the Titans* (MGM) with Ursula Andress, Burgess Meredith, Harry Hamlin, Flora Robson, Claire Bloom, Maggie Smith, Sian Phillips, Judi Bowker, Susan Fleetwood, Pat Roach, Tim Piggot-Smith; prod. Charles H. Schneer and Ray Harryhausen; dir. Desmond Davis

Television

LORD MARCHMAIN in *Brideshead Revisited* (UK: Granada TV) (adapted from Evelyn Waugh by John Mortimer) with Anthony Andrews, Jeremy Irons, Claire Bloom; dir. Charles Sturridge

SANDOR LUKACS in *Wagner* with Richard Burton, John Gielgud, Ralph Richardson, Vanessa Redgrave, dir. Tony Palmer

1982 *Television*

CLIFFORD MORTIMER in Mortimer's *A Voyage round my Father* (UK: Thames Television) with Alan Bates, Elizabeth Sellars, Jane Asher;

dir. Alvin Rakoff
Published memoirs: *Confessions of an Actor*

1983 *Television*

LEAR in *King Lear* (UK: Granada TV) with Colin Blakely, Diana Rigg, Dorothy Tutin, John Hurt; dir. Michael Elliott

MR HALPERN in Goldstein's *Mr Halpern and Mr Johnson* with Jackie Gleason; dir. Alvin Rakoff

DR WAINWRIGHT in Choderov and Panama's *A Talent for Murder* (BBC) with Angela Lansbury; dir: Alvin Rakoff

1984 *Films*

ADMIRAL HOOD in *The Bounty* with Mel Gibson, Anthony Hopkins, Edward Fox; dir. Roger Donaldson

Television

HENRY BREASLEY in Fowles's *The Ebony Tower* (UK: Granada TV) (adapted for Granada television by John Mortimer); dir. Robert Knights

GAIUS in *The Last Days of Pompeii* with Ned Beatty, Brian Blessed, Ernest Borgnine, Nicholas Clay, Lesley-Anne Down, Olivia Hussey, Siobhan McKenna, Franco Nero, Anthony Quayle; adapted for ABC television from Edward Bulwer Lytton's novel by Carmen Culver; dir. Peter Hunt

1985 *Films*

SIR GERALD SCAITH in *The*

Jigsaw Man with Michael
Caine, Robert Powell, Susan
George; dir. Terence Young
RUDOLF HESS in *Wild Geese II*
with Scott Glenn, Edward Fox,
Stratford Johns; prod. Euan
Lloyd; dir. Peter Hunt; *last film
role*

Television
KING WILLIAM III in *Peter the
Great*

1986   *Television*
HARRY BURRARD in Priestley's
Lost Empires (Granada TV); *last
television role*

Theatre
AKASH (a "portrayal" in
hologram form) in *Time* with
Cliff Richard (later David
Cassidy), produced by Dave
Clark at the Dominion Theatre,
London
Published *Olivier on Acting*

Notes

Direct quotations from Laurence Olivier in the text come from his memoirs, *Confessions of an Actor* (Weidenfeld & Nicolson, 1982), unless otherwise identified below or in the text itself. Publication details of books cited in these source notes are to be found in the bibliography on pages 482–91. Quotations from contemporary reviews are usually sourced in the text; further details are provided here only to guide the reader to valuable further reading in critical anthologies, etc., especially in the case of Olivier specialists such as Kenneth Tynan. Other direct quotations not identified in these source notes are clearly signposted in the text itself.

Foreword

1 Laurence Olivier, letter to the author, 16 July 1978
2 Garry O'Connor (ed.), Introduction to *Olivier: In Celebration*
3 Peter Ustinov, *Dear Me*

Prologue

1 Richard Meryman, "First Lord of the Stage", *Life* magazine, New York, 12 August 1972
2 Mark Amory, interview, and in contribution to O'Connor (ed.), *op. cit.*
3 Joan Plowright, quoted in LO, *Confessions of an Actor*

4 Robert Speaight, *Shakespeare on the Stage*
5 Author's interviews with members of the cast
6 LO, quoted by Derek Granger in contribution to O'Connor (ed.), *op. cit.*
7 LO, quoted by Michael Caine in contribution to *ibid*.
8 Garson Kanin, *Tracy and Hepburn*
9 Peter Ustinov, in contribution to O'Connor (ed.), *op. cit.*
10 Kathleen Tynan, *The Life of Kenneth Tynan*
11 Sir Peter Hall, interview, and in contribution to O'Connor (ed.), *op. cit.*.

12 Derek Jacobi, interview
13 Ian Holm, interview
14 John Osborne, in Logan Gourlay (ed.), *Olivier*
15 Thomas Kiernan, *Sir Larry*
16 Sir Peter Hall, interview
17 J. B. Priestley, *Particular Pleasures*

1: 1907–24

1 The author is grateful to Lord McCarthy for writing to point out this reference from Laurence Irving's biography of his grandfather, after reading material from a draft of this book published in the *Observer* in May 1987, on the occasion of Olivier's eightieth birthday.
2 Ustinov, *op. cit.*
3 Lord Wilson, interview
4 Sybille Olivier furnished a family history to Felix Barker for his biography of LO and Vivien Leigh, *The Oliviers* (1953). I am grateful to Mr Barker for permission to make use of that material in this chapter.
5 LO, maiden speech in the House of Lords, *Hansard*, 20 July 1971
6 *Daily Telegraph*, 14 May 1939
7 *Manchester Guardian*, 3 April 1947
8 *Two Hundred Years of Dorking Cricket, 1766–1968* (published privately, 1968). I am grateful to Desmond Cecil, then skipper of neighbouring Claygate CC, for help in obtaining a copy.
9 LO, interviewed by Kenneth Tynan on BBC TV, 23 June 1967; later published in Hal Burton (ed.), *Great Acting*
10 *Birmingham Post*, 17 July 1958
11 *Daily Telegraph*, 14 May 1937
12 Kiernan, *op. cit.*
13 Richard Findlater (ed.), *At The Royal Court*

14 *Sunday Times*, 16 November 1953
15 *Manchester Guardian*, 3 April 1947
16 *Sunday Times*, 16 November 1953
17 There is some confusion over this, the first stage role in which LO was cast, even if he did not play it. In 1952 he told Felix Barker that it was First Citizen, but in 1982 in his own memoirs he wrote Second Citizen. I have opted for the version of a memory thirty years younger.
18 *Sunday Express*, 26 March 1964
19 BBC Radio, 16 December 1969
20 Kiernan, *op. cit.*
21 *Life* magazine, 12 August 1972
22 Kiernan, *op. cit.*
23 Michael Billington, in contribution to O'Connor (ed.), *op. cit.*
24 *Manchester Guardian*, 3 April 1947
25 *Ibid.*
26 Denys Blakelock, *Round the Next Corner*
27 W. A. Darlington, *6001 Nights: Forty Years a Dramatic Critic*

2: 1924–8

1 Marion Cole, *Fogie: The Life of Elsie Fogerty*
2 *Ibid.*
3 LO, in conversation with Kenneth Harris, *Observer*, 2 and 9 February 1969
4 Irving Wardle, *The Theatres of George Devine*
5 Athene Seyler, interview
6 Cole, *op. cit.*
7 *Ibid.*
8 O'Connor (ed.), *op. cit.*
9 *Birmingham Post*, 3 November 1956
10 Denys Blakelock, *op. cit.*
11 Lillian and Helen Ross, *The Player: Profile of an Art*
12 Ralph Richardson, in contribution to Sheridan Morley (ed.), *Theatre*

'73, extracted in the *Sunday Times*, 21 October 1973
13 Laurence Naismith, interviewed on BBC TV's *Olivier*, 1985
14 J. C. Trewin, *The Birmingham Repertory Theatre, 1913–63*
15 Blakelock, *Round the Next Corner*
16 *Observer*, 12 March 1962
17 Jessica Tandy, interview
18 Gwen Ffrangcon-Davies, interview
19 Harold Hobson, *Ralph Richardson*
20 Sir John Gielgud, interview, and in contribution to Findlater (ed.), *op. cit.*
21 J. C. Trewin, *The Gay Twenties: A Decade of the Theatre*
22 Esmond Knight, interview
23 Findlater (ed.), *op. cit.*
24 Denys Blakelock, *Advice to a Player: Letters to a Young Actor*

3: 1928–31
1 R. C. Sherriff, *No Leading Lady*
2 Basil Dean, *Mind's Eye: An Autobiography 1927–72*
3 Darlington, *op. cit.*
4 Dean, *op. cit.*
5 LO, interviewed by Sewell Stokes in *Theatre Arts*, New York, December 1945
6 Robert Speaight, *The Property Basket*
7 Jack Hawkins, *Anything for a Quiet Life*
8 W. Macqueen-Pope, *The Footlights Flickered*
9 Sheridan Morley, *A Talent to Amuse*
10 *Daily Herald*, 22 May 1930
11 *Sunday Dispatch*, 30 April 1961
12 *The Times*, 26 July 1930
13 *Evening Chronicle*, Manchester, 13 September 1930
14 Noël Coward, *Present Indicative*
15 *Ibid.*
16 John Mills, *Up in the Clouds, Gentlemen, Please*

17 Nora Swinburne, interview
18 Esmond Knight, interview
19 LO, interviewed by Kenneth Tynan on BBC TV; reprinted in Burton, *op. cit.*
20 Charles Castle, *Noël*
21 *Ibid.*
22 John Mason Brown, *Seeing Things*
23 Brooks Atkinson, *Broadway, New York*

4: 1931–5
1 Sheridan Morley, *Tales from the Hollywood Raj*
2 J. B. Priestley, *Midnight on the Desert*
3 Rudy Behlmer (ed.), *Memo from David O. Selznick*
4 LO, interviewed by Terry Coleman, "Olivier Now", *Show* magazine, June 1970
5 Douglas Fairbanks Jr, interview
6 Thomas Quinn Curtis, *Von Stroheim*
7 Douglas Fairbanks Jr, interview
8 Dean, *op. cit.*
9 Harold Hobson, *Theatre in Britain*
10 Sheridan Morley, *Gladys Cooper*
11 Norman Zierold, *Garbo*
12 LO, on *The Dick Cavett Show*, New York, 1973
13 John Cottrell, *Laurence Olivier*
14 Zierold, *op. cit.*
15 Martin Gottfried, *Jed Harris: The Curse of Genius*
16 Kanin, *op. cit.*
17 Stark Young, *Immortal Shadows: On Dramatic Criticism*
18 Cottrell, *op. cit.*
19 John Gielgud, *Early Stages*
20 Brian Aherne, *A Proper Job*
21 Cole Lesley, *The Life of Noël Coward*
22 Audrey Williamson, *Theatre of Two Decades*
23 Blakelock, *Round the Next Corner*
24 Emlyn Williams, in contribution to O'Connor (ed.), *op. cit.*

5: 1935

1 Sir John Gielgud, interview
2 Graham Greene, *Spectator*, 15 November 1935; later collected in *The Pleasure Dome*
3 Wardle, *The Theatres of George Devine*
4 Percy Harris and Elizabeth Montgomery (surviving members of Motley), interview
5 James Agate, *Brief Chronicles*
6 Barker, *op. cit.*
7 Gielgud, *op. cit.*
8 Letter from Richardson to LO, first quoted in Barker, *op. cit.*
9 Sir John Gielgud, interview
10 Peggy Ashcroft, in contribution to Gourlay (ed.), *op. cit.*
11 Gielgud, *op. cit.*
12 *Ibid.*
13 *The David Frost Show*, New York, 11 December 1970
14 LO, quoted in Ronald Hayman, *Playback*
15 LO, *On Acting*
16 LO, interviewed by Kenneth Tynan on BBC TV; reprinted in Burton, *op. cit.*
17 Kenneth Tynan, *He That Plays the King*
18 Elisabeth Bergner, interview
19 Bernard Grebanier, *Then Came Each Actor*
20 *Spectator*, 11 September 1936; reprinted in Greene, *op. cit.*
21 Robert L. Daniels, *Laurence Olivier: Theatre and Cinema*
22 Anne Edwards, *Vivien Leigh*

6: 1936

1 Mr Tarquin Olivier unfortunately decided against granting an interview for the purposes of this volume, though we have met socially. The portrait of him is compiled from conversations with friends and acquaintances, and writers who *have* interviewed him, as well as his father's own account of their relationship.
2 There are numerous different accounts of LO's first meeting with Vivien Leigh. After interminable investigation of published and unpublished evidence, I have settled for this as the nearest we will now ever get to the truth. Interviewed by Felix Barker for their official biography, the couple referred only to the wait for a taxi – but then they were being less than honest with Mr Barker about many such incidents in their recent and less recent lives.
3 Edwards, *op. cit.* The author is most grateful to Miss Edwards for her help in conversations about LO and Vivien Leigh, and her generous permission to make use of published and unpublished material.
4 *Daily Express*, 17 August 1960
5 Paul Tabori, *Alexander Korda*
6 Janet Dunbar, *Flora Robson*
7 James Mason, *Before I Forget*
8 *Spectator*, 26 February 1937
9 Author's source requests anonymity

7: 1937

1 Peter Roberts, *The Old Vic Story*, which provides an excellent portrait of Lilian Baylis, though an even fuller one can be found in Richard Findlater, *Lilian Baylis: The Lady of the Old Vic*
2 Findlater, *ibid.*
3 Barker, *op. cit.*
4 The author was kindly entertained there by Anthony Hopkins
5 Ernest Jones, *Oedipus and Hamlet,*

Essays in Applied Psychoanalysis

6 James Forsyth, *Tyrone Guthrie*

7 Michael Redgrave, *In my Mind's Eye*

8 Tyrone Guthrie, *A Life in the Theatre*

9 Speaight, *Shakespeare on the Stage*

10 Audrey Williamson, *Old Vic Drama*

11 Ustinov, *op. cit.*

12 Harcourt Williams, *The Old Vic Saga*

13 Forsyth, *op. cit.*

14 Redgrave, *op. cit.*

15 Gourlay (ed.), *op. cit.*

16 Stuart Burge, interview

17 Jessica Tandy, interview

18 J. C. Trewin, *Shakespeare on the English Stage*

19 Herbert Farjeon, *The Shakespearean Scene*

20 Jessica Tandy, interview, and in Cottrell, *op. cit.*

21 Laurence Kitchin, *Mid-Century Drama*

22 Forsyth, *op. cit.* Other accounts of the excursion to Elsinore are to be found in Guthrie's own memoirs and the writings of the various critics present, notably Bishop, Brown, Darlington and Speaight.

23 George W. Bishop, *My Betters*

24 Ivor Brown, *Shakespeare*

25 I am grateful to Hugo Vickers for information in this and several other areas while he was still working on his forthcoming biography of Vivien Leigh

26 Dean, *op. cit.*

27 *Ibid.*

28 *Spectator*, 12 January 1940

29 C. A. Lejeune, *Thank You for Having Me*

8: 1937–9

1 Behlmer (ed.), *op. cit.*

2 Roberts, *op. cit.*

3 Guthrie, *op. cit.*, and Forsyth, *op. cit.*

4 Guthrie, *ibid.*

5 Garry O'Connor, *Ralph Richardson: An Actor's Life*

6 John Casson, *Lewis and Sybil: A Memoir*

7 Arthur Marx, *Goldwyn: The Man behind the Myth*

8 Gourlay, *op. cit.*

9 David Niven, *The Moon's a Balloon*

10 Marx, *op. cit.*

11 Gourlay (ed.), *op. cit.*

12 There are many different versions of this famous story; Olivier's own is here reconciled with numerous other published accounts.

13 Behlmer (ed.), *op. cit.*

14 Bob Thomas, *Selznick*

15 *Spectator*, 5 May 1939

16 O'Connor, *Ralph Richardson*

17 LO, interviewed by Kenneth Harris, *Observer*, 2 and 9 February 1969

18 Behlmer (ed.), *op. cit.*

19 *Ibid.*

20 *Ibid.*

9: 1939–41

1 Douglas Fairbanks Jr, interview

2 Sir Cedric Hardwicke, *A Victorian in Orbit*

3 Niven, *op. cit.*

4 Behlmer (ed.), *op. cit.*

5 Donald Spoto, *The Life of Alfred Hitchcock*

6 Percy Harris and Elizabeth Montgomery, interview

7 Lord Lothian, cable to Foreign Office, 8 June 1940

8 Hayman, *op. cit.*

9 Michael Balcon, *Sunday Dispatch*, 25 August 1940

10 Lord Lothian, cable to Foreign Office, 31 August 1940

11 Cary Grant, quoted in Herbert Wilcox, *Twenty-Five Thousand Sunsets*
12 Edwards, *op. cit.*
13 Kanin, *op. cit.*
14 Sherriff, *op. cit.*
15 Paul Tabori, *Alexander Korda*
16 Barker, *op. cit.*
17 Behlmer (ed.), *op. cit.*

10: 1941–4

1 Forsyth, *op. cit.*
2 Richardson, in contribution to Morley (ed.), *Theatre '73*; extracted in the *Sunday Times*, 21 October 1973
3 Hayman, *op. cit.*
4 Gourlay (ed.), *op. cit.*, and *New York Times*, 10 March 1976
5 Alan Wood, *Mr Rank*
6 LO, interviewed by Kenneth Harris, *Observer*, 2 and 9 February 1969
7 Sir John Mills, interview
8 Susana Walton, *William Walton: Behind the Façade*
9 Wood, *op. cit.*
10 Kiernan, *op. cit.*
11 GBS, quoted in many different accounts of this scene
12 Edwards, *op. cit.*

11: 1944–5

1 O'Connor, *Ralph Richardson*
2 Wendy Trewin, *All on Stage: Charles Wyndham and the Alberys*
3 LO's own account confirms that of Guthrie himself, *In Various Directions*, and his biographers
4 Graham Payn and Sheridan Morley (eds), *The Noël Coward Diaries*, subsequently referred to throughout these notes as Coward, *Diaries*

5 Sir John Mills, interview
6 Kenneth Tynan, revised for publication in *He That Plays the King*
7 Speaight, *The Property Basket* and *Drama since 1939*
8 Ronald Harwood, *Sir Donald Wolfit CBE*
9 The best recent account of the formation of the Old Vic management may be found in O'Connor, *Ralph Richardson*, to supplement Guthrie's in *A Life in the Theatre*, and Forsyth, *op. cit.*
10 John Mortimer, interview, and *In Character*
11 Eric Bentley, *In Search of the Theatre*
12 Guthrie, *A Life in the Theatre*
13 Laurence Kitchin, *Shakespeare in the Modern Theatre*
14 Williams, *op. cit.*
15 Richard Buckle (ed.), *Cecil Beaton, Self Portrait with Friends: Diaries 1926–74*
16 Behlmer (ed.), *op. cit.*
17 LO's own account confirms theatrical folklore
18 Kenneth Tynan, *A View of the English Stage*
19 Richardson to Melvyn Bragg, *The South Bank Show*, London Weekend Television, 1982
20 Casson, *op. cit.*

12: 1945–7

1 Richardson interviewed in *Vogue* (US), 1971, quoted in William C. Young, *Famous Actors and Actresses on the American Stage*
2 Sir John Mills, interview
3 Williams, *op. cit.*
4 LO, quoted by John Mortimer, interview, and *In Character*
5 Donald Sinden, *A Touch of the Memoirs*

6 Hobson, *Ralph Richardson*
7 Edwards, *op. cit.*
8 John Mason Brown, *Seeing Things*
9 Olivier's financial support of his first wife continued for many years.
10 J. C. Trewin, *Peter Brook: A Biography*
11 Kitchin, *op. cit.*
12 Coward, *Diaries*
13 Bentley, *op. cit.*
14 O'Connor, *Ralph Richardson*, confirmed by other accounts
15 *Ibid.*
16 LO, in numerous interviews
17 LO, "An Essay in Hamlet", in Brenda Cross (ed.), *The Film Hamlet: A Record of its Production*
18 Ronald Hayman, *John Gielgud*
19 Buckle (ed.), *op. cit.*
20 Alan Dent, "Text Editing Shakespeare", in Dent (ed.), *Hamlet: The Film and the Play*
21 Wood, *op. cit.*
22 Bentley, *op. cit.*
23 Jean Renoir, quoted in Jack J. Jorgens, *Shakespeare on Film*
24 Mason Brown, *Dramatis Personae*
25 Bernard Grebanier, *The Heart of Hamlet*
26 Wood, *op. cit.*
27 Cross (ed.), *op. cit.*
28 Dent (ed.), *op. cit.*
29 James Agee, *Agee on Film*

13: 1947–8

1 Garry O'Connor, *Darlings of the Gods*. Mr O'Connor's book is a *locus classicus* on the Oliviers' tour of Australia and New Zealand, as is Felix Barker's *The Oliviers*, which first published LO's own journal of the trip. This account is indebted to both and to an interview with Terence Morgan and Georgina Jumel.

2 Buckle (ed.), *op. cit.*
3 O'Connor, *Darlings of the Gods*
4 Barker, *op. cit.*
5 LO, *Confessions of an Actor*
6 Forsyth, *op. cit.*
7 Jean Batters, *Edith Evans: A Personal Memoir*
8 Trewin, *Shakespeare on the English Stage*
9 T. C. Worsley, *The Fugitive Art: Dramatic Commentaries 1947–51*
10 O'Connor, *Ralph Richardson*
11 O'Connor, *Darlings of the Gods*

14: 1948–52

1 Williams, *op. cit.*
2 *Spectator*, 12 December 1948
3 Harold Hobson, *Theatre in Britain*
4 Buckle (ed.), *op. cit.*
5 Hugo Vickers, interview, and in *Cecil Beaton: The Authorized Biography*
6 Edwards, *op. cit.*
7 *Daily Express*, 13 October 1949
8 *The Mail on Sunday*, 24 October 1982
9 Tynan, *He That Plays the King*
10 Alexander Walker, *Vivien*
11 Harold Clurman, *Lies Like Truth*
12 Sir John Mills, interview
13 "The Oliviers in Hollywood", *New York Times* magazine, 22 October 1950
14 Gourlay (ed.), *op. cit.*
15 Walker, *op. cit.*
16 *Ibid.*
17 Coward, *Diaries*
18 O'Connor (ed.), *op. cit.*
19 Richard Findlater, *Michael Redgrave: Actor*
20 Redgrave, *op. cit.*
21 Michael Korda, *Charmed Lives*
22 Edwards, *op. cit.*

15: 1952–5

1 Casson, *op. cit.*

2 Wilcox, *op. cit.*
3 Bentley, *The Dramatic Event*
4 Pauline Kael, *The New Yorker*; reprinted in *I Lost It at the Movies*
5 Trewin, *Peter Brook*
6 Elaine Dundy, *Finch, Bloody Finch*
7 David Niven and Danny Kaye's published remarks on this episode are here reconciled with Olivier's own
8 Gourlay (ed.), *op. cit.*
9 BBC Radio, 19 November 1969
10 Graphically described by Bernard Hepton in the BBC TV series, *Olivier*, 1985
11 LO, *On Acting*

16: 1955

1 John Barber, *Daily Express*, 8 June 1955
2 The *locus classicus* on this and most other major moments in the last 100 years of Shakespeare performance at Stratford is Sally Beauman, *The Royal Shakespeare Company: A History of Ten Decades*
3 M. Darlow and G. Hodson, *Terence Rattigan: The Man and his Work*
4 Sir John Gielgud, interview
5 Gielgud, *An Actor and his Time*
6 Kenneth Tynan's review in the *Observer*, as summarized by LO in *Confessions of an Actor*
7 Tynan, *A View of the English Stage*
8 LO to various interviewers
9 Trewin, *Peter Brook*
10 *Ibid.*
11 Tynan, *A View of the English Stage*
12 Speaight, *Shakespeare on the Stage*
13 Tynan, *A View of the English Stage*
14 Coward, *Diaries*, the basis for all direct quotation in this passage

17: 1955–6

1 LO, *On Acting*

2 The author is extremely grateful to Harry Andrews (who was to have played Macduff in the film) for lending him his own cherished copy of the screenplay for an inordinate length of time.
3 Gourlay (ed.), *op. cit.*
4 *Ibid.*
5 Darlow & Hodson, *op. cit.*
6 Buckle (ed.), *op. cit.*
7 Sandra Shevey, *The Marilyn Scandal*
8 Arthur Miller, *Timebends: A Life*
9 Cottrell, *op. cit.*
10 Korda, *op. cit.*
11 Coward, *Diaries*
12 Edwards, *op. cit.*
13 There are many conflicting versions of this story. That offered here is the nearest the author can get to reconciling the conflicting versions of Miller, Osborne, Devine and Olivier himself.

18: 1956–8

1 LO, in Findlater (ed.), *At the Royal Court*
2 John Osborne, in *ibid.*
3 John Osborne, preface to *The Entertainer* (Faber & Faber, London, 1961)
4 Gourlay (ed.), *op. cit.*
5 *Ibid.*
6 Findlater (ed.), *At the Royal Court*
7 *Ibid.*, and Gourlay (ed.), *op. cit.*
8 *Ibid.*
9 Findlater (ed.), *op. cit.*
10 Tynan, *A View of the English Stage*
11 Kiernan, *op. cit.*
12 Wardle, *op. cit.*, plus various interviews with Osborne and Richardson
13 The author is grateful to Maxine Audley, a member of the company on that tour, for much of the description which follows.

14 Kenneth Tynan, *Tynan Right and Left*

15 Coward, *Diaries*

16 *Daily Herald*, 23 May 1958

17 Donald Edgar, *Evening Standard*, 2 September 1959

18 Harwood, *op. cit.*

19 *Daily Mail*, 20 November 1958

20 *The Times*, 20 November 1958

19: 1958–62

1 LO's preface to William Hobbs, *Techniques of the Stage Fight*

2 Jessica Tandy, interview

3 Coward, *Diaries*

4 Ustinov, *op. cit.*

5 Quoted in Cottrell, *op. cit.*

6 *Ibid.*

7 Ustinov, *op. cit.*

8 Quoted in Cottrell, *op. cit.*

9 Gourlay (ed.), *op. cit.*

10 Sam Wanamaker, interview

11 Sir Peter Hall, interview

12 Kitchin, *op. cit.*

13 Ian McKellen, interview

14 Tynan, *A View of the English Stage*

15 Quoted in Ronald Hayman, *Techniques of Acting*

16 Constance Cummings (Benn Levy's widow), interview

17 Charlton Heston, interview

18 Felix Barker, *Evening News*, 18 May 1960

19 Barbara Leaming, *Orson Welles*

20 *Observer*, 8 May 1960

21 Edwards, *op. cit.*

22 Virginia Fairweather, *Cry God for Larry*

23 Cottrell, *op. cit.*

24 *Ibid.*

25 Gourlay (ed.), *op. cit.*

26 Cottrell, *op. cit.*

27 Zero Mostel, interview

28 Arthur Kennedy, interview

29 Reports of the Olivier and Gage divorce proceedings in *The Times* and the *Daily Herald*, 2 December 1960

20: 1962–3

1 Esmond Knight and Nora Swinburne, interview

2 Nora Swinburne, interview

3 Source requests anonymity

4 Coward, *Diaries*

5 Hume Cronyn, interview

6 Edwards, *op. cit.*

7 The following section on the Chichester Festival Theatre is based on the author's interview with Leslie Evershed-Martin, supplemented by his book *The Impossible Theatre*, and Ronald Hayman's study of Chichester, *The First Thrust: Chichester Festival Theatre*. Some direct quotes from LO come from the introduction he wrote to Evershed-Martin's book.

8 LO, introduction to Evershed-Martin, *ibid.*

9 David Susskind, interview

10 Fairweather, *op. cit.*

11 Kenneth Tynan, "Olivier: The Actor and the Moor", published in *The Sound of Two Hands Clapping*

12 Gourlay (ed.), *op. cit.*

13 Kenneth Tynan, *Observer*, 15 July 1962; reprinted in *A View of the English Stage*

14 Fairweather, *op. cit.*

15 Redgrave, *op. cit.*

16 Leslie Evershed-Martin, interview

17 John Elsom and Nicholas Tomalin, *The History of the National Theatre*

18 Jonathan Miller, interview

19 Gourlay (ed.), *op. cit.*

20 John Russell Taylor, *Anger and After*

21 Gourlay (ed.), *op. cit.*

22 Burton's version of this popular story is quoted in Cottrell, *op. cit.*

Many others abound.
23 Fairweather, *op. cit.*
24 Kenneth Pearson, *Sunday Times* magazine, 23 September 1962

21: 1963–4

1 Guthrie's remarks on *The Brains Trust* were reprinted in *Encore*, summer 1956
2 Elsom and Tomalin, *op. cit.*
3 *Ibid.*
4 Guthrie, *In Various Directions*
5 *Ibid.*
6 Geoffrey Whitworth, *The Making of a National Theatre*
7 Sir Peter Hall, interview, and in *Peter Hall's Diaries*
8 Elsom and Tomalin, *op. cit.*, which gives a much fuller account of this period (officially "approved" by LO in his memoirs), as does Beauman, *op. cit.* There is also an excellent discussion of the two companies' contrasting methods and styles in Ronald Hayman, *The Set-Up: Anatomy of the English Theatre Today*
9 Elsom and Tomalin, *op. cit.*
10 Wardle, *op. cit.*
11 J. W. Lambert, interview, and in *Drama in Britain, 1964–73*
12 Nicholas Wapshott, *Peter O'Toole*
13 Sir John Gielgud, interview, and Hayman, *John Gielgud*. LO's failure to bring his abiding friend Richardson to the National Theatre has never been satisfactorily explained, either by writers, colleagues or the two men themselves.
14 Esmond Knight, interview
15 Tynan, *He That Plays the King*
16 Kathleen Tynan, *op. cit.*
17 *Olivier*, interviews by Melvyn Bragg, London Weekend

Television, 1982
18 Gourlay (ed.), *op. cit.*
19 Wapshott, *op. cit.*
20 Joseph McCrindle (ed.), *Behind the Scenes: Theatre and Film Interviews* from the *Transatlantic Review*
21 Redgrave, *op. cit.*
22 Tynan, "Olivier: The Actor and the Moor", in *The Sound of Two Hands Clapping*
23 Gourlay, (ed.), *op. cit.* Mr Gaskill was one of Olivier's few professional colleagues to decline, without explanation, the author's request for an interview.
24 John Elsom (ed.), *Post-War British Theatre Criticism*
25 Harold Clurman, *The Divine Pastime*
26 Tynan, *Tynan Right and Left*
27 *Observer*, 9 February 1969
28 Tynan, "Olivier: The Actor and the Moor", in *The Sound of Two Hands Clapping*
29 F. R. Leavis, *The Common Pursuit* (Chatto & Windus, London, 1952)
30 *Sunday Times*, 26 April 1964
31 *Life* magazine, 1963
32 LO, quoted by Harold Hobson in *Sunday Times*, 3 November 1963
33 *The David Frost Show*, New York, 11 May 1970
34 Laurence Kitchin, "Othello as Hipster", in *Drama in the Sixties*
35 Tynan, "Olivier: The Actor and the Moor", in *The Sound of Two Hands Clapping*
36 Hayman, *Playback*
37 Guthrie, *In Various Directions*
38 *Evening Standard*, 22 November 1963

22: 1964–7

1 Harry Andrews, interview
2 *Sunday Times*, 3 November 1963
3 Redgrave, *op. cit.*

4 *Observer*, 27 November 1964;
reprinted in Ronald Bryden, *The
Unfinished Hero and Other Essays*
5 Lesley, *op. cit.*
6 Keir Dullea, interview
7 *Observer*, 1 May 1964
8 Stuart Burge, interview
9 *Sunday Times*, 24 October 1965
10 Tynan, address to the Royal
Society of Arts, 1964; reprinted in
A View of the English Stage
11 Lambert, *op. cit.*
12 Tynan memorandum to LO,
quoted in LO, *Confessions of an Actor*
13 Sir Peter Hall, interview
14 Elsom and Tomalin, *op. cit.*
15 *Ibid.*
16 Hugh Willatt, *Sunday Times*,
30 April 1967, quoted
approvingly by LO in a letter
to *The Times*, 8 May 1967
17 Kathleen Tynan, *op. cit.*
18 Edwards, *op. cit.*
19 O'Connor, *Darlings of the Gods*
20 *New York Times* magazine,
25 March 1979

23: 1967–73
1 Wardle, *op. cit.*
2 *Sunday Telegraph*, 20 July 1969
3 Fairweather, *op. cit.*
4 *Daily Express*, 27 January 1968
5 *Observer*, 21 January 1968
6 Trewin, *Peter Brook*
7 *Daily Express*, 27 January 1968
8 *Sunday Telegraph*, 20 July 1969
9 Jonathan Miller, interview
10 Meryman, "First Lord of the
Stage", *Life* magazine, New York,
12 August 1972
11 Quoted in Gourlay (ed.), *op. cit.*
12 Elizabeth Sprigge, *Sybil Thorndike
Casson*
13 Sir Richard Attenborough,
interview

14 Alexander Walker, *Evening
Standard*, quoted in Margaret
Morley, *The Films and Faces of
Laurence Olivier*
15 Margaret Hinxman, *Sunday
Telegraph*, in *ibid.*
16 David Robinson, *Financial Times*, in
ibid.
17 Ronald Hastings, *Daily Telegraph*,
27 May 1971
18 Denis Quilley, interview
19 Michael Blakemore, interview
20 Constance Cummings, interview
21 Denis Quilley, interview
22 *Hansard*, 20 July 1971
23 The following sequence of events is
based on the author's interview
with Sir Peter Hall and the
evidence in Hall's published
diaries, as well as Olivier's own
written account and the author's
interviews with other participants.
24 Sir Richard Attenborough,
interview; and letter from LO to
Burton, to be published in the
forthcoming biography by Melvyn
Bragg
25 Laurence Evans, interview
26 Hall, *op. cit.*
27 Lord Rayne, letter to the *Sunday
Telegraph*, 3 October 1982. Rayne
declared himself appalled by the
bitter account of these events given
by Olivier in his memoirs.
28 Sir Richard Attenborough,
interview
29 Jeremy Isaacs, interview

24: 1973–83
1 A composite of Michael Caine's two
remembered versions of this letter,
in O'Connor (ed.), *op. cit.*, and
William Hall, *Raising Caine*. This
account of *Sleuth* is indebted to
both.

2 Sir John Mills and Sir Richard Attenborough, interviews
3 *Olivier*, BBC Television, prod. Bridget Winter, 1985; and William Goldman, *Adventures in the Screen Trade*
4 Charlton Heston, interview
5 *Bergen Record*, New Jersey, 7 October 1976
6 Sir Richard Attenborough, interview
7 Hall, interview, and *op. cit.*
8 O'Connor (ed.), *op. cit.* Mr Granger declined the author's request for an interview.
9 Helen Mirren, interview
10 *TV Guide*, USA, 21 October 1978
11 Natalie Wood, quoted in the *Bergen Record*, New Jersey, 5 December 1976
12 Jack Kroll, *Newsweek*, 1978
13 Daniel Petrie, interview
14 NT press conference, 13 March 1973
15 *New York Times* magazine, 25 March 1979

16 John Badham, interview
17 Richard Fleischer, interview
18 John Mortimer, interview
19 *Reputations*, an appraisal of Kenneth Tynan by Anthony Howard, BBC TV, 1982
20 Lord Rayne, letter to *Sunday Telegraph*, 3 October 1982
21 Lord Miles, interview
22 Lord Miles, quoted in LO, *Confessions of an Actor*
23 Laurence Evans, interview
24 Gawn Grainger, interview

25: 1983–7
1 Richard Meryman, *Life* magazine, 1983
2 *Observer*, 10 April 1983
3 See page 333
4 Source requests anonymity
5 Laurence Evans, interview
6 Gawn Grainger, interview
7 *New York Times* magazine, 25 March 1979
8 Meryman, *op cit.*
9 Ustinov, *op. cit.*

Bibliography

The following is a selective list of books and articles consulted by the author in the course of his research. He is grateful to the authors and publishers of those quoted, as identified in the source notes.

1: Books

ACKLAND, Rodney, *The Celluloid Mistress* (Wingate, London, 1954)

AGATE, James, *Brief Chronicles* (Jonathan Cape, London, 1943)

AGATE, James, *Red Letter Nights* (Jonathan Cape, London, 1944)

AGATE, James, *The Contemporary Theatre, 1944–1945* (Harrap, London, 1946)

AGEE, James, *Agee on Film* (McDowell Obolensky, New York, 1958)

AHERNE, Brian, *A Proper Job* (Houghton Mifflin, Boston, 1969)

ALPERT, Hollis, *The Barrymores* (W. H. Allen, London, 1964)

ATKINSON, Brooks, *Broadway, New York* (Macmillan, New York, 1970)

BACALL, Lauren, *By Myself* (Knopf, New York, 1978)

BAINBRIDGE, John, *Garbo* (Frederick Muller, London, 1955)

BARKER, Felix, *The Oliviers* (Hamish Hamilton, London, 1953)

BARKER, Felix, *Laurence Olivier* (Spellmount, Tunbridge Wells, 1984)

BARTHOLOMEUSZ, Dennis, *Macbeth and the Players* (Cambridge University Press, Cambridge, 1969)

BATTERS, Jean, *Edith Evans: A Personal Memoir* (Hart-Davis, London, 1977)

BAXTER, Beverley, *First Nights and Footlights* (Hutchinson, London, 1955)

BAXTER, Beverley, *First Nights and Noises Off* (Hutchinson, London, 1966)

BAZIN, Andre, *What is Cinema?*, vol. I (University of California Press, Berkeley, 1974)

BEATON, Cecil, *The Happy Years: Diaries 1944–48* (Weidenfeld & Nicolson, London, 1972)

BEAUMAN, Sally, *The Royal Shakespeare Company: A History of Ten Decades*

(Oxford University Press, Oxford, 1982)

BEHLMER, Rudy (ed.), *Memo from David O. Selznick* (Viking, New York, 1972)

BENTLEY, Eric, *In Search of the Theatre* (Vintage, New York, 1955)

BENTLEY, Eric, *The Dramatic Event* (Beacon Press, Boston, 1956)

BETTS, Ernest, *The Film Business* (Pitman, New York, 1973)

BILLINGTON, Michael, *The Modern Actor* (Hamish Hamilton, London, 1973)

BISHOP, George W., *My Betters* (Heinemann, London, 1957)

BLAKELOCK, Denys, *Finding my Way* (Hollis & Carter, London, 1958)

BLAKELOCK, Denys, *Advice to a Player: Letters to a Young Actor* (Heinemann, London, 1958)

BLAKELOCK, Denys, *Round the Next Corner* (Gollancz, London, 1967)

BLOOM, Claire, *Limelight and After* (Weidenfeld & Nicolson, London, 1982)

BRAGG, Melvyn, *Laurence Olivier* (Hutchinson, London, 1984)

BROOK, Donald, *A Pageant of English Actors* (Macmillan, New York, 1950)

BROOK, Peter, *The Empty Space* (McGibbon & Kee, London, 1968)

BROWN, Ivor, *Shakespeare* (Collins, London, 1949)

BROWN, Ivor, *Theatre 1954–5* (Max Reinhardt, London, 1955)

BROWN, Ivor, *Shakespeare Memorial Theatre 1954–6* (Max Reinhardt, London, 1956)

BROWN, Ivor, *Shakespeare and the Actors* (Coward McCann, New York, 1970)

BRYDEN, Ronald, *The Unfinished Hero and Other Essays* (Faber & Faber, London, 1969)

BUCKLE, Richard (ed.), *Cecil Beaton, Self-portrait with Friends: Diaries 1926–*

74 (Weidenfeld & Nicolson, London, 1979)

BURTON, Hal, *Great Acting* (BBC, London, 1967)

CALLOW, Simon, *Being an Actor* (Methuen, London, 1984)

CALLOW, Simon, *Charles Laughton* (Methuen, London, 1987)

CARLISLE, Carol Jones, *Shakespeare and the Green Room* (University of North Carolina, North Carolina, 1969)

CASSON, John, *Lewis and Sybil: A Memoir* (Collins, London, 1972)

CASTLE, Charles, *Noël* (W. H. Allen, London, 1973)

CLUNES, Alec, *The British Theatre* (Cassell, London, 1964)

CLURMAN, Harold, *Lies Like Truth* (Grove Press, New York, 1958)

CLURMAN, Harold, *The Naked Image* (Macmillan, New York, 1966)

CLURMAN, Harold, *The Divine Pastime* (Macmillan, New York, 1974)

COLE, Marion, *Fogie: The Life of Elsie Fogerty* (Peter Davies, London, 1967)

COLE, Toby, and CHINOY, Helen Krich, *Actors on Acting* (Crown, New York, 1977)

COLE, Toby, and CHINOY, Helen Krich, *Directors on Directing* (Bobb-Merril, Indianapolis, 1963)

COLVIN, Ian, *Flight 777* (Evans Bros, London, 1957)

CONNELL, Brian, *Knight Errant: A Study of Douglas Fairbanks Jr* (Hodder & Stoughton, London, 1955)

CONRAD, Earl, *Billy Rose, Manhattan Primitive* (World Publishing, New York, 1968)

COOK, Judith, *The National Theatre* (Harrap, London, 1976)

COTTRELL, John, *Laurence Olivier* (Weidenfeld & Nicolson, London, 1975)

COWARD, Noël, *Present Indicative*

(Heinemann, London, 1937)

COWARD, Noël, *Future Indefinite* (Heinemann, London, 1954)

CROSS, Brenda (ed,), *The Film Hamlet: A Record of its Production* (Saturn Press, London, 1948)

CURTIS, Thomas Quinn, *Von Stroheim* (Angus & Robertson, London, 1971)

DANIELS, Robert L., *Laurence Oliver: Theatre and Cinema* (Tantivy, London, 1980)

DARLINGTON, W. A., *The Actor and his Audience* (Phoenix House, London, 1949)

DARLINGTON, W. A., *6001 Nights: Forty Years a Dramatic Critic* (Harrap, London, 1960)

DARLINGTON, W. A., *Laurence Olivier* (Morgan Grampian, London, 1968)

DARLOW, M., and HODSON, G., *Terence Rattigan: The Man and his Work* (Quartet, London, 1979)

DAUBENY, Sir Peter, *My World of Theatre* (Jonathan Cape, London, 1971)

DEAN, Basil, *Mind's Eye: An Autobiography 1927–72* (Hutchinson, London, 1973)

DE BANKE, Cecil, *Shakespeare Production, Then and Now* (Hutchinson, London, 1954)

DENT, Alan, *Preludes and Studies* (Macmillan, London, 1942)

DENT, Alan, *Hamlet: The Film and the Play* (World Film Publishing, London, 1948)

DENT, Alan, *Vivien Leigh: A Bouquet* (Hamish Hamilton, London, 1969)

DONALDSON, Frances, *The Actor-Managers* (Regnery, Chicago, 1970)

DU MAURIER, Daphne, *Gerald, A Portrait* (Gollancz, London, 1934)

DUNBAR, Janet, *Flora Robson* (Harrap, London, 1960)

DUNDY, Elaine, *Finch, Bloody Finch* (Michael Joseph, London, 1980)

DURGNAT, Raymond, *A Mirror for England: British Movies from Austerity to Affluence* (Praeger, New York, 1971)

ECKERT, Charles W., *Focus on Shakespearean Films* (Prentice-Hall, New Jersey, 1972)

EDWARDS, Anne, *Vivien Leigh* (W. H. Allen, London, 1977)

ELSOM, John, *Theatre Outside London* (Macmillan, London, 1971)

ELSOM, John, *Post-War British Theatre Criticism* (Routledge & Kegan Paul, London, 1981)

ELSOM, John, and TOMALIN, Nicholas, *The History of the National Theatre* (Jonathan Cape, London, 1978)

EVERSHED-MARTIN, Leslie, *The Impossible Theatre* (Phillimore, Chichester, 1971)

FAIRWEATHER, Virginia, *Cry God for Larry* (Calder & Boyars, London, 1969; US title: *Olivier: An Informal Portrait* [Coward McCann, New York, 1969])

FARJEON, Herbert, *The Shakespearean Scene* (Hutchinson, London, 1949)

FAULKNER, Trader, *Peter Finch: A Biography* (Angus & Robertson, London, 1979)

FERRIS, Paul, *Richard Burton* (Weidenfeld & Nicolson, London, 1981)

FINDLATER, Richard, *Michael Redgrave: Actor* (Heinemann, London, 1956)

FINDLATER, Richard, *The Player Kings* (Weidenfeld & Nicolson, London, 1971)

FINDLATER, Richard, *Lilian Baylis: The Lady of the Old Vic* (Allen Lane, London, 1975)

FINDLATER, Richard (ed.), *At the Royal Court* (Amber Lane Press, London, 1981)

FINDLATER, Richard, *These Our Actors* (Elm Tree Books, London, 1983)

FORBES, Brian, *Notes for a Life* (Collins, London, 1974)

FORBES, Brian, *Ned's Girl: A Biography of Dame Edith Evans* (Elm Tree Books, London, 1977)

FORBES, Brian, *That Despicable Race* (Elm Tree Books, London, 1980)

FORSYTH, James, *Tyrone Guthrie: The Authorized Biography* (Hamish Hamilton, London, 1976)

FRENCH, Philip, *The Movie Moguls* (Weidenfeld & Nicolson, London, 1969)

GASSNER, John, *The Theatre in our Times* (Crown, New York, 1954)

GEDULD, Harry M., *Filmguide to Henry V* (Indiana University Press, Indiana, 1973)

GIELGUD, John, *Early Stages* (Macmillan, London, 1939)

GIELGUD, John, *Stage Directions* (Heinemann, London, 1963)

GIELGUD, John, *An Actor and his Time* (Sidgwick & Jackson, London, 1979)

GIELGUD, Val, *Years in a Mirror* (Bodley Head, London, 1965)

GOLDMAN, William, *Adventures in the Screen Trade* (Warner, New York, 1983)

GOODMAN, Randolph (ed.), *Drama on Stage* (Holt, Rinehart, New York, 1961)

GORDON, Ruth, *An Open Book* (Doubleday, New York, 1980)

GOTTFRIED, Martin, *Jed Harris: The Curse of Genius* (Little, Brown, Boston, 1984)

GOURLAY, Logan (ed.), *Olivier* (Weidenfeld & Nicolson, London, 1973)

GREBANIER, Bernard, *The Heart of Hamlet* (Apollo Books, New York, 1967)

GREBANIER, Bernard, *Then Came Each Actor* (McKay, New York, 1975)

GREENE, Graham, *The Pleasure Dome* (Secker & Warburg, London, 1972)

GROSSE, Gordon, *Shakespearean Playgoing, 1890–1952* (Mowbray, London, 1953)

GUINNESS, Alec, *Blessings in Disguise* (Hamish Hamilton, London, 1985)

GUTHRIE, Tyrone, *A Life in the Theatre* (Hamish Hamilton, London, 1960)

GUTHRIE, Tyrone, *In Various Directions* (Michael Joseph, London, 1965)

GUTHRIE, Tyrone, *Tyrone Guthrie on Acting* (Studio Vista, London, 1971)

HALL, Sir Peter, *Peter Hall's Diaries* (Hamish Hamilton, London, 1983)

HALL, William, *Raising Caine* (Sidgwick & Jackson, London, 1981)

HANKEY, Julie (ed.), *Richard III, "Plays in Performance"* (Junctions Books, London, 1981)

HARDWICKE, Sir Cedric, *Let's Pretend* (Grayson & Grayson, London, 1932)

HARDWICKE, Sir Cedric, *A Victorian in Orbit* (Methuen, London, 1961)

HARRISON, Rex, *Rex* (Macmillan, London, 1974)

HARWOOD, Ronald, *Sir Donald Wolfit CBE* (Secker & Warburg, London, 1971)

HARWOOD, Ronald, *All the World's a Stage* (BBC/Secker & Warburg, London, 1984)

HAWKINS, Jack, *Anything for a Quiet Life* (Elm Tree Books, London, 1973)

HAYMAN, Ronald, *Techniques of Acting* (Holt, Rinehart, New York, 1969)

HAYMAN, Ronald, *John Gielgud* (Heinemann, London, 1971)

HAYMAN, Ronald, *Playback* (Davis-Poynter, London, 1973)

HAYMAN, Ronald, *The Set-Up: Anatomy of the English Theatre Today*

(Methuen, London, 1974)

HAYMAN, Ronald, *The First Thrust: Chichester Festival Theatre* (Davis-Poynter, London, 1975)

HESTON, Charlton, *The Actor's Life: Diaries* (Dutton, New York, 1978)

HIRSCH, Foster, *Laurence Olivier* (Twayne, Boston, 1979)

HOBBS, William, *Techniques of the Stage Fight* (Studio Vista, London, 1967)

HOBSON, Harold, *Ralph Richardson* (Rockliff, London, 1958)

HOBSON, Harold, *Theatre in Britain* (Phaidon, London, 1984)

HOUSTON, Penelope, *The Contemporary Cinema* (Penguin, London, 1963)

HUNTLEY, John, *British Film Music* (Skelton Robinson, London, 1947)

HYAMS, Joe, *Bogie: The Authorized Biography* (W. H. Allen, London, 1971)

JONES, Ernest, *Oedipus and Hamlet, Essays in Applied Psychoanalysis* (New York, 1923)

JORGENS, Jack J., *Shakespeare on Film* (Indiana University Press, Indiana, 1977)

KAEL, Pauline, *I Lost It at the Movies* (Little, Brown, Boston, 1965)

KAEL, Pauline, *Deeper into Movies* (Warner, New York, 1969–73)

KAEL, Pauline, *5001 Nights at the Movies* (Elm Tree Books, London, 1982)

KANIN, Garson, *Tracy and Hepburn* (Viking, New York, 1971)

KAUFMAN, Stanley, *A World on Film* (Harper & Row, New York, 1966)

KAUFMAN, Stanley, *Persons of the Drama* (Harper & Row, New York, 1976)

KEMP, J. C., *The Birmingham Repertory Theatre* (Cornish Bros, London, 1943)

KEOWN, Eric, *Peggy Ashcroft* (Rockliff, London, 1955)

KERR, Walter, *Thirty Plays Hath*

November (Simon & Schuster, New York, 1965)

KIERNAN, Thomas, *Sir Larry* (Times Books, New York, 1981)

KITCHIN, Laurence, *Mid-Century Drama* (Faber & Faber, London, 1960)

KITCHIN, Laurence, *Drama in the Sixties* (Faber & Faber, London, 1966)

KORDA, Michael, *Charmed Lives* (Random House, New York, 1979)

KORDA, Michael, *Queenie* (Simon & Schuster, New York, 1985)

KOTT, Jan, *Shakespeare our Contemporary* (Methuen, London, 1965)

KULIK, Karol, *Alexander Korda* (Arlington House, New York, 1975)

LAMBERT, J. W., *Drama in Britain, 1964–73* (Longmans, London, 1974)

LANCHESTER, Elsa, *Charles Laughton and I* (Faber & Faber, London, 1938)

LANDSTONE, Charles, *Offstage* (Elek, London, 1953)

LASKY, Jessie L. Jr (with SILVER, Pat), *Love Scene: The Story of Laurence Olivier and Vivien Leigh* (Crowell, New York, 1978)

LEAMING, Barbara, *Orson Welles* (Weidenfeld & Nicolson, London, 1985)

LEJEUNE, C. A., *Thank You for Having Me* (Hutchinson, London, 1964)

LENBURG, Jeff, *Dustin Hoffman* (St Martins, New York, 1983)

LESLEY, Cole, *The Life of Noël Coward* (Jonathan Cape, London, 1976)

LESLIE, Cole, PAYN, Graham, and MORLEY, Sheridan, *Noël Coward and his Friends* (Weidenfeld & Nicolson, London, 1979)

MACQUEEN-POPE, W., *St James: Theatre of Distinction* (W. H. Allen, London, 1958)

MACQUEEN-POPE, W., *The Footlights Flickered* (Herbert Jenkins, London, 1959)

MANVELL, Roger, *Shakespeare and the Film* (Dent, London, 1971)

MAROWITZ, Charles, *Confessions of a Counterfeit Critic* (Methuen, London, 1973)

MAROWITZ, Charles, and TRUSSLER, Simon (eds), *Theatre at Work* (Methuen, London, 1967)

MARSHALL, Norman, *The Other Theatre* (John Lehmann, London, 1947)

MARX, Arthur, *Goldwyn: The Man behind the Myth* (Bodley Head, London, 1976)

MASON, James, *Before I Forget* (Hamish Hamilton, London, 1981)

MASON BROWN, John, *Seeing Things* (McGraw-Hill, New York, 1946)

MASON BROWN, John, *Dramatis Personae* (Viking, New York, 1963)

MATTHEWS, Bache, *A History of the Birmingham Repertory Theatre* (Chatto, London, 1924)

MCCARTHY, Mary, *Sights and Spectacles* (Farrar Strauss & Giroux, New York, 1956)

MCCARTHY, Mary, *Theatre Chronicles (1937–62)* (Farrar Strauss & Giroux, New York, 1963)

MCCRINDLE, Joseph (ed.), *Behind the Scenes: Theatre and Film Interviews* (Pitman, London, 1971)

MILES, Bernard, and TREWIN, J. C., *Curtain Calls* (Lutterworth, London, 1981)

MILLER, Arthur, *Timebends: A Life* (Methuen, London, 1987)

MILLS, John, *Up in the Clouds, Gentlemen, Please* (Weidenfeld & Nicolson, London, 1980)

MORE, Kenneth, *Happy Go Lucky* (Robert Hale, London, 1959)

MORLEY, Margaret, *The Films and Faces of Laurence Olivier* (LSP Books, Surrey, 1978)

MORLEY, Sheridan, *A Talent To Amuse* (Heinemann, London, 1969)

MORLEY, Sheridan (ed.), *Theatre '73* (Hutchinson, London, 1973)

MORLEY, Sheridan (ed.), *The Theatre Addict's Archive* (Elm Tree Books, London, 1977)

MORLEY, Sheridan, *Gladys Cooper*, (Weidenfeld & Nicolson, London, 1979)

MORLEY, Sheridan, *Gertrude Lawrence* (Weidenfeld & Nicolson, London, 1981)

MORLEY, Sheridan, *Tales from the Hollywood Raj* (Weidenfeld & Nicolson, London, 1983)

MORLEY, Sheridan, *The Other Side of the Moon: The Life of David Niven* (Weidenfeld & Nicolson, London, 1985)

MORTIMER, John, *In Character* (Allen Lane, London, 1983)

MUIR, Kenneth, and SCHOENBAUM, Samuel (eds), *A New Companion to Shakespeare Studies* (Oxford University Press, Oxford, 1971)

MULLIN, Michael, *Macbeth Onstage: An Annotated Facsimile of Glen Byam Shaw's 1955 Promptbook* (University of Missouri, Missouri, 1976)

NIVEN, David, *The Moon's a Balloon* (Hamish Hamilton, London, 1972)

NIVEN, David, *Bring on the Empty Horses* (Hamish Hamilton, London, 1975)

O'CONNOR, Garry, *Ralph Richardson: An Actor's Life* (Hodder & Stoughton, London, 1982)

O'CONNOR, Garry, *Darlings of the Gods* (Hodder & Stoughton, London, 1984)

O'CONNOR, Garry (ed.), *Olivier: In Celebration* (Hodder & Stoughton, London, 1987)

OLIVIER, Laurence, *Confessions of an Actor* (Weidenfeld & Nicolson, London, 1982)

OLIVIER, Laurence, *On Acting* (Weidenfeld & Nicolson, London, 1986)

PAYN, Graham, and MORLEY, Sheridan (eds), *The Noël Coward Diaries* (Weidenfeld & Nicolson, London, 1982)

PEARSON, Hesketh, *The Last Actor Managers* (Methuen, London, 1950)

PERRY, George (ed.), *Forever Ealing* (Pavilion, London, 1981)

PRIESTLEY, J. B., *Midnight on the Desert* (Heinemann, London, 1937)

PRIESTLEY, J. B., *Particular Pleasures* (Stein & Day, New York, 1975)

REDFIELD, William, *Letters from an Actor* (Cassell, London, 1966)

REDGRAVE, Sir Michael, *In my Mind's Eye* (Weidenfeld & Nicolson, London, 1983)

ROBERTS, Peter, *The Old Vic Story* (W. H. Allen, London, 1976)

ROBOZ, Zsuzsi, and GEBLER DAVIES, Stan, *Chichester 10: Portrait of a Decade* (Davis-Poynter, London, 1975)

ROBYNS, Gwen, *Light of a Star* (Leslie Frewin, London, 1968)

ROSS, Lillan and Helen, *The Player: Profile of an Art* (Simon & Schuster, New York, 1962)

RUSSELL TAYLOR, John, *Anger and After* (Methuen, London, 1962)

ST JOHN, Adela Rogers, *The Honeycomb* (Doubleday, New York, 1969)

SANDERSON, Michael, *From Irving to Olivier: A Social History of the Acting Profession in England, 1890–1980* (Athlone, London, 1984)

SHERRIFF, R. C., *No Leading Lady* (Gollancz, London, 1968)

SHEVEY, Sandra, *The Marilyn Scandal* (Sidgwick & Jackson, London, 1987)

SHINDLER, Colin, *Hollywood Goes to War* (Routledge & Kegan Paul, London, 1979)

SINCLAIR, Andrew, *Spiegel: The Man behind the Pictures* (Weidenfeld & Nicolson, London, 1987)

SINDEN, Donald, *A Touch of the Memoirs* (Hodder & Stoughton, London, 1982)

SPEAIGHT, Robert, *The Property Basket* (Harvill, London, 1970)

SPEAIGHT, Robert, *Shakespeare on the Stage* (Collins, London, 1973)

SPENCER, T. J. B. (ed.), *Shakespeare: A Celebration* (Penguin, London, 1964)

SPIEL, Hilda, *Sir L. Olivier* (Rembrandt-Heihe Buhne & Film, Berlin, 1958)

SPOTO, Donald, *The Life of Alfred Hitchcock* (Collins, London, 1983)

SPRAGUE, A. C., *Shakespearean Players and Performances* (A & C Black, London, 1954)

SPRAGUE, A. C., and TREWIN, J. C., *Shakespeare's Plays Today* (Sidgwick & Jackson, London, 1970)

SPRIGGE, Elizabeth, *Sybil Thorndike Casson* (Gollancz, London, 1971)

STANISLAVSKI, Constantin, *My Life in Art* (New York, 1924)

STANISLAVSKI, Constantin, *Building a Character* (Max Reinhardt, London, 1950)

STOKES, Sewell, *Without Veils: An Intimate Biography of Gladys Cooper* (Peter Davies, London, 1953)

SWINDELL, Larry, *Spencer Tracy* (World Publishing, New York, 1969)

SWINDELL, Larry, *Charles Boyer* (Doubleday, New York, 1983)

TABORI, Paul, *Alexander Korda* (Oldbourne/Heinman, New York, 1959)

TANITCH, Robert (ed.), *Ralph Richardson: A Tribute* (Evans, London, 1982)

TANITCH, Robert, *Olivier, The Complete Career* (Thames and Hudson, London, 1985)

THORNDIKE, Russell, *Sybil Thorndike*

(Eyre & Spottiswoode, London, 1950)

THOMAS, Bob, *Selznick* (Doubleday, New York, 1970)

TREWIN, J. C., *We'll Hear a Play* (Carroll & Nicholson, London, 1949)

TREWIN, J. C., *The Theatre Since 1900* (Dakers, London, 1951)

TREWIN, J. C., *A Play Tonight* (Elek, London, 1952)

TREWIN, J. C., *Edith Evans* (Rockliff, London, 1954)

TREWIN, J. C., *The Birmingham Repertory Theatre 1913–63* (Rockliff, London, 1963)

TREWIN, J. C., *Shakespeare on the English Stage* (Rockliff, London, 1964)

TREWIN, J. C., *Drama in Britain 1951–64* (Longmans, London, 1965)

TREWIN, J. C., *Robert Donat: A Biography* (Heinemann, London, 1968)

TREWIN, J. C., *Peter Brook: A Biography* (Macdonald, London, 1971)

TREWIN, J. C. (with MANDER, Raymond, and MITCHENSON, Joe), *The Gay Twenties: A Decade of the Theatre* (Macdonald, London, 1958)

TREWIN, J. C. (with MANDER, Raymond, and MITCHENSON, Joe), *The Turbulent Thirties: A Further Decade* (Macdonald, London, 1960)

TREWIN, Wendy, *All on Stage: Charles Wyndham and the Alberys* (Harrap, London, 1980)

TRUFFAUT, François, *The Films in my Life* (Allen Lane, London, 1980)

TYNAN, Kathleen, *The Life of Kenneth Tynan* (Weidenfeld & Nicolson, London, 1987)

TYNAN, Kenneth, *He That Plays the King* (Longmans, London, 1950)

TYNAN, Kenneth, *Alec Guinness* (Rockliff, London, 1953)

TYNAN, Kenneth, *Curtains* (Longmans, London, 1961)

TYNAN, Kenneth (ed.), *The Recruiting Officer, the NT Production* (Hart-Davis, London, 1965)

TYNAN, Kenneth (ed.), *Othello, the NT Production* (Hart-Davis, London, 1966)

TYNAN, Kenneth, *Tynan Right and Left* (Longmans, London, 1967)

TYNAN, Kenneth, *The Sound of Two Hands Clapping* (Jonathan Cape, London, 1975)

TYNAN, Kenneth, *A View of the English Stage* (Davis-Poynter, London, 1975)

TYNAN, Kenneth, *Show People: Profiles in Entertainment* (Weidenfeld & Nicolson, London, 1980)

USTINOV, Peter, *Dear Me* (Heinemann, London, 1977)

VAN THAL, Herbert (ed.), *James Agate: An Anthology* (Hart-Davis, London, 1961)

VICKERS, Hugo, *Cecil Beaton: The Authorized Biography* (Weidenfeld & Nicolson, London, 1985)

WALKER, Alexander, *Hollywood UK* (Stein & Day, New York, 1974)

WALKER, Alexander, *Vivien* (Weidenfeld & Nicolson, London, 1987)

WALTON, Susana, *William Walton: Behind the Façade* (Oxford University Press, Oxford, 1988)

WAPSHOTT, Nicholas, *Peter O'Toole* (New English Library, London, 1983)

WARDLE, Irving, *The Theatres of George Devine* (Jonathan Cape, London, 1978)

WEATHERBY, W. J., *Conversations with Marilyn* (Robson Books, London, 1976)

WEBSTER, Margaret, *The Same Only Different* (Gollancz, London, 1969)

WESTMORE, F., and DAVIDSON, M., *The Westmores of Hollywood* (W. H. Allen, London, 1976)

WHITWORTH, Geoffrey, *The Making of a National Theatre* (Faber & Faber, London, 1951)

WILCOX, Herbert, *Twenty-Five Thousand Sunsets* (Bodley Head, London, 1967)

WILLIAMS, Harcourt, *The Old Vic Saga* (Winchester Publications, London, 1949)

WILLIAMSON, Audrey, *Old Vic Drama* (Rockliff, London, 1948)

WILLIAMSON, Audrey, *Theatre of Two Decades* (Rockliff, London, 1951)

WILLIAMSON, Audrey, *Old Vic Drama No. 2* (Rockliff, London, 1957)

WILSON KNIGHT, G., *Shakespearian Production* (Routledge & Kegan Paul, London, 1968)

WOOD, Alan, *Mr Rank* (Hodder & Stoughton, London, 1952)

WORSLEY, T. C., *The Fugitive Art: Dramatic Commentaries 1947–51* (John Lehmann, London, 1952)

YOUNG, Stark, *Immortal Shadows: On Dramatic Criticism* (Scribners, New York, 1948)

YOUNG, William C., *Famous Actors and Actresses on the American Stage*, vol. II (Bowker Co., New York, 1975)

ZIEROLD, Norman, *Garbo* (Stein & Day, New York, 1969)

2: Articles in Scholarly Periodicals

BABCOK, R. W., "George Lynn Kitteridge, Olivier and the Historic Hamlet", *College Journal*, XI (1950)

BROWN, John Russell, "The Study and Practice of Shakespeare Production", *Shakespeare Survey 18* (1965)

BROWN, John Russell, "Three Kinds of Shakespeare", *Shakespeare Survey 18* (1965)

BYRNE, Muriel St Clare, "Fifty Years of Shakespeare Production", *Shakespeare Survey 2* (1949)

CANARIS, Volker, "*Die Erstern Juden, Dic Ich Kannte, Warem Nathen und Shylock*", *Theater Heute*, XIV (1973)

DAVID, Richard, "The Tragic Curve", *Shakespeare Survey 9* (1956)

EVANS, Gareth Lloyd, "Shakespeare and the Actors: Notes towards Interpretation", *Shakespeare Survey 21* (1968)

FISHER, H. K., "*Antony and Cleopatra* at the Piccadilly", *Life and Letters Today*, LXX (1947)

FOULKES, Richard, "Henry Irving and Laurence Olivier as Shylock", *Theatre Notebook*, XXVII (1973)

GLICK, Claris, "Hamlet in the English Theatre: Acting Texts 1676–1963", *Shakespeare Quarterly*, XX (1969)

HOPE-WALLACE, Philip, "Stratford-on-Avon: *Titus Andronicus*", *Time and Tide*, XXXVI (1955)

LUNARI, Gifi, "Laurence Olivier", *Documenti di Theatro 7* (1959)

MELCHINGER, Siegfried, "*Shakespeare Auf Dem Modernen Welttheater*", *Theater Heute*, XII (1964)

MULLIN, Michael, "*Macbeth* at Stratford-on-Avon", *Shakespeare Studies*, IX (1976)

RYLANDS, George, "Elizabethan Drama in the West End", *Shakespeare Survey 1* (1948)

SANDERS, Norman, "The Popularity of Shakespeare: An Examination of the Royal Shakespeare's Repertoire", *Shakespeare Survey 16* (1963)

SPEAIGHT, Robert, "Shakespeare in Britain", *Shakespeare Quarterly*, XV (1964)

SPEAIGHT, Robert, "Shakespeare in Britain", *Shakespeare Quarterly*, XVIII (1967)

SPEAIGHT, Robert, "Shakespeare in Britain", *Shakespeare Quarterly*, XX (1969)

SULLIVAN, Patrick, "Strumpet Wind – the National Theatre's *Merchant of Venice*", *Educational Theatre Journal*, 26 (1974)

VENESKY, Alice, "Shakespeare Conquers Broadway: The Oliviers' *Antony and Cleopatra*", *Shakespeare Quarterly*, III (1952)

3: Miscellaneous

Who's Who in the Theatre (Isaac Pitman & Son, London)

STIFF, Rev. Neville, *The Church in Dorking and District* (privately, 1912)

Two Hundred Years of Dorking Cricket, 1766–1968 (privately, 1968)

The Roll of St Edward's School, 1863–1949, 6th ed (St Edward's School Society, 1951)

A History of St Edward's School, 1863–1963 (St Edward's School Society, 1962)

Index

LO stands for Sir Laurence Olivier, NT for the National Theatre

Actors' Orphanage, 306
Adding Machine, The (Elmer Rice): LO in, with Birmingham Rep, 41–2
Adrian, Max, 338, 370, 372, 374, 427
Advertisement, The (Natalia Ginzburg), 408
After All (John van Druten): LO in (1929), 56
Agate, James, 197; quoted, 51, 53, 61, 79, 83, 84, 85, 88, 89, 91–2, 92, 97, 107, 119, 131, 134, 135, 192–3, 193, 197, 203, 204, 205, 210, 212; mentioned, 409
Agee, James, quoted, 180, 222
Aherne, Brian, 81, 153, 162
Albery, Bronson, 35, 84, 89, 187
Albery Theatre, *see* New Theatre
Alexander, Sir George, 258
Allen, Adrienne, 60, 61, 61–2, 63
All Saints school, 17–20
All's Well That Ends Well: LO in, with Birmingham Rep, 41
Amory, Mark, 444
Amphitryon 38 (Giraudoux), 416
Anderson, Daphne, 272
Anderson, Judith, 131, 335

Andrews, Dana, 275
Andrews, Harry, 246, 265, 384
Anna Karenina (film), 218
Antigone (Anouilh): LO in (1949), 242, 251, 253, 255
Antony and Cleopatra: LO in (1951), 265–7, 268–70
Apted, Michael, 440
Arlen, Stephen, 370, 390, 427
Arms and the Man (Shaw): LO in, with Old Vic (1944–5), 186, 187, 189
Arthur, Jean, 141
Arts Council, 224, 248, 249, 365, 417
As You Like It: all-male production, at NT, 395; film version, LO in, 95–7
Ashcroft, Dame Peggy, 31, 32, 37, 84, 92, 136, 137, 450
Asher, Irving, 274–5
Asherson, Renee, 175
Ashwell, Lena, 34–5
Asquith, Anthony, 173, 177
Atkins, Eileen, 361
Atkinson, Brooks, quoted, 65, 77, 145, 156
Attenborough, Richard, 415, 416, 422, 432, 435
Australia: Old Vic tour of (1948), 225–6, 227–41, 244, 247
Ayliff, Henry, 42, 43

Aylmer, Felix, 56, 217

Bacall, Lauren, 261, 330
Back to Methuselah (Shaw): LO in, with Birmingham Rep, 43; at NT, 408
Baddeley, Angela, 36–7
Bader, Douglas, 25
Badham, John, 443
Baker, Stanley, 283
Balcon, Michael, 160–1
Banks, Leslie, 86, 110, 127
Barber, John, quoted, 287, 292–3, 298, 317
Barber and the Cow, The (D. T. Davies): LO in, with Birmingham Rep, 40
Barker, Felix, 235, 267–8; quoted, 389
Barrault, Jean-Louis, 271; quoted, 211
Barrie, Sir James Matthew, 82, 96
Barrie, Wendy, 104
Barrymore, Ethel, 221
Barrymore, John, 30, 69, 72
Barrymore, Lionel, 69
Bates, Alan, 440
Bateson, Timothy, 283
Bats in the Belfry, 124
Battersby, Martin, 252
Battle of Britain (film): LO in, 415–16
Battle of Shrivings, The (Peter Shaffer), 407

492

Baur, Harry, 86, 87
Baxter, Beverley, quoted, 207, 211–12, 212, 250, 253, 267
Baylis, Lilian, 113–15, 115, 120, 122, 125, 130–1
Beaton, Cecil, 210, 215–16, 226, 251–2, 306; quoted, 195, 215, 216
Beau Geste (P. C. Wren): LO in (1929), 48–9, 51–3
Beauman, Sally, quoted, 288
Beaumont, Hugh ("Binkie"), 170, 255, 403, 421, 427
Because We Must, 124
Beck, Reginald, 174, 216; quoted, 221–2
Becket (Anouilh): LO in (1960), 346–8
Beddington, Jack, 173
Bees on the Boat-Deck (Priestley): LO in (1936), 97–8
Beggar's Opera, The (film): LO in, 31, 272–4
Bel Geddes, Barbara, 440
Beldon, Eileen, 44; quoted, 42
Bennett, Arnold, quoted, 42, 61
Bennett, Joan, 142
Benny, Jack, 306
Benson & Hedges Ltd, 4
Benthall, Michael, 265
Bentley, Eric, quoted, 179, 193, 220, 273
Bergman, Ingmar, 334
Bergner, Elisabeth, 95–7, 170
Berliner Ensemble, 374, 376
Best, Edna, 54
Betsy, The (film): LO in, 441–2
Betts, Ernest, quoted, 179
Bill of Divorcement, A (film), 71–2
Billington, Michael, quoted, 22–3, 410, 412, 419
Biography (S. N. Behrman): LO in (1934), 78–9, 103
Bird in Hand (John Drinkwater): LO in, with Birmingham Rep, 41, 47–8, 55
Birmingham Post, quoted, 41
Birmingham Repertory Company, 37–45, 47
Bishop, George W., 126
Blackburn, Aubrey, 106
Blakelock, Denys, 24, 38, 41, 83; quoted, 24, 37–8, 39, 45, 83

Blakely, Colin, 370, 375, 408, 447–8
Blakemore, Michael 418, 421
Bliss, Sir Arthur, 272
Blithe Spirit (film), 174
Bloom, Claire, 283, 284
Bogarde, Dirk, 400, 435
Bogart, Humphrey, 261
Born Yesterday (Garson Kanin), 216
Bothwellians, The, 80
Bower, Dallas, 173–4, 174, 175
Bowra, Maurice, 205
Boxgrove School, 12
Boyd, Dorothy, 56
Boys from Brazil, The (film): LO in, 442
Bracken, Brendan, 174
Brando, Marlon, 257, 261, 429
Breen, Joseph, 165
Brideshead Revisited (TV film): LO in, 444
Bridge Too Far, A (film): LO in, 435, 440
Bridges-Adams, William, 38
Bridie, James, 268
Brien, Alan, quoted, 379
Brighton: LO's house at, 384
British Quota Act, 56
Broken Heart, The (John Ford): LO in, at Chichester (1962), 355–6
Brook, Peter, 272–4, 288–9, 295–7, 405–7
Brown, George, 284–5
Brown, Ivor, quoted, 56, 78–9, 82, 97, 114, 120–1, 126, 135, 253, 266, 292, 294
Brown, John Mason, quoted, 65, 145, 194, 208, 220–1
Brown, Katharine, 129
Brown, Pamela, 283
Browne, Maurice, 51, 82
Bruce, Nigel, 150
Bryden, Ronald, quoted, 385, 388
Buchanan, Jack, 282
Buckmaster, John, 102, 276–7
Build the Broken Walls (film), 173
Bundy, Bill, 231
Bunny Lake Is Missing (film), 387
Burchett's Green: LO's house at, 102
Burge, Stuart, 120, 368, 388
Burnett, Mina, 56

Burrell, John, 185, 189, 192, 211, 237–40, 247
Burton, Richard, 63, 88, 124, 330, 334, 337, 349, 369, 443
Bushell, Anthony, 68, 217, 258, 282–3
Byron (Alice Law): LO in (1924), 31

Caan, James, 435
Cadogan, Sir Alexander, quoted, 166
Caesar and Cleopatra (Shaw): LO in (1951), 265–7, 268–70; Pascal's film, 170, 181–2
Cahoon, Helen, 272
Caine, Michael, 3, 428–9, 435, 438, 449
Campbell, Mrs Patrick, 61
Cannan, Denis, 272
Captain Carvallo (Denis Cannan), 260, 263
Cardiff, Jack, 308–9
Carroll, Sydney, 106, 124
Casson, Sir Lewis, 35–6, 135, 135–6, 358
Cat on a Hot Tin Roof (Tennessee Williams): LO in TV version, 439, 440–1
Cenci, The (Shelley): LO in (1926), 36
Central School of Speech Training and Dramatic Art, 27–9, 31–2, 82
Chances, The (Villiers): LO in, at Chichester (1962), 355–6
Chandos, Lord (formerly Oliver Lyttelton), 224, 364, 365, 367, 394, 396, 397, 413–14, 427
Chatterton, Ruth, 68
Chekhov, Anton, 31
Chevalier, Maurice, 86
Cheyne Walk: LO's house in, 79
Chichester Festival Theatre, 3, 351–2, 353, 355–9, 368, 391
Chifley, Ben, 233, 234
Church, Esme, 116
Churchill, Sir Winston, 158, 166, 169, 267, 322, 387
Cinema, The, quoted, 70
Circle of Chalk, The (Klabund and Laver): LO in (1929), 53–4
Claire, Ina, 78
Clash of the Titans (film): LO in, 443

Clements, John, 170, 392
Clive, Colin, 51, 53, 55, 68
Clunes, Alec, 115, 283
Clurman, Harold, quoted, 375–6
Colefax, Lady (Sibyl), 202, 213
Colleano, Bonar, 257
Collection, The (Pinter): LO in TV version, 439, 440
Collier, Lionel, quoted, 110
Colman, Ronald, 52, 151, 162, 162–4
Come Back Little Sheba (TV film), 441
Commonweal, quoted, 145
Compton, Fay, 356, 358
Conachy, Dr Arthur, 310
Connery, Sean, 154, 435
Conquest of the Air (film): LO in, 86
Cons, Emma, 113
Consul, The (Menotti), 263
Contessa, La (Paul Osborn), 400
Conway, Harold. quoted, 250
Cooper, Alfred Duff, 157, 158
Cooper, George, 237
Cooper, Gladys, 30–1, 73, 74
Cooper, Louie, 349
Cooper, Melville, 41
Coote, Robert, 150
Coriolanus: LO in. at Old Vic (1938), 135; LO in, at Stratford (1959), 338–41
Cornell, Katharine, 81, 143, 144, 145, 160
Cottesloe, Lord, 365
Cottrell, Cherry, 116
Cottrell, John, quoted, 190
Courtenay, Tom, 370
Coward, Noël, 31; relations with LO, 57, 61–5, 78, 80–1, 131, 210, 214, 263, 299–300, 304, 326, 335, 349, 387–8; Private Lives, 57, 61–5; on LO, 62, 64, 79, 188–9, 189, 211; Biography, 78; in Second World War, 157, 158, 174; knighthood, 214; and Vivien Leigh, 257, 270, 278, 279, 299–300, 310, 311, 338, 341, 400; death, 427; mentioned, 34, 305, 306, 386
Craig, Edith, 32
Craig, Edward Gordon, 198–9
Crawford, George, 219

Crawford, Joan, 68, 141
Cripps, Sir Stafford, 213
Critic, The (Sheridan): LO in, with Old Vic (1945–6), 204–7 passim
Cronyn, Hume, 335
Crucible, The (Arthur Miller), 387
Cruickshank, Andrew, 131, 283
Cukor, George, 76, 142, 144, 148, 155, 430
Culver, Roland, 54
Cummings, Constance, 170, 418, 419
Cunningham, Dan, 227–8, 232, 235, 244–5
Curtis, Tony, 335
Curzon, George, 206
Cusack, Cyril, 170, 335, 352, 370
Cushing, Peter, 227, 232
Cushman, Robert, quoted, 448
Cyrano de Bergerac, 211
Czinner, Paul, 95, 96

Dacre, Lord (Hugh Trevor-Roper), 396
Daily Express, quoted, 51, 287, 292–3, 325, 329, 354, 379
Daily Herald, 58
Daily Mail, 443; quoted, 297, 362
Daily Telegraph, 33; quoted, 25, 97, 126, 190, 212
Dale, James, 78
Damascus Blade, The (Bridget Boland), 260
Damita, Lily, 68
Dance of Death, The (Strindberg), 392–3, 403–4
Daniels, Marc, 352
Daniels, Robert L., quoted, 97
Daphne Laureola (James Bridie), 254, 258; TV version, 439, 441
Dark Journey (film), 124
Darlington, W. A., quoted, 25, 51, 52, 89, 92, 190, 212, 294
Darlow, Michael, quoted, 305
Davenport, Bromley, 56
David Copperfield (film): LO in, 416
Davis, Bette, 137, 141, 142
Davis, Sammy, Jr, 381
de Banzie, Brenda, 259

de Havilland, Olivia, 143
de Lissa, Arthur, 79
de Valois, Ninette, 114
Dean, Basil: casts LO as Beau Geste, 48–9, 51–2; rejects Journey's End, 51; casts LO in The Circle of Chalk, 53, 54; on LO, 73, 248; directs Vivien Leigh, 105–6, 127–8; in Second World War, 172, 198
Deep Blue Sea, The (Rattigan), 290
Dehn, Paul, quoted, 302
del Giudice, Filippo, 174, 176, 180, 214, 215, 216
Delysia, Alice, 34
Demi-Paradise, The (film): LO in, 173, 177
Denham studios, 86, 104, 177
Denmark: Hamlet performed in, 123–4, 124–6
Dent, Alan, 131, 173, 216, 256, 283, 321–2; quoted, 119, 135, 211, 216, 222, 256
Devil's Disciple, The (film): LO in, 324, 327
Devine, George: relations with LO, 79, 137, 255, 272, 314, 315, 319, 326, 368, 392, 403; leaves Old Vic for Stratford, 288; founds and manages English Stage Company at Royal Court, 288, 314, 315, 368; death, 392, 403; mentioned, 87
Dexter, John, 368, 370, 376, 380, 393–4, 395, 424
Dieterle, William, 151, 275
Dignam, Mark, 246
Dillon, Carmen, 173, 216, 221, 283
Disney, Walt, 78
Divorce of Lady X, The (film), 130
Dix, Dorothy, 116
Dixon, Campbell, quoted, 97
Doctor's Dilemma, The (Shaw), 170–1
Donat, Robert, 85, 110, 161, 178, 210, 268, 288
Donlan, Yolande, 216
Douglas, Kirk, 324, 327, 335–7
Dracula (film): LO in, 443
du Maurier, Sir Gerald, 30–1, 31, 82
Duel of Angels, 330, 343
Duke, Patty, 352
Duncan, Frank, 171

Dundy, Elaine, 275
Dunlop, Frank, 407, 413
Durham Cottage, Chelsea, 120, 264, 320
Duvall, Robert, 433

Ealing Studios, 72
Eames, Clare, 41–2
Ebony Tower, The (TV film): LO in, 449
Eden End (Priestley), 424, 431
Edinburgh Festival, 126
Edwards, Anne, quoted, 107, 195, 289
Elephant Walk (film), 274–7
Eliot, T. S., quoted, 295–6
Elizabeth, Princess (later Queen Elizabeth II), 132
Elliott, Denholm, 259, 335
Elsom, John, quoted, 364, 403
English Ballet Company, 114
English Stage Company, *see under* Royal Court Theatre
ENSA, 160, 198
Entertainer, The (Osborne): LO in (1957), 314–18, 319–20, 324, 326; film version, 317, 341
Ervine, St John, quoted, 42, 44
Esher, Lord, 237–8, 246–9, 365
Esmond, H. V., 47
Esmond, Jill: meets LO, 47–8; various stage roles, 47, 48, 55, 57–8; arranges to marry LO, 54–5; marriage, 57–60; views on marriage, in *Daily Herald*, 58; son (Tarquin Olivier, *q.v.*), 60, 101–2; in *Private Lives* with LO, 63, 64, 65; in Hollywood with LO, 65, 67, 69, 71–2; returns to England with LO, 72; in *No Funny Business* with LO, 72; in *The Green Bay Tree* with LO, 77; with LO in Chelsea, 79; in *Ringmaster* with LO, 82; in *Twelfth Night* with LO, 121; LO leaves her for Vivien Leigh, 126–7; divorce, 147, 153, 162; takes Tarquin to Canada (1939), 164; mentioned, 76, 111, 209

Evans, Dame Edith, 31, 81, 91, 92, 115, 137, 254, 338, 386
Evans, Laurence, 421, 445
Evans, Maurice, 52
Evans, Monica, 345
Evening News, 267
Evening Standard, quoted, 42, 74, 207, 250, 282, 287, 327, 360, 375
Evershed-Martin, Leslie, 351–2, 353, 359
Eyre, Richard, 421

Fading Mansions, 258
Fairbanks, Douglas, Jr, 68, 70, 150, 210, 330
Fairweather, Virginia, 353, 361, 404, 407
Farjeon, Herbert, quoted, 92, 122, 265
Farmer's Wife, The (Phillpotts): LO in, with Birmingham Rep, 39, 40
Farrington, Robin, 325
Fay, W. G., 41, 42
Feldman, Charles K., 260
Festival of Britain, 249, 265
Ffrangcon-Davies, Gwen, 43, 79, 80; quoted, 45, 79, 92
Fields, Gracie, 105–6, 160
Film Weekly, quoted, 130
Filumena (Eduardo de Filippo), 443
Finch, Peter, 235, 236, 254, 255, 260, 264, 269, 274–7, 299, 301–2, 326
Findlater, Richard, 363; quoted, 294, 297, 318
Finlay, Frank, 2, 88, 370, 376, 380, 388, 443, 450
Finney, Albert, 339, 341, 437
Fire Over England (film): LO and Vivien Leigh in, 108–11, 169
Fitzgerald, Geraldine, 335
Flea in her Ear, A (Feydeau): LO in, with NT, 404
Fleischer, Richard, 443
Fleming, Victor, 144
Flower, Sir Fordham, 365
Flynn, Errol, 68
Fogerty, Elsie, 27–9, 30, 31, 32, 107
Fontaine, Joan, 153
Fontanne, Lynn, 199
Forbes, Ralph, 68
Forbes-Robertson, Sir Johnston, 20, 85
Forsyth, James, 239; quoted, 262–3, 408

49th Parallel (film): LO in 170
Fox, Edward, 435
Frank, Julian, 33
Frankenstein (film), 68
Fraser, Lovat, 258
Friends and Lovers (film): LO in, 68–9, 71
Fripp, Lady, 59
Front Page, The, 417
Fry, Christopher, 13, 259, 272
Furse, Margaret, 173
Furse, Roger, 173, 215, 216, 221, 258, 283, 302, 337–8, 355

Gage, Roger, 326, 348
Gambon, Michael, 370
Garbo, Greta, 74–6
Gardner, Cyril, 72
Garson, Greer, 83, 155
Gaskill, William, 318, 368, 370, 374–6, 393–4, 395
Gazzara, Ben, 440
General Motors, 286
General Strike, 39
Genn, Leo, 121, 175
Gentleman's Agreement (film), 105
Ghost Train, The (Arnold Ridley), 33
Gielgud, Sir John: as actor, 4, 24, 85, 87, 92, 93, 94, 95, 132, 212; on LO, 4, 92–3, 291–2; with Birmingham Rep, 33; with Old Vic, 63, 80; as Hamlet, 84, 85; with LO in *Romeo and Juliet*, 84–95; in *Secret Agent* film, 87, 90; declines to film *Hamlet*, 95, 215; and Vivien Leigh, 108, 170, 289, 292, 400; in *School for Scandal*, 132; declines to help direct Old Vic, 185; gives Kean's sword to LO, 192; as Lear, 212; knighthood, 214; in LO's *Richard III* film, 283, 290–1; directs LO in *Twelfth Night*, 289, 290–2; with NT, 370, 405, 408, 437; a Companion of Honour, 412; plays scene with LO and Richardson, 443; mentioned, 28, 43, 123–4, 136, 210, 251–2, 265, 279, 415, 442
Gilbert, John, 75, 76
Gillan, Sir Angus, 225
Gingold, Hermione, quoted, 192

Gleason, Jackie, 449
Glenville, Peter, 346, 347, 354
Gliddon, John, 104–5, 106
Goddard, Paulette, 141
Golden Arrow (Victor Cunard): LO in, 82–3, 86
Goldwyn, Sam, 137, 138, 139–40, 152, 220, 225
Gone with the Wind, 128, 129, 141–4, 154
Goodman, Lord, 366–7, 411–12, 413
Goolden, Richard, 59
Gordon, Ruth, 115
Goring, Marius, 116, 121, 137
Gould, Elliott, 435
Grainger, Gawn, 437–8
Granada Television, 438
Granger, Derek, 398, 438–9; quoted, 438, 440, 441
Granger, Stewart, 276–7
Grant, Cary, 66, 161–2
Granville-Barker, Harley, 92
Grebanier, Bernard, quoted, 156, 221
Green Bay Tree, The (Mordaunt Shairp): LO in (1933), 77–8
Green Sash, The, 105
Greene, Graham, 127; quoted, 86–7, 96–7, 111, 128, 145
Greene, Milton, 304, 307, 309
Greenwood, Joan, 356, 358
Griffith, Hugh, 272
Guardian (formerly *Manchester Guardian*), 187; quoted, 297, 361, 379, 410, 419
Guinness, Sir Alec: with the Old Vic in 1930s, 39, 115, 116, 120, 121; on LO, 120; guest of LO, 210, 330; with the Old Vic, 1946–7, 211; mentioned, 265, 341, 430
Gullan, Cambell, 80
Guthrie, Sir Tyrone, 111, 115; at Old Vic in 1930s, 39, 90, 111, 115–26 *passim*, 132–4, 142; on LO, 90, 116–17, 121; persuades LO to play Hamlet, 111; directs LO in *Hamlet*, 115–21; theatre-in-the-round, 126, 351; doubts Vivien Leigh's abilities, 127, 170; and Old Vic post-war, 184–5,

194, 204; advice to LO, 187–8; feud with LO, 204, 239; resumes control of Old Vic (1951), 249; failure with *Top of the Ladder*, 262–3; candidate to direct NT, 262, 363–4; midwife to Chichester Festival Theatre, 351–2; critical of LO as NT director, 364, 382–3; works with NT, 408; mentioned, 210
Guthrie Theatre, Minneapolis, 126
Guys and Dolls (musical), 413, 420–1

Hackett, James, 24
Hale, Lionel, quoted, 131
Hall, Sir Peter: on LO, 4, 6, 395; his Stratford debut, 296; at the Arts Theatre, 318–19; directs LO at Stratford, 338–9; and plans for NT–Stratford alliance, 365, 366, 366–7; succeeds LO at NT, 398, 417, 420, 421–2, 423, 424, 436–8; knighthood, 438; in tribute to LO, 450
Hamilton, Hamish, 268
Hamlet: modern-dress productions, 39; actor's age, 85; Gielgud as Hamlet, 84–5; Guinness as Hamlet, 265, 267; LO as Hamlet, with Old Vic (1937), 111, 115–21, tour of Denmark, 123–4, 124–6; O'Toole as Hamlet, with NT (1963), 369, 371, 372–4; LO's film, 118, 176, 214–22, 234, 254–5, 371
Hannen, Nicholas ("Bead"), 186
Happy Hypocrite, The, 108
Harding, Ann, 70
Hardwick, Paul, 311
Hardwicke, Sir Cedric: in Birmingham Rep, 40; on LO, 40; in Hollywood, 66, 151–2; and Second World War, 151, 151–2, 161, 162; with the Old Vic, 240, 247; in LO's *Richard III* film, 283; quoted, 99
Harewood, Lord, 317–18
Harold (Tennyson): LO in, with Birmingham Rep, 43–4

Harris, Jed, 77–8
Harris, Julie, 352
Harris, Percy and Sophie, *see* Motley
Harris, Robert, 38
Harris, Rosemary, 342, 356, 370
Harrison, Rex, 124, 270, 311, 341, 400
Hartford, Huntington, 328
Hartley, Ernest, 103
Hartley, Gertrude, 103, 143, 147, 150, 164, 167, 289, 302
Hartley, Vivian, *see* Leigh, Vivien
Harvey, Lilian, 56
Hawkins, Jack, 36, 53, 59, 330; quoted, 55
Hawthorne, Nigel, 188
Hay Fever, 386, 387
Hayes, Helen, 83, 283
Hayman, Ronald, quoted, 385
Hazlitt, William, quoted, 208
Heald, Father Geoffrey, 19, 23
Hecht, Harold, 327
Heller, Otto, 283
Helpmann, Robert, 132, 178, 265, 345–6
Henry IV: LO in Part II (1925), 31; LO in Parts I and II, with Old Vic (1945–6), 203–4, 208
Henry V: LO in, with Old Vic (1937), 122–3; LO's film, 32, 169, 173–81, 209, 220
Henry VIII: LO in (1925), 36–7; LO in BBC radio production, 282
Hepburn, Katharine, 71–2, 77, 78, 163–4, 430
Hepple, Jeanne, 386
Her Strange Desire (film), *see* *Potiphar's Wife*
Herlie, Eileen, 218
Heston, Charlton, 342, 434
Hewitt, Muriel, 37
Hicks, Sir Seymour, 160
Hindle Wakes (Stanley Houghton): TV version, 439, 441
Hippodrome, Brighton, 33–4
Hitchcock, Alfred, 87, 90, 148, 152, 153–4, 160
Hitler, Adolf, 169
Hobbs, Carleton, 156

Hobson, Harold, 384; quoted, 43, 73–4, 97–8, 206, 249, 250, 254, 256, 294, 373, 379, 380, 393, 410–11, 424
Hobson's Choice, 371, 389
Hoffman, Dustin, 432, 433–4
Holden, William, 341
Holloway, Stanley, 217, 272, 273
Holm, Eleanor, 269
Holm, Ian, 4, 339
Holman, Leigh: marries Vivian Hartley (later Vivien Leigh), 102; daughter Suzanne, 102; resents Vivien's acting career, 103–4, 105, 107–8; Vivien leaves him, 126–7; divorce, 147, 162; granted custody of Suzanne, 159; in Second World War, 164; remains close to Vivien, 323; Suzanne's wedding, 325
Holman, Suzanne, 102, 126–7, 159, 164, 167, 195–6, 323, 325
Holman, Vivian, *see* Leigh, Vivien
Home and Beauty (Maugham): LO in, 408
Home and Colonial (Coward), 263, 309
Hope, Bob, 306
Hope-Wallace, Philip, quoted, 297, 361, 379
Hopkins, Anthony, 399, 435
Horne, David, 105
Horsebridge Green: LO's house at, 384
Howard, Leslie, 66, 143, 168, 170
Howard, William K., 110
Howe, George, 116
Hughes, Ted, 405
Hume, Benita, 162
Hunt, Hugh, 249
Hussey, Olivia, 415
Huxley, Aldous, 154
Hyde White, Wilfrid, 265, 269
Hyson, Dorothy, 142

I Stand Condemned (film), *see Moscow Nights*
Ibsen, Henrik, quoted, 331
In Which We Serve (Coward), 174
Inchon (film): LO in, 443
Incorporated Stage Society, 49

"Into Battle" (radio programme), 173
Irving, Ellis, 131
Irving, Sir Henry, 9, 43, 84, 85, 192–3, 268
Isaacs, Jeremy, 422–3
Ivanov (Chekhov), 400
Ives, Burl, 440

Jackson, Sir Barry, 37–43 *passim*, 47, 51, 186
Jacobi, Derek, 4, 370
Jazz Singer, The (film): LO in, 443
Jeans, Isabel, quoted, 32
Jessel, George, 345
Jesus of Nazareth (TV film): LO in, 435
Jigsaw Man, The (film): LO in, 449
John, Evan, 115
John Gabriel Borkman (Ibsen): LO in, on TV, 328–9
Jones, Dr Ernest, 115, 116, 118–19, 132–3
Jones, Griffith, 175
Jones, Jennifer, 260
Journey's End (Sherriff): LO in, 49–51, 53, 54; film version, 55
Julius Caesar: LO in, at school, 19–20; LO in, with Lena Ashwell Players, 35
Jumel, Georgina, 227, 234
Jumpers (Tom Stoppard), 417
Juno and the Paycock (O'Casey), 392

Kael, Pauline, quoted, 273–4, 388
Kanin, Garson, 163–4, 216, 413
Karloff, Boris, 68
Kaye, Danny, 230, 261, 269, 276, 277, 282
Kazan, Elia, 256
Kean, Edmund, Coleridge on, 452
Keith-Johnston, Colin, 82
Kempson, Rachel, 115, 259, 358
Kennedy, Arthur, 347
Kennedy, John F., 348, 383
Kenny, Sean, 355, 372
Kentish, David, 258
Khartoum (film): LO in, 392
King Lear: LO in, with Old Vic (1946), 210–13; LO contemplates appearing in, 409; LO in TV version, 446–8

King of Nowhere, The (Bridie), 134–5
Kingsley, Ben, 450
Kingsway Theatre, 38
Kitchin, Laurence, quoted, 7, 123, 194, 211, 339, 340, 381–2
Knight, Esmond, 283, 311, 370; quoted, 44, 62
Knox, Alexander, 156
Korda, Sir Alexander, 86, 104; meets Vivien Leigh, 104, 106, 107–8; *Fire Over England*, 108–10; more parts for Vivien, 127–8, 129–30; worries about Oliviers' marriage, 158, 159; *Lady Hamilton*, 158, 159, 165–6; his war work, knighthood, 159, 166; joins Laurence Olivier Productions, 258; further relations with Vivien, 266, 274, 290; and LO's film of *Richard III*, 282, 286; death, 303; mentioned, 210
Korda, Michael, 309
Korda, Vincent, 165
Krasker, Robert, 173
Kretzmer, Herbert, quoted, 379
Kroll, Jack, quoted, 441–2
Kruger, Hardy, 435
Kubrick, Stanley, 336

Lady Caroline Lamb (film): LO in, 416
Lady Hamilton (film; US title *That Hamilton Woman*): LO and Vivien Leigh in, 158, 159, 164–6, 169
Lake, The (Massingham and Macdonald), 77
Lambert, J. W., quoted, 369, 381, 389, 393
Lancaster, Burt, 324, 327
Landi, Elissa, 56, 69
Lang, Robert, 356, 413, 421
Lansbury, Angela, 449
Lasdun, Denys, 383
Last Days of Pompeii, The (TV film): LO in, 449
Last Enemy, The (Frank Harvey): LO in (1929), 56
Lauder, Harry, 34
Laughton, Charles: relations with LO, 10, 123, 136, 337, 434; in Hollywood, 66, 151, 335, 337; in films with Korda, 86, 110, 130; at Stratford, 337, 338

Laurence Olivier
Productions Ltd, 236, 242,
254, 257, 258, 263, 342,
400
Laurie, John, 283, 370
Lawrence, Gertrude, 57, 65,
72
Lawrence, T. E., 61 .
Lawton, Frank, 56, 59
Leaming, Barbara, quoted,
343
Lean, David, 174, 178
Leaver, Philip, 35
Leavis, F. R., 380
Lee, Baroness, 412, 413
Leggatt, Alison, 59
Leigh, Vivien (formerly
Holman, née Hartley;
LO's second wife): birth
and early life, 102; first
marriage to Leigh
Holman, 102, 103–4, 105,
106, 107–8; daughter, see
Holman, Suzanne; begins
acting career, 103–7;
becomes "Vivien Leigh",
104, 106; acting ability,
107, 124, 156, 170, 197,
242, 250–1, 253, 266–7,
289, 293, 298; falls in love
with LO, 98, 103; meets
LO, 102; in Fire Over
England with LO, 108–11;
furtive relationship with
LO, 112, 124, 126; minor
stage roles, 124; Ophelia
in Old Vic Hamlet's
Danish tour, 124, 125,
127; leaves Holman for
LO, 126–7; in Twenty-One
Days with LO, 127–8; as
Scarlett O'Hara in
Selznick film, 128, 129,
141–4, 154; in A Yank at
Oxford, 129; Titania in
Midsummer Night's Dream
at Old Vic, 132, 141, 142;
life with LO, 132, 136,
146–7; "living in sin",
disapproved of, 132, 143,
154; considered for
Wuthering Heights film,
136–8; lonely in London,
140–1; not cast as
Rebecca, 147–9; divorce
in prospect, 147; outbreak
of war, 150; LO anxious
to marry her, 152–3;
Oscar for Best Actress (as
Scarlett O'Hara), 154;
recognizes LO's
superiority as actor, 154,

158, 182, 195, 234, 300;
not chosen for Pride and
Prejudice film, 154–5; in
Romeo and Juliet with LO,
155–7; in Lady Hamilton
with LO, 158–60, 164–5,
166; early problems in
relationship with LO,
158–9; divorced, 162;
marries LO, 162–4; meets
mother and daughter in
Canada, 164, 167; dispute
over contract with
Selznick, 167, 175, 182,
195–6; returns to Britain
with LO, 167–8; in The
Doctor's Dilemma, 170–1;
physical health
deteriorates, 171, 198; not
able to play in Henry V
film, 175; deteriorating
relationship with LO,
181, 195; miscarriage,
181, 182; Cleopatra in
Caesar and Cleopatra film,
181–2; mental illness
develops, 182–3, 186, 202,
207, 218, 227; directed by
LO in The Skin of our Teeth,
195–8, 199; develops TB,
199; neglected by LO,
199–200; and Notley,
201–2, 207–8, 210, 264–5,
338; in New York with
LO (1945), 208, 209–10;
in Italy with LO, 216; in
film of Anna Karenina, 218;
in Australia with LO and
Old Vic, 225, 226, 227–37
passim, 240–5; relations
with LO in Australia, 226,
228, 235, 243; young
admirers, 232, 235, 244–5;
and LO's knighthood,
226, 235; relations with
Tarquin Olivier, 227, 324,
400; and Peter Finch, 235,
254, 255, 274–7, 299, 301–
2, 326; and LO's New
Theatre company, 242,
250–5; LO thought to
have "played down" to
her level, 250, 253, 266–7,
281, 298; no longer loves
LO, 253–4; in Streetcar,
255, 256–8, 259, see also
film, below; "tipped . . .
over into madness", 256;
misses Venus Observed, 259;
to Hollywood with LO,
for Streetcar film, 260–2;
façade of happy marriage

maintained, 262, 267–8;
two Cleopatra roles for
Festival of Britain, 265,
266–7; manic-depressive,
or schizophrenic, 269–70;
in Elephant Walk, 274–6,
277; breakdown, 275–9; in
The Sleeping Prince (1953),
279–82; uneasy modus
vivendi with LO, 289; in
The Deep Blue Sea, 290; in
Twelfth Night, 290, 292; in
Macbeth and Titus
Andronicus (1955), 33, 290,
298–9; relations with LO,
and mental condition,
deteriorating, 298–300,
301–2, 303, 310–11; and
visit of Marilyn Monroe,
309–10, 312, 312–13;
another miscarriage, 310,
311; LO resolves to
change his life, 319; LO
keeps her out of The
Entertainer, 319–20;
European tour of Titus,
320–1; fails to save
St James's Theatre, 321–2;
matrimonial troubles
publicly aired, 322–4; she
and LO lead separate
lives, but shun divorce,
325, 326–7, 329–30; in
Duel of Angels, 330, 343; in
love with Jack Merivale,
330; more "ghastly
scenes", 335; not
reconciled to LO's
departure, 338, 341, 345–
6; divorce, 344–5, 348;
view of Joan Plowright,
349, 401; taken over by
Merivale, 350, 386, 400;
death, 399–402; her
importance to LO, 112,
401; mentioned, 131, 172,
188, 215, 272, 282, 287
Leighton, Margaret, 186
Lena Ashwell Players, 34–5
Leonard, Robert Z., 155
Levin, Bernard, quoted, 297,
344, 362, 375
Levy, Benn, 170, 342
Life magazine, quoted, 335
Lillie, Beatrice, 330
Lindo, Olga, 54
Little Romance, A (film), 442
Littlewood, Joan, 318–19
Liverpool Repertory
Company, 38, 48
Livesey, Roger, 131
Logan, Joshua, 305, 311

London County Council, 365–6, 366
London Palladium, 306
Long Day's Journey into Night (O'Neill): LO in, with NT, 417, 418–20
Look Back in Anger (Osborne), 312–13, 318
Look Up and Laugh (film), 105–6
Lord Chamberlain, 80, 257, 394, 406
Los Angeles Times, quoted, 441
Lost Empires (TV film): LO in, 450
Lothian, Lord, 151–2, 157–8, 161–2
Love Among the Ruins (TV film): LO in, 430
Love for Love (Congreve), 389
Love's Labour's Lost, NT production, 408
Lunt, Alfred, 199, 269
Lupino, Stanley, 19
Lyttelton, Oliver, *see* Chandos, Lord
Lytton, Lord, 130, 185, 248

Macbeth: LO in (1924), 33; LO in, with Birmingham Rep (1928), 42–3; LO in, with Old Vic (1937), 130–7; LO in, at Stratford (1955), 287–8, 288–9, 290, 293–5, 298; LO's plan for film, 301, 302–4, 323, 324, 327–8
McCormick, F. J., 217
McCowen Alec, 450
MacDonagh, Donagh, 258
McDowell, Malcolm, 440
McEwan, Geraldine, 326, 392, 421, 450
Mackay, Rev. H. F. B., 19, 57
McKechnie, Donald, 408
McKell, William, 233
McKenna, Siobhan, 258
Macqueen-Pope, William, quoted, 56
Mailer, Norman, quoted, 382
Malleson, Miles, 204, 389
Mamoulian, Rouben, 75
Manchester Guardian, see *Guardian*
Mann, Jean, 323
Marathon Man (film): LO in, 432–3, 433–4, 436
Margaret, Princess, 132
Marie-Louise, Princess, 59

Marowitz, Charles, quoted, 410
Marshall, Herbert, 54
Marvellous History of Saint Bernard, The (Ghéon): LO in, with Birmingham Rep, 38, 39
Mask of Virtue, The, 106–7
Mason, James, 79, 110
Massey, Daniel, 63
Massey, Raymond, 68, 73, 82, 86, 110, 170
Master Builder, The (Ibsen): LO in, with MT, 371, 385–8
Matheson, Muir, 283
Maturin, Eric, 42
Meet a Body, 282
Menges, Herbert, 258
Menjou, Adolphe, 68
Merchant of Venice, The: LO in, at drama school, 31–2; LO in, with NT, 409–11; transferred to West End, 413
Merivale, John (Jack), 159, 197, 330, 350, 400
Merman, Ethel, 269
Messel, Oliver, 132
MGM, 67, 74–7, 129, 154–5
Michell, Keith, 236, 356
Middleton, Edgar, 62
Midsummer Night's Dream, A: LO in, at school, 25–6; Vivien Leigh in Old Vic production, 132, 141, 142
Miles, Lord, 444
Miles, Sarah, 354
Milland, Ray, 66
Miller, Arthur, 306, 306–7, 307, 309, 311, 312–13, 319, 407
Miller, Jonathan, 409–10, 438; quoted, 359
Miller, Ruby, 33, 34
Mills, Sir John, 62, 132, 178, 189, 190, 203, 210, 260, 262–3, 306, 415, 431–2
Milton, Robert, 70
Mirren, Helen, 440
Mitchell, Stephen, 248
Monckton, Sir Walter, 196
Monroe, Marilyn, 301–2, 304–10, 311–13, 319
Montgomery, Elizabeth, *see* Motley
Montgomery, Robert, 67, 70
Monthly Film Bulletin, quoted, 72
Moon and Sixpence, The (Maugham): LO in, on TV, 329, 335

Moore, Eva, 47
Moore, Peter, 275
Moore, Robert, 440
More, Kenneth, 290
Morell, Andre, 356
Morgan, Charles, 105
Morgan, Terence, 217, 227
Morley, Sheridan, quoted, 62, 66
Morning's at Seven (Paul Osborn), 439
Mortimer, John, 387, 404; quoted, 388
Moscow, NT at, 389
Moscow Nights (film; US title *I Stand Condemned*): LO in, 31, 86–7
Mostel, Zero, 347
Motley (Elizabeth Montgomery and Percy and Sophie Harris), 79, 87, 130, 155, 156
Mr Halpern and Mr Johnson (TV film): LO in, 449
Much Ado About Nothing, Zeffirelli's production, 390
Murder for Sale (film), *see Temporary Widow, The*
Murder on the Second Floor (Frank Vosper), 54, 55
Mutiny on the Bounty (film): LO in, 449

Naismith, Laurence, quoted, 17–18, 23
Napier, Diana, 104
Narizzano, Silvio, 441
Nathan, George Jean, quoted, 208–9
National Health, The (Peter Nichols), 418
National Theatre: early plans for (from 1848), 364–5; failure to establish Old Vic as first home of, 213, 224–5, 226, 238, 249; foundation-stone laid (1951), then moved, 268, 363; LO tipped to be director, 356–7, 359, 362, 363–5, 366; plans for NT–Stratford alliance, 365–7; new plan for nucleus of NT at Old Vic, 366, 367–8; LO appointed founder-director (1963), 113, 115, 367–8; first season at Old Vic, 369–83, 385; LO's "statement of intent", 371; opening night, 373; architect for new building

National Theatre—*contd.*
appointed, 383; second
season at Old Vic, 385–7,
389; tour to Moscow, 389;
stocktaking, 390–1;
management problems,
393–6; the *Soldiers*
controversy, 396–8; LO's
illness, 398–9; tour of
Canada, 403, 404; finance
for new building
approved (1968), 405;
Peter Brook at NT, 405–
7; LO considers
resignation, 407–8;
building work begins, 408;
US tour (1970), 409; LO
as Shylock, 409–11; Lord
Chandos removed from
chairmanship, 413–14;
criticism of LO and of NT,
416–17; LO in *Long Day's
Journey into Night*, 417,
418–20; box office
successess, 417–18; LO
replaced by Peter Hall,
398, 417, 420, 421–2, 423,
424, 436–8; new building
topped out (1973), 423;
LO's record at the NT,
423–4; LO's last roles,
424–5; NT's last night at
Old Vic, 437; opening of
new theatre by the Queen,
437–8; entertainment in
honour of LO (1987), 450
NBC, 439
Negri, Pola, 69
Nesbitt, Cathleen, 56, 82
Neville, John, 88, 356
New Statesman, quoted, 248,
419
New Theatre (now the
Albery), 84, 187, 188, 242,
249
New York Herald Tribune,
quoted, 335, 348
New York Theater Guild,
170
New York Times, quoted, 69,
70, 72, 77, 145, 209, 269,
335, 348, 354, 416
New Yorker, quoted, 273–4,
388
New Zealand, Old Vic tour
of (1948), 225, 241–4
Newcastle, Duke of, 19
Newman, Paul, 154, 440
News Chronicle, quoted, 119,
179, 211, 302
Newton, Robert, 110, 116,
175

Nicholas and Alexandra (film):
LO in, 414, 416
Night of a Hundred Stars, 306
Nightingale, Benedict,
quoted, 419
Nine Till Six, 58
Niven, David, 138, 150, 152,
178, 202, 210, 276–7
No Funny Business (film): LO
in, 72
No, No, Nanette, 31
No Man's Land (Pinter), 437
No Time for Comedy
(Behrman): LO in (1939),
143–4, 144–5, 146
Norman, Norman V., 33, 36
Notley Abbey, 201–2, 207–
8, 210, 264–5, 274, 338,
384
Nunn, Trevor, 420

Oberon, Merle, 86, 104,
129–30, 136, 137, 138–9,
140
O'Brien, Edmond, 156
Observer, quoted, 42, 44, 56,
79, 86, 120–1, 191, 253,
266, 292, 344, 356, 385,
388, 448
O'Casey, Sean, 31
O'Connor, Dan, 225–6
O'Connor, Garry, 242, 249;
quoted, 45, 135, 401
Odd Man Out (film), 174
"Oedipuff", 204–7, 208
Oedipus (Seneca), at NT,
405–7
Oedipus Rex (Sophocles): LO
in, with Old Vic (1945–
6), 204–7 *passim*, 208
Oh! What a Lovely War (film):
LO in, 415
Old Vic Theatre, 113–15;
1936–7 season, 111, 115–
23; in Denmark with
Hamlet, 123–6; LO's
second season, 130–6;
itinerant after 1941
bombing, 184;
triumvirate of directors
(Richardson, LO,
Burrell), 184–5; 1944–5
season, in Manchester,
185–8; at New Theatre,
London, 185, 186–95;
European tour (1945),
198–9; 1945–6 season,
202–7; New York tour,
208–9; 1946–7 season,
210–13, 216; as home for
NT, *see under* National
Theatre; Australian tour,

225–37, 240–5; dismissal
of the triumvirate, 237–40,
246–9; LO to have New
Theatre for 1948–9
season, 242, 244, 246;
Llewellyn Rees takes over,
249; theatre in Waterloo
Road rebuilt (1950), 249;
Theatre Centre and
School closed (1951), 288;
LO's rebuilding "ruined"
the Old Vic, 372;
mentioned, 63
Olivier, Agnes (née
Crookenden; mother), 12–
17, 18, 21–3
Olivier, Gerard Dacres
("Dickie"; brother): born,
12; on his father, 14;
childhood theatricals, 15;
school, 17, 18, 19, 23; on
LO, 18, 23; to India, 26;
manages Notley, 310, 329;
death, 329
Olivier, Rev. Gerard Kerr
(father), 10, 11–16, 20–2,
24; first marriage, 12; two
elder children, 12; enters
the church, 12; third child
(LO) born, 13;
encourages LO's
theatrical career, 26, 28,
29; second marriage, 30,
55; attends LO's wedding,
59; death, 145–6
Olivier, Isobel Buchanan
(stepmother), 30, 55
Olivier, Julie-Kate
(daughter), 393
Olivier, Sir Laurence (Lord
Olivier): as actor, 5, 22–
3, 88–90, 92–4, 97, 116–
17, 145, 189–92, 294–5,
296–7, 317, 334, 339–40,
344, 428–9; as airman,
160; appearance, 31, 38,
45, 116; awards and prizes,
180, 211, 254–5, 335, 429,
442; biography, *see* Barker,
Felix; birth, 13; childhood
and education, 13–26;
country seat, *see* Notley;
debut at Brighton, 33–4;
as director, 5–6, 83, 195,
291–2; at drama school,
28–33; end of his acting
career, 450; Englishness, 4,
10, 101; family, 10–13;
feminine streak, 22; on
film acting, 140; first film
roles, 56–7; first London
part, 31; first visit to the

theatre, 19; garden at Steyning, 439; honorary degree, 180, 209; House of Lords, only speech in, 420; as impresario, *see* Chichester Festival Theatre, Laurence Olivier Productions, St James's Theatre, *and under* National Theatre *and* Old Vic; injuries, 333; Kean's sword received from Gielgud, 192; knighthood, 213–14, 222, 226, 235; last stage appearance, 424–5; luck, extremes of good and bad, 222–3; marriages, *see under* Esmond, Jill, Leigh, Vivien, Plowright, Joan; memoirs, 443–4; Order of Merit, 444; peerage, 9–10, 404–5, 411–12; Polaroid advertisement, 426, 430; religion, sense of guilt, 60, 334; and Second World War, 147, 150–2, 157–8, 160–2, 167–8, 169, 171–3; television, introduction to, 328–9; working methods, 2–3, 281

Olivier, Richard (son), 353, 412, 451
Olivier, Sybille (sister), 12, 15–16, 29, 121
Olivier, Sydney (uncle; later Baron Olivier), 11, 49
Olivier, Tamsin (daughter), 368
Olivier, Tarquin (son): birth, 60; relations with LO, 101–2, 127, 197, 227, 323, 324; to Canada in 1939, 159, 164; returns to England, 197; description of Notley, 207; relations with Vivien Leigh, 227, 324, 400; at Christ Church, 324; Richard Olivier's godfather, 353; works in Tanzania, 393; his son Tristan, 393; mentioned, 209
Olivier, Tristan (grandson), 393
Olivier family, 10–11
"Olivier's Horse", 11
One More River, 342
O'Neill, Ryan, 435
Osborne, John, 4, 313, 314–15, 316, 318, 320, 385
Oscar, Henry, 31, 110

O'Sullivan, Maureen, 129
Othello: LO as Iago, with Old Vic (1938), 132–4; Orson Welles in, at the St James's, 269; LO in, with NT, 2, 371, 376–82, 390, 392, 403; in Moscow, 389; filmed, 388
O'Toole, Peter, 369–70, 372–4

Palmer, Lilli, 270, 311
Paramount, 67, 305
Paris Bound: LO in (1929), 54
Parker, Cecil, 83
Parker, Dorothy, quoted, 77
Parsons, Louella, 276
Party, The (Trevor Griffiths): LO in (1973), 424
Pascal, Gabriel, 170, 181–2
Patrick, Nigel, 82
Peacock, Walter, 38
Pearl Harbor, 166
Peaslee, Richard, 406
Peck, Gregory, 154, 442
Peer Gynt (Ibsen): LO in, with Old Vic (1944–5), 185, 188
Penley, Derrick, 244
People, The, quoted, 179
Perfect Understanding (film): LO in, 72, 73
Perkins, Anthony, 154
Peter the Great (TV film): LO in, 450
Petherbridge, Edward, 450
Petrie, Daniel, 442
Phoenix Theatre, 61
Pickup, Ronald, 418, 419
Picturegoer, quoted, 68, 69, 70, 110
Plowright, David, 438
Plowright, Joan: meets LO, 314; in *The Entertainer* with LO, 326; on LO, 2, 334; in film of *The Entertainer,* 341; holiday in France with LO, 341; in *Rhinoceros* with LO, 343, 344, 345; affair with LO becomes known, 344, 345; in *A Taste of Honey,* 346, 347; various opinions of her, 349; marries LO, 349; first child (Richard Olivier, q.v.), 353–4; in *The Chances,* 356; and Tynan's appointment to NT, 357; in *Uncle Vanya* with LO, 358, 368; in *Saint Joan,* 368; first daughter

(Tamsin), 368; in *The Master Builder* with LO, 386; miscarriage, 386; second daughter (Julie-Kate), 392, 393; in *The Three Sisters* with LO, 399, 408; provides stability for LO, 401, 452; aims to reduce LO's work-load, 403; LO's tour of Canada, 403, 404; LO's peerage, 405, 411; CBE, 408; in *The Merchant of Venice* with LO, 409; and NT management, 413; in *Saturday, Sunday, Monday* with LO, 424; and LO's final appearance in, 424; various later roles, 431, 441, 443; mentioned, 330, 355, 438
Plummer, Christopher, 2
Pollock, Ellen, 57
Pommer, Erich, 110
Porter, Cole, 269
Portman, Eric, 170
Potiphar's Wife (film; US title *Her Strange Desire*): LO in, 62
Powell, William, 147
Power, Hartley, 216
Power, Tyrone, 81, 269, 306
Power and the Glory, The (Greene); LO in, on TV, 352–3
Preminger, Otto, 387
Pride and Prejudice (film): LO in, 154–5
Priestley, J. B., 97, 161; quoted, 6, 66–7
Prince and the Showgirl, The (film of Rattigan's *Sleeping Prince*), 301–2, 304–10, 311–12
Private Lives (Coward), 57, 60–2, 62–5, 67
Providence (Alain Resnais), 442
Purnell, Louise, 370, 399

Q Planes (film), 137
Q theatre, 105
Quartermaine, Leon, 96
Quayle, Anthony, 86, 265, 288
Queen Christina (film), 74–6
Queen of Scots (Gordon Daviot): LO in (1934), 79–80, 103
Quilley, Denis, 418, 419–20, 421
Quinn, Anthony, 346–8, 414
Quinn, Patsy, 105

Rains, Claude, 66, 182
Rakoff, Alvin, 444
Ramsdell, Roger, 173
Rank, J. Arthur, 176, 179,
  213–14, 219–20
Rathbone, Basil, 81, 162
Rats of Norway (Keith
  Winter): LO in (1933),
  73–4
Rattigan, Terence, 263, 272,
  280–1, 290, 304–5, 307,
  400
Ray, Cyril, quoted, 247–8
Rayne, Lord (Sir Max
  Rayne), 414, 420, 421–2,
  444
Reagan, Ronald, 448
Rebecca (film): LO in, 147,
  148–9, 152–4
Recruiting Officer, The
  (Farquhar): LO in, with
  NT, 371, 374–6
Redford, Robert, 435
Redgrave, Lynn, 370
Redgrave, Sir Michael: with
  Old Vic in 1936–7, 115,
  116, 120; on LO's Hamlet,
  118, 120; as Hamlet, 120;
  declines part in *Henry V*
  film, 174; a Notley visitor,
  210, 358; Festival of
  Britain plans, 265; on
  LO's Antony, 265;
  supposed rival of LO, 358;
  in *Uncle Vanya* with LO, at
  Chichester, 358–9; with
  NT, 370, 373, 385, 386;
  contracts Parkinson's
  Disease, 385; mentioned,
  124, 137, 154, 161, 415
Redgrave, Vanessa, 338–9,
  358
Redington, Michael, 227–8,
  243
Redman, Joyce, 186, 370,
  388
Reed, Carol, 36, 174, 282
Rees, Llewellyn, 249
Regent Theatre, 38
Relph, George, 186, 227,
  232, 253
Renoir, Jean, quoted, 220
Rhinoceros (Ionesco): LO in,
  at Royal Court Theatre,
  342–4, 345, 347
Richard III: LO in, with Old
  Vic (1944–5), 189–93;
  Australian tour, 228, 230,
  232, 234, 237, 244; LO in,
  at New Theatre (1949),
  242, 252–3; LO's film,
  282–6, 302

Richard of Bordeaux (Gordon
  Daviot), 80
Richardson, Muriel, 40
Richardson, Sir Ralph:
  friendship with LO, 37,
  43, 80, 210, 213–14, 432;
  in Birmingham Rep, 37,
  40, 43, 44–5; as motorist,
  9, 40, 49–50, 185; on LO,
  5, 40, 90, 171, 222–3;
  performances with LO,
  44–5, 97–8, 130, 132–4,
  137, 188, 193–4, 203–4,
  206, 286, 333, 443; joins
  Old Vic, 63; in films with
  Korda, 86, 130, 137;
  advice to LO, 91, 111, 122,
  137; as Othello, 132–4; as
  actor, 134, 188, 204; in
  Second World War, 169,
  171; directs Old Vic with
  LO and Burrell, 184–8,
  193–5, 198, 202–4, 208–9,
  211, 224–5, 237–40, 246–
  9; as Peer Gynt, 188; as
  Uncle Vanya, 193–4; as
  Falstaff, 202–4, 208–9;
  knighthood, 213; in
  Hollywood, 225, 239; in
  LO's *Richard III* film, 283,
  286; not invited to NT by
  LO, 370; last
  performance, 443; death,
  451; mentioned, 3, 55, 59,
  79, 95, 137, 145, 218, 415,
  437
Richardson, Tony, 315, 317,
  320, 341, 358, 360
Ridley, Arnold, 33
Ringmaster (Keith Winter),
  81, 82
RKO Radio, 67–8, 70–1
Roar Like a Dove, 330
Robards, Jason, 434
Roberts, Rachel, 400
Robeson, Paul, 338
Robey, Sir George, 34, 174
Robson, Flora, 108, 110, 138
Rodgers, Richard, 269
Romeo and Juliet: LO in
  Gielgud's 1935
  production, 39, 84, 85,
  87–95; LO and Vivien
  Leigh in, in New York
  (1940), 155–7; Zeffirelli's
  film, 415
Rose, Billy, 268–9, 270
Rossiter, Leonard, 360
Royal Academy of Dramatic
  Art (RADA), 27
Royal Court Theatre: Barry
  Jackson and, 38; English

Stage Company at, 288,
  312, 314, 317–19, 368, 406
Royal Hunt of the Sun, The, 390
Royal Shakespeare Theatre,
  Stratford, *see under*
  Shakespeare Memorial
  Theatre

Sadler's Wells Theatre, 114,
  366, 367
St Christopher's School, 32–
  3
Saint-Denis, Michel, 130,
  131, 204, 255, 427
St Edward's school, 24, 25
St James's Theatre, 258–9,
  263, 265, 271, 321–2
Saint Joan (Shaw), 368, 374
St Martin's Lane (film), 136,
  137
Samson, Beryl, 104
Saturday, Sunday, Monday
  (Eduardo de Filippo): LO
  in, with NT, 424; TV
  version, 439, 441
Saturday Night Fever (film),
  426
Saved (Edward Bond), 406
Saville, Victor, 124
Savoy Theatre, 51
Scacchi, Greta, 449
Scaife, Isobel, 115
Schell, Maximillian, 435
Schertzinger, Victor, 68
Schlesinger, John, 432, 433–4
School for Scandal, The
  (Sheridan): Gielgud in,
  with Old Vic, 132; LO in,
  with Old Vic in Australia
  (1948), 215, 228, 229, 230,
  235, 241, 242–3; LO in, at
  New Theatre, 242, 250–2;
  at NT, 417
Scofield, Paul, 353, 416
Scott, George C., 352
Second World War, 147,
  150–2, 157–8, 159–62,
  166–8, 169, 171–3
Secret Agent, The, 87, 90–1
Selznick, David O., 67, 69–
  70, 70–1, 129, 141–4, 147,
  147–9, 153–4, 167, 175,
  182, 195–6
Selznick, Irene, 256
Selznick, Myron, 141–2
Semi-Detached (David
  Turner): LO in (1962),
  360–2
Serena Blandish, 141
Serlin, Oscar, 129
Seven Per Cent Solution, The
  (film): LO in, 433

Seyler, Athene, 31, 56, 86, 133–4
Shakespeare Memorial Theatre, Stratford-upon-Avon: LO at original theatre, 24; in 1920s, 38; in 1950s, 288, 338; Royal Shakespeare Theatre/Company, 365–7, 417, 420
Shaw, George Bernard, 27, 41, 170, 181–2, 365
Shaw, Glen Byam, 79–80, 89, 287–8, 291, 295
She Stoops to Conquer (Sheridan): LO in, with Birmingham Rep, 40
Shearer, Norma, 67
Sheldon, Dr Joanna, 431
Sher, Anthony, 450
Sherriff, Paul, 173
Sherriff, R. C., 49, 50, 53, 158, 165, 166
Sherwood, Robert, 148
Shifting Heart, The, 342
Ship of Fools (film), 400
Shoes of the Fisherman, The (film): LO in, 414–15
Shulman, Milton, quoted, 282, 375
Silver Box, The (Galsworthy): LO in, with Birmingham Rep, 41
Simmons, Jean, 218, 335
Sinatra, Frank, 348
Sister Carrie (film): LO in, 260–1, 274
Skin of our Teeth, The (Thornton Wilder), 195–8, 199, 228, 230, 231
Sleeping Prince, The (Rattigan): LO in, 272, 279–82; film version, *see Prince and the Showgirl*
Sleuth (film): LO in, 427–9
Smith, Barry, 377
Smith, C. Aubrey, 68
Smith, Maggie, 370, 375, 385–6, 388, 390
Soldiers (Rolf Hochhuth), 396–8
Something to Talk About (Phillpotts): LO in, with Birmingham Rep, 41
South Sea Bubble (Coward), 309–10, 311
Southern, Terry, 3
Spanier, Ginette, 200
Spartacus (film): LO in, 330, 335–8
Speaight, Robert, 135; quoted, 53, 117, 135, 192,

294, 297
Spectator, quoted, 86–7, 96–7, 111, 128, 145, 247–8
Sphinx Has Spoken, The (film), *see Friends and Lovers*
Spiegel, Sam, 303
Spoto, Donald, quoted, 154
Spring Awakening (Wedekind), 394
Stamp, Terence, 354
Stanislavsky, Konstantin, 40
Stannard, Heather, 259
Star! (film), 63
Steinbeck, John, 269
Stephens, Robert, 370, 375, 390, 399, 407
Stokes, Sewell, 53
Stoll Theatre, 352
Storm in a Teacup (film), 124
Stranger Within, The: LO in (1929), 54
Strasberg, Paula, 307, 308
Strasberg, Susan, 327
Stratford, Ontario, 2, 126, 351
Stratford-upon-Avon, *see* Shakespeare Memorial Theatre
Stratton, Arthur, 56–7
Streetcar Named Desire, A (Tennessee Williams): Vivien Leigh in (1949), 255–8, 260; film version, 260, 261–2; TV production, 439
Stride, John, 370
Stroheim, Erich Von, 68, 69, 151
Sullivan, Francis L., 116
Sunday Dispatch, 160
Sunday Express, quoted, 387
Sunday Telegraph, quoted, 379
Sunday Times, 394; quoted, 51, 83, 192–3, 197, 254, 369, 373, 410–11
Sunderland, Scott, 44
Susskind, David, 335, 352
Swaffer, Hannen, quoted, 51
Swanson, Gloria, 71, 72
Swinburne, Mercia, 79, 227
Swinburne, Nora, 59, 62
Sydney, Basil, 217, 219

Talent for Murder, A (TV film), 449
Tamburlaine, 437
Taming of the Shrew, The: LO in, at school, 23–5; LO in, with Birmingham Rep, 44–5
Tandy, Jessica, 121, 335; quoted, 43, 88, 123, 334

Taste of Honey, A (Sheelagh Delaney), 346, 347
Taylor, Elizabeth, 63, 277, 440
Taylor, Robert, 129, 155
Taylor, Rod, 154
Tempest, Dame Marie, 81
Temple, Bishop (later Archbishop), 20
Temporary Widow, The (film; US title *Murder for Sale*): LO in, 56
Tennant, Cecil, 227, 234, 235–6, 236–7, 242, 258, 268, 275, 276, 277, 305, 352, 353, 404
Tennent (H. M.) Ltd, 170
Tennyson, Alfred, Lord, 43
Term of Trial (film): LO in, 354, 360
Terry, Ellen, 19–20, 23, 199
That Hamilton Woman (film), *see Lady Hamilton*
Theatre Royal (Ferber and Kauffman): LO in (1934), 80–2, 98, 103
This Happy Breed (film), 174
Thorndike, Canon, 35
Thorndike, Russell, 283
Thorndike, Dame Sybil, 31, 35, 188; sees LO perform at school, 19–20, 24; on LO, 20, 24, 135–6, 271–2, 359; performances with LO, 37, 135, 135–6, 358; advises LO to go to Birmingham, 37, 38; with Old Vic, 186, 188, 208; and Marilyn Monroe, 208, 309, 311; Companion of Honour, 412; mentioned, 36, 198, 282, 293
Thornton, Michael, quoted, 387
Three Sisters, The (Chekhov): NT production, 399, 408; film version, 408
Through the Crack (Blackwood and Pearn), 32
Tickerage Mill, 400
Time (musical), 5, 448
Time magazine, quoted, 145, 155, 180, 392, 433
Times, The, 58; quoted, 24–5, 52, 54, 56, 105, 131, 211, 257, 292, 297, 317, 329, 340, 373, 375, 380, 392, 419

Titus Andronicus: LO in, at Stratford (1955), 287–8, 288–9, 290, 295–8, 299; European tour, 199–200, 320–1; at the Stoll Theatre, 320, 322

Too Many Crooks (film): LO in, 56–7

Top of the Ladder (Tyrone Guthrie), 262–3

Tovarich (musical), 400

Toynbee, Arnold, quoted, 380

Tracy, Spencer, 3, 261

Tree, Lady, 19

Tree, Sir Herbert Beerbohm, 27, 36

Trevor-Roper, Hugh, *see* Dacre, Lord

Trewin, J. C., quoted, 41, 44, 84, 89, 121–2, 131, 134–5, 135, 190, 191, 193, 197, 239–40, 267, 294, 297. 361, 406; mentioned, 260

Troughton, Patrick, 283

Trumbo, Dalton, 336

Tumbler, The (Benn Levy), 342

Turner, David, 360

Tutin, Dorothy, 272, 321, 447

Twelfth Night: LO in, at school, 20; LO in, with Old Vic (1937), 121–2; Old Vic production (1948), 246–7; LO in, at Stratford (1955), 289, 290–2

Twenty-One Days (film), 127–8

Tynan, Kathleen, 371, 398

Tynan, Kenneth Peacock, 370–1; appears in *Hamlet*, 267; empathy towards LO, 293; NT's literary manager, 357, 370–1, 374–5, 376–8, 380, 391, 393–5, 396–8, 406, 409, 416–17; protests at delay in building NT, 363; leaves NT, 398; quoted, 3, 21–2, 94, 94–5, 180, 180–1, 191–2, 197, 212, 257, 266–7, 269, 292, 293, 294, 296–7, 298, 299, 317, 319, 321, 339, 340, 344, 347–8, 354, 356, 358, 360–1, 371, 376, 427; mentioned, 21, 443–4

Ullmann, Liv, 435

Ulster Television, 328

Uncle Vanya (Chekhov): LO in, with Birmingham Rep, 41; LO in, with Old Vic (1944–5), 186, 193; LO in, at Chichester (1962–3), 355, 357–9, 368; at NT, 374; filmed, 388

Unfailing Instinct, The (Julian Frank): LO in, at Brighton (1925), 33

Unsworth, Geoffrey, 388

Ustinov, Peter, 264, 335–6; quoted, 3, 9, 118, 264, 337, 452–3

Variety, quoted, 65, 388, 440

Veidt, Conrad, 124

Venice Preserved (Otway), 296

Venus Observed (Christopher Fry), 258, 259–60, 270

Village Squire, The (film), 105

Village Voice, quoted, 410

Volpone (Jonson), at NT, 408

Vosper, Frank, 54

Voyage round my Father, A (John Mortimer): LO in, 444–5

Wagner (TV film): LO in, 443

Wagner, Robert, 440

Waiting for Gillian, 282

Wakhevitch, Georges, 272

Walbrook, Anton, 170

Walker, Alexander, quoted, 262, 360, 387

Walton, Sir William, 173, 178–9, 217, 283

Wanamaker, Sam, 338–9

Wanger, Walter, 76

Ward, Barbara (later Baroness Jackson), 247

Ward, Penelope Dudley, 86

Wardle, Irving, quoted, 419

Warner Brothers, 257

Washbourne, Mona, 361

Waterloo Bridge (film), 155

Wattis, Richard, 311

Webster, Ben, 156

Webster, Margaret, 59, 79

Weidenfeld, Lord, 443

Weissberger, Arnold, 349

Welles, Orson, 81, 269, 343–4

Westward Passage (film): LO in, 70, 71

Whale, James, 49, 68

Wheldon, Huw, 351

Whitelaw, Billie, 370

Whiting, Leonard, 415

Whitty, Dame May, 82, 156

Wilcox, Herbert, 272–4

Wilcox, Toyah, 449

Wild Geese II (film): LO in, 449–50

Wilde, Cornel, 156

Wilder, Billy, 311

Willatt, Hugh, 397

William III, King, 10

Williams, Clifford, 395, 408

Williams, Emlyn, 83, 330

Williams, Harcourt, 87, 111, 118, 186, 193, 194–5, 203–4, 246

Williams, Hugh, 138

Williams, Tennessee, 257–8

Williamson, Audrey, quoted, 82, 88, 122; mentioned, 134

Williamson, Nicol, 433

Wilson, Beatrice, 33

Wilson, Harold, 9–10, 404–5, 411–12

Wilson, Jack, 78

Wilson, Professor John Dover, 265–6

Wimperis, Arthur, 167

Winchell, Walter, quoted, 64

Winnington, Richard, quoted, 179

Wolfit, Sir Donald, 186, 192, 210, 265, 328

Wong, Anna May, 53, 66

Wontner, Arthur, 36

Wood, Alan, quoted, 221

Wood, Natalie, 440–1

Wood, Sam, 144

Woodward, Joanne, 441

Wooland, Norman, 217, 370

Woollcott, Mr and Mrs Alexander, 160

Workhouse Donkey, The (John Arden), 368

World at War, A (TV series): LO and, 422–3

World-Telegram, quoted 146

Worsley, T. C., quoted, 240, 261, 263

Wray, Maxwell, 106

Wrede, Caspar, 329

Wuthering Heights (film): LO in, 136–40, 145

Wyler, William, 137, 138, 140, 174, 261, 304

Yank at Oxford, A (film), 129

Yellow Passport, The (film): LO in, 69

Young, Stark, quoted, 77

Young, Terence, 174

Yvonne Arnaud Theatre, 385

Zeffirelli, Franco, 382, 390

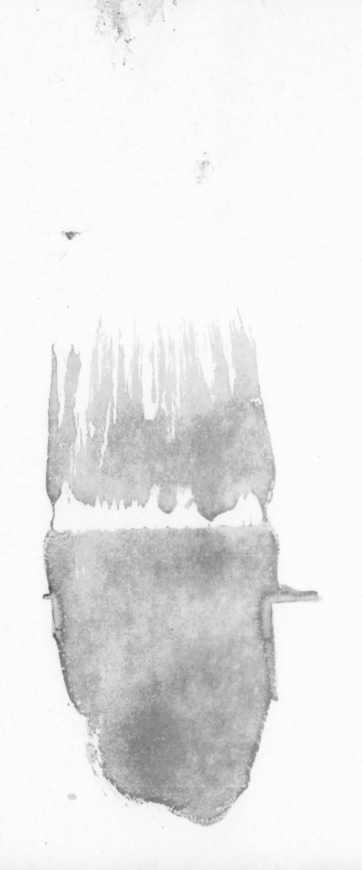